A GUIDE TO THE WORLD ANTI-DOPING CODE

Third Edition

The law relating to anti-doping changes rapidly. The World Anti-Doping Code was first adopted in 2004 to provide a common set of anti-doping rules applicable across all sport worldwide. The Code has evolved and changed significantly through two major processes of review. This third edition provides essential guidance and commentary on the 2015 Code which replaces the 2009 Code. The 2015 Code contains many significant changes in the core Articles of the Code, particularly in the regime on sanctions for anti-doping rule violations, and in the amended International Standards. The text outlines how the current law has developed from anti-doping rules and principles in operation before the Code and explains the central role of the Court of Arbitration for Sport in this development and in applying the current Code. This third edition will be an important single resource for any reader working or studying in the field.

PAUL DAVID QC is a barrister practising from Eldon Chambers, Auckland. He has acted as independent counsel to Drug-Free Sport New Zealand for 15 years. He is included on the list of arbitrators at the Court of Arbitration for Sport.

A GUIDE TO THE WORLD ANTI-DOPING CODE

The Fight for the Spirit of Sport

THIRD EDITION

PAUL DAVID QC BA HONS LLM
(CANTAB) BARRISTER

CAMBRIDGE
UNIVERSITY PRESS

CAMBRIDGE
UNIVERSITY PRESS

University Printing House, Cambridge CB2 8BS, United Kingdom

One Liberty Plaza, 20th Floor, New York, NY 10006, USA

477 Williamstown Road, Port Melbourne, VIC 3207, Australia

4843/24, 2nd Floor, Ansari Road, Daryaganj, Delhi - 110002, India

79 Anson Road, #06-04/06, Singapore 079906

Cambridge University Press is part of the University of Cambridge.

It furthers the University's mission by disseminating knowledge in the pursuit of education, learning, and research at the highest international levels of excellence.

www.cambridge.org
Information on this title: www.cambridge.org/9781107175860
DOI: 10.1017/9781316809624

First published by Cambridge University Press 2008
Second edition published by Cambridge University Press 2013
Third edition published by Cambridge University Press 2017

Printed in the United Kingdom by Clays, St Ives plc

A catalogue record for this publication is available from the British Library

ISBN 978-1-107-17586-0 Hardback

CONTENTS

FIGURES

vii

PREFACE TO THE THIRD EDITION

I worked on this third edition of this text over the 2015 Christmas break – a time of tranquil repose in New Zealand, when the weather is usually good and you can relax with family and friends, eat and drink *al fresco* and swim in the sea if you are so inclined. But for a sports lover, even one on a holiday break, this was a very troubling time. Many claim with some justification that 2015 was one of the worst for sport and its management, with FIFA corruption and doping scandals dominating the media. 2016 seemed to continue the same way.

Since the second edition, we have seen several significant doping issues in sport, which have generated increasing awareness of the scale of the problem facing it. The ending of the Armstrong saga in terms of the imposition of sanctions in the sport of cycling produced a report by the Independent Commission for Cycling revealing the extent of the systemic issues which the sport had to address and caused Union Cycliste Internationale (UCI) to adopt a range of measures to try and address them. The long-running investigation into alleged doping at National Rugby League (NRL) and Australian Football League (AFL) clubs in Australia came to a close in the Court of Arbitration for Sport (CAS), at least, with the decision that thirty-two Essendon players had used a prohibited substance and were to be subject to a two-year period of ineligibility. Later in 2016, there was a further final unsuccessful appeal to the Swiss Federal Tribunal, which saw the bans maintained.

Perhaps most disturbing were the investigations commissioned by WADA into allegations of systemic doping and the covering up of doping violations by Signatories to the Code. The content of the reports created great difficulty for the sporting organisations involved and affected athletes in the short time-frame before the Rio Olympics, producing a hurried response by way of rule-making by international sporting organisations and subsequent challenges by athletes to eligibility decisions before the CAS Ad Hoc Division sitting in Rio. The whole affair raised concerns about the general effectiveness of the anti-doping system. The dust is now settling after the publication of a further final report at the end of 2016, and the result seems likely to be a more coherent anti-doping regime, with clearer proportionate sanctions where non-compliance by Signatories to the Code is established.

A casual reader of the world's sporting media over the past two years might be forgiven for thinking that, to borrow from the Roman historian Tacitus, writing about life under some Roman emperors, corruption in sport has become the fashion of the day. Certainly, it seems very naive to think that any elite competitive sport based on physical performance is free from doping in any form. Add to this increasing concerns about the way in which developing young athletes in sports like rugby appear to be obtaining prohibited substances such as steroids (often over the Internet) in order to make the grade.

The current disturbing picture highlights the importance of sports having good clear rules to combat corrupt practices which participants understand and a good system to enforce them. While this text does contain some comment on the effectiveness of the rules under the Code, and makes some suggestions for change in its concluding chapter, its focus is on providing a guide to the operation of the rules for those working with them.

Since the second edition, the 2009 Code and International Standards have been amended under the review process required by the Code. After a very extensive process, the 2015 Code introduced significant changes in several important areas – notably, in relation to sanctions under a completely refashioned Article 10, one of the main themes of which is the introduction of tougher penalties for those who might be called 'real cheats'. The nature of current problems has emphasised the need for investigations which go beyond testing (and may well involve 'whistle-blowing' informants as a source of intelligence and information). This shift in anti-doping activities, which has been gathering momentum for some time, is recognised in changes in the Code and Standards.

Previous editions were published when the Code was about to be amended, but I thought that this third edition would best serve its purpose as a guide to a much changed 2015 Code if it appeared about two years after that Code had started to operate.

While recent events emphasise the continued relevance of the fight against doping and the role of the anti-doping rules in the Code in that fight, this work does not conduct the fight. Nor does it discuss how the fight should best be conducted. The aim of this text remains to provide comment and practical assistance on the rules contained in the Code in order to help all those operating under the Code interpret and apply its provisions in an efficient, fair and effective manner.

As the anti-doping area becomes more complex, as the rules change to meet current challenges and are regularly reviewed, it is important to keep in mind that the purpose of any decision-making process under the Code is to provide a reasoned decision in a timely manner which is truly accessible to those who are subject to the rules in the Code.

While there is no doubt that the Code has become more detailed and that many more CAS awards and tribunal decisions applying its provisions are being produced, the aim of this work (notwithstanding the regretted increase in length required to cover and comment on the Code regime) remains to keep things as simple as possible. This approach is consistent with the aim of the Code: to create a set of sport-specific rules for anti-doping which can stand alone and be interpreted without recourse to national law, and which provide a certain predictable set of rules for use by a range of participants in sport.

Regrettably, some written decisions applying the Code and some of the wide-ranging comment on them seem to lose sight of the need to provide straightforward reasoned decisions for those who are most affected by the rules under the Code – usually, the athletes. The accessibility of the law under the Code is very important, and there is a risk of this being lost if decisions become too long and involved as a result of the attempt to set out and review case law (which often does no more than provide examples of the application of the Code in different factual situations).

Many decisions which apply the Code to particular circumstances are inherently factual, and the task of the tribunal is the familiar one of interpreting the provisions of the Code correctly on the basis of the words used and applying them to the facts of the case. In providing commentary on the Code – in particular, on the key Articles which set out the elements of the violations, the requirements for proof and the applicable sanctions – I have tried to provide comments which can be considered and applied in a straightforward way in order to elucidate the meaning of a provision before applying it in the circumstances of a particular case. This approach seems particularly relevant where decisions under the Code are most likely to be made by tribunals at national level or tribunals established by international federations – a hearing before CAS should be the exception, if the system is working well. The idea of the case summaries (which have been revised, with some removed and about thirty added) is to provide examples of the Code's provisions in action in order to assist all those who operate and make decisions under the Code in the process of applying the Code.

I believe that in this sporting world, where the effective and fair application of uniform rules to combat doping – the Code – has never been more important, this work can contribute most effectively if it remains faithful to the aim expressed for the first edition in 2008: to provide a practical guide to the rules for those working with the Code.

PREFACE TO THE SECOND EDITION

Recently, an anti-doping expert with many years' experience in the field told me that he had encountered more difficult issues in his work in the past twelve months than in the past twelve years. This comment and others like it, together with my own experiences in working with the legal issues arising in the anti-doping area has prompted the writing of the second edition of this guide to the World Anti-Doping Code.

While the regulation of doping in sport has been a fast moving field over the past decade, there has been a quickening of the pace in the last three years, since the publication of the first edition of this text. The obvious change in the regulatory framework since the first edition has been the adoption, from 1 January 2010, of the 2009 Code by Signatories to the Code. The significant changes brought about by the 2009 Code, in particular in relation to the imposition of sanctions, means that the process of hearing and determining particular periods of ineligibility has become complex. The new Code has been accompanied by revised International Standards and Guidelines. However, the increase in activity in the field is not simply the result of changes in the rules. Rather, several factors have worked together to produce an increase in investigative work and inquiries by anti-doping organisations and more allegations before sports tribunals and the Court of Arbitration for Sport (CAS) in which the provisions of the 2009 Code and operation of new Standards and Guidelines have had to be considered. Anti-doping organisations have focussed increasingly on the investigation of violations under the Code which are not established by testing alone, and new rules in Standards and Guidelines relating to matters such as athlete whereabouts and biological passports have provided more data on which these investigations can be based. State authorities have also become increasingly involved in anti-doping regulation and investigation under applicable national laws, whether sport-specific criminal or general public health legislation. This has made more information available to anti-doping organisations under the Code and given greater impetus to their investigations, as well as giving rise to difficult legal issues where the provisions of national law and the rules under the Code come into potential conflict. In addition, in the area of testing, the development of effective tests for particular performance-enhancing substances such as the latest variants of erythropoietin (EPO) and human growth hormone (hGH) has caught more athletes who had been prepared to take the risk and take performance-enhancing substances. These developments have meant that there is more regulation to be understood and operated by those working in the area and more material available to anti-doping organisations upon which allegations can be based.

Whether there is in fact more or less doping in sport is hard to assess, but there has been a significant increase in the efforts to detect doping and bring forward anti-doping allegations against the athletes and support persons involved. While the vast majority of athletes young and not so young, professional and amateur, are dedicated to competing clean, the demands of modern sport and the ready availability of performance-enhancing substances for sale (particularly over the Internet) mean that the temptation to cheat is ever present. It would seem, from the decided cases which more wide-ranging investigations by anti-doping organisations are producing, that this temptation is one that some athletes find hard to resist.

Today, those who have to deal with anti-doping issues are confronted by more complex regulatory issues, an increasing number of investigations and allegations involving complex evidence, a complex decision-making process under the Code, in particular as regards the imposition of sanctions, and a wide range of decisions under the Code from various sporting tribunals around the world, from CAS and national courts, in particular the Swiss Federal Tribunal.

This second edition of the text retains the approach and structure adopted in the first. It seeks to explain and comment on the provisions of the 2009 Code and the principles which are applied in making decisions under it. The important points are again illustrated by summaries of key decisions by sporting tribunals at national level and CAS and from national courts, in particular the Swiss Federal Tribunal, where appeals from CAS under the Code will be brought. Some thirty new summaries have been added to the text.

While each chapter of the first edition has been the subject of amendment, the most significant legal developments have, perhaps, taken place in the area of the proof of use of prohibited substances by other evidence, apart from positive tests, including data obtained and evaluated under biological passport regimes, the rules established to assist in obtaining such evidence, and in the sanctions regime under the 2009 Code. The process of a tribunal imposing a sanction under the Code now more frequently involves a more difficult evaluation of the degree of fault in connection with a violation.

In the past two years, there have been significant wide-ranging anti-doping investigations in many jurisdictions often involves both State and sporting authorities. Several are currently ongoing. The level of resource and commitment to the fight against doping in sport from both anti-doping organisations operating under the Code and States supporting the Code in accordance with their obligations under the UNESCO Convention appears likely to increase. This second edition again seeks to provide an up-to-date guide to the Code and its operation for those working in a rapidly developing area.

TABLE OF CASES

xv

INTRODUCTION

The last two decades of the twentieth century saw many doping scandals concerning the major sporting events and leading athletes. Events such as the 1988 Olympic 100m final, where a steroid-assisted Ben Johnson won the gold medal in startling fashion, are etched in the sporting memories of many fans as tarnished magic moments.[1] However, it was the doping affair concerning the Festina cycling team during the 1998 Tour de France which highlighted the need for more coordinated global action against doping. The foundation of the World Anti-Doping Authority (WADA), which was established as a private foundation under the laws of Switzerland on 10 November 1999 to promote, coordinate and monitor the fight against doping in sport in all its forms, was the most significant response to this need.

While doping investigations and scandals continue in the sporting world,[2] WADA remains a highly visible player in efforts to combat doping. The World Anti-Doping Program, introduced by WADA, which has

1 This run and the outcry in Canada produced the Dubin Commission of Inquiry into the Use of Drugs and Banned Practices Intended to Increase Athletic Performance, which led to significant changes in the organisation of testing for prohibited substances in Canada and other countries. Ultimately, Mr Johnson was banned for life under the IAAF Rules when he committed a further doping violation. For the decision in the Ontario Court (General Division) rejecting the challenge to this life ban, see *Johnson v. Athletics Canada and IAAF* [1997] No. 3201 (Chapter 10, page 505).

2 The cycle of scandals producing reports that produce calls for reform and indeed rule changes has continued. Athletics and cycling have perhaps continued to provide the most prominent headlines in the media. The recent reports commissioned by WADA contained findings which significantly affected the integrity of sporting competition ahead of the Rio Olympics. The first, two-part report by the WADA Independent Commission was focussed on evidence of systematic doping and the corrupt covering up of positive tests in athletics. The second report concerned systematic doping and avoidance of the return of positive tests. See Chapter 10, pages 530–4 for more detail on the position surrounding the Rio Olympics and related CAS awards. It should be noted that the various decisions made in relation to sports rules introduced as a result of the reports' findings related not to sanctions imposed under the Code, but rather to rules implemented by sporting organisations such as the IOC, IPC and IAAF because a Signatory was alleged to have not complied with its

the World Anti-Doping Code ('Code') at its centre as a uniform set of anti-doping rules, has been at the heart of these efforts. This book seeks to provide a guide to the Code, and to the International Standards which operate together with it, for all those who work with the Code, whether as administrators, advisers or participants in sport.

Origins of WADA and the Code

The International Olympic Committee (IOC) convened the World Conference on Doping in Sport which took place in Lausanne in February 1999. As a result of a proposal from the Conference, WADA was established as an independent body[3] intended to create and maintain unified standards for anti-doping testing and the imposition of sanctions for doping violations, and to coordinate the efforts of sports organisations, anti-doping organisations and governments in combating doping in sport.

Until WADA was founded, the IOC had taken the lead role in implementing measures to prevent doping in sport.[4] Olympic sports, and sports outside the Olympic movement, had adopted the Olympic Movement Anti-Doping Code (OMADC), which was produced and refined by the IOC. WADA took over this role and sought to build a wider acceptance throughout the global sporting community for a standard approach to the detection and punishment of doping. WADA assumed the role of producing the list of prohibited substances and methods from the IOC and

obligations under the Code. The second part of the report from the WADA Independent Commission was published in December 2016.

Cycling has seen a number of scandals, lengthy investigations and results management processes, which led to a report by the Cycling Independent Reform Commission in February 2015 as the sport sought to reform. This report made a range of recommendations for the better conduct of anti-doping procedures by UCI and for reform of the governance of the body.

3 The governance structure of WADA is outside the scope of this text. The make-up of the WADA Foundation Board – the supreme decision-making body at WADA – which has a fifty/fifty split in its composition between Government and IOC appointees has been the subject of criticism on grounds that IOC appointees may have conflicts of interest in addressing certain issues and that this might undermine the independence of WADA. At a recent WADA Foundation Board meeting on 20 November 2016 the Board appointed a working group to examine strengthening WADA's governance structure to ensure its independence from governments and sporting organisations.

4 The IOC initially established its Medical Code under the Olympic Charter. This Code sought to provide for prohibited substances, sanctions and such matters, and to harmonise the approach to doping across international federations and national Olympic committees.

developed the Code,[5] in pursuit of its main objective of developing harmonised rules, disciplinary procedures and sanctions.

The Code aims to produce international harmony by fostering agreement between the organisations which are Signatories to it. It contains key Articles relating, primarily, to doping violations, proof of violations and sanctions, which Signatories have to implement without significant amendment in order to accept the Code. Other Articles provide for standards relating to the handling of anti-doping matters. Signatories have to meet these, but are allowed to do so in different ways. Implementation occurs by the adoption of rules which apply to members or to those taking part in sporting competition. Because of the manner in which it operates, the effectiveness of the Code depends on those who agree to comply with it and to apply its terms meeting their obligations. While the Code does provide for its implementation by Signatories to be monitored by WADA, and does contain some general sanctions where there is non-compliance by Signatories, those sanctions are limited, and the focus of the Code is on establishing a regime which regulates the conduct of individuals and which sanctions those individuals who breach the provisions of the regime.[6]

Adoption of the Code

The Code was the product of an extensive consultation and drafting process, and was unanimously adopted by the World Conference on Doping at Copenhagen in March 2003. Since its adoption, the Code has been accepted by Signatories around the world. The organisations which can accept the Code as Signatories (in addition to WADA itself) include the IOC, national Olympic committees, the International Paralympic Committee (IPC), national paralympic committees, international federations, national anti-doping organisations (NADOs) and major event organisations. The number of Signatories in these categories is currently

5 For the full text of the 2004, 2009, and 2015 Codes, see the WADA website, www.wada-ama .org. The version of the 2015 Code redlined with the changes from the 2009 Code is of real assistance in understanding the significant changes made.

6 The Foundation Board meeting on 20 November 2016 agreed to grant WADA authority to impose proportionate sanctions on Signatories who were proven not to have complied with their obligations under the Code. This proposed new sanctions regime will be developed after consultation with stakeholders. It will represent a significant development of the Code and the role of WADA under it.

approaching 100 per cent.[7] Through agreement by Signatories to apply the
Code, an interlocking structure of agreements containing the Code's key
Articles and other provisions which fulfil its standards has been created
throughout the world of sport at both international and national level.

Neither governments nor national sporting organisations (NSOs) can
be Signatories to the Code. NSOs and their members become bound to the
Code through the agreements made by and with Signatories which adopt
the Code, such as international federations and NADOs. NSOs are either
bound by their membership of other organisations which are Signatories,
or enter into specific agreements with Signatories. Individual participants
in a sport become bound as members of a sporting organisation which has
implemented the Code, or when they agree to the terms on which an event
is held at national or international level. Although they cannot agree to
the Code, governments have an important part to play in supporting it by
implementing the UNESCO Anti-Doping Convention. The Convention
has secured global acceptance and provides important State-level support
for the Code.

The Code and the International Standards

In the last decade, the Code has become the central rallying point for the
fight against doping in sport, and its existence has received widespread
media coverage. Together with the International Standards concerning the
Prohibited List, Testing and Investigations, Laboratories, Therapeutic Use
Exemptions (TUEs) and, most recently, the Protection of Privacy and Personal Information and the model Guidelines for Signatories produced by
WADA,[8] the Code makes up the World Anti-Doping Program, which is
intended to bind participants in sport in the same way as the rules of the
sport themselves. This programme encompasses both the key substantive
elements of the anti-doping regime, such as the violations and sanctions,
and the technical operational procedures (provided primarily by the International Standards) by which anti-doping rule violations, in particular the

7 For the current position on the acceptance of the Code, see www.wada-ama.org. International federations outside the Olympic movement were slower to adopt the Code (see
  e.g. the lengthy process by which FIFA adopted the Code) but, again, acceptance is now
  widespread. The process of acceptance by FIFA included obtaining an advisory opinion
  from CAS on the compatibility of provisions of the Code with fundamental principles of
  Swiss law (see CAS 2005/C/976 & 986, *FIFA and WADA* in Chapter 10, pages 499–501).
8 For more on the International Standards, which are a mandatory aspect of the Code, and
  the various Guidelines published by WADA, see Chapter 2.

presence of prohibited substances or methods in bodily samples given by athletes, will be detected, such as sampling and testing.

Some idea of the scope of the WADA programme is provided by the fact that some 283 304 samples were collected and analysed in 2014.[9] In addition, anti-doping organisations are now devoting more time and resources to the gathering of accurate whereabouts information from elite athletes, to test planning and target testing and to the investigation of doping violations, such as trafficking, which are not established by positive tests, but by obtaining and presenting other evidence.[10] A significant development in recent years has been the use of the Athlete Biological Passport (ABP), which allows sporting organisations to adopt biological passport regimes under which doping can be detected by the analysis and expert evaluation of blood or urine values for an athlete over time. Again, WADA has published and amended Guidelines for the operation of the ABP.

The practical result of the acceptance of the Code is that both national- and international-level athletes who are bound by the Code can be subject to both testing for the presence of prohibited substances and prohibited methods in their bodily samples in-competition and out-of-competition (and to the various related obligations connected with a testing programme, such as the provision of information concerning their whereabouts) and to investigation in respect of various violations[11] which do not require adverse analytical findings or the analysis of bodily samples. In addition, the conduct of other persons bound by the Code, such as athlete support personnel, who may commit anti-doping rule violations, such as trafficking or administering prohibited substances, may be investigated by the anti-doping organisations responsible for administering the Code, at both national and international level. Investigations will be carried out by the anti-doping organisation which has jurisdiction under the Code over the athlete or other person. An investigation may lead to the bringing of allegations by the organisation responsible for managing the results of an investigation, and, where a violation is established, to the imposition of sanctions by the tribunal which hears the allegation.[12] The tribunal

9 See 2014 Anti-Doping Testing Figures Report on the WADA website.
10 For the ABP Guidelines, the proof of such violations and case summaries, see Chapter 5, pages 205–24.
11 The Code uses the phrase 'anti-doping rule violations'. In the text, this or the abbreviation 'violation' is used.
12 See Chapter 7, pages 292–4 for the position on which organisation has responsibility for investigation and results management.

hearing an allegation will be either a national- or an international-level sporting tribunal or the Court of Arbitration for Sport (CAS), depending on the rules and policies of the particular anti-doping organisation which manages the results.[13]

The aim of the Code is to provide for the process of investigating and hearing doping violations to be carried out in a consistent and coordinated way throughout the sporting world. The central place of CAS – an arbitral institution established by the Olympic movement in the mid-1980s to hear sports-related disputes – in interpreting and applying the Code is important in bringing about a consistent approach to its application. However, to a significant extent, the Code operates and is applied at either national level or in international federations, with many decisions on the application of the Code being made by tribunals functioning at this level.[14]

While governments cannot be Signatories to the Code, most have declared their support for it. The International Convention against Doping in Sport was developed and adopted by the General Conference of UNESCO at its 33rd Session on 19 October 2005. This Convention has come into effect and has been widely ratified in a short period of time.[15] The Convention provides a means by which State parties can commit themselves to take steps to support the Code.[16] It is again important, however, to note that the Code's legal enforceability is not derived from this State-level commitment or from legislative acts by individual States, but, as with the anti-doping regimes which the Code replaced (and, indeed, other disciplinary regimes in sport), from the agreement by sporting organisations, their members and participants in sport to apply it.

Other Methods of Regulation

The Introduction to the Code specifically provides that it is enforceable by agreement and forms a sport-specific set of rules, and that it is not

13 Tribunals will have jurisdiction by agreement over the hearing of alleged violations under the Code and may well be regarded as functioning as arbitral bodies in considering the allegations brought (see Chapter 10, pages 485–7).

14 By way of example, for consideration of the way in which Code decisions are made at the national level in New Zealand, see Paul David QC, 'Hearing Anti-Doping Cases in New Zealand' in *Doping in Sport and the Law* (Hart Publishing, 2016). The establishment of independent tribunals by the State to hear anti-doping allegations under the Code at national level (as opposed to those allegations being heard by internal domestic tribunals set up by the sporting organisations themselves) is becoming more common.

15 On 17 November 2010, Fiji became the 150th country to ratify the Convention. At the time of writing, over 200 countries have ratified it. Since the Convention came into force on 1 February 2007, it has been one of UNESCO's most rapidly implemented treaties.

16 See Chapter 2, pages 88–90 for an outline of the main provisions of the Convention.

intended to be subject to the national requirements of criminal or civil law.[17] Doping in sport can be made subject to the provisions of criminal or civil law by national governments, and some States have enacted specific anti-doping legislation criminalising doping in sport. In many jurisdictions, however, there is no criminal or other legislation which is specifically concerned with the problem of doping in sport. Criminal allegations in the context of doping in sport have been relatively rare, although increased political awareness of the problem of drugs in sport has seen more countries enact specific anti-doping laws (with Germany being the most recent). Where criminal allegations are brought, they are usually made under legislation which is concerned with the regulation of the supply of prescription medicines or with customs control, or under general misuse of drugs provisions, where the use of substances which are prohibited in sport falls within the terms of the legislation.

The Code functions at a transnational level, independently of the national laws of States. In some instances, while an outcome reached under national law will be applied within a particular State, the agreement of an athlete to the application of the Code (and, as a consequence, decisions made under the Code by the tribunals with responsibility for hearings) can mean that, internationally, in the world of sport, the outcome in disciplinary proceedings may differ from the outcome of proceedings in State courts.[18]

Liaison with State Authorities

The Code functions as an international agreement across national boundaries and seeks to bring about a coordinated approach among Signatories. The investigation of anti-doping rule violations under the Code may also involve liaison between anti-doping organisations operating under the Code and the State authorities responsible for enforcing criminal law or customs legislation (or, perhaps, other bodies responsible for professional disciplinary matters). The extent to which this kind of liaison

---

17 The Code will be subject to the legal principles which protect fundamental rights in national courts, and the Introduction to the 2015 Code records at p. 17 that the Code is intended to be applied in a way which respects the principles of human rights and proportionality. For the purposes of the application of fundamental rights, it is submitted that the better view is that regimes under the Code, and in particular its sanctions, are not criminal in nature.

18 See further Chapter 2, pages 80–1 for a case summary which provides an example. There are many examples of CAS awards reaching decisions under anti-doping regimes which are binding internationally in sport but differ from decisions made by national sporting bodies or, indeed, national courts in relation to the same conduct.

and reporting occurs will depend on the rules and policies of the organisation responsible for investigation and results management under the Code, and the relevant national legislative provisions which are potentially applicable.[19] The territorial nature of criminal law has meant that there has, to date, been relatively little international coordination by authorities responsible for the application of laws concerning such matters as trafficking in prohibited substances. However, WADA is now seeking to promote greater cross-border cooperation between States in the light of growing concern at the large scale of the criminal activity involved in the trafficking of performance-enhancing drugs and methods. This area of the possible international criminal regulation of doping in sport lies outside the Code (and the general scope of this book, until specific rules or Guidelines for Signatories to the Code are developed), but has to be kept in mind by those involved in investigations and those operating under the Code, both from the point of view of sharing information with State authorities and in relation to the conduct of investigations concerning possible violations under the Code, where athletes or other persons may also be subject to criminal proceedings related to the matters under investigation.

The Challenges for the Code

The Need for Consistency

As with any instrument which seeks to produce a standard, harmonised approach in an area of wide-ranging international activity, the Code faces considerable challenges. Perhaps the main areas where constant effort is required, if the Code is to achieve its goals, are the challenges presented

19 The investigation and criminal prosecutions and anti-doping violation proceedings relating to the Bay Area Laboratory Cooperative run by Mr Conte (the 'BALCO affair') provide a good early example of the interaction between the criminal law of a State and the disciplinary system agreed to by athletes under the Code. Mr Conte and others involved in a wide-ranging doping conspiracy were subject to criminal punishment for charges involving trafficking in drugs under the US misuse of drugs legislation, while a number of high-profile athletes received periods of ineligibility of up to eight years under the rules of the USATF/IAAF following hearings before the American Arbitration Association (AAA) and CAS, to which they were bound. Several recent doping cases have started with searches carried out by police in criminal investigations (see e.g. Operatión Puerta in Spain, in which a search of a medical facility by police revealed bags of blood for use in blood transfusions). The case against the cyclist Alejandro Valverde provides an interesting example of the issues which can arise where the application of national laws and sporting rules across territorial frontiers is involved. See Chapter 2, pages 82–7 for a summary of the various proceedings.

by the need for the consistent application and interpretation of the Code's provisions by tribunals hearing anti-doping violations around the sporting world, and by the need for those who are bound by the Code to be aware of the principles concerning liability for, and punishment of, anti-doping rule violations under the Code. While WADA, governments, the various Signatories to the Code (in particular, the NADOs and international federations) and NSOs devote considerable energy to the education of sporting participants (and the Code is often referred to in the sporting media), the cases which come before national tribunals and CAS still continue to show that there remains a good deal of ignorance among many sporting participants, their coaches and their advisers, at both national and international level, concerning the nature of the anti-doping regime under the Code (in particular, the high level of obligation imposed on athletes by the strict liability regime under the Code) and the consequences of violations.

Access to Decisions under the Code

In the area of decision-making under the Code, CAS occupies a central position in its interpretation and application. CAS Panels have emphasised the need for consistency in their awards. The goal of harmonisation is relatively difficult to achieve when many tribunals (particularly at the national level) may well not be aware of the decisions made and principles applied in interpreting and applying Articles of the Code by other sporting tribunals or CAS. In recent years, access to decisions has improved significantly, with CAS providing an online database of decisions going back to 1986 and regularly publishing the most recent decisions.[20] However, the production of a range of decisions worldwide by various sporting tribunals and CAS makes the task of consistent decision-making harder. This book seeks to assist by providing a guide to the fundamental principles of the Code for those involved in sport, whether as participants in sporting competitions, sports administrators, advisers or decision-makers. In key areas, the operation of the provisions of the Code is illustrated by reference to summaries of decisions by CAS and other sporting tribunals.

20 The CAS website (www.tas-cas.org) reproduces the most recent decisions (generally, six decisions are posted at a time, with different decisions appearing on the French and English parts of the site) and provides an online library of past decisions. Digests of CAS awards dating back to 1986 have also been produced: see Digest of CAS decisions I (1986–88), II (1998–2000) and III (2001–03). References to CAS awards in the period 1986–2003 in the text refer to the references in the Digests.

Outline of the Text

After a short description of the development of anti-doping measures in the area of sporting activity, the book outlines the legal principles relating to liability for doping which were developed before the advent of the Code and which are, to a significant extent, carried forward into the Code. The text then outlines, by reference to decisions of CAS Panels and national courts, the lack of harmony in the approach to doping (in particular, as regards the imposition of sanctions) which the Code was produced to address. An overview of the Code and the World Anti-Doping Program follows, before a commentary on the interpretation and application of the key Articles of the Code by reference to decisions made by tribunals and CAS.[21]

The structure of the book broadly follows that of Part One of the 2015 Code[22] and provides an explanation of, and commentary on, the Articles, with summaries of relevant CAS awards and sporting tribunal decisions set out after the Articles to which they apply or at the end of each chapter. The Code has been the subject of two review processes, in accordance with its terms, which produced the 2009 Code (which considerably amended the 2004 Code) and the 2015 Code (which again considerably amended the 2009 Code, in particular as regards the regime of sanctions for anti-doping rule violations). References to the Code in the text are to the 2015 Code unless otherwise stated. The full texts of the 2004 and 2009 Codes are available on the WADA website. It is still quite possible that allegations will

---

21 The liberty given to sporting organisations in relation to managing results means that there are many different sporting tribunals which have to interpret and apply the Code. Additionally, at the national level, in some jurisdictions, tribunals which are independent of NSOs have been established to hear sports-related disputes by agreement with NSOs. An example is the New Zealand Sports Tribunal (www.sportstribunal.org.nz). In other jurisdictions, established arbitration bodies provide the first-instance decision-making tribunal for anti-doping rule violations (see e.g. the AAA in the US anti-doping regime). The United Kingdom has established an independent tribunal to hear doping allegations: the United Kingdom Anti-Doping Tribunal. The text refers to CAS awards and decisions in the courts and to the decisions of sporting tribunals at the national and the international level, where the decisions assist in understanding the operation of the provisions of the Code. Many anti-doping allegations under the Code will be decided by national-level tribunals or by tribunals established by the relevant international federation.

22 The text also outlines, in Chapter 2, the provisions of the Code concerning the roles and responsibilities of Signatories under Part 3, but as noted, the focus of the rules in the Code and of sanctions under it is on the conduct of individuals. The Code depends upon its Signatories doing all they can to implement and enforce it, and sanctions for non-compliance are limited.

have to be considered under the 2009 Code,[23] and for this reason, and for comparison with related provisions in the 2015 Code, the text retains some of the material relevant to the application of the 2009 Code and comments on the changes made in the 2015 Code. The text seeks to focus on the key Articles of the 2015 Code, but in order to understand the operation of specific Articles, the reader must also understand the background to the Code, how it becomes effective in a legal sense, the operation of the International Standards essential to its operation and incorporated into it, the hearing system which it creates and the relationship between the rules under the Code and external legal principles under national legal systems. The text tries to bring these elements together in order to explain how this set of sports rules functions and what they mean for participants who are bound by them.

Chapter 1 provides a brief summary of the history of doping and the development of anti-doping regimes, then outlines the key principles developed in relation to doping liability before the Code. It explains the role of CAS in developing the principles applied in anti-doping matters and in interpreting and applying the Code on appeals, and outlines the current 2016 CAS procedural rules applicable in anti-doping matters.

Chapter 2 gives a general overview of the provisions of the Code and the International Standards, and explains how they operate together to form the World Anti-Doping Program. The chapter also contains a summary of the main provisions of the International Convention against Doping in Sport 2005, by which State parties agree to take action to support the Code.

Chapter 3 outlines the central role of the International Standard Prohibited List and the system of testing for anti-doping violations in more detail, and explains how substances are included in the Prohibited List by WADA. It explains the contents of the current International Standards.

Chapter 4 discusses the general principles and provisions relevant to the interpretation and application of the Code.

Chapter 5 comments on Articles 1 and 2 of the Code, which contain the key provisions outlining the anti-doping rule violations.

Chapter 6 discusses the burden and standard of proof applicable to anti-doping rule violations under Article 3 of the Code and the burden and standard applicable in other situations for athletes and others who may have to prove various matters under the Code.

23 Where a violation is discovered which occurred before 1 January 2015, the 2009 Code will apply to it.

Chapter 7 reviews the provisions of the Code relating to results management, reporting and hearings by Signatories. It outlines certain national systems for results management and hearings and explains the provisions of the Code concerned with the responsibility for testing and investigation, confidentiality and reporting, provisional suspension and the mutual recognition of the decisions of other Signatories.

Chapter 8 continues with commentary on the Articles of the Code, explaining the application of Articles 9 and 10, the key Articles relating to the imposition of sanctions, with reference to decisions of CAS and of various national and international tribunals. It outlines the operation of the significantly amended regime for assessing sanctions under the 2015 Code.

Chapter 9 comments on Article 13 of the Code, which provides for appeal rights to national appeal tribunals and CAS. It then discusses the possible grounds for further appeals against CAS awards to the courts.

Chapter 10 discusses the possibility of challenges to the enforceability of the Code before national and supranational courts. It begins by outlining the grounds for challenging CAS awards under Swiss law, then outlines possible challenges to decisions under the Code in national courts. It considers potential civil claims against anti-doping organisations which undertake testing, investigation and results management and discusses possible claims by clean athletes against competitors who are found to have doped. It summarises decisions by the Swiss Federal Tribunal and other national courts on challenges to the Code. In addition, it considers the issues which arise when organisations adopt rules and regulations which can be interpreted as providing further consequences for anti-doping rule violations in addition to the sanctions under the Code.

Chapter 11 explains the process by which the provisions of the Code are reviewed and amended, and discusses areas where the regime under the Code faces challenges. The chapter considers the effectiveness of the Code to date, and how the Code measures up to its stated aims.

Appendix 1 contains some text and case summaries on Article 10.4 of the 2009 Code, drawn from the second edition. Appendix 2 provides Figures 5–8 from the second edition of this text. Appendix 3 reproduces the final chapters of the first and second editions. Like Chapter 11 of this edition, those chapters are concerned with the possible development of the Code as it goes through review, and the material is included to provide some context for and comment on the changes which have taken place in the Code over its evolution.

The Sources of Law in Relation to the Interpretation of the Code

CAS awards produced both before and after the Code are of central importance in understanding the principles which underpin it. The awards also provide those with responsibility for administering and applying the Code with valuable examples of its provisions in action in differing factual circumstances. In addition to publishing the various documents which make up the WADA programme, WADA has developed a legal section on its website which contains the CAS appeals in which WADA has been a party (and those cases where there have been further challenges before the Swiss Federal Tribunal).[24] Beyond this, there are a number of websites which provide the decisions of national-level tribunals, arbitration panels and international sporting federation tribunals on doping matters.[25] The decisions of tribunals established by national anti-doping organisations and international federations also have significance and value, because it is at this level that many decisions under the Code will be made. In addition, from time to time, national courts (in particular the Swiss Federal Supreme Court) and supranational tribunals and courts (such as the European Commission and the European Court of Justice) have considered challenges to findings on doping violations and sanctions, in decisions which are reported in the law reports. The various sources of decisions are diffuse. The goal of harmonisation and consistency has been considerably assisted by the development of the CAS database of cases, but more might, perhaps, be done to provide a coherent commentary and fuller collection of decisions on the Code.[26]

The text refers to decisions from these sources. Agreement to the Code is now widespread in the sporting world, and there is a proliferation of decisions by different CAS Panels and sporting tribunals in areas such as the application of the Code's provisions on sanctions. The text seeks to

24 See Chapter 9, pages 477–8 for the standing of WADA to appeal findings by tribunals and CAS. See also the legal section of the WADA website, www.wada-ama.org, for the cases in which WADA was directly involved. This is a small proportion of the number of CAS awards in the doping area. For an example, see Chapter 9, pages 475–6.
25 See e.g. sporting federations: www.itftennis.com (tennis), www.fina.org (swimming), www.horsesport.org (equestrianism), www.irb.com (rugby) and www.iaaf.org (athletics); NADOs: www.usantidoping.org (USADA); www.adrsportred.ca, www.cces.ca (Sport Dispute Resolution Centre of Canada) and www.uksport.gov.uk (UK Sport).
26 Much in the manner of UNCITRAL in relation to the conventions which it has promoted or is responsible for: see the CLOUT database on the UNCITRAL website, www.uncitral.org.

state the principles applicable under the Code by interpreting the relevant provisions, and to illustrate the principles in action by reference to some relevant decisions, but it cannot and does not reproduce or comment on all the decisions in which a particular provision of the Code has been considered. Indeed, in certain important areas, recourse to a wide range of decisions with differing factual bases is unlikely to assist a tribunal considering a particular matter on its facts. It is the correct interpretation and application of the provisions of the Code to the particular circumstances which is important for the production of accessible reasoned decisions in a timely manner. Clearly, CAS awards and tribunal decisions which interpret Articles of the Code or which set out principles that are relevant to the case before a tribunal will help, but no doctrine of strict precedent applies, and in many cases other decisions do no more than provide examples of the application of provisions of the Code in other factual circumstances. In such cases, a tribunal is more likely to operate effectively and produce a clear accessible decision if it adopts an approach which finds the facts of the particular case before it and applies the relevant provisions of the Code to them.

At the time of finalising the text, in mid to late 2016, the 2015 Code has been in force for approaching two years, and there has, as yet, been relatively limited consideration by tribunals of some of the significant changes it makes. In these areas, the focus of the commentary is on the interpretation and application of the text of the Code, but where possible case summaries applying the 2015 Code are included.

This book does not attempt to engage in any moral or ethical debate over the use of doping to enhance performance in sport, but, rather, to provide a guide to the Code for administrators, participants, their support persons and their advisers. Like most who love sport and the challenges and spectacle which it provides, I have no difficulty in accepting the fundamental premise of the World Anti-Doping Program and the Code. Sport is completely devalued where performance is achieved as a result of taking prohibited substances or using prohibited methods, and ultimately loses its attraction and value, leaving spectators and participants feeling deceived and cheated.

Some recent doping scandals have caused certain people to write despairingly of the death of sport, where the spectator can no longer believe that the athlete's struggle is not artificially aided, and to suggest that the fight against doping may be lost or not worth the effort. There are also those who are prepared to allow sport to drift slowly away, until it becomes a vast doping 'free-for-all' dedicated only to providing spectacle at any cost. In recent times, while doping stories continue and scandals seem to intensify on a daily basis, there does appear to be an ever more coordinated push in and outside sport to have drug-free competitive play. I am content to leave moral and ethical debate to others, and I am happy to endorse the aims of the Code and the need to take every step possible to uphold honest competition. It is still too early to say whether the fight against doping in sport can be won, but the Code has given it considerable impetus, and it does not seem too much to hope that, while cheating will probably always be present in some form where humans compete, the values which underpin true sporting competition may come more strongly to the fore in the years ahead. The challenge is to ensure that the anti-doping rules are clear and are consistently applied, so that doping is tackled by clear, predictable and fair means and those participating in sport know where they stand.[27] I hope that this book can assist in providing a guide to the 'rules of the game' established under the 2015 Code, with illustrations of the rules in action drawn from relevant decisions, which will benefit all involved with or affected by the operation of the rules under the Code.

27 For an early statement from CAS on the need for clear rules if strict liability for doping is to be imposed, see CAS 94/129, *Quigley* v. *UIT* Award 23 May 1995, CAS Digest I, pp. 193 and 194. See Chapter 1, pages 50–2.

1

The Early Development of Principles Relating to Anti-doping Regimes: the Role of the Court of Arbitration for Sport

Background

Disqualification and the imposition of disciplinary sanctions as a response to the offence of doping has been a part of the sporting world for many years. From the 1970s onwards, most sporting bodies, at both national and international level, had rules under which their members submitted to drug testing, and to the imposition of sanctions (primarily in the form of the disqualification of results and a period of ineligibility from competition) in the event that they were found to have committed a violation of the rules. To a significant degree, doping was regulated internationally by the IOC, the body which leads and manages the Olympic movement. The OMADC, produced by the IOC, was applicable to 'the Olympic Games, the various championships to which the IOC granted its patronage and to all sports practiced within the context of the Olympic Movement, including pre-competition preparation periods'.[1] The OMADC was the fore-runner of the WADA Code, and many of the substantive features of the OMADC were adopted by the Code.

OMADC

The IOC anti-doping rules were amended and refined over the years. OMADC 1999, which came into force on 1 January 2000, contained many of the elements which are still found in the WADA Code and the International Standards. Certain important anti-doping principles, such as the concept of the strict liability of the athlete for the presence of any substance or method designated as prohibited in a bodily sample, had been a

---

1 See Preamble to OMADC 1999, which applied to the 2000 Sydney Olympic Games. For the list of international federations which are part of the summer and winter Olympic movement, see Olympic Charter, Rule 46.

feature of earlier versions of the OMADC, and the anti-doping regimes of many sporting organisations, for many years.

OMADC contained provisions relating to the accreditation of laboratories, testing and sampling, the Prohibited List of substances, violations and appeals to CAS against decisions made by the IOC, an international federation, a national Olympic committee or any other sporting organisation. The provisions in relation to sanctions differentiated between certain specified substances and other substances, and laid down a standard minimum period of suspension of two years for doping with a substance which was not one of the specific substances (where a specified substance was detected, a lesser sanction was available). For offences which were more serious, including intentional doping and refusal, OMADC contained a wider range of possible sanctions, including suspension from competition for between two and eight years.[2] For a second offence committed within ten years after an earlier offence, the period of suspension was between four years and life. Fines were also part of the sanctions regime. Consistent with the principle of strict liability, any case of doping in-competition led to the invalidation of the result obtained in the competition where the doping had been detected. OMADC provided that competent international federation bodies could evaluate 'specific exceptional circumstances' so that there might be a possible modification of the standard two-year sanction. As will be outlined later, the 2004 Code changed this regime in important areas, particularly as regards the approach to the imposition of sanctions, but a review of OMADC illustrates the extent to which the Code built on what had been developed over a period of time by the Olympic movement.

Different Approaches

International federations and national Olympic committees which formed part of the Olympic movement had to adopt OMADC. OMADC was also accepted by sports outside the Olympic movement. There were, however, many sporting organisations, at both national and international level, which had their own anti-doping regimes defining and regulating anti-doping violations and sanctions. While, over time, some sports adopted provisions which referred appeals in doping matters under their

---

2　The 2015 Code has in effect reintroduced a separate penalty for certain intentional breaches. See Chapter 8, pages 346–72 for consideration of 'intentional conduct' under the 2015 Code in imposing sanctions, as well as case summaries.

anti-doping policies to CAS, many still continued to hear doping viola-tions in their own tribunals, with, often, internal appeal rights. The differ-ent anti-doping regimes, and the different tribunals which heard allega-tions under them, led, inevitably, to different outcomes for athletes across sports as regards, in particular, sanctions for doping violations.

Court Challenges

In addition to pursuing internal processes and CAS appeals, athletes aggrieved by the decisions of sporting tribunals from time to time brought legal claims before national courts and supranational tribunals such as the European Court of Justice, seeking to strike down anti-doping rules on the basis that they were invalid as being contrary to legal principles protecting such fundamental rights as the right to work, the right to pri-vacy or the right to be free from discrimination. Challenges were relatively rare and usually concerned the legality of the principle of strict liability, under which the presence of a prohibited substance in the bodily sample of an athlete constituted a doping violation without the need to establish any intentional or, indeed, negligent conduct by the athlete, and the sanc-tions imposed for violations under doping regimes. The question raised on behalf of the athletes in such challenges, which were brought under the principles relating to the judicial review of domestic tribunals or as appeals against arbitration awards which applied in the particular jurisdiction, was whether strict liability and/or the particular fixed sanction was in accor-dance with the fundamental principles of human rights applicable in the jurisdiction in question.[3] In some countries, State-funded NADOs were established by legislation to carry out testing and to make determinations

---

3 See e.g. the decision in *Krabbe* v. *IAAF*, Decision of the OLG Munich, 28 March 1996, where the fixed sanction of four years for doping applicable under IAAF Rules at the time was declared to be an infringement of fundamental rights under the German Constitution. This decision is widely seen as the source of the standard two-year period of ineligibility in many anti-doping regimes, which was adopted in the 2004 Code. The *Krabbe* decision represents a rare example of a successful challenge to one aspect of an anti-doping regime on the basis that it infringes fundamental rights. See Chapter 10, where the nature of such challenges to doping regimes is reviewed in more detail. A period of ineligibility of four years was introduced under the 2009 Code where aggravating circumstances were estab-lished in connection with certain anti-doping violations. This provision has been removed under the 2015 Code, and a new standard period of ineligibility of four years has been introduced for intentional breaches of Articles 2.1, 2.2 and 2.6 of the Code. See Chapter 8, pages 346–72 for commentary on 'intentional conduct' in the context of sanctions and gen-erally for commentary on the sanctions regime under Article 10 of the Code.

as to the occurrence of doping violations. In some such national systems, an athlete had the right under the applicable legislation to challenge a determination by the NADO that there had been a doping violation in the national courts, with the relevant NSO handling the result if there was no challenge or no successful challenge.[4]

International Developments

In the domain of public international law, outside the sport-specific rules which operated as a matter of private contract law between sporting bodies and their members, international conventions were produced under which State parties agreed to take measures to combat doping in sport. An early example was the 1989 European Convention on Doping.

Criminal Law: Principles Generally Inapplicable

As has already been noted, conduct which amounts to a doping violation under an anti-doping regime (or the Code) may also give rise to criminal[5] liability under national law. The private disciplinary nature of

4 For an example of testing and investigation by NADOs established under statute, see the position under the earlier Australian and New Zealand legislation, the Australian Sports Anti-Doping Act 2005 and the New Zealand Sports Drug Agency Act 1994. The Australian statutory system continues in force. This system allows for appeals against decisions by the NADO (ASADA) in relation to the commission of anti-doping violations under the Code, addressed to the Administrative Appeals Tribunal (AAT) under the national legal system. This national system sits alongside the hearing process for alleged violations under the Code before sporting tribunals – in Australia, CAS at first instance and on appeal. The New Zealand statutory regime was changed by the enactment of the Sports Anti-Doping Act 2006 and the implementation of the Sports Anti-Doping Rules (SADR) 2007 – currently SADR 2016, which implements the 2015 Code and current international standards. This change removed the process by which the NADO (Drug Free Sport New Zealand) made a determination that a doping infraction had been committed under its statutory functions, which could be appealed in the courts. The position under the current legislation is that the DFSNZ will carry out testing and investigations under the SADR and present evidence in support of an alleged violation of the SADR/Code before the Sports Tribunal, an independent tribunal established by the State. NSOs agree to the application of the Code and to the jurisdiction of the Sports Tribunal by agreeing to the application of the SADR. There is no separate process of determination by DFSNZ with appeal rights to the courts. For a review of the hearing processes under the Code in New Zealand, see David, 'Hearing Anti-Doping Cases in New Zealand'.
5 At the time of writing (mid-2016), there is an increase in the criminalisation of doping in national legal systems and/or political interest in this approach, arising no doubt from the increasing concern over corruption in sports governing bodies. In Germany, proposed criminal legislation governing sports doping and dealing in doping products has recently

doping rules in sport was generally recognised by national courts and CAS at an early stage, with the result that anti-doping regimes were held to function by agreement on an international basis outside national legal systems. Given the nature of anti-doping rules, the fundamental principles of criminal law were generally held by CAS not to be applicable to the process of proving and hearing an anti-doping rule violation under sports anti-doping regimes: what mattered was not the criminal law of a State and the approach which a criminal court would adopt to the proof of an allegation, but the interpretation and application of the terms of the rules of the particular disciplinary regime to which an athlete or other person had agreed. While the point is not entirely free from doubt, it would seem that the anti-doping proceedings are not criminal in nature for the purpose of the application of the principles in the European Convention on Human Rights (ECHR), but should be viewed as civil proceedings of a disciplinary nature.[6] This has a significant effect, because in criminal proceedings, the person who is subject to a charge will usually have a range of protections in respect of fundamental rights in the investigation and trial process (as a result of the consequences to the individual of criminal conviction) which are not available to the same extent in civil or disciplinary proceedings.

Development of Common Principles

While different anti-doping regimes were in operation and were producing different outcomes, over a period of time, through the work of those who drafted anti-doping regimes such as the OMADC and the decisions made by CAS on doping appeals concerning the application of various anti-doping regimes, common principles relating to the interpretation and application of sporting anti-doping rules were developed. The decisions of national courts, when athletes mounted challenges to tribunal decisions, also considered the principles by which doping is regulated in sport, and largely upheld the autonomy and enforceability of anti-doping regimes as

passed into law. See Chapter 2, pages 81–2 for a general consideration of the position where criminal investigation and investigations under the Code coincide. See Chapter 10, pages 524–30 for some examples of civil cases which have come before national courts in the context of anti-doping rule violations.

6 See Chapter 10 for challenges to the Code based on fundamental rights and consideration of the legal characterisation of the regime under the Code. For a discussion of this question, see Jean-Paul Costa, 'Legal Opinion Regarding the Draft 3.0 Revision of the World Anti-Doping Code', https://www.wada-ama.org/sites/default/files/resources/files/WADC-Legal-Opinion-on-Draft-2015-Code-3.0-EN.pdf, as outlined in Chapter 10, page 486, note 6.

a matter of private contract law, which were binding on members of the association in question and did not infringe the fundamental rights of the individual protected by law. Given the central role of CAS in interpreting and applying anti-doping policies, and the role which it is now given under the Code,[7] perhaps the most important court decisions are those of the Swiss Federal Supreme Court dismissing appeals against CAS awards, where it was submitted that the awards, which applied the provisions of sports anti-doping regimes such as OMADC, infringed Swiss public policy in violating fundamental principles relating to fundamental rights.[8]

The Role of the Court of Arbitration for Sport

Starting with its initial decisions in 1986, CAS played an increasingly influential role in the interpretation and application of anti-doping regimes as the number of sporting organisations adopting exclusive appeal rights to CAS increased. From a relatively early stage, well before the advent of the Code, CAS arbitration panels, while not bound by any general doctrine of precedent, sought to build a coherent body of principle relating to the key elements of anti-doping regulation by reference to the decisions of other CAS Panels.[9] The central role which CAS now has in the interpretation of the Code is reinforced by the appeal process under the Code, which makes CAS the mandatory appeal court for international-level athletes and an obvious option for appeal procedures for Signatories for appeals by national-level athletes.[10] When the Code was first implemented in 2004, it sought to build on the principles established by the earlier decisions of CAS on substantive provisions of anti-doping rules and to address areas of uncertainty in the approach to the interpretation and application of those

7 See Chapter 9 for the system of appeals to CAS under Article 13 of the Code.
8 See e.g. *G* v. *FEI*, 1st Civil Division of the Swiss Federal Tribunal, 15 March 1993, CAS Digest I 1986–88, p. 545; *N* v. *FEI*, 1st Civil Division of the Swiss Federal Tribunal, 31 October 1996, CAS Digest 1986–88, p. 585; *N, J, Y, W* v. *FINA*, 2nd Civil Division of the Swiss Federal Tribunal, 31 March 1999, CAS Digest 1998–2000, p. 767; *A and B* v. *IOC and FIS*, 1st Civil Division of the Swiss Federal Tribunal, 27 May 2003, CAS Digest 2001–03, p. 674. These cases all concern appeals to the Swiss Federal Supreme Court seeking to set aside CAS awards, which are international arbitration awards under the Swiss Code on Private International Law. For summaries of these and more recent decisions, as well as further discussion of the nature of the challenges, see Chapter 10.
9 For a consideration of the approach of CAS in this area, see Gabrielle Kaufmann-Kohler, 'Arbitral Precedent: Dream, Necessity or Excuse?' *Arbitration International*, 23(3) (2007), 357.
10 See Chapter 9.

earlier rules, particularly in relation to the imposition of sanctions, which were also reflected in the decisions of various CAS Panels. In the light of the central role CAS has played in the development of general principles in the doping area, and the position which it now occupies in interpreting and applying the Code in its appellate jurisdiction, the development of CAS and its main features as an arbitral institution are now outlined.

The role of CAS in doping cases and whether it functions with sufficient independence was the subject of much discussion in 2015 as a result of the decision in the Munich Higher Regional Court in *Pechstein* v. *DESG and ISU*. This court found that the then applicable CAS Rules were contrary to German competition law and refused to stay proceedings in the national courts brought by Ms Pechstein in which she claimed that a period of ineligibility imposed by CAS for the use of a prohibited method established by analysis of her ABP (and affirmed by the Swiss Federal Court) was illegal under national law. The CAS Rules have been amended since the decision in an effort to address the issue raised. Subsequently, in June 2016, the German Federal Court of Justice reversed the decision of the Higher Regional Court of Munich and held that the agreement to refer an anti-doping allegation to CAS was valid, that CAS was a true court of arbitration and that as a result its award was valid before the German courts. The decisions of both courts are summarised and discussed further in Chapter 10, pages 513–17.

CAS Rules

CAS is an arbitral institution providing arbitral and mediation services to sporting organisations in accordance with established procedural rules.[11] CAS was founded, as a result of an initiative from the IOC, as a court devoted specifically to sports disputes. In 1983, the IOC ratified the statutes of CAS. The statutes came into force in 1984 when the court started to operate. As with any arbitral method of resolving disputes, the jurisdiction of CAS over a dispute depends on the agreement of the parties to refer disputes to CAS, and without such an agreement, CAS will have no jurisdiction.[12] Initially, CAS offered first-instance arbitration only,

---

11 CAS now operates under the Code of Sports Related Arbitration (2017 edition). This is the most recent edition of the CAS Code. The amendments from the 2016 Code are relatively minor.

12 For case summaries where there was no jurisdiction to hear an appeal brought before CAS because there was no agreement to submit the matter to CAS, see Chapter 2, pages 72–7. Similarly, a party cannot be joined to an arbitration before CAS without its agreement. See e.g. CAS 2009/A/1870, *WADA* v. *Jessica Hardy and USADA*, in Chapter 8, pages 413–14.

together with a procedure for giving advisory opinions, which is no longer available.

Gradually, international federations began to use the standard CAS arbitration clauses giving exclusive jurisdiction to CAS for sports-related disputes where such disputes could not be settled amicably.

An appeals arbitration jurisdiction (and a standard arbitration clause) was developed, and as a result, more doping cases came before CAS in the form of appeals from the decisions of sporting tribunals.[13] From the early 1990s onwards, a good deal of the work of CAS has involved doping appeals. The central position of CAS in hearing appeals brought by international-level athletes in respect of anti-doping rule violations is now confirmed by Article 13.2.1 of the Code.[14]

Independence of CAS

The degree of connection between CAS and the IOC, both under the CAS Procedural Rules and in a practical sense,[15] led to comment by the Swiss Federal Tribunal, on an appeal against a CAS award, concerning the possible lack of independence of CAS where the IOC was a party to a dispute (although that was not the position in the particular case before the court for decision).[16] This concern led to the reform of CAS in 1994 and the creation of the International Chamber of Arbitration for Sport (ICAS), a body of twenty high-level jurists appointed by the international federations, the Association of National Olympic Committees (ANOC) and the IOC, and by the jurists appointed by those organisations. ICAS members are appointed for renewable periods of four years. They cannot appear on the list of CAS arbitrators, nor act as counsel in CAS proceedings. ICAS has 'the aim of ensuring the protection of the rights of the parties before CAS and the absolute independence of this institution'.[17] Like CAS, the seat of ICAS is in Lausanne, Switzerland.

---

13 In 2003, disciplinary cases accounted for 40 per cent of the work of CAS, most of which were doping matters. See Matthieu Reeb (ed.), *Recueil des sentences du TAS: Digest of CAS Awards III 2001–3* (The Hague: Kluwer Law International), pp. xxvii–xxxv for a summary of the development of CAS, with a summary of the types of dispute submitted to it from its establishment until 2003 at p. xxxiii. In the same volume, at pp. 771–2, the statistics for cases referred to CAS from its establishment until 2003 are set out.
14 See Article 13.2.1 of the WADA Code, and see Chapter 7, where the hearing of appeals under the Code is outlined and discussed.
15 At the time, the IOC financed CAS, could modify CAS Statutes and had considerable powers to appoint arbitrators to CAS.
16 *G v. FEI* (see note 8); Chapter 10, pages 506–7.
17 For the operation of ICAS in relation to CAS, see Statutes 6–11 of the CAS Procedural Rules. ICAS or the Board of ICAS is exclusively responsible for handling any challenges

After the reorganisation of CAS and the creation of ICAS, a further challenge to the independence of CAS where the IOC was a party to proceedings was made by disqualified Olympic cross-country skiers who brought a public law appeal under the Swiss Federal Code on Private International Law[18] against a CAS award. This appeal was rejected by the Swiss Federal Court.[19]

> The plaintiffs submit ...that the CAS is not an independent tribunal in a dispute in which IOC is a party. On the basis of Article 190, paragraph 2(a) LDIP, in conjunction with Article 6, paragraph 1 ECHR and Article 30, paragraph 1 of the Constitution, they argue that the two awards in which IOC named as a party should be set aside ...Under the terms of Article 13.2.1 of the new WADA Code, the CAS is the appeals body for all doping-related disputes related to international sports events or international-level athletes. This is a tangible sign that States and all parties concerned by the fight against doping have confidence in the CAS. It is hard to imagine that they would have felt able to endorse the judicial powers of the CAS so resoundingly if they had thought that it was controlled by the IOC.
>
> *To conclude it is clear that the CAS is sufficiently independent vis-à-vis the IOC as well as other parties that call upon its services, for decisions in cases involving the IOC to be considered true awards, equivalent to the judgments of State Courts.* [emphasis added]

The recent *Pechstein* case raised again the question whether the CAS process guaranteed sufficient independence in its appointed arbitrators given the position of athletes facing anti-doping rule violations under the Code. P contended that the process of appointment of arbitrators to the CAS List created a bias towards sports governing bodies, with the result that insisting on agreement by athletes to such an arbitral process infringed German competition law. This argument was rejected on appeal, as outlined earlier. The German Federal Court of Justice did not find that this method of appointing arbitrators created an appearance of bias, particularly where athletes and sporting organisations could be expected to have aligned interests generally in relation to combating doping in sport.

Discussion of the broader policy issues raised by this kind of challenge is beyond the scope of this text, which focusses on the interpretation and operation of the rules under the Code. However, it is difficult to see

---

to an arbitrator appointed on the grounds of legitimate doubts over the arbitrator's independence (see Rule 34 of the Code of Sports Related Arbitration). See pages 25–6.

18 Known in English as PILA. See Chapter 10, pages 487–9 for a discussion of the nature of various challenges to CAS arbitration awards.

19 *A and B* v. *IOC and FIS* (see note 8).

challenges to the referral of allegations under the Code to CAS which are based on general allegations of unfairness in the procedures, succeeding, where CAS, like the Code itself, has broad support from sporting organisations and from State parties to the UNESCO Convention which agree to support the Code, which has CAS as the central hearing body. It is suggested that, under the current rules, there is no unfairness which is likely to lead to a national court finding that fundamental rights are engaged to the extent that they require a reference to CAS to be disregarded and/or an award to be set aside and not upheld. In general terms, the acceptance of an arbitral court as the tribunal responsible for decisions under the Code is consistent with the general movement to support the use of arbitration. Sport long ago chose to refer disputes to specialist tribunals (whether internal or external to the sporting organisations involved), and it seems that only a specialist independent arbitral forum is capable of providing the kind of dispute resolution process which sport requires to meet its needs. CAS has operated for over thirty years in that role, and has been given a specific appellate role under the Code since the Code was first accepted in 2004. It seems likely that CAS will continue in the role, with any necessary procedural or structural reform being carried out in order to address any issues as to the process before it.

Code for Sports Related Arbitration

CAS functions under a Code for Sports Related Arbitration and Mediation ('CAS Procedural Rules'). The fifth edition of the CAS Procedural Rules came into force on 1 March 2013. These rules have been the subject of amendment, and the 2016 edition came into force on 1 January 2016.[20] They state that CAS and ICAS were created 'in order to settle sports-related disputes through arbitration and mediation'.[21] The Rules contain Statutes relating to the functions and operation of both ICAS and CAS, the jurisdiction of CAS and the procedural rules governing the conduct of arbitrations in the ordinary arbitration jurisdiction and in

20 The text refers to the 2016 Edition of the CAS Code. The amendments in 2016 are relatively few in number, although they do make a change to the way in which arbitrators are appointed to the CAS List in S14. For a detailed review of the CAS Procedural Rules, see Despina Mavromati and Matthieu Reeb, *The Code of the Court of Arbitration for Sport: Commentary, Cases and Materials* (Philadelphia, PA: Wolters Kluwer, 2015). Further minor amendments have been made, and they are effective from January 1 2017 – see CAS website, www.tas-cas.org.

21 S1.

the appeals arbitration jurisdiction (as well as the CAS Mediation Rules). Appeals in doping matters are heard under the appeals arbitration jurisdiction. While it is more common for doping allegations to be heard in national-level sports tribunals at first instance, they may be heard before CAS in its ordinary jurisdiction if it has been agreed in particular sporting rules to adopt this course. Allegations may also be heard before CAS in the *Ad Hoc* Jurisdiction where they arise during a major sporting event at which CAS has established an *Ad Hoc* Panel. Recently, at the Rio Olympics, CAS established two separate Ad Hoc Divisions for the first time and appointed arbitrators to both a general Ad Hoc Division and a specialist Ad Hoc Doping Division.[22]

Role of the International Council of Arbitration for Sport

ICAS is the governing body of CAS. Its purpose is to facilitate the resolution of sports-related disputes and to safeguard the independence of CAS and the rights of the parties to it.[23] ICAS is composed of twenty experienced jurists, who are appointed as follows. Four members are appointed by the International Sports Federations, four by the ANOC, four by the IOC, four by the twelve ICAS members appointed by the international federations, national Olympic committees and IOC 'with a view to safeguarding the interests of athletes' and four by the sixteen ICAS members appointed 'from among personalities independent of the bodies designating the other members of ICAS'.[24] Appointments are for four years and can be renewed, with nominations taking place in the last year of the four-year cycle. On appointment, members of ICAS have to sign an undertaking as to total objectivity and independence, and they are bound by the obligations of confidentiality under the CAS Procedural Rules. Members of ICAS are not permitted to be on the list of CAS arbitrators or mediators and cannot act as counsel for any party in proceedings before CAS.[25]

---

22 The two panels sat under rules for each jurisdiction and heard and decided twenty-eight cases. Most were concerned with the eligibility issues involving Russian athletes which were heard in the ordinary Ad Hoc Division – they did not concern sanctions for violations of the Code, but rather the interpretation and application of rules made by sporting organisations which affected the eligibility of athletes who were bound by those rules. See further Chapter 10, pages 530–4.

23 S2.

24 It is this appointment procedure which was said to create the unfairness in the appointment of arbitrators relied on in *Pechstein*. It was contended that the fact that sporting organisations appoint more members of ICAS, who in turn appoint the arbitrators to the CAS List, meant that there was a structural bias against athletes. See Chapter 10, pages 513–17 for the case summary.

25 SS4–5.

Under its Statutes, ICAS elects a President, two Vice-Presidents, one President of the CAS Ordinary Arbitration Division and one President of the CAS Appeal Arbitration Division (and two deputies) from among its twenty members every four years. ICAS functions either by itself in plenary session or through its Board, which comprises the elected President and two Vice-Presidents, the President of the Ordinary Arbitration Division and the President of the CAS Appeals Arbitration Division. ICAS cannot delegate its functions in electing officers and approving the ICAS budget and CAS accounts to its Board. ICAS is responsible for the adoption and amendment of the Code for Sports Related Arbitration, the appointment of arbitrators and mediators to the CAS List,[26] the resolution of challenges to arbitrators, the appointment of the Secretary General of CAS, the financing and supervision of CAS offices and the setting up of regional or local, permanent or *ad hoc* arbitration structures. Perhaps most importantly, ICAS has the general power to take such action as it deems necessary to protect the rights of the parties to an arbitration and, in particular, best guarantee the total independence of its arbitrators, as well as to promote the settlement of sports-related disputes through arbitration.[27]

ICAS has to meet whenever the activity of CAS so requires it, and at least once a year. Quorum at a meeting is ten members. Any modification of the CAS Procedural Rules requires a two-thirds majority of the ICAS members. The elected President of ICAS is also the President of CAS. The Board of ICAS meets at the invitation of the ICAS President, and the CAS Secretary General takes part in ICAS Board meetings as Secretary to the Board and has a 'consultative' voice.

Where ICAS is called upon to resolve a challenge to an arbitrator, a member of ICAS or the Board may be challenged where the circumstances cast doubt on his or her independence in relation to any party to the arbitration with which the challenge is concerned. A member of ICAS has to disqualify him or herself where ICAS is called upon to make a decision in respect of an arbitration where a party is a sporting body to which the ICAS member belongs or where a member of a law firm to which the member belongs is acting as counsel or arbitrator.[28]

CAS Composition and Organisation

Under its Statutes, CAS constitutes Panels from persons designated by ICAS as arbitrators and mediators which have the responsibility of resolving disputes in sport by arbitration and/or mediation. CAS is composed of

26 See SS13–19.   27 SS6–7.   28 SS8–11.

two divisions – the Ordinary Arbitration Division and the Appeals Arbitration Division – and arbitration proceedings submitted to CAS are assigned to the appropriate Division by the Court Office. Each Division is responsible, through its President or deputy, for the smooth running of proceedings which are referred to it under the CAS Procedural Rules.

CAS provides the infrastructure to conduct arbitrations and oversees the efficient conduct of proceedings. CAS has a Court Office with a Secretary-General and counsel. The Court Office assigns proceedings submitted to CAS to one or other of the Divisions according to the nature of the proceedings. The assignment of the proceedings is not capable of challenge by the parties. The proceedings may be reassigned to another Division by the Court Office in the event of a change of circumstances after consultation with the Panel.

The President of a Division may be challenged where the circumstances give rise to legitimate doubts with regard to his or her independence in relation to one of the parties to an arbitration assigned to the Division. The President must disqualify him or herself where arbitration proceedings assigned to the Division involve a sports body to which he or she belongs or if a member of a law firm to which the President belongs is acting as arbitrator or counsel. ICAS will decide on the challenge. If there is a successful challenge, the Deputy President will assume the responsibility for the proceedings. The mission of CAS is to set in operation Panels which have the task of providing, by arbitration and/or mediation, for the resolution of disputes within the field of sport in accordance with the Procedural Rules.

The list of CAS arbitrators and mediators is established by ICAS. ICAS appoints persons to the list of arbitrators who have appropriate legal training, recognised competence in sports law and/or international arbitration, a good knowledge of sport in general and a good command of at least one of the CAS working languages (French and English). Such persons' names are brought to the attention of ICAS by the IOC, international federations and national Olympic committees and by the athletes' commissions of the IOC, international federations and national Olympic committees, among other sources.[29]

---

29 S14. The 2016 amendments add the reference to referral by athletes' commissions, presumably as a result of the point raised in *Pechstein* concerning the dominant influence of sports' governing bodies on the appointment of arbitrators. However, the structural point relied on by the Court in *Pechstein* relied on the rules for the composition of ICAS, which meant that the governing bodies appointed twelve ICAS members. This led, according to the Munich Higher Regional Court, to those governing bodies having a decisive influence

The CAS Statutes further provide that in establishing the list, ICAS has to ensure a distribution of appointees which reflects the various sources of persons proposed for it. It must also ensure a fair representation of the continents and different juridical cultures. Statute 18 requires that those who agree to appointment to the list sign a declaration that they will exercise their functions personally, with objectivity and independence. Those appointed to the CAS List are not permitted to act as counsel for a party before CAS. CAS arbitrators and mediators are bound by a duty of confidentiality and cannot disclose any information relating to CAS proceedings to any third party. ICAS has the power to remove an arbitrator or mediator who acts contrary to the CAS Procedural Rules or in a manner which affects the reputation of ICAS or CAS. An arbitrator may also be removed if he or she refuses to or is prevented from carrying out his or her duties or fails to fulfil his or her duties in a reasonable time.[30]

Outline of CAS Procedural Rules 2016

General Procedural Rules

The CAS Procedural Rules contain general provisions which apply to all arbitrations and specific provisions which apply to the Ordinary Arbitration Division and the Appeals Arbitration Division. In summary, the general rules provide as follows:[31]

- The Procedural Rules apply where the parties have agreed to refer a sports-related dispute to CAS, whether by an arbitration clause inserted into a contract or, where there is an appeal against a decision by a sports-related body, where the rules of the body provide for an appeal to CAS. This provision identifies the central requirements for jurisdiction: that there is agreement to arbitrate the dispute before CAS and that the dispute is 'sports-related'.[32]
- The seat of CAS and of each Arbitration Panel is Lausanne, Switzerland. The hearing can be held in another place should the President of the Panel or the President of the CAS Division so decide, but this will not change the seat of the arbitration.[33]

---

on the appointment of arbitrators to the CAS List, thereby putting the independence and neutrality of CAS in issue. This point was found to be without merit on appeal by the German Federal Court of Justice. For a case summary, see Chapter 10, pages 513–17.

30 The requirement to fulfil duties in a reasonable time was included in the amendments to the Code which came into effect on 1 January 2012. The provision is in Rule 35 of the CAS Procedural Rules 2016.

31 Articles R27–37.   32 Article R27.   33 Article R28.

- The CAS working languages are English and French. In the absence of agreement between the parties as to the language to be used in the arbitration, the President of the relevant CAS Division will select one of the two languages as the language of the arbitration. The parties can request that another language be used, and this can be the language of the arbitration provided the Panel and the CAS Court Office agree. The language chosen or directed to be used in the arbitration will be used during the entire proceedings. An order on the language to be used in proceedings will usually be made at the beginning of the proceedings.[34]
- Parties may be represented or assisted by persons of their choice in arbitration before CAS. Those chosen as representatives need not be lawyers, although generally the increasing complexity of work before CAS means that parties are represented by lawyers. Where a party is represented, he or she has to provide written confirmation of that representation to the CAS Office. ICAS has established Guidelines for the administration of a Legal Aid Fund and parties to arbitrations may apply for the assistance of *pro bono* lawyers. A decision on whether to grant legal aid to a party is made by the President of ICAS and is not subject to appeal.[35]
- Notifications and communications by CAS or the Panel for the parties are made through the CAS Office by sending them to the addresses set out in the documents filed in the proceedings.
- Orders and decisions made by CAS and the Panel can be notified by courier and/or facsimile and/or electronic mail provided the method used permits proof of receipt.
- The request for arbitration, the statement of appeal and any other written submissions have to be filed by courier delivery by the parties at the CAS Court Office. Documents annexed to written submissions may be filed electronically. Written submissions themselves may be filed in advance by facsimile or email to the official CAS email address. The filing is valid for the purposes of timing on receipt of the facsimile and email by the CAS Office provided that the written submission and copies are also filed by courier by the first subsequent business day after the applicable time limit.

---

34 Article R29. There have been several recent CAS arbitrations concerning doping allegations where other languages, such as Spanish and Italian, have been used by agreement between the parties and CAS. See e.g. the CAS award in relation to the Italian cyclist Riccardo Riccò, TAS 2008/A/1698. English has been used in about 75 per cent of all arbitration procedures before CAS up to August 2014. See statistical graph in Mavromati and Reeb, *The Code*, p. 89.
35 Article R30.

- There is specific provision for electronic filing of submissions, but this method of filing can only be activated after the filing of the request for arbitration or the statement of appeal, which must be done by courier delivery.[36]
- The running of time under the Rules begins from the day after the date of notification to CAS. Holidays and non-working days are included in the calculation of time. A time limit will be met where the communications are sent before midnight at the place where the notification has to be made on the day when the time limit expires. Where a time limit would expire on a holiday or non-business day in the place where notification is to be made, it will be extended to the end of the next business day. Time limits may be extended by the President of the Division, if warranted by the circumstances, and provided the time limit has not already expired. The time limit for the filing of the statement of appeal is an exception and cannot be extended. Failure to file the statement of appeal in time in the correct way will mean that the appeal is inadmissible.[37]
- Arbitrators must remain independent of the parties and must disclose any circumstance likely to affect their independence. Every arbitrator has to be taken from the list of arbitrators drawn up by ICAS and must have a good command of the language of the arbitration and be available to complete the arbitration expeditiously. The independence of an arbitrator can be challenged under the CAS Procedural Rules within seven days of the ground of the challenge becoming known. The determination of a challenge to an arbitrator's independence is a matter within the exclusive power of the ICAS Board, which may either decide the challenge itself or refer it to ICAS in plenary session. A determination on a challenge by the ICAS Board or ICAS will be made after the challenged arbitrator and the other arbitrators appointed have been asked to provide written comment. Brief reasons have to be given for the decision, and the decision may be published by ICAS.[38] If ICAS refuses to give a decision on a removal, the question can be referred to the Swiss Federal Tribunal under the applicable Swiss legislation.
- In addition to the power of ICAS and its Board to rule on a challenge to an arbitrator, ICAS may remove an arbitrator if he or she does not carry out his or her duties in a reasonable time. Removal on this basis is

36 Article R31. 37 Article R32. For further considerations of appeals, see Chapter 9.

38 Articles R33–34. For an example of a decision by ICAS on a challenge to the independence of an arbitrator, see CAS 2012/A/2012, *Brescia Calcio S.p.A.* v. *West Ham United FC*. For further consideration of the obligations of independence and impartiality of arbitrators as part of the right to a fair hearing under Article 8 of the Code, see Chapter 7, pages 321–4.

a matter for ICAS and cannot be requested by a party to the arbitration. Where removal for this reason is considered, the parties and the arbitrator in question, as well as other arbitrators, will make written comments. ICAS will provide brief reasons for its decision. An arbitrator who has been successfully challenged or removed or who has died or resigned from his or her appointment will be replaced and the proceedings will continue without repeating any steps taken before replacement.[39]

- Applications can be made for provisional or conservatory measures provided all internal legal remedies available under the rules of the sporting body concerned in the proceeding have been exhausted. Where the parties have agreed to submit a dispute to arbitration before CAS, whether in the ordinary or the appeal arbitration procedure, they agree to waive their rights to request provisional or conservatory measures from State authorities.[40] Applications for provisional measures will usually be made at the beginning of proceedings. They will be considered by either the President of the relevant Division of CAS or the CAS Panel (where the file has been transferred to the Panel). On an application being made, the CAS Court Office Fee of CHF 1000 has to be paid. The time for a response to an application for provisional measures is ten days, or less if the circumstances require. In ruling on an application, the President or Panel first determines whether CAS has jurisdiction over the case. If CAS has jurisdiction, the President or Panel must decide whether the relief sought is necessary to protect the applicant from irreparable harm, consider the likelihood of success on its merits and determine the balance of interests between the applicant for the orders and the respondent.

Ordinary Arbitrations: Special Provisions

The special provisions applicable to the Ordinary Arbitration Procedure begin with provision for the form of the Request for Arbitration and the material which has to be filed by the party referring the dispute to arbitration in order to start the arbitration proceedings. On filing its

---

39 Articles R35–36.
40 Article R37. Applications for provisional measures in doping cases are likely to involve applications for an athlete to train and/or compete pending a hearing of either the initial allegation or an appeal. Such applications can of course arise in doping cases in ordinary proceedings where CAS is used for first-instance hearings or in the appeal jurisdiction where an athlete challenges a ban or an anti-doping organisation challenges a decision. For an example of an application for provisional measures in a doping matter which has been dismissed, see CAS 2000/A/274, S v. FINA, 26 May 2000, CAS Digest II 1998–2000, p. 755. For further consideration of these applications, see Chapter 7, pages 310–12.

request, the Claimant must pay the Court Office Fee under Rule 64.1. This fee, which is payable in all CAS arbitration proceedings, has recently been increased to CHF1000. The fee is not refunded at the conclusion of the arbitration but is taken into account when the Panel assesses the final amount of costs in the arbitration. The documents which have to be filed to start an ordinary arbitration include a brief statement of the facts and legal argument concerning the issue which is to be submitted to CAS, the contract containing the arbitration agreement and any relevant information about the number and choice of arbitrators, including the name and address of the arbitrator chosen by the Claimant. If the requirements for the documents to be filed are not fulfilled when the Request for Arbitration is filed, a short extension may by granted to remedy the position, but if the requirements remain unsatisfied, the Request for Arbitration will be deemed withdrawn. Filing has to be by courier to the CAS Court Office in accordance with Article R31. The arbitration proceedings will start when the CAS Court Office receives the complete request for arbitration.

Unless there is clearly no arbitration agreement referring the dispute to CAS, and thus no jurisdiction for the proceeding before CAS, the CAS Court Office has to take all appropriate steps to set the arbitration in motion. It will ask the Respondent for its position on the law applicable to the dispute and on the number of arbitrators and choice of arbitrator – in particular, its appointee from the CAS List. It will direct the filing of an answer to the Request for Arbitration and will set time limits for the process. There is no specific time limit for the filing of an answer, and the Respondent can ask for the time to be extended until after the applicant has paid the advance of the arbitration costs required under Article R64.2. The answer has to contain a brief statement of defence, any defence of lack of jurisdiction and any counterclaim.[41]

If a jurisdictional objection is raised, the Panel has power to rule on its own jurisdiction and will do so after the parties have presented written submissions. Any ruling will be by way of a preliminary decision or in an award on the merits. This determination will be made irrespective of any legal action pending before a State court unless substantive grounds require a suspension of the arbitration proceedings.

---

41 A claim that there is no jurisdiction for the arbitration should be made before any defence on the merits is filed because, if a defence on the merits is filed, there will be a deemed waiver of jurisdictional challenge under the Swiss Private International Law Act (PILA) (which reflects the principles under the UNCITRAL Model Law on Commercial Arbitration).

Appointment of Arbitrators

The Panel will be formed by the appointment of arbitrators in accordance with the arbitration agreement. If there is no provision for the number of arbitrators in the arbitration agreement, the President of the Division will determine whether the Panel will be one or three arbitrators, taking into account the nature of the dispute. If the parties have not agreed on the manner of appointment of the arbitrators, the process of appointment under the Rules will apply. If a sole arbitrator is to be appointed, the parties have to make the appointment by mutual agreement within a time limit of fifteen days from the time of the receipt of the request for arbitration. If the parties cannot agree, the appointment will be made by the President of the Division.

If three arbitrators are to be appointed, the Claimant and the Respondent have to provide their appointments within the time limits set by the CAS Court Office. If no appointment is made, the President of the Division will make the appointments. The two arbitrators appointed then select a President for the Panel within a further period of time set by the CAS Court Office. Again, the President of the Division will appoint if the two arbitrators fail to do so. Where arbitrators are nominated by the parties, they have to be confirmed in their appointment by the President of the Division, who must ascertain that the arbitrators meet the requirements under the Rules. Upon the formation of a Panel, the CAS Court Office will fix the amount which must be paid by the parties as an advance on the costs of the arbitration under Rule 64.2 and will fix a time for payment of the sum to the CAS Court Office. Once a Panel has been formed by this process, the CAS Court Office will transfer the file to the arbitrators. This step will not be taken if the parties have not paid the advance for the costs of the arbitration, which is fixed by the CAS Court Office under Rule 64.2.

Where multi-party arbitrations are concerned, the provisions applicable in the ordinary arbitration procedure under Rule 41 are applicable in the Appeal Division. If the Request for Arbitration names several Claimants and/or Respondents, the Panel will be formed in accordance with the number of arbitrators and method of appointment agreed to by the parties. If there is no such agreement, the President of the Division will decide on the number of arbitrators.[42]

---

42 For an example of a multi-party arbitration, see CAS *Yegorova and Others* v. *IAAF* in Chapter 5, pages 245–6.

Where three arbitrators are to be appointed, and there are several Claimants and/or Respondents, the Claimants and/or Respondents will jointly nominate an arbitrator. In the absence of a joint nomination, the nomination will be made by the President of the Division. Where there are three or more parties with diverging interests, the arbitrators will have to be appointed either in accordance with the agreement of the parties or by the President of the Division. In all cases, the appointed arbitrators will then choose the President of the Panel in the normal way. An *ad hoc* clerk may be appointed to assist the Panel, and the fees of this clerk will be included in the arbitration costs.

Third-Party Joinder and Intervention

Where a Respondent intends to have a third party participate in the arbitration, it has to refer to this in its answer to the appeal and give reasons for the intended joinder. The CAS Office will send a copy of the Respondent's answer on the appeal to the third party, giving the third party a time limit to provide a response to the proposed joinder and its substantive response in the case. The CAS Office must also provide for a period of time in which for the Claimant to express its position on the proposed participation of the third party.

Where a third party wishes to intervene as a party to the arbitration, it has to make an application with reasons for the proposed intervention within ten days of the arbitration becoming known to it. This application must be made before the hearing, or before the close of the evidentiary proceedings if no hearing is held. Again, the CAS Office will communicate the making of the application to the parties to the arbitration, giving them a time within which to express their position on the proposed intervention and file any substantive answer.

A party can only be joined or intervene in the arbitration if it is bound by the arbitration agreement or if it and the parties to the arbitration agree in writing to this course. After the time for responses to an application for joinder or intervention has passed, the President of the Division or the Panel (if one has been appointed) decides on the participation of the third party, taking into account the existence of any arbitration agreement. If the President makes a decision on this question, any Panel which is subsequently formed can make a fresh decision on the question of joinder or intervention.

If the President accepts the participation of the third party, CAS will proceed to form a Panel in accordance with the agreement of all the parties. In the absence of agreement, the President will decide on the number of arbitrators in accordance with the Rules previously outlined.

Where the participation of a third party is permitted, the Panel has to make the necessary related procedural directions and decide on the third party's rights in the proceedings. The Panel may allow parties which are joined or intervene in the arbitration to file *amicus curiae* briefs.

Conciliation

Before the transfer of the file to the Panel, the President of the Division may seek to resolve the dispute by conciliation. After the file has been referred to the Panel, the Panel may also seek to do this. A resolution reached by conciliation may be contained in an arbitration award issued by consent.[43]

Procedure before CAS Panel

The procedure before the Panel places considerable emphasis on the exchange of written material. The parties have to exchange written submissions and written evidence in advance of a hearing. After the submissions and written evidence have been exchanged, the parties cannot produce further written evidence, save by agreement of the parties or if the Panel permits this, in exceptional circumstances. The written submissions by the parties will contain a statement of claim and the response. The documents can contain claims which are not in the original reference to arbitration and response – however, after these documents have been filed, neither party may raise further claims without the consent of the other. The aim of the process is to limit the cases to the arguments and evidence contained in the written documents. The oral submissions made at the hearing and the witnesses heard are limited to the matters and witnesses specified in the written material.

The Panel may give directions for the hearing of witnesses and experts by telephone or video conference and can permit evidence to be received by written statement with the appearance of a witness being excused. The Panel may dispense with the need for a hearing and decide the matter on the basis of the written material after consultation with the parties, if it considers that it is sufficiently well informed about the case. The Panel has power to order a party to produce documents in its custody or control

---

43 Article R42.

on the request of another party where the documents can be shown to be relevant and under the control of the party in question. The Panel can also of its own motion order the production of documents by the parties, hear further witnesses or appoint and hear experts. Where the Panel wishes to appoint an expert, it has to consult with the parties about the appointment and the terms of reference for the expert.

Expedition

Where the parties consent, the President of the Division or the President of the Panel may decide to proceed on an expedited basis. Where the Claimant fails to submit its written submissions, the reference will be deemed withdrawn. Where the Respondent is in default, the Panel may proceed with the arbitration and deliver an award. Similarly, where a party does not appear at a hearing, the Panel may proceed with the hearing and deliver an award.

The Arbitration Award

The award will be written, dated and signed and will contain reasons for the decision. While an award may be made by majority, dissenting opinions are not recognised by CAS and will not be notified to the parties. The law applicable to the merits of the dispute will be the law chosen by the parties or, in the absence of such choice, will be Swiss law. The parties may authorise the Panel to decide the dispute *ex aequo et bono* ('according to principles of fairness and equity'). Proceedings are confidential and the awards are not made public, unless an award provides for publication or all parties agree.[44]

Costs

The costs of arbitration in the Ordinary Division are determined under Rule 64. Upon the formation of a Panel, the CAS Court Office will fix a sum as an advance on the costs of arbitration, which is to be paid by the parties in equal shares. At the end of the proceedings, the CAS Panel determines in its award which party shall bear the arbitration costs and in what proportion. Generally, an award in the Ordinary Division grants the

---

44 For further consideration of the nature of hearings at first instance, and of appeal under the Code, see Chapters 7 and 8.

prevailing party a contribution to its legal fees and other expenses, taking into account the outcome of the proceedings, as well as the conduct and financial resources of the parties.

Special Provisions Applicable to the Appeal Arbitration Procedure

The special provisions applicable to the Appeal Arbitration Procedure provide for an appeal to be filed against the decision of a federation, association or sports-related body, where the rules of the body so provide, or where the parties have concluded a specific arbitration agreement, and provided the appellant has exhausted the legal remedies under the rules of the sport-related body prior to making the appeal.[45]

As in the Ordinary Division, the CAS Code contains provisions relating to the appointment of the arbitrator and the procedure on the appeal. Under the appeal procedure, the appellant has to submit a statement of appeal containing certain specified information and nominating an arbitrator from the CAS List. When the statement of appeal is filed in the CAS Court Office, the appellant has to pay the Court Office fee of CHF1000. The time limit on an appeal is twenty-one days from the receipt of the decision appealed against, unless the rules of the body whose decision is under appeal provide otherwise.[46] As already noted, this time limit is strict and cannot be extended. The running of time will be calculated as set out in Rule 32, with official holidays and non-working days not included in the calculation. A time limit will be met if the relevant documents are sent by midnight on the last day of the time limit at the place where notification has to be made. Where the last day of the time limit falls on an official holiday or on a non-business day, the time limit will expire at the end of the first subsequent business day.

The Statement of Appeal has to contain the name and full address of the Respondent, a copy of the decision appealed against, the appellant's request for relief, the name of the arbitrator nominated by the appellant (unless the appointment of a sole arbitrator is requested), any application to stay the execution of the decision appealed against, with reasons in support, and a copy of the statutes and regulations which provide for the appeal to CAS.[47]

An appeal will be submitted to a Panel of three arbitrators, unless at the time the appellant's statement of appeal is lodged the appellant establishes that the parties have agreed to a sole arbitrator or the President of the

---

45 Article R47.   46 Article R49.   47 Article R48.

Appeal Division decides to submit the appeal to a sole arbitrator given the circumstances of the case. Where two or more cases clearly have the same object, the parties can be invited to refer them to the same Panel by the President of the Appeal Division. If the parties do not agree to this course, the President will decide whether the cases should be referred to the same Panel.[48]

Within ten days of the end of the time limit on the lodging of the statement of appeal, the appellant has to file its appeal brief. This document sets out the applicant's full case on the facts and the law, contains all the exhibits relevant to the appeal and specifies the evidence on which the appellant will rely. It includes witness statements. The appellant may inform the CAS Office in writing that the statement of appeal is to be considered as the appeal brief where it wishes to adopt this course. If an appeal brief is not filed or no statement is made that the statement of appeal is the appeal brief within the time limit, the appeal is deemed to be withdrawn.[49]

Unless it is clear that there is no binding arbitration agreement referring the appeal to CAS, or that the arbitration agreement relied on does not cover the dispute raised such that there is no jurisdiction for the appeal, CAS will set the arbitration in motion after the filing of a statement of appeal and the appellant's brief.

The CAS Court Office will provide the statement of appeal to the Respondent, and the President of the Appeal Division will form a Panel to hear the matter. The President also has to decide promptly on any application for a stay of any order appealed against. This involves a consideration of whether the requirements for the grant of provisional measures have been fulfilled. CAS will also send a copy of the statement of appeal and appeal brief to the body which has issued the decision challenged on appeal. The President of the Division may make directions for the appeal to proceed in an expedited manner where that is appropriate.

Unless the parties have agreed on a sole arbitrator or the President considers that the appeal is an emergency and must be submitted to a sole arbitrator, the Respondent has to nominate an arbitrator within ten days of receiving the statement of appeal.

If a hearing by a sole arbitrator has been agreed to by the parties or ordered by the President, the President formally appoints the sole arbitrator on receipt of the statement of appeal. If the appeal is to be heard by a Panel of three arbitrators (as is usually the case on appeals under the Code), the President of the Division appoints the President of the Panel

48 Article R50.   49 Article R51.

after the Respondent has nominated its arbitrator. The President consults with the two arbitrators appointed by the parties as to the nomination of the President of the Panel. The appointment of the arbitrators will only occur in the formal sense when the President confirms it. Before confirming the appointment, the President has to check that the arbitrators are qualified and independent, as required by Rule 33.

When a Panel has been formed to hear the appeal, this is noted by the CAS Court Office and the case file is transferred to the arbitrators. This step can only occur if the parties have paid the advance of the CAS costs required under Rule 64.2. An *ad hoc* clerk can be appointed to assist the Panel. The fees of the clerk will be included in the arbitration costs.

The provisions of Rule 41, with appropriate amendment relating to multiple Claimants and Respondents, as well as joinder and intervention, are applicable to the appeal procedure.

The Respondent has to file its substantive answer to the appeal within twenty days of receiving the appeal brief. This response has to contain a statement of defence on jurisdiction (if applicable) and substance, listing the various documents, exhibits and evidence which will be relied on by the Respondent.[50] If an objection is raised by the Respondent as to CAS's jurisdiction, the Panel (if constituted) or the CAS Court Office must invite the parties to make written submissions on this question and may rule on this point in a preliminary decision or in a final award on the merits.

If the Respondent fails to provide a brief in answer to the appeal brief, the Panel may proceed with the arbitration and deliver an award.

Where the appeal brief and Respondent's answer have been filed, the parties are not permitted to supplement their cases or produce new exhibits or specify further evidence, save where they agree to this course or the President of the Panel so orders on the basis of exceptional circumstances. While the time limit for filing documentary material is very important in bringing about prompt hearings, a Panel may decide to receive late submissions or evidence if there are substantiated exceptional circumstances justifying this course. This will involve a substantiated explanation as to why the further submissions or evidence are relevant and why they have to be filed late. The Panel can at any time seek to resolve the dispute by conciliation. If it does so, the settlement reached may be the subject of a consent arbitral award.[51]

---

50 Article R55.   51 Article R58.

On the hearing of the appeal, the Panel has full power to review the facts and the law on an appeal under Article R57. This provision has had particular importance in doping appeals, in providing the means to address complaints that an allegation has not been the subject of a fair hearing before a sporting tribunal.[52]

The law applicable to the merits of the appeal will be the law chosen by the parties, or, in the absence of such a choice, the law of the country in which the federation, association or sports-related body which has given the decision under appeal is domiciled, or else the rules of law which the Panel deems appropriate.[53] The award will be expressed to be final and binding on the parties, and may not be challenged on the basis that the parties have no domicile, habitual residence or business establishment in Switzerland, or that they have expressly excluded all setting-aside proceedings in the arbitration agreement.

As already noted, dissenting opinions are not recognised by CAS and are not notified. The Panel can communicate the operative part of the award before giving its reasons. The award has to state brief reasons. The Rules contain no specific provision for confidentiality in the appeal process, although it is submitted that, as with arbitrations generally, the procedure and hearings will be confidential, unless the parties have agreed otherwise. Under the Rules for an appeal, the arbitration award, a summary and/or a press release will be published by CAS, unless the parties agree to the contrary. Generally, CAS appeal awards, including athletes' names, are published where the anti-doping rule violation is established.[54] Once the award has been rendered in proper form and notified to the parties, it is final and binding between the parties and can be enforced. The award can be the subject of further challenge by way of a proceeding applying to the Swiss Federal Tribunal to set it aside. The available grounds of challenge are narrow under the applicable Swiss legislation: the Swiss Private International Law Act (PILA).[55]

---

52 Article R57 has often been relied on in doping matters by CAS Panels, allowing them to re-hear a matter and 'cure' alleged defects in the initial hearing process, where an appellant alleges that there were breaches of natural justice in the proceedings which led to the making of the initial decision. See Chapter 9, pages 479–81.
53 Article R58.
54 Article R59, last paragraph. As regards anti-doping rule violations, Rule 59 reflects the requirements for publication under Article 14.3.2 of the Code where the commission of an anti-doping rule violation has been established. See Chapter 7, pages 315–16.
55 See Chapter 10, pages 487–95 for more detail on challenges to CAS awards to the Swiss Federal Tribunal and issues of enforceability. See Mavromati and Reeb, The Code, pp. 589–95 for statistics on challenges against CAS awards to the Swiss Federal Tribunal.

Cost of Arbitration Proceedings

Under Rule 65, where an appeal is against a decision which is of a disciplinary nature by an international federation or sports body, the fees and costs of the arbitrators are borne by CAS and the arbitration is free of charge to this extent. Rule 65 will apply in doping appeals where the appeal is from a tribunal established by an international federation or a sports body. Rule 65 would appear not to apply to appeals in doping cases heard by independent tribunals, to which NSOs refer allegations under the Code by agreement. It is difficult to justify this restriction on the application of Rule 65 on a principled basis where the independent tribunal in effect replaces a tribunal established by a sporting organisation in the hearing process.

The filing fee of CHF1000 is non-refundable and the funds are kept by CAS. The costs of the parties, expert witnesses and interpreters in the arbitration are advanced by the parties and the Panel must decide which party will bear them, and in what proportion, taking into account the outcome of the proceedings, as well as the conduct and financial resources of the parties. Legal costs will be borne by the parties themselves. The President of the Appeals Division has a discretion to allow the general regime as to costs in the Ordinary Division to apply in an appeals arbitration by his or her own decision or on request of the President of the Panel. This discretion may be exercised in doping appeals where the conduct of one of the parties justifies such an approach. Usually, this will involve a party acting in bad faith or significantly misconducting itself in the proceedings.

Where CAS hears a doping matter in its Ordinary Division, the general provisions as to the costs of arbitration proceedings under Rule 64 will apply. The arbitral award will determine which party will bear the arbitration costs and in what proportion. As a general rule, the prevailing party will be awarded a contribution towards its legal fees and expenses in the proceeding.

Advisory Opinions

Until the amendments to the CAS Code which came into force on 1 January 2012, the CAS Code contained further provisions allowing the IOC, international federations and national Olympic committees to request an advisory opinion on any legal issue with respect to the practice or development of sports or any sports- or sport-related activity.[56] This procedure

---

56 See R60–62 and 66 in the 2012 Code – all now abrogated.

was used in relation to questions raised by international federations concerning the enforceability and compatibility of the anti-doping regime in the Code with legal principles protecting fundamental rights under national legal systems, and other significant issues arising in relation to anti-doping regimes.[57] Under the procedure, the CAS President reviewed a request for an advisory opinion and decided whether the question raised could properly be the subject of an opinion. If it could, the President formed a Panel of one or three arbitrators and designated the President of the Panel. The CAS President formulated the questions arising from the request and forwarded them to the Panel. Where such proceedings were brought, the cost was borne by the party requesting the opinion. The opinion was non-binding and did not constitute a binding arbitration award. In 2012, amendments to the CAS Rules removed this procedure. From a historical perspective, opinions under the procedure have, from time to time, contributed to the understanding and development of the Code. By way of example, the origins of the application of the doctrine of *lex mitior* to the imposition of sanctions in doping violations can be traced to an early CAS advisory opinion.

The CAS *Ad Hoc* Jurisdiction

CAS has developed an *ad hoc* jurisdiction under which it sits during major sporting events such as the Olympic Games, the Fédération Internationale de Football Association (FIFA) World Cup and the Commonwealth Games and decides disputes which arise during and in the ten-days immediately prior to the opening of the event, under specific rules.[58] All competitors agree as a condition of entry to such events that disputes (and appeals from decisions by the IOC, national Olympic

---

57 For examples of advisory opinions, see CAS 94/128, *UCI and CONI*, Advisory Opinion (opinion on competence to establish rules for testing as between international federation as NSO and *lex mitior* principle); CAS 2005/C/976 & 986, *FIFA and WADA*, Advisory Opinion (opinion on questions relating to compatibility of certain provisions of 2004 Code with fundamental principles of Swiss Law); for a fairly recent significant example of the use of this procedure, see CAS 2011/O/2442, *USOC v. IOC*, where the parties sought an advisory opinion on Rule 45 of the Olympic Charter, which bars any athlete who has received a doping sanction of more than six months' ineligibility from competing in the next Olympic Games and Olympic Winter Games. For the content of the CAS advisory opinion, see Chapter 10, pages 523–4. The reason for the removal of the procedure was that it was unilateral. ICAS considered that the process was being used to obtain opinions on existing disputes and that it would be better for such disputes to be subject to adversarial process.

58 Where the arbitration relates to a decision made by the IOC, a national Olympic committee, an international federation or the organising committee of the event, the Claimant

committee, international federation or organising committee of the event) arising during the period of the event will be referred to the jurisdiction of CAS.[59] There have been a number of cases involving alleged doping violations under the Code which have arisen in the context of a major sporting event and have been considered by CAS in its *Ad Hoc* Jurisdiction. For the Rio Olympics in 2016, the CAS Ad Hoc Division sat in two divisions – the Anti-Doping Division and the General Division – under two sets of similar procedural rules based on the CAS Code. The Anti-Doping Division was responsible for hearing at first instance anti-doping rule violations under the Code which occurred during the period of the Games. The General Division considered all other disputes, including eligibility, disqualification and disciplinary cases, usually as an appeal body against decisions made by international federations.[60] The Anti-Doping Division replaced the earlier procedure under which anti-doping rule violations alleged to have been committed during the Games were dealt with by the IOC after recommendations from the CAS Ad Hoc Division. Under the system at Rio, the CAS Ad Hoc Division was solely responsible for the hearing of an allegation under the Code. The sanctions which it could impose were limited to the consequences at the Games (disqualification and loss of result, and exclusion from the Olympic Games), with the period of ineligibility for any breach established being referred to the relevant international federation.[61]

CAS Rules: Particular Aspects of Appeals in Doping Matters under the Code

The procedural rules which govern CAS are of great importance in the context of the Code, because CAS is given exclusive jurisdiction by the

has to exhaust internal remedies, unless the time required for this would make the CAS appeal ineffective.

59 Ad Hoc Divisions of CAS have been convened for the Summer Olympic Games since 1996, for the Winter Games since 1998, for the Commonwealth Games since 1998, for the UEFA European Championships since 2000 and for the FIFA World Cup since 2006. The jurisdiction is expanding: by way of example, there was an Ad Hoc Division of CAS at the 2014 Asian Games. For a description of the operation of the Ad Hoc Division at the Sydney Olympics 2000, see Gabrielle Kaufmann-Kohler, *Arbitration at the Olympics: Issues of Fast-Track Disputes Resolution and Sports Law* (The Hague: Kluwer Law International, 2001).

60 This meant that the various eligibility questions which had to be determined in relation to Russian athletes were under the jurisdiction of the General Division.

61 For a summary of the rules governing the two CAS *ad hoc* tribunals at the Rio Olympics and a discussion of the some of the decisions from a procedural perspective, see Despina Mavromati, 'The Rules Governing the CAS Anti-Doping and Ad Hoc Divisions at the Olympic Games', https://ssrn.com/abstract=2816482.

Code over appeals by international athletes in relation to decisions under the Code, and it may also be chosen as either a first-instance or appeal tribunal for hearings concerning national-level athletes under the Code. Depending on its terms, an agreement to the application of the Code by an individual athlete or an organisation (and its members) is also likely to function as an agreement to the application of the procedural rules of CAS.[62]

The choice of arbitration by an institution with its juridical seat in Switzerland as the method for hearing appeals under the Code has important consequences. Generally, in most jurisdictions which have domestic legislation based on the UNCITRAL Model Law on International Commercial Arbitration ('Model Law') and the 1958 New York Convention on the Enforcement of Foreign Arbitration Awards ('New York Convention'), any challenge to an arbitration award made by CAS that is brought before the courts will only be available on limited grounds, and, where the seat of the arbitration is Switzerland and the arbitration is international in nature, any appeal will properly be a matter for the courts of Switzerland. Under Swiss law, the grounds for challenging arbitration awards (whether domestic or international) reflect the grounds in the Model Law and the New York Convention.[63] Where the arbitration is an international arbitration under Swiss law (which will be the case in many doping appeals where one party is not resident in Switzerland), the rights of appeal will be governed by the Swiss Federal Code on Private International Law (PILA).[64]

Substantive Law Governing Dispute on Appeal

On a doping appeal, CAS will decide the substantive dispute in accordance with the law chosen by the parties, or, in the absence of such a choice, according to the law of the country in which the federation, association or sports body which gave the challenged decision is domiciled, or by such other rules of law as CAS decides should apply to the dispute.[65] CAS Panels, in considering whether a doping regime is enforceable as a matter of public policy, have considered arguments based on the law governing the substantive merits of the dispute, and on the provisions of the legal

---

62 Article 13.2.1 of the Code provides that international athletes may appeal decisions to CAS in accordance with the provisions applicable before CAS. See Chapter 9, pages 472–4.

63 See Chapter 10, pages 487–9 for more on the possible grounds of challenge to CAS awards.

64 See Chapter 10, pages 487–95 on Articles 190–192 PILA and for case summaries and discussion of appeals to the Swiss Federal Supreme Court against CAS awards.

65 In accordance with Article R58.

system to which the sporting organisation concerned or CAS award is subject (Swiss law or the legal system to which the rules of the sporting organisation before CAS are subject).[66] Procedural issues, where they arise in an arbitration, will, unless the parties have agreed on the application of a particular legal system, be determined by the procedural principles applicable by Swiss law to a domestic or international arbitration.

The Development of Fundamental Principles in Anti-Doping Matters by CAS before the Code

CAS began to handle anti-doping cases in increasing numbers during the 1990s, as international federations began to incorporate standard arbitration clauses into their rules and regulations which referred disputes in doping and other matters to CAS. In addition, the Olympic movement, by its Charter,[67] provided for all disputes arising in relation to the Olympic Games to be submitted to CAS. The result of the ever-increasing number of decisions made by CAS in anti-doping matters was that CAS Panels developed and applied a number of key principles concerning the interpretation of anti-doping regimes, the proof of allegations and the imposition of sanctions. The Code, when it was first implemented in 2004, codified certain of the principles which had been adopted by CAS Panels and further developed and refined them.

In disputes concerning doping in connection with Olympic sports, CAS applied and interpreted OMADC. In other cases, CAS interpreted and applied the anti-doping regimes of international federations. By the end of 2003, all Olympic international federations and approximately ten non-Olympic international federations officially recognised CAS as an appeals body, and included in their statutes an arbitration clause in favour of CAS.

The Key Principles Developed by CAS in Doping Cases before the Code

The main principles developed and applied by CAS in anti-doping cases in the period before the adoption of the Code in 2004 can be summarised as follows:

---

66 See e.g. the CAS award in *Eder* in Chapter 10, pages 510–11 and CAS 2010/A/2230, *UK Anti-Doping and Simon Gibbs* in Appendix 1, pages 557–9, where the arbitrator considered arguments concerning the legality of the approach under Article 10.4 of the 2009 Code by reference to the provisions protecting fundamental rights under EU law.
67 Article 74 of the Olympic Charter (now Article 61).

- The application of an anti-doping policy was a question of interpreting the policy in order to determine its intent and effect. CAS Panels noted that they were required to interpret doping policies and rules in a purposive manner, which 'seeks to discern the intention of the rule-maker not to frustrate it'.[68] However, where there was no provision which could be interpreted to have the desired effect or meaning in the anti-doping policy, no purposive approach to the text could fill the gap.[69] In this context, CAS Panels noted that it was incumbent on those who wished to impose strict liability for doping on athletes to do so with clear rules.[70]

- The principle of strict liability was established and applied in relation to many anti-doping regimes, including the OMADC. In the doping context, strict liability meant that the initial burden of proving the presence of a prohibited substance in the body of the athlete fell on the organisation bringing the allegation, whether an international federation, the IOC or another organisation. The presence of a prohibited substance was a matter which had to be considered and determined objectively on the results of the testing process. If the organisation bringing the allegation discharged this burden, the principle of strict liability created a presumption that a doping offence had been committed (provided the provisions of the relevant anti-doping regime were adequately drafted to achieve this). There was no need to prove an intention to cheat by enhancing[71] sport performance through the use of the substance. This approach was endorsed on the ground that imposing a burden on the sporting organisation to prove an intention to enhance sporting performance on the part of the athlete would make the task of fighting drugs in sport impossible, particularly where anti-doping organisations had no coercive powers which might be used in an investigation.

- The counter-balance to the general acceptance of strict liability was that, in matters of interpretation, sporting rules and regulations had to be clear if strict liability were to be imposed on participants. This followed

---

68 See CAS 96/149, *AC* v. *FINA*, relied on in CAS 2000/A/312, *L* v. *FILA*, 22 October 2001.

69 See e.g. CAS 99/A/230, *B* v. *International Judo Federation*, where there was no provision for sanctions for out-of-competition testing in the then rules of the International Judo Federation (IJF) and a suspension was set aside.

70 See CAS 94/129, *USA Shooting and Quigley* v. *UIT* at pages 50–2. This statement has been endorsed many times by CAS Panels over the ensuing years.

71 See e.g. CAS 2000/A/310, *L* v. *International Olympic Committee*, Award of 22 October 2001, CAS Digest of III, 2001–03, p. 127, and various awards cited at p. 132 of this award.

from the severe potential consequences of a strict liability regime for those who could be liable without fault.[72]

- Given the consequences of an adverse finding, the evidentiary standard required of the party bringing an anti-doping allegation was high – this standard was held to be lower than the criminal standard, but higher than the ordinary civil standard. The objective elements of the offence of doping had to be 'established to the comfortable satisfaction of the Court bearing in mind the seriousness of the allegation made'.[73]

- If the party bringing the allegation established the objective elements of the offence of doping to the required standard, the burden of proof shifted to the athlete, who had to produce clear evidence showing, for example, that the required procedure for collecting the sample had not been followed, the chain of custody of the sample had been broken, or there were laboratory errors which called into question the result of the sample analysis.[74] However, in order for errors in procedure to affect the laboratory finding that there was an adverse analytical finding (and, as a consequence, a doping offence), they had to be material in the sense of being capable of affecting the result of the test. This question was approached by asking whether such a material effect on the reliability of the test was a reasonable conclusion to draw from the failures established. Certain aspects of the testing and analysis process, such as the athlete's rights in relation to the B sample opening and analysis, were treated differently and were held to be fundamental safeguards by CAS Panels, which, if not provided, meant that there could be no finding that there had been a positive test and a doping violation on that basis.[75]

- There was no need for the IOC or any other party bringing an anti-doping allegation to prove that the athlete intended to cheat or was at fault in order to establish the offence of doping. If the athlete was found

---

72 See also *USA Shooting and Quigley* v. *UIT*; see note 70.

73 See CAS 2000/A/310, *L* v. *International Olympic Committee* and CAS 98/208, *N, J, Y and W* v. *FINA*, CAS Digest II, p. 234. There are many CAS decisions which have adopted this 'sport-specific' standard of proof, and it is codified in Article 3 of the Code. The standard formerly also applied under the 2009 Code, where the athlete bore an evidential burden in certain circumstances, but this approach has been removed by the amendments in the 2015 Code, and the standard now only applies where an anti-doping organisation carries the burden of proof (see Chapter 6, pages 277–9).

74 See, again, *L* v. *International Olympic Committee* (see note 73) and the cases at p. 133, para. 24 of the Award.

75 See e.g. CAS 91/86, *S* v. *FEI*, Award of 25 June 1992; CAS 2002/A/385, *T* v. *FIG*, Award of 23 January 2003; and CAS 98/184, *P* v. *FEI*, Award of 25 September 1998, pp. 45–6. See also Chapter 5, pages 191–5 for the cases on B sample rights under the Code.

to have a prohibited substance in his or her system, then a violation was established and the athlete had to be disqualified from the competition in which the test took place. This approach was mandated by sporting fairness to other competitors.[76]

- The question whether an athlete had intentionally or negligently committed the offence of doping was held to be relevant to the assessment of the disciplinary sanctions which might be imposed upon the athlete. Some CAS Panels held that they had the general power to vary the sanctions which were set down in anti-doping regimes in order to provide for the particular circumstances of an individual case. As a result, while strict liability always applied to the disqualification of results, CAS Panels, from time to time, held that they were able to vary the period of ineligibility under an anti-doping regime to reflect the circumstances of a particular case.[77]

- From an early stage, CAS adopted and applied the principle of *lex mitior* to the adjudication of anti-doping matters where substantive rules had changed between the time of the commission of the alleged violation and the hearing of the allegation by a tribunal. Generally, an anti-doping allegation will be governed by the rules in force at the time of commission of the alleged anti-doping rule violation (*'tempus regit actum'*). However, where new substantive rules as to sanction come into force after the commission of the alleged anti-doping rule violation which are more favourable to the athlete and are in force at the time when the allegation is heard or there is a hearing as to sanction, then those new rules will be applied.[78]

- CAS tribunals consistently upheld the disciplinary nature of doping regimes (and sanctions undertaken) which were enforceable as a matter of private law, and held that fundamental legal principles

---

76 CAS 94/129, *USA Shooting and Quigley* v. *UIT*, CAS Digest, p. 187 (see pages 50–2).

77 See e.g. CAS 2000/A/317, *A* v. *FILA*, Award of 9 July 2001.

78 See e.g. UCI and CONI Advisory Opinion CAS 94/128, p. 507, relying on the principle 'as a fundamental principle of any democratic regime' by reference to Swiss Law Article 2, para. 2 the Penal Code and Italian Law Article 2 Penal Code. For examples of the application of this principle, see CAS 96/149, *AC* v. *FINA*; CAS 2000/A/289, *UCI* v. *C and FCC*; and CAS 2003/A/507, *Strahya* v. *FINA*, where new FINA Rules giving a two-year suspension were applied despite a four-year period of ineligibility having been mandated at the time of the violation. This principle is important in a regime where the rules are regularly reviewed and changed, and is expressly referred to in the transitional provisions in Article 25.2 of the Code. See further pages 56–7 for two case summaries and Chapter 8, pages 455–7 for comment on the application and operation of transitional provisions in imposing sanctions for breaches of the Code.

established in national legal systems associated with criminal law were not applicable.[79] The Swiss Federal Supreme Court also held, on various appeals, where it was contended that CAS arbitration awards should be set aside on the grounds that they were contrary to (Swiss) public policy, that anti-doping regimes, and the approach taken by CAS to their interpretation and application, did not infringe fundamental principles of human rights and public policy under Swiss law.[80]

Pre-Code CAS Awards Illustrating Fundamental Principles

Strict Liability: Rationale and Need for Clear Rules

CAS 94/129, *USA Shooting and Quigley* v. *International Shooting Union (UIT)*, Award of 23 May 1995, CAS Digest I, p. 187

Q competed as a member of the USA Shooting team in the men's skeet event. He felt ill and took cough mixture prescribed by a doctor. The doctor was shown the list of banned drugs and said that the drug given was not banned.

The cough mixture turned out to contain ephedrine, which was a banned substance. Q won a gold medal. USA Shooting said it did not wish to take up the right to have a third party represent it in the testing of the B sample. It agreed to the nomination by UIT of an observer. The B sample confirmed ephedrine to reasonably high levels. The decision was made by International Shooting to suspend Q for the inadvertent use of medication for three months, disqualify his results and order the return of his medal. As a result, because the event had been designated as an event in which Olympics quota places could be earned, USA Shooting lost a country quota place.

The particular international federation doping rules provided, at the time, that doping meant the use of one or more substances mentioned in an anti-doping list 'for the aim of obtaining an increase in performance'.

79 An exception to this approach is to be found in the application of the doctrine, derived from the criminal law of a number of jurisdictions, of *lex mitior* to the imposition of sanctions as outlined.

80 See e.g. *N, J, Y and W* v. *FINA*, 31 March 1999, 2nd Civil Division of Swiss Federal Tribunal, where an appeal against a CAS award by four Chinese swimmers was dismissed on the grounds that the principle of strict liability, with the shifting of the onus to the athlete, could not be said to infringe the fundamental principles of Swiss law and gave grounds to set aside the CAS award on the basis that it was contrary to public policy. For a summary of the decision, see Chapter 10, page 508.

CAS held that there was no doping violation on the words used in the rules. The decision by the international federation was reversed and the sanction set aside. If strict liability were to be imposed then the wording had to be clear. The anti-doping regulations in question required, on their true construction, that the organisation bringing the allegation establish an intention to increase performance, and no such intention had been established in this case. The justification for strict liability set out in the *Quigley* award, which has been carried through many international federation rules, CAS awards and the Code (see notes to Code under Article 2.1 at page 9 of the Code) was expressed as follows:

> It is true that a strict liability test is likely in some sense to be unfair in an individual case, such as that of Q, where the athlete may have taken medication as the result of mislabelling or faulty advice for which he or she is not responsible – particularly in the circumstances of sudden illness in a foreign country. But it is also in some sense 'unfair' for an athlete to get food poisoning on the eve of an important competition. Yet in neither case will the rules of the competition be altered to undo the unfairness. Just as the competition will not be postponed to await the athlete's recovery, so the prohibition of banned substances will not be lifted in recognition of its accidental absorption. The vicissitudes of competition, like those of life generally, may create many types of unfairness, whether by accident or the negligence of unaccountable persons, which the law cannot repair.
>
> Furthermore, it appears to be a laudable policy objective not to repair an accidental unfairness to an individual by creating an intentional unfairness to the whole body of other competitors. This is what would happen if banned performance-enhancing substances were tolerated when absorbed inadvertently. Moreover, it is likely that even intentional abuse would in many cases escape sanction for lack of proof of guilty intent. And it is certain that a requirement of intent would invite costly litigation that may well cripple federations – particularly those run on modest budgets – in their fight against doping.
>
> For these reasons, the Panel would, as a matter of principle, be prepared to apply a strict liability test. The Panel is aware that arguments have been raised that a strict liability standard is unreasonable, and indeed contrary to natural justice, because it does not permit the accused to establish moral innocence. It has even been argued that it is an excessive restraint of trade. The Panel is unconvinced by such objections and considers that in principle the high objectives and practical necessities of the fight against doping amply justify the application of a strict liability standard.
>
> But if such a standard is to be applied, it must be clearly articulated. This is where we reach the heart of the problem of this case.

The award also refers to some further points of importance in doping cases. It was argued that the provisions for testing procedures were not properly followed as required by the IOC Charter which was applicable at the time. The Panel held that breaches of specific requirements need to be sufficiently material as to 'call into question the validity and correctness of the positive result'. The Panel emphasised that, if strict liability is adopted, 'it becomes even more important that the rules for the testing procedure are crystal clear, that they are designed for reliability, and that it may be shown that they have been followed'.

The award is also important for its observations on one of the grounds of the appeal: the lack of due process before the tribunal. The appellant relied on the provisions of the IOC Charter against doping in sport concerning hearings, and argued that he had not had a proper hearing. While CAS did not have to decide the issue, given its finding on the interpretation of the rules, it observed that an accused can be accorded a right to be 'heard' by being given the opportunity to make written submissions. It also noted that, as long as an appeal to CAS by way of re-hearing is available, a deficiency in the initial hearing process can be 'cured' by the appeal hearing.[81]

Strict Liability Justification for Disqualification: Flexibility in Fixed Sanctions?

Arbitration CAS 95/141, C v. FINA, Award of 22 April 1996

C won a long-distance swimming event and underwent doping control. On analysis, her sample was found positive for etilefrine. C explained in writing that she did not have control over food and drink given immediately before and during a race. The coach admitted that he had accidentally given her a capsule of effortil during later stages of the race. The FFN Disciplinary Tribunal 'abandoned' the idea of punishing her. The International Swimming Federation (FINA) reviewed the matter and imposed a sanction of two years under FINA Rules. On appeal to CAS by C, strict liability for the presence of a banned substance in the body of an athlete was upheld. Disqualification for the event in question could not be questioned but, as regards the level of disciplinary sanction,

---

81 See further Chapter 7 on the requirements for a fair hearing and Chapter 8 on the nature of hearings on CAS appeals.

subjective elements in each case must be taken into consideration. The award expresses the tension between strict liability for the offence and the discretionary flexibility as to sanctions which was developed by some CAS Panels:

> The Panel is of the opinion that the system of strict liability of the athlete must prevail when sporting fairness is at stake. This means that, once a banned substance is discovered in the urine or blood of an athlete, he must automatically be disqualified from the competition in question, without any possibility for him to rebut this presumption of guilt. *It would, indeed, be shocking to include in a ranking an athlete who had not competed using the same means as his opponents, for whatever reason.* [emphasis added]
>
> In conjunction with such a sporting sanction, a disciplinary sanction may also be involved in a doping case. In a majority of cases this is a suspension of the athlete who tested positive. The Panel believes that the different sports rules on sanctions and doping cases should make allowance for an appreciation of the subjective elements in each case for it is, indeed, the task of the sports authorities to establish the guilt of an *athlete in order to fix a just and equitable sanction.* Such flexibility is, moreover, also advocated by the IOC ...The principle of presumption of the athlete's guilt may remain but ...the athlete must have the possibility of shifting the burden of proof by providing exculpatory evidence.
>
> *The Panel believes that a fixed rate system governing sanctions in doping cases is not desirable and the more flexible system, which provides a sliding scale of suspension periods depending on the level of fault of the athlete, is preferable.* [emphasis added]

The Panel found that the penalty was not in proportion to the circumstances of the case given 'the excellent morality and earlier conduct of C in general'. In addition, the circumstances of the case and, in particular, the obscure behaviour of the coach, extenuated the fault of the appellant. The Panel found that suspension from 28 January 1995 to 12 March 1996 was sufficient.

The case is an early example of CAS adopting a flexible approach to the imposition of sanctions in order to arrive at a sanction which it considered to be proportionate. CAS Panels varied in their approach in this area in the period before the adoption of the Code.[82]

---

82 See further pages 57–8.

Review of Fixed Sanctions in Anti-Doping Policies

Arbitration CAS 95/150, V v. FINA, Award of 28 June 1996

Swimmer R took a headache tablet given to her by her coach, V. The tablet contained a banned substance. The coach did not check the contents. R competed. R was warned by FINA, with no further sanction. V was found to have acted 'recklessly' and was suspended (after consideration by FINA) for one year. The coach argued, on appeal to CAS, that he had to have a guilty mind to be responsible for committing a doping offence under FINA Rules. The Panel found that helping or advising a competitor in misuse did not necessarily have to involve a guilty mind in the sense of intending that the competitor would obtain an advantage by using a prohibited substance.

The coach submitted to CAS that the FINA sentence was manifestly excessive. FINA argued that the Panel should not review the suspension provided it was made in conformity with the law, and that all relevant aspects were taken into account. CAS found that it had authority to vary the sanction, and this was not ultimately disputed. The Panel said it was reluctant to intervene with the sanction. The swimmer trusted the coach. R said that she would have satisfied herself if the tablet had been provided by anyone other than the coach or the team doctor. The conduct of the coach was found to fall well below the standard of care and vigilance required of him as a professional and a coach. The coach cooperated fully and was a professional relying on coaching for a living. He could not attend Olympic Games as a result of the offence and would have to bear the stigma of the finding. The suspension was reduced to seven months on the basis of the discretion in the CAS Panel.

CAS 98/214, B v. FIJ, Award of 17 March 1999

B, a French judo player, tested positive for nandrolone. He was a member of the French Judo Federation, which was a member of International Judo Federation (IJF). Two years' suspension, with the second year suspended, was imposed by the French Judo Federation based on French public law. The French Minister for Youth in Sport took the matter to the National Anti-Doping Commission. The minister ordered by decree that B be suspended for a period of one year. The sanction imposed by the Ministry in France did not comply with the IJF's regulation. The IJF increased the suspension. The judo player appealed to CAS, which found the IJF's decision had been taken without reason and without hearing. However, the defects in that decision-making process were cured by appeal.

> A complete investigation by an appeal authority which has full power to hear the case remedies the flaws in the procedure at first instance such as the violation of the right to a hearing.

The appellant challenged whether the analysis supported the finding that there was a prohibited substance. This turned on analysing the approach in relation to testing for levels of nandrolone. CAS held that the evidence supported the finding that a prohibited substance was in the appellant's body and that it had not been produced naturally.

The sentence of the IJF did not have a finite period. It simply stated that it took effect on 2 October 1997 and had to run until the next meeting of the executive of the IJF. The provision of the IJF Anti-Doping Regulations was for a fixed penalty of two years for a first offence. Notwithstanding the provision for a fixed sentence, the CAS Panel found that it had discretion to change the sanction.

> It is undesirable to have a fixed tariff system governing the sanctions in doping cases, a more flexible system being preferred that makes allowance for suspensions with periods whose ranges vary as a function of the athlete's culpability.

The Panel found that a two-year suspension would be disproportionate to the circumstances of the case given the appellant's excellent ethical record, certified by the French authorities and his GP. The appellant was considered to have ingested prohibited substances 'in an isolated case, in unexplained circumstances and/or unexplained reasons'. The Panel imposed a fifteen-month suspension because it would prefer not to impose two years.

Testing Processes, Procedural Failures, B Sample and Application of Lex Mitior Doctrine

CAS 98/184, *P* v. *International Equestrian Federation,*
Award of 25 September 1998, CAS Digest II, p. 197

The CAS Panel found that, in every case where it was alleged there had been departures from procedures, it was important to study the facts.

> If the Panel is satisfied that the sample tested came from the person or horse in question, and that the chain of custody is established, that no question of contamination arises, that the equipment used to test was appropriate and the results were correctly interpreted, then it should not be deterred

from upholding a verdict as to the presence of a prohibited substance merely
because some departure from procedure may be proven, still less because of
matters irrelevant to the validity of the test. [emphasis added]

The Panel rejected most of the complaint relating to the testing process. However, there was an initial negative blood test in addition to the positive urine test of which the appellant was not informed. Had the appellant been informed of the negative blood test, she would have asked for the B sample to be analysed. Without the information, she did not do so. She could not be said to have waived the B sample analysis where she had not been given the information. The Panel found it unfair in the circumstances to rely on the analysis of the A sample alone. The Panel found that the Fédération Équestre Internationale (FEI) was under a duty to allow the appellant all the information required to make an informed choice as to whether to request a B sample. Without B sample analysis, no positive finding of doping could be made. The appeal was upheld.

Application of Lex Mitior *Doctrine*

TAS 94/128, *UCI and CONI* (Italian National Olympic Committee)

CAS gave an advisory opinion on various aspects of doping rules (which pre-dated the Code). In answering one of the questions raised as to the application of new rules, the Panel explained that new rules would be applicable to an allegation against an athlete in relation to matters which had occurred before the new rules came into force where those rules would bring about a more favourable outcome on sanctions for the accused. In giving this opinion, the Panel adopted the principle of *lex mitior* as a fundamental principle of every democratic regime. It gave as examples of the protection of this principle from criminal law, Swiss Law (Article 2 Rule 2 of the Criminal Code) and Italian Law (Article 2 of the Criminal Code). This principle was to be applied to anti-doping proceedings, given their penal character. The principle should apply where a period of ineligibility had been imposed unless it had been entirely served.

TAS 2001/A/318, *V v. Fédération Cycliste Suisse*

Professional cyclist V was subject to criminal process as a result of the search of a team car at the Tour de France in 1998. V made admissions in that process. On the basis of the admissions, Swiss cycling imposed a suspension of nine months without any suspended period under the then applicable rules of the sport. CAS found that nine months' suspension was not excessive given the nature of the doping admitted to by the rider – regular use of EPO, steroids and other substances – and that it could not increase the sanction. There was no breach of the principle of equal treatment under the Swiss Constitutional provisions where V's conduct was more serious than that of three other cyclists sanctioned as a result of the same inquiry. There was no basis to allow a suspension of the period of ineligibility, although this was technically available on *lex mitior* principles.

Different Approaches by CAS Panels to Discretion in Relation to Fixed Sanctions

As the awards in the previous section illustrate, before the adoption of the Code in 2004, CAS Panels adopted different approaches to the application of provisions in anti-doping rules which imposed fixed violations. Several CAS Panels held that they had a broad power to vary a fixed sanction in a sport's anti-doping rules, so as to impose a sanction which they considered appropriate in the circumstances of the case, while other Panels were less receptive to a flexible approach to sanctions.[83] This more flexible approach to sanctions was applied by CAS Panels on the basis of fundamental principles applicable under Swiss law (and other legal systems) relating to the protection of human rights, under which a limit on a person's fundamental rights had to be justifiable as a reasonable, proportionate limitation. In some cases, by way of contrast, CAS Panels upheld very severe sanctions under sports rules, such as the imposition of a life ban from sport for a first doping offence, on the basis of the private nature of doping rules, where the provisions of the particular rules were clear and the possible sanction had been expressly acknowledged by athletes.[84] Whether one approach or the other would be followed by CAS was difficult to predict, and the differences between doping sanctions in various regimes and in the approach to the imposition of sanctions by sporting tribunals and CAS led to concerns about inconsistent results across different sports. Ultimately, this unevenness was one reason for the development of the Code, and, in particular, for the Articles of the Code imposing fixed sanctions, with

---

83 See e.g. CAS 2000/A/312, *L v. FILA*, Award of 22 October 2001, CAS Digest III, 2001–03, p. 148, where a CAS Panel found it just and equitable to reduce a two-year suspension to one year where a wrestler had inadvertently consumed nandrolone precursors in a food supplement.

84 See CAS 2001/A/330, *R v. FISA*, CAS Digest III, 2001–03, p. 197, a case involving an oarsman who was subject to a life ban by FISA, which was upheld by CAS on appeal. See page 59 for case summary.

elimination or reduction of a sanction only available in limited, exceptional circumstances. To an extent, the Code was amended in both 2009 and 2015 to provide for greater flexibility in imposing sanctions for doping violations. The history of the Code and its development over time might be said to reflect an ongoing tension between the competing ideas of certainty and flexibility in the imposition of sanctions which was present in early pre-Code CAS decisions.

The four pre-Code decisions described in the next section illustrate differing approaches to the level of sanction in anti-doping regimes established by differing international federations, conflict between approaches in tribunals at national and international level and different approaches by CAS Panels to the question of whether a fixed sanction could be reduced to ensure that the period of ineligibility was a proportionate response to the fault (or otherwise) of the athlete. Before the Code there were, perhaps, more CAS awards where Panels, when faced with possible grounds on which to reduce a fixed sanction, decided that CAS had a discretion to reduce the period of fixed ineligibility than there were awards where Panels applied a fixed sanction contained in the relevant international federation rules or policy, where the sanction might be seen as imposing a disproportionate penalty. The problem created by the different approaches was that it was difficult to predict when a principle, such as the principle of proportionality, might be relied on by a CAS Panel to reduce a sanction which appeared to be fixed under the particular doping policy that had been agreed to by those involved in the sport. The different approaches were productive of inconsistency and injustice between athletes and between sports. One of the main goals of the Code was and remains to address this lack of certainty and harmony by establishing a common set of rules to govern doping (and sanctions in particular) with a clearly stated purpose of achieving harmony, such that the Rules can be interpreted and applied in the light of that purpose.

Lack of Harmony Relating to Sanctions between Anti-doping Regimes before the Code

CAS 2001/A/318, V v. Fédération Cycliste Suisse (Swiss Cycling), Award of 23 April 2001, CAS Digest III, p. 185

V, a professional cyclist, admitted long-term doping along with other team members in criminal proceedings. Swiss Cycling, a national federation, at the request of the international cycling federation, Union Cycliste

Internationale (UCI), ordered a nine-month suspension under the particular sport rules. V appealed to CAS to have the beginning of the suspension run from an earlier date. V also sought to argue that a nine-month suspension was excessive. CAS held that the period of suspension should run from the most recent infringement. There was no basis to say that the suspension period was excessive and no justification for deferring the sanction because of V's admission: the rider only admitted infractions at a late stage.

This decision and the suspension period can be contrasted with a CAS award at about the same time in relation to the sport of rowing.

CAS 2001/A/330, R v. FISA, Award of 23 November 2001, CAS Digest III, p. 197

FISA imposed a life ban on an international oarsman who tested positive for anabolic steroids. On appeal, CAS held that the life ban was valid. The provisions under the FISA Rules were predictable and well known to all rowers, and had provided the possibility of a life ban for a first doping offence for more than twelve years. In addition, the appellant had signed the 'rower commitment', which confirmed doping violations in the sport of rowing were punishable with a life ban for a first offence. In summary, CAS held that the sanction was not impeachable under Swiss law, nor could it be said to be disproportionate.

> While it is clear to the Panel that many international federations have decided that a two year suspension is appropriate for a first doping offence, it is equally clear that other International Federations, such as FISA, have chosen to impose higher minimum standards as a demonstration of the determination and commitment to the eradication of doping in that sport.
>
> Although the issue has never been directly considered or decided, either by CAS Panels or by the Swiss Federal Tribunal, in rulings or in CAS decisions, it seems to the Panel, as a matter of principle, that a life ban can be considered both justified and proportionate in doping cases; see the decision of the Swiss Federal Tribunal in N, J, Y, V. That is so even if the ban is imposed for a first offence.

In addition to different approaches by CAS Panels occasioned in part, at least, by different doping regimes, in some cases, decisions reached under national legal systems could differ from those reached by the international federations and CAS.

CAS 2001/A/337, B v. FINA, Award of 22 March 2002, CAS Digest III, p. 206

B, a New Zealand swimmer, was tested by the New Zealand Sports Drug Agency, the NADO established by legislation, under the national rules which bound B as a member of New Zealand Swimming. The A and B samples were found to contain 19-norandrosterone (NA). An appeal was available to the athlete before the New Zealand courts under the statutory regime applicable at the time. The determination by the NADO that a doping infraction had been committed was ultimately set aside by the New Zealand Court of Appeal, on the grounds that there had been a delay in the transportation of the samples to the testing laboratory. This was a material flaw in the procedure laid down by the statutory regulations which prevented, the Court of Appeal held, the NADO from relying on the results of the laboratory analysis to determine that there had been a doping infraction. The New Zealand courts did not have to address the question of whether the delay had been likely to cause a deterioration of the sample because the breach of the statutory regulation was enough to invalidate the determination made under the legislation.

The New Zealand Swimming Federation decided, after the New Zealand court decisions, that there was, in effect, no doping violation because of the failure to follow the process set down in the statutory regulations. However, FINA found that the expert evidence before the New Zealand courts, which was produced before it, was sufficient to justify a finding under the FINA anti-doping rules that there had been a doping offence. A ban of four years was imposed.

On appeal by B against the FINA decision, CAS held that the international federation could impose a sanction independent of the outcome of proceedings concerning sanctions at the national level (see also CAS 99/156, F v. FINA, Award of 6 October 1997). Unlike the New Zealand courts under the national legislative regime, CAS and FINA had to consider whether the failure to follow procedures had affected the result obtained from testing of the sample under the applicable anti-doping rules. FINA Rules at the time provided that a departure from the rules had to cast genuine doubt on the reliability of a finding. The CAS Panel found that none of the breaches in relation to the sample affected the test result (including the fact the B sample had not been examined by a different person). Scientific evidence established that the level of NA exceeded the threshold of 2 ng/ml, and this resulted in an adverse analytical finding. FINA Rules at the time provided for a minimum suspension of four years, with cancellation of all results during the six months prior to suspension – in fact, a four-and-a-half-year suspension. The Panel held that the minimum sanction of four-and-a-half years for a first offence was inappropriately excessive in the case and allowed a reduction for the special circumstances. The Panel adopted a two-year suspension for a first-time doping offence as legally acceptable.[85] A period of ineligibility of two years was imposed from the time of initial suspension.

CAS Ad Hoc OWG Salt Lake City, P and Latvian Olympic Committee v. IOC

P was a bobsleigh captain who tested positive for nandrolone. His international federation imposed a three-month period of ineligibility, which would allow him to compete in the Olympic Games. Under the relevant international federation rules, the period of suspension should have been two years. The IOC sought to exclude P from the Games after he had been selected by his national Olympic committee. CAS held that, once P had been dealt with by his international federation and had completed the ban, he had a legitimate expectation that he would be able to compete freely in all competitions open to him. CAS noted that the IOC had no right to appeal the sanction by the international federation. CAS found that it was wrong for the IOC to exclude P from the Games, and reversed the decision.

---

85 Contrast CAS 2002/A/399, *P* v. *FINA*, Award of 31 January 2003, where the CAS Panel found that a four-and-a-half-year ban under the applicable FINA Rules was proportionate.

2

Overview of the Code and the World Anti-Doping Program

Purpose

This World Anti-Doping Program is a complex set of standard-form agreements which Signatories adopt to provide a comprehensive anti-doping regime. The Program is made up of the Code, the International Standards (which are expressly incorporated into the Code) and Models of Best Practice or Guidelines (which are developed by WADA and provided for Signatories to assist them in carrying out their obligations under the Code and International Standards). It is not mandatory for Signatories to follow Guidelines, but compliance with the Code (which also must involve operating in accordance with the International Standards given the way in which the Standards operate as part of the Code) is mandatory for a Signatory to comply with its obligations.[1] Most of the Guidelines are closely connected to operations under the Code and International Standards, and will be followed by Signatories.

The Program has the expressed aim of protecting athletes' fundamental right to participate in doping-free sport and of promoting health, fairness and equality for athletes worldwide and ensuring harmonised, co-ordinated and effective anti-doping programmes, at the international and national level, with regard to the detection, deterrence and prevention of doping.[2] While functioning as a result of the voluntary agreement of

---

1 For WADA's powers to monitor compliance with the Code, see Article 23.5. WADA compliance reports are forwarded to the WADA Foundation Board, which makes its finding on the question of whether a Signatory is compliant at a meeting at which the Signatory is given the opportunity to submit written arguments on its position to the Board. A decision by the Board that a Signatory is not compliant can be appealed to CAS under Article 13.6. As at 21 November 2016, the following Signatories had been declared to be non-compliant with the Code: Azerbaijan Anti-Doping Agency, Brazilian Anti-Doping Agency, Indonesian Anti-Doping Agency, Spanish Anti-Doping Agency and Russian Anti-Doping Agency.
2 See the Introduction to the Code.

Signatories, the Code (and Program) can be described as a kind of international law of sport in the anti-doping area.[3]

While they operate in a different sphere of activity, the Code (and Program) function in much the same way as voluntary international instruments in areas such as international trade and commerce. The voluntary rules which govern the operation of bankers' documentary credits and the conventions which govern the carriage of goods by sea are good examples. The Uniform Customs and Practice for Documentary Credits (UCP) functions by agreement or incorporation, and might, like the Code, be described as a body of 'soft' international law which has been generally adopted so as to bring about a common approach in a particular area of activity. In the case of the Code, the aim is to provide a common, harmonised approach to the regulation of doping in sport.[4]

The Parts of the Code

The Code is made up of four parts. Part One contains the key provisions relating to doping control as it is defined by the Code. These provisions will be adopted by Signatories to provide their common anti-doping policies. Under the Code, the expression 'doping control' is defined as covering all parts of the process of determining whether doping or any other anti-doping rule violation has occurred, from test distribution planning or initial investigation of an anti-doping rule violation to the ultimate disposition of any appeal and all the steps in between, including the provision of whereabouts information,[5] sample collection and handling, laboratory analysis, TUEs, the management of results and hearings. The organisations which can accept the Code are referred to as 'Signatories' or 'anti-doping organisations' in the Code. A Signatory is an entity which signs and agrees to comply with the Code. An anti-doping organisation is a

---

3 For the status of the Code and its interpretation as an independent text, see Article 24.3 and Chapter 4, pages 158–61.

4 Similarly, while the Hague–Visby Rules, which regulate the carriage of goods by sea, can apply either by force of law or by contract, they are regularly incorporated by commercial parties into contractual documents such as bills of lading and charter parties, and form a standard liability regime concerning the carriage of goods by sea.

5 See the definition of doping control in the Code. The scope of doping control is important in considering the circumstances in which the violation of tampering under Article 2.5 may be committed. See Chapter 5, pages 241–6.

Signatory responsible for adopting rules initiating, implementing or enforcing any part of the doping control process.

Part Two of the Code sets out the essential education and research functions of Signatories. Part Three provides, in general terms, for the roles and responsibilities of Signatories and the individuals – athletes and athlete support personnel – who are bound by the Code. State parties cannot be Signatories to the Code, but Article 22 in Part Three of the Code provides that the commitment of governments to the Code is to be evidenced by each government signing the Copenhagen Declaration on Anti-Doping in Sport of 3 March 2003, ratifying the International Convention against Doping in Sport adopted by UNESCO on 19 October 2005 (UNESCO Convention) and taking affirmative measures to support the Code.[6]

Part Four contains the provisions concerning the ways in which Signatories will formally accept and implement the Code, how compliance with the operation of the Code will be monitored by WADA, the consequences for non-compliance by Signatories and the process by which the Code will be monitored and modified.[7]

Part Four specifically identifies the Articles of the Code which must be implemented without substantive change by Signatories. These Articles represent the core of the anti-doping regime under the Code, which must be adopted if a common approach is to be created. The specified Articles are: Article 1 (Definition of Doping), Article 2 (Anti-Doping Rule Violations), Article 3 (Proof of Doping), Article 4.2.2 (Specified Substances), Article 4.3.3 (WADA's Determination of the Prohibited List), Article 7.11 (Retirement from Sport), Article 9 (Automatic Disqualification of Individual Results), Article 10 (Sanctions on Individuals), Article 11 (Consequences to Teams), Article 13 (Appeals) with the exception of 13.2.2, 13.6 and 13.7, Article 15.1 (Mutual Recognition of Decisions), Article 17 (Statute of Limitations), Article 24 (Interpretation of the Code) and Appendix 1 – Definitions. Article 23.2.2 further provides that a Signatory cannot add additional provisions to its rules which change the effect of the Articles set out previously. While other Articles of the Code are not the subject of the specific obligation that they be adopted without substantive change, they also impose standards and requirements which must be met

---

6 See Article 22 for the involvement of governments in complying with the UNESCO Convention and for more detail, see pages 87–8.
7 The Code has now been through two reviews, which have seen the production of the 2009 and 2015 Codes. See further Chapter 11 for some general comment on the overall effect of the process of regular review.

if a Signatory is to comply with its obligations under the Code. As further outlined in Chapter 3, the International Standards also make detailed provision for various aspects of doping control which must be followed by Signatories if their processes are to be Code-compliant. Part Four also contains important provisions on the interpretation of the Code and provides in Article 25 for the application of the Code in transitional situations – this is an important aspect of the operation of the Code, because each revision has seen significant changes, particularly in relation to the sanctions for violations.[8]

The International Standards provide the details of prohibited substances and methods, the grant of exemptions so that athletes can be permitted to take prohibited substances on therapeutic grounds, the process of planning and carrying out the testing and analysis of bodily samples by WADA-accredited laboratories, the general process of gathering intelligence and investigating anti-doping rule violations by anti-doping organisations, the collection of whereabouts information and the protection of privacy and of personal information collected and held by anti-doping organisations.[9]

The International Standard for the Prohibited List is of central importance in that it defines the scope of the violations covered by the Code by providing, on an annual basis, for the substances and methods which are prohibited under the Code and which can, as a result, give rise to potential liability for anti-doping rule violations under the Code.

The most significant recent changes in the International Standards have, perhaps, involved the amendment of the International Standard for Testing and Investigations (ISTI) to include Articles obliging anti-doping organisations to carry out intelligence-gathering and investigations into possible anti-doping rule violations. These amendments are linked to changes in the 2015 Code which provide for the obligations of anti-doping organisations in relation to investigations.[10] Before these recent

---

8 See further Chapter 8, pages 455–7.
9 The International Standard for the Prohibited List 2017 (which will be in force from 1 January 2017), the International Standard for Therapeutic Use Exemptions (ISTUE) June 2016, the International Standard for Testing and Investigations (ISTI) January 2017, the International Standard for Laboratories (ISL) June 2016 and the International Standard for the Protection of Privacy and Personal Information 2015. For more detailed consideration of the contents of the International Standards, see Chapter 3.
10 Articles 5.1.2 and 5.8 2015 Code. See also Guidelines Information Gathering and Intelligence Sharing 2015, which aim to assist anti-doping organisations in carrying out their obligations in respect of the investigation of anti-doping rule violations that do not arise from the analysis of samples.

amendments, while the Code has since its initial acceptance contained a range of anti-doping rule violations, most of which can only be established by evidence other than positive tests,[11] there was little express provision in the Code and Standards concerning the investigation of violations not involving testing.[12] Most of the provisions in the International Standards were concerned with the process of sampling and analysis used to support allegations of doping by detecting the presence of a prohibited substance or method. While WADA has given investigation and intelligence-sharing much greater impetus and provided general guidance for anti-doping organisations, Signatories still remain largely responsible for the practical detail and resourcing required to establish the policies and processes by which they will conduct and manage investigations into those violations which may be established, not by test results, but by obtaining other reliable evidence. Unlike the process of testing, investigations into other violations may take a wide range of different forms.[13]

Over several years, WADA has sought to develop its own ability and that of Signatories to investigate the more serious anti-doping rule violations which can be central to coordinated doping schemes such as trafficking and the administration of prohibited substances. The proof of these violations may require the discovery and presentation of a diverse range of evidential material. In order to assist in obtaining such evidence, WADA has sought to bring about greater coordination between itself and anti-doping organisations and international and national law-enforcement agencies relating to investigations and the sharing of information. As long ago as 2008, WADA entered into a memorandum of understanding with the International Criminal Police Organization (Interpol) to establish a framework for cooperation which allows exchanges of information and expertise so as to bring about the prevention and suppression of doping and trafficking in doping. NADOs are encouraged to enter into similar arrangements with State agencies in the WADA Guidelines for Coordinating Investigations and Sharing Anti-Doping Information and Evidence, produced in 2011. There have been a number of investigations around the world in which anti-doping organisations have worked with national authorities in investigating the possible commission of criminal offences

---

11 See Chapter 5, pages 177–9 for the elements of the violations.
12 Those violations which do not involve the presence of a prohibited substance in a sample, the use of a prohibited substance or refusal to submit to sample analysis.
13 See Chapter 5 for commentary on the different violations under Article 2 of the Code and case summaries.

relating to substances on the Prohibited List, and this kind of collaborative investigation is seen by WADA as a vital aspect of investigating and preventing doping practices and fulfilling the purpose of the Code.[14]

This emphasis on investigation and the gathering of intelligence is also reflected in the amended 'substantial assistance' provisions in the 2015 Code and the greater discretion given to WADA to agree on suspensions of periods of ineligibility where athletes and others bound by the Code provide assistance which leads to anti-doping proceedings against others. WADA has recently expressed its support for greater protection and incentives for 'whistleblowers'.[15]

In conjunction with these developments, the Code and Standards also provide for more focussed targeted testing using information held by anti-doping organisations and for the operation of ABP programmes. The ABP involves the longitudinal profiling of athletes by reference to biological markers in blood and urine samples. Analysis of the profile built up for an individual athlete can be used to determine by expert analysis whether an athlete is taking prohibited substances such as EPO or steroids.[16] Evidence obtained by evaluating the ABP may be used in support of allegations that an athlete has used a prohibited substance or method, or as the basis for targeted out-of-competition testing.

In each of the preceding areas, WADA and anti-doping organisations collect and hold private information.[17] The development of the Privacy Standard, which was first introduced in 2011, can be seen as a response to the need to ensure that information provided to anti-doping organisations under the Code will be held in accordance with legal standards established under national law.

14 While WADA actively supports collaboration with State agencies responsible for investigating and prosecuting criminal offending, its view is that criminalising doping in sport under national criminal law is not the answer to the problem of doping in sport.

15 The two-part Independent Commission Report on compliance with the Code by Russian Athletics and the Russian Anti-Doping Agency, released in November 2015 and June 2016, and the further McLaren Report, were the result of evidence provided by the Russian athlete Yuliya Stepanova, who was subject to a reduced period of ineligibility of three years, five months for providing 'substantial assistance'. Under an agreement reached with WADA, the period of ineligibility was reduced by seven months. See WADA statement.

16 For more detail on the ABP and for case summaries involving proof of violations relying on ABP analysis, see further Chapter 5, pages 204–24. The ISTI contains specific provision for the testing and custody of blood in order to provide samples to the ABP.

17 Information collected by anti-doping organisations and WADA will be held in the Anti-Doping Administration and Management System (ADAMS), a database used for data entry, storage and sharing.

Acceptance by Signatories

The effect of the acceptance of the Code by Signatories – the IOC, national Olympic committees, the IPC, national paralympic committees, international federations, major event organisations, NADOs and WADA – has been to create a network of agreements regulating the anti-doping area across sports at the international and national level. If Signatories carry out their responsibilities as required by the Code, the agreements which they enter into with their members and other organisations will contain the key Articles of the Code relating to such matters as the definition of doping, anti-doping rule violations, proof of doping, sanctions and appeals without significant amendment[18] and other provisions which meet the standards in the Code, and provide that the Signatories will follow the WADA International Standards in carrying out their functions. This process of implementation aims to establish a common approach to the detection of doping and the management of allegations through the medium of a standard agreed set of provisions.

The responsibility for testing and investigation in relation to persons who are bound by the Code will fall on Signatories as provided for by the Code. The Signatory responsible for testing and investigation will be responsible for the management of the results obtained.[19] In certain situations, more than one Signatory under the Code may potentially be responsible for testing, investigation or results management, because athletes may be bound by different policies and rules.[20] The Code contains specific provisions allocating responsibility for testing, investigation and results management which aim to avoid conflicts between Signatories, and WADA has also produced a Guideline for the process, to be followed where there is a possible conflict between anti-doping organisations in relation to testing.[21]

Figure 1 sets out in simple terms the way in which the Code has effect by international agreement.

By providing for a single set of substantive anti-doping rules applicable throughout sport, the Code provides the essential foundation for a

18 For the list of Articles, see Article 23.2.   19 See further Chapter 7.
20 For an example of an athlete being bound by different sets of rules, see the award of the CAS Panel in *Baggeley* at pages 78–80, where an appeal to CAS was held to be out of time under the limit under the CAS Procedural Rules by which B had become bound by agreement. In many situations, an athlete will be subject to the rules of both a national and an international organisation, but, where the Code has been properly adopted and implemented by both organisations, there should be consistency in the rules of the sporting bodies in all the areas covered by the Code.
21 See Chapter 7.

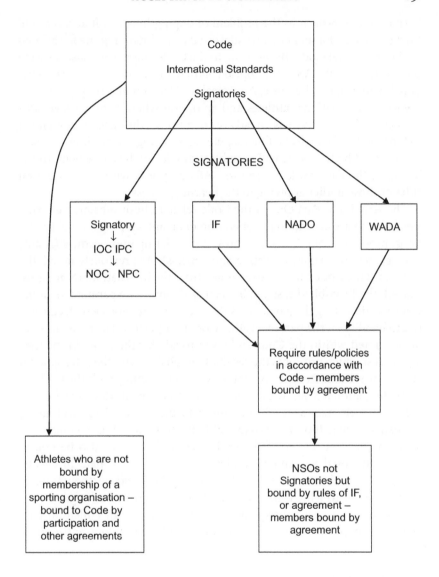

Outside scope of agreement

1.   Sporting organisations and their members which have not accepted Code.

2.   General law of States which may make doping in sporting context criminal, or establishes other legal regimes for anti-doping within State.

3.   Convention on Doping in Sport by which States agree to support Code at the international level.

Figure 1 General overview of how the Code works by agreement

harmonised approach to the problem of doping in sport. It also seeks to further the development of a standardised disciplinary regime for all who are bound by the Code. By agreeing to the Code, Signatories also agree to the central role of CAS as the appeal tribunal for decisions by sporting tribunals which apply the Code. An appeal to CAS is compulsory for appeals involving international athletes and an option where national-level athletes are involved.[22] As has already been outlined, the effect of agreement to the Code will usually be that disputes concerning the disciplinary matters covered by the Code will be subject to referral, by agreement, to tribunals at the national level, and to CAS on appeal, with the procedural rules of those bodies applying to the hearing process.

The Articles of Part One of the Code relate to both substantive provisions, which are central to the operation of an anti-doping regime (violations, proof and sanctions), and provisions relating to procedure (results management, hearings, reporting and appeals). As previously noted, the Articles of the Code cannot be separated from the International Standards. Indeed, the Prohibited List can be seen as defining the parameters of the Code by stipulating the particular substances and methods which can give rise to liability on the part of an athlete or other person. The Standards are incorporated within the Code and also provide for the detail in the testing process which produces the results. Compliance with the International Standards is mandatory if a Signatory wishes to comply with the Code.

At the national level, while NSOs cannot be Signatories to the Code, they and their members will be bound to the Code. NSOs will agree, by their membership of international federations which are Signatories, to the application of the Code. Individual athletes may also be bound by the individual agreements under which they participate in events. Whether an athlete is bound to the Code will depend on the nature of the agreement to which they are subject and its terms. Such agreements may be inferred as a consequence of the conduct of an athlete in participating in-competition.[23] In addition, NSOs may adopt anti-doping

---

22 See Chapter 9 on appeals.

23 It may be possible to infer that a contract has been entered into from evidence of the acts and conduct of the parties. See J.A. McHugh in *Integrated Computer Services Pty Ltd v. Digital Equipment Corporation Aust. Pty Limited* (1988) 5 BPR 11, 110, at 11, 117: 'A contract may be inferred from the acts and conduct of the party as well as or in the absence of their words ... the question in this class of case is whether the conduct of the parties would, in the light of the surrounding circumstances, show a tacit understanding or agreement.' See also, in the sporting context, *Raguz v. Sullivan* (Chapter 10, page 506). A tribunal will need to be comfortably satisfied that an athlete is bound to the relevant anti-doping rules

policies provided or supported by NADOs which are based on the Code, and which, if properly adopted under the NSO rules, bind their members. The manner in which an individual is said to have become bound to the Code may have to be considered by a tribunal in the context of a challenge to its jurisdiction.[24]

The agreement-based system has significant advantages and generally reflects the way in which sporting organisations both large and small have operated as private bodies and regulated their affairs in the past by passing rules which bind their members by contract. The way in which the Code functions by way of voluntary agreement under the rules of private organisations means that challenges to its validity on the grounds that it contravenes fundamental human rights may be met with the contention that the disciplinary rules of a private organisation should not generally be invalidated by reference to the general principles protecting fundamental rights under a particular legal system, or, at least, that the courts should be reluctant to interfere with the autonomy of such private associations on this basis.[25] However, the way in which the Code operates also means that jurisdiction over an individual depends on the existence of an agreement which is binding on the individual. A person or participant who has not agreed to the Code will not be bound by it, or by the processes under the Code. While the Code has now been accepted by Signatories throughout the sporting world, there have been several instances where CAS has held that the Code's provisions did not apply to allegations brought against individual athletes because there was no binding agreement to the application of the Code or to the jurisdiction of CAS in the particular circumstances of the case. Where such jurisdictional questions arise, they will be determined by the arbitral tribunal considering the allegation in accordance with the rules of the system of law applicable to the arbitration. Under Swiss law (and the law in other jurisdictions which have adopted the UNCITRAL Model Law), CAS arbitrators have jurisdiction to decide whether they have jurisdiction in the arbitration.[26]

for jurisdiction to be established. For the proof of anti-doping rule violations, see Chapter 6.

24 For examples of CAS awards considering whether an athlete is bound to an arbitration agreement referring a matter to CAS, see case summaries in *Busch* and *Dodô* at pages 72–6, where the issue was considered by the Swiss Federal Supreme Court in considering challenges to CAS awards.

25 See Chapter 10 on challenges to anti-doping regimes and the Code.

26 The doctrine is called *Kompetenz-Kompetenz* in civil jurisdictions. See e.g. *N* v. *FEI*, where the Swiss Federal Court dismissed an appeal from a CAS award and found that an equestrian competitor was bound to the CAS arbitration, even though the agreement he had

Where there is agreement by athletes to the application of the Code, whether individually or through their membership of a sporting organisation, the agreement will usually have the effect of incorporating the provisions of the various International Standards which are incorporated into the Code and the relevant results management and hearing rules under the Code. This follows from the way in which the Code itself incorporates the Standards and provides for the jurisdiction of CAS on appeals.[27] The effect of such an agreement will generally be that an athlete agrees to the process of testing, analysis and investigation, the Code's substantive rules on violations and sanctions and the process of results management and hearings (and the related CAS procedural rules). The provisions on these substantive and operational or procedural matters are found in various documents (the Code, the Standards and Tribunal and CAS Procedural Rules), but usually agreement to the Code will bring with it the wider agreement to the processes required for the Code to provide a functioning system. The scope of the agreement by the athlete will depend on the interpretation of the particular agreement in question, but generally an agreement incorporating the Code will be interpreted broadly in accordance with its purpose and will have this broad effect.

Illustrations: Jurisdiction – the Importance of Agreement

Agreement to Testing and CAS Jurisdiction on Appeal

CAS 2008/A/1738, *WADA v. DEB and Busch*;
CAS 2008/A/1564, *WADA v. IIHF and Busch*;
Busch v. WADA, Swiss Federal Tribunal, 4A-358/2009,
Judgement of 6 November 2009

B was an international German ice hockey player who played for the national team in several international competitions and for several years competed at the Ice Hockey World Championships. On 6 March 2008, a doping control officer (DCO) attended his home to carry out an out-of-competition test. B refused to submit to sample collection, saying he was too often disturbed by frequent doping testing and criticised the way

---

signed did not refer to an arbitration clause, because he was well aware generally of the referral of disputes to arbitration in his sport. Similarly, at national level, where tribunals have jurisdiction by agreement, the first issue in doping allegations can be whether there is a binding agreement to the jurisdiction of the tribunal.
27 See Chapter 9 (Article 13.2.1 Code).

athletes were selected for out-of-competition testing. After warnings as to severe consequences, B refused the test.

After contact with the German national anti-doping agency (NADA), B changed his mind. Later in the day, a test was performed, which was negative. The NADA informed the Deutscher Eishockey Bund (DEB) of the refusal. DEB decided, in the circumstances of the case, to sanction B with a public warning with a three-month ban and, in the case of a further violation, a fine of €5000 and fifty-six hours' community work. This decision was communicated to the International Ice Hockey Federation (IIHF). WADA was also informed of the decision by the NADA. WADA asked IIHF to take steps against B under its regulations, requesting that the IIHF directorate at the World Championships provisionally suspend B. IIHF did not provisionally suspend B, nor take any steps under its regulations. It refused to take further steps against B and prevent him competing at the World Championships because there was an appeal process under the German Anti-Doping Code available which had to be used before IIHF could interfere in decisions of the DEB member body. WADA sought advice from DEB as to its appeal rights. DEB informed WADA that, under its rules, there was an appeal process to the National Court of Arbitration for Sport, which would be replaced by the Ad Hoc Court of Arbitration of the German Sports Confederation until the National Court of Arbitration was established. WADA appealed to the Ad Hoc Court of Arbitration of the German Olympic Sports Confederation. The Ad Hoc Court of Arbitration held that there had been an intentional refusal by B but that DEB had failed to implement the NADA Code and failed to bind B to its rules by declaration. As a result, there was no basis upon which B could be sanctioned. WADA appealed the decision of IIHF not to take steps against B to CAS. It also appealed the decision of the Ad Hoc Court of Arbitration.

The two WADA appeals were heard by the same CAS Panel. WADA contended that the Ad Hoc Court of Arbitration had failed to apply the rules and regulations of IIHF and the anti-doping rules under those regulations. While WADA accepted that DEB had not implemented the WADA Code, it argued that B was bound to the Code by signing the IIHF Player Entry Form for the World Championships, under which he agreed to abide and observe the IIHF statutes, by-laws and regulations at all times. DEB and B, after he had applied to intervene, submitted that there was no binding agreement to the jurisdiction of the Ad Hoc Court of Arbitration.

The CAS Panel held that the IIHF Player Entry Form fulfilled the basic requirements for a valid arbitration clause or arbitration agreement.

The Player Entry Form signed by B at the IIHF Championship provided as follows:

> I, the undersigned, declare on my honour that:
>
> (a) I am under the jurisdiction of the national association I represent ...
>
> (l) I agree to abide by and observe the IIHF statutes, by-laws and regulations (including those related to medical doping control) and the decisions of the IIHF and the Championship Director in all matters including disciplinary measures, not to involve any third party whatsoever outside of the IIHF in the resolution of any dispute whatsoever arising in connection with the IIHF Championship and/or the statutes, by-laws and regulations and decisions made by the IIHF relating thereto excepting, where having exhausted the appeal procedures under the IIHF, in which case I undertake to submit any dispute to the jurisdiction of the Court of Arbitration for Sport in Lausanne, Switzerland for definitive and final resolution.

The CAS Panel approached the interpretation of the Entry Form by reference to Swiss law by reason of the seat of IIHF being in Switzerland. Under Swiss law, if a party contended that he or she had understood the clause in a different manner from the other party to the agreement, under the principle of confidence, the will of the parties had to be established by deciding how the clause could be and must have been understood bona fide by the addressee of the declaration in question. The Panel held that the clause applied to bind players to IIHF decisions on disciplinary matters including matters outside the World Championships and to the jurisdiction of CAS for appeals after IIHF procedures had been exhausted. However, while the parties had entered into a valid arbitration agreement and agreed to the jurisdiction of the Ad Hoc Court of Arbitration for Sport, there had been no express agreement to a possible appeal to CAS from that tribunal. The award of the Ad Hoc Court of Arbitration was expressed to be final and binding and not subject to appeal. This meant that there was no further right of appeal to CAS from that tribunal.

In the appeal against the decision of IIHF not to institute disciplinary proceedings against B, CAS held that the decision by the IIHF not to take steps was a decision capable of being appealed and that the Player Agreement gave jurisdiction under the Code for WADA to appeal to CAS.

On the substance of the case, the Panel found that there was, indeed, a refusal to submit to sample collection. The matters that B relied on – annoyance at the number of tests that he had to undergo, intrusions into his privacy, hard training before the test, intrusion in his home life – did not amount to any exceptional circumstances so as to support a plea of no significant fault or negligence, even if it were available. A sanction of two years was imposed.

B appealed to the Swiss Federal Tribunal as provided by Swiss law under Article 190 PILA on the ground that CAS had wrongly held that it had jurisdiction in the matter. The Swiss Federal Tribunal disagreed with CAS on the interpretation of the Player Entry Form. It agreed on the general principles of Swiss law which were applicable to the interpretation of the Player Entry Form and held that, on its proper interpretation, the form was limited to disputes arising in relation to the Championship. WADA could show no connection between the out-of-competition test and the requested period of two years' ineligibility and the IIHF World Championship. The Player Entry Form, while forming a valid arbitration agreement, did not give rise to an arbitration agreement covering disputes which were not connected with the World Championships. Accordingly, where there was no connection between the testing which B refused and the World Championships, there was no arbitration agreement covering the sanctioning for B's refusal to submit to that testing. Nor could jurisdiction be maintained on a basis that B had confirmed that he belonged to a national federation which was subject to IIHF statutes and regulations. Notwithstanding the generous approach to the question of the validity of arbitral agreement in international arbitration, the Federal Court did not find that B was bound to an arbitration agreement on this basis. Accordingly, the decision by CAS was set aside.

CAS 2007/A/1370, *FIFA v. STJD, CBF and Dodô* – Player Bound to Rules Incorporating Code – Jurisdictional Challenge Fails *Dodô v. FIFA and WADA*, Swiss Federal Tribunal, 4A_460/2008

D, a professional footballer, belonged to the Brazilian Football Confederation. He played at international level. He tested positive after a Brazilian championship match for a stimulant, fenproporex. Before the highest sports court in Brazilian football, the Superior Tribunal de Justiça Desportiva (STJD), D was acquitted because the tribunal accepted his argument that he had been the victim of innocent contamination and that he had not been negligent.

On notification of the decision, FIFA and WADA appealed to CAS. CBF and D argued that there was no jurisdiction to hear the appeal (notwithstanding that CBF and D were bound to respect the statutes of FIFA) because the decision by STJD was made by a wholly independent judicial body from which there could be no appeal. The CAS Panel considered that STJD was part of the organisation CBF, although an independent body, which meant that its decisions had to be considered as the decisions of CBF. While there was appeal under national law against the decision, under the applicable international rules of FIFA, there was an appeal to CAS. The decision had to be considered a doping-related decision by a national federation and, accordingly, there was jurisdiction to hear WADA and FIFA's appeal under the FIFA statutes. The CAS Tribunal further held that there was jurisdiction over the player where he had expressly agreed in his employment contract to respect the rules of CBF. The CBF statutes provided that CBF players had to abide by the rules of FIFA. The FIFA statutes incorporated the WADA Code and this was sufficient to establish the jurisdiction of CAS over the player by the application of Article 13 of the Code. CAS held that a violation had clearly been committed and the player could not establish on the evidence how the substance had come to be in his system as he contended.

Even if the player had discharged the burden on him of showing how the substance had entered his system, the Panel held that the no fault or no significant fault defence was not applicable. Even on the facts alleged by the player, the player's conduct showed a significant disregard of his positive duty of caution.

On appeal to the Swiss Federal Tribunal, D argued that the arbitration award should be set aside under Chapter 12 PILA. The appeal raised the ground that CAS had no jurisdiction, relying on Article 190(2)(b) PILA. The tribunal upheld the conclusion that CAS had jurisdiction because CBF is a member of FIFA and the CBF statutes, which bound D, expressly incorporated the FIFA rules which provided for CAS appeals where a judicial body of a member gave a decision. The player had expressly acknowledged in his employment contract that he was bound by the FIFA rules and this included Article 61 of the FIFA statutes, under which both FIFA and WADA had standing to appeal the final doping decisions of its members. The conclusion that STJD was, as a matter of fact, an organ of CBF with the result that its decisions could be appealed to CAS under the FIFA statutes was not capable of challenge before the Federal Tribunal on appeal because such a factual finding had to be accepted on an appeal under Article 190. Accordingly, the appeal against the CAS award was dismissed.

CAS 2006/A/1190, *WADA* v. *PCB and Akhtar and Asif*

Two Pakistani test cricketers tested positive for a steroid metabolite. They were found not to have committed a doping offence by the Pakistan

Cricket Board (PCB) Appeals Committee. Under the right to appeal provided by Article 13 of the Code, WADA sought to appeal against the decision of the Appeals Committee to CAS. CAS dismissed the appeal on the basis that it had no jurisdiction to entertain the appeal. The CAS Panel accepted that it had power to decide on its own jurisdiction under Swiss law, which governed the conduct of the arbitration as an international arbitration (Article 186 PILA).

PCB submitted that WADA had no right of appeal as the statutes and regulations of the PCB did not provide for any appeal to CAS. As a result, the fundamental basis for jurisdiction referred to in Rule 47 of the CAS Code of Arbitration, namely, that the statutory regulations of the association had to include a specific arbitration agreement, was not made out. There could be no jurisdiction where PCB had not agreed to the Code.[28]

The CAS Panel felt compelled to reach the conclusion (with regret) that there was no appeal right for WADA. It noted that:

> the fight against doping would be severely hampered if International Federations, such as the ICC and national governing bodies such as the PCB do not ensure that their anti-doping rules are able to avoid unsatisfactory decisions as the majority decision of the PCB Appeals Committee in this case.

Agreement to Investigation Powers

CAS 2004/O/645, *United States Anti-Doping Agency* v. *Montgomery*; CAS 2004/O/649, *United States Anti-Doping Agency* v. *Gaines*

The proceedings arose from the BALCO investigation. As a preliminary issue, the athletes facing the allegations raised the question of the jurisdiction of the United States Anti-Doping Agency (USADA), the independent body established to conduct the anti-doping programme for Olympic sports in the United States, to investigate and bring anti-doping rule violation proceedings against them (other than allegations based on positive tests). The athletes were members of USA Track and Field (USATF), a member of the International Association of Athletics Federations (IAAF). They argued that the agreement between USADA and the United States Olympic Committee (USOC), under which USADA was given authority

---

28 See also e.g. CAS 2005/A/953, *Ashley Cole* v. *FA Premier League*, for a similar finding in the context of a commercial dispute in soccer.

to investigate and prosecute alleged doping violations (the USADA Protocol), did not bind them, nor, in any event, on its true construction, provide jurisdiction for USADA to investigate and prosecute in respect of 'non-analytical positive' (other violations apart from doping) cases. The CAS Panel considered the jurisdictional argument and held that the athletes were clearly bound to the USADA Protocol under the USATF regulations which were binding on them, and that the USADA Protocol, on its true construction, extended to allow USADA to investigate the kind of case against the athletes and prosecute it. The Panel further held that, as a result of being bound by the Protocol, the athletes had agreed to submit disputes concerning 'non-analytical positives' to the jurisdiction of the Panel. The challenge to the power of USADA to bring the case, and the Panel to hear it, was held to fail when the relevant contractual documents were interpreted according to both their 'spirit and letter'.

Effect of Agreement to the Jurisdiction of CAS: CAS Code of Sports Related Procedure and Time Limits Applicable

CAS 2006/A/1168, *Baggeley* v. *International Canoeing Federation*

An appeal brought by Mr Baggeley, the leading Australian Olympic canoeist, against a decision by the International Canoeing Federation (ICF) to impose a two-year period of ineligibility in relation to an anti-doping rule violation (on review of a first-instance CAS award imposing a period of fifteen months in proceedings brought by national organisations to whose rules Mr Baggeley was subject, on the grounds that the canoeist had established no significant fault or negligence). The CAS Panel found on the appeal from the ICF decision, which had been reached unilaterally without Mr Baggeley being heard, that, on the construction of the CAS Rules, which the appellant had agreed governed the appeal, the appeal was filed out of time and there was, as a result, no jurisdiction to hear the appeal under the CAS Rules. There could be no jurisdiction in CAS other than the jurisdiction established by agreement, and the agreement to the jurisdiction of CAS included the CAS time limit for filing the appeal under the CAS Procedural Rules.[29]

---

29 For some criticism of the effect of the incorporation of the CAS procedural rules by agreement to the jurisdiction of CAS by accepting the Code, see J. E. Marshall and Amy Catherine Hale, 'Unilateral Unappealable Doping Sanctions', *International Sports Law Review*, 7 (2007), 39.

The Consequences of the Agreement-Based System

The fact that the Code and the International Standards (and related provisions) can only bind persons by agreement has important basic consequences:

- Those who have not agreed to the Code, whether through their membership of organisations which have agreed to the Code or individually under the terms under which they compete or participate in sport, cannot be subject to the provisions of the Code.
- The rights and obligations of those who agree to the Code are limited to the rights and obligations contained in the Code and the International Standards. By way of example, anti-doping organisations acting under the Code can only investigate in relation to substances which are on the Prohibited List and possible violations which are in the Code. Without specific provisions, whether under other rules or under the general law, attempts by NADOs to conduct wider investigations will not be possible and are likely to be unlawful.
- A person or organisation which is subject to the Code by agreement can also be subject to other obligations imposed by other bodies, whether the State or other sporting organisations, at national or international level, whether under the general law or by private agreement. The operation of the different sets of obligations can produce different outcomes. By way of example, there may be different processes and sanctions at national level under a particular policy of a sporting body or State regime, and at international level under the Code. A sanction under the Code may be enforceable at international level while a different outcome prevails at national level. While such situations are detrimental to the harmony which the Code seeks to create, an athlete may be prevented from competing internationally while free to compete within his or her own country, or an athlete may be subject to different periods of ineligibility from NSOs and international sporting organisations.
- The private nature of the tribunals (whether national tribunals or CAS) which, by agreement, will determine alleged violations under the Code will mean that their decisions may be subject to challenge in national courts or before supranational tribunals on the grounds that they infringe fundamental rights protected by national or international legal principles. While the presence and nature of the appeal right to CAS under Article 13 of the Code can be seen as limiting the avenue for challenge because it makes the hearing subject to Swiss law on

international arbitration, the agreement-based nature of the system for the hearing of allegations under the Code means that the challenge of Code decisions to national courts and/or supranational tribunals will remain possible. This is because tribunals operating under the Code are not State courts but tribunals which are subject to possible review to State courts on national legal principles.[30]

The Possibility of Significant Differences at National and International Level where the Code Is Not Adopted or Not Properly Applied at National Level

CAS 2006/A/1149 and 2007/A/1211,[31] WADA v. FMF and Mr Alvarez

A was a Mexican footballer. He had previously been suspended for one year by his national federation, the Federation of Mexican Football (FMF), when he tested positive for a prohibited substance. He tested positive again for stanozolol in 2006. While his club was notified of the positive test, he was not. Under the FIFA Rules, he would have had forty-eight hours to request a B sample analysis. The failure to notify meant that he could not do this. The FMF Disciplinary Committee dismissed the allegation because it was wrongly informed that the B sample had been destroyed so that the procedural error could not be cured. In fact, the WADA-accredited laboratory still had the sample. FMF appealed to the Mexican State Appeal Body (CAAD). CAAD dismissed the appeal against the dismissal of the allegation. WADA appealed to CAS.

The player faced a possible lifetime ban. He presented a number of arguments. He contended that the national process could not be overruled by CAS on an appeal. The CAS Panel underlined that a national-level arbitral appeal, or, indeed, a decision under national law, would not affect a decision made as a consequence of a player being a member of an international federation:

---

30 Challenges are rare and have been unsuccessful since the implementation of the Code. There are currently two cases before the ECHR challenging CAS processes as breaching fundamental rights protected under Article 6 of the ECHR. It appears that one, the *Pechstein* case, is likely to continue before the ECHR after the decision in the German Federal Supreme Court. See further Chapter 10, pages 513–17.

31 For a further example, see TAS 2006/A/1120, *UCI v. Jiminez and RFEC*, where the Panel considered the legal position in Spain did not invalidate the international arbitration process before CAS, and that, as a consequence, there was nothing to prevent a CAS award under the Code being made and binding the athlete in the world of sport.

National associations have vested authority in international federations, precisely in order to eliminate unfair competition and, in particular, to remove the temptation to assist national competitors by over-indulgence.

In effect, the exercise of WADA appeal rights under the FIFA regulations was part of this structure. The general principle could apply to national-level disciplinary decisions by sporting tribunals and by national public authorities (CAS 96/156, *F* v. *FINA*, Award of 10 November 1997 and CAS 98/214, *B* v. *FIJ*, CAS Digest II 1998–2002, p. 291).

The Panel noted that it was quite possible to have different outcomes at national and international level (although this is undesirable), where an athlete is bound to two different systems (see e.g. CAS 2005/A/872, *UCI* v. *Munoz and FCC*).

While at national level, a State may impose its decisions, there is nothing to prevent the award of a CAS Panel governing the international position under the rules of the relevant international federation which bind the player. Usually, the position will be complementary, particularly where a State supports the Code, but conflict is certainly possible.

The player was ultimately found to have committed a second violation. The WADA appeal was upheld. He was banned for life under the FIFA regulations.

Investigations by State Agencies and Anti-doping Organisations

Issues

As previously noted, WADA has continued to try to increase the coordination between State authorities conducting investigations and seeking to bring allegations under national criminal law and anti-doping organisations operating under the Code. Agreements between such organisations do not create obligations under the Code, but the exchange of information between State agencies and anti-doping organisations means that national courts and sporting arbitral tribunals such as CAS may have to consider questions relating to information and evidence which involve possible conflicts between national law and the position in sporting arbitration. Before the national courts, such matters have to be determined under national law. Before sporting arbitral tribunals, the issues will be determined under the principles of the legal system governing the dispute resolution process. Usually, before CAS, matters such as the admissibility of evidence obtained from an investigation by a State agency will be decided under Swiss law relating to international arbitration.

The ability of State authorities to share information with anti-doping organisations will be a matter for the applicable national legal system. Such sharing of information is expressly encouraged under the Code. Article 22 expressly provides that governments will put in place legislation, policies or practices for cooperation and sharing information with anti-doping organisations. Generally, there has been a significant increase in information provided by State agencies to anti-doping organisations which can be used as the basis for investigations and anti-doping allegations.

The proceedings in the Spanish courts, before CAS and in the Swiss Federal Tribunal in relation to the investigation and allegations involving the Spanish cyclist Alejandro Valverde Belmonte illustrate the factual, procedural and substantive legal issues which can arise where both national law-enforcement authorities and NADOs are involved in investigating alleged doping activities and bringing forward allegations. The potentially complex interplay between processes under State law and national-level tribunal proceedings and/or arbitral proceedings before CAS can make the prompt provision of reasoned decisions under the Code (which is a fundamental requirement in the sporting context, as provided for in Article 8 of the Code) difficult to achieve.

Illustrations

CAS 2007/A/1396 & 1402, *WADA and UCI* v. *Valverde and RFEC*; TAS 2009/A/1879, *Alejandro Valverde* v. *CONI, WADA, UCI*; *Valverde* v. *CONI, WADA, UCI*, Swiss Federal Tribunal, 4A 234/2010, 29 October 2010; *Valverde* v. *WADA, UCI*

The various CAS awards and the decisions in the Swiss Federal Supreme Court in the case against the Spanish professional cyclist, Mr Valverde, had their origins in a criminal investigation undertaken by the Spanish Civil Guard called 'Operatión Puerta', which began in May 2004. In 2006, a Spanish doctor, Dr Fuentes, and other individuals were arrested and charged with violating Spanish public health legislation. UCI was permitted to review the file and some of the evidence gathered in the investigation. After this review, it requested the Spanish National Cycling Federation (RFEC) to initiate disciplinary proceedings against V. This request was based upon the evidence gathered in the Operatión Puerta inquiries, which included a blood bag labelled 'blood bag no. 18', which was reported to belong to V. The competent body for doping matters within the RFEC made a decision not to open a disciplinary file against V in September

2007. In January 2009, the Spanish court closed the criminal investigations and held that criminal complaints should be filed against several individuals, including Dr Fuentes and his sister. V was not charged in these criminal proceedings.

Italian Proceedings

The cycling authorities in Italy also pursued V. The Italian authorities issued letters rogatory to the Spanish court requesting the release of blood bag no. 18. This request was granted in January 2009 by a Spanish judge, who authorised the Italian authorities to collect samples for their own use, drawn from blood bag no. 18. In January 2009, representatives of the anti-doping organisation responsible for investigating and prosecuting anti-doping violations within Italy, CONI UPA, and two officers of the Italian police attended and collected the samples. In February 2009, CONI, the body responsible for bringing anti-doping rule violation allegations in Italy, commenced proceedings against V and summoned him for questioning regarding his involvement in Operatión Puerta. Italian judicial authorities also began separate criminal proceedings against V for violations of Italian law. The evidence relied on by CONI included a sample from V taken when he was racing in Italy and DNA analysis of the blood from blood bag no. 18. The evidence was said to provide a 'match' between the DNA in the sample and that found in the blood bag, thereby identifying the blood in the bag as V's.

A hearing took place in the Italian proceedings in May 2009 and the Italian National Anti-Doping Tribunal found that V had committed a violation of Article 2.2 of the Code – the use or attempted use of a prohibited substance or a prohibited method. As a result, V was banned for two years from participating in any events organised under the auspices of CONI or related NSOs in Italy. V appealed this decision to CAS. In CAS 2009/A/1879, CAS dismissed V's appeal in relation to the Italian proceedings. During this time, V continued to compete in events around the world, but not in Italy, where the two-year period of ineligibility imposed by the Italian tribunal was applicable.

In the Spanish criminal proceedings, the initial investigating magistrate had closed the file against V in March 2007 on the grounds that doping was not an offence under Spanish law at the time of the alleged activity. The order closing the file was appealed by UCI, WADA and RFEC, and this appeal was allowed, with the Madrid Court of Appeal ordering that the file be reopened.

Analysis of the blood bags by the Barcelona laboratory revealed that nine, including blood bag no. 18, contained EPO. In October 2006, the Spanish investigating magistrate had also made an order prohibiting the use of material obtained in criminal proceedings in administrative proceedings. In his appeal to CAS in relation to the Italian proceedings, V submitted that CONI had no jurisdiction over the matter. It was submitted that a foreign-affiliated rider had to be dealt with by UCI, that the CONI proceedings prejudiced the athlete's rights to defence in the Spanish criminal proceedings and that, as a result of the orders made by the investigating magistrate in the Spanish proceedings, the evidence from those proceedings could not be used in the Italian disciplinary proceedings. In any event the evidence, if admissible, was not sufficient to prove an anti-doping rule violation which would permit the sanctioning of V.

Admissibility of Evidence from Criminal Process

Applying the national anti-doping rule in force at the time of the alleged violation (May 2006), CAS held that CONI had jurisdiction over a non-affiliated foreign rider in so far as V participated in sporting competitions in Italy. The CAS Panel held that the evidence obtained from the Spanish criminal process was admissible. The question of the admissibility of the evidence was procedural in nature and subject to the procedural rules applicable before CAS. As a matter of Swiss law relating to international arbitration, the discretion of the Panel to admit evidence was limited only by procedural public order. The Panel held that there was no relevant breach of the legal assistance process in the way in which the evidence had been obtained by judicial cooperation in the criminal process. The letters rogatory were valid because they had been endorsed by the public prosecutor of Rome. The order of revocation was limited in its effect to Spain and did not bind the Panel. The order could create no legal effect outside Spain and, in any event, by the time of the order of revocation, the process of blood bag no. 18 leaving Spanish territory and being analysed by the Italian police had already taken place. As had been held in the other arbitration proceedings before CAS, the Panel found that the orders made by the Spanish judge did not prohibit the production and use of Operatión Puerta documents in the CAS arbitration. The only limit in the power of the CAS Panel as a matter of international arbitration law relating to the admissibility of evidence was the concept of procedural public order under Swiss law. The alleged violations of the rules relating to judicial cooperation put forward on behalf of V did not amount to any violation of Swiss public order. Under Swiss law, the admissibility of evidence

allegedly obtained in an illegitimate manner was a balancing exercise and
there was no basis for not admitting the evidence obtained from the Spanish criminal proceedings. The argument that the analysis of the contents
of blood bag no. 18 would breach V's rights relating to the protection of
personality under Swiss law was also rejected. While the protection of personality was a part of public order and could limit the admissibility of evidence, a breach of personality rights is not considered illicit under Swiss
law when it is justified by the consent of the victim or by private or public
interests or by law.

CAS found that the fight against doping constituted a sufficient private
and public interest to justify the breach. The athlete's objections to CONI's
right to use blood collected in the 2008 Tour de France was also rejected.

The Panel then assessed the evidence against V. It rejected a challenge to
the chain of custody of the bags found in Spain and the samples collected
during the Tour de France. It rejected a challenge to the credibility of the
DNA match between V's DNA and the blood in the bag. The Panel held
that the DNA match was sufficient to prove, at the very least, an attempt to
use a doping method. It did not find it necessary to go further and consider
the presence of EPO in the bag. Other evidence also supported the finding against V. V was accordingly prohibited from assuming any function
within CONI and participating in any competitions in Italy for a period
of two years.[32]

Appeals to the Swiss Federal Supreme Court

V subsequently appealed this decision to the Swiss Federal Supreme
Court. He challenged the decision by CAS in relation to the Italian tribunal's ruling and sought to annul the award on the grounds set out in
Articles 190–192 PILA. In the appeal, he alleged that the composition of
the CAS Panel was irregular and that his right to be heard by an unbi-
ased tribunal had been breached. He alleged that the relationship of one
of the arbitrators to WADA gave rise to impartiality or an appearance of

32 It should be noted that DNA matching of blood bags obtained as a result of Operatión
Puerta and other evidence allowed proceedings to be brought under the Code against several other riders. The most recent CAS decision concerns the German former Tour de
France winner Jan Ullrich. The investigation is still continuing today, over ten years after
it started in the Spanish courts. In mid-2016, a Spanish appeals court allowed an appeal
by WADA and others against a court order to destroy the blood bags at the centre of the
investigations. The bags have been handed over to WADA and UCI. Any allegations under
the Code are likely to face arguments that they are time-barred under the limitation provisions.

impartiality. After consideration of the details of the arbitrator's work for WADA, the tribunal held, on an objective consideration of the established circumstances, that there was no appearance of bias, particularly given the nature of international sports arbitration. It also found that there was no basis for the claims that V had been denied his rights in the hearing by being refused the opportunity to carry out a further DNA test or by not being given sufficient time to review the documents provided for the hearing.

Appeal by WADA against RFEC Not to Bring
Disciplinary Proceedings

In CAS 2007/A/1396 & 1402, CAS heard the appeal brought by WADA and UCI against the decision by the RFEC in September 2007 not to open disciplinary proceedings against V as a result of the evidence found in the Operatión Puerta inquiry. In this appeal, WADA and UCI contended that RFEC had a duty to consider the merits of the claim against the athlete. It was submitted for V that the consideration of the Panel should be limited to the review of the decision and that if the decision was incorrect, the matter should be remitted to the RFEC so that it could decide whether or not to institute disciplinary proceedings.

The Panel held that it had full power to review the decisions by RFEC under the CAS Rules and that it could also determine whether, on the evidence before it, an anti-doping rule violation had been committed. In a pre-trial order, the Panel had held that the evidence collected in the course of Operatión Puerta investigation could be used in the arbitration, notwithstanding the orders in the Spanish courts to the contrary. The Panel then proceeded to review the evidence and held that it supported a finding that V had used a prohibited substance. It partially upheld the appeals and imposed a two-year period of ineligibility on V, starting 1 January 2010. This applied worldwide, extending the orders made in the Italian proceedings.

V also sought to annul this award in proceedings before the Swiss Federal Supreme Court on the basis that CAS had no jurisdiction to entertain an appeal against the decision by RFEC not to bring disciplinary proceedings. He also sought to appeal a decision by the President of the CAS Panel not to address the merits of a request to interpret and correct the CAS award. In two separate decisions, the Swiss Federal Supreme Court held that the appellant had no legal interest in the appeal against the refusal to review and correct the award, as its aim was the same as the

appeal against the CAS award. This meant that the jurisdiction to consider an appeal against a decision not to review an award did not have
to be decided. On the substantive appeals, the court held that the award
should not be annulled on the ground that the Panel giving the decision
had been improperly constituted where a party-appointed arbitrator had
withdrawn, with the remaining two members of the Panel producing the
award, and that, while the principle of *ne bis in idem* was part of Swiss
public policy, the principle had not been breached where the Italian proceedings against V and the proceedings on the appeal to CAS from the
refusal by RFEC to bring disciplinary proceedings were concerned with
different subject matters: ineligibility from competition on Italian soil and
worldwide ineligibility under the internationally applicable rules of the
sport. With the imposition of a two-year period of ineligibility applicable worldwide, this long journey through sporting tribunals, CAS and the
Swiss Supreme Court came to an end.

General International Support for the Code: the UNESCO International Convention against Doping in Sport

While the Code has its effect by voluntary agreement between private
organisations, it provides, in general terms, for governments to play a
role. Article 22 of the Code states that governments will show their commitment to the Code by signing the Copenhagen Declaration on Anti-
Doping in Sport and by taking all actions and measures to comply with
the UNESCO Convention. Amendments to Article 22 in the 2015 Code
emphasise that governments which have committed to the Code will
put in place legislation, policies or administrative practices for cooperation and sharing of information with anti-doping organisations and will
encourage the timely lawful sharing of information by all public services
and agencies with anti-doping organisations where that would be useful
in the fight against doping. The expectation is that this obligation will have
been met by governments by 1 January 2016. The other obligations, which
should already have been met, involve governments respecting arbitration as the preferred means of resolving doping-related disputes (subject
to human and fundamental rights and applicable national law), establishing a NADO where one does not exist,[33] respecting the autonomy and

33 The participation of Kenya in the 2016 Rio Olympics required it to pass laws creating a
NADO. Kenya was declared non-compliant with the Code, but this declaration was lifted
before the Games.

independence of the NADO and not interfering in its operation. The Article contains what Signatories expect of governments, but the only obligations binding on governments are that they will fulfil the requirements of the UNESCO Convention. A failure to accept the Convention or to comply with it may result in ineligibility to bid for events and other consequences.

The International Convention against Doping in Sport was signed in Paris on 19 October 2005 under the auspices of UNESCO ('the Doping Convention'). The Doping Convention builds on the earlier European Anti-Doping Convention (and its additional Protocol), and provides for State parties to support the purposes of the Code by adopting appropriate measures at national and international levels. The Convention explicitly recognises the need for public authorities and organisations responsible for sport to 'have complementary responsibilities to prevent and combat doping in sport'. The purpose of the Doping Convention is expressed as being to 'promote the prevention of, and the fight against, doping in sport with a view to its elimination'.[34]

The Convention: Summary

The Convention contains general provisions by which State parties commit themselves to the principles of the Code as the means of carrying out the purpose of the Convention. State parties agree to adopt appropriate measures, which might be legislation, regulation, policies or administrative practices,[35] to restrict the availability of prohibited substances and methods; to encourage sporting organisations and anti-doping organisations to adopt such measures; to take measures or encourage sporting organisations and anti-doping organisations to adopt measures aimed at athletes' support personnel who commit anti-doping violations; to encourage producers and distributors of nutritional supplements to establish best practices in the marketing and distribution of nutritional supplements;[36] to provide funding to support national testing

---

34 Article 1 of the Convention – the purposes are similar to those of the earlier European Anti-Doping Convention.
35 See Articles 4 and 5 of the Convention.
36 CAS awards reveal that contaminated nutritional supplements have, on many occasions, been, or have been claimed to be, the cause of positive tests. Given the general knowledge of the risk, an athlete testing positive as a result of taking a contaminated supplement has found it difficult to establish the basis for a reduction of the applicable sanction. The 2015 Code now contains specific provisions in Article 10.5.1.2 for the reduction of the applicable

programmes; and to withhold sport-related financial support from ath-letes or athletes' support personnel who are suspended from sports organ-isations and from anti-doping organisations which do not comply with the Code. State parties also agree to facilitate doping controls by organisations from other States. The Convention contains further provisions relating to international cooperation,[37] by which State parties agree to facilitate coop-eration between anti-doping organisations, public authorities and sports organisations in their jurisdiction and those within the jurisdiction of other State parties in order to achieve, at the international level, the pur-pose of the Convention. State parties undertake to support WADA and its funding and to facilitate the task of WADA and anti-doping organisa-tions in carrying out doping control across borders, where that is appro-priate and in accordance with domestic law and procedures. The Conven-tion further provides for State parties to take steps to support education and training programmes for anti-doping and to promote and encourage research. There is provision for the monitoring of the Doping Convention by a conference of the parties to it. WADA is an advisory organisation to that conference. The Convention entered into force on its thirtieth ratifi-cation, and as at 31 July 2015 it had been ratified by 182 countries.[38]

The Doping Convention represents 'soft' international law (like the Code itself) which encourages State parties to support the Code in var-ious ways. The Convention reinforces the high level of international com-mitment to the elimination of doping in sport, and this international unity can be relied on to support the Code as an agreed response to the problem of doping. Against this international backdrop, which presents a strongly united front against doping, the restriction of an athlete's individual per-sonal and economic rights by the Code's provisions on strict liability and sanctions is more readily seen as a justifiable response to the problem of doping in sport which is not contrary to public policy.[39]

   sanction where the athlete can show that a prohibited substance detected in a sample came
   from a contaminated product. See further Chapter 8, pages 398–400.
37 Articles 13–18, which relate to facilitating cooperation between anti-doping organisations
   and sports organisations in the jurisdiction of a State party.
38 The Fifth Conference of the Parties to the Convention took place on 29–30 October 2015,
   in Paris. WADA attended in an advisory capacity. Other key bodies, such as the IOC and
   European Commission, attended in the capacity of observers.
39 See e.g. the various opinions obtained by WADA on whether the Code complies with fundamental rights referred to in Chapter 10, page 486, note 6 and the advisory opinion from
   CAS requested by WADA and FIFA (Chapter 10, pages 499–501). See also *Meca-Medina
   and Majcen* v. *Commission of European Communities and Republic of Finland* (Chapter 10,
   pages 503–4) for the decision by the European Court of Justice holding that anti-doping

Compliance with the UNESCO Convention is monitored as determined by the Conference of the State Parties to the Convention following consultation with the State parties and WADA. A failure by a State party to meet its obligations under the Convention (a matter which might be difficult to establish) could lead to a reference to the conference of the parties to the Convention. WADA has the primary responsibility of monitoring compliance with the Code. Non-compliance with the Code by Signatories may lead to steps being taken by WADA under the Code itself in its role of monitoring compliance with the Code.[40]

provisions are a justifiable restriction on the economic freedoms protected under EU law, and Chapter 10 for further consideration of similar challenges to the Code.

40 See Articles 23.4–23.5 for compliance with the Code and monitoring compliance with the Code, and UNESCO Convention and Chapter 7, pages 320–1 for compliance by mutual recognition of decisions by Signatories. WADA had declared various Signatories non-compliant as at 21 November 2016; see note 1.

The International Standards in More Detail

The Role of International Standards

The Code functions together with the WADA International Standards and various Guidelines or Models of Best Practice which may be adopted by anti-doping organisations in relation to the processes contained in the Standards. Although Guidelines cover many important areas of the sample collection and testing process, they are not mandatory, whereas Signatories must apply and comply with the International Standards in order to fulfil their obligations under the Code. The Standards (and related Technical Documents) are an indispensable part of the regime under the Code, and the Articles of the Code make direct reference to the Standards where testing and investigations, the analysis of samples to prove doping, the designation of prohibited substances and methods and the grant of TUEs are referred to.[1] Article 4 (Prohibited List and TUE), Article 5 (Testing and Investigations) and Article 6 (Laboratories) of the Code, which have been the subject of some amendment in the 2015 Code, contain general provisions relating to the operation of the Standards which explain their purpose, role and operation in the regime. The same provisions and other provisions of the Code also serve to incorporate the operation of the Standards into the Code. The Code cannot function as a set of rules regulating the misuse of drugs in sport without the operation of the Standards.

The Standards allow WADA to provide for and develop a harmonised anti-doping regime which is binding worldwide on Signatories to the Code. Recently, a good deal of the development in the Standards, Technical Documents and Guidelines has been concerned with the general processes by which anti-doping organisations conduct their anti-doping operations.

---

1 In contrast to the pre-Code regime under OMADC, the Standards are contained in separate documents, whereas OMADC contained all the elements of the doping regime.

The most obvious example of the essential role of the Standards is in establishing the violation of doping under Article 2.1. Testing for a substance or method identified as prohibited under the Prohibited List has to be carried out in conformity with the ISTI (Article 5.2 Code). The sample obtained has to be analysed by a WADA laboratory accredited under the International Standard for Laboratories (ISL) if doping is to be established (Article 6.1 Code and notes). There can only be a doping violation if a prohibited substance or method designated under the International Standard Prohibited List is detected, and on review of a positive test, the anti-doping organisation responsible for results management will have to ascertain whether the substance detected is subject to a TUE granted under the International Standard for Therapeutic Use Exemptions (ISTUE). The entire process of obtaining a sample and a result from the analysis of that sample which supports an allegation under Article 2.1 is contained in the applicable Standards. In addition, in obtaining, processing and storing information through this process, an anti-doping organisation has to operate under the International Standard for the Protection of Personal and Private Information.

In general terms, the Code provides the framework for the processes, key obligations and sanctions and for results management, while the Standards provide the all-important detail of the processes which have to be followed by anti-doping organisations and athletes. An anti-doping organisation which agrees to the Code, and an athlete or other person who is bound to it, will agree to the application of both the Code and the Standards. Non-compliance with the provisions of an applicable Standard will mean that a party is in breach of its obligations under the Code. The consequence will depend on the particular provision in the Standard and the circumstances. The Standards contain a mix of obligations. Some provisions impose obligations which anti-doping organisations have to fulfil if they are to meet their general obligations under the Code. Other provisions are specifically concerned with the detail of the particular processes which an anti-doping organisation must follow in order to establish a violation of the Code. Further provisions in the Standards impose obligations on participants who are bound by the Code.

The consequence of a breach of a provision of the ISTI or ISL will depend on the nature of the provision. Non-compliance with requirements for sampling and analysis under the ISTI and ISL may mean that an anti-doping organisation cannot establish that the process has been carried out which is necessary to prove an anti-doping rule violation. In this area, the defence of an alleged anti-doping violation under the Code may involve the detailed consideration of the Standards applicable to the process of testing and analysis (and related Technical Documents concerning such matters as the method of analysing samples for specific prohibited substances or methods)[2] in order to determine whether the anti-doping organisation has carried out its obligations properly so as to be able to prove the allegation.[3]

Non-compliance with provisions in the ISTI relating to the provision of whereabouts information may mean that an athlete has committed an anti-doping rule violation or a breach of the whereabouts requirements. Non-compliance with other obligations under the Standards may simply put an anti-doping organisation in breach of its obligations under the Code and make it potentially liable to be declared non-compliant by WADA, as opposed to being directly relevant to the proof of a violation of the Code by an individual bound by it. This chapter seeks to outline the various obligations imposed in the Standards.

The Current International Standards

As at 1 January 2017, the International Standards in force were:

- the Prohibited List 2017;[4]
- the International Standard for Therapeutic Use Exemptions (ISTUE), January 2016;
- the International Standard for Testing and Investigations (ISTI), January 2017;
- the International Standard for Laboratories 7.0 (ISL), 2 June 2016; and

---

2 An early example would be the various CAS awards concerning the effectiveness and scientific soundness of testing methods used to detect the presence of EPO in samples in its various synthetic forms. The WADA Technical Document TD2009EPO sought to harmonise testing for recombinant erythropoietin (i.e. epoetin) and its analogues (e.g. darbepoetin and methoxypolyethylene glycol-epoetin beta). More recently, the decision limits set out in the Guidelines applicable to testing for hGH were the subject of challenges in proceedings before CAS on the basis that they were not reliable – the cases led to the publication of new Guidelines. The proof of use of prohibited substances by means of evidence derived from ABP regimes has meant that CAS Panels have had to consider the admissibility and reliability of evidence obtained by such regimes. See Chapter 5, pages 206–15 for an outline.

3 For examples of this kind of case, see Chapter 5, pages 195–204.

4 This Standard has to be changed no less than annually by WADA under the process contained in the Code. The Prohibited List 2017 came into force on 1 January 2017. It made some relatively minor changes to the Prohibited List 2016.

- the International Standard for the Protection of Privacy and Personal Information (ISPPPI), January 2015.

In addition to the Standards themselves, there are a number of further documents published by WADA which form part of the ISL. These Technical Documents, which are regularly reviewed and revised, relate to a significant degree to the process of testing, analysing and reporting by laboratories.[5] In this area, Technical Documents are under regular development in order to provide for the detection of new forms of prohibited substances and methods used by athletes. The best examples are perhaps the testing processes developed and designed to detect synthetic forms of EPO and the use of human growth hormone.[6] Guidelines for anti-doping organisations have also been published covering important aspects of the testing and results management process which are not mandatory.[7] Perhaps the most significant are the Athlete Biological Passport Operating

---

5 See the WADA website for the following Technical Documents: Blood Analytical Requirements for the ABP TD2015BAR, Decision Limits for the Confirmatory Quantification of Threshold Substances TD2014DL, Detection of Synthetic Forms of Endogenous Anabolic Androgenic Steroids by GC-C- IRMS TD2014IRMS (see now TD2016IRMS), Endogenous Anabolic Androgenic Steroids Measurement and Reporting TD2014EAAS (see now TD2016NA), Harmonisation of Analysis and Reporting of 19-Norsteroids Related to Nandrolone TD2015NA, Harmonisation of Analysis and Reporting of Erythrpoiesis Stimulating Agents (ESAs) by Electrophoretic Techniques TD2014EPO, Human Growth Hormone (hGH) Isoform Differential Immunoassays for Doping Control Analyses TD2015GH, Identification Criteria for Qualitative Assays Incorporating Column Chromatography and Mass Spectrometry TD2015IDCR, Laboratory Document Packages TD2009LDOC, Laboratory Internal Chain of Custody TD 2009 LCOC, Minimum Required Performance Levels for Detection and Identification of Non-Threshold Substances TD 2015 MRPL.
6 See e.g. CAS 2009/A/1931, *Iourieva and Akhatova* v. *IBU*, where the application of the new TD 2009 EPO to the evaluation and interpretation of results in the detection of biosimilar EPO was considered by the CAS Panel. At the time, the new Technical Document was necessary to provide for the method of detecting the various new forms of recombinant EPO being used by athletes. The Panel noted that it had been advised that there were some eighty variations of the substance available on the market.
7 The WADA site lists Guidelines in force in the different areas: Information Gathering and Intelligence December 2015, Guidelines for Optimising Collaboration between International Federations and NADO February 2016, Guidelines for implementing an Effective Testing Program October 2014, International Cooperation by NADOs June 2014, Reporting and Management of hCG and LH Findings in Male Athletes December 2016, HGH Biomarkers Test April 2016, Blood Sample Collection September 2016, Urine Sample Collection October 2014, Breath Alcohol Testing October 2014, Sample Collection Personnel, Major event testing February 2016, Therapeutic Use Exemptions Jan 2016, ABP Operating Guidelines 1 January 2017, Education and Information to Prevent Doping in Sport May 2016, Results Management Hearings and Decisions October 2014, TUE Enquiries by Accredited Laboratories June 2009 and Laboratory Test Reports January 2008.

Guidelines, which provide guidance for the running of an ABP regime.[8] These documents also include Guidelines for Coordinating Investigations and Sharing Anti-Doping Information and Evidence, which seek to assist anti-doping organisations in creating and developing partnerships with the national agencies responsible for law enforcement so that cooperation and the exchange of relevant information can be improved, which should make the investigation of non-analytical anti-doping violations more effective.[9] Similarly, there are non-mandatory Guidelines which seek to assist anti-doping organisations (and the committees formed by them) in their consideration of applications for TUEs under the TUE Standard.[10] The various documents referred to in this section, whether binding or non-binding, form part of the World Anti-Doping Program. In each of these areas, the Guidelines seek to provide assistance to anti-doping organisation in carrying out mandatory obligations under the Code.

While, for the most part, the International Standards and the related Technical Documents, and many of the published Guidelines, are still concerned with the identification of prohibited substances and methods and the process of sampling and testing for the presence of prohibited substances in bodily samples taken from an athlete, the greater focus on the investigation of the violations under Articles 2.2–2.8 which do not involve positive tests has seen the amendment of the Code and ISTI and the implementation of related Guidelines to impose obligations and provide guidance to Signatories for the conduct of such investigations and the management of results obtained in them.[11] However, for the most part, the nature

---

8 An ABP programme is linked to mandatory testing and analysis processes under the Code and Standards. The Guidelines annex mandatory Technical Documents for the analysis of samples which return adverse passport findings. For an outline of the operation of an ABP programme, see Chapter 5, pages 204–10, where the operation of the programme in connection with the relevant violation – the use of prohibited substances and methods – is considered with relevant case summaries.

9 See WADA website. The Guidelines were produced in May 2011. More recently, in February 2016, WADA produced Guidelines for Optimising Collaboration between International Federations and National Anti-Doping Organisations.

10 See e.g. Therapeutic Use Exemption Guidelines January 2016, which are non-mandatory Guidelines from WADA providing anti-doping organisations with a model of best practice to assist them in carrying out their obligations in considering TUE applications under Article 4.4 of the Code and the ISTUE. For more on applications for TUEs, see pages 112–24.

11 There have been a number of changes since the second edition of the text in 2012. At that time, the Guideline on Results Management contained a section on managing the results of investigations into anti-doping rule violations apart from doping under Article 2.1 of the Code, but these provisions and the provisions of the Code were very limited

of investigations into non-analytical violations means that obligations and Guidelines in this area have to be expressed in quite general terms.

The Prohibited List

The Prohibited List[12] fulfils the fundamental role under the Code of identifying the substances and methods which are prohibited under the Code and are the subject of testing by anti-doping organisations. Without this list of designated substances and methods, the obligations and violations under the Code would have no purpose. The Prohibited List can be regarded as the foundation on which the Code is built. Apart from the violation of doping under Article 2.1, which involves detection of the presence of a prohibited substance or method or its metabolites or markers in the bodily sample of an athlete, the other violations in Article 2 of the Code involve avoiding or interfering with the process of doping control in some way, carrying out acts in relation to prohibited substances or methods or failing to meet obligations under the Standards (the whereabouts obligations under the ISTI).[13] The violations involving use, possession, attempted administration and trafficking generally require an anti-doping organisation to establish that a prohibited substance or method was involved in the violation, although they do not involve proof of the presence of a prohibited substance in the bodily sample of an athlete by testing and analysis.[14] While a doping violation under Article 2.1 requires sample analysis by a WADA-approved or authorised

and much was left to the anti-doping organisation handling the investigation. Anti-doping organisations now have much clearer obligations and more guidance in this area under the Code itself, the applicable Standard (the ISTI) and the relevant Guidelines (Optimising Collaboration between IF and NADO, Information Sharing and Intelligence Gathering and Implementing an Effective Testing Program).

12 The current Prohibited List 2017 came into force on 1 January 2017. The List is published in English and French, and, as with the interpretation of the Code, in the event of conflict between the English and French versions of the Code, the English version will prevail.

13 See Chapter 5 for an outline of the violations under Article 2 and the elements of each violation.

14 See Chapter 5 for the proof of the elements of the violations in Article 2. In many circumstances, where violations are investigated, it will be necessary for an anti-doping organisation to have a substance analysed by a laboratory in order to determine that the conduct alleged does, indeed, relate to a prohibited substance or method. If such a substance or method is not involved, generally there can be no violation under the Code, although there can be an attempt to use a prohibited substance or method where the athlete has the intention to use a prohibited substance or method but the substance or method which she intends to use is in fact not prohibited. See Chapter 5, pages 215–17.

laboratory (and anti-doping organisations operating under the Code are likely to use WADA-approved laboratories for analytical work), the status of substances involved in other violations under the Code might be established by analysis carried out by non-WADA laboratories, provided the evidential results produced were proven to be reliable.

The Consequence of Inclusion on the Prohibited List

The nature of the WADA programme means that no allegation can be brought or investigation carried out in relation to a substance or method which is not included in the Prohibited List, even if it can be shown that a particular substance or method has a performance-enhancing effect or otherwise might meet the requirements for inclusion in the Prohibited List. A sporting organisation may be able to investigate and bring an allegation under its own rules if the use of a substance or method which is not on the List can be said to breach those rules. Similarly, where an anti-doping organisation has the power to investigate anti-doping rule violations under the Code, it will not be able to investigate allegations which do not relate in some way to the use of substances which are on the Prohibited List, other than where it seeks to assist WADA under the monitoring programme, according to which particular substances which are not on the Prohibited List are monitored in order to detect any patterns of misuse in sport by anonymous testing.[15]

Review of the Prohibited List

The limitation on the application of the Code to the detection of substances and methods in the Prohibited List highlights the importance of the regular review of the List by WADA so that it covers, as far as possible, the prohibited substances and methods which may be used by athletes to enhance performance. Under Article 4.1 of the Code, WADA is obliged to publish the List as an International Standard as often as is necessary, and no less often than annually. WADA has the power to amend the List as required. The effect is that the content of the List is under review, with

---

15 See Article 4.5 of the Code, the 2016 Monitoring Programme, which came into force at the same time as the 2016 Prohibited List. The programme provided that certain stimulants and narcotics were to be monitored in-competition, that the use of glucocorticosteroids by certain routes of administration would be monitored both in- and out-of-competition and that the use of telmisartan would be monitored both in- and out-of-competition. Certain narcotics and stimulants have been added to the 2017 Monitoring Programme.

changes made as required, at least on an annual basis. Where WADA proposes to amend the List, it has to distribute the proposed amended List to all Signatories and governments for comment and consultation. When the List has been adopted, WADA must publish the List on its website and distribute it promptly to the Signatories for distribution to their members.[16] The rules of each anti-doping organisation specify that, unless the List provides otherwise, the List will go into effect under the rules of the anti-doping organisation within three months of the List being published by WADA.

Considerations

The List has to identify the prohibited substance and methods which are prohibited at all times and the substances and methods which are prohibited in-competition only. International federations can recommend the expansion of the List to provide that particular substances are prohibited in a particular sport.

Specified and Non-specified Substances

The List makes the important distinction between specified and non-specified substances. The classes of substances which are designated as specified substances under the List were significantly extended as part of the changes implemented by the 2009 Code. While before the 2009 Code, specified substances were expressly referred to on the List as substances 'which were particularly susceptible to unintentional anti-doping rule violations because of their general availability in medicine or products or which are less likely to be successfully used as doping agents', the List no longer contains this comment.[17] The comment to Article 4.2.2 of the 2015 Code now states that 'specified substances should not in any way be considered less important or less dangerous than other doping substances. Rather they are simply substances which are more likely to have been consumed by an athlete for a purpose other than the enhancement of performance'. This provision makes a similar point about the innocent taking of specified substances, although it seeks to make sure that detection of specified substances is not assumed to involve a lesser form of breach of

16 See Article 4.1 of the Code. The 2016 Prohibited List came into effect on 1 January 2016 and is published on the WADA website. The 2017 Prohibited List (and 2017 Monitoring Program) came into effect on 1 January 2017.
17 See Article 4.2.2 of the Code and Prohibited List 2016.

the Code. The expansion of the class of specified substances means that the class contains a number of substances which may well be used in doping for performance enhancement. Article 4.2.2 provides that specified substances are all prohibited substances except those which fall within the classes of anabolic agents and hormone antagonists and modulators, as identified on the Prohibited List. Prohibited methods cannot be specified substances.

The question whether a substance detected in a sample is specified or not has always been important in relation to the imposition of sanctions. Under the 2015 Code, where a violation of Article 2.1, 2.2 or 2.6 involves a specified substance, the period of ineligibility will be two years unless intentional conduct as provided for in Article 10.2.3 is established by the anti-doping organisation.[18] Generally, where a violation of Article 2.1, 2.2 or 2.6 involves a specified substance and there is no intentional conduct, if the person who committed the violation establishes no significant fault or negligence under Article 10.5.1.1, the period of two years may be replaced with a sanction ranging from a warning to two years' ineligibility.[19]

Provisions

The speed with which new performance-enhancing substances are developed, often from known listed substances, means that the List has to cover substances related to prohibited substances if it is to catch the range of prohibited substances in use in a meaningful way. The List seeks to do this through forms of generic listing and by including a 'catch-all' clause at the ends of its sections. The List has also included (since 2011) a section which seeks to catch substances which are not currently approved for human therapeutic use by any governmental regulatory authority.[20]

18 The fact that the sanction for the presence, use or possession of a specified substance can increase to four years where an anti-doping organisation establishes intentional conduct recognises that specified substances may well be used intentionally in breach of the Code to enhance performance.

19 See Chapter 8, pages 353–369 for further comment and case summaries. Previously, under the 2009 Code, the presence of a specified substance meant that the more flexible regime on sanctions under Article 10.4 was applicable. Article 10.4 has been removed in the 2015 Code as part of the complete re-casting of Article 10 on sanctions. While the range of sanctions is the same under the 'no significant fault' provision under the 2015 Code as under Article 10.4 of the 2009 Code, the requirements for the application of the provision are different. Appendix 2 contains the text from the second edition, which reviews the application of Article 10.4 of the 2009 Code and provides relevant case summaries. This material is largely of historical relevance.

20 For more detail, see pages 102–3.

How is a Substance or Method Included on the List?

The question whether a substance or method should be prohibited is determined by the WADA List Committee (which comprises eleven scientists) by reference to the criteria contained in Article 4.3 of the Code. Where the Committee considers that a substance or method should be included on the List, it reports to the WADA Health Committee, which makes the final decision on inclusion.

A substance or method will be considered for inclusion in the List if WADA considers that two of the following three criteria are met:

- medical or other scientific evidence, pharmacological effect or experience that the substance or method alone or in combination with other substances or methods improves sport performance;
- medical or other scientific evidence, pharmacological effect or experience that use of the substance or method represents an actual or potential health risk to the athlete;
- WADA's determination that the use of the substance or method is contrary to the spirit of sport as described in the Introduction to the Code.

If two of the three criteria are satisfied, WADA can decide whether to include the substance or method in the Prohibited List. The addition of the words 'in its sole discretion' in the 2015 Code emphasises that the decision whether the criteria are established and whether to include a substance or method in the List is solely a matter for WADA. A substance or method will also be included on the List if WADA determines that there is medical or scientific evidence, pharmacological effect or experience that the substance or method has potential to mask the use of prohibited substances or methods.[21] The reason for the inclusion of a substance or method on the List is not recorded on the List, nor is the reason made available publicly. Where WADA places a substance or class of substances on the List, it will also decide whether it will be classed as a specified substance or not and whether it will be prohibited in-competition only or both in-competition and out-of-competition.

Generally, where a substance is included on the List, it is prohibited across all sports which adopt the Code. Similarly, the detection of any quantity of a prohibited substance will establish a violation unless a specific threshold requirement for an adverse analytical finding is imposed

21 See Article 4.3.2 of the Code.

under the List and/or the relevant Technical Document.[22] The Prohibited List, and the violations under Article 2.1 where prohibited substances are detected, operate in accordance with the principle of strict liability for the detected presence of any quantity of a prohibited substance, regardless of any intent to improve sporting performance (or, indeed, of any possibility of such improvement or intent to break the code).[23]

No Challenge to List Status

Where a substance or method has been included on the Prohibited List, that decision cannot be challenged by an athlete facing an anti-doping rule violation by claiming that the substance or method does not, in fact, satisfy the criteria for inclusion.[24] As a CAS Panel observed in CAS 2005/A/921, *FINA* v. *Kreutzmann and the German Swimming Federation*:

> Once a substance has been put on the List, it is the fact that such a substance has been detected in the athlete's body that is deciding. The List and the

22 Some substances have such a threshold requirement before an adverse analytical finding can be made; see TD 2017DL. The problem of the regular detection of cannabis in the samples of athletes given in-competition who used the drug recreationally outside competition was addressed in a practical way by increasing the decision limit for the reporting of an adverse analytical finding from 15 ng/ml to initially 175 ng/ml, then 180 ng/ml (for technical reasons). It is important to distinguish any applicable threshold requirement for the detection of a substance at a particular level before an adverse analytical finding can be made and the minimum required performance levels for laboratories for the purposes of accreditation under the ISL. While for certain substances there can only be an adverse analytical finding if specified decision limits are exceeded, the fact that a laboratory can detect the presence of a substance at lower levels than those required by way of minimum performance does not affect the making of an adverse analytical finding for the substance detected. (See e.g. CAS 2009/A/1805, *IAAF* v. *RFEA and Onyia* – low level of clenbuterol detected. CAS Panel concluded wrong to treat minimum detection level required for a laboratory to be accredited with limit on detection level for a positive test.)

23 The question whether there was 'intention' as defined in Article 10.2.3 of the 2015 Code involved in taking or using a prohibited substance or method will now arise under the provisions imposing the four-year period of ineligibility under the 2015 Code. See further Chapter 8, pages 346–72.

24 See Article 4.3.3 of the 2015 Code. The provision also states that the classification of the substance under the List and its classification as a substance prohibited at all times or in-competition only is final and not subject to challenge 'based on an argument that the substance or method was not a masking agent or did not have the potential to enhance performance, represent a health risk or violate the spirit of sport'. While the expressed grounds of challenge are not really applicable to classification decisions, the intention of the Article is clear, and it would be interpreted as making final and not subject to challenge any decision by WADA concerning the inclusion and classification of substances and methods in the Prohibited List.

agreed procedure for its elaboration and enforcement leaves no room for a
counter-analysis to determine whether a substance was effectively used as
a masking agent or not.

This kind of impermissible challenge to the inclusion of a substance or
method (and related decisions as to the classification of the substance or
method under the List) should be distinguished from the situation where
the athlete claims that the determination that a particular substance or
method has been detected is invalid because the testing and/or analysis
has been incorrectly performed, or where an athlete claims that a substance detected is not a substance included on the List because it is not,
on proper scientific analysis of its chemical composition, a substance identified on the List or a substance which is 'similar' to substances in a class
of prohibited substances on the List. Such contentions can be raised by
athletes facing an anti-doping rule violation as defences to the allegation.

What Does the List Include?

As with previous versions of the List, the 2017 Prohibited List distinguishes between substances which are prohibited at all times, both in- and
out-of-competition, and those prohibited in-competition only. The general groups of substances which are prohibited in-competition and out-
of-competition are non-approved substances, anabolic agents, peptide
hormones, growth factors and related substances and mimetics, beta-2
agonists, hormone and metabolic modulators, diuretics and other masking agents.

The methods which are prohibited at all times in-competition and out-
of-competition are the manipulation of blood and blood components,
chemical and physical manipulation and gene doping. These substances
and methods are generally those which are employed by athletes who
intend to improve their sporting results by chemical means – those who
might in common parlance be described as deliberately cheating.

Under S0 (which was a new provision introduced in the 2011 List and
amended in the 2012 List, and included in the section on Prohibited Substances to make it clear that it does not refer to prohibited methods), the
2017 List prohibits non-approved substances in- and out-of-competition.
A 'non-approved' substance is generally defined as any pharmacological
substance which is not addressed by any of the subsequent sections of
the List and which has 'no current approval by any governmental regulatory health authority for human therapeutic use'. Examples given are

drugs under pre-clinical or clinical development, discontinued designer drugs and drugs only approved for veterinary use. The section is generic in nature, and no specific substances are identified. The provision itself makes it clear that S0 can only be applied where a substance does not fall within another section of the List, whether by express designation or by the application of a 'catch-all' provision. The provision can be criticised as not designating prohibited substances with sufficient certainty, with the result that the rules to which athletes are subject lack the predictability which has been held to be required in anti-doping regimes.[25]

The substances which are prohibited in-competition only are stimulants, narcotics, cannabinoids and glucocorticoids. It is important to note that stimulants are broken up into listed identified stimulants, which are non-specified stimulants, and the broader category of specified stimulants, which includes a list of identified stimulants and those stimulants with a similar chemical structure or similar biological effect. Alcohol and beta-blockers are prohibited in-competition in certain designated sports only.

Similar Substances: Catch-All Provisions

Several categories of substances prohibited under the List are expressed to include 'other substances with a similar chemical structure or similar biological effect'. This 'catch-all' provision avoids substances falling outside the List purely because they are not specifically named in a particular category. Such a provision is found in the following parts of the List: Section 1 (anabolic androgenic steroids (AAS), exogenous[26] AAS), Section 2

25 J. E. Marshall and A. C. Jennings, 'When Will WADA Get It Right? The 2011 WADA List', *Commentator of ANZSLA* (2010), 81. To date, this provision on the List does not appear to have been relied on in any proceedings which have reached CAS or any sporting tribunal. This probably reflects the broad scope of the List, the effectiveness of the 'catch-all' provisions in the List and the regular review of the substances which are included in the List.

26 The List distinguishes between substances which occur naturally in the body (endogenous) and those which come from outside the body (exogenous). Earlier versions of the List contained provisions relating to further investigation and analysis where an endogenous substance was detected in a sample which might have come from an exogenous source and give rise to an adverse analytical finding. Under the ISL the presence of prohibited substances which can be produced endogenously may in certain circumstances be reported as an atypical finding to the responsible anti-doping organisation. After receiving such a report the anti-doping organisation will have to review the atypical finding under Article 7.4 of the Code and carry out the required further investigation or direct such further investigation in order to determine whether the atypical finding will be brought forward

(prohibiting hormones and related substances), Section 4 (diuretics and marketing agents) and Section 6b (specified stimulants). Under the List, substances are identified by technical scientific name, International Non-proprietary Name (INN) and International Union of Pure and Applied Chemistry (IUPAC) nomenclature – the latter where further clarity is necessary. The List also uses common names for prohibited substances where this is considered helpful in communicating the substances covered by the List. The List cannot as a result be approached as a wholly technical scientific document; rather, it is a document which seeks to identify and describe the substances and classes of substance which are the subject of regulation in sport as comprehensively and clearly as possible for the wide range of persons who are bound by the regime created by the Code or who have to consider its application.

Reason for 'Catch-All' Provisions

The rationale for the use of 'catch-all' provisions was explained by the arbitrator in the award relating to the doping allegations against the British athlete, Dwain Chambers, which arose from the US BALCO investigation:

> The reason for the drafting of the list in the form of example substances is derived from the complexity of the subject matter, the continuing advances in scientific understanding and the need for a rule which is comprehensive, fair and clear. It would be impracticable to identify all forms of steroids in the list of prohibited substances, and it is always possible for new substances to be synthesized. It would be unfair to some athletes, and detrimental to the health of others, to permit athletes to experiment with novel forms or derivations of steroids until such time as the rule makers detected the new compounds and moved to add them to the list of identified substances. To restrict the prohibition to certain named substances would be both unfair and detrimental to the interests of the sport and athletes.

As has been noted, an athlete facing an allegation of doping can challenge the claim that a substance which is not specifically identified on the List is prohibited because it has a similar chemical structure or similar biological effect to a group of substances on the List.[27] Such a challenge raises the scientific question whether a particular substance is, in fact, related to the class of prohibited substances in question, and that question

---

as an adverse analytical finding. See pages 110–11 for discussion of atypical findings under the Code. See Chapter 7 for results management.

27 See CAS 2005/A/726, *Calle Williams* v. *IOC* at pages 107–9.

will be determined by a consideration of expert scientific evidence on the nature of the substance by the tribunal hearing the allegation. Where the issue is raised by the evidence, the burden of showing that the substance is 'similar' will fall on the anti-doping organisation bringing the allegation, and the standard of proof will be the standard which applies to the proof of any violation – proof to the comfortable satisfaction of the tribunal.[28]

A substance specifically identified by its chemical name may well have many closely related metabolites and compounds which will be impractical to list individually. The 'catch-all' provision makes the individual listing of all such compounds unnecessary.

In other parts of the List, while the 'catch-all' provision is not used, substances are described in a generic way (e.g. 'insulins', 'all beta 2 agonists', etc.); other parts of the List make it clear that the substances listed in a section are examples of the generically named substance by adding 'including but not limited to'.

Where substances are more generally described, all substances which fall within the description used when it is interpreted in the scientific context will, it is submitted, be covered by the description, provided it can be shown by the anti-doping organisation bringing the allegation that the substance comes within the description. Where a section of the List contains no 'catch-all' provision (or other provision permitting a broader interpretation of the terms used in the section) and substances are specifically listed by their chemical names, the substances prohibited will be limited to the specifically identified substances. In such a section, no 'catch-all' provision can be implied and the proper approach is, it is submitted, to interpret the List as being limited to the designation of the specific chemical compounds listed. Most areas of the List contain some provisions which extend the scope of the particular section beyond the designated substances. S1b of the 2017 List specifies certain endogenous AAS and provides that they are prohibited when administered exogenously. While endogenous AAS are specified because only certain AAS are produced endogenously, the metabolites and isomers (which, if detected, will lead to an adverse analytical finding) form an open list because the list of metabolites and isomers is prefaced by the phrase 'including but not limited to'.

Those stimulants which are not within the class of specified substances are specifically identified and listed. All other stimulants (save imidazole

28 For the burden and standard of proof, see further Chapter 6.

derivatives for topical use and the stimulants included in the monitoring programme) will be prohibited as specified substances. In most sections of the List, where generic listing and/or a 'catch-all' or other provision is used, the wording of the List means that the sections should be interpreted more broadly to cover all substances which are not specified by name but which can be shown to fall within the scope of the provisions which broaden the application of the section.

Specified Substances

The List has always identified specified substances in accordance with the Code. Under earlier Lists, these substances were said to be designated as specified substances because, while prohibited, they were 'particularly susceptible to unintentional anti-doping rule violations because of their general availability as medicinal products or …less likely to be successfully abused as doping agents'. This explanation is no longer in the 2017 List, but as set out earlier, the notes to Article 4.2.2 of the 2015 Code contain text which includes a similar warning. As the notes to the now removed Article 10.4 of the 2009 Code stated, the increase in the number of specified substances under the 2009 Code meant that specified substances would not necessarily be less serious doping agents than non-specified substances. Of course, the consequence of the broadening of the category of specified substances under the 2009 Code was that the maximum period of ineligibility for a violation involving a specified substance where the requirements of Article 10.4 were met was increased from one year under the 2004 Code to two years, and the requirements under the 2009 Code for a reduced sanction for an anti-doping violation involving a specified substance were changed to impose a significantly higher burden of proof on an athlete seeking the reduced sanction.[29] While the provisions relating to sanctions for specified substances have been altered fundamentally under the 2015 Code, the provisions on the periods of ineligibility for violations involving specified substances reflect the approach taken when the category was broadened under the 2009 Code.

Again, the designation of specified substances is carried out by WADA, and, as with the designation of prohibited substances generally, the designation of a substance as a specified substance, or a failure to so designate a substance, cannot be challenged by an athlete.

---

29 See Appendix 1 for the requirements under Article 10.4 and summaries of relevant decisions.

Illustrations of Issues Relating to Identification of Prohibited Substances

Is the Substance Detected Similar?

CAS 2005/A/726, *Calle Williams* v. IOC   W was tested after the women's points race at the Athens Olympics. She noted on the doping control form that she had taken neosaldina. The analysis of the sample showed the presence of heptaminol. WADA (which was responsible for testing at the Games) wrote to the IOC informing it that heptaminol was a substance with a similar chemical structure or similar pharmacological effects to the listed substances. The IOC was informed of an adverse analytical finding on the A sample. The B sample was tested on request by the athlete and confirmed the A-sample result. The matter was considered by the IOC Disciplinary Commission.

It was established at the hearing that W had been prescribed neosaldina for a headache by a doctor attached to the Colombian Olympic team. She was disqualified from the race and ordered to return her bronze medal. UCI was directed by the IOC to consider any further action. Ms Williams started CAS proceedings to appeal the IOC decision.

The central issue was straightforward: did the result of the analysis of the sample show the presence of a substance which was within the Prohibited List as a substance 'with similar chemical structure or similar pharmacological effect' to the substances named as S1 stimulants on the Prohibited List?

The medicine taken contained isometheptene. The evidence was that this substance metabolised into desmehyl isometheptene, which, in the test tube in the laboratory, transforms into heptaminol. This scientific process was accepted on both sides.

CAS held, on the scientific evidence, that isometheptene was not a prohibited substance under the IOC Rules. It acknowledged the importance of the 'related substances' extension on the Prohibited List as a means of identifying and sanctioning 'the use of substances not expressly listed as prohibited but nonetheless related to a prohibited substance by its pharmacological actions or chemical structure'. Without this extension, an athlete could take a drug which was only slightly different from the drugs on the List and which had similar effects, but escape sanction.

CAS rejected an argument from the IOC that, as with the inclusion of a substance on the List, no challenge was available to a finding by the anti-doping organisation that a substance was related to a substance on the List. With a substance which was said to be similar to a prohibited substance (as opposed to the decision whether to include a substance on the List), there was no process of consideration by experts from all interested groups, and allowing no challenge on a ruling that a substance was similar to a listed substance would place too much responsibility with WADA alone.

On a consideration of the expert evidence, CAS found that the substance detected was not similar to a listed substance. It was not sufficient that the substance could be said to have the same effect as the group of substances and be a stimulant. By a majority, the Panel found that WADA had not discharged the burden of proof and shown to their 'comfortable satisfaction' that the substance detected had the necessary similarity with any of the substances listed.

The Panel also considered that, even if a substance were found to be similar to substances on the List, it would still have to be satisfied that the criteria for the inclusion of a substance on the List were satisfied before it could be treated as prohibited.

CAS 2002/A/376, *Baxter* v. *IOC*   B was a skier for the British team who was awarded a bronze medal in the 2002 Olympic Games in slalom. He had a long-standing problem with nasal congestion and had a non-prescription Vicks Vapour inhaler. The Vicks inhaler was included on the list of permitted substances issued by the UK Sports Council. The US Vicks inhaler had a different formulation to the one sold in the United Kingdom: the US version contained levomethamphetamine. B bought a US Vicks inhaler and did not consult with the doctor, because it seemed to be the same as the UK product. He did not read the back of the package, which said that levomethamphetamine was an active ingredient.[30] When tested after winning his medal, the laboratory reported the presence of methamphetamine from the inhaler. At the Olympics, B was disqualified from the skiing event and had his bronze medal and diploma withdrawn by the IOC. He was further suspended for three months as a result of the positive test by the Fédération Internationale de Ski (FIS).[31] He appealed to CAS.

The question raised was whether the ingredient in the Vicks inhaler fell within the reference in the OMADC to methamphetamine. Methamphetamine has two isomers: levomethamphetamine, which is found

---

30 This case is one of many where an athlete has suffered serious consequences as a result of not being careful enough in purchasing non-prescription medicines.
31 For the subsequent CAS hearing on the successful appeal by B against the way in which the three-month sanction was ordered to be served, see CAS 2002/A/396, *Baxter* v. *FIS*, CAS Digest III, p. 373.

in decongestants, and methamphetamine, which is found in 'speed'. B claimed that only the methamphetamine isomer was intended to be included on the List. The Panel held that, on the proper construction of the List, the term 'methamphetamine' included both isomers of methamphetamine, including levomethamphetamine, or, at a minimum, that levomethamphetamine fell under the group 'amphetamines' in the OMADC List. The argument that levomethamphetamine in the Vicks inhaler was a separate substance from methamphetamine was rejected on the expert evidence, on the basis that, from a scientific perspective, the term 'methamphetamine' denotes both isomer forms.

As a result, the unusual request for further specific testing from B to determine which isomer had been detected was refused. The Panel decided that the disqualification from the Olympics was correct, and represented a proper application of the principles of strict liability for doping to the results obtained.

General Scientific Challenges to Test Results

Where a finding that a bodily sample contains a prohibited substance is challenged on the basis either that the testing was incorrectly carried out or that the conclusion that a prohibited substance was not produced naturally by the athlete was incorrect, the hearing process will involve the consideration of expert testimony concerning the procedures by which the adverse analytical finding was reached.[32] An example of the scientific issues which can be raised in such a case is *USADA* v. *Landis*, where challenges were made to several aspects of the laboratory process by which samples were analysed to determine whether they showed an elevated ratio of testosterone to epitestosterone (T/E ratio) and/or the presence of exogenous testosterone by isotope ratio mass spectrometry (IRMS).[33] Where anti-doping rule violations are defended on this basis, the facts relating to the testing and analysis process carried out under the applicable Standards and Technical Documents will have to be considered by reference to the specific rules of proof in Article 3 of the Code concerning alleged departures from International Standards.[34]

---

32 There have been many cases where a challenge to an adverse analytical finding has involved the consideration of complex conflicting scientific evidence relating to the laboratory analytical processes. See Chapter 5, pages 193–204 for relevant examples in case summaries.
33 See Chapter 5, pages 195–7 for the case summary.
34 See further Chapter 6, pages 280–2.

Prohibited Methods

Prohibited methods include all forms of external manipulation involving artificial enhancement of oxygen transfer, tampering with samples during doping control in order to alter their integrity by such methods as the use of catheters or urine substitution,[35] intravenous infusions (save for legitimate medical treatment) and gene doping.

Prohibited Substances which Occur Naturally in the Body

Where a sample is analysed and a substance is detected which is capable of being produced naturally by the body, a further investigation may be required to decide whether an adverse analytical finding should be made because the substance is not of endogenous origin.[36] While under the 2004 Code the Prohibited List contained notes referring to the process of further investigation which might be required, the List now makes no specific provision for such matters.[37] The Technical Documents which are concerned with the analysis of samples for the measurement and reporting of endogenous anabolic steroids which have been administered exogenously and for the measurement and reporting of human growth hormone provide for the testing of samples to determine the presence of synthetic forms of endogenous anabolic steroids. In certain circumstances, the testing process may be inconclusive, and this will lead to the reporting of an atypical finding. An atypical finding is defined in the Code as 'a report from the laboratory or other WADA approved entity which requires further investigation as provided by the International Standard for Laboratories or related Technical Documents prior to the determination of an adverse analytical finding'. Under Article 7.4 of the 2015 Code, the anti-doping organisation responsible for managing the result will have to conduct the required investigation into such a finding. The nature of that investigation

---

35 This conduct may also give rise to a violation for tampering with doping control under Article 2.5. See Chapter 5, pages 241–6 for the elements of the violation under Article 2.5 and relevant case summaries.

36 'Endogenous' refers to a substance which is capable of being produced by the body naturally, while 'exogenous' refers to a substance which is not ordinarily capable of being produced naturally by the body.

37 The change appears to reflect a desire on the part of WADA for the List to be concerned with the designation of substances rather than the process of determining whether a prohibited substance or method is present in a sample.

will depend on the circumstances of the particular case.[38] After the investigation has concluded, the athlete will be notified whether or not the atypical finding will be brought forward as an adverse analytical finding. An atypical finding will not be notified to any party, including the athlete, before the conclusion of the required investigation and the decision whether to take the atypical finding forward as an adverse analytical finding, save where the anti-doping organisation decides that the B sample will be analysed before the end of the investigation or receives a request from the organiser of a major event or a sport body selecting a team for an international event to disclose whether an athlete in a list provided by the organiser or sport body has a pending atypical finding. Disclosure can only be made to a major event organiser or sport body under these provisions after the athlete has been notified of the finding.[39]

Testosterone and Other Endogenous Steroids

Technical Documents provide for a two-stage analytical process to be carried out by laboratories in respect of the reporting of endogenous AAS. The TD2014EASS provides for the process by which laboratories measure and report endogenous AAS in urine, including the measurement and reporting of data used in relation to the steroidal module of the ABP. TD2014IRMS sets out the analytical method to be used by the laboratory to detect the presence of synthetic forms of endogenous AAS by gas chromatography–combustion–isotope ratio mass spectrometry (GC-C-IRMS). GC-C-IRMS will be carried out as a confirmation procedure where initial testing shows a suspicious steroid profile or an atypical passport finding. A laboratory can also be requested to carry out GC-C-IRMS

---

38 The notes to Article 7.4 provide the example of a situation where it has been previously established that an athlete has a naturally elevated testosterone level and the atypical finding is consistent with this. In that situation, the anti-doping organisation would declare that the result was negative after the athlete's previous testing results and profile had been considered. However, there may be other circumstances where it is necessary for the anti-doping organisation to carry out a more extensive investigation. Such an investigation could take different forms but is likely to involve further no-notice testing to allow for further analysis and profiling. The investigation of an atypical finding or of an adverse passport finding is the responsibility of the anti-doping organisation which had the testing conducted and/or which was responsible for results management. The anti-doping organisation may have to provide further information to WADA concerning the atypical finding. See ISTI 12.2. For more on the ABP and atypical passport findings, see Chapter 5, pages 204–10.
39 Article 7.3.1. See Chapter 7 for results management.

by an anti-doping organisation with responsibility for testing or by an Athlete Passport Unit or WADA where the 'markers' in the steroid profile are normal. Where the GC-C-IRMS is inconclusive, the laboratory will report the result as an atypical finding, and this will lead to further investigation under Article 7.3 of the Code. The Technical Document for the harmonisation of testing and analysis to detect human growth hormone contains a similar obligation to report inconclusive samples as atypical findings or atypical passport findings.

The International Standard for Therapeutic Use Exemptions (ISTUE)

The ISTUE was initially derived by WADA from a review of the various procedures and protocols of international federations, the IOC and NADOs in relation to the permitted use of prohibited substances or prohibited methods for therapeutic reasons. The Standard sets out the conditions for the grant of a TUE, the responsibilities of anti-doping organisations in making and communicating TUE decisions, the process of applying for a TUE and the process by which a TUE obtained is recognised, the obligations of WADA in reviewing TUE decisions and the confidentiality obligations applicable in respect of information collected in the TUE process. The effect of the Code and Standard is to provide for a harmonised process for granting TUEs across sports and countries.[40] The ISTUE reflects the basic principle that the use of any drug in sport should be limited to 'medically justified indications', and provides for the process by which athletes are allowed to use prohibited substances where there is a medically justified reason.[41]

Article 4.4 of the Code provides in general terms that there will be no anti-doping rule violation where the presence of a prohibited substance, its use or attempted use or its possession, administration or attempted administration is consistent with a TUE granted under the ISTUE.

Article 4.4.5 of the 2015 Code now permits NADOs to allow athletes who are not international- or national-level athletes who are using prohibited substances for therapeutic reasons to apply for retroactive TUEs if they are tested and return positive tests. This is because anti-doping organisations have a discretion whether to test these athletes and are permitted not to require advance TUEs for them.

---

40 See Introduction and Scope to ISTUE.
41 See Title to Prohibited List 2008. The phrase no longer appears in the Prohibited List 2017, but it remains an appropriate summary of the aim of the TUE system.

Article 4.4 of the Code

The general provisions concerning the jurisdiction to grant TUEs (and for appeals) are set out in Article 4.4 of the Code. The substantive considerations for the grant of TUEs are contained in the ISTUE, and there are also WADA Guidelines to assist anti-doping organisations in the operation of the system under the ISTUE.[42]

Article 4.4 was significantly re-cast in the 2015 Code to clarify the jurisdiction over TUE decisions and the recognition and review of TUEs, and to provide more clearly for appeal rights in relation to TUE decisions. Article 13 now confirms that all TUE appeals are regulated by Article 4.4, not Article 13.

Under Article 4.4.2, an athlete who is not an international-level athlete has to apply to his or her NADO for a TUE. If the TUE is not granted, the athlete has the right to appeal to the appeal body at national level.[43]

Under Article 4.4.3, an international-level athlete has to apply to his or her international federation for a TUE. If an international-level athlete has a TUE from his or her NADO which meets the ISTUE criteria then the TUE has to be recognised by the international federation. If the international federation refuses to recognise the TUE because it does not in its view meet the criteria then it has to notify the athlete and national doping organisation of this promptly and give reasons. The athlete and NADO then have twenty-one days to refer the TUE to WADA for review. If there is no referral, the TUE becomes invalid on the expiry of the period of twenty-one days for referral for review. If the TUE is referred to WADA for review, it remains valid at national level and for out-of-competition testing but is not valid for international-level competition. If an international-level athlete has no national-level TUE, he or she must apply directly to his or her international federation as soon as the need for a TUE arises. If the application is declined, the international federation must notify the athlete with reasons. If the TUE is granted, both the athlete and his or her NADO must be notified. Again, if the NADO considers that the TUE granted does not meet the criteria under the ISTUE then it can refer the question to WADA for review. Pending WADA's decision on the review, the TUE remains valid for international-level competition but not for national-level

---

42 WADA TUE Guidelines and Medical Information to Support the Decisions of TUEC are available on the WADA website. They are to be used to assist members of a Therapeutic Use Exemption Committee (TUEC) in applying the TUE criteria.

43 Articles 13.2.2 and 13.2.3 for appeals at national level. See further Chapter 9, page 477.

competition. Similarly, if there is no referral for review, the TUE becomes valid at national level as well as at international level when the twenty-one-day period for review ends.

Under Article 4.4.4, a major event organisation may require athletes to apply for TUEs if they wish to use a prohibited substance or method in connection with an event it is responsible for. The major event organisation has to ensure that there is a process in place for applications to be made by athletes who do not have a TUE. If a TUE is granted, it will be valid for the event only. There are similar provisions for the recognition of TUEs already held by athletes by major event organisations and for notification and appeal to an independent body established by the major event organisation if the major event organisation does not recognise the TUE (usually, this appeal body will be CAS).

Under Article 4.4.5, where, under the testing plan adopted, an anti-doping organisation chooses to collect samples from athletes bound by the Code who are neither national- nor international-level athletes and who do not have to apply for advanced TUEs under its testing plan, the anti-doping organisation may permit an athlete who tests positive to apply for a retroactive TUE.

WADA is under an obligation to review any international federation decision not to recognise a national TUE and any decision by an international federation to grant a TUE referred to it by any NADO. WADA may also review any other TUE decision at any time, whether on request or on its own initiative, and reverse the decision if it does not comply with the criteria under the ISTUE.

Any decision by an international federation on a TUE which WADA chooses not to review or which it reviews and does not reverse can be appealed by the athlete or anti-doping organisation exclusively to CAS. The decision under appeal will be the decision of the international federation, not WADA's decision on review, but the time for the appeal will not begin to run until the date when WADA communicates its decision on review. A decision to reverse a TUE decision by WADA on review can be appealed by the athlete, anti-doping organisation or international federation affected exclusively to CAS; a failure to make a decision on a properly submitted application for the grant or recognition of a TUE is considered to be a denial of the application and will give rise to rights of appeal.

Any athlete bound by the Code may wish to apply for a TUE. As outlined, NADOs, international federations and major event organisations may have to consider an application for a TUE. Each organisation has to have an advertised process for making and considering TUE applications and a TUE Committee (TUEC) made up of at least three physicians with experience in clinical sports exercise medicine, which will consider TUE applications. The majority of the physicians must have no political responsibility within the sporting organisation which appoints them. The ISTUE sets out the information which has to be included in an application for a TUE and the time-frames for the application and for a decision by the TUEC.

As has been noted, WADA has in some circumstances an obligation to review TUE decisions, and in others it has the power to review decisions if it wishes to, whether upon request by those affected by the decision or on its own initiative. WADA has to have a TUEC for this purpose. If WADA decides not to refer a request to review a TUE decision to its TUEC, that decision cannot be appealed. The original TUE decision may be appealed to CAS.

Application for TUE and Criteria for Grant

Under the ISTUE, a TUE may be granted to an athlete with any of the required conditions, permitting the use of a substance or method contained in the Prohibited List at a specified dose. The application will be made on the standard form and must be accompanied by a statement from the athlete's physician supporting the need to take the substance for therapeutic reasons and by a complete medical history, including the original diagnosis of the condition requiring the therapeutic treatment. The application for a TUE has to be made as soon as possible, and where it is for the use of a substance prohibited in-competition, at least thirty days before the competition, unless the application is made in an emergency or under exceptional circumstances. The application is made through the Anti-Doping Administration and Management System (ADAMS). The TUEC has to make its decision as soon as possible and (unless there are exceptional circumstances) within twenty-one days of the application. Where a TUE is granted, it has to include the permitted dosages, any conditions and a time for expiry. If the TUE is declined, the TUEC has to give reasons. The decision whether to grant or decline an application will be notified to the athlete, to the other affected anti-doping organisations and to WADA through ADAMS.

The specified criteria under the ISTUE which an application for a TUEC must satisfy are:

- The prohibited substance or method is needed to treat an acute or chronic medical condition such that the athlete would experience a significant impairment of health if the prohibited substance or method were to be withheld.
- The therapeutic use of the prohibited substance or method is highly unlikely to produce any additional enhancement of performance beyond what might be anticipated by a return to the athlete's normal health following the acute or chronic medical condition.
- There is no reasonable therapeutic alternative to the use of the prohibited substance or method.
- The necessity to use the prohibited substance or method is not a consequence in whole or in part of the previous use of a prohibited substance or method (without a TUE) which was prohibited at the time of such use.[44]

The applicant for the TUE has to satisfy the TUEC that the criteria are met. The ISTUE 2016 amended the Standard to make it clear that an applicant for a TUE has to establish the requirements to the balance-of-probabilities standard. The comment to Article 4.1 makes it clear that on any decision in relation to recognition or on review, the question is whether the applicant for the TUE has established the requirements for a TUE under Article 4.1 ISTUE on the balance of probabilities.

The Application of the Criteria

While those who are members of TUEC established by anti-doping organisation to assess TUE applications will consider the health of the athlete in the course of considering the application of the criteria for the grant of a TUE set out in the previous section, there is no general residual discretion to deny a TUE, where the criteria under the Standard have been established, on the grounds that allowing the athlete to take part in the sporting activity with the TUE exemption will endanger the health of the athlete.[45] There may be exceptional cases where there is strong evidence that the athlete's health will be damaged by competing with a TUE, with the result

---

44 See ISTUE Article 4.1(a)–(d). The provisions have undergone some minor amendment in the 2015 revision of the ISTUE.
45 CAS 2004/A/717, *International Paralympic Committee* v. *Brockman and WADA*. The Code and ISTUE provisions in relation to the review of TUEs by WADA make it clear that the question whether to grant or decline a TUE is a matter of considering the criteria under the ISTUE and does not involve any broader consideration of the welfare of the athlete.

that 'a reasonable therapeutic alternative to the use of the prohibited substance' under the criteria is for the athlete to withdraw from competition and not take part. However, generally, the consideration of the general fitness of the athlete to take part in the sport is a different matter from the consideration whether to grant a TUE, and the fact that the athlete might be incapable of playing the sport without the TUE is not a matter which a TUEC should consider in deciding whether to grant a TUE.[46] By contrast, where a decision on the fitness of an athlete to take part is considered under the general eligibility rules of a sport, it will be necessary to consider the effect of the use of any prohibited substance taken under the TUE on the athlete. There is an obvious link between the processes by which the general fitness of an athlete to take part in the sport under its eligibility rules and the question whether to grant a TUE are considered – a TUE application might make it clear to the sporting organisation that the athlete is no longer fit for competition under its eligibility rules. This would arise in the case of a chronic disease where a TUE is denied on the basis that the TUEC considered that the reasonable therapeutic alternative for the athlete was not to take the prohibited substance and so not take part in the sport, because the effects of the substance would seriously impair the health of the athlete. Such a decision by a TUEC on the TUE application might well be followed by a decision by the sporting organisation to prevent the athlete competing on the ground that his or her health would be endangered under the general competition rules of the sport.

Approach to TUE Appeals

As noted, decisions by international federations may be the subject of an appeal to CAS under Article 4.4.7 of the Code.[47] Under Rule 57, CAS has a broad general power to review decisions on fact and law in its appeal jurisdiction, which has frequently been relied on by CAS arbitrators in appeals in anti-doping matters.[48] However, a decision in relation to an application

---

46 CAS 2004/A/709, *B v. UCI and WADA* at para. 51.
47 Article 13.4 in the 2015 Code now provides that TUE decisions may be appealed exclusively as provided in Article 4.4. Article 4.4.7 reverses the decision in *Berger* where the CAS Panel held that Article 13.4, on its interpretation, did not provide an appeal for an athlete whose application for a TUE had been denied by the TUEC of the international federation and this decision was confirmed by WADA. The appeal was heard because the parties had agreed to jurisdiction. See pages 122–4 for a summary of the case.
48 See Chapter 9 on appeals and Article 57 of the CAS Procedural Rules for the power to re-hear a matter on the facts and law on appeal.

for a TUE by a TUEC represents a form of expert determination, and it was held by a CAS Panel in *Bouyer*[49] that the jurisdiction of CAS on an appeal against such a decision was limited. The approach taken was that CAS should not substitute itself for the TUEC of an anti-doping organisation and reconsider a TUE decision. The Panel held that it should only consider whether the application has been properly considered by reference to the criteria under the Standard and whether the Standard has otherwise been properly applied.[50] This approach was, however, not followed by a CAS Panel in *Berger* v. *WADA* (see pages 122–4), which saw no reason why it could not reconsider the refusal of a TUE by considering the medical evidence under its powers on appeal under Rule 57. While accepting that the Panel had to give the views of medical experts respect and appropriate weight, the Panel took the position that it would not shrink from taking a different view if that was appropriate on the evidence 'as a matter of logic and commonsense'. This is consistent with the general approach on appeals by CAS, although the fact that a TUEC is a body of experts and must have a majority of members with no involvement with the sporting organisation might be said to support a more deferential approach. The same approach was also taken by a CAS Panel in a later appeal against the reversal of a decision by the WADA TUEC to deny a TUE.[51] It should also be noted that, as is the case in relation to the consideration of anti-doping violations under the Code, an appeal in relation to a TUE cannot consider whether a substance has been properly included in the Prohibited List, thereby making an application for a TUE necessary.

Retroactive TUE Applications

The ISTUE sets out the circumstances in which an application can be made for a TUE on a retroactive basis. The basic position is that the athlete who is subject to the Code must apply for a TUE before using a

---

49 For a summary of the decision in CAS 2004/A/709, *Bouyer*, see pages 121–2.
50 See para. 50 of the CAS Award in *Bouyer*.
51 CAS 2013/A/3437, *ISSF* v. *WADA*, where the ISSF appealed against a decision by the WADA TUEC to reverse the ISSF decision to deny a TUE application made by a shooter who sought a TUE for atenolol – a prohibited beta-blocker. The WADA TUEC decision to grant a TUE was set aside by CAS because the evidence could not discharge the second requirement of the criteria under the ISTUE in force at the time and show that therapeutic use would produce no additional enhancement of performance other than that which might be anticipated by a return to a normal state of health following treatment of a legitimate medical condition.

prohibited substance or method if he or she wishes to use the substance or method for therapeutic reasons and avoid committing an anti-doping rule violation.

A TUE can only be granted on a retroactive basis where emergency treatment or treatment of an acute medical condition was necessary, where exceptional circumstances meant that there was insufficient time for the athlete to apply for a TUE or for the TUEC to consider an application before sample collection, where the applicable rules require a retroactive application[52] or where WADA and the anti-doping organisation to which an application for a TUE was or would be made agree that fairness requires that a TUE be granted retroactively.

Given that the effect of a retroactive TUE will be to remove an anti-doping rule violation committed in-competition where competitors are entitled to assume that fellow competitors will not compete with prohibited substances in their systems, the requirements must, it is submitted, be considered as imposing strict limitations for the grant of a retroactive TUE. Such a TUE is generally reserved for unusual circumstances which can be shown to have prevented the athlete from making an application before competing as required by the ISTUE. If the required circumstances for a retroactive application can be established, the application will be considered against the same requirements as a standard application for a TUE.[53]

The ISTUE contains provisions requiring the applicant to consent to the disclosure of their medical information to the TUEC and scientific experts for the consideration of the application and for the applicant's physician to release any further medical information required for the same purpose. All information supplied can only be used for the purposes of considering the application for the TUE or in relation to possible anti-doping rule violation proceedings. The standard forms for applications are annexed to the ISTUE.

TUE applications will be made using the WADA Web-based data-management system ADAMS, where the information supplied will be held and through which decisions on TUE applications will be notified to the affected parties. The collection, storage, processing, disclosure and retention of personal information under the ISTUE have to comply with the requirements of the ISPPPI. Anti-doping organisations also have to

---

52 This will apply where an anti-doping organisation tests athletes who are not national- or international-level athletes and so are not required to have advance TUEs.
53 Article 4.3(a) and (b) of the ISTUE.

maintain private information obtained in this process and other aspects of their operations in accordance with any applicable national privacy laws.

General Process

Where an adverse analytical finding is made after a sample has been analysed, the anti-doping organisation responsible for results management will carry out an initial review of the finding to determine, among other things, whether an applicable TUE has been granted before deciding to notify the results as an adverse analytical finding.[54]

The process of applying for a TUE has often been misunderstood by athletes and their advisers and not correctly followed. As a result, there have been a number of findings that doping violations have been committed by athletes who might have obtained a TUE for the prohibited substance detected if an application had been made before the event. The generally strict limits on retroactive approval should be borne in mind by athletes and their advisers.

As with the inadvertent use of prohibited substances, athletes and their advisers carry a significant responsibility to exercise care in ensuring that proper applications for TUEs are made. Ignorance of the rules or simply forgetting to apply for a TUE will not constitute the kind of exceptional circumstance which might justify an application for retroactive approval after doping control has been carried out. In exceptional circumstances, problems with TUE applications before a sample produces a positive test may provide a basis for a plea of no significant fault, but such situations will be very uncommon.[55] Where an athlete is able to apply for a retroactive TUE under the testing regime adopted by a NADO by reason of the level at which they compete they should have the relevant medical information available. Their application will need to meet the usual criteria for the grant of a TUE (not the specific requirements for a retroactive TUE, which would apply to an athlete who was required to have a TUE in advance); if it does not, the athlete will be subject to the usual consequences attached to a violation of the Code.

54 Article 7.1 of the Code and Chapter 7 of the present volume.
55 For a case where problems with obtaining a TUE were part of the circumstances in which an athlete was able to raise a defence of no fault in connection with a refusal to submit to sample collection, see CAS 2007/A/1416, *WADA v. USADA and Scherf*. A no-significant-fault plea in such a case would not now be available under the 2015 Code.

Illustrations

Application of Criteria: General Fitness to Compete Irrelevant

CAS 2004/A/717, *IPC* v. *Brockman and WADA* A CAS Panel dismissed an appeal brought by IPC against the grant of a TUE to a British paralympic dressage rider of international level. The IPC had decided not to grant the TUE on the grounds that the health of the athlete would be detrimentally affected by competing. WADA had reversed this decision on the grounds that there was no general health ground for denying a TUE, while not disagreeing with the general power of a sporting organisation to exclude athletes from competition whereby they were unfit to take part. CAS found that the approach of IPC was not in accordance with the International Standard. The award discussed the situations in which the health of the athlete will be considered under the criteria, and how, in certain circumstances, it would be possible for a TUEC to conclude that one reasonable therapeutic alternative to the grant of the TUE would be that the athlete does not compete, given the effect of competing while taking the prohibited substance. This did not apply in this case.

Establishing the Criteria for a TUE on the Evidence

TAS 2004/A/769, *Franck Bouyer* v. *UCI and AMA*; TAS 2005/A/965, *UCI* v. *AMA and Bouyer* B had been a professional cyclist for ten years. In 2002, he began to notice symptoms while riding and was diagnosed with a particular condition for which he was prescribed a prohibited substance. He applied for a TUE. The UCI TUEC found that the criteria were not made out, because it was impossible to guarantee that the substance would not improve performance beyond the level which might be anticipated by a return to normal health following the treatment of the condition.

The WADA TUEC confirmed this decision that the requirements of Article 4.3 of the Standards had not been met. The Committee also found that the requirements of Article 4.2 did not appear to have been met. Before CAS, there was an initial procedural argument as to whether there was a right of appeal from the WADA decision or whether the decision of the UCI TUEC had to be the subject of an appeal. The parties, however, agreed on the CAS tribunal having jurisdiction in relation to the UCI TUEC, with no point on the time limit for the appeal being taken.

The Panel held that the burden lay upon the athlete to show that he was entitled to the TUE. It found that new factual material and evidence was not admissible before CAS. The Panel held that Mr Bouyer had given no tangible proof of his 'feeling' that the prohibited substance did not improve his performance beyond that which would amount to a return to normal health. Although the Panel heard further medical evidence on behalf of Mr Bouyer, it rejected the appeal. On jurisdiction, the Panel considered that it was not in a position to put itself in the position of the TUEC and make medical assessments. It should only proceed on the probative material put forward in support of the application. In making its finding on the appeal, the Panel noted that Mr Bouyer was able to reapply for a TUE.

Subsequently, Mr Bouyer did reapply for a TUE. His position was that he could only continue as a cyclist if he was allowed to take the prohibited substance. Tests were carried out after the first hearing in an effort to establish the absence of performance enhancement in using the substance. Again, the UCI TUEC did not grant the TUE. The WADA TUEC, however, granted the TUE subject to monitoring, and reversed the UCI TUEC decision. UCI appealed to CAS. The Panel found that there was no discretion in the decision whether to grant a TUE. The question was whether the criteria had been met. If the prohibited substance might have a performance-enhancement effect beyond bringing the athlete back to a state of normal health, then the TUE had to be refused.

The WADA TUEC had found that the performance-enhancing potential of the drug was not clear on information before it on the TUE file. The Panel held that the criteria had not been properly applied by the WADA TUEC in the light of its own medical conclusions as to the effect of the substance which Mr Bouyer had to take. In effect, the WADA TUEC had given a TUE while finding that the performance-enhancing effect had not been excluded. Accordingly, no TUE could properly be granted.[56]

Approach to TUE Criteria

CAS 2009/A/1948, *Berger* v. *WADA* Mr Berger was an international paraplegic shooter. He had been taking a beta-blocker called metoprolol for many years to treat a significant heart disease. If he did not take metoprolol, his life would be endangered. Metoprolol is a prohibited substance in- and out-of-competition in shooting under the Prohibited List.

Mr Berger initially applied to the international federation for a TUE. His application was rejected. This was confirmed by the WADA TUEC on the basis that Article 4.3 of the Standard was not met, because Mr Berger had

---

56 In 2010, Mr Bouyer returned to competition in cycling successfully. Apparently, a treatment had been developed for his condition which did not involve him taking a prohibited substance.

not shown that the metoprolol would produce no additional enhancement to performance other than that which might be anticipated by a return to a normal state of health. The WADA TUEC based its decision on the scientific literature on the effect of beta-blockers. On appeal to CAS, it was contended that evidence obtained in monitoring Mr Berger's heart showed that, while the beta-blocker had a therapeutic effect, the heart rate was not lowered significantly. In those circumstances, it was contended, on behalf of Mr Berger, that there was no additional enhancement of performance or increased steadiness.

The CAS Panel was not prepared to accept that there was jurisdiction for the appeal on the wording of Article 13.4 where the WADA TUEC had confirmed the decision of the IPC TUEC as opposed to denying the TUE. Article 13.4 was limited on its words to decisions 'reversing' the TUE decision. However, the parties had agreed to the appeal proceeding in the event that the tribunal was not persuaded that there was a right of appeal under the Code.

Contrary to the approach taken by the CAS Panel in the *Bouyer* decision, the Panel was prepared to review the evidence and, notwithstanding the expert evaluation by the TUEC, it held that the usual extensive powers of review conferred on a CAS Appeal Panel by Rule 57 of the CAS Procedural Rules were applicable, which meant that there could be no restriction on the power of a Panel to review the facts and the law.

> There is no reason to suppose that merely because the members of the Panel may not be physicians that they are not competent to decide matters of a medical nature assisted by expert evidence. Just as in cases coming before courts of law, medical issues frequently arise in cases before CAS Panels whose members have no medical qualifications. They frequently arise in cases of alleged anti-doping violations under the WADC. The Panel will give the views of persons with appropriate qualifications the utmost respect and weight which is due but will not shrink from taking a different view if, on the totality of the evidence before the Panel, a different conclusion is more compelling as a matter of logic and commonsense.

The Panel agreed that there was no residual discretion to decline the TUE if the criteria under the Standards were met. On the central substantive issue, the Panel reviewed the evidence in relation to the effect of the beta-blocker on Mr Berger. It found that, while the evidence showed that the beta-blocker did not have a significant effect on Mr Berger's heart rate, the effect on hand tremor could not be discounted. This secondary effect of metoprolol was, the CAS Panel concluded, supported by studies on the effects of beta-blockers. The evidence of likely reduction in hand tremor was capable of being relied on. The Panel concluded:

> Considering the medical evidence as a whole, we take the view the appellant has not demonstrated that the therapeutic use of the Prohibited Substance would produce no additional enhancement of performance other than that which might be anticipated by return to a state of normal health following the treatment of a legitimate medical condition. Thus we have reached the conclusion that the athlete in this case, at this time, on the basis of all the evidence before us, has not discharged the burden resting upon him to establish this entitlement to the TUE for the use of metoprolol whilst participating in his chosen sport of shooting.

The International Standard for Testing and Investigations (ISTI)

The ISTI and ISL are concerned with the process by which an athlete is tested and a sample is collected (by an anti-doping organisation with jurisdiction by agreement over the athlete) for analysis by WADA-accredited laboratories in order to determine whether the sample contains a prohibited substance or provides evidence of the use of a prohibited method. The important general principle set out in Article 6.1 of the Code is that violation of doping under Article 2.1 can only be established by sample analysis carried out by a WADA-accredited or WADA-approved laboratory. Both Standards provide mandatory requirements for the testing and analytical process.[57] While there are specific provisions of the Code which operate to prevent inconsequential departures from the Standards from invalidating test results, the general position is that anti-doping organisations have to comply with the rules they have set themselves for the collection and analysis of samples if they are to be able to impose strict liability for doping or the use of prohibited substances or methods on the athlete.[58]

The ISTI was significantly amended in its January 2015 version (with limited amendment of the provisions concerning ABP processes in the January 2017 version) in order to reflect the greater emphasis placed on investigations into other anti-doping rule violations apart from those involving the presence or use of prohibited substances. This extended

---

57 See Article 5.5 for the requirement to carry out testing in compliance with the ISTI, and Article 6.4 for the analysis of samples in conformity with ISL.
58 See Chapter 6 for a more detailed consideration of the presumption in relation to analysis by WADA-accredited laboratories and the effect of departures from the processes under the International Standards.

range of anti-doping work and purposes is reflected in Article 5 of the Code.

The ISTI is now expressed to have two main purposes: the planning of intelligent and effective testing and maintenance of the integrity of samples collected; and the efficient gathering, assessment and use of anti-doping intelligence and efficient and effective conduct of investigations into possible anti-doping rule violations. The second purpose reflects the way in which the work of WADA and of anti-doping organisations generally has developed. While there is no doubt that there will be a continuing increase in the effort to investigate non-analytical anti-doping violations, the process of testing athletes in- and out-of-competition in order to determine whether they have committed violations of Articles 2.1 and 2.2 of the Code will always remain central to the operation of the Code.[59] Indeed, the testing of athletes on a targeted basis may well be the culmination of an intelligence-led investigation. It should also be noted that several violations are closely linked to the process of testing and are concerned with protecting the integrity of the testing process (refusal to submit to sample collection, tampering or attempting to tamper with doping control).

The whereabouts regime, which is provided for in Article 5.6 of the Code and set out in detail in ISTI Annex I, involves the provision of whereabouts information by designated athletes so that they are available for testing out-of-competition. Again, these whereabouts requirements and the violation under Article 2.4 for breach of the requirements form an important part of the testing regime under the Code and reflect the focus under the Code on unannounced out-of-competition testing.[60]

Article 5: Testing and Investigations

Article 5 provides for the important general limitation on the purposes of testing and investigation that these processes can only be undertaken for anti-doping purposes. An anti-doping organisation which acts outside the scope of the Code would be likely to breach national law (in the absence of other powers under national law). Anti-doping purposes cover testing which has to be carried out to obtain analytical evidence relating

59 NADOs are currently having to assess the extent to which they allocate resources to investigations not involving testing. The first step where a general investigation is conducted may be to target test athletes who are suspected of being involved in committing violations.
60 See Chapter 5, pages 233–241 for further detail on Article 2.4 and case summaries. See Chapter 8, page 431 for sanctions for breach of Article 2.4.

to an athlete's compliance with the obligations under Articles 2.1 and 2.2 and investigations into other violations of the Code. The provisions of the Code and the ISTI combine obligations which anti-doping organisations must fulfil if they are to comply with the Code and obligations as to the process which anti-doping organisations must fulfil if they are to be able to put forward evidence to prove an allegation of breach of the Code. In recent times, much of the added provision in the Code and Standards has related to the steps which anti-doping organisations must take to meet their obligations in testing and investigations under the Code.

Investigations have to be undertaken where testing results show an atypical finding or an adverse passport finding in order to find out whether there has been a breach of Article 2.1 or 2.2, and, more generally, in order to determine whether other violations under the Code have been committed.

Anti-doping organisations have to ensure that they are able to collect anti-doping intelligence to establish 'patterns trends and relationships' that may assist in determining anti-doping strategy. They have to use information to develop an effective test distribution plan, to plan target testing and to provide the basis for investigations, to assist in investigating atypical findings and adverse passport findings and to assist in investigating analytical and non-analytical information which may establish possible anti-doping rule violations.

Article 5.2 sets out the fundamental principle of the testing regime that an athlete may be required to provide a sample for analysis at any time, in any place, by an anti-doping organisation with authority to test him or her. Various anti-doping organisations may have jurisdiction to test an athlete. The general principle of testing at any time is limited to an extent by the notes to Article 5.2, which require an anti-doping organisation to have 'serious and specific' suspicion that an athlete may be engaged in doping before testing them between 11 pm and 6 am unless the athlete has given a time in that period as a testing window under the whereabouts regime or has consented to testing in that period. The notes also provide that a challenge by the athlete to the adequacy of suspicion cannot be a defence to an alleged violation based on a test carried out at that time.[61] This limitation on testing at any time was no doubt included in the notes to address concerns as to compliance with fundamental protections such

---

61 An athlete who wished to bring a claim in relation to the timing of a test and/or the basis for a test would have to bring his or her claim under national law. Such a claim would not affect the position under the Code.

as the guarantee of the right to respect of private and family life.[62] Testing has to be carried out in compliance with the ISTI. NADOs, international federations, major event organisations and WADA all have testing authority in certain circumstances. The Code sets out when this jurisdiction is available.

Article 5.4 expressly refers to the Technical Document for Sport Specific Analysis (TDSSA) under the ISTI. This requires a specific risk-assessment process which anti-doping organisations must carry out in order to develop an effective test distribution plan. Such a plan has to prioritise between disciplines, athletes, the type of testing and sample analysis. The TDSSA must be followed by anti-doping organisations, and they have to provide a copy of the current test distribution plan to WADA on request. This kind of assessment and planning involves the use of a range of information which anti-doping organisations obtain.

Article 5.6 of the Code[63] requires athletes who have been included in a registered testing pool to provide whereabouts information to their international federation or NADO as specified by the ISTI (ISTI Annex I contains the detailed requirements). Article 5.6 requires coordination between organisations in relation to the athletes identified and included in a registered testing pool and the whereabouts information supplied through the ADAMS database. The Article also underlines that the information will be used exclusively for the anti-doping activities under the Code and that the information will be maintained in strict confidence and will be destroyed when no longer required for the purposes under the Code, as required by the ISPPPI. Article 5.7 contains specific provisions for athletes who wish to return to competition from retirement to make themselves available for testing by giving six months' notice before returning to international or national events.

Article 5 of the Code sets out the overall framework for testing and investigations, and the ISTI provides the detail. The consideration of an allegation that an athlete has committed a violation of Article 2.1 or 2.2 will often, where the allegation is denied, involve an examination of the process which produced the reported positive test. While successful challenges to the process are relatively uncommon, a review of the sampling and testing process and relevant documentation to reach a view on whether the

62 See Costa, 'Legal Opinion', pp. 23–5 for consideration of the issues.
63 This Article was previously in substance Article 14.5 of the 2009 Code. It is now more appropriately placed in Article 5, given the close relationship between the provision of whereabouts information and the testing of athletes.

ISTI and ISL have been complied with is an important part of advising an athlete on his or her rights in relation to an alleged violation.

The ISTI in Detail

Part Two of the ISTI sets out the process for planning effective testing. Article 4.0 details the process by which an anti-doping organisation should use the TDSSA (as provided by Article 5.4) to assess the risk that particular prohibited substances and methods are likely to be abused in particular sporting disciplines in order to develop its test distribution plan. The aim is to fulfil the requirement of implementing a testing plan which is proportionate with the risk of doping in the athletes who are under the jurisdiction of the anti-doping organisation. The testing plan developed by an anti-doping organisation has to be documented and filed with WADA where an anti-doping organisation seeks to have samples analysed using a less extensive menu than is set out in the applicable Technical Document. WADA can ask to inspect an anti-doping organisation's current plan.

In order to comply with its obligations under the Code, an anti-doping organisation has to be able to show to WADA that it has made a proper assessment of the relevant risks and has adopted an appropriate test distribution plan. This part of the ISTI also recognises that anti-doping organisations may not have the resources to deal with very large pools of athletes who may fit the criteria for inclusion in a registered testing pool. The definition of 'athlete' under the 2015 Code allows NADOs to limit who will be subject to national anti-doping programmes to those athletes who compete at the national level. Similarly, international federations can focus their programmes on those athletes who compete regularly at international level. Anti-doping organisations are free to decide on the criteria which will be used to classify athletes as national- and international-level performers. The definition of 'athlete' also allows anti-doping organisations discretion whether to apply anti-doping rules to athletes who are neither international- nor national-level athletes. An anti-doping organisation may choose to conduct limited testing or no testing in relation to athletes who are neither international- nor national-level athletes. However, where testing is carried out and a violation is committed by any athlete over whom the anti-doping organisation has authority because they are bound by the Code, the consequences under the Code must be applied.

In summary, the provisions of ISTI and the Code permit anti-doping organisations to narrow the focus of their testing in a practical targeted manner, but they cannot be relied on by an athlete who is in fact subject to the Code to say that he or she should not have been subject to the Code because the anti-doping organisation ought to have exercised its power not to apply the Code's provisions.

Part Two Section 4.0 ISTI further provides for prioritising between different athletes, between different types of testing for target testing (which is a priority) and between different types of testing (in-competition and out-of-competition, blood urine and testing under the ABP). The ISTI provides that, save in exceptional and justifiable circumstances, all testing has to be no-advance-notice testing.[64] This first part of the ISTI also makes general provision for the collection of whereabouts information as part of effective testing.[65] The collection of whereabouts information is stated to have the aim of allowing efficient no-advance-notice testing. The ISTI provides for an anti-doping organisation to allow whereabouts information to be collected from a team and not from individual athletes during periods of team activity. As with testing, an anti-doping organisation can adopt a pyramid or tiered approach, which requires more whereabouts information from some athletes, as a result of the risk analysis conducted under the ISTI as part of the test distribution planning, and less information from others. The amount of whereabouts information sought will depend on the priority given to testing particular athletes or groups of athletes and the amount of information which the anti-doping organisation considers is required to test athletes effectively. The top tier of athletes will contain high-profile athletes, athletes in ABP programmes and athletes who are considered by the anti-doping organisation to be at the highest risk of doping. These athletes will be within a registered testing pool, with the result that the provisions of Annex I and Article 2.4 of the ISTI will apply to them. This flexible approach to the provision of whereabouts information is also intended to allow anti-doping organisations to seek information from athletes which would not meet the requirements under Annex I and bring Article 2.4 into play, but which is useful for testing purposes because it provides sufficient information to allow

64 This is testing which takes place with no advance warning to the athlete and where the athlete is continuously chaperoned from the time of notification through sample collection. See the definition of 'no advance notice' in the ISTI. For consideration of this important aspect of the testing regime in the context of arguments under the whereabouts regime, see CAS 2014/A/2, *DFSNZ* v. *Gemmell* in Chapter 5, pages 238–40, where CAS reversed a decision by the NZ Sports Tribunal that there was no breach of the whereabouts requirements because the DCO seeking to locate the athlete had not taken the step of calling the athlete's mobile phone.
65 The detail of the whereabouts information scheme is set out in Annex I of the ISTI. For further detail and case summaries, see Chapter 5, pages 233–41. For sanctions, see Chapter 8, page 431.

appropriate out-of-competition testing on a no-advance-notice basis. Where athletes who are not in the registered testing pool fail to meet particular whereabouts requirements which are applicable to them, the anti-doping organisation should consider moving the athletes into the registered testing pool. The presumption is that where an anti-doping organisation plans to collect three or more samples a year from an athlete, the athlete has to be put in the registered testing pool.

The overall approach to the collection of whereabouts information under ISTI Article 4.8 is intended to allow greater discretion to anti-doping organisations regarding the inclusion of athletes in registered testing pools, which will have the effect of making Article 2.4 applicable. The exercise of this discretion is linked to the testing planning of the anti-doping organisation and involves considering how much particular athletes will be subject to testing and how much whereabouts information is required to permit effective no-advance-notice testing. Generally, where an anti-doping organisation intends to test in out-of-competition periods, it must have a registered testing pool of athletes unless it can show that it is able to locate those athletes for no-advance-notice testing during all out-of-competition periods without whereabouts information, as provided for in ISTI Annex I and Article 2.4. The question whether the approach taken by an anti-doping organisation to testing and collecting whereabouts information complies with the ISTI will be assessed by WADA. On any assessment, the anti-doping organisation will have to show that it has made a proper assessment of the relevant risks and adopted appropriate criteria for testing athletes and for their inclusion in registered testing pools. The requirement for no-advance-notice out-of-competition testing is central to the Code and underpins the whereabouts regime, and the approach of an anti-doping organisation to the collection of whereabouts information will no doubt be assessed with this requirement in mind if questions of non-compliance arise.

The names of athletes in registered testing pools will be available to WADA and other anti-doping organisations where information is collected through ADAMS. If ADAMS is not used, anti-doping organisations have to make the criteria for including athletes in a registered testing pool or the list of athletes included available to WADA and other anti-doping organisations with testing authority over the athletes. Registered testing pools have to be reviewed regularly, with athletes who do not meet the criteria removed and athletes who do added.

Article 4.9 ISTI contains general provisions requiring anti-doping organisations to coordinate testing efforts where they have overlapping testing responsibility. Agreement has to be reached on roles in event testing, and WADA has to resolve the position where no agreement can be reached, as provided by Annex J ISTI. Anti-doping organisations have to share information on completed testing with other relevant anti-doping organisations without delay. They also have to consult with one another, with WADA and with relevant State authorities in obtaining and sharing information which may be useful in planning the distribution of tests. Anti-doping organisations may enter into contracts with other anti-doping organisations and third parties to carry out sample collection and may stipulate how any discretion given to a sample collection authority under the ISTI may be exercised.

Section 5.0 ISTI contains the provisions relating to the notification of athletes who are to be tested. These provisions are part of the requirements for carrying out a valid test. The provisions seek to ensure that athletes are properly notified of sample collection, that the athletes' rights are maintained, that there are no opportunities to manipulate the sample and that notification is properly documented. The anti-doping organisation must use trained personnel for the testing process. A DCO will manage the sample collection session. Sample collection personnel are responsible for the process of notifying the athlete and directing the athlete through the process of providing a sample. They will notify the athlete selected for testing, accompany the athlete to the doping control station and verify the provision of the sample. Notification in terms of the ISTI is required before there can be a requirement to submit to doping control, and an absence of notification would provide a defence to an allegation of refusing to submit to sample collection. Doping control personnel may play an important role as witnesses if any allegation of refusal arises from sample collection.

ISTI 5.3 again emphasises that, save in exceptional and justifiable circumstances, no-advance-notice testing has to be the method of sample collection. The note to this Article underlines that it is not acceptable, given the requirement for no-advance-notice testing, for a sporting body to insist on being given advance notice so that it can have a representative present at sample collection.

The detailed provisions of Articles 5.2–5.4 ISTI provide for the requirements for notification, the appointment of sample collection personnel, the validation of the identity of the athlete to be tested, the planning of notification, the recording of the notification and the consideration of those circumstances where a third party has to be notified of the testing before the athlete (testing minors and persons with impairments).

Article 5.4 ISTI sets out the requirements for notification. When initial contact is made with an athlete selected for testing, the sample collection personnel must inform the athlete of his or her responsibilities and various rights. The rights include the right to have a representative and, if required, an interpreter, the right to ask for additional information about the sample collection process, the right to request a delay in reporting to the doping control station for valid reasons, and the right to request modifications in the process where an athlete is disabled. The athlete must also be informed of specific responsibilities – namely, to remain within the sight of the drug control officer or chaperone from the time of notification until provision of the sample, to produce identification in accordance with the requirements of the ISTI so that this can be documented and to comply with sample collection procedures. Non-compliance with the obligations may result in a violation of refusal being reported to the anti-doping organisation responsible for the testing process. The athlete has to be warned that non-compliance will be reported. Failures to comply with the processes will be investigated as provided for by Annex A ISTI – Investigating Possible Failure to Comply.

Article 6.0 ISTI contains detailed provision governing the preparation for a sample collection session and Section 7.0 ISTI sets out the steps required to conduct a sample collection session in an effective manner in order to ensure the integrity, security and identity of the sample and respect for the privacy of the athlete. There are specific provisions for the method of collection of urine and blood samples in Annexes D and E ISTI. Annex K was added to the ISTI 2017 and makes specific provision for the collection, storage and transmission of blood samples for an ABP.

Articles 8.0 and 9.0 ISTI provide for the proper storage of samples and of sample collection documentation collected at a doping control station and for their transportation to the relevant anti-doping organisation. Anti-doping organisations must use a transportation system for samples and documentation which protects their integrity, identity and security. The anti-doping organisation responsible for the process has to check on the chain of custody and, if receipt of samples or sample collection documents are not confirmed at their destination, or a sample's integrity may have been compromised during transport, must consider whether to declare the sampling process void.[66]

Article 10.0 ISTI provides that samples collected from an athlete are owned by the testing authority and that ownership of the samples may be transferred by that authority to an authority responsible for results

66 See 9.3.5 IST.

management or to another anti-doping organisation on request. The effectiveness of this provision is difficult to assess, but where an athlete is bound to the Code and Standards, the basic position would be that he or she has agreed to this position on the ownership of any samples he or she gives.

Part Three Article 11.0 ISTI was added in the review of the IST in 2014. It is concerned with the gathering, assessment and use of intelligence in anti-doping investigations. While the requirements for testing are specific in their content, the provisions relating to the standards for the efficient and effective gathering of intelligence for the purpose of planned and targeted testing and as the basis for the investigation of anti-doping rule violations are general in nature. They are directed at the development of effective investigation procedures by anti-doping organisations.

Anti-doping organisations have to do all they can to collect intelligence from all available sources. They have to have policies and procedures in place to handle the information securely and confidentially so that sources of intelligence are protected and the risk of leaks and inadvertent disclosure is addressed. Anti-doping organisations have to be able to collate and assess intelligence to establish whether it provides a reasonable cause to suspect that an anti-doping rule violation has been committed. Intelligence may also be used to develop testing plans or to carry out targeted testing. Anti-doping organisations must also develop policies and procedures for sharing intelligence with other anti-doping organisations and regulatory authorities.

Section 12.0 ISTI provides, in general terms, for the standards required of anti-doping organisations in the conduct of investigations into atypical and adverse passport findings, into other analytical or non-analytical information where there is reasonable cause to suspect that an anti-doping rule violation may have been committed and into whether athlete support personnel and other persons may have been involved in a violation committed by an athlete. ISTI 12.2 emphasises that atypical findings and adverse passport findings have to be investigated confidentially by the anti-doping organisation with responsibility, in accordance with Articles 7.4 and 7.5 of the Code and under the ISL. Information from this kind of investigation has to be provided to WADA on request.

Section 12.3 ISTI provides that anti-doping organisations have to be able to carry out confidential investigations into other possible anti-doping rule violations. WADA has to be notified where an investigation is commenced, and must be kept informed of its status. An anti-doping organisation has general obligations to gather all relevant information, to develop that information into admissible and reliable evidence and to ensure that investigations are carried out fairly, objectively and impartially.

All possible resources should be used in the conduct of investigations, whether they are at the disposal of the anti-doping organisation itself or come from law enforcement and regulatory agencies.

It is important to emphasise that the content of these obligations in relation to intelligence gathering and investigations, while mandatory and important for the proper implementation of the Code by anti-doping organisations, is general. ISTI contains no sanction for anti-doping organisations which do not meet the obligations, although non-compliance by a Signatory may mean that it is declared non-compliant under the Code by WADA.

In contrast, the requirements relating to sample collection and compliance with those requirements can be of central importance where an athlete defends an allegation of breach of the Code based on a positive test on the ground that there has been a failure to follow the applicable procedures. Similarly, an allegation of refusal or evasion – or, indeed, tampering – may be decided by considering whether the requirements for sample collection were properly followed.

If a breach of the ISTI can be established which could reasonably have caused an adverse analytical finding, it will be for the anti-doping organisation to show that the breach was not causative of the violation.[67] The outcome in such cases will depend on the particular circumstances and the particular breach of the ISTI. With some breaches, it may simply not be possible for the athlete to establish that the breach could reasonably have caused an adverse analytical finding. Where a causal connection between breach and adverse analytical finding can be established (where, for example, a breach of the chain of custody is established), it may be difficult for the anti-doping organisation to prove the negative, and show that the breach did not cause the violation to the required standard of the 'comfortable satisfaction' of the tribunal, as required by the Code.

A failure to follow the ISTI in the process of asking an athlete to provide a sample may also be relied on to say that there could be no valid test or to claim that an athlete was justified in refusing the test. Where attempts are made to obtain a sample in clear breach of the requirements of the ISTI, the athlete may be able to show that there was compelling justification to refuse to submit to doping control.[68]

---

67 See Chapter 6, pages 280–2 for the evidential presumptions available under the Code and the rebuttal of these presumptions.

68 For the violation of refusing, failing or otherwise evading sample collection under Article 2.3 of the Code, see Chapter 5, pages 224–33.

The Whereabouts Regime under the Code and ISTI

The creation of whereabouts rules which are intended to function in a uniform way as between anti-doping organisations is seen as a fundamental aspect of an effective anti-doping regime. Such a regime allows athletes who are subject to the rules to be located for testing at any time. The rules were previously contained in Article 11.0 IST, with the provisions setting out the general obligations to provide whereabouts information in Article 14.3 of the 2009 Code. As previously noted, the general provisions concerning the purpose of collecting whereabouts information and the tiered approach to the collection of the information by anti-doping organisations are now set out in Article 5.6 of the Code and Articles 4.8.6 and 4.8.7 ISTI.

The detailed requirements for the collection of whereabouts requirements from athletes who are in registered testing pools and are subject to the 'full' application of the whereabouts regime are set out in Annex I to the ISTI. The obligations imposed under Annex I are important because they are the basis for possible allegations that an athlete has committed breaches of the whereabouts regime which may lead to a violation of Article 2.4.

Athletes chosen to be in a registered testing pool will be international- or national-level athletes who are subject to focussed testing in- and out-of-competition and, as a result, have to provide whereabouts information as provided by Article 5.6 of the Code and the ISTI. International federations and NSOs have to coordinate the identification of athletes in their registered testing pools and the collection of their whereabouts information and provide a list identifying the athletes in their registered testing pools through ADAMS.

Where an athlete fails to file whereabouts information as required or is not available for testing at a given whereabouts location, he or she will commit a whereabouts failure. Three whereabouts failures in any twelve-month period will amount to a violation of Article 2.4.[69] While an individual whereabouts failure cannot be a violation under Article 2.4, it may, depending on the way in which the failure occurred, be a breach of either Article 2.3 (evasion of sample collection) or Article 2.5 (tampering or attempted tampering with doping control).

An athlete who has been included in a registered testing pool has to make quarterly whereabouts filings. The information filed has to provide

---

69 See Chapter 5, pages 233–41 for the operation of Article 2.4 and case summaries and Chapter 8, page 431 for sanctions.

complete information about the athlete's whereabouts in the forthcoming quarter. This information has to identify where the athlete will be living, training and competing during the quarter. In the filing, the athlete has to specify a location where he or she will be available for testing in a specific sixty-minute time slot each day. The provision of this information does not limit the general obligation of an athlete under Article 5.2 of the Code to be available for testing at any time. Nor does it qualify or diminish the obligation to provide the full information required on a quarterly filing. If the athlete is not available for testing in the sixty-minute time slot (and the conditions for a finding of breach are met), he or she will commit a whereabouts failure.[70]

The information which has to be provided by athletes in the registered testing pool must be filed as specified by the anti-doping organisation in advance of each quarter. This information has to include specific daily detail for training and working locations and the athlete's competitive schedule, including the specified sixty-minute time slot. It is the athlete's responsibility to file accurate whereabouts information in sufficient detail to allow any anti-doping organisation to locate him or her for testing at any time during the quarter, including but not limited to the sixty-minute time slot. The information has to be sufficient for the DCO to find the location, gain access and find the athlete.

Filing Failures

Failing to provide adequate information may be considered to be a filing failure. If the information filed becomes inaccurate, it is the athlete's responsibility to file updates as soon as possible. Anti-doping organisations have to provide mechanisms for this, such as text messaging, and have to check for updates to the whereabouts information. Athletes can only be found to have committed a filing failure if the anti-doping organisation managing the whereabouts regime can establish that the athlete had been notified of his or her inclusion in the registered testing pool and of the requirements and consequences of failure to comply, that the athlete failed to comply with the filing requirements by failing to file

---

70 The sixty-minute window was as the notes to Annex I Article 1.1.b make clear a compromise between different approaches to the obligation to be available for testing under different whereabouts regimes before 2009. The compromise is that the athlete has to give whereabouts information for all times every day of the quarter but is only liable for a missed test in the sixty-minute time slot.

or by filing inadequate information and, where the failure is a second or third failure, that notice of the previous failure had been given and the athlete's failure to comply with the filing requirements was at least negligent. There is presumption of negligence against the athlete, which he or she has to rebut, where it is proved that the athlete was notified of the requirements but failed to comply with them.

Missed Tests

The other central element of the whereabouts regime is that the athlete must be at the locations given and available for testing in the specified sixty-minute time slot. If he or she is not available in this period, this has to be pursued as a missed test by the anti-doping organisation. A missed test, like a filing failure, is a breach of the whereabouts regime and will count as a breach of the regime in the same way. A failure to be at a location specified outside the sixty-minute time slot will not be breach of the whereabouts regime, although the athlete is obliged to submit to testing at any time and in any place at the request of an anti-doping organisation. A failure to be present for testing outside the specified sixty-minute time slot, while not a whereabouts violation, may, depending on the circumstances, amount to a violation of evading or tampering with doping control. The aim of the sixty-minute time slot is to make it clear when an unsuccessful attempt to test an athlete will count as a missed test and to provide for a location where the athlete can certainly be tested at least once a day. The information provided by athletes regarding their sixty-minute time slots may also be used in anti-doping investigations. An anti-doping organisation may decide to try and target-test an individual at other locations in- or outside the sixty-minute time slot where the athlete makes regular last-minute changes to his or her time slot or location for the sixty-minute time slot.[71]

Conditions for Declaring a Missed Test

The anti-doping organisation responsible for results management can only declare a missed test if the athlete was given notice of his or her potential liability for a missed test (this would be on joining the RTP and coming under the obligation to submit whereabouts filings), if he or she

---

71 See *DFSNZ* v. *Ciancio* in Chapter 5, pages 240–1 for an example of last-minute changes amounting to tampering.

was unavailable at the location specified in the whereabouts information during the sixty-minute time slot, if a DCO tried to test the athlete by going to the location specified at the time specified in the whereabouts information filed, if the DCO did what was reasonable to locate the athlete at the specified location and, if the possible breach was a second or third breach, if any previous breach had been notified to the athlete and if the athlete's failure to be available for testing was at least negligent. There is a presumption that the failure of an athlete to be available is negligent if the other requirements for a missed test are met, which may only be rebutted by the athlete establishing that no negligent behaviour on his or her part caused or contributed to the missed test.

Results Management

Results management will be carried out by the anti-doping organisation with which the athlete filed the whereabouts information. The process of results management involves obtaining any reports, reviewing the documentary file and deciding whether the requirements for a filing failure or missed test are established. If the anti-doping organisation decides that one of the requirements has not been met, it has to notify WADA, the relevant international federation or anti-doping organisation and the anti-doping organisation which uncovered the whereabouts failure. Reasons have to be given for the decision, and a decision not to record a breach of the whereabouts requirements can be appealed under Article 13 of the Code.[72]

If the organisation with results management authority decides that the requirements for a whereabouts failure are met, it has to give notice to the athlete within fourteen days providing details of the alleged failure and giving the athlete a reasonable time-frame in which to decide whether to reply admitting the breach or to say why he or she does not admit it. The notice has to advise of the consequences of three whereabouts failures in a twelve-month period and note the position as regards any other failures. With a filing failure, the notice has to be given that the athlete must file any missing whereabouts information by a specified deadline.

If the breach is admitted or the athlete does not respond, the notified whereabouts failure has to be recorded against the athlete. If a response is

72 The appeal is expressly provided for in Annex I ISTI but not expressly referred to in Article 13.

provided, the anti-doping organisation has to consider whether the athlete's explanation changes the decision that the requirements for recording a whereabouts failure have been established. If the anti-doping organisation changes its original decision, it has to advise WADA, the international federation and NADO, and that decision can be appealed under Article 13 of the Code. If the original decision stands, the anti-doping organisation has to notify the athlete of his or her right to request an administrative review of the decision. If no administrative review is requested, the whereabouts failure will be recorded. If a review is requested, it will be carried out by one or more persons not connected with the assessment of the failure. The review is on the papers only, and its purpose is to consider afresh whether the requirements for a whereabouts failure have been met. Again, if the review concludes that the requirements have not been met, WADA, the relevant international federation and NADO and any anti-doping organisation which found the whereabouts failure have to be notified. Each notified organisation has a right of appeal against the decision under Article 13 of the Code.

If the review decides that the requirements for the whereabouts failure have been met, the athlete has to be notified and the failure recorded against the athlete. Decisions to record a whereabouts failure will be reported to WADA and all other anti-doping organisations under the Code by putting the information into ADAMS or another similar system approved by WADA. Information concerning apparent whereabouts failures can be given to other anti-doping organisations at an earlier stage of the results management process on a strictly confidential basis where the anti-doping organisation responsible considers this appropriate for anti-doping investigation or testing. There can be no public disclosure of whereabouts failures, whether by reference to individual athletes or to sports, before a decision in proceedings in respect of an alleged breach of Article 2.4.

As already noted, the organisation with results management authority must bring proceedings for a breach of Article 2.4 against an athlete who has three whereabouts failure recorded against him or her within any twelve-month period. If this step is not taken within thirty days of WADA receiving notice of the recording of the third whereabouts breach, the inactivity will mean that there is a deemed decision that no violation has occurred for the purposes of appeal rights under Article 13.2. This will allow WADA and the other relevant anti-doping organisations to bring an appeal.

There are general provisions at the end of Annex I ISTI permitting agreements for the delegation of some or all of the responsibilities between the various organisations which are responsible for implementing and managing whereabouts regimes. Where there is no appropriate national anti-doping organisation in existence, the whereabouts responsibilities under Annex I will be assumed by the relevant national Olympic committee. If WADA determines that an international federation or NADO is not performing some or all of its whereabouts responsibilities, it can decide to delegate some or all of those responsibilities to any other anti-doping organisation which it considers appropriate.

Athletes in individual or team sports can delegate the provision of whereabouts filings to a third party, such as a manager or coach. It is important to note that the athlete still remains responsible for any filing failure or missed test which occurs notwithstanding the cause of the failure or missed test was the failure of the third party in carrying out its role as delegate of the athlete. Annex I contains specific provision that the failures of a third-party delegate will not be a defence against an alleged whereabouts breach by an athlete under Article 2.4. It is unclear how this provision relates to the consideration of the question whether the athlete can show that no negligence on his or her part caused or contributed to the failure. It seems doubtful, without clear provision to that effect, that it would be interpreted as attributing the negligence of a third party to the athlete. It is unclear whether a proper delegation of the whereabouts filing by an athlete can provide a defence to a whereabouts failure or whether it will only be relevant to the fault of the athlete in imposing sanction. It is submitted that, given the terms of the provision, where an athlete has chosen a responsible person to make filings and that person has been properly instructed in that regard, this may allow the athlete to establish that no negligence on his or her part caused or contributed to the violation. If there is some causative negligence on the part of the athlete in the delegation or in the steps taken to instruct the delegate, there will be a whereabouts breach, but the circumstances of the breach will be relevant in determining the level of fault of the athlete in relation to the breach and the period of ineligibility.

As can be seen, the components of the whereabouts regime in Annex I are directly relevant to the proof of alleged breaches of Article 2.4. A violation of Article 2.4 involves two distinct processes, which are both relevant to any determination of breach and possible sanction. This makes for a potentially complicated process where a violation is alleged. Advising on such allegations involves a review of the application of Annex I to each alleged whereabouts breach notwithstanding that the breaches may already have been the subject of review in the results management process carried out by the anti-doping organisation.

The International Standard for Laboratories (ISL)

The ISL was amended at the same time as the IST. The current version of the ISL came into force in June 2016. This version is not significantly different to the one which came into force in January 2015 (and replaced the version of January 2012). The ISL has not been as extensively amended as the ISTI. As with other International Standards, the role of the ISL is specifically identified in the 2015 Code. The ISL seeks to provide a harmonised approach across the accredited WADA laboratories which operate to provide testing and analysis of samples obtained from athletes. This is fundamental to the creation of a system which all involved in sport can rely on to produce fair, consistent results.

Samples taken from athletes under the ISTI have to be analysed in WADA-accredited or WADA-approved laboratories for the purposes of determining whether there has been a breach of Article 2.1 – the presence of a prohibited substance in the sample of the athlete. The addition of the phrase 'WADA- approved laboratories' allows WADA to approve rather than accredit laboratories where considerations of cost and access mean that particular analyses have to be carried out in particular laboratories which are not WADA accredited. The important point is that if WADA does approve a laboratory, the presumption that the laboratory has carried out an analysis in compliance with the Standard will apply as it does to an accredited laboratory. This requirement for analysis in a WADA-accredited or -approved laboratory only applies to establishing proof of violations under Article 2.1. Where analysis is required in any other alleged violation, elements of violations can be established by results from other laboratories, as long as they can be shown to operate reliably and produce reliable results.

2015 Code: General Provisions on Sample Analysis

Article 6.2 of the Code confirms that the analysis of samples must only be carried out for legitimate anti-doping purposes – to detect prohibited substances or methods under the Prohibited List (or substances on the monitoring programme) in order to assist an anti-doping organisation in profiling relevant parameters in a urine, blood or other matrix, including

DNA and genome profiling. This form of analysis of an athlete's individual biological profile is now more common because of the increasing use of ABPs. The analysis does not seek to detect a particular prohibited substance, but rather to build a profile for the athlete which can be used to detect abnormal values which may be indicative of doping. Samples can be collected and stored for future analysis. Samples can only be used for research with the athlete's written consent.

Article 6.4 of the 2015 Code contains new provisions concerning analysis based on the particular risk of doping assessed as arising in particular sports. This is part of the development and extension of the principle of intelligent testing. The TDSSA establishes particular menus for particular sports, which direct the substances for which analysis will be conducted. Anti-doping organisations can request more extensive testing than is set out in the menus in the Technical Document; they may also request a less extensive analysis, as long as WADA is satisfied that this is appropriate. Article 6.4.3 confirms that, as provided in the ISL, laboratories can test samples for substances not on the menu under the Technical Document.

The changing nature of substances used in doping and the development of testing processes means that later testing of stored samples may reveal anti-doping violations committed at a time when the substances could not have been detected. Article 6.5 provides for the further analysis of samples before the A and B sample results have been notified. Samples may be stored and subjected to further analysis in conformity with the requirements under the ISL at any time at the direction of the anti-doping organisation responsible for collection or of WADA.[73]

ISL Provisions

The ISL imposes a common standard on WADA laboratories by reference to the obligation to meet the ISO/IEC 17025 as it relates to the testing processes carried out by the laboratory. Compliance with this standard must be verified and monitored by an accreditation body which is a full member of the International Laboratory Accreditation Cooperation (ILAC) (and which is a party to the ILAC Mutual Recognition Arrangement) and by WADA itself.

Part Two of the ISL governs the accreditation of laboratories and the conduct of sample analysis by WADA-accredited laboratories. The overall aim is to harmonise the process of analysing samples and obtaining results

---

73 The re-testing of samples provided at the 2008 and 2012 Olympic Games has resulted in a number of disqualifications and impositions of periods of ineligibility.

and to ensure the production of valid reliable test results by the network of WADA laboratories around the world.

WADA took over the role of accrediting laboratories from the IOC. As has been noted, samples taken by Signatories to the WADA Code must be analysed at WADA-accredited or -approved laboratories if a doping violation under Article 2.1 is to be established, and only analysis by a WADA-accredited or approved laboratory can create the presumption under the Code that the process of testing has been carried out in accordance with the International Standards.[74]

The ISL sets out the standards which must be met in order to be granted and to maintain WADA accreditation, and contains the relevant requirements and operating standards in its main provisions and in annexes and Technical Documents. The process of accreditation involves an application, an initial report by WADA, a probationary period and a final accreditation process under which the laboratory is assessed by WADA and the relevant accreditation body for compliance with ISO/IEC 17025.[75] Compliance with specific requirements of ISO/TEC 17025 for the analysis of urine and blood doping control samples is an important part of the accreditation process. In making its application for accreditation, a laboratory has to provide an official letter of support from a relevant national public authority responsible for the national anti-doping programme, or a similar letter of support from either the national Olympic committee or NADO. The supporting letter must contain, at a minimum, a guarantee of financial support annually for a minimum of three years, a guarantee of a sufficient number of samples annually for three years and a guarantee of the provision of necessary analytical facilities and instrumentation, where applicable. In order to be accredited, the laboratory must have professional liability risk insurance cover to the value of US$2 million.

The process of maintaining accreditation involves continuing to meet the standards, and the laboratory is subject to annual audit by WADA and the accreditation body. The process for monitoring and evaluating the performance of a laboratory is set out in Annex A ISL – WADA External Quality Assessment Scheme. In summary, this process involves the assessment of the performance of the laboratory in the analysis of blood or urine samples supplied periodically by WADA, in order to test the capability of the laboratory to detect prohibited substances and methods. A range of

74 See Chapter 6 on the burden of proof under the Code, in particular pages 280–2 on the shifting burden of proof where departures from a relevant International Standard are established. There are currently thirty-three WADA-accredited laboratories.
75 For the detail of the requirements, see ISL 4.1 and 4.2.

factors is considered in evaluating the performance of a laboratory and assigning it a points score. The reporting of a false positive in this EQAS process may result in the laboratory being suspended or having its accreditation revoked. Suspension may be based on other matters too, including other evidence of serious ISL deviations arising from analysis of doping control samples. The period of suspension up to a maximum of six months has to be proportionate to the seriousness of the performance failures. In the period of suspension, the laboratory has to correct non-compliance. If it does so, it can get its accreditation back. If it does not do so (and the period of suspension can be extended to up to twelve months), its accreditation will be revoked. WADA has a broad general power to remove the accreditation of a laboratory in order to protect the interests of the anti-doping community.

Adherence with the ISL and Technical Documents is mandatory if accredited laboratories are to provide a unified system worldwide which can be trusted to provide reliable results.

An accredited laboratory can modify and develop existing procedures or develop new procedures for analysis (if the procedures are within the technology accredited) without approval from the accreditation body, provided the laboratory has appropriate documentary processes for validation in its document management systems. Where the laboratory develops new procedures which are outside the scope of the accreditation, the procedures must be assessed and approved by WADA as fit for purpose before being used. After approval by WADA, the laboratory must obtain accreditation for the procedures from the relevant accreditation body. If a new analytical method is included within the laboratory's scope of ISO/IEC 17025 accreditation, this establishes that the method is fit for purpose and the laboratory does not have to provide documentation to validate the method in support of an adverse analytical finding made using the method. A finding using such an approved new analytical method would be presumed valid and a party seeking to challenge this presumption would have to give notices under Article 3.2.1 of the 2015 Code (see Chapter 6, pages 281–2).

The detail of the analytical and technical process for the testing of urine and blood samples is set out in the ISL. The ISL contains specific provisions, but, where not specifically provided for in the ISL, technical processes are governed by ISO/IEC 17025 and ISO 9001, as applied to the analysis of doping control samples. This covers receiving and handling samples, preparing samples for testing, analysing A and B samples, reviewing results, documenting the process and results and preparing the required laboratory documentation packages to support the results. A laboratory must have documented procedures to ensure that it maintains a coordinated record relating to each sample analysed. The documentary record must be such that, in the absence of an analyst, another competent analyst could evaluate what has been performed and interpret the data. The steps in the analysis process have to be traceable to the person who performed them.

The ISL also contains provision for the retention of samples for possible re-testing. The Annexes to the ISL contain provision for proficiency tests of the laboratory (Annex A), the ethics of laboratories (Annex B), the list of Technical Documents which form part of the ISL and requirements which must be followed in particular circumstances. The Code of Ethics in Annex B to the ISL has to be adhered to by laboratory personnel, and each year the director of the laboratory has to sign a document attesting that the laboratory and staff operate in accordance with this code of ethics. Under the code of ethics, laboratory personnel cannot engage in conduct which is detrimental to the WADA anti-doping programme.

Athlete confidentiality is emphasised as a key consideration under the ISL, and there are particular provisions aimed at communication by methods which are likely to maintain confidentiality.[76] The ISL contains further provisions relating to the maintenance of quality by management processes and audits, and the provision of ISO/IEC 17025 will also be applicable to this process. Laboratories have to develop, validate and document testing methods for compounds on the Prohibited List and related substances which are fit for the purpose. Equipment has to be listed and maintained to the ISO 17025 standard.

The process for obtaining accreditation is set out in the ISL, and laboratories can be audited at any time. WADA must review compliance with the Standards required for analysis and accreditation on an annual basis. WADA accreditation can be suspended or revoked on written notice. Where accreditation is revoked by WADA, there is a right of appeal to CAS.[77]

76 Articles 5.2.6 and 13.1–13.4. See also Annex C ISL.
77 CAS has dismissed an appeal by a Malaysian laboratory under Article 13.6 of the Code against the revocation of its accreditation by WADA. This was the first time WADA had revoked the accreditation of a laboratory. See CAS 2010/A/2162, *Doping Control Centre Universiti Sains Malaysia* v. *WADA*. As a result of the WADA Independent Commission report into the conduct of the Russian anti-doping organisation and the WADA-accredited laboratory in Moscow (among others), the accreditation of the Moscow laboratory was removed by WADA. Article 4.4 was amended in the ISL 2016 to include some more

Where an athlete challenges an adverse analytical finding, the laboratory must provide the documentary package in support of the finding in accordance with its obligations under the ISL and the related Technical Document. Earlier versions of the ISL provided that the laboratory was not required to provide any documentation not listed for inclusion in the ISL in the documentary package and sought to bar discovery requests relating to standard operating procedures, general quality-management documents and other documents not required by the Technical Document on Laboratory Documentation Packages. This provision is no longer contained in the ISL. Generally, such documents will be irrelevant where an adverse analytical finding is challenged, but, if an athlete can establish the relevance of a request to claims of a breach of the ISL, a tribunal cannot, it is submitted, be barred from ordering the discovery of the documents where the tribunal has power to do this under its procedural rules.[78]

There are many provisions in the ISL which are expressed in mandatory terms, particularly in relation to the carrying out of analysis and testing. In challenges to adverse analytical findings, compliance with such provisions by the laboratory will often be the subject of intense scrutiny. However, a breach of such a mandatory provision will only lead to an adverse analytical finding being set aside if the athlete first establishes that the breach could reasonably have caused the adverse analytical finding and the anti-doping organisation fails to comfortably satisfy the hearing body that the breach did not cause the adverse analytical finding.[79] As previously noted, in connection with breaches of the ISTI, it is necessary to consider the evidence relating to the possible consequences of the particular breach, in order to determine whether the anti-doping organisation has proved that the breach did not cause the adverse analytical finding, to the standard required under the Code.

The Presumption in Favour of WADA Laboratories

Under the Code, as already noted, a result from an accredited laboratory gives rise to a presumption that the analysis and other processes have

---

detailed provision on the circumstances in which accreditation may be removed and given back by WADA.

78 In *USADA* v. *Landis* (see Chapter 5, pages 195–7), in a pre-hearing ruling, the AAA tribunal ordered the production of documents not falling within the documentary package where they were relevant to the case.

79 For an example of a consideration of this in the context of a challenge to an adverse analytical finding, see again *USADA* v. *Landis* at pages 195–7.

been properly carried out in accordance with the Standards. Article 6.1 of the 2015 Code, together with its notes, provides that only an analysis by a WADA-accredited/approved laboratory can prove a doping violation under Article 2.1. If a laboratory produces a test result but is not accredited at the time of the test, the result can still be used to prove another violation under the Code apart from a violation under Article 2.1, provided the process of analysis and the consequent results can be proven to be reliable. The anti-doping organisation responsible would have to prove that the testing procedure was properly carried out and was in accordance with established scientific practice to the required standard of proof of the comfortable satisfaction of the tribunal, if the test result was to be considered.[80]

Scientific Tests

Notwithstanding the general presumption in favour of the test result from an accredited laboratory, an athlete may seek to challenge the particular analytical process which the laboratory has carried out in reaching the result on the basis that it represents a departure from the procedures or, indeed, make a more fundamental challenge to the scientific test used to detect the particular prohibited substance or method by claiming that it is ineffective and/or inaccurate on established scientific principles. In either situation, the burden will lie on the athlete to establish the alleged failure or deficiency on a balance of probabilities. Where a new or evolving testing method has been used to detect a prohibited substance or method, or where there are different scientific views about the effectiveness of a test, an athlete may seek to show by expert scientific evidence that the method is deficient. If an athlete succeeds in establishing that a method is deficient, it is submitted that the test result will not stand because the result obtained will not have scientific value. This would not be a departure from the procedure in the ISL but a fundamental failure in the scientific method, which would directly affect the result of the analysis. Such challenges were largely unsuccessful in pre-Code cases where it was contended that the test for rEPO (and mimetics of the drug such as darbepoetin) was deficient.[81]

---

80 See *Modahl* v. *BAF and IAAF* (Chapter 10, pages 525–6), where Lord Hoffmann expressed the view, when the House of Lords struck out the damages claim by M in civil proceedings which relied on a claim for breach of contract for testing by a non-accredited laboratory under the system run by the IAAF at the time, that the fact that a laboratory was not accredited could not invalidate an otherwise properly conducted test.

81 See e.g. CAS 2002/A/370, *Lazutina* v. *IOC*; CAS 2002/A/374, *Muehlegg* v. *IOC*, approval of direct urine test to detect rEPO. Other methods can be used and have been considered

Where a testing method could be shown to be new and not accredited, the anti-doping organisation would have to satisfy the tribunal of its reliability in scientific terms, but there is no bar on the use of new tests because a violation can be established by any reliable means.

As previously noted, if a departure from the analysis and custodial procedures in the ISL which could reasonably have caused an adverse analytical finding is established by an athlete or person facing an allegation, the burden will then fall on the anti-doping organisation bringing the allegation to show that the departure was not causative of any adverse analytical finding or any other anti-doping violation.[82] Whether this burden can be discharged will depend upon the nature of the breach and the evidence relating to its possible effect on the test result. It may be difficult for an anti-doping organisation to discharge the burden of proof to the high standard required – the comfortable satisfaction of the tribunal. It should be noted that procedural failings in relation to B sample rights, which affect the rights of an athlete to have the A sample finding confirmed by requesting the analysis of the B sample, are treated differently from breaches of the ISTI and ISL relating to the process of sample-taking, custody and analysis, and will generally lead to the A sample result being invalidated as a means of proving a violation under Article 2.1.

The International Standard for the Protection of Privacy and Personal Information (ISPPPI)

Signatories to the Code obtain and will hold a wide range of personal information obtained in carrying out their functions. In many situations, this information will be sensitive personal information relating to such matters as the medical conditions and health of an athlete. In most jurisdictions in which the Code operates, national law will seek to protect the privacy rights of individuals in relation to this kind of information through specific legislation and/or under the general principles of the law. Signatories to the Code have to operate in compliance with the provisions of national law in this area and in accordance with the ISPPPI, to which

and accepted as reliable after consideration of the scientific issues. Recently, a successful challenge to the decision limits in testing for hGH led to changes in the relevant Technical Document. Under Article 3.2.1, WADA-approved analytical methods or decision limits are presumed scientifically valid. A challenge is not barred, but if an athlete wishes to rebut the presumption, he or she will have to give notice to WADA if the challenge is to be heard by CAS.

82 See Articles 3.2.1 and 3.2.2 of the Code and page 109.

they are bound by agreement to the Code. The ISPPPI has been formulated with the general principles found in international instruments protecting privacy and the processing of personal data in mind (e.g. the EC Directive 95/46 EC on processing and free movement of personal data).

The ISPPPI seeks to ensure that personal information processed in connection with anti-doping activities is protected and that the privacy of the person supplying this information is preserved. The Standard initially came into force on 1 January 2009. An amended Standard was adopted and came into force on 1 June 2009. As part of the review of the Code which produced the 2015 Code, the ISPPPI was also reviewed. The current Standard in force is dated 1 January 2015.

National anti-doping organisations today operate more broadly than was the case previously under the Code, particularly in the areas of investigations and the collecting of information relating to athletes who are in registered testing pools. All Signatories to the Code obtain and process an increasing amount of private personal information, and all must have systems in place to meet the requirements of national law and the ISPPPI. Where the rights of individuals in relation to their private information are infringed, the Code gives no express individual rights, although a breach of the ISPPPI could lead to a finding that a Signatory is non-compliant or conceivably affect the proof of an allegation of breach of the Code. By contrast, national law is likely to provide both a statutory remedy for any breach of privacy laws and to allow civil claims for infringement of privacy rights and for the wrongful release of confidential information by the individuals affected.

Information Held

Signatories to the Code will retain and hold private personal information relating to athlete whereabouts, medical histories relevant to TUE applications, doping control and testing data. In particular, WADA acts as a central clearing house for doping control, testing data, whereabouts information and ABP data. Anti-doping organisations have to report all in-competition and out-of-competition tests using ADAMS in order to assist with the planning of testing. This information will be made available to the athlete (where appropriate), the international federation and national anti-doping organisation and any other anti-doping organisation with testing authority over the athlete (Article 14.5). WADA and other Signatories will also hold a range of further information concerning such matters as investigations into anti-doping rule violations.

Code Provisions on Private Information

WADA has developed a computer-based programme called ADAMS. ADAMS holds the private information of athletes and others persons supplied to WADA under the Code. Article 14.5 of the 2015 Code provides that private information regarding athletes, athlete support personnel and others held by WADA, in ADAMS and otherwise, has to be maintained by WADA in strict confidence and in accordance with the ISPPPI.

Under the Code, anti-doping organisations are permitted to collect, store, process and disclose personal information relating to athletes and other persons where this is necessary and appropriate to conducting their anti-doping activities under the Code and International Standards. They have to comply with the ISPPPI and national law in dealing with personal information (Article 14.6 of the 2015 Code).

Application of the ISPPPI

The ISPPPI applies to the activities specified by the Code and International Standards which are to be carried out by anti-doping organisations and their third-party agents for the purpose of establishing whether anti-doping rule violations have taken place, including collecting whereabouts information, conducting testing, performing results management, determining whether an athlete's use of a prohibited substance or method is strictly limited to legitimate and documented therapeutic purposes, educating participants on their rights and responsibilities, conducting investigations into anti-doping rule violations and initiating legal proceedings against those who are alleged to have committed such violations. The Standard applies to all personal information. Within the general category of personal information, the Standard identifies a category of 'sensitive personal information', which is personal information relating to a participant's racial or ethnic origin, commission of offences (criminal or otherwise), health and genetic information.

Relationship between the ISPPPI and National Law

Article 4 of the ISPPPI sets out the minimum requirements for the processing of personal information by anti-doping organisations and their third-party agents. All anti-doping organisations must comply with the Standard, even where its requirements exceed the requirements under national privacy law. If compliance with the Standard would cause an anti-doping organisation to breach other applicable laws, then the national laws must prevail. Where data protection and privacy laws and regulations impose requirements that exceed those arising under the Standard, anti-doping organisations must comply with those data protection and privacy laws.

Processing Relevant and Proportionate Personal Information

Article 5 ISPPPI provides that anti-doping organisations are only permitted to process personal information where it is relevant[83] to the conduct of anti-doping activities under the Code and International Standards or where otherwise required by applicable law, regulation or compulsory legal process. The organisations are not entitled to process personal information where such processing is not relevant or appropriate, or where it is unnecessary in the context of their anti-doping activities. In such matters as the assessment of whether an athlete's use or possession of a prohibited substance or method is legitimate under a TUE, the performance of testing, the carrying out of an investigation or results management, anti-doping organisations should only process the personal information which is required for the particular activity. Article 5 also provides that anti-doping organisations may process personal information for other specified purposes provided that the purposes relate exclusively to the fight against doping and are found to be relevant following an appropriately documented assessment performed by the anti-doping organisation. The examples given of such other purposes are the improvement of testing, planning and procedures. Given the importance of privacy rights and obligations, anti-doping organisations will need to proceed with caution if they seek to rely on this provision to process personal information.

Accuracy of Information

Personal information processed by an anti-doping organisation has to be accurate, complete and up to date, and anti-doping organisations have to correct and amend information which is not accurate as soon as possible.

---

83 'Relevant' replaced the phrase 'necessary and appropriate' in one amendment to the ISPPPI in 2016. It is submitted that this makes no substantive difference to the nature of the obligation under Article 5.

Grounds to Process Information: Consent

Personal information can only be processed by anti-doping organisations on valid legal grounds or with the informed consent of a participant (save in exceptional circumstances). In order to obtain consent and process personal information with consent, anti-doping organisations have to provide adequate information to the participant so that informed consent is obtained before or at the time of collection. The information which has to be provided is set out in Article 7 ISPPPI. Participants also have to be informed of the consequences that could arise from a refusal to participate in doping controls and a refusal to consent to the processing of personal information for that purpose. In exceptional circumstances, notice of the information to be provided before or at the time of collection can be delayed or suspended where giving notice might jeopardise an investigation or undermine the integrity of the anti-doping process. The reason for the delay has to be recorded and the information has to be provided as soon as reasonably possible.

Anti-doping organisations can process personal information in the absence of a participant's consent in certain circumstances. They have to inform participants that regardless of a refusal to grant or a withdrawal of consent, they may still need to process personal information where that is necessary to commence or pursue investigations into suspected anti-doping rule violations relating to the participant, to conduct or participate in proceedings involving suspected anti-doping rule violations relating to the participant and to establish exercise or defend legal claims relating to the anti-doping organisation and/or the participant. These exceptions are intended to avoid participants refusing to grant consent or withdraw consent for the processing of personal information in order to block anti-doping procedures.

Information to be Given Concerning Processing of Information

Anti-doping organisations have to inform participants or persons to whom personal information relates about the processing of their personal information. This is required in order to obtain the informed consent of the person to whom the information relates. Article 7 ISPPPI provides that the information has to include the identity of the anti-doping organisation collecting the information, the type of information that may be processed, the purposes for which the information may be used, for how long the information will be retained, other possible recipients of the information (including anti-doping organisations in other countries), the possibility and circumstances under which personal information may be publicly disclosed, the participant's rights under the International Standard in relation to the personal information and any other information necessary to ensure the handling of personal information remains fair (such as information about the regulatory authorities overseeing the processing of the information by the anti-doping organisation). This information has to be communicated to participants or other persons before or at the time at which personal information is collected. Usually, anti-doping organisations will seek to provide the required information concerning the use and processing of the information and its possible disclosure to third parties in written form to the person supplying the information, who will be asked to sign a written acknowledgement or agreement. Anti-doping organisations are also required to be responsive to any questions or concerns of participants in relation to the processing. Where anti-doping organisations receive the personal information from third parties and not directly from the participant, they have to communicate the information to the participant as soon as possible, without unnecessary delay.

Disclosure of Information

Under Article 8 ISPPPI, anti-doping organisations can only disclose personal information to other anti-doping organisations where that disclosure is necessary to allow the anti-doping organisations receiving the information to fulfil obligations under the Code, and where the disclosure is in accordance with applicable privacy and data protection laws. Information cannot be disclosed to other anti-doping organisations where the anti-doping organisation cannot establish a right, authority or need to obtain the personal information, where there is evidence that the anti-doping organisation does not comply with the ISPPPI, where the anti-doping organisation is prohibited from disclosing the personal information by applicable law or where the disclosure would seriously compromise the status of an ongoing investigation. Personal information can be disclosed to other third parties, apart from anti-doping organisations, where disclosure is required by law, where it takes place with the informed express and written consent of the participant or where disclosure is necessary to assist law enforcement or government authorities in the detection, investigation or prosecution of a criminal offence or breach of the Code, provided the information requested is reasonably relevant to the offence in question and cannot otherwise be obtained by the authorities.

Maintaining Security of Information

Under Article 9 ISPPPI, anti-doping organisations have to maintain the security of personal information and have to designate a person who is accountable for compliance with this obligation. All necessary security safeguards have to be implemented to protect information. These have to be commensurate with the sensitivity of the personal information, and a higher level of security is applicable to sensitive personal information. Where personal information is disclosed to third-party agents in connection with anti-doping activities, anti-doping organisations have to ensure that the third-party agents are subject to controls, including contractual controls, in order to protect the confidentiality and privacy of the personal information. This obligation is ongoing. Under Article 9.6, added in the ISPPPI 2016, in the event of a security breach which significantly affects the interests of participants or other persons, the anti-doping organisation has to give them notice of the breach, setting out its nature, its possible negative consequences and the steps taken or to be taken to remedy it.

Retention of Information

Personal information can only be retained where it remains relevant to ful-filling the obligations of the anti-doping organisation under the Code or the ISPPPI. When personal information no longer serves this purpose, it has to be deleted, destroyed or permanently anonymised. Generally, sensitive personal information requires more compelling reasons and justification for its continued retention. Anti-doping organisations have to establish clear retention times to govern the processing of personal information and have to develop specific plans and procedures to ensure secure retention and eventual destruction. Different retention times are applicable to different types of personal information, taking into account the purposes for which the information is processed. Annex A of the ISPPPI sets out the retention times and criteria for particular kinds of information.

Rights of Persons whose Personal Information is Processed

Participants and other persons whose personal information is obtained have the right to obtain confirmation whether or not personal information has been processed in relation to them. They have the right to have the information provided to them when it is collected and to obtain a copy within a reasonable time-frame in a readily intelligible format, unless providing a copy would plainly conflict with the anti-doping organisation's ability to plan or conduct no-advance-notice testing or to investigate and establish anti-doping rule violations. Requests from participants or persons concerning access to personal information must be addressed by anti-doping organisations, save where meeting the request would impose a disproportionate burden on the anti-doping organisation as regards cost and effort given the nature of the information in question. The comment to Article 11.1 ISPPPI states the save in exceptional circumstances, the time-frame for a response to a request should be six to eight weeks.[84] When an anti-doping organisation refuses to allow a participant access to his or her personal information, it has to give reasons for the refusal as soon as is practicable. Where information is shown to be inaccurate, incomplete or excessive, the information has to be appropriately amended or deleted.

Rights to Bring Complaint

In addition to the rights of a participant under any applicable national law, under the ISPPPI a participant has to be permitted to initiate a complaint against an anti-doping organisation where he or she has a reasonable good-faith belief that the organisation is not complying with the Standard. Anti-doping organisations must have procedures in place for dealing with such complaints in a fair and impartial manner. If a complaint cannot be satisfactorily resolved, the parties may notify WADA and/or submit a complaint to CAS. CAS will determine whether a violation of the Standard has occurred. If the International Standard has not been adhered to, the anti-doping organisation in breach will be required to rectify the breach of the Standard.

The Standard was produced after extensive consultation with Signatories to the Code and national governments. It is broadly consistent with privacy legislation in many jurisdictions. The contractual nature of the Code and the Standards means that anti-doping organisations have to adhere both to the ISPPPI and to any applicable national law relating to privacy. As previously noted, while giving rise to remedies under the provisions of the ISPPI and possibly the Code, the acts or omissions of an anti-doping organisation in relation to personal information may give rise to

---

84 Aspects of national law relating to the provision of official information or privacy may apply in some jurisdictions and impose different time-frames for the provision of information on request by anti-doping organisations.

breaches of national law, and it is more likely that an individual aggrieved by a breach involving the abuse of private information will seek recourse under national law.

Breach of ISPPPI and Admissibility of Evidence

The obtaining of information in breach of the ISPPPI or other conduct which breaches the provisions of the Standard may give rise to potential argument about the admissibility of evidence put forward in support of allegations under the Code before tribunals or CAS. Neither the Code nor the ISPPPI contains any provision relating to the effect of breaches of the ISPPPI in proceedings brought alleging violations under the Code. The nature of the obligations under the ISPPPI means that it is unlikely that a breach will have a causative link to an adverse analytical finding or, indeed, the commission of any other anti-doping rule violation. Where information is tendered before a tribunal or CAS which has been obtained in breach of the ISPPPI, the tribunal may need to determine whether the material is admissible. The Code contains no provisions as to the admissibility of evidence. A question of this kind will be determined under the law applicable to the tribunal or arbitration proceedings and any particular provision of the rules of the tribunal.[85]

---

85 For an example of CAS considering admissibility issues by reference to the principles of international arbitration law applicable under Swiss law, see the *Valverde* case summary in Chapter 2, pages 82–7. See also *UCI and WADA* v. *Contador* in Chapter 8, pages 385–90, where the CAS Panel considered the proposed tender of evidence from a witness who was to remain anonymous by reference to Swiss law.

4

The Nature of the Code and Its Interpretation and Application

Effect of Global Acceptance

As has been outlined, the acceptance of the Code by Signatories creates agreements binding sporting organisations and their members, which have the support of States through the Anti-Doping Convention. The Convention does not make the Code part of the law of Signatory States but, rather, commits States to take steps in order to support the Code to reinforce the regime formed by the Code and International Standards. While the Code operates in an area of significant public interest and importance and might be likened to a private legislative regime for sport, it functions as a contractual arrangement by which sporting organisations and associations regulate themselves in the anti-doping area. One of the challenges presented by this interlocking international network of agreements regulating anti-doping in sport is how to ensure a harmonised approach to its interpretation and application.

It is important to bear in mind that, while there are a significant number of common features in anti-doping regimes which accept the Code (as the Code requires), there will also be a number of areas where sporting organisations will continue to establish and maintain their specific policies by developing and adopting rules concerning such matters as the investigation of anti-doping rule violations (not involving testing and analysis), sanctions for teams, the management of results, reporting and confidentiality. While many of the rules in these areas will have to meet the mandatory standards set by the applicable Articles of the Code and will be based on them, there may well be other aspects of anti-doping policies which function outside the Code, such as the imposition of other sanctions (e.g. financial penalties).[1] Rules covering such matters may, just like the

---

1 Article 10.10 of the Code allows for anti-doping organisations to provide for the proportionate recovery of costs and for financial sanctions for anti-doping rule violations. Financial sanctions can only be imposed where the maximum period of ineligibility has been imposed and where the principle of proportionality is satisfied. See further Chapter 8, pages

provisions of the Code and International Standards, have to be interpreted by tribunals and CAS, applying principles which are applicable to the interpretation of private agreements.

The risk with the exercise of interpreting the various rules which operate by agreement is that different approaches to the exercise of interpretation of rules may lead to inconsistency and lack of harmony. To an extent, the use of CAS as an appeal court under the Code is intended to bring about a consistent approach to the interpretation and applicable of the Code. However, the most important feature of the Code is that it contains specific provisions relating to its interpretation which are intended to address and remove this risk.

Interpreting and Applying the Code

Initial Agreement to Jurisdiction

The contractual nature of the arrangements created by the Code means that, in some disputes, there may be a threshold question as to whether there has been an agreement which, on its true construction, binds an individual athlete to the Code or to the arbitral process under the Code.[2] Such a question of construction will be determined according to the rules of the tribunal hearing the matter and by reference to the law of the legal system applicable to that question, and tribunals will usually have jurisdiction to rule on whether they have jurisdiction over the matter which is before them under the applicable national law.[3]

If jurisdiction is established under the applicable agreement, questions regarding the correct interpretation of a particular provision in the anti-doping rules or policy which has been agreed to may then arise, whether in relation to Articles of the Code which have been included in the rules or

448–9 and Chapter 10, pages 497–9 for consideration of the requirements of proportionate measures generally and for a relevant case summary.

2 See Chapter 2, pages 72–7 for examples of cases where this essential prerequisite for the application of the Code was considered. For a recent example of different views between CAS and the Swiss Federal Supreme Court on the interpretation of an agreement said to bind an athlete to testing, see the case summary of *Busch* in Chapter 2, pages 72–5.

3 Under the law relating to arbitration in countries which have adopted the UNCITRAL Model Law on Arbitration, arbitral tribunals will have jurisdiction to rule on their own jurisdiction. This will usually involve deciding whether a person is bound by an arbitration clause and/or whether the dispute falls within the scope of the arbitration clause. The CAS Code specifically provides for the Panel to rule on its own jurisdiction (Rule 39). The position under Swiss law (under the Swiss PILA 1987 Article 186) applying to CAS arbitration under the Code is that CAS has jurisdiction to determine whether it has jurisdiction.

policy without significant amendment, the provisions by which the organisation seeks to follow the standards set by the Code or the International Standards.

Such questions of construction are familiar to courts and arbitrators in contractual disputes around the world. The general principles of contractual interpretation are a well-established feature of contract law in most, if not all jurisdictions. While there has been considerable debate over certain aspects of the principles of contractual interpretation in common law jurisdictions (largely concerning the extent to which background information can be considered), the essential applicable principles involve ascertaining the intention of the parties to the agreement in the objective sense, by reference to the natural ordinary meaning of the words used in the agreement. The court or arbitrator has to consider what a reasonable person in the position of the parties to the contract would have understood the contract to mean at the time it was entered into. The meaning will be considered against the general background or factual matrix of the contract. Where there is dispute over the meaning of the words, the court or arbitrator may consider how a suggested interpretation fits with the purpose of the contract. While modern contractual interpretation adopts a 'purposive' approach, with courts and arbitrators concerned to arrive at a meaning for a disputed term which best fits with the purpose of the parties as revealed by an objective examination of background material, the focus remains on interpreting the contract in accordance with the meaning of the words which the parties have used. This all-important focus on the text of the agreement has been recently underlined by the UK Supreme Court in important general comments on contract interpretation.[4] The principles of the interpretation of contracts applicable in civil law jurisdictions such as Switzerland are formulated differently, with significantly more emphasis on finding the subjective contractual intention of the parties. The principles require that the court find the actual intentions of the parties and, if that cannot be determined, that the contract be interpreted by reference to the principle of good faith, which involves asking what a reasonable person in the place of the contracting parties would have considered to be the contractual intention.

While this difference in approaches appears to offer the potential for differences of outcome regarding the interpretation of contracts, the application of Swiss law to questions of contract interpretation before CAS does

---

4 See *Arnold* v. *Britton and ors [2015] UK SC 36*, in particular Lord Neuberger at paragraphs 17–23.

not appear to have made a significant difference to decisions on interpreting sporting rules. In relation to the interpretation of the Code, the
approach which the Code itself requires focusses on principles of interpretation which are generally accepted and not on particular national legal
principles.

Purpose of the Code

Anti-doping regimes operate in a particular sporting context, and the
Code represents a sporting consensus which has the clearly stated purposes of protecting athletes' fundamental right to participate in doping-
free fair competition and ensuring harmonised and effective anti-doping
measures at national and international level. The clearly stated aims of the
Code must, it is submitted, be used where questions of interpretation arise,
although the starting point for the exercise of interpretation is the examination of the words of the rules or policy in order to arrive at the meaning
that they convey to a reasonable reader.

Clarity and Certainty

In deciding cases involving the interpretation of anti-doping regimes, the
need for 'clarity and certainty'[5] or 'predictability'[6] in anti-doping rules
where, if athletes are found to have committed violations, they may lose
their sporting careers has been emphasised by CAS Panels throughout the
period in which CAS has considered doping matters. CAS Panels have
also warned of the need to keep the purpose of anti-doping regimes in
mind, and to construe them in a manner which will 'discern the intention of the rule maker', rather than frustrate it.[7] Whether terms will be
pronounced ineffective for lack of clarity or ambiguity or construed in a
manner which gives effect to the purpose of an anti-doping policy will
depend on the words used in the particular provisions under consideration. The principle of interpreting a rule which lacks clear meaning against
the party which has produced the rule has been relied on by CAS Panels in
declaring that a rule is ineffective or should be interpreted in a particular
way.

5 See e.g. CAS 2000/A/312, L v. FILA, CAS Digest III.
6 See e.g. CAS 2008/A/1545, Anderson & others v. IOC.
7 See e.g. CAS 96/149, AC v. FINA, CAS Digest I, p. 251; CAS 2001/A/317, A v. FILA (see
note 4).

It is submitted that the Code, by its provisions and explanatory intro-duction and notes, provides, for the most part, the necessary clarity and certainty of meaning in key areas, particularly in relation to the key Arti-cles which have to be adopted without significant amendment. As noted, the Code also contains clear statements of its purpose, which can be referred to where different interpretations are under consideration.

The acceptance of the Code has led to a reduction in the diversity of anti-doping policies. The refinement of the key elements of anti-doping policies in such areas as strict liability and the imposition of sanctions by the adoption of the key Articles of the Code means that the policies have a clear, consistent meaning in relation to the fundamental princi-ples. The most likely areas of difficulty with the central provisions of the Code lie not, perhaps, within the area of construction in the strict sense, but in the application of general phrases such as 'fault' and 'no signif-icant fault or negligence' – which require an evaluation of conduct by tribunals – to particular factual situations. In these areas, the aim and purpose of the provisions are set out in the Code and in the notes in a manner which should assist in promoting a consistent approach to the questions raised, although the definitions of the key phrases are general in nature, and many inquiries will be fact-specific.

Role of Applicable Law

An anti-doping policy which implements the Code may contain a choice-of-law clause by which the parties choose the legal system which is to apply to the interpretation of the policy. In the absence of such a provision, the CAS Procedural Rules contain a provision permitting a CAS Panel to have reference to the legal system of the jurisdiction where a sports organisation has its seat. As many international sporting federations have their seats in Switzerland, Swiss law is likely to apply in many disputes.

At a national level, anti-doping regimes may also be subject to local legislation and potentially to the interpretative approach of a national legal system. However, the law which governs the policy or rules should not have any significance influence on questions of the interpretation of the Code, in light of the increasing assimilation of the principles of contractual interpretation across many jurisdictions, including both common law and civil systems, and more particularly the provision of Article 24 of the Code relating to interpretation. This provision has a significant effect on the approach to interpretation, and it is, perhaps, more likely that the legal system governing an anti-doping policy and the system to which the sporting organisation involved in the matter is subject will need to be considered by a tribunal or CAS (or indeed a court) in the context of arguments that the provisions of an anti-doping policy are contrary to the fundamental rights protected under that legal system.[8]

Article 24 of the Code

The possible impact of the principles of interpretation established by a particular legal system on the interpretation of the Code is significantly reduced or removed by the presence of Article 24. This Article, which must be adopted without substantive change by Signatories, provides that questions of interpretation are to be approached in a manner which underlines the international nature of the text as a Code which is intended to function outside the constraints of a particular legal system. Article 24.3 provides that the Code is to be interpreted as 'an independent and autonomous text' and not 'by reference to the existing law or statute of the signatories or governments'. This important provision emphasises for all tribunals which have to consider the interpretation of the Code that principles of interpretation which are generally accepted internationally are to be applied, rather than particular principles of interpretation and law derived from one particular national legal system. The focus in interpreting the Code should, accordingly, be on the principles of interpretation which are common to all legal systems. If that approach is adopted, it is more likely that the Code will be interpreted and applied in a consistent manner. It is suggested that the general principles of contractual construction set out in this chapter represent the principles which will be applied. Tribunals and CAS Panels are also likely to refer to international documents which contain statements of common principles of contract law, such as the Unidroit Principles of International Commercial Contracts 2010.[9] It is submitted that this general approach should apply to the interpretation of all rules which implement the Code and International Standards because the Standards are an integral part of the Code (as confirmed in the Purpose to the Code) and have the same international nature.

---

8 See Chapter 10, pages 510–13 for examples of CAS Panels considering such questions under the laws of a particular State.

9 See Articles 4.1–4.8 of the Unidroit Principles for the principles of interpretation. For an example of a CAS Panel referring to the Unidroit Principles, see CAS 2009/A/1752, *Dvyatovskiy* v. *IOC* in Chapter 5, pages 199–201.

The Purpose of the Code

The Introduction to the Code contains clear statements as to the Code's purpose[10] (which should be considered by tribunals to arrive at the meaning of doping policies), and the Code also contains annotations which explain the Articles and their aims. While the annotations in the 2015 Code have been reduced, they remain fairly extensive, particularly in relation to the central Articles on violations, the burden and standard of proof and the imposition and elimination or reduction of sanctions. Article 24.2 confirms the important status of the notes of the Code by providing that the notes have to be used to interpret the Code. The annotations are, at various places, the equivalent of a detailed statement of the purpose and intent of the Code (particularly in the area of the imposition of sanctions) and provide statements which are clearly intended to guide any tribunal interpreting and applying the provisions. By way of example, while reduced in scope, the notes to Article 10.4 provide clear statements as to the circumstances which will not provide the basis for a 'no fault' plea by an athlete.

The International Approach to Interpretation

In summary, the effect of the provisions in Article 24.3 and the application of general principles of contractual interpretation is that the meaning of the Code and the policies which implement it should be determined by tribunals in a straightforward way by approaching the words used in the Article under consideration, together with the notes to the Code, and asking what meaning a reasonable person would give to the words under consideration in the context of the Code overall. Where different interpretations are under consideration, the purpose of the Code as expressed in the Code itself (e.g. the introduction and notes) should be considered, and where possible an interpretation which better meets that purpose should be adopted. While amendments to the Code will frequently have been the subject of consideration at WADA meetings and a significant volume of background material may be available, it is submitted that the intention of Article 24.3 is that tribunals should not generally review this kind of material in an effort to ascertain the drafters' intent.[11] At all times, a tribunal

---

10 See p. 1 of the Introduction to the Code and Chapter 2, pages 62–3.
11 The practical burden of this kind of approach – the fact that it leads tribunals away from the objective interpretation of the words and rarely produces certain answers or scores a 'bulls-eye' on deciding meaning – is good reason not to approach the interpretation of the

(or court) should, it is submitted, seek to avoid considering a question of construction by reference to specific national legal principles by reason of the provision in Article 24.3.

The Code can be likened to international instruments and agreements which operate in areas such as international trade, and provide a code for rights and liabilities in relation to the carriage of goods by sea or air, or seek to establish uniform commercial practice concerning documentary credits, which will apply in a wide range of legal systems.[12] In mercantile law, courts and arbitral tribunals have been conscious of the need for such international agreements to be interpreted and applied in a manner which emphasises uniformity, achieves comity and is 'consistent with broad principles of general acceptation', rather than by reference to particular national legal principles or case law.[13] This approach should be applied to the interpretation of the Code and the International Standards, and Article 24.3 endorses it. Generally, it is submitted that CAS and tribunals applying the Code should be extremely wary of arguments which seek to advance particular interpretations of the Code based on the application of particular principles of contract interpretation in national law.

Where provisions in an anti-doping policy seek to implement the standards contained in the Articles of the Code in the areas where Signatories do not have to adopt provisions without significant amendment, tribunals should, it is submitted, seek to interpret the provisions in a manner which upholds the purpose of the Code as set out in the Articles (and notes), where the words used permit such an interpretation.

Code in this way. The uncertainty of arriving at an intention as to meaning from the many divergent views expressed in the review process again provides a sound basis to remain focussed on the text of the Code as drafted.

12 See e.g. international conventions and codes such as the Hague–Visby Rules, which govern liability for the carriage of goods by sea, and the Uniform Customs and Practice for Documentary Credits (UCP), which provides a code for the operation and use of letters of credit in international trade.

13 See e.g. Lord Macmillan in *Bank of England* v. *Vagliano Brothers* [1932] AC 328 and 344; *Fothergill* v. *Monarch Airlines Ltd* [1981] AC 259; *Buchanan & Co. Ltd* v. *Babco Forwarding and Shipping (UK) Ltd* [1978] AC 141; *J. I. MacWilliam Co., Inc.* v. *Mediterranean Shipping Co. SA* [2005] UKHL 11, per Lord Steyn. See also *Hatzvl* v. *XL Insurance Co Ltd* [2009] EWCA 223, where L. J. Collins says in relation to interpreting an international convention: 'The starting point is to consider the natural meaning of the language used in the provision in question. But it is necessary to consider the convention as a whole and give it a purposive interpretation. The language of an international convention should be interpreted constrained by technical rules of English law or by English legal precedent but on broad principles of general acceptance.' This, it is submitted, should be the general approach to the interpretation of the Code.

The Central Role of CAS in Interpretation

CAS Panels have often emphasised the need for a consistent approach to the interpretation and application of the provisions of the Code in a manner which accords with its purpose. The need for consistency and comity has, perhaps, to date been most emphasised in the difficult areas of the interpretation and application of Articles relating to the imposition of sanctions – Articles 10.5.1 and 10.5.2 of the 2004 Code and Article 10.4 of the 2009 Code, under which the fixed period of ineligibility for violations may, in certain circumstances, be reduced or eliminated.[14]

CAS Panels have also had to consider whether particular provisions of the Code and the outcome of their application are compatible with the fundamental rights protected under the legal system to which a particular sporting policy or sporting organisation is subject, or under the system of law which governs a challenge to the CAS award in the matter. CAS Panels have upheld the legality and enforceability of the Code's provisions in the context of such fundamental rights in the same manner as the Swiss courts.[15] In exceptional circumstances, where the provisions of the 2004 Code contained a 'gap' in its provisions concerning sanctions which, in the opinion of the CAS Panel hearing the matter, brought about a harsh, disproportionate sanction for an athlete who had committed two violations each involving no significant fault, a CAS Panel held that the effect of the provisions of the Code should be mitigated under the principle of proportionality, with the result that the sanction which would have applied under the Code for a second violation, by reason of the 'gap' in the Code's provisions, was reduced to one which, the Panel considered, was proportionate. This technique, which involves interpreting the Code in a manner which produces an outcome which aligns with the fundamental rights and protections or public policy of a particular legal system, can only possibly be applied in those rare cases where the Articles of the Code can truly be

---

14 The division between CAS Panels in relation to the interpretation and application of Article 10.4 of the 2009 Code and the broad discretion available if the requirements for a possible reduction of the two-year period were met made this a problematic Article from the perspective of predictability and consistency. The 2015 Code no longer contains this provision.

15 See Chapter 10, pages 483–93, where the grounds on which CAS and the courts have found that the Code is not contrary to fundamental rights are outlined. See e.g. the CAS award in *Eder* in Chapter 10, pages 510–11, where the anti-doping regime of the Austrian Skiing Federation, which implemented the Code and was subject to Austrian law, was held to be valid and not contrary to fundamental rights protected under Austrian law, Swiss law and the principles of the ECHR.

said not to have provided for a particular situation, and where a wholly disproportionate outcome would result from the literal application of the provisions of the Code.[16] This approach, while undertaken in the context of the rules of a private association by an arbitral tribunal, can be likened to the application of the principle of statutory interpretation applicable in many jurisdictions: that a statutory provision will be interpreted, wherever possible, in a manner which complies with constitutional or fundamental rights. The changes brought about by the 2009 Code, which introduced greater flexibility in relation to sanctions, meant that it was generally not possible to maintain that the Code did not provide fully for proportionality. The 2015 Code now makes specific reference to the principles of proportionality and human rights in its Introduction by stating that the provisions of the Code, while not limited by national legal requirements relevant to criminal law, are intended to be applied in a manner which respects the principles of proportionality and human rights. This reference raises the possibility that a tribunal might rely on this provision, in a particular case where the fundamental principles of proportionality or human rights would in its view be infringed by the result reached on the application of the Code's provisions, to make a decision on the interpretation of the Code which it considered was consistent with those principles and which reduced the sanction under the Code. It is submitted that this possibility could only arise in an exceptional case and that the statement in the Introduction is intended to be declaratory of the way in which the Code's provisions have been drafted and operate.[17]

16 See *Puerta* v. *ITF* in Chapter 8, pages 406–7, where the provisions relating to sanctions under the 2004 Code meant that a player who had committed two violations involving no significant fault, one before the Code, the other under the Code, would face a ten-year ban on the literal application of the provisions of the Code. The CAS Panel relied on the principle of proportionality to reduce the period of ineligibility to two years. This award should be viewed, it is submitted, as an exceptional decision. The 2009 Code contains clearer and fuller provisions in relation to sanctions for second violations which fill the 'gap' in the 2004 Code. The 2015 Code makes specific reference to fundamental rights and proportionality, and this appears to leave open the possibility that the principles might be relied on to address a particular exceptional case.

17 By way of example, it seems possible that tribunals might be taxed with arguments based on proportionality where certain violations attract four years' ineligibility in circumstances where it may be difficult to describe a person's conduct as involving an intention to break the rules and/or to cheat. See e.g. the discussion on the imposition of a four-year period of ineligibility where an athlete alleged to have committed the violation of refusal cannot establish a compelling justification for the refusal in Chapter 8, pages 342–4.

5

Articles 1 and 2 of the Code: Anti-doping Rule Violations under the Code

Introduction

Article 2 is a central provision of the Code, which Signatories must implement without significant amendment, and will be reproduced verbatim in all Code-compliant doping policies. The Article sets out the violations which may be committed by athletes and other persons who are bound by the Code, and which anti-doping organisations will seek to investigate and establish before tribunals. Those tribunals, whether established at national level by NADOs or at international level by international federations, will have to decide whether violations under Article 2 have been established to the required standard of proof. CAS will also carry out the same exercise where it either has been chosen as the first-instance tribunal by a national anti-doping organisation or international federation or acts as an appellate tribunal as provided for by Article 13 of the Code.

Doping is defined by Article 1 as the occurrence of one or more of the anti-doping rule violations in Article 2.1. While collectively defined as doping by Article 1, the violations in Article 2 extend beyond the violations of 'doping' (in the sense of an athlete having a prohibited substance or its metabolites or markers in his or her bodily sample or using a prohibited method) and refusal to submit to testing for the presence of prohibited substances in the athlete's system, which were largely the focus of anti-doping investigations and proceedings as the Code developed, and include violations which involve various forms of intentional conduct relating to prohibited substances or the testing process. This general range of violations was present in the OMADC and in many sports anti-doping policies before the Code, but the enforcement of anti-doping regimes focussed, to a considerable degree, on the detection of the presence of prohibited substances and methods through the collection of bodily samples for testing. The establishment of WADA, and the increasing awareness of the scope of the problem of doping in sport over the period of its existence, has seen greater attention given to the need to investigate and establish other violations as a means of combating doping in sport generally. For example, violations such as administering and trafficking in prohibited substances can, if detected and established at a hearing, be brought against those involved in providing doping products to athletes.

The investigation of the non-analytical violations under the Code has received much greater attention from WADA and anti-doping organisations in recent years. Various agreements and understandings have been entered into with national and international law enforcement agencies.[1] Under those agreements, anti-doping organisations seek to increase cooperation in investigations and facilitate the exchange of relevant information and evidence. The amendments in the 2015 Code and the ISTI 2017 underline this important shift in emphasis.[2] Several significant anti-doping investigations have been pursued by anti-doping organisations in collaboration with State agencies, and, increasingly, information on the illegal importation of prohibited substances from agencies such as customs agencies is used by anti-doping organisations to pursue investigations and bring allegations against athletes and other persons who are subject to the Code.[3]

Investigations into Other Violations

The successful investigation of violations which rely on evidence apart from positive tests poses significant challenges for anti-doping organisations. However, ultimately, such investigations, and the hearings which result from them, will involve the well-established process of the production and consideration of evidence before a tribunal in order to prove the allegation made.[4] This was acknowledged early in the development of the

1 For an example, see the cooperation agreement between WADA and Interpol dated 2 February 2009, under which the parties agree to cooperate and exchange information in the area of anti-doping. This illustrates the increasing importance attributed to this area. See also the document produced by WADA to assist anti-doping organisations in establishing and developing relationships with State law enforcement agencies referred to in Chapter 2, pages 66–7. The increasing trend towards the criminalisation of doping under national legal systems has increased activity by law enforcement agencies, which is likely to produce more information that can be used by anti-doping organisations conducting investigations under the Code.
2 See Chapter 3, pages 124–41 for more detail, and page 94, note 7 for the relevant WADA guideline.
3 For examples of cases which have arisen from such investigations, see pages 170–7.
4 The increase in such investigations by anti-doping organisations at national and international level has seen longer, more wide-ranging hearings before tribunals where the evidence relating to conduct over considerable periods of time and more varied and complex

Code by the CAS Panel in *USADA* v. *Montgomery*,[5] where the allegations against Mr Montgomery arose from the BALCO investigation into systematic organised doping by leading track and field athletes. The Panel observed, adopting a statement from the Italian Olympic Committee in an earlier decision, as follows:

> The Panel would add, in conclusion, that there is no reason to believe that the world of sport has seen the last of this sort of 'no adverse analytical finding' case. It must constantly be borne in mind, as noted above, that doping offences can be proved by a variety of means. In this regard, the Panel concurs with the observation expressed in the Comitato Olimpico Nazionale Italiano ('CONI') matter, that 'in anti-doping proceedings other than those deriving from positive testing, sports authorities do not have an easy task in discharging the burden of proving that an anti-doping rule violation has occurred, as no presumption applies'. However, the Panel also concurs wholeheartedly with the exhortation of the CONI Panel, which wrote as follows in the concluding passage of its Award, a declaration that this Panel adopts as its own:
>
> > In any event, the undeniable circumstance that the conviction for doping offences is more difficult when the evidence is other than positive testing must not prevent the sports authorities from prosecuting such offences as already marked, with the utmost earnestness and eagerness, using any available method of investigation. In the end, it will be up to the adjudicating body having jurisdiction over the matter – which, according to Article 8 of the WADC, must always be a 'fair and impartial hearing body' – to determine case by case whether the standard of proof of Article 3.1 of the WADC has been met and the burden of proof has been discharged, or not, by the prosecuting sports authority.

Since this early statement, WADA has urged anti-doping organisations and sporting organisations to pursue the investigation of non-analytical violations. Although such investigations present various challenges for anti-doping organisations in terms of their investigatory powers, resources and expertise, there has been a steady increase in the number of investigations and resultant allegations involving non-analytical violations. The WADA document on information sharing contains a summary

anti-doping violations has to be examined. CAS has maintained the position established in many CAS awards that an appeal will involve a full re-hearing of the evidence. Although in some decisions CAS Panels have adopted a more limited approach to the consideration of an appeal from a discretionary decision, this was not the general position, and the *de novo* approach is the established procedure and is expressly emphasised by the provisions of the 2015 Code on appeals. See Chapter 9, pages 479–81.

5 For a summary of the decision, see pages 170–2.

of a number of anti-doping investigations,[6] which gave rise to a range of allegations of anti-doping rule violations against athletes and others bound by the Code and involved individuals being investigated and prosecuted under national law by State agencies. Since that time, investigations into systemic doping in cycling and athletics have produced similar outcomes.

Illustrations

The Investigation and Proof of 'Non-analytical Positive' Violations

CAS 2004/O/645, USADA v. Montgomery   This case arose from the BALCO investigation (as did several others). M, a world and Olympic champion at 100 metres, was charged by USADA, the agency responsible for doping control in the United States, with various doping offences under the IAAF anti-doping rules, including using prohibited substances, aiding others to use prohibited substances and trafficking.

M was alleged to have used one or more substances in the 'anabolic steroids class, Testosterone/Epitestosterone cream, EPO, growth hormone and Insulin'. USADA sought a lifetime ban under the IAAF Rules. M waived the domestic hearing process before the American Arbitration Association (AAA) and the parties agreed to an arbitration before CAS in the Ordinary Division. There were various procedural disputes which were the subject of rulings before the hearing.

The Standard of Proof   On the standard of proof, the parties disagreed on whether the IAAF Rule, which was in force when the alleged use began and which required proof beyond a reasonable doubt, or the Code provision, which came into force during the period of the use and required proof

---

6 See Chapter 2, pages 81–2. The document lists many investigations, including the 1998 Festina raids at the Tour de France, the 2002 Salt Lake City Olympics seizure of blood transfusion material, the 2003 BALCO investigation into trafficking in the United States, the 2004 oil-for-drug investigation in Italy, the 2006 Operatión Puerta investigation in Spain, the large-scale seizure by customs officials of anabolic steroids and growth hormones in Finland, the 2007 Operation Raw Deal in the United States and the 2009 investigation into the professional cycling team Lampre in Italy. The latest investigation carried out by WADA involves Russian athletics and the Russian anti-doping laboratory and agency, and is largely based on information obtained from a 'whistle-blower', or informant. For the report into this, see *The Report by the Independent Commission into Doping in Athletics* Parts 1 and 2, December 2015 and January 2016. See Chapter 8, pages 436–8 for 'substantial assistance' under Article 10.6.1.

to the comfortable satisfaction of the tribunal, applied. The Panel found that with such serious allegations, the difference in the formulation of the standard made little or no difference to the requirements for proof of the allegations.

> [I]n view of the nature and gravity of the allegations at issue in these proceedings, there is no practical distinction between the standards of proof advocated by USADA and the Respondents. It makes little, if indeed any, difference whether 'beyond a reasonable doubt' or 'comfortable satisfaction' standard is applied to determine the claims against the Respondents ... Either way USADA bears the burden of proving by strong evidence commensurate with the serious claims it makes, that the Respondents committed the doping offences in question.

The Range of Evidence Produced   As the hearing on the merits progressed, the broad, more serious violations against M, including trafficking, were dropped, and the charge pursued was the use of the prohibited substances. A wide range of evidence was produced in order to prove this charge to the required standard of proof, including various documents from the files seized at BALCO, blood test results which were said to be abnormal (although they had not led to a positive test), various newspaper reports in which M is said to have admitted using various prohibited substances in grand jury testimony, and evidence of admissions of using a cream called 'Clear' made to another athlete, Kelly White. The admissibility and reliability of all the evidence was challenged.

Proof by Admission   The Panel did not rule on the issues raised because it was unanimously of the view that the evidence of admissions made by M to Ms White of the use of prohibited substances, given by Ms White, was credible. The Panel noted that 'the fact that the Panel does not consider it necessary to analyse and comment on the mass of other evidence against the athlete is not to be taken as an indication that it considers that such other evidence could not demonstrate that the Respondent is guilty of doping. Doping can be proved by a variety of means: and this is nowhere more true than in "non-analytical positive" cases such as the present.'

With the withdrawal of the trafficking charges, USADA reduced the sanction sought to four years. However, the IAAF Rules provided for a two-year period of ineligibility, and this was the period imposed, together with disqualification of results.

The Panel observed, in conclusion, 'that there is no reason to believe that the world of sport has seen the last of this sort of "no adverse analytical finding case". This has certainly proved true, and such cases are now seen as central to the fight against doping, because they provide a better opportunity to catch those who are involved in concerted schemes to dope and/or provide prohibited substances to athletes.

An Example of the Proof of a Range of Violations Arising as a Result of Material Found after a Search by State Authorities[7]

CAS 2007/A/1286, *Eder* v. *IOC*; CAS 2007/A/1288, *Tauber* v. *IOC*; CAS 2007/A/1289, *Pinter* v. *IOC*   These proceedings were an appeal to CAS from a decision of the IOC Executive Board.[8] E, T and P had been ordered to be permanently ineligible for all future Olympic Games by the IOC Executive Board as a result of recommendations made by the IOC Disciplinary Committee.

The IOC Disciplinary Committee had investigated potential anti-doping rule violations under the IOC Anti-Doping Rules (which are based on the Code) arising from the discovery of a range of material at a house occupied by the Austrian cross-country skiing team at the 2006 Turin Winter Olympics. E, T and P shared the house with another member of the team, D. The coach and manager of the team were also at premises in the same village (as was M, a former coach who had been banned for life from participation at the Olympic Games as a result of his role in performing blood transfusions at the previous Winter Games in Salt Lake City). The International Federation of Skiing announced before the Games that it would be imposing five-day protective bans at the Games where athletes tested with haemoglobin (HGB) levels over 17 g/dl.

Material Found on Search   When the house was searched by the Italian police, a range of equipment was found in the possession of E, T and P and seized. T had a haemoglobinmeter (a device for measuring HGB levels),

---

7 For another example of an early case arising from a search where the anti-doping organisation faced difficulties in proving the alleged violations, see *French* v. *Australian Sports Commission and Cycling Australia* in Chapter 6, pages 288–9.

8 There was a further related appeal in CAS 2007/A/1290, *Deithart* v. *IOC*, in which D, another member of the team found with similar items in his possession, brought an appeal against the IOC decision to impose a life ban on competing in the Olympic Games. His appeal against the finding that he had committed violations was dismissed, but the majority of the Panel held that the life ban on participation in the Olympics was disproportionate given D's role in the matter and reduced the period of ineligibility to four years. This would prevent D from appearing at the Olympics again as an active athlete, but not from participating in the Olympics in some other capacity in the future.

various used and unused needles and an infusion pack. P had used and unused syringes. E had an intravenous drip with a needle containing saline solution. The other athlete in the house, D, was in possession of syringes, infusion device packs, a box of black pills, and four jars for HGB testing. The coach and manager were also found to be in possession of similar items of equipment. Used items had traces of blood on them. A subsequent analysis of the haemoglobinmeter showed that values for HGB had been measured fifty-nine times in a period of nine days before the search.

E admitted that he had given himself an intravenous infusion of saline. E said he did this when he had diarrhoea. He had consulted the team doctor and had carried out the infusion himself after the team doctor had failed to arrive at the house and he had called his own doctor, who said he should self-administer the infusion. This admission led to E being the subject of anti-doping proceedings before Ski Austria, in which he was found to have used a prohibited method and ordered to be ineligible for one year after a finding of no significant fault or negligence.[9] E also explained that his naturally high HGB levels necessitated the use of the infusion. In the IOC hearing, he also admitted administering another infusion. As a result of the material discovered (and the admissions in the case of E), E, T and P were found by the IOC to have committed violations of the IOC Anti-Doping Rules under Article 2.2 (the use or attempted use of a prohibited substance or method), Article 2.6.1 (the possession of a prohibited method) and Article 2.8 (the administration or attempted administration of a prohibited method to any athlete, or assisting, encouraging, aiding, abetting, covering up or any other type of complicity involving an anti-doping rule violation or any attempted violation). E, T and P claimed that they had a legitimate reason to possess the items which were found in their possession, and that, in any event, the items which they each individually possessed could not be said to be prohibited methods. They appealed to CAS against the lifetime ineligibility from attending the Olympic Games.

Arguments for E, T and P   E claimed that he had in his possession an intravenous infusion kit and saline in case he was attended by a doctor who did not have such equipment with him should he need intravenous infusion. He admitted the use of an intravenous infusion but said this was by way of legitimate medical treatment. T said that he had the haemoglobinmeter in his possession to check his HGB levels. He claimed that he had naturally high levels and was concerned to ensure that those

9 See CAS 2006/A/1102, *Eder* v. *Ski Austria* in Chapter 10, pages 510–11.

levels did not reach a level at which he could not compete when he was at altitude. P explained that he had various syringes in his possession in order to administer non-prohibited substances and also to scratch his fingertip in order to obtain blood to check his HGB levels on the haemoglobin-meter.

E, T and P all submitted that the hearing process before the IOC was flawed in the procedural sense.

Legal Submissions E also submitted that he had been previously dealt with for using a prohibited method when he had been found to have used a prohibited method and was banned for twelve months by Ski Austria. He submitted that the further IOC proceeding was null and void under the ECHR as being a second trial on the same matter. He further submitted that the standard of proof required should be beyond reasonable doubt. T and P also claimed that the standard of proof should be higher than that contained in Article 3.1 of the Code, given the gravity of the sanction. E submitted that there was insufficient evidence to demonstrate that he had used a prohibited method and that, in any event, before there could be a breach of Article 2.2, a subjective intent on his part to achieve increased performance had to be established. He also submitted that the circumstances in which he had administered a saline infusion qualified as 'legitimate acute medical treatment', which meant that there was no use of a prohibited method.

E, T and P submitted that the items which they had in their possession did not amount to the possession of a prohibited method, whether this was the enhancement of oxygen transfer, blood doping or intravenous infusions. They argued that, for there to be possession of a prohibited method, there had to be an intention to enhance performance, and, in any event, they did not each possess the items found in the possession of the others, with the result that they could not be said to possess sufficient items to possess the prohibited method. T and P each claimed, like E, that they had the items which they had to protect health rather than enhance performance, or, alternatively, that they had acceptable justification for possessing the materials.

Each athlete further submitted that a lifetime ban was disproportionate.

Findings of the Panel The Panel found that any challenge to due process before the IOC Board was cured by the further hearing before it. On E's submission under the ECHR, it found that Article 4 of the ECHR was not applicable to proceedings of the kind before the Panel but was limited to criminal proceedings. In any event, E was subject to a sanction for two further violations in addition to the one which had already been heard by Ski Austria (Articles 2.6.1 and 2.8) and the evidence in the earlier proceedings was different from the evidence before CAS in the current proceedings. On the standard of proof, the Panel applied Article 3.1 and the standard of 'comfortable satisfaction', and said that, in any event, there was little practical difference between the 'balance of probabilities standard' and the 'beyond a reasonable doubt standard' if those standards were applied as required by Article 3.1: 'bearing in mind the seriousness of the allegation which is made'.

At a general level, the Panel was concerned at the frequency of the coincidences which the appellants relied on in support of their possession of the various items found in their possession. The overall coincidence was that each member of the ski team had arrived at the accommodation reserved for them at the Olympic Games with parts of a kit which could be used for administering a prohibited method, namely, blood doping. The Panel did not accept the medical justifications for the athletes having the items.

The Panel found that E had admitted using a prohibited method by carrying out two infusions. There was no need, under Article 2.2 of the Code and the IOC Anti-Doping Rules, for the anti-doping organisation to prove that the athlete intended subjectively to enhance his or her performance. The Panel went on to conclude that these infusions did not constitute 'legitimate acute medical treatment'.

Possession of a Prohibited Method   On the allegation of possession of a prohibited method, the Panel was of the view that the concept of possession had to be considered in light of all the surrounding circumstances. The possession of a prohibited method would be established where it could be shown to the comfortable satisfaction of the Panel that, in all the circumstances, an athlete was in possession, either physical or constructive, of items which would enable the athlete to engage in a prohibited method. The Panel found that the appellants were all in possession of a prohibited method, namely, intravenous infusions, as described under the Prohibited List. Given the arrangements under which the premises were occupied, each athlete was in constructive possession of the items in the actual possession of the others (and of those items in the possession of D, the coach and the manager). There was no need to establish an intent to use a prohibited method to enhance performance. There was no 'acceptable justification or TUE' to justify the possession of the prohibited method. At the very least – and the Panel did not have to make a finding of possession of the prohibited method of blood doping (although it concluded that there was a strong likelihood that E, T and P were in possession of the prohibited method) – each athlete was in possession of the prohibited method of intravenous infusions without any TUE or other acceptable justification.

Article 2.8: Complicity in Violations   On the violation under Article 2.8, the Panel applied the broad words of the Article, which made it clear that any action falling within the Article might be sufficient to show complicity. The Panel also noted that the possible application of the violation was not limited to conduct involving athletes – it could apply to conduct with any person bound by the Rules, which included a coach or support staff member. The Panel found that, in the absence of physical assistance, there could also be a violation of Article 2.8 where there was psychological assistance in the form of encouragement to commit a violation. It drew upon provisions in the Swiss Code of Obligations in support of this. The Panel found that T's provision of the haemoglobinmeter was the key to the administration of the prohibited method. It found that T had assisted E and P by making the haemoglobinmeter available, thereby violating Article 2.8. E and P had violated Article 2.8 by engaging in the possession of a prohibited method and thereby encouraging and providing mental support to fellow athletes to possess the prohibited method. In summary, the athletes were found to have carried out the use of a prohibited method as part of a scheme in which they actively encouraged their fellow athletes in anti-doping rule violations, namely, the possession of prohibited methods.

Claims by the athletes that there was no fault or no significant fault on their parts were rejected. As to sanctions, the Panel found that the decision to ban the appellants from all future participation at the Olympic Games was proportionate in the circumstances of the conduct. The appellants had to take responsibility for their acts of complicity in the various offences and the Panel was not prepared to reduce the lifetime ban to one of ten years, which would have allowed the athletes to take part in the Olympic Games in the future as coaches or support staff.

Since these early decisions, it has gradually become more common for anti-doping organisations to bring allegations of trafficking in prohibited substances relying on evidence obtained by their own investigations and, often, evidence received from State agencies, such as the police and customs. The websites of national anti-doping tribunals feature a growing number of cases where multiple violations, including trafficking, arise from the operations of enterprises which buy prohibited substances (often over the Internet) and distribute them to customers.[10] Collaboration with State agencies is essential to the conduct of these investigations, because those agencies will often have statutory power to obtain evidence, in particular by exercising powers of search and seizure, where anti-doping organisations do not.

The Elements of the Violations in Article 2

For those involved in administering the investigation and results management processes under the Code, or advising in relation to them or deciding on allegations made under the Code, a sound knowledge of the elements of each violation in Article 2 is important.

The 2015 Code has expanded the number of anti-doping rule violations from eight to ten. This expansion includes the logical step of splitting the violation of complicity from Article 2.8 (which previously included both the administration of a prohibited substance or method and complicity in the anti-doping rule violation of another) to provide, in a new Article 2.9, for a separate violation. The substantive addition to the violations in Article 2 of the 2015 Code is the inclusion of a new Article 2.10 which prohibits athletes and other persons bound by the Code from associating with athlete support persons in certain circumstances. The addition of this Article was considered to be an important step in addressing the problems which arise from support persons who provide coaching and advisory services when subject to periods of ineligibility or other equivalent orders which will involve athletes working on regimes which put them in breach the Code.

The violations in Article 2 cover a wide range of possible activities by athletes and support personnel, from a significant conspiracy to supply and administer doping products to a group of athletes or team, as revealed by the BALCO investigation in the United States, to a straightforward in-competition test which returns an adverse analytical finding after laboratory analysis. The evidence required to prove a violation and the required investigation and hearing process will vary considerably.

The 2015 Code now provides separately in Article 10 for sanctions to be increased in relation to certain violations where 'intentional conduct', as

---

10 Some examples from the United Kingdom and New Zealand are *UKAD* v. *Tinklin SR/180201*; *UKAD* v. *Colcough SR/120105*; *DFSNZ* v. *Milne ST11/14*; *RFU* v. *Peters* Rugby Football Union Appeal Panel 27 May 2014. See Chapter 8, pages 432–4 for sanctions for trafficking and related violations and case summaries.

defined in Article 10.2.3, is present. This element is not referred to in Article 2 as an element of the violation and is expressed as a factor relevant for the imposition of sanctions only. It means that in considering violations where the provisions in Article 10 apply – Articles 2.1 (doping), 2.2 (use or attempted use) and 2.6 (possession) – tribunals will have to consider this additional component of 'intentional' conduct in arriving at the sanction. In effect, Articles 2.1, 2.2 and 2.6 become different violations, attracting more significant sanctions, where a further element is established under the rules. This important change needs to be kept in mind when the components of the violation set out in Article 2 are considered.

The additional element of intentional conduct in Article 10.2 is specifically expressed in Article 10.2.3 to identify those athletes who commit a violation in order to cheat, but it is submitted that this does not form part of the definition of 'intentional conduct' which has to be applied.[11] The violations in Article 2 remain expressed without reference to this provision on intentional conduct, and generally proof of an intention to obtain a sporting advantage by the conduct which is in breach of the Code or to cheat is not a requirement for the proof of a violation.

On the wording of Article 2, it can still be said that the violations are divided between a doping violation based on a positive test contrary to Article 2.1, where strict liability applies to establish the commission of the violation and no intentional or negligent behaviour has to be established as an element of the violation, and the violations where an element of intentional or negligent conduct on the part of the person charged has to be proved to establish the violation. In relation to the violations under Article 2 which require that some element of negligent or intentional conduct on the part of the person alleged to be in breach be proved, it should, however, be emphasised that while intentional conduct in the sense of deliberate action in relation to specified substances or methods or doping control will often need to be established to prove the violations, none of the violations requires proof that the conduct which constitutes the violation (whether deliberate or inadvertent) was in fact characterised by an intention to enhance sport performance or to cheat. The provisions of Article 10.2 which refer to proof of intentional conduct (or proof that conduct was not intentional) in the sense of identifying athletes who cheat apply only to sanctions for violations under Articles 2.1, 2.2 and 2.6 and do not change the requirements for the proof of other violations which require

11 See Chapter 8, pages 353–60 for more detailed consideration of 'intentional conduct' under Article 10.2.3.

intentional or deliberate conduct but not an intention to cheat (although, with violations such as administering, trafficking and complicity, the proof of the elements of the violation will often involve conduct which involves an intention to cheat).

Agreement to the Code: a Fundamental Requirement

In dealing with any alleged breach of Article 2, it must be kept in mind that all the violations share the fundamental requirement that the investigation, and bringing, of an allegation must concern an athlete or other person who is bound by the Code, whether by specific individual agreement in some form, or through the agreement of an organisation to which the person or athlete belongs. As has been outlined,[12] without agreement to the application of the Code, there will be no jurisdiction for an anti-doping organisation to conduct any investigation or to bring proceedings in respect of an alleged violation. This can be a difficult threshold issue in some cases where the status of the person alleged to be in breach of the anti-doping rules is unclear. The question whether there is a binding agreement is an objective one and involves examining the circumstances and determining whether an agreement to the application of the rules has been entered into. Under the general law, in most jurisdictions where a person is a member of a sporting organisation and that organisation has adopted anti-doping rules incorporating the Code, he or she will be bound by contract (or applicable statutory provisions governing the organisation as a company or incorporated association) as a member to the provisions of the Code as per the rules of the organisation. Under the Code, Signatories have general obligations to require participants to agree to be bound by rules which incorporate the Code's provisions.[13] This can be accomplished in different ways, but Signatories will often have those who participate enter into specific agreements to be bound by the Code and accept the jurisdiction of the relevant sports tribunal and CAS. More rarely, in the absence of a specific agreement, an agreement to a sport's rules, and thereby the Code, may also be found to exist where a person's conduct amounts to an acceptance of the rules under which a sport is conducted.[14]

---

12 See Chapter 2 for relevant case summaries.
13 See Article 20 for the obligations of Signatories – e.g. Article 20.3.3 for the obligation of an international federation.
14 There are cases where an agreement to the Code/anti-doping rules has been inferred from the conduct of the person allegedly in breach. See e.g. *UKAD* v. *Tinklin* in Chapter 8, page 434, where the father of a boxer was found to have accepted the anti-doping rules of the

Whether an anti-doping organisation can establish that a person is subject to the Code will depend upon interpretation of the legal documents which are said to bind them to the Code. The interpretation of these contractual documents will be decided according to the principles of the legal system which is applicable to the question in the particular arbitration. Before CAS, Swiss law provides that the arbitral tribunal is competent to rule on its own jurisdiction.[15] The parties may have chosen the law applicable to such questions of interpretation, but this is unlikely, and the legal system applicable is likely to be the law of the place where the sporting federation which gave the challenged decision has its domicile. In many cases involving international federations, this approach this will lead to the application of the principles of Swiss law to the interpretation of documents said to provide for jurisdiction, because many international sporting federations are domiciled in Switzerland. In general terms, the principles of interpretation under Swiss law, while differing in some respects, are unlikely to produce different results from those which apply in common law jurisdictions.[16] Where CAS rules on its jurisdiction, the decision of CAS will be within the scope of an appeal to the Swiss Federal Tribunal.[17] Where such a question arises before a sports tribunal at national level, generally that tribunal is likely to have jurisdiction to decide on its own jurisdiction, whether expressly under its rules or by implication under the agreement applicable to the proceedings. Where tribunals only operate at national level, with no appeal to CAS (as might be the case with allegations involving national-level athletes), they are likely to be subject to the supervisory jurisdiction of the national courts, whether they function as a domestic tribunal or as a form of arbitration. The scope of any likely review will be narrow, but it would generally encompass a decision by the tribunal that it had jurisdiction over an athlete and/or the allegations made against him or her under the relevant rules.

---

sport by his involvement as a support person at an event. It seems difficult to support the finding that a contract was to be inferred in the *Tinklin* case on the facts.

15 Article 186 PILA. This is confirmed by the CAS Procedural Rules.

16 See Chapter 4 for the interpretation of the Code and pages 159–60. The finding that there is an agreement with an athlete and the interpretation of the scope of any arbitration agreement or indeed the interpretation of the Code are different exercises. While a broad purposive approach should be adopted to the Code and any arbitration clause which submits disputes to CAS, a decision on the existence of an agreement which creates jurisdiction over the athlete is likely to be more strictly approached.

17 For an example of a successful challenge to a finding by a CAS Panel that it had jurisdiction over an allegation that an athlete had committed a violation under the Code, see CAS 2008/A/1738, *WADA v. DEB and Busch* in Chapter 2, pages 72–5.

Who can Commit Anti-doping Rule Violations?

The anti-doping rule violations under Articles 2.1 (presence of a prohibited substance), 2.2 (use or attempted use),[18] 2.3 (evasion) and 2.4 (whereabouts information filing failures and missed tests) can only be committed by athletes. Article 2.6 (possession) contains specific provision for the violation to be committed by an athlete or an athlete support person.[19] There is no specific provision in Articles 2.5 (tampering), 2.7 (trafficking) or 2.8 (administration) stating whether both athletes and others who are bound by the Code can commit the violation. The provisions concerning the sanctions for violations of Articles 2.7 and 2.8 and the nature of the violations themselves indicate that the violations can be committed by athletes or athlete support personnel or by other persons bound by the Code.[20] Similarly, the violations of complicity under Article 2.9 and prohibited association under Article 2.10 can be committed by any person bound by the Code. While there is no specific provision in the Code regarding the violation of tampering with doping control under Article 2.5, it is submitted that, while allegations will usually relate to the conduct of an athlete, this violation can be committed by any person who is bound by the Code. This approach to and interpretation of Article 2.5 is consistent with the wide range of conduct covered by the definition of 'tampering' and with the purpose of the Code in providing for effective doping control.[21]

Violations of Article 2.4 will arise where there are breaches of the whereabouts requirements as set out in Annex I ISTI. While an athlete can

18 The wording of the violation in Article 2.2 has been changed to make this clear.
19 'Athlete support personnel' is broadly defined to cover 'any coach, trainer, manager, agent, team staff, official, medical, paramedical personnel, parent or any other *Person* working with, treating or assisting an *Athlete* participating in or preparing for sport *Competition*'. It could be contended that the violation under Article 2.6 should be interpreted as applying to any person bound by the Code. This would involve a purposive approach to the Code and Article, and a broad reading of the definition of 'athlete support personnel', but it seems difficult on the specific words used. A limited approach does not make sense given the aims of the Code, in that it might allow a person who does not work with the athletes or team but is part of an organisation to be in possession of prohibited substances or methods.
20 See Article 10.3.2 on the lifetime period of ineligibility where the violation is committed by an athlete support person and involves a minor, and also the definition of 'trafficking', which indicates that the violation is potentially applicable to 'athlete support personnel'.
21 There is support for this in the general definition of 'attempt' applicable to attempted tampering under Article 2.5, which refers to attempts by both athletes and other persons. In addition, the specific references to allegations of tampering being brought against those who provide misleading/fraudulent information in an investigation under ISTI indicate that the violation is intended to apply to any person who is bound by the Code.

delegate the provision of whereabouts information and the information may be given on a collective basis on behalf of teams, Annex I.6.4 ISTI makes it clear that it is the athlete's responsibility to provide the necessary whereabouts information and be available for testing as provided in that information, and that it will be the athlete who commits the violation under Article 2.4. Where a person is given responsibility for filing whereabouts information by an athlete, he or she may be subject to disciplinary process under the rules of the sporting organisation if he or she fails to discharge this responsibility properly, but he or she cannot commit a violation under Article 2.4. However, if a third party who is bound by the Code becomes involved in assisting an athlete to provide fraudulent whereabouts information in order to avoid testing, that person may be liable under Article 2.5 (tampering) or Article 2.9 (complicity) in respect of his or her conduct.

Article 2.1: Presence of a Prohibited Substance or its Metabolites or Markers in an Athlete's Bodily Specimen

Article 2.1 provides for the violation, which is founded on the principle of strict liability for the presence of a prohibited substance in an athlete's bodily specimen. This violation has been a feature of anti-doping regimes since the initial efforts to combat the use of performance-enhancing substances in sport.[22] Notwithstanding the increase in investigations into the conduct of athletes and other persons bound by the Code, which may lead to allegations that violations have been committed which do not rely on adverse analytical findings, positive tests in- or out-of-competition will remain the basis for many allegations against athletes. It is likely that there will always be a considerable focus on testing athletes for the use of prohibited substances and methods (with greater emphasis on targeted 'no-notice' out-of-competition testing where anti-doping organisations have the information required to make decisions on which athletes to target test).[23] Wide-ranging investigations into athlete conduct involving the

---

22 See Chapter 1, pages 46–50 for the development of this principle in anti-doping regimes, as well as the early CAS award in *USA Shooting and Quigley* v. *UIT* (Chapter 1, pages 50–2). See also Chapter 10 for the decisions in the Swiss and other national courts which have upheld the principle of strict liability under anti-doping regimes and the Code as not being contrary to fundamental rights protected by the law.

23 The development of the whereabouts requirement, which is now set out in Annex I ISTI, is an important aspect of no-notice out-of-competition testing. Planned and targeted testing is emphasised by the provisions of the ISTI. See further Chapter 3, pages 128–34.

consideration of a range of evidence gathered may ultimately lead to the targeted testing of an athlete or a group of athletes out-of-competition and to reliance on any positive tests obtained rather than the bringing of allegations in respect of other violations on the basis of other evidence discovered in the investigation.

As the note to Article 2.1 makes clear, Articles 2.1.1–2.1.3 reflect the position established by earlier CAS decisions under anti-doping regimes relating to strict liability for the presence of a prohibited substance in an athlete's sample. As many CAS decisions have underlined, often in cases where an athlete sought to obtain a reduced period of ineligibility under the Code by explaining a positive test on the basis that the prohibited substance has been mistakenly ingested in a nutritional supplement,[24] the regime established by Article 2.1 is one based on the personal responsibility of the athlete, under which the athlete has to exercise all reasonable care to avoid the ingestion of prohibited substances. The nature of the regime generally explains the very narrow scope for the operation of the defence of 'no fault' and the relatively narrow scope for the defence of 'no significant fault' under Article 10 of the Code. Although the circumstances in which those defences will apply have changed under the 2015 Code, the definitions of 'no fault' and 'no significant fault' have been retained in the same form as under the 2009 Code.

Elements of Violation

There are two elements to a violation of Article 2.1:

- the person alleged to have committed the violation must be an athlete; and
- a prohibited substance or its metabolites or markers must be present in the athlete's bodily specimen.

Under the 2015 Code, the definition of 'athlete' has been simplified. An athlete is defined as any person who competes in sport at the

---

24 For examples of cases where athletes sought to rely on the defences under Articles 10.5.1 and 10.5.2 in either the 2004 or the 2009 Code where a positive test was said to arise from a contaminated or mislabelled nutritional supplement, see Chapter 8, pages 401–11. The defences under the 2015 Code have been significantly revised, but Article 10 still contains defences which are based on the athlete showing 'no fault' or 'no significant fault'. There is a specific 'no significant fault' defence under Article 10.5.1.2 where the prohibited substance is shown to come from a contaminated substance as defined in the Code. See Chapter 8, pages 398–400 for more detailed consideration of the sanctions regime where a contaminated substance produces the violation.

international level (as defined by each international federation) or national level (as defined by each NADO). The definition further provides for an anti-doping organisation to have a discretion to apply anti-doping rules to athletes who are neither international- nor national-level athletes. An anti-doping organisation may elect to conduct limited testing or no testing, to analyse samples for a more limited menu of prohibited substances, to require no or limited whereabouts information and to not require advance TUEs from athletes who are not designated as international- or national-level athletes. Where an athlete who has not been designated as an international- or national-level athlete returns a positive test, the national anti-doping organisation may permit the athlete to apply for a retroactive TUE. However, where an athlete who is bound to the Code but is not designated as an international- or national-level athlete commits a violation under the Code, the consequences under the Code must apply (apart from the requirements for publication of the decision under Article 14.3.2). Further, for the purposes of the violations of administration and complicity, and for anti-doping education, any person who participates in sport under the authority of any organisation accepting the Code will be an athlete.

The criteria which will be applied to decide whether an athlete is an international- or a national-level athlete are for the international federations and national anti-doping organisations to determine, in a manner which is consistent with the ISTI.

In most situations, the way in which anti-doping rules are implemented by sporting organisations at national and international level will mean that a wide range of athletes are subject to the rules which implement the Code by contract as members of sporting organisations or as participants in sporting events and activities. It will then be for the international federation and/or national anti-doping organisation to determine which athletes fall within the national- and international-athlete categories and what approach will be taken to athletes who, while bound to the rules as a matter of contract, do not fall within those categories. The alternative approach, which would involve specifically identifying across all sports on a regular, changing basis the individual athletes who have to agree to anti-doping rules and entering into agreements only with those athletes (with all others standing outside the rules unless they subsequently agree to them), would be both impractical and ineffective. Such an approach would also not fit with the minimum requirement in the definition of athlete, which requires national anti-doping organisations to ensure that all those participating in sport under the authority of any sporting organisation implementing the Code are athletes for the purposes of Articles 2.8 and 2.9.

The definition also makes it clear that each national anti-doping organisation is free to expand the application of its anti-doping programme to lower levels of competition, and even to those who only participate in fitness activities without competing. While those who compete under the authority of an organisation which has accepted the Code will be subject to the consequences under the Code if they commit a breach, where the application of the Code is extended to persons who are not members of or under the authority of a sporting organisation and do not compete, the question whether the sanctions under the Code should be applied would be a matter for the particular rules and agreements implemented by the anti-doping organisation which chooses to extend the application of its programme in this way.

In many sets of rules implementing the Code at national and international level, the position will be that, while many recreational-level or masters athletes are bound by contract to the Code by their membership of a sporting organisation, the national anti-doping organisation will develop rules which modify the anti-doping requirements as regards athletes at these competitive levels. The definition makes it clear that this is a matter for the relevant organisation. However, in the absence of particular rules varying the standard position, the contractual obligations undertaken by the athlete in relation to the Code will simply apply as provided by the terms of the agreement under which he or she is bound to the Code on an objective approach to the terms. Where an athlete is bound to the obligations under the Code and commits a violation, the level at which they are competing is generally not relevant to the imposition of sanctions. However, where a consequence of the athlete's level of competition is that he or she has had no or little anti-doping education, this may be relevant to the assessment of the athlete's fault as defined under the Code in applying the fault-based defences under Article 10.[25]

Further elements of the violation under Article 2.1 are defined in the definitions in the Code. A sample or specimen is any biological material

---

25 In assessing the fault of an athlete for the purposes of the defences under Article 10 of the 2015 Code, the fact that an athlete competes largely at a recreational level may mean that they have not received any or adequate anti-doping education – a factor which may explain the departure from the standard of conduct required from athletes under the Code and which may be relevant in assessing the degree of fault in the exercise of arriving at the applicable sanction under Article 10. For consideration of sanctions under Article 10, see Chapter 8.

collected for the purposes of doping control. At present, only blood and urine tests are carried out under the Code, and the ISTI sets out, in its Annexes, Guidelines for the conduct of such tests.[26] The violation under Article 2.1 only applies to prohibited substances, not to the detection of prohibited methods. Where the use of a prohibited method is detected or established by evidence, this will provide the basis for an allegation of use of a prohibited method under Article 2.2.

Article 2.1.1 confirms that strict liability is the basis for the violation under Article 2.1 by expressly providing that there is no need to prove any intent, fault, negligence or knowing use on the part of the athlete – the presence of a substance, its metabolites or its markers in the athlete's sample is sufficient. This is enough to establish that the prohibited substance has entered the athlete's body, and Article 2.1.1 underlines that it is the athlete's personal duty to 'ensure that no prohibited substance enters his or her body'.[27] This strict duty is the basis for the automatic disqualification of results under Article 9 in the competition in which the violation was detected, where an athlete commits violation of Article 2.1 in-competition. The duty also explains why an athlete faces a significant burden if he or she wishes to establish that there are grounds to eliminate or reduce the period of ineligibility applicable to a violation under Article 2.1 under Article 10 of the Code.[28] The notes to Article 2.1.1 under the 2009 Code referred to the balance in the Code between the automatic disqualification of results for the benefit of all 'clean' athletes[29] and fairness to individual athletes, which allows, in exceptional circumstances, for a reduction or elimination of the period of ineligibility. Although the notes to the Article have been shortened and this text has been removed in the 2015 Code, it is submitted that the general point made about the balance in the Code remains good.

Detection of Prohibited Substances

The detected presence of any quantity of a prohibited substance or its metabolites or markers in an athlete's sample constitutes an anti-doping

---

26 See Chapter 3, pages 124–41 for an outline of the provisions of the ISTI.
27 The general obligation on participants in sport who are bound by the Code is further underlined in Article 21.1.3 of the Code.
28 See Chapter 8 for more detailed consideration of the requirements for the reduction or elimination of a period of ineligibility.
29 The argument that results should not be disqualified if there is no strict proof of performance-enhancing effect was consistently rejected before the implementation of the Code, and the provision of the Code reflects the position reached in the earlier cases. See e.g. CAS 2002/A/376, *Baxter v. IOC*.

rule violation. The Prohibited List determines the substances which are prohibited, whether they are prohibited in-competition only or at all times both in-competition and out-of-competition and whether the substances fall within the category of 'specified substances'. In the case of certain substances, there is a quantitative minimum reporting threshold in the Prohibited List which must be exceeded before there can be an adverse analytical finding by the laboratory.[30] It should be noted that, where a WADA laboratory has to be able to detect substances at certain levels in order to show that it can perform to the standard required for accreditation by WADA,[31] the level imposed by way of a performance standard for the laboratory does not amount to a threshold for the purpose of finding that a violation has occurred. It is simply the detection of a prohibited substance which is relevant. If a laboratory can detect a prohibited substance more accurately than is required for accreditation (i.e. in lower quantities), in a reliable manner, and does so, an adverse analytical finding can be established (provided there is no relevant threshold for a positive test under the Prohibited List). The detection of substances identified on the Prohibited List which can be produced naturally within the body may require further investigation and assessment by the anti-doping organisation and WADA laboratory before there can be a report of an adverse analytical finding.[32]

Where a substance which is prohibited in-competition only is detected outside competition, there will be no violation under Article 2.1. If there is a positive test in-competition for a substance which is prohibited in-competition, it is no defence for the athlete to say that the positive test relates to out-of-competition use, because the violation is committed where a prohibited substance is present in a sample taken in-competition, not by the use of a substance out-of-competition. In the Code, 'in-competition' is defined as the period from twelve hours before a competition in which the athlete is scheduled to participate until the end of the

---

30 For the thresholds in relation to specific substances, see WADA TD2017DL Decision Limits for the Confirmatory Quantification of Threshold Substances. CAS previously held that a threshold set for the reporting of a positive test for nandrolone could not be called into question before it; see CAS 2000/A/310, *L v. IOC*, p. 127, CAS Digest III and CAS O.G 00/015, *Melinte v. IAAF*, CAS Digest II, p. 69. The current substances for which there is a threshold for the reporting of an adverse analytical finding are 19-Norandrosterone, Carboxy-THC, Salbutamol, Formoterol, Glycerol, Morphine, Cathine, Ephedrine, Methylephedrine and Pseudoephedrine. The decision limit for Carboxy-THC (cannabis) was increased significantly to the current level as a practical way of addressing the prevalence of violations involving low levels of recreational use in certain jurisdictions. There is also a decision limit in the detection of hGH.

31 See Chapter 3, pages 141–8 for the ISL.

32 See Chapter 3, pages 109–12 for more detail on possible investigation and the reporting of atypical findings under the 2015 Code.

competition and of the sample collection process related to the competition. This definition applies unless the rules of an international federation or ruling body of the event apply. Often, the question whether an athlete is 'in-competition' will be a matter of the rules applied by the international federation or event organiser.[33]

The Prohibited List changes, and substances may be taken by athletes when not prohibited and later result in positive tests after they have been included on the List. In such circumstances, the violation under Article 2.1 will be committed as a result of the presence of the prohibited substance in the sample. Depending on the circumstances in which the substance was taken, the athlete may be able to rely on the no fault or no significant fault defences under Article 10 to eliminate or reduce the period of ineligibility. The inclusion of Meldonium on the 2016 Prohibited List after it had previously been on the Monitoring Programme produced a number of positive tests. Uncertainty over the rate at which the drug would be removed from an athlete's body led to a specific notice from WADA recommending the approach to results management and adjudication for positive tests for the substance.[34]

If a test reveals the presence of a metabolite for a prohibited substance which is also capable of being produced from a substance which is not prohibited, it is submitted that it will be for the athlete to establish that he or she did not ingest the prohibited substance. The presence of a metabolite of a prohibited substance establishes the violation on the words of Article 2.1.1. The athlete will have to establish the grounds for exoneration on the balance of probabilities.

The proof of a violation under Article 2.1 relies on the process of testing and analysis by an accredited WADA laboratory[35] to prove the presence of

---

33 See e.g. CAS 2009/A/1926, *Gasquet* v. *ITF* in Chapter 8, pages 391–2, where the argument that the player was not in-competition under the ITF Rules was rejected.

34 See WADA Notice Meldonium – the Notice provides for stays in the results management process where excretion studies are required to ascertain whether the substance was taken before 1 January 2016. Where that position is established, the Notice accepts that an athlete could not reasonably be expected to have known or suspected that the substance would still be in his or her system after 1 January 2016 and would be able to establish no fault or negligence. In cases where the substance was taken after 1 January, results management has to proceed in the normal way. For an example of a case where the substance was taken after 1 January 2016, see *Sharapova* v. *ITF*, summarised in Chapter 8, pages 420–3. There have been a number of no fault findings by anti-doping organisations under this WADA Notice for meldonium – see, for example, decisions on the USADA website (www.usada .org) under 'Results Management.'

35 There is a network of thirty-two such WADA-accredited laboratories worldwide. For a short summary of the provisions relating to accreditation under the ISL, see Chapter 3, pages 142–6.

a prohibited substance or prohibited method in the sample[36] taken from the athlete. The anti-doping organisation responsible for results management will present the finding of a WADA-accredited laboratory to the tribunal hearing the allegation to prove the violation after the steps required to confirm the initial result and manage the result in accordance with the Code have been carried out.[37]

The findings from a WADA-accredited laboratory will be presumed to have been reached by a proper process under the relevant International Standards unless the athlete shows at a hearing that there has been a departure from an applicable International Standard which could reasonably have caused an adverse analytical finding, in the sense that it would be reasonable to conclude that an adverse analytical finding could have been caused by the departure.[38] If the athlete establishes such a departure and the required causative link to the adverse analytical finding, the anti-doping organisation must then show that the irregularity was not causative of the violation.[39] The athlete will have to establish any alleged departure from the relevant International Standard and its possible causative effect, on the balance of probabilities, while the anti-doping organisation will have to prove its case and disprove the effect of any departure established by the athlete to the comfortable satisfaction of the tribunal.[40] Where a departure from an applicable International Standard has been established in terms of Article 3.2.2, the anti-doping organisation faces the potentially difficult task of proving a negative, namely, that the departure had no causative effect on the adverse analytical finding. However, it should be noted that the requirement under Article 3.2.2 that the alleged departure could reasonably have caused the adverse analytical finding means that the athlete faces a considerable initial burden. The provisions of the

---

36 The definition of a sample covers both blood and urine samples. The ISTI contains Guidelines in its Annexes for the taking of blood and urine samples. There are additional requirements concerning the collection of information from an athlete where samples are collected for the compilation of an ABP. The ABP information will contain the results of tests taken specifically for the passport and of general tests under the Code/ISTI. ISTI 2017 has an added Annex K governing the collection of samples for an ABP.

37 See Chapter 7 for an outline of the results management process.

38 See Article 3.2.2 of the 2015 Code for the presumption and its rebuttal by an athlete through establishing that there has been a departure from the Standard. See pages 204–24 for examples of challenges to the analytical processes which seek to rebut the presumption in favour of the result from the WADA laboratory. For a consideration of the construction of this provision, see CAS 2012/A/2791, *Campbell Brown* v. *JAA* – summary at pages 203–4.

39 See Article 3.2.2. The requirement that the athlete establish the causative link was introduced by the 2009 Code. The approach is consistent with the approach by CAS Panels before the adoption of the Code.

40 See further Chapter 6 for more on the burden and standard of proof under the Code.

Code largely continue to reflect the position reached by CAS Panels before the 2004 Code, which held that, to be material, an irregularity had to be something which could reasonably be said to affect the test result.

Possible Defences

Challenges may be made in respect of each element of a violation under Article 2.1. Although the areas for possible defences fall within a relatively narrow compass, they can involve hearings incorporating complex scientific evidence, particularly in relation to testing methods and processes. The anti-doping organisation will have to show that the substance or method identified by testing and analysis is on the Prohibited List, although, as already outlined, the athlete cannot contest the decision by WADA's List Committee to include a particular substance on the List.[41] However, the question whether a particular substance is within the types of substance listed (if not specifically identified on the List), or whether it is a substance 'with a similar chemical structure or similar biological effect' to the substances listed, can be raised.[42] Such questions involve construing the Prohibited List by considering the meaning of the words used in the general context of the purpose of the List and the Code and considering any relevant scientific evidence as to the nature of the substance detected.

The athlete may also challenge the testing methods used by the laboratory and claim that the processes (particularly newly devised tests) were inadequate and inappropriate given the state of scientific knowledge. Where an evidential basis for such a challenge has been laid, the tribunal is likely to have to consider expert evidence in relation to the testing methods. Ultimately, the anti-doping organisation bringing the allegation will have to satisfy the tribunal that the tests were reliable according to the state of scientific knowledge. It should be noted that a new Article 3.2.1 has been inserted in the 2015 Code to include a new presumption in relation to analytical methods. This Article provides for a presumption that analytical methods and decision limits approved by WADA after consultation within the relevant scientific community and which have been peer-reviewed are scientifically valid and imposes conditions as to formal notice if an athlete wishes to challenge a WADA decision and rebut this presumption.[43]

---

41 See Chapter 3, pages 101–2.
42 See Chapter 3, pages 102–3 for the parts of the Prohibited List where this applies to particular classes of substance.
43 Article 3.2.1 of the Code. See Chapter 6, pages 280–2 for further comment.

If the testing method itself is appropriate, the athlete may contend that the method or related procedures were not properly carried out, usually by reference to the processes required by the ISL or the ISTI. Challenges to the process for testing and analysis, on the basis that the procedures in the ISTI and ISL have not been followed, are, perhaps, the most common form of defence put forward by athletes facing violations of Article 2.1 arising from a positive test.

Areas of Non-scientific Challenge to Testing and Analytical Processes

As far as the process of sampling and testing is concerned, perhaps the most common non-scientific areas of challenge relate to the chain of custody and the rights of the athlete in relation to the B sample. Both areas have been the focus of investigation and inquiry by athletes and those representing them since the early days of drug testing in sport. Defects in the chain of custody of a sample may provide a reasonable basis to say that the sample has been contaminated or may have degraded. Where there is such a defect in the chain of custody, there will be a breach of the ISTI which may be considered as establishing a causative link to the adverse analytical finding required under Article 3.2 of the Code. If this is the case, as previously noted, it will be difficult for an anti-doping organisation to prove, to the comfortable satisfaction of the tribunal, that an adverse analytical finding was not caused by the departure from the International Standard. However, this will depend on the facts surrounding the break in the chain of custody and the expert evidence on the possible effect on the test result.[44] Confirmation of an A sample analysis by the properly carried out analysis of a B sample will establish that a breach of the chain of custody in relation to the A sample was not causative of the adverse analytical finding on the A sample test.

B Sample Rights

The rights of the athlete in relation to the B sample, which are set out in Article 7.3 of the Code, give rise to different considerations and have been held to be a fundamental part of the process for the athlete, and they have been treated differently from other breaches of the testing and

---

44 See e.g. CAS 2005/A/908, *WADA v. Wium*, where CAS found that a break in the chain of custody did not cast sufficient doubt on the reliability of the test results to show that the detection of the prohibited substance in the urine sample was not sufficient to establish a doping violation to the comfortable satisfaction of the Panel.

analytical requirements.[45] Several CAS Panels have held that, if an athlete is not properly afforded the rights to attend the opening of a B sample, or the rights to have a B sample tested are in some way denied to the athlete, there can be no confirmation of the A sample. As a matter of principle, a defect in the B sample analysis process is different from a failure to give the B sample rights. A distinction should be drawn between a denial of the proper B sample process to an athlete and a failure to carry out the analysis of the B sample properly. Where the athlete is not given the rights in the proper manner, CAS awards establish that such a failure will be fatal to the process of confirmation of the A sample, so that there can be no violation under Article 2.1. Where there is a departure from the process of handling or analysing the B sample, so that the athlete establishes a breach under Article 3.2.2, while it is likely to be difficult for the anti-doping organisation to prove the negative proposition that the departure from the standard did not cause the adverse analytical finding to the required standard of comfortable satisfaction, that will be a matter which has to be decided in the particular circumstances of the case. CAS Panels have also been strict in relation to defective processes relating to the B sample, and have, in a number of awards, held that a defect in the process of analysing the B sample[46] means also that the B sample analysis is invalid. There is, perhaps, a tendency in the decisions to find that the B sample process must be correctly carried out if the result is to stand, but the approach to a departure from the proper process of analysis (as opposed to the giving of the B sample rights to the athlete), where this is established by the athlete as required by Article 3.2.2, should be that the tribunal considers, on the evidence, whether the anti-doping organisation has established, to the required standard, that the departure from proper process did not cause the B sample test result.

Where a B sample does not confirm the A sample, or where there are other problems with the B sample process which invalidate the analysis, while there will be no violation under Article 2.1, it may still be possible to establish a violation for using a prohibited substance under Article 2.2

---

45 Article 7.3 is concerned solely with the procedural process in relation to the B sample and contains no provision concerning the consequence of a failure in relation to the athlete's B sample rights.

46 See e.g. CAS 2006/A/1119, *UCI* v. *Landaluze*, where the B sample was analysed by the same analyst as the A sample, in breach of the ISL in force at the time, and the CAS Panel found that the international federation could not satisfy the onus on it of showing that the departure did not cause the analytical finding. The ISL has now been changed. In any event, this case might well be decided differently under the current Article 3.2.2.

if the evidence from the A sample (and any other evidence) is found to establish use to the required standard. Similarly, it may also be possible to establish a violation for 'use' under Article 2.2 by reference to the B sample only. Alternatively, there may be other evidence arising from the investigation carried out by the anti-doping organisation which supports another violation under the Code.[47]

Tribunals hearing an allegation under Article 2.1 should not enquire in a general way into the accreditation of the WADA laboratory, or whether laboratory processes meet certain general standards such as ISO/IEC standards. Such matters can only be relevant where they have a direct bearing on the analytical process used in relation to the sample which is the subject of the positive result. The evidence put forward has to show a specific departure from mandatory aspects of the Standards which are applicable to the process. CAS Panels have, however, often had to consider expert evidence relating to the adequacy of the particular testing methods used as a means of determining the presence of the particular prohibited substance detected. Article 6.1 and its notes establish that a violation under Article 2.1 can only be established by sample analysis carried out by a WADA-accredited or WADA-approved laboratory. An analysis by another, non-approved or unauthorised laboratory can support an allegation that another violation has been committed, provided the testing has been carried out in a reliable manner. Where analysis by a non-approved or unauthorised laboratory is in issue, the burden of showing that the testing was carried out in a reliable fashion will fall on the anti-doping organisation from the outset, and there will be no presumption in favour of the laboratory result.[48]

Illustrations

Failure to Provide an Athlete with Rights in Relation
to a B Sample

CAS 2008/A/1607, *Varis* v. *IBU*   V appealed a decision of the International Biathlon Union (IBU), which had found V had committed a

---

47 See notes to Article 2.2 of the Code, which refers to the proof of the violation on either the A or B sample alone where the anti-doping organisation provides a satisfactory explanation for the absence of confirmation in the other sample. See also CAS 2002/A/385, *T v. FIG*, CAS Digest III, where, notwithstanding the athlete not being given her right to attend an opening of the B sample, which meant that there would be no adverse analytical finding and no violation under the equivalent of Article 2.1, her admission of use led to a finding that the violation of using a prohibited substance had been established.

48 See e.g. CAS 2003/A/452, *IAAF v. Boulam*.

second anti-doping rule violation under the Code and had imposed a lifetime period of ineligibility. V asserted that the decision of the IBU executive board should be overruled. The appeal concerned the athlete's right to have the B sample analysed in the presence of her representative.

In May 2003, V had been banned for two years after testing positive for the presence of EPO. V resumed competition after the period of ineligibility had come to an end. In January 2008, the A sample taken from the athlete in an in-competition test showed the presence of recombinant EPO. V requested that the B sample be opened and tested. This took place in the absence of the appellant at the Lausanne laboratory. The B sample confirmed the A sample analysis.

The ISL changed between 2008 and 2009, reducing the time for the B sample to be analysed. IBU refused a request for postponement by the athlete on the basis that IBU had made reasonable efforts to accommodate the athlete's desire to have a representative at the opening and testing of the B sample. IBU considered that it had to go ahead because it seemed unlikely the athlete would be able to make arrangements for a representative to attend within the seven-day period set down for B sample analysis under ISL.

V contended that her right to attend, or have her representative attend, the B sample opening analysis was fundamental. Nothing had been done to accommodate the athlete's request for a different testing date. The evidence suggested the athlete obtained no explanation as to why her request could not be accommodated. Whichever version of ISL applied, the Panel considered that the IBU had acted unreasonably in not attempting to accommodate the appellant's request for the opening and testing of the B sample on another date. The tribunal concluded that neither the IBU Anti-Doping Rules nor the International Standard had been followed correctly.

> We also find that the IBU acted with unreasonable haste and lack of accommodation having regard to the legitimate requests by the appellant and her lawyer for different arrangements to be made so that a representative of the athlete could be present for the opening and testing of her B sample.

IBU contended that this departure from the International Standard did not cause the adverse analytical finding. For the Panel, the question was not whether the presence of the appellant's representative at the B sample analysis would have made any difference to the outcome, but whether the failure to follow the applicable rules by making reasonable attempts to accommodate the appellant's request invalidated the B sample results.

The Panel found the reasoning in CAS 2002/A/385, *Tchachina* v. *FIG* was applicable. In *Tchachina*, a CAS Panel had concluded that the failure to notify the athlete of the right to attend the opening and analysis of the B sample had compromised the 'limited rights of an athlete to such an extent that the results of the analysis of the "B" sample and thus the entire urine test must be disregarded'.

The Panel allowed V's appeal, set aside the lifetime ban and concluded as follows:

> In coming to this conclusion we are of the view that an athlete's right to be given a reasonable opportunity to observe the opening and testing of a B sample is of sufficient importance that it needs to be enforced even in situations where all of the other evidence available indicates that the appellant committed an anti-doping rule violation.

Challenges to Testing/Analytical Processes under the 2004 Code

North American Court of Arbitration for Sport, AAA Panel Case No. 30 190 00847 06, *USADA* v. *Floyd Landis* L challenged the USADA decision that he had committed an anti-doping rule violation arising from a reported adverse analytical finding for elevated testosterone levels after a test carried out at the end of stage 17 of the 2006 Tour de France. USADA alleged that the analysis of the samples showed a T/E ratio in excess of 4:1 and that testosterone in the sample had not been produced naturally within L's body. The issue, in a lengthy contested hearing (which featured a number of pre-trial interlocutory applications and a ten-day hearing after the case had taken over a year to come to the hearing), was whether the laboratory analysis which led to the adverse analytical finding had been properly carried out in accordance with the ISL and the related Technical Documents. L sought to establish that there had been a departure from the ISL, so as to rebut the presumption in favour of the WADA laboratory that the analysis had been carried out in accordance with the Standard. The challenges related to both the process by which an elevated T/E ratio had been identified by gas chromatography/mass spectrometry (GCMS) and the further IRMS testing used to establish that the sample contained testosterone which had not been produced naturally in L's body.

On the T/E ratio testing, all the arbitrators agreed that the testing had been carried out in a manner which contravened the Technical Document relevant to the testing, because the laboratory had not carried out the testing to confirm the T/E ratio by using the proper diagnostic method in the

Technical Documents. It was no answer to this failure to say that the laboratory had the relevant ISO accreditation for the process. The particular process concerned was defective. This meant that, as regards this test, the presumption in favour of the laboratory was rebutted, and the arbitrators concluded that USADA could not comfortably satisfy the tribunal that the departure from the ISL had not caused the adverse analytical finding. All the arbitrators agreed in dismissing the charge made on the basis of the T/E ratio.

On the IRMS testing, which, earlier CAS awards have established, can still be applied where the T/E ratio test is unreliable, and can stand alone to establish that the testosterone detected was not naturally produced,[49] a number of errors were put forward by those representing L. The errors related to departures from the relevant technical standard. The majority of the arbitrators found that, on all but one of the alleged errors, the presumption that the laboratory had properly carried out the analysis was not rebutted. On the error which the majority arbitrators held was a departure from the standard – the failure to check the instruments in accordance with the relevant linearity standard – the majority held that USADA had satisfied the burden on it to show that the failure to comply with the standard did not cause the adverse analytical finding. On further alleged errors relating to poor chromatography, failure to record changes to recorded data and deletion of data, the majority found that there was no departure from the standard. Further non-scientific issues were raised relating to the chain of custody and errors in documentation. The majority found that there was no breach shown by the chain of custody documents, and that, in any event, the fact that the B sample analysis confirmed the A sample meant that any breach in the chain of custody did not cause the adverse analytical finding. They also decided that, while there were errors in the documentation which rebutted the presumption in favour of the WADA laboratory, the errors did not cause the adverse analytical finding because it could, in fact, be shown by USADA that, at all times, the correct sample was being analysed. The majority decided that the charge of doping based on the IRMS analysis was established.

On a further issue raised by the evidence produced by USADA, the arbitrators found that the statements made by L to the former Tour de France winner, Greg LeMond, could not be interpreted as admissions of doping.

---

49 See e.g. CAS 1999/A/239, *UCI v. Moller*, CAS 2000/A/274, *S v. FINA*, CAS Digest II, p. 389.

The minority arbitrator dissented on the finding that the IRMS testing process result should be accepted. He found that the WADA laboratory had not been 'trustworthy'. He based his decision primarily on the defects in the documents recording the steps in the analytical process, which he concluded showed that data had been 'cherry-picked' and the steps in the analytical sequence mixed up. This was a breach of the ISL, and there was no evidence from USADA which could satisfy the arbitrator that the failures were not causative of the adverse analytical finding reached at the end of the process of analysis. He also found that the flaws in the chain of custody and the failures to record corrections in the documents correctly made the laboratory process unreliable. He concluded his dissenting opinion:

> Given the plethora of laboratory errors in this case, there was certainly no reliable scientific evidence introduced to find that Mr Landis committed a doping offence.

The result was that, by a majority, L was found to have committed a doping violation and was banned for two years from the time at which he voluntarily ceased competing.

CAS 2007/A/1394, *Landis* v. *USADA*   On appeal to CAS, the full range of challenges to the laboratory analysis of the sample were again considered on a re-hearing. The challenges related to quality control, linearity, peak identification, manual integration of IRMS test results, chromatography, electronic data file reprocessing, the chain of custody, GCMS issue, validation of positivity criteria, data-recording requirements under ISL, documentary errors, the spirit of the same operator rule and steroid metabolism. All the challenges were rejected. While finding that the allegations did not prove a departure from the Standard, in many cases the Panel also found that, in any event, the alleged discrepancy would not cause the violation. In addition, the Panel rejected wide-ranging allegations of forgery and cover-up by the laboratory and bias on the part of witnesses. It also found that, in some areas, the experts called for L had crossed the line into advocacy in an unacceptable way.

The Panel rejected allegations of misconduct on the part of the Respondent, USADA, and found that the approach taken on the appeal, which had involved a wide-ranging re-examination on appeal of multiple defences, entitled the Respondent to some compensation for part of its attorney's fees and costs, and awarded US$100 000 in favour of the Respondent.[50]

Use of a Prohibited Method: Contested Scientific Tests

CAS 2005/A/884, Hamilton v. USADA and UCI   H is a US cyclist and won the 2004 Olympic time trial. He challenged the finding that he had tested positive for a homologous blood transfusion after a sample was taken at the Vuelta Espagnol – blood doping being a prohibited method under the List. A test called the homologous blood transfusion test using a technique called flow cytometry was used by the WADA-accredited laboratory to identify mixed red blood cell populations. After a first arbitration hearing before the AAA, at which H was found to have committed a doping violation, H appealed to CAS under the UCI Regulations. He challenged the testing method used by the WADA laboratory as unreliable. After re-hearing detailed expert evidence on the reliability of the method and the chances of false positives, CAS dismissed the appeal. The Panel observed that there was no requirement that a particular test be used by a WADA laboratory. A finding from a WADA laboratory was sufficient to provide evidence of a violation. However, where new tests are used by a laboratory not specifically accredited to carry them out, the anti-doping organisation has to show that they were carried out in accordance with the proper standards of the scientific community if there is a challenge to their reliability.

After a number of matters advanced to claim that the test was unreliable had been considered, CAS held on the scientific evidence that the test was reliable and had been scientifically validated. After considering the possible explanations for the presence of mixed red blood cell populations (chimerism or some other cause), the Panel found that the only explanation for the results was blood doping, and it was comfortably satisfied that H had used a prohibited method contrary to the UCI Rules (which adopted the Code).

---

50 Subsequently, a challenge to the finding of CAS in the US courts by L was settled. L returned to racing, then retired. After denying the allegations, he ultimately admitted doping during his career and provided evidence against Lance Armstrong, with whom he rode in teams in the 1990s. Ultimately, the evidence of H and other riders led to the decision by USADA that A had committed serious anti-doping rule violations which warranted a lifetime ban under the Code. H and other riders who had provided sworn evidence against Mr Armstrong received six-month periods of ineligibility because they had provided 'substantial assistance' under Article 10.6.3 of the 2009 Code. USADA produced a reasoned decision in which Mr Armstrong was found to have committed various violations of the Code. See USADA v. Lance Armstrong Reasoned Decision 10 October 2012.

Successful Challenges to a Positive Test

CAS 2009/A/1752, *Dvyatovskiy* v. *IOC*; CAS 2009/A/1753, *Tsikhan* v. *IOC* D and T were Belarusian hammer throwers who placed second and third in the Olympic hammer throw final in 2008. Samples taken in doping control were analysed and found to contain T/E ratios of 8.1 and 7.8, in excess of the authorised T/E ratio of 4.1 under the Prohibited List. B samples confirmed that the permitted ratios had been exceeded. The IOC Disciplinary Commission heard the allegations against the athletes and disqualified both from the hammer throw event.

The athletes appealed to CAS. They challenged the analysis by the Beijing laboratory which had produced the T/E ratios. They also claimed GC-C-IRMS measurements had been improperly carried out. They claimed that the T/E analytical procedure in respect of each B sample was undertaken by the same laboratory assistant who had been heavily involved in the analysis of the A sample, in breach of the ISL, paragraph 5.2.4.3.2.2, which was in force at the time. There were also no positive or negative quality control samples within the confirmation run of the T/E analyses, again in breach of ISL. It was further claimed that there were a number of defects in relation to the IRMS analysis. Two analysts performed the procedures on both the A and the B sample, in violation of ISL. Documents and information provided in the information package for each athlete were incomplete and incomprehensible, and indicative of human error and/or equipment malfunction. It was claimed that the failings and breaches of the ISL individually and together meant that there was an insufficient basis to conclude either that the athletes had a T/E ratio above 4.1 or that the testosterone in their bodies was of exogenous origin.

The parties disagreed on the burden of proof. The Panel held that the IOC had acted in conflict with the Code in departing from the words of Article 3.2.1 of the Code and in placing the burden on the athlete to establish that there had been a departure from an International Standard and that it had reasonably caused the adverse analytical finding. In the Panel's view, the contradiction between the IOC Rules and the 2004 Code was to be resolved by interpreting the applicable rules against the IOC (*contra proferentem*). This approach was based on *Unidroit Principles on International Commercial Contracts*. The Panel chose to apply the provisions of Article 3.2.1 as set out in the 2004 Code.

After a summary of the testing process, and the way in which the ratio in excess of 4.1 has to be confirmed by another reliable analytical method, such as IRMS, the Panel considered the various technical challenges to the IOC decision and heard expert evidence from both sides. The Panel concluded that several of the values in each of the athletes' IRMS analyses fell outside acceptable ranges for testing in accordance with the ISL. Accordingly, the athletes had met the burden of proof of establishing a departure.

The Panel went on to find that the variability between values in the B sample did not justify the nullification of the entire test. The Panel declined to admit the athletes' general steroid profiles. The Panel found a further discrepancy in the sequence filing in which an automatic computer programme had identified the position of vials for analysis. The sequence file provided in the documentation package had been reconstructed and was not the original file. The Panel did not consider there was an adequate explanation for this. The Panel held that the interruption of the pre-programmed sequence for testing to alter the positioning of the vials manually gave rise to risk that the results from one sample might be incorrectly attributed to another. The risk was greater when it was known that the analyses reported on the file were part of a wider batch from which other athlete samples were tested.

The Panel was not satisfied with the records produced, given the obligations to document procedures under ISL. This was a further departure from the ISL. The Panel further concluded that the Beijing laboratory did not properly document quality control procedures and so was in breach of the ISL. However, the Panel relied on expert evidence to decide that a range of quality control activities was available and found that the requirements had been met overall, even if documentation in the packages was missing.

On the completeness of documentation, the refusal of the laboratory to produce a specific requested documentary item concerning the procedure for quality control meant that the appellants could not be asked to bear the burden of proof where evidence critical to their defence had not been disclosed.

On the breach of the Different Analyst Rule, the Panel applied a strict approach. Any analyst involved in the A sample analysis, whether the activity of that analyst involved direct interaction with the open or accessible sample or not, could not be involved in any activity with the B sample. The change in the Standard was not applicable and the strict approach under the earlier version of the ISL applied.[51]

---

51 The Panel applied CAS 2006/A/1119, *UCI* v. *Landaluce*; AAA 30 190 001 9907, *USADA* v. *Jenkins*.

In conclusion, the Panel found that, in the case of both athletes, there had been breaches of the requirements for documentation and reporting under the ISL and a breach of the Different Analyst Rule. The reconstruction of the sequence file meant that the transparency of the testing process had been denied to the athletes. In the Panel's view, if there was a breach, the test results should be annulled. In this difficult and complex matter, the Panel found in favour of the athletes and set aside the decision of the IOC.

Unsuccessful Challenge to Analysis

CAS 2010/A/2185, *Alberto Blanco* v. *USADA*   B, a professional cyclist competing for a US team, was tested during a stage race in China. The sample was analysed by a WADA-accredited laboratory in Beijing. At the time of analysis, ISL 5.0 was in force. The samples were analysed under TD EAAS 2004. This required IRMS when the concentration of DHEA was over 100 ng/ml and that of etiocholanolone was over 10 000 ng/ml. The laboratory found concentrations of substances in excess of the limits, so that under TD EAAS 2004, IRMS analysis had to be carried out. This showed the presence of exogenous testosterone. B requested analysis of the B sample, which was analysed using the same procedure as for the A sample. By the time of analysis of the B sample, the ISL 2009 version 6.0 had come into force. The B sample confirmed the A sample.

B challenged the chain of custody. He also contended that the same analyst had carried out parts of the analysis of the A and B samples, in breach of Article 5.2.4.3.2.2 of the ISL 2008, and that the results for the A and B sample analyses exceeded the acceptable measure of uncertainty required under Articles 5.2.4.3.2.3 and 5.2.6.1 of the ISL 2008. There were lengthy disputes about the discovery of documents. Ultimately, the Beijing laboratory was ordered to produce the documents requested.

The AAA Panel found that the anti-doping rule violation had been proved to the required standard. There was no breach of the Two Analyst Rule because the same-analyst prohibition was not present in the ISL version 6.0. The fact that the same two chemists analysed the A and B samples did not violate the ISL. This finding was not challenged on appeal to CAS.

Before CAS, B sought the production of further documents from the laboratory. USADA contended that no further documents should be produced because of the stipulation agreed between the parties. The CAS Panel ordered the production of further documents by the laboratory.

The parties were in disagreement as to whether Article 3.2.1 of the 2004 Code or the amended Article of the 2009 Code was applicable. The amended Article of the 2009 Code imposed a heavier burden on the athlete where it was alleged that there had been a departure from the ISL, and required the athlete to show that the departure could reasonably have caused the adverse analytical finding before the burden would shift to the NADO to prove that the breach did not cause the adverse analytical finding. B contended that the provision of the 2009 Code was substantive in nature and could not apply because that would violate the principle that substantive legal changes should not be retroactive, as provided in Article 24.5 of the 2009 Code. B contended that USADA could not meet the requirement under the 2004 Code of showing that the violations of the ISL did not cause the adverse analytical finding.

The CAS Panel noted that the argument on the application of the provisions relating to the burden of proof arose only if a violation of the ISL could be established. B submitted that the results obtained by the laboratory for his samples lacked robustness, and that they were not reliable because they did not meet the measurement of uncertainty required by the ISL.

The central question for the Panel was, accordingly, whether the evidence showed that there had been a departure from the relevant International Standard – the ISL. The Panel found that the absence of negative controls by the laboratory did not amount to a departure from the ISL because, on the proper interpretation of the ISL, this was not a mandatory step for the IRMS analysis, but was rather a matter for the process by which the laboratory was accredited.

The Panel considered the requirements under the ISL that the method of detection should produce consistent analytical results. It found that the variances between the results of the A and B samples in the IRMS analysis did not bring into question the results of the tests. The results were not near the threshold for reporting a positive test under TD EAAS 2004, and there was no concern regarding the robustness of the test results. Unlike the results in the D and T case, the variances were consistent.

The Panel considered that it was not persuaded that there had been a departure from the ISL, and, as a result, it concluded that an anti-doping rule violation had been committed. It rejected the appeal and maintained the two-year period of ineligibility imposed on B. It did not, in the circumstances, have to decide whether the provision of the 2004 Code or the 2009 Code on the alleged departure from the ISL applied.

The Panel did note that neither the TD EAAS nor the ISL contained provisions establishing the level of uncertainty in the IRMS process and other testing processes, and it recommended that these measurements should be included in the ISL. It also recommended that more guidance be given by WADA to laboratories on the running of negative controls and that laboratories be required to run such controls.

Challenge to a Positive Test – Effect of Failure to Follow the International Standard for Testing – No Violation under Article 2.1

CAS 2012/A/2791, *Campbell Brown* v. *JAA*   CB provided a sample after a competition which returned a positive test for HCT, which is a specified substance. It is often contained in medicines prescribed for high blood pressure.

CB could only produce a partial sample. The DCO did not follow the mandatory requirements for handling a partial sample under IST, which involves using a partial sample kit. CB's partial sample was put in a covered but unsealed container and left on the ground. CB waited to provide a sufficient sample in the sample collection area, where there were other athletes, for about forty minutes. She washed her hands and stretched while waiting. She did not watch the container at all times.

There was a clear breach of the IST by the DCO. Expert evidence was called for the athlete. This was to the effect that HCT could be present in small quantities in sweat or water and that the sample could have been contaminated because it was unsealed. Expert evidence for WADA challenged this opinion.

The Panel interpreted Article 3.2.1 of the 2009 Code as requiring the athlete to show that it was reasonable to conclude on the facts established that the adverse finding could have been caused by the departure from the IST. However, the Panel said that the burden on the athlete should not be set too high, because of the importance of anti-doping organisations following the rules. By a majority, the Panel found that, on the evidence, the adverse analytical finding could possibly have been caused by the departure from the IST, because there was a reasonable possibility in the circumstances of environmental contamination of the unsealed container holding the partial sample. As a result of this finding, the JAA had to prove to the comfortable satisfaction of the Panel that the breach did not have any effect on the result. It had effectively to exclude the possibility of contamination – in reality, this meant that it had to show that the prohibited substance had been taken – and could not do so. The allegation that there had been a violation of Article 2.1 was dismissed.

Article 2.2: Use or Attempted Use by an Athlete of a Prohibited Substance or a Prohibited Method

This violation does not require that an anti-doping organisation proves an adverse analytical finding from a sample taken from an athlete, although often testing and analysis will be the method of establishing the use of prohibited methods such as blood doping. Article 2.2 contains two potential violations: use and attempted use. The violations can potentially be established by a wide range of evidence. The evidence must be reliable and sufficient to discharge the burden of proof on the anti-doping organisation under the Code.[52] As previously noted, the Code provides that only an athlete can commit this violation.

Use

The two elements of use of a prohibited substance or a prohibited method are:

- the use, application, ingestion, injection or consumption by any means whatsoever[53]
- of any prohibited substance or prohibited method.

Prohibited substances and prohibited methods are identified on the Prohibited List. It is important to note the wide range of prohibited methods, which includes the various forms of blood doping, tampering and attempting to tamper with the integrity and validity of samples and the use of 'intravenous infusions and/or injections of more than 50 mL per 6 hour period except for those legitimately received in the course of hospital admissions, surgical procedures or clinical investigations'.[54]

---

52 The Code makes no further provision concerning the admissibility and quality of evidence required to prove a violation. See further Chapter 6, pages 282–3.
53 See the definition of 'use' in the Code, and the *Hamilton* case at page 198.
54 See Prohibited List 2017 Prohibited Methods M2. Where the use of an intravenous infusion in breach of M2 is established, it will be for the athlete to prove on the balance of probabilities that the infusion was received in the course of legitimate medical treatment. The List refers expressly to legitimately receiving infusions in hospital admission, surgical procedures or clinical investigations.

Intent

There is no need to prove any intent, fault, negligence or knowing use in order to establish an anti-doping rule violation for use of a prohibited substance or prohibited method.[55] It will, accordingly, not be necessary to prove that an athlete knew that a substance being used was a prohibited substance. It will be sufficient if the substance used was, in fact, prohibited under the List.

An athlete will not breach Article 2.2 if he or she uses a substance out-of-competition which is not prohibited out-of-competition. As previously noted, whether use occurs out-of-competition will depend on the particular circumstances and, quite possibly, the rules of the particular competition.

The definition of 'use' is broad. It covers the 'utilisation, application, ingestion, injection or consumption by any means whatsoever of any prohibited substance or prohibited method'. Use can be established by any reliable evidence. There have been many examples of violations of Article 2.2 being established by evidence of admissions, documentary evidence, reliable analysis of either an A or a B sample (provided that there is a satisfactory explanation for the absence of confirmation from the other sample) and other analytical information which does not satisfy the requirements necessary to establish a violation of Article 2.1. Where an athlete is subject to an ABP programme, the analysis and expert evaluation of the data collected in his or her passport may be used to support an allegation under Article 2.2.

Analytical Evidence from ABPs

Perhaps the most significant development in anti-doping investigation has been the introduction of the ABP for certain elite athletes. The concept of an ABP was first proposed by WADA in 2002, and the first Guidelines were published in 2009 (and the most recent in January 2017). The ABP is an important method for the detection of doping substances and methods. In recent years, it has become apparent that doping has become more scientifically planned, with some athletes using low doses of prohibited substances or prohibited methods in a systematic way, which may go undetected even where anti-doping organisations carry out well-planned 'no-notice' out-of-competition testing.

---

55 Article 2.2.1 of the 2015 Code.

The idea of the ABP is to establish a profile of an individual athlete covering the variables in his or her blood and the markers for specific classes of substance, in order to allow anti-doping organisations to establish when the athlete is manipulating his or her physiological variables through the use of prohibited substances and/or methods. There are now two standardised modules under the ABP, which follow similar administrative procedures – the haematological and the steroidal modules. The haematological module collects information from an athlete's samples on the biological markers relevant for the detection of blood doping, whether by the use of hormones stimulating erythropoeisis or blood transfusions. The steroidal module collects information from urine samples on the biological markers relevant for the detection of anabolic steroids and other anabolic agents. The values for these markers provide a profile of the particular athlete. Where samples reveal departures from the established profile, this may indicate doping when the results are subjected to statistical analysis. The operation of the ABP programme is directly linked to potential allegations under Article 2.2.

Outline of the ABP Programme

The process for the operation of the ABP programme is set out in the Code, the ISTI and the ABP Guidelines. The aim is to provide a coordinated process under which athletes chosen for inclusion in the ABP programme by an anti-doping organisation have an individual biological passport which is held in ADAMS, operated by WADA. For each ABP, an anti-doping organisation will be the passport custodian. This will be the organisation responsible for following up on adverse passport finding.

The information on the biological markers from samples obtained from an athlete will be added to his or her ABP in ADAMS. ADAMS contains an adaptive model. This is a mathematical statistical tool which calculates the probability for the occurrence of marker values in an athlete's profile on the basis that the athlete has a normal profile. Where the adaptive model detects atypical values for T/E values in the steroidal module, the sample will be subject to confirmation procedures as set out in the applicable Technical Document in the normal way. If the presence of an anabolic steroid is confirmed by the laboratory procedures, the usual results management process for a positive test will be followed. If the confirmation procedure is negative or inconclusive, the anti-doping organisation will be advised on further testing or possible expert review.

Where the haematological module of the ABP produces an adverse passport finding, there must be an expert review. An expert reviews the passport anonymously and reports back to the athlete passport management unit – the person at the anti-doping organisation responsible for the management of the biological passports – with an evaluation of the passport. The passport is reviewed anonymously. If the passport is normal, the normal testing pattern continues. If the passport is suspicious, target testing will be signalled and other recommendations will be made. If the expert considers that it is highly unlikely that the longitudinal profile is the result of a normal physiological or pathological condition and that it may be the result of the use of a prohibited substance or prohibited method, the passport will be referred to two further experts for review. If the expert considers on the basis of the information in the passport that the athlete has a pathological condition, this will be communicated to the athlete by the anti-doping organisation or the passport will be sent to two other experts for review.

Where a passport is sent for further review, this review will be carried out by the initial expert and two further experts chosen from the expert panel maintained by the passport management unit. The experts should have the experience necessary to review passports in the two different areas. The two new experts use the same approach as the initial expert. If they unanimously conclude that, considering the information contained in the passport at the time of review, it is highly likely that a prohibited substance or prohibited method has been used and unlikely that the position in the passport is the result of any other cause, the passport management unit will have to prepare a documentary package which includes the key information, as well as laboratory documentary packages for the tests within the passport which the experts deem essential. The key information for both modules includes age, gender, sport and discipline, type of test, sample code and internal laboratory number, biological data and results obtained by the adaptive model, competition information, chain of custody documentation and information from doping control forms for each sample collected in the period covered by the passport, as determined by the expert panel and passport management unit. Where the expert review concerns the haematological module, further information on the possible exposure of the athlete to altitude for the period defined by the expert panel, on whether the athlete has received a blood transfusion or suffered significant blood loss in the previous three months, on temperature conditions during transport of the blood samples and on laboratory documentation (including blood results and scattergrams) must be included. Where the expert review concerns the steroidal module information on the pH and specific gravity of the urine sample, laboratory documentation, the results of any further GC-C-IRMS confirmation procedures, indications of ethanol consumption, bacterial activities and a list of medications taken by the athlete which might influence his or her steroid profile have to be included.

The expert panel then reviews its finding on the review of the passport, after reviewing the further information in the ABP package. If the panel maintains its view that the information in the passport shows that it is highly likely that a prohibited substance or method has been used, the passport management unit will declare that there is an adverse passport finding. The process takes place on a strictly confidential process and will be anonymous, although the Guidelines acknowledge that information provided to the experts may allow the athlete to be identified and declare that this shall not invalidate the process.

The adverse passport finding will be reported to the anti-doping organisation responsible for the passport by the passport management unit. The anti-doping organisation will then advise the athlete and WADA that it is considering bringing an anti-doping rule violation against the athlete, provide the ABP documentation package to the athlete and invite the athlete to provide his or her own explanation for the data provided to the anti-doping organisation. There is no time limit for the athlete's explanation, but it has to be given in a timely manner. The anti-doping organisation will refer any explanation from the athlete to the expert panel for consideration. The panel will then consider the athlete's information and any further information which it considers necessary to give its final opinion in conjunction with the anti-doping organisation and the passport management unit. At the end of the process, the panel can either maintain its original view and decide unanimously that it is highly likely that the athlete used a prohibited substance or prohibited method (and that it was unlikely to find the passport abnormal assuming any other cause[56]) or decide that it is unable to reach an opinion unanimously. If the panel does not maintain its original view and cannot reach a view on the passport, it can recommend further investigation or testing.

---

56 The language of the Guideline is a little convoluted, but it is intended to mean that in the Panel's view, the only reason for the abnormal passport is that it is highly likely that the athlete used a prohibited substance or prohibited method.

Where the expert panel does maintain its view on the passport, the anti-doping organisation will proceed to give the athlete notice of the violation under Article 7.5 of the Code or the rules which provide for results management.

As can be seen, the process of evaluating the information in an ABP involves scientific assessment and evaluation of the data obtained and held. The process of evaluation also involves receiving and considering any explanation from the athlete. While this process is not one of final adjudication, an anti-doping organisation should ensure that it is conducted fairly, in a manner which allows the athlete the opportunity to give a proper response within the constraints of timely procedures.

In many cases, initial adverse passport findings may not permit experts to reach a conclusive view on the passport, but a suspicious profile is likely to lead to further target testing and investigation. This is an important aspect of a biological passport programme.

Where an allegation that an athlete has used a prohibited substance or method is brought on the basis of the evaluation of his or her ABP, the athlete will be able to challenge the evidence put forward by the anti-doping organisation in support of the allegation. Generally, while the athlete is able to challenge the collection and analysis of samples in the same way as in any other testing case, the focus of ABP cases tends to be on the related questions of whether the anti-doping organisation can show that the profile is, in fact, abnormal for the particular athlete and whether, if it is, the profile can be explained by some other cause apart from the taking of a prohibited substance or method. The anti-doping organisation has to satisfy the tribunal to the standard of comfortable satisfaction that the analysis of the passport profile establishes a breach of Article 2.2. While the athlete will have to introduce evidence to support his or her explanation for the profile shown by the passport, he or she does not carry a probative burden and it will be for the anti-doping organisation to rebut any suggested explanations and to prove to the comfortable satisfaction of the tribunal that the passport profile establishes the violation of Article 2.2. While the Guideline does not expressly require the expert panel to be comfortably satisfied in its opinion on the passport, the requirement for the panel's unanimous opinion is, it is submitted, consistent with the standard of proof required under the Code.

The ABP does not provide direct evidence of doping in the same way as a positive test, but requires the expert analysis of changes in a profile built up from the analysis of samples obtained over time. If it is determined by a panel of experts that there is a departure from the established profile for an athlete which cannot, in their opinion, be explained by other circumstances (e.g. illness or the effect of a particular training regime), the ABP data will provide evidence to support an allegation of the use of a prohibited substance or method.

The development of the ABP is regarded as a significant step in the fight against doping, and in recent times, several international sporting federations have adopted ABP regimes for their leading athletes, with cycling being perhaps the most notable example. The early cases in which evidence obtained from an ABP regime has been used to prove allegations that an athlete has used a prohibited substance or method are summarised in the next section.[57] Where an ABP regime does not, after expert evaluation of the data obtained, provide firm evidence of doping which can be used to support an allegation before a tribunal, questionable blood values revealed by the programme may lead to target testing of the athlete under the ISTI.

Illustrations

Using the ABP to Establish Use

CAS 2009/A/1912, *Pechstein* v. *ISU*   P was an international speed skater and elite performer who, since 1988, had won five gold and two Olympic bronze medals and several world, European and national championships. She was one of the most successful winter sports athletes of all time. Between 4 February 2000 and 30 April 2009, P underwent numerous in-competition and out-of-competition anti-doping controls. She had never tested positive.

The International Skating Union (ISU) collected many blood samples as part of its blood profiling programme. In particular, from 20 October 2007 to 30 April 2009, twenty-seven blood samples were collected from P. Blood parameters were measured. The haematological parameters of P's blood showed significant variation. P was informed that the values were abnormal. After review of the blood profile, the ISU filed a statement of disciplinary complaint accusing the athlete of having used a prohibited substance and/or a prohibited method (i.e. some form of blood doping) in breach of the Code. The ISU Disciplinary Commission held that P had breached Article 2.2, disqualified her results and imposed a two-year period of ineligibility. P appealed to CAS. She was granted

---

57 For decisions on the ABP, see pages 210–17.

provisional measures by CAS to allow her to practise and train in an endeavour to qualify for the Olympic Games.

The CAS Panel heard a significant number of expert witnesses evaluating the blood sample data. P contended that she had not committed any anti-doping rule violation.

P claimed that the use of longitudinal profiling was not permitted before 1 January 2009, when WADA introduced its ABP Guidelines. On this approach, only blood samples after 1 January 2009 could be used against her. She further claimed that the ISL and IST were applicable to the sampling process under the blood profile regime and that none of her samples had been analysed at a WADA-accredited laboratory, rendering the evidence inadmissible. P also challenged the upper limit on the haematological levels adopted by the ISU's experts. She contended that the data collected by the ISU were unreliable. She submitted that the ISU had not met the burden of proof which lay on it.

The ISU contended that it was perfectly permissible for it to initiate its own blood profiling programme before the implementation of the WADA Guidelines. It submitted that it had kept to all necessary procedures.

The CAS Panel held that blood samples obtained before the WADA Guidelines for longitudinal profiling came into effect could be used in evidence to support longitudinal profiling, provided the evidence was reliable (as provided by Article 3.2 of the Code). The resort to new evidentiary methods could not be struck down on the basis that it represented the retrospective application of substantive law. The longitudinal profiling was an evidentiary or procedural method and the only issue was whether the information provided by it was reliable. There was no presumption available that tests had been carried out properly as there would be with tests at a WADA laboratory, with the result that the reliability of the testing and analysis had to be established by the ISU.

The Panel concluded that it was comfortably satisfied that the blood values from P could be relied upon. It considered the expert evidence in relation to P's haematological values, which, it held, established that they were very high and abnormal. The Panel did not accept the position put forward by the appellant and her experts that the abnormally high values seen were not abnormal for her. A mean value of 2.1 for P was derived from a sequence of tests. The Panel concluded that the values recorded in February 2009 (3.49, 3.54 and 3.38) were abnormal even in comparison with the athlete's own individual values. There was no valid explanation for the high blood values, and the possibility of blood disease was safely excluded. The Panel found that the abnormal values recorded in February

2009 (and the subsequent sharp drop in the values) could not be explained by any congenital or developed abnormality. They had to result from the athlete's illicit manipulation of her own blood.

As a result, P was found to have used a prohibited method, namely blood doping, in breach of Article 2.2. This decision has been the subject of appeals to the Swiss Federal Tribunal, and the athlete has pursued civil proceedings claiming damages in the German courts. After the Swiss Federal Tribunal dismissed P's appeal from the CAS award in 2010, she pursued civil proceedings in the German courts. On appeal, the Munich Higher Regional Court Civil Division declined to enforce the CAS award and stay the German proceedings, leaving the damages claim against the national sporting organisation and international federation to proceed. The decision of the Munich Higher Regional Court was reversed by the highest German court – the German Federal Tribunal (GFT) – on June 7 2016.[58] The GFT upheld the CAS award and rejected a challenge to CAS on competition law grounds.

TAS 2010/A/2178, *Pietro Caucchioli* **v.** *CONI & UCI*   C, an Italian cyclist, was part of the UCI ABP programme. The UCI expert panel considered that his blood profile, as shown by thirteen samples taken in the 2008–09 season, could only be explained by the use of a prohibited method. An allegation under Article 2.2 was brought before the national tribunal, which found the allegation proved, and imposed a two-year period of ineligibility.

C appealed to CAS. He submitted that samples taken before the publication of the WADA Guideline on ABP could not be relied on because analysis under the ABP could not have retrospective effect, that the sample analysis was unreliable because of breaches of the International Standards and that his blood profile could not be attributed to the use of a prohibited method when it was properly evaluated.

While acknowledging the basic principle that the alleged violation was subject to the substantive rules of law applicable at the time when it occurred, and that new substantive rules could not have retrospective effect, the Panel held that using new methods of analysis did not infringe this principle, because it did not involve a new substantive legal rule but rather an improved method of proceeding to detect violations. The relevant substantive legal rule in issue, namely the anti-doping rule violation

---

58 See *Pechstein* v. *DESG and ISU* U1110/14/Kart and the summary of the decisions in the German courts in Chapter 10, pages 513–17.

of using a prohibited method, was in force at the time of the alleged violation. The Panel also dismissed the challenge to the independence of the UCI expert panel on the basis that it was paid by UCI. Payment did not undermine independence, particularly where the experts carried out their analysis of profiles on an anonymous basis under the relevant rules. While there were some possible irregularities in some of the analyses, they showed fluctuations in levels of the relevant blood markers which could only be consistent with blood transfusions. C's appeal was dismissed.

TAS 2010/A/2306, *Pellizotti* v. *CONI and UCI*   P, an Italian professional cyclist, was in the UCI ABP programme. In December 2009, the panel of nine experts appointed by UCI to review ABP data concluded that it was highly probable that the rider's samples showed that he had taken a prohibited substance or used a prohibited method. After the athlete had provided his response, a panel of three experts concluded that the athlete's explanation of the values was not satisfactory and recommended the bringing of anti-doping rule violation proceedings against P.

The Italian national tribunal (TNA) considered that the allegation had to be proved as provided by Article 3 of the Code. It held that the ABP did not infringe the principle of non-retroactivity. It did not introduce a new substantive violation but, rather, a method of establishing the existence of a violation. There were no anomalies in the analysis of the athlete's samples and the analysis by a WADA-approved laboratory was presumed to be valid under Article 3.2.1 of the Code. The ABP was a reliable method of detecting doping, but, in this particular case, the analyses did not prove the violation to the required standard under Article 3.

On Appeal to CAS   UCI appealed to CAS. CAS confirmed the TNA decision that there was no infringement of the principle of retroactivity as set out in the 2009 Code. The introduction of the ABP was the introduction of a new detection method rather than any change in substantive law.

The ABP identified specific values for HGB reticulocytes (RETs) and a ratio expressing the relationship between the concentration of HGB and RET (the 'off-score'). The three values obtained created a range of values for the athlete tested, which could be used statistically to establish whether variations were likely to be the result of doping or not.

A challenge to the independence of the UCI experts by P failed.

The Panel analysed the reliability of the results. It found that the athlete had not been able to displace the presumption in favour of analysis by WADA-accredited laboratories under Article 3.2 of the Code. The analytical irregularities identified by the athlete did not affect the quality of the results. On the results, CAS concluded that two sets of values, which were explained by the athlete as being the result of resting after heavy training and his presence at altitude (and heavy training) at the time the samples were taken, did not establish to the required standard that the athlete had been doping. UCI had not succeeded in excluding the possibility that the values were the result of the circumstances outlined by the athlete. However, further values in the samples taken at the 2009 Giro d'Italia and the 2009 Tour de France were held to show the use of a prohibited method, namely blood doping. The samples during the Giro showed HGB values increasing, notwithstanding heavy physical effort. The conclusion was supported by comparing the values with those obtained at the previous year's Giro, particularly where the HGB value just before the event was similar in both years. Again, the variations in the values in the samples during the course of the 2009 Tour de France proved blood doping. They showed an extremely high value immediately before the event and a levelling off during it which could not be attributed to altitude or other explanations put forward by P.

The Panel concluded that the athlete had used a prohibited method contrary to Article 2.2 of the Code.

UCI sought the imposition of a four-year period of ineligibility on the basis that aggravating circumstances were present. It also sought a financial penalty against P of a little over €400 000, being seventy per cent of P's income (in accordance with the UCI rules). The Panel found that €250 000 of the income came from a prize in a race. P's basic salary was €328 000. The Panel reduced the financial penalty further to take into account P's age and his limited prospects at the end of the period of suspension. It imposed a financial penalty of €115 000 under the UCI rules. The Panel did not consider that the circumstances justified any increase in the standard sanction and imposed a period of two years' ineligibility on the athlete.

Assessment of the Explanation for an Abnormal Profile

UK Anti-Doping v. *Jonathan Tiernan-Locke*, **National Anti-Doping Panel 15 July 2014 SR 0000120108**   T, a professional cyclist, was charged with using ESA or blood doping to boost HGB. The evidence in support came from an expert analysis of his ABP profile, which provides values in relation to blood HGB and RET percentages. A formula combines these values to produce a 'score' for the particular athlete.

T gave an initial sample after entering the programme when he joined a leading professional team, then four more samples to build up his profile. The expert review panel considered that the first sample showed irregular values when the profile shown by all his samples was considered. They concluded that the values were indicative of doping to increase HGB levels in the period before he joined the team.

T gave the explanation that he had gone on an alcoholic binge about thirty-two hours before the sample had been taken and had not eaten the next day. He had gone out to celebrate signing his major professional contract. The question raised by T was not whether his values were not irregular when set alongside the profile in his passport, but whether the alcoholic binge could account for the readings from the sample so that there was an innocent explanation for them. The Panel heard expert evidence on both sides. The NADO had to disprove the explanation put forward by the athlete, supported by his expert evidence, and establish that the explanation put forward by its own scientific experts was correct. The Panel considered the evidence of the athlete, the expert evidence in support of that evidence and the expert evidence called by the NADO to support the evaluation of the results as showing the use of prohibited substances or methods. The Panel did not accept the athlete's explanation that he was severely dehydrated when the sample was taken because, even if he had been on a drinking binge, he was training normally for the World Championships, which were to take place the next day. As a result of this factual finding, the Panel rejected the scientific opinion based on the athlete being extremely dehydrated. The Panel found that the NADO had shown that the athlete's explanation was wrong and had proved the violation to the 'comfortable satisfaction' standard under the Code on the basis of the scientific evidence put forward.

Attempt to Use   The three elements of an attempted use of a prohibited substance or a prohibited method are:

- purposely engaging in conduct that constitutes a substantial step in a course of conduct planned to culminate in[59]
- the application, ingestion, injection or consumption by any means whatsoever
- of any prohibited substance or prohibited method.

59 See the definition of 'attempt' in the Code.

The definition further provides that there shall be no anti-doping rule violation based solely on an attempt to commit a violation if the person who made the attempt renounces it prior to its being discovered by a third party not involved in the attempt.

Mental Element   A mental element on the part of the athlete charged with a violation under Article 2.2 must be proved in order to establish an anti-doping rule violation for the attempted use of a prohibited substance or prohibited method. It must be shown, to the comfortable satisfaction of the tribunal, that the athlete purposely engaged in the conduct that constitutes a substantial step in the course of conduct planned to culminate in the use of a prohibited substance or prohibited method. It is submitted that the intention need relate only to the acts or other conduct relating to the planned use, and an intention to enhance sport performance need not be proved (although in most cases the acts carried out may well be linked to such an intention).[60]

Impossibility   The violation under Article 2.2 is expressed in terms of the use of prohibited substances or prohibited methods as defined in the Code, and Article 2.2.1 also refers to an athlete's personal duty to ensure that prohibited substances do not enter his or her body. The question which arises in connection with the violation of attempted use is whether the violation can be committed where an athlete intends to use a prohibited substance or method but the substance or method with which the attempt is concerned turns out not, in fact, to be a prohibited substance or method at all. While it can be contended that the Code is only concerned with the actual use or attempted use of prohibited substances as defined, and that the use of the italicised definitions in the wording of Article 2.1 supports the limitation of the violation to situations where prohibited substances and methods are, in fact, involved, a CAS Panel has held that there can be an attempt to use a prohibited substance where the substance which the athlete attempted to use is not, in fact, a prohibited substance, provided the athlete has the necessary intent and carries out the necessary steps which are planned to culminate in the commission of an anti-doping rule violation.[61]

It can be suggested that an interpretation which limits the application of the Code to situations where prohibited substances are, in fact, involved

---

60 See *E, T and P v. IOC* on pages 172–7.
61 See CAS 2008/A/1664, *IRB v. Troy and ARU* at pages 220–1.

reflects the nature of the Code as an agreement under which persons agree to be subject to investigations and proceedings for alleged violations relating to the use of substances and methods which are, in fact, on the Prohibited List. While under the criminal law in many jurisdictions an attempt to commit a criminal offence can be established where it was impossible on the facts for the accused to commit the criminal offence, the position under the Code could be considered to be different given its contractual nature, particularly where the Code is expressly not intended to be subject to the standards applicable in criminal proceedings. The broader interpretation of Article 2.2 is, however, consistent with the general purpose of the Code of preventing doping in sport. It has been adopted by CAS, is consistent with the well-established principle that an interpretation of the Code which furthers its purpose should be adopted where that is available on the words used and should now be regarded as the established position.

The definition of 'attempt' expressly provides that if a person[62] renounces an attempt prior to its being discovered by a third party not involved in the attempt, then that person shall not have committed an anti-doping rule violation based solely on that attempt. Whether a person has renounced an attempt will (like the question whether the conduct in question amounts to an attempt) be a question of fact. It is submitted that evidence of a clear, unequivocal renunciation will be required.

Again, it should be noted that it is not necessary to establish that an athlete or person used or attempted to use a prohibited substance or method with the intention of enhancing sport performance. The notes to the Code make clear that the violation does not extend the Code to make the use of substances out-of-competition which are prohibited in-competition only into a violation.[63]

Can an Attempt be Proved on the Facts?

CAS 2007/A/1426, *Giuseppe Gibilisco* v. *CONI*   G was a professional pole vaulter who belonged to the Italian Military Corps. He was subject to the jurisdiction of the Italian Olympic Committee.

---

62 See the definition of 'attempt'. The reference to 'person' in the attempt cannot refer to an attempt under Article 2.2, which can only be committed by an athlete, but would be applicable to an attempt by a person apart from an athlete to tamper with doping control under Article 2.5.

63 The notes to Article 2.2 also explain that the presence of a prohibited substance in an in-competition test will be a violation of Article 2.1 regardless of when the substance may have been ingested or administered. This note might be more appropriately placed in Article 2.1.

In 2004, a criminal investigation called 'Oil for Drugs' was begun by the State Prosecutor's Office in Rome. This involved an investigation into a particular doctor who was suspected of providing prohibited substances to athletes. The doctor had previously been suspended by the Italian Cycling Federation.

In May 2004, a unit of the military police recorded by wire-tap a conversation between the doctor and G at the doctor's office, in which they spoke of diet, medicines and supplements and testovis, which is a product containing testosterone and growth hormones. A search was carried out of G's home by the police. A personal schedule was found with the letters 'A-P-G' written against the months of January and February. It was claimed that the letters referred to three prohibited substances which other cyclists involved in the investigation had also been prescribed by the doctor.

In a separate investigation, a cyclist had admitted that he had been advised by the doctor to take prohibited substances and that the doctor used letters to indicate the substances.

When G was asked about the result of the search by the police, he admitted that he had been in contact with the doctor for a period of months because he was unhappy with the doctors who were then taking care of him. He also admitted that he had not told his military superiors of the visits to the doctor in order to avoid his results being associated with doping (this was after G had heard about the doctor's involvements in doping matters). He also admitted having requested information from the doctor about doping substances and that he had been advised by the doctor to take growth hormones. However, he insisted he had never taken any substances and said that the pills found during the search containing caffeine had been given to him by another athlete at a meeting. He said the letters 'A-P-G' written down in his schedule referred to training programmes.

In further interviews with CONI, the athlete confirmed his earlier statement to the police. The criminal investigation in respect of G was closed in 2005. In July 2007, a sports tribunal imposed a two-year period of ineligibility on G for the attempted use of prohibited substances. After an appeal to the Appeal Committee of the Federazione Italiana Di Atletica Leggera (FIDAL), the decision was set aside and G was acquitted. UPA-CONI appealed this decision to the Appeal Tribunal of CONI.

Appeal Tribunal The Appeal Tribunal held that the matter was governed by the Code, not Italian criminal law. The concept of attempt had to be assessed by reference to the definition in the Code, not that in the criminal code. In allowing the appeal, CONI held that it was not credible that G had visited the doctor to ask about nutritional supplements. The tribunal took into account a range of matters – G's admission that he had known about the doctor's previous involvement in doping cases and yet continued calling on him, that he had not informed his coaches and his military superiors of his visits to the doctor, that he had said that the doctor had advised him to take growth hormones, that he had refused to reveal the name of the person who had given the contact details of the doctor and the tape recording of the conversation between the doctor and G. Generally, the tribunal concluded that the doctor would never have given the advice concerning prohibited substances in the conversation if the athlete had not asked for it. To these matters, the tribunal added the letters and the schedule and the fact that there had been no plausible explanation presented establishing the training programmes the letters were said to refer to. It overturned the decision and found the allegation proved.

Before CAS G appealed to CAS. After challenges to the independence of arbitrators had been considered, the Panel examined the facts that had been established, namely that G called on the doctor on several occasions after he had become aware he had been involved in doping matters, that they had talked about prohibited substances in the doctor's office, that he had never informed his military superiors or the doctors at FIDAL about his visits, that G had contradicted himself in his statements before the authorities and that no convincing explanation had been given about the letters in the schedule. The Panel held that, while the facts gave rise to a considerable degree of suspicion and provided some indication the applicant may have been involved in doping practices, they were not sufficient to prove to the required standard the athlete's intent to commit a violation so as to establish an attempt in terms of Article 2.2 of the Code. The proven facts, whether taken individually or together, could not, in the Panel's opinion, be considered as conduct constituting a substantial step in a course of conduct planned to culminate in the commission of anti-doping rule violations. A request by the CONI representative for G to be found guilty of using the assistance of a medical person who was suspended contrary to the sport's rules was also considered. The Panel decided that this subsidiary motion was not capable of being considered because such an allegation had not been made before the Italian sports authorities nor dealt with in any way in the appealed decision. Notwithstanding the wide-ranging powers of the Panel on appeal, it could only consider matters which were legitimately the subject of the appeal. The allegation was dismissed and the two-year period of ineligibility set aside.

Attempted Use where Substances are not Shown to be Prohibited Substances

CAS 2008/A/1664, *IRB* v. *Troy and the ARU* T was an amateur rugby player under the jurisdiction of the Australian Rugby Union (ARU). Australian customs seized two packages addressed to T from the United Kingdom and the United States containing a concealed container of packets labelled as containing testosterone and one bottle of capsules labelled DHEA 200. The seizure notice informed T of his rights under the customs legislation. T did not claim the goods and they were subsequently destroyed in the customs warehouse. T was notified of violations under the Code by the Australian Sports Anti-Doping Authority (ASADA) – an attempt to use prohibited substance and the possession of prohibited substances. T admitted placing orders but said at no time prior to receiving notification from customs was he aware that they contained prohibited substances. ASADA passed its notice on to the ARU and IRB. The ARU sent T an infraction notice making the allegations of breaches of the Code against him. The ARU Judicial Committee dismissed the allegations and declined to make a finding that there had been a breach by the Respondent.

The IRB and WADA lodged appeals to CAS. There was common ground that T had agreed to observe the ARU's anti-doping by-laws. T had admitted that he ordered the goods over the Internet, paid for them by credit card and imported them into Australia. He had never physically had possession of the goods.

T's evidence was that he had never intentionally ordered products containing testosterone or DHEA. He had not heard of the substance DHEA until he received the customs correspondence. The Panel did not accept this, based on his interviews with ASADA. T's evidence that the product ordered was not the same as the one seized was also rejected. The Panel was comfortably satisfied that in respect of the products ordered, T believed that they contained testosterone or DHEA. However, the substances had not been analysed and there was no proof that the items ordered in fact contained the prohibited substances. It was not possible to prove constructive possession because T could not have known of the presence of the prohibited substances at the time they had been seized.

On the allegation of attempted use, the Panel held that the violation could be committed where it was not established that a prohibited substance was, in fact, involved, provided it was proved that the athlete had purposely engaged in conduct planned to culminate in the use of a prohibited substance as provided in the Code. It relied on the purpose of the Code, the wording of the definition of attempt in the Code and the criminal law in Australia (and other jurisdictions) to decide that conduct which could not, in fact, have brought about the use of a prohibited substance could still amount to an attempt to use a prohibited substance on the proper interpretation of Article 2.2.

Proof of Article 2.2 Violation   This violation does not require proof by the testing process. An anti-doping organisation may establish that a prohibited substance or method has been used by means of a wide variety of possible evidence, including admissions by the athlete, provided that the evidence is reliable, as required by Article 3 of the Code.[64] As noted, evidence based on the evaluation of an ABP may be used to establish this violation. In several recent decisions, CAS has upheld the reliability of evidence obtained from the evaluation of an athlete's ABP. Each case will, however, turn on the particular ABP in question and on the expert evidence evaluating the results obtained in the passport regime which is presented to the tribunal.[65]

Where a B sample is not analysed or properly analysed, the result of an A sample analysis may still be relied on to show use of a prohibited substance, even though the absence of the B sample analysis means that there can be no positive test and breach of Article 2.1. In such cases, the tribunal would need to be comfortably satisfied by the analysis of the A sample alone, and by the explanation for the absence of a B sample analysis, that a violation under Article 2.2 had been committed. Similarly, B sample analysis alone might be relied on.

Use of an A Sample Alone as Reliable Evidence

CAS A3/2007, ASADA v. *Van Tienen*   VT was an Australian weightlifting representative. She had competed for Australia in the United States. She provided a sample at the competition, which was analysed and found to be negative. In accordance with standard practice with such a result, the sample was discarded. However, the testing data were retained. The sample was not tested for a stimulant called benzylpiperazine (BZP). (At the time, BZP was prohibited in-competition.)

In October 2005, four weightlifters from Australia tested positive for BZP. An investigation was carried out into the positive tests. VT was

---

64 See e.g. *USADA* v. *Montgomery* and *Gaines* at pages 289–90.
65 See case summaries, pages 210–24.

interviewed. She worked for a supplement company and had been supplying and selling a product called Fortius Syneprine to other athletes. The other athletes were banned for two years.

After this, and during the investigation, the computer data files from the A sample analysis of the sample provided by VT were reviewed by an expert. He found that the peaks recorded clearly showed the presence of BZP. There was no issue as to the chain of custody or that the analysis of the data had not been carried out by established scientific methods.

The athlete argued that, in the absence of a B sample, the analysis of the A sample could not be relied on. The CAS arbitrator held that use of a prohibited substance was established by the expert evidence relating to the data file. The evidence was reliable and the absence of a B sample did not mean that evidence as to the result of the A sample should be rejected where the allegation was one of use. ASADA could not rely on the presumption under the Code, but it could still use the evidence to establish the violation, if it was reliable. The arbitrator also found on the evidence that the athlete had probably taken the same product as had been taken by the other athletes who had tested positive.

Use of Prohibited Methods   The violation covers the use of prohibited methods as identified in the Prohibited List, including the use of intravenous infusions and/or injections under M2 of the List. Under M2, infusions or injections of more than 50 ml per six-hour period are prohibited 'except for those legitimately received in the course of hospital admissions, surgical procedures or clinical investigations'. If a prohibited substance is used in such a situation, this will lead to an anti-doping rule violation, whether under Article 2.1 or under Article 2.2 (unless the athlete can obtain a TUE on a retroactive basis), although the athlete might, in the particular circumstances of the violation, be able to establish no fault or no significant fault so as to eliminate or reduce the period of ineligibility. Where a prohibited method such as an intravenous infusion which does not involve using a prohibited substance is used, the athlete or other person will not commit a violation if the use of the infusion was a legitimate medical treatment as set out in M2 of the Prohibited List. While neither the Code nor the List makes specific provision in relation to the burden of proof with regard to the question whether the use of an intravenous infusion is a legitimate medical treatment, it is submitted that, if the anti-doping organisation establishes that an intravenous infusion was used, it will be for the athlete or other person facing the allegation to show, on the balance of probabilities, that the use was in circumstances which meant that there was no violation by reason of the legitimate-medical-treatment exception on the Prohibited List.[66] While the exception in M2 is specifically worded, it is submitted that it can be interpreted to cover any situation where the infusion is received as part of a legitimate medical treatment. Where an athlete self-administers an intravenous infusion, there can be no acute medical situation in a formal sense and no legitimate medical treatment unless the actions of the athlete can be shown to have been carried out under the direction of a medical professional, although the situation might, depending on the facts, support a plea that there was no significant fault on the part of the athlete.[67]

The Effect of Article 10.2   As already outlined, Article 10.2 applies to violations of both Article 2.1 and Article 2.2 (and to Article 2.6). This means that first violations which do not involve specified substances will attract a period of ineligibility of four years unless the athlete establishes that the anti-doping violation was not intentional. The athlete will have to prove absence of intent as defined in Article 10.2.3 on the balance of probabilities if the four-year period of ineligibility is not to apply. If he or she does establish the absence of intent, the period of ineligibility will be two years. Where an alleged violation of Article 2.1 or 2.2 involves a specified substance, a violation will attract a period of ineligibility of two years unless the anti-doping organisation proves that the anti-doping rule violation was intentional according to the definition in Article 10.2.3. If intentional conduct under Article 10.2.3 is not established, the period of ineligibility will be two years. Intention is defined in Article 10.2.3 (the Code contains no definition in the definition section) in terms of actual knowledge (the athlete knowing that his or her conduct constituted an anti-doping rule violation) or conscious risk-taking (the athlete knowing that there was a significant risk that his or her conduct might constitute or result in an anti-doping rule violation and manifestly disregarding that risk). Overall,

---

66 See Chapter 6, pages 279–80 for the burden on the athlete generally under Article 3.1.
67 See *WADA* v. *Eder and Ski Austria* in Chapter 10, pages 510–11, where the use of an intravenous infusion of saline by the athlete was considered on the appeal brought to CAS. The CAS Panel in CAS 2002/A/389/390/391/392/393, *Mayer* v. *IOC* set out a test by which to determine whether medical treatment was legitimate. Although this decision was made before the Code came into force, its criteria were used by the CAS Panel. These criteria are that the medical treatment was necessary to cure an illness or injury, there was no valid treatment which would not fall within the definition of doping available, that the treatment was not performance-enhancing, that before treatment there was some form of medical diagnosis, that the treatment was applied by qualified medical personnel in an appropriate medical setting and that there are adequate records of the treatment available.

the term 'intentional' is described as being intended to identify those athletes who cheat. The effect of the provisions is considered further in Chapter 8.[68]

The effect of Article 10.2.1 is that where either intentional conduct is established or the presumption of intentional conduct is not rebutted, violations under Articles 2.1, 2.2 or 2.6 are treated more seriously as regards sanctions. In the case of a violation of attempted use, the anti-doping organisation has to prove deliberate intentional conduct planned to culminate in the commission of an anti-doping rule violation in order to establish the violation under Article 2.2. It is submitted that Article 10.2.3 is intended to create a further requirement before a four-year period of ineligibility can be imposed. Establishing the violation of attempted use under Article 2.2 does not involve proving the kind of intentional conduct referred to in Article 10.2.3 because, it is submitted, the proof of an attempt does not require proof of intentional or reckless conduct (as defined in Article 10.2.3). Establishing attempted use in breach of Article 2.2 involves the proof of deliberate conduct which the athlete intended would culminate in circumstances which, as a matter of fact, amount to an anti-doping rule violation. However, where an attempt to use a prohibited substance (which is not a specified substance) or prohibited method is established, it will be difficult for an athlete to establish that the attempted use, which involves deliberate acts, was not intentional or reckless in terms of Article 10.2.3. Where the attempt to use involves a specified substance, the anti-doping organisation will have to prove that the intentional conduct described in Article 10.2.3 is present (in addition to the conduct required to establish an attempt) in order for a four-year period of ineligibility to apply.

Article 2.3: Evading, Refusing or Failing to Submit to Sample Collection

Article 2.3 provides for three ways in which a violation of Article 2.3 can be committed, all of which require that an anti-doping organisation is carrying out anti-doping sample collection as authorised by the Code. Article 2.3 establishes the three violations and the required elements as follows:

- evading sample collection;
- refusing to submit to sample collection without compelling justification after notification of the obligation to submit to sample collection; or

---

68 See Chapter 8, pages 353–72 for case summaries involving the proof or disproof of intentional conduct under Article 10.2.3.

- failing to submit to sample collection after notification of the obligation to submit to sample collection.

Evading sample collection will require proof of intentional conduct in that the athlete is shown to have deliberately avoided sample collection. This will require that the athlete is aware of the sample collection which an anti-doping organisation is seeking to carry out and sets out to avoid it, but will not require formal notification of the need to submit to sample collection.

Establishing a 'refusal' to submit to a sample collection will require an anti-doping organisation to prove an intentional act (or intentional omission) on the part of the athlete after he or she has been notified under the ISTI of the obligations to submit to sample collection and to comply with his or her obligations.[69] Such an intentional act or omission will not necessarily be required to prove a 'failure' to submit to sample collection without compelling justification – this violation can be committed by either intentional or negligent conduct. As with refusal, failing to submit to sample collection can only be alleged once there has been notification of the athlete's obligation to submit to sample collection as required by the relevant rules in the ISTI.[70] However, in order to prove these violations, it is not necessary to prove that the athlete acted with intent in the sense of having knowledge of the rules and consequences of refusal and intending to avoid them, or indeed that the athlete acted to avoid being tested in order to cover up the taking of prohibited substances. It is unclear whether the full notification of all the rights and obligations under the ISTI in a formal manner and of the consequences of not complying is required for the violation of refusal or failure to submit to be established. The athlete who departs before full notification can be completed will, if full formal notification is required to found an allegation of refusal under the ISTI, evade sample collection.

The Defence of Compelling Justification

A determination by a tribunal as to whether a violation under Article 2.3 has been established to the required standard will be a question of fact. If a refusal or failure to submit to sample collection has been established on the facts, there will be no violation if there is a 'compelling' justification for

---

69 ISTI 5.4 (a) sets out the notification to the athlete of the fundamental obligation to undergo sample collection and ISTI 5.4 sets out the obligation to comply with the process, breach of which may lead to an allegation of refusal after investigation.
70 See Chapter 3, pages 128–34.

the refusal or failure. It is submitted that the athlete bears the burden of establishing the existence of 'compelling justification' on his or her part, to the standard of the balance of probabilities, as required by Article 3 of the Code.[71] The use of the word 'compelling' means that the justification relied on will have to be of an overwhelming nature. This approach accords with the important place of the violation under Article 2.3 in upholding the testing regime under the Code. Overall, the testing regime under the Code depends on athletes submitting to sample collection wherever that is practically possible.

The requirement to submit to sample collection unless there is compelling justification to refuse has been described in one CAS award as requiring the athlete to provide a sample 'wherever physically, hygienically and morally possible'.[72] This statement reflects the strict approach to the defence in Article 2.3 established by CAS awards, but the question whether an athlete can show compelling justification is ultimately a matter of fact for the tribunal, which has to apply the provisions of the violation to the particular circumstances established by the evidence.

The athlete will have to establish very clear compelling reasons for his or her conduct in refusing to submit to doping control in order to meet the requirements imposed for a valid justification. It is suggested that the question should be approached by asking whether the reasons for the refusal have their origins in factual circumstances which make the refusal a reasonable course for the athlete, notwithstanding his or her clear obligation to submit to sample collection, and the importance of that obligation. The Code makes no provision concerning the extent to which the assessment of the justification for refusal is subjective. It is submitted that the assessment is objective, and involves considering the conduct of the athlete by reference to the conduct of a hypothetical reasonable athlete in the position of the athlete facing the allegation. As with establishing the violation itself, a subjective belief on the part of an athlete that he or she is no longer obliged to submit to testing when, in fact, he or she is so obliged, cannot provide justification for a refusal.[73] This approach to the circumstances in which an athlete may establish a defence reflects the importance of the violation of refusal under the regime established by the Code – the testing regime requires the cooperation of athletes who are subject to the

---

71 See Chapter 6, pages 279–80.   72 CAS 2005/A/925.
73 Of course, an athlete who refuses, claiming that he or she is, in fact, no longer subject to testing when this is correct, will not commit a violation because there would be no jurisdiction over the athlete.

Code and cannot function without this. It is vital that the requirements for a violation under Article 2.3 are interpreted and applied in a robust way where the provision so permits, if the testing system and overall purpose of the Code is not to be undermined.

The 2015 Code expressly says in the comment to Article 10.5.2 that the no significant fault defence in Article 10.5.2 is potentially applicable to any violation apart from those which have an element of intent. The examples of violations to which the defence would not apply given in the comment to Article 10.5.2 are the violations of tampering, trafficking, administration and complicity, as well as any violation where intent is part of the sanction, as in Article 10.2.1. It is submitted that where a violation under Article 2.3 involves deliberate conduct in evading sample collection or refusing or failing to submit to sample collection with no compelling justification for the refusal, Article 10.5.2 cannot apply.[74] In other situations where the violation of Article 2.3 involves failing to submit to sample collection and results from carelessness by the athlete, it may, in exceptional circumstances, be possible for the athlete to establish no significant fault as a basis for reducing the period of ineligibility.

The sanction for a violation of Article 2.3 has been increased by the 2015 Code in line with the sanctions for breaches of Articles 2.1, 2.2 and 2.6 under Article 10.3. As with those violations, the athlete will be subject to a period of ineligibility of four years. The four-year period of ineligibility for a breach of Article 2.3 can be reduced by proof that the conduct was not intentional (as that is defined in Article 10.2.3) where the breach involves failing to submit to sample collection, but for other forms of the violation under Article 2.3 (evasion or refusal) only prompt admission under Article 10.6.3 can reduce the four-year period down to a minimum of two years.[75] The provision allowing the athlete to establish that the violation is not intentional is limited expressly to cases of failing to submit to sample collection and appears to prevent an athlete who has refused or evaded a test without compelling justification from attempting to show that the refusal or evasion was not intentional in terms of Article 10.2.3. This means that the treatment of a violation under Article 2.3 is arguably stricter than the treatment of violations under Articles 2.1, 2.2 and 2.6. Only in cases of negligent failure to submit to sample collection will it be

---

74 For consideration of the application of Article 10.5.2 in cases involving a breach of Article 2.3, see Chapter 8, pages 370–2.

75 See Chapter 8, pages 430–1 on sanctions for breach of Article 2.3 and pages 440–1 for consideration of the prompt admission provision in Article 10.6.3.

possible to argue for a two-year period of ineligibility and/or any reduction for no significant fault. This approach in effect treats the intentional conduct involved in evasion and refusal as showing an intentional conduct of the kind defined in Article 10.2.3 which cannot be rebutted (presumably on policy grounds). Whether the application of this four-year period of ineligibility may be challenged on the ground that it is a disproportionate penalty in certain circumstances or whether tribunals will reduce the period of ineligibility of four years applying the principle of proportionality where the athlete establishes an innocent intention in refusing is an open question. The person who intentionally refuses to submit to sample collection after notification for religious or cultural reasons, and who cannot establish compelling justification for the refusal, may be subject to four years' ineligibility in circumstances where their conduct was not intentional as defined under Article 10.2.3 and they had no intention to avoid the detection of doping.

Illustrations

Failure to Prove Notification by a Testing Authority on Facts

CAS 2008/A/1551, *WADA v. CONI, FIGC and Cherubin*   C was an Italian football player in Serie A. After a game in which his team lost 3:0, he was selected for drug testing. After being notified, he left the DCOs and went back into the team changing room, where heated discussions were being carried out with the president and coach of the club concerning the team's performance in the match. He was out of sight for about half an hour and then came back and was tested. The test was negative.

In the Italian National Tribunals, C was sanctioned for breaches of the rule about not assisting the Anti-Doping Commission rather than breaches of the Code. A one-month period of ineligibility was imposed.

WADA appealed that decision to CAS, where it contended that the player should have been charged and sanctioned under Article 2.3 of the Code. It submitted that a violation of Article 2.3 could be based on negligent or intentional conduct by the athlete. The Panel held that the allegation had not been made out on the facts. There were factual issues as to what had occurred at the end of the match. On the evidence, the Panel was not satisfied that C had been notified in the required manner that he was not to leave the anti-doping station. This meant that he had not been clearly told in a way which enabled him to understand that he would be in breach of his duties and would be refusing if he did so. The evidence did not clearly show that the player had been spoken to before he went off on his own initiative to be involved in the after-match discussions in the changing rooms.

Failure to Submit – No Compelling Jurisdiction

AAA No. 30 190 00814 02, *Ina* **v.** *United States Anti-Doping Agency (USADA)*   I was an elite ice skater who USADA was to test on a no-advance-notice basis. After a first attempt had been declared a missed test, I provided daily faxes of her schedule. A DCO went to her house at 10.30 pm. She refused to provide a sample. On a further occasion, I provided a sample, which, on analysis, produced a negative analytical finding. USADA proposed a four-year suspension under the ISU Anti-Doping Code which applied for a refusal at the time. I claimed that there were procedural defects, that the late-night visit was a breach of her privacy and that she had not been clearly informed by the DCO of the possible sanction so that her refusal was not absolute. On the facts, the AAA Panel found that, on the wording of the ISU violation, there had been a refusal and that none of the points justified the refusal. There was no 'compelling justification' for a refusal under Article 2.3.

CAS 2004/A/714, *Fazeckas* **v.** *IOC*   F was tested after winning the discus at the 2004 Athens Olympic Games. Despite a 'plurality of attempts', F did not provide an adequate sample. He said he did not feel good and did not accept the opportunity to go to the medical centre to finish the process. The IOC decided that there had been a refusal. F was disqualified and had to return his gold medal. He appealed to CAS (in its Ad Hoc Division) on the basis of defects in the IOC hearing and the testing notification process. He also claimed that he had justification to refuse the sample because of 'psychological factors caused by the conduct of the witnesses and the mood of doping control'. CAS heard all the witnesses to the process and further new evidence in exercising its power to carry out a full review of the facts and law on appeal. CAS adopted the established position that such a process on appeal would cure any defect in the process before the IOC, although CAS found that the process had been carried out properly in accordance with the IOC Athens Rules. Where a partial sample was provided, there was a failure to submit to sample collection and, on the facts, the athlete could show no 'compelling justification' for the failure.

Evading Doping Control

CAS 2004/A/718, *Annus* v. *IOC*   CAS, sitting in the Ad Hoc Division established for the Athens Olympics, heard an appeal by a Hungarian hammer-thrower, A, who had won the hammer-throw at the Games. A provided a urine sample after the Olympic final, and there was no adverse analytical finding. He left the Olympic Village to drive home by car to Hungary. At that time, the organising committee for the Games sought to serve a doping control notification on A but could not do so. Whereabouts information was requested by the IOC from the Hungarian Olympic Committee, and telephone numbers were provided. Home details were also given and two DCOs drove to A's home in Hungary to carry out testing. They were met by a crowd of fans and felt threatened. They returned the next day, when A had left. They gave a further notification to the Hungarian Olympic Committee giving a time for doping control at the local police station. The athlete did not come. The IOC decided to disqualify A and remove his medal under the Olympic Charter, and held that disciplinary proceedings would continue into an allegation of tampering with doping control. A submitted that he had not refused a doping test and had not committed any doping violation. A appealed to CAS under the IOC doping rules relating to the Olympics. CAS held that A's conduct between the end of the competition and his failure to attend doping control was, on the facts, an evasion of doping control and that the violation had been made out.

Impossibility and Use and the Possible Application of Article
10.5.2 to Refusal under the 2004 Code

RYA Anti-Doping Tribunal, *Royal Yachting Association (RYA)* v. *Christine Johnston*   The Royal Yachting Association (RYA) alleged that J, a board sailor, had committed doping offences under its anti-doping rules, namely, the use of a prohibited substance and refusing to submit to sample collection. J had refused to submit to anti-doping control in February 2007, at a time when she regarded herself as retired. She had also signed the doping control form after refusing, indicating that she was using a cream for eczema which she believed contained a prohibited substance.

J had been looking to retire at the end of 2006. She sold her equipment in early 2007. She wrote to the RYA asking to be released from her obligation to give whereabouts information. The RYA replied by email that, as she was still in the world Top 20, she would have to continue to provide the information. By February 2007, she was no longer in the world Top 20 and regarded herself as retired. J took the email from the RYA to mean that she was no longer required to be within the testing regime when she fell outside the Top 20. At about this time, she saw her doctor and was prescribed an eczema cream which she believed contained a prohibited substance. J began using the cream in February 2007, when she believed that she was no longer subject to the drug-testing regime. When J was asked to provide a sample in an out-of-competition test in March 2007, she refused to submit to doping control.

Impossibility   As a matter of fact, the cream did not contain a prohibited substance. There could, accordingly, be no violation of using a prohibited substance. The RYA sought to establish an attempt. On the alleged attempt to use a prohibited substance, the tribunal considered whether it was possible to attempt to use a prohibited substance where the substance used was not a prohibited substance. The tribunal did not decide this point, but found that an attempt could not be proved where J did not believe that she was in the anti-doping regime and, in the circumstances, could not be said to have made an intentional knowing attempt. The Anti-Doping Tribunal found that there was common ground that there was a refusal, and that J was, in fact, still subject to the anti-doping regime. She had to show 'compelling justification' for the refusal. The email exchange, which concerned whereabouts information, could not be interpreted as providing 'compelling justification' for the refusal.

No Significant Fault or Negligence   On the question whether the fixed sanction of two years could be reduced because there was no significant fault or negligence, the tribunal held that, where there was an intentional refusal, it would be a very rare case where an athlete could establish no significant fault or negligence. J's belief that she was retired was not capable of satisfying the requirements for establishing no significant fault or negligence. This approach confused the reason for the refusal with the refusal itself, and the claim that there was no significant fault had to relate to the refusal itself. There could be no reduction in the period of ineligibility on the basis that J was not significantly at fault or negligent.

No Justification and No Defence under Articles 10.5.1 and
10.5.2 of the 2009 Code

Irish Anti-Doping Appeal Panel, *WADA* v. *Irish Sport Anti-Doping Disciplinary Panel and Julie McHale*, 29 July 2010   M was a very experienced and successful kick-boxer. She was subject to the Irish Anti-Doping Rules. On 8 September 2008, anti-doping officers called unannounced at her home at about 5.50 pm. M declined to furnish a sample as requested because she was on her way to a meeting with a very important customer of her employer. She had recently begun a new job and had a potential new client. She did not want to be late for the meeting. She offered to give a sample later, at 8.00 pm. The anti-doping officers explained the possible consequences of refusal and suggested that they could accompany her to the meeting and she could give the sample afterwards.

It was alleged that there had been a breach of Article 2.3 of the Irish Anti-Doping Rules. The decision of the Irish Anti-Doping Disciplinary Panel was to the effect that a breach had occurred, but the athlete had established no fault or negligence. This Panel imposed a three-month period of ineligibility.

On appeal to the Irish Sport Anti-Doping Panel, the Panel held that the 2007 Rules applied to the matter. In the 2007 Rules, the provision required the athlete to establish justification for the refusal rather than 'compelling justification'.

Under the 2007 Rules, the provision dealing with no fault or negligence appeared according to the Appeal Panel to be limited and not applicable to a violation of Article 2.3. Under the 2009 version of the Rules, the provision was not so confined. Accordingly, on the principles of *lex mitior*, M was entitled to have the question whether she had shown no fault or negligence or no significant fault or negligence considered.

The Panel first held that it was not possible to exercise a discretion as to the period of ineligibility if no fault was established – the sanction of three months' ineligibility was not available. If the athlete did establish no fault or negligence, then the period of ineligibility had to be eliminated. On consideration of the evidence, the Panel held that it was very difficult to work out how the idea of no fault or negligence could ever apply where the athlete deliberately refused to give a sample and had no compelling justification for this. The tribunal accepted that the defences under Articles 10.5.1 and 10.5.2 might possibly apply, but held that they could not be established in the circumstances of this matter. The circumstances were not exceptional and M's fault in refusing the test could not be regarded as sufficiently small as not to be significant. The tribunal held that there was no further residual discretion in the matter (in dealing with an argument based upon the principle of proportionality based on the CAS award in *Puerta v. ITF*). A two-year period of ineligibility was imposed from a date which took into account some delay in the process of having the matter heard.

Article 2.4: Whereabouts Failures

The violation under Article 2.4 requires consideration of the rules set out in Annex I of the ISTI. The violation will be committed where an athlete who is in a registered testing pool commits any combination of three missed tests and/or filing failures as defined in Annex I ISTI within a period of twelve months.[76] The requirements for this violation can only be understood by reference to the provisions in Annex I ISTI, which set out the requirements for the provision of whereabouts information, for missed tests and filing failures and for results management in relation to those breaches in detail. The whereabouts regime is an important part of the testing regime under the Code and operates to support one of the important aims of the Code – testing athletes on a no-advance-notice basis.

The detail of the obligations to file whereabouts information and to be available for testing in a sixty-minute time slot are set out in detail in ISTI and have been outlined in Chapter 3, pages 135–8.

Where an allegation of a breach of Article 2.4 is brought, the anti-doping organisation has to prove each whereabouts breach before the relevant tribunal to the required standard of comfortable satisfaction under Article 3.1.

It is submitted that the conditions applicable before a filing failure or missed test can be recorded, which are set out in ISTI Annex I 3.6 (a)–(d) and 4.3 (a)–(e), are mandatory requirements which the national anti-doping organisation must establish in order to prove a breach (if the findings recorded after the results management process under Annex I are challenged) before the tribunal hearing the allegation of breach of Article 2.4.

Only athletes who have been included in a registered testing pool by an anti-doping organisation can commit a whereabouts violation. An athlete remains responsible for his or her whereabouts filing where he or she has delegated the task to another person (although the delegation may provide the basis for the athlete to rebut the presumption of negligence). The third

---

76 The period for counting violations has been shortened in the 2015 Code from eighteen to twelve months. The transitional provision in the ISTI seek to give athletes the full benefit of the change in the Code by providing that any missed test or filing failure which occurred before 1 January 2015 will no longer count for the purposes of a breach of Article 2.4 twelve months after the date on which it occurred. See ISTI I1.4.

party who has been given the responsibility cannot be liable for a whereabouts breach, but could be liable for other violations – such as tampering with doping control under Article 2.5 or complicity under Article 2.9 – if he or she was involved in assisting the athlete in avoiding whereabouts requirements.

An athlete included in a registered testing pool has to be notified of his or her inclusion in the pool, the whereabouts requirements which he or she must comply with and the consequences of non-compliance. Athletes in registered testing pools have to file whereabouts information as specified in the ISTI on a quarterly basis and must be available for testing in the sixty-minute time slot which they specify in the information filed. An athlete may commit a filing failure by not filing the required information or by filing inadequate information.

A filing failure can only be declared where the athlete was duly notified of his or her inclusion in the registered testing pool, of the whereabouts requirements and of the consequences of non-compliance, where there was a failure to provide the required whereabouts information, where the failure to comply was at least negligent and, in the case of a second or third failure, where the athlete has been given notice of the previous failure (and, where deficient whereabouts information had been provided, has been given notice of the obligation to file the required whereabouts information by a specific deadline to avoid further filing failures). The occurrence of the failure is presumed to be negligent where the athlete has been notified of the requirements but has not complied with them, unless the athlete proves that no negligence on his or her part caused or contributed to the failure.

There will be a whereabouts failure in the form of a missed test where an athlete is not available for testing at the location and in the sixty-minute time slot specified in the whereabouts filing. Again, a missed test can only be declared by the organisation managing the whereabouts information if the athlete received notice of inclusion in the registered testing pool and was informed that he or she would be liable for a missed test if he or she was unavailable for testing in the sixty-minute time slot, if a DCO attempted to test the athlete in the sixty-minute time slot on a given day at the place specified in the whereabouts information, if the DCO did what was reasonable to try and locate the athlete at the specified location in the time slot (short of giving the athlete advance notice of the test), if the athlete has received notice of any previous unsuccessful attempt (if the alleged missed test was within a sixty-minute time slot during which there had been a previous unsuccessful attempt to locate the athlete) and if the athlete's failure was at least negligent. Again, if the other conditions for a missed test are established, the failure of the athlete will be presumed to be negligent. This presumption can be rebutted by the athlete if he or she establishes that no negligent behaviour on his or her part caused or contributed to the failure to be available.

Each alleged breach will be subject to a results management process by the anti-doping organisation with which the athlete files his or her whereabouts information. This process, which is outlined in Chapter 3, can involve an administrative review of the decision to record a whereabouts breach.

Where three whereabouts failures are recorded against the athlete in a twelve-month period, the organisation which has responsibility for the whereabouts information must bring an allegation of breach of Article 2.4 against the athlete.[77] If this is not done within thirty days of WADA receiving notice of the third finding, this is deemed to be a decision that there had been no violation committed for the purpose of the appeal rights under Article 13.2.

An athlete who is alleged to have committed a breach of Article 2.4 has a right to a full hearing of the allegation. The previous determinations of breaches made by the organisation managing the whereabouts information and any administrative review are not binding on the tribunal hearing the allegation. The athlete is free to challenge any of the alleged breaches and to have a full hearing on every aspect of each alleged breach. The anti-doping organisation will have to prove the requirements for the findings of breach under Annex I to the comfortable satisfaction of the tribunal, although the presumption of causative negligence which is established where the other conditions for a finding are met will mean that, in most cases, the athlete will carry a burden of showing that he or she was not negligent in any way which can be said to be causative of the breach.

77 It is submitted that the anti-doping organisation has no discretion whether to bring forward an anti-doping rule violation under the ISTI if, after the required results management processes have been carried out, there are three breaches in twelve months. The language of the ISTI is mandatory ('shall'), and this absence of discretion is consistent with the general position that where an anti-doping organisation concludes that in its view a violation has been committed after it has reviewed the results of testing or an investigation, it has no discretion to decide not to bring the allegation forward. It is submitted that this is the general position under the Code. Where an anti-doping organisation reaches the view that it has evidence which it considers will establish an anti-doping rule violation, it must bring the allegation forward before the relevant tribunal. See further Chapter 7, pages 306–10.

As has been outlined,[78] the ISTI provides the detailed regime for the provision of whereabouts information and for the management of results by anti-doping organisations where failures to provide the information or missed tests under the regime are reported. This standard approach, mandated by the ISTI, has replaced a variety of differing whereabouts regimes in sports rules.

Article 2.4 covers a wide range of conduct – both intentional (e.g. deliberately failing to provide whereabouts information to avoid testing) and negligent (e.g. simply forgetting to provide whereabouts information). Where deliberate conduct is involved, the whereabouts failures may also provide the basis to prove violations of evading sample collection or tampering with doping control under Articles 2.3 and 2.5.[79]

If one or other of the alleged filing failures or missed tests is not proved, there will be no violation under Article 2.4, although those filing failures or missed tests which are proved will continue to count against the athlete until such time as they stop counting by the running of time.

Delegation to a third party of the responsibility to file whereabouts information under the ISTI by an athlete does not mean that a national anti-doping organisation or international federation can satisfy its obligations to notify alleged breaches of the whereabouts requirements to the athlete by notifying the third party. As has been outlined, the athlete remains responsible for whereabouts obligations, and it is the athlete who has to be notified for there to be a breach which counts under Article 2.4.

Illustrations

Early Case – Negligent Failures Leading to Missed Tests

CAS 2006/A/1165, *Ohuruogu* v. *UK Athletics Ltd* O was an international 400 metres runner in the registered testing pool of UK Athletics (UKA). O gave her schedule details to UKA as required, but changed the schedule and did not notify changes on three occasions, and was not available for testing where her schedule indicated she would be. She was found guilty of an anti-doping rule violation by a UKA committee. She was declared ineligible for competition for one year in accordance with the

---

78 See Chapter 3, pages 135–41.
79 For an example of engaging in deliberately misleading whereabouts filings so as to avoid testing and committing violations under Articles 2.3 and 2.5, see *DFSNZ* v. *Ciancio* ST 03/14 at pages 240–1.

UKA rules.[80] She appealed to CAS, under IAAF Rules (as an international-level athlete, she was entitled to appeal the UKA decision to CAS). O submitted that the rules should be interpreted as not being triggered simply by a failure to attend tests, but rather by the athlete being notified of three failures to attend after evaluation by UKA. In support of this, it was submitted that rules should be strictly construed, given their penal nature. It was also submitted that the sanction in the UKA rules was disproportionate and not in line with the penalties for such violations under other sports rules. For UKA, it was submitted that, while the athlete was notified of each missed test evaluation, it was not a requirement that each test be notified before there could be a further evaluation in relation to another missed test. The Panel held that an evaluation of three missed tests by UKA was all that was required on construction of the rules. There was no requirement that the athlete had to be notified of evaluation for a missed test before a further missed test could be declared.

The Panel held that the sanction was not disproportionate or inappropriate, given the importance of out-of-competition testing and the need for athletes to provide accurate whereabouts information and attend for tests if the anti-doping regime were to be effective.

> The Panel concludes by noting that the burden on an athlete to provide accurate and up-to-date whereabouts information is, no doubt, onerous. However, the anti-doping rules are necessarily strict in order to catch athletes that do cheat by using drugs and the rules can sometimes produce outcomes that may be considered unfair. *The case should serve as a warning to all athletes that the relevant authorities take the provision of whereabouts information extremely seriously as they are a vital part of the fight against drugs in sport.* [emphasis added]

Intentional Breaches of Whereabouts Rules – Amounting to Tampering

CAS 2008/A/1612, *Rasmussen v. FMC and UCI*   R was in a pool of athletes who had to provide whereabouts information. He failed to provide

---

80 A further consequence of this violation for Ms Ohuruogu was that she was banned from Olympic participation for life by the rules of the British Olympic Association (BOA). This is an example of further contractual rules applying to an athlete in addition to the Code. An appeal against the life ban to a BOA tribunal has recently been allowed. For further consideration of the question of additional sanctions imposed by sporting bodies and, in addition, the effectiveness of By-Law 45 of the Olympic Charter, see Chapter 10, pages 523–4.

whereabouts information on four occasions between May 2007 and January 2008. He was notified of the failures by the NADO and UCI. UCI asked the NADO to bring allegations of a violation of Articles 2.4 and 2.5 (tampering) against R. A tribunal held that R had deliberately provided false whereabouts information. It imposed a two-year period of ineligibility.

On appeal to CAS, CAS rejected the argument that the NADO was not competent to carry out the out-of-competition test and request the information because this should have been done by the NADO of the country where R was resident. An athlete's national NADO and the NADO of the country where he or she lives are both competent under the Code. In addition, R was subject to the rules of the international federation. Challenges to the individual breaches were rejected. R was held to have been aware of the consequences of failure to meet his obligations, and it was held that he had deliberately lied about his location. His conduct had directly led to avoiding tests.

In those circumstances, R, in addition to his failure to provide whereabouts information, was guilty of tampering with doping control contrary to Article 2.5. R's plea for a reduced sanction on the basis he had provided assistance in relation to conduct by team members was rejected.

Requirements for a Missed Test under the IST

CAS 2014/A/2, *DFSNZ* v. *Gemmell*   G was charged with a breach of Article 2.4 in 2014 after three breaches of whereabouts requirements in eighteen months under the IST Annex I (the provisions under the 2009 Code).

The dispute before the NZ Sports Tribunal concerned one of the breaches and the requirement to establish a breach under the applicable provisions of IST. The Sports Tribunal held that because the DCO had not tried to call the athlete's mobile at the end of the sixty-minute time slot, the anti-doping organisation had not done what was reasonable to locate the athlete, so that one of the requirements for a whereabouts breach for a missed test had not been established. As a result, the tribunal held that there was no violation of Article 2.4 because only two breaches of the whereabouts rules had been established.

The national anti-doping organisation appealed to CAS. CAS held that the tribunal had proceeded on an incorrect interpretation of the whereabouts regime in the IST. The regime was expressly based on the need for no-advance-notice testing. On the proper interpretation of the IST, there was no mandatory obligation on the DCO to try and call the athlete's mobile to meet the requirements of taking reasonable steps to locate the athlete at the address given in his whereabouts filing. Interpreting the IST as requiring that the athlete be called on a mobile was inconsistent with the requirement for no-advance-notice testing which underpinned the Code, the IST and the whereabouts rules. While making a mobile phone call could be an option which an anti-doping organisation might adopt, there was no failure to meet the requirements under the IST in the anti-doping organisation's not instructing the DCO to take this step.

In the circumstances (on the basis that the athlete was at the given whereabouts address), it was the responsibility of the athlete to be available for testing, and the DCO had taken reasonable steps to locate him by ringing the bell and waiting for sixty minutes. Accordingly, there was a whereabouts breach in the athlete's not being available for testing.

G also argued that he should have the benefit of the provisions of 2015 Code and be exonerated because the 2015 Code, when it came into force, would amend Article 2.4 to provide that a violation would be committed where there were three breaches of the whereabouts regime in twelve months, not eighteen months. At the time of the breaches, the 2009 Code was in force, and the position was the same at the time of the hearing of the allegation. The Sports Tribunal and CAS both found that G could not have the benefit of the new Article 2.4 in the 2015 Code where it was not yet in force. G's offending had to be considered on the rules applicable at the time of the breaches. The doctrine of *lex mitior* could not apply where the new rules were not in force. Further, CAS confirmed that it had only ever applied the doctrine of *lex mitior* to changes in the rules which changed the sanctions for a violation, as opposed to the substantive requirements for a violation.

CAS held that three breaches of the whereabouts requirements had been proven, and accordingly a violation of Article 2.4 was established.

On considering the nature of the whereabouts breaches in order to arrive at the period of ineligibility, CAS held that two of the breaches involved understandable carelessness rather than being inexcusable, which meant that CAS had to assess the seriousness of the violation overall. CAS imposed a period of fifteen months' ineligibility by reference to the seriousness of the violation.

Subsequently, after the coming into force of the 2015 Code, G applied to the New Zealand Sports Tribunal for a reduction of the period of ineligibility under the transitional provisions in Article 25.3 of the 2015 Code. This application was granted by the Sports Tribunal, which held that the application under Article 25.3 was available. Article 25.3 was not limited to cases where the doctrine of *lex mitior* was applicable. The tribunal considered that it was appropriate to reduce the ban to twelve months.[81]

Evading and Tampering with Sample Collection by Filing False Whereabouts Information – Second Violation under the 2015 Code

DFSNZ v. *Ciancio* ST 03/14 24 June 2015   C was a weightlifter in the registered testing pool of his NADO. On several occasions, he had provided last-minute updates to his whereabouts information, changing his sixty-minute time slot from a city address to a country address 100 km away, which could not be reached from the city address in the sixty-minute slot. The relevant anti-doping organisation attended both addresses, as well as the address given as his training address, simultaneously during the athlete's sixty-minute slot, but C could not be located at any of them. The rural property given as a work address appeared to be unoccupied. On investigation, neighbours who shared a driveway said that they had never seen C there.

C was charged with breaches of Articles 2.3 (evading) and 2.5 (tampering). Both allegations were made on the basis that C had provided misleading whereabouts information over a four-month period, during which time he had updated his whereabouts information some thirty-five times to give the rural property as his work address at or around the time of his daily sixty-minute time slot. After several adjournments for the completion of other anti-doping proceedings against C, the Sports Tribunal considered the evidence against C and found the violations proved. The tribunal concluded that the 'inevitable and irresistible conclusion was that C was engaged in a systematic plan to avoid the requirements to which he was subject'.

Second Violation – 2015 Code – Lex Mitior   C's violations were second violations – a period of ineligibility of seven years had been imposed for the earlier violations of possessing and trafficking in prohibited substances, starting from 24 November 2012.

C was held to be entitled to be dealt with under the 2015 Code, which was in force at the time of the hearing. His conduct (he had sought several adjournments of the hearing) did not disqualify him from relying on *lex mitior*. Under the 2009 Code (which was in force at the time of the violations), he would have received a lifetime period of ineligibility for his

81 *Gemmell* v. *DFSNZ* ST 01/15 26 January 2015.

second violation. Under the 2015 Code, the period of ineligibility for the second violation was assessed in accordance with Article 14.7.1 and was held to be eight years (double the period for the violation treated as a first violation). The period of ineligibility could not be made to run consecutively under the Code/rules and was ordered to start from the time of the hearing – June 2014.

No Violation under Article 2.4 where Athlete not Notified of Breaches

CAS 2011/A/2499, *Albert Subirats* v. *FINA* S, a swimmer and a member of the registered testing pool of his international federation, FINA, submitted his whereabouts form to his national swimming federation (VSF). VSF failed to forward its forms in 2010. FINA notified VSF of the failure. VSF only notified S after the third violation. The FINA doping panel held that S had committed a violation and imposed a one-year period of ineligibility and disqualified his results.

Before CAS, the finding was set aside. While S was responsible for the failure to file the forms, notwithstanding the delegation of the task to VSF, it was not sufficient for notice to be given to VSF. FINA had to notify S personally. The delegation of the obligation to file the information did not, on the application of the IST, extend to the giving of notices of failure.

Article 2.5: Tampering or Attempted Tampering with any Part of Doping Control

This violation prohibits conduct which subverts the doping control process in any way, but which is not within the definition of prohibited methods under the Prohibited List. The elements of this violation are:

- altering for an improper purpose or in an improper way, bringing improper influence to bear, interfering improperly, obstructing, misleading or engaging in any fraudulent conduct to alter results or prevent normal procedures from occurring or purposely engaging in conduct that constitutes a substantial step in a course of conduct planned to culminate in the occurrence of one of the above
- any part of the process of doping control which includes all steps and processes from test distribution planning to ultimate disposition of any appeal including all steps and processes in between such as the provision of whereabouts information, sample collection and handling, laboratory analysis, TUE, results management and hearings.

Article 2.5 (in wording added by the 2015 Code into the Article itself) confirms that tampering includes, without limitation, intentionally interfering or attempting to interfere with a doping control official, providing fraudulent information to an anti-doping organisation and intimidating or attempting to intimidate a potential witness. This express provision reflects the importance placed in the 2015 Code and ISTI on the conduct of investigations by anti-doping organisations and the importance of maintaining the integrity of those investigations.

The broad scope of doping control as defined in the Code and the definition of tampering in Article 2.5 means that this violation can cover a very wide range of conduct which interferes with any aspect of the operations of an anti-doping organisation under the Code. The words added in the 2015 Code highlight conduct which might involve bribery or deliberate fraudulent conduct in the context of testing or investigations – this could cover putting forward a position or case which is intentionally misleading to investigators or a tribunal which hears an allegation. The provisions of the ISTI also expressly state that those who provide misleading information in the course of an investigation should be the subject of charges of tampering or attempted tampering in breach of Article 2.5.[82]

Conduct by athletes which generally involves tampering with the testing process is referred to in the Prohibited List under Prohibited Methods M2 and would give rise to a violation under Article 2.2.[83] Some further examples of conduct that would fall under Article 2.5 would be altering identification numbers on a doping control form,[84] bribing or threatening members of an anti-doping organisation considering a charge of a doping violation and deliberately misleading anti-doping organisations by providing false information as to whereabouts.[85] The text of the Article contains no express provision concerning the persons who may commit the violation. Although tampering which falls within the scope of the prohibited method under the List can only be committed by an athlete, the

---

82 ISTI 12.3.5. While Article 2.5 contains no express provision, it is submitted that the intentional nature of the violation of tampering means that in the context of making statements in investigations a person should be given express notice that giving a false statement in an interview will amount to tampering before an allegation of tampering by providing fraudulent information can be brought.

83 Use of devices to 'doctor' urine samples would lead to an adverse finding and a doping violation for using a prohibited method under Article 2.2.

84 See also the notes to Article 2.5.

85 See e.g. the *Rasmussen* case at pages 237–8. Annex I ISTI expressly provides for this possibility at I.3.4.

violation under Article 2.5 can be committed by any person who is subject to the Code.[86]

The nature of the violation means that an element of intentional conduct must be established to prove a violation of Article 2.5. It is submitted that this does not require an intention to interfere with the process of doping control in order to conceal doping violations or affect the results, but simply an intention to interfere deliberately with any part of the doping control process so as to prevent it from taking its normal proper course. By way of example, an athlete who did not believe in drug testing would commit a violation under Article 2.5 if he or she interfered with some aspect of doping control as a protest.[87]

As with attempted use under Article 2.2, where an allegation of attempted tampering is brought, there will be a mental requirement in the violation. The anti-doping organisation must prove that the athlete or other person purposely engaged in conduct that constitutes a substantial step in the course of conduct planned to culminate in tampering with any part of doping control. If a person renounces an attempt prior to the attempt being discovered by a third party not involved in the attempt, then that person will not have committed an anti-doping rule violation based solely on that attempt.

Illustrations

Manipulation as a Prohibited Method Established by Drawing Inferences: Pre-Code CAS Awards

CAS 98/211, _B_ v. _FINA_, Award of 7 June 1999, CAS Digest II B was alleged to have manipulated a sample by pouring whisky into it. The evidence from the sample collection session was found to support the allegation of manipulating a sample by pouring whisky into it. The laboratory analysis showed 'unequivocal signs of alteration. The content of alcohol in the sample is in no way compatible with human consumption and the sample shows a very strong whisky odour.' In circumstances where

---

86 This is supported by the definition of 'attempt' applicable to an attempt to tamper with doping control, which contains a reference to a 'person' as well as an athlete.

87 The penalty for the violation of tampering is a four-year period of ineligibility. This period of ineligibility can be reduced to a minimum of two years under the specific prompt admission provision which applies under Article 10.6.3. The defence of no significant fault has no application because the violation involves intent. For an example of tampering in the context of the provision of whereabouts information, see _DFSNZ_ v. _Ciancio_ at pages 240–1.

the athlete had not been observed at all times during the sampling process (as B should have been), the appellant had had the opportunity to manipulate the sample. The inference drawn was that the sample had been contaminated by the athlete. B was found to have committed a violation of the FINA Rules. The report from the laboratory also suggested the administration of some metabolic precursor of testosterone and recommended a follow-up. The appeal from the FINA Panel decision to CAS was dismissed. It should be noted that the general standard of proof was confirmed in this award. The CAS Panel held that to adopt a criminal standard 'at any rate where the disciplinary charge is not a criminal offence' is to confuse the public law of the State with the private law of an association.

CAS 2004/A/607, Galabin Boevski v. IWF B was a Bulgarian weightlifter. He and other weightlifters were tested out-of-competition by an international DCO of the International Weightlifting Federation (IWF). Samples of urine were taken from the athletes. The urine samples from B and two others, which were sealed and sent to the laboratory, were found to be the same urine. B had been the subject of a previous sanction of two years' ineligibility. The IWF determined that the samples had been manipulated, and notified the BWF of its finding. The BWF appealed to the IWF and, after an obviously deficient process, the BWF agreed that two of the athletes would receive an eighteen-month ban and B would be given an eight-year ban (instead of the life ban provided for in the rules). B appealed to CAS. CAS re-heard the allegation of manipulation by hearing the witnesses afresh, thereby curing the defective process in the inferior tribunals. The CAS Panel had to decide whether the allegation of manipulation had been established. The choice lay between manipulation from the time of the passing of the sample until the sealing of the samples in Berlingerei jars and manipulation while the samples were in the custody of the anti-doping organisation in the jars. The Panel held that, as the athletes had not been constantly observed, there had been no check for the use of any device by B or another athlete at the time of sampling which might have provided other urine as the sample and there was no evidence that the Berlingerei jars had been tampered with after sealing, the Panel was comfortably satisfied that the manipulation had been carried out by B in the period before the samples were sealed. The appeal was dismissed. The eight-year period of ineligibility was maintained.

Use of a Prohibited Method – Investigation
of Manipulation of Samples

CAS 2008/A/1718, *IAAF* v. *All Russia Athletic Federation and Yegorova and Others* The IAAF became concerned at irregularities in the out-of-competition testing programme conducted in Russia. The irregularity concerned certain Russian athletes in the registered testing pool. The athletes had suspicious blood profiles and there were significantly lower numbers of missed tests in out-of-competition testing among the Russian athletes when compared with other national groups. The IAAF was concerned that the requirement for no-notice out-of-competition testing was not being fully observed in Russia, leaving the doping control process open to manipulation.

The IAAF investigated the possible manipulation of samples collected under the out-of-competition testing regime. It compared the DNA profiles of out-of-competition urine samples with DNA profiles from in-competition samples from selected athletes. DNA analysis revealed that, for seven female athletes, the out-of-competition and in-competition samples presented different genetic profiles, which excluded the possibility that the same person had provided the samples.

The Russian Federation dealt with the matter and decided that it would suspend the athletes for two years from the date of the out-of-competition testing which was the foundation for the IAAF investigation. The IAAF appealed to CAS against the sanction imposed and submitted that a period of four years' ineligibility should be imposed. The athletes sought to raise new issues on the appeal and to claim that there ought not to have been a finding that they had committed an anti-doping rule violation under the IAAF Rules. This was based on challenges to the process of sample collection and DNA analysis. Those challenges were rejected on the evidence.

In support of its submission that a period of up to four years' ineligibility should have been imposed, the IAAF relied on the nature of the violation committed by the athletes and on additional evidence as to the blood profile data of the athletes, and submitted that an increased sanction of up to four years was consistent with the 2009 Code, which did not apply to the events which were subject to the allegations. It also submitted that increased sanctions of this kind were needed if the fight against doping in sport were to be successful.

CAS confirmed the general scope of the Panel's power of review on appeal and did not accept an argument that it should limit the scope of review to show deference to the decision of the tribunal which was under appeal. CAS held that, notwithstanding the absence of direct evidence of tampering, there was a clear case based on the DNA results which supported an inference of tampering. This was supported by circumstantial evidence of significant probative value. In the absence of any explanation from the athletes as to how the DNA differed between the out-of-competition and in-competition samples, CAS was entitled to find that tampering had occurred. After reviewing other tampering cases, the tribunal held, on the facts of this case, that an increased period of ineligibility of up to four years was not warranted. The scope of any doping scheme had not been uncovered. Given the uncertainties, the Panel did not consider it just and equitable to go to the upper limits of discretion as regards the length of the period of ineligibility.

The Panel decided that the appropriate sanction for the athletes was a period of ineligibility of two years and nine months. The athletes' results were disqualified from the time of the competition at which an out-of-competition sample had been tampered with.

Article 2.6: Possession of Prohibited Substances and Methods

Article 2.6 contains two principal violations at 2.6.1 and 2.6.2: possession by an athlete and possession by athlete support personnel. The sanction for the violation under Article 2.6 has been changed by Article 10.2 of the Code and, depending on whether intentional conduct as defined in Article 10.2.3 is present in the commission of the violation or not (whether deemed and not disproved or proven), the sanction for a first violation will be either four or two years' ineligibility.[88]

The requirements for the violation reflect the general approach to the concept of possession established in the criminal law of many jurisdictions, which treats possession as the intentional exercise of physical custody over a thing. Under the definition in the Code, the concept of possession encompasses both actual possession and constructive possession. The violation will be established where the anti-doping organisation proves:

- actual physical possession of a prohibited substance or prohibited method; or
- constructive possession by means of exclusive control over a prohibited substance or prohibited method or by means of exclusive control

88 See Chapter 8, pages 353–60.

over the premises in which a prohibited substance or prohibited method exists; or

- constructive possession (where there is no exclusive control) by knowledge of the presence of a prohibited substance or prohibited method coupled with an intention to exercise control over it; or
- purchase of a prohibited substance or method (including by electronic or other means).

Actual Possession

In order to establish actual possession, the anti-doping organisation will have to show the intentional exercise of physical custody over the prohibited substance or method.

Constructive Possession

Exclusive control or an intention to exercise exclusive control can establish constructive possession. There is no definition of the element of 'exclusive control', but it is submitted that this involves establishing that the person charged had complete control over the substance or method or over the premises or part of the premises in which the prohibited substance or method exists, to the exclusion of all others, or else an intention to exercise such complete control. If exclusive control is established, constructive possession can be established without proof of knowledge and intention to exercise control. Where there is no actual possession or exclusive control, the anti-doping organisation will have to establish constructive possession on the basis of an intention to exercise control over the prohibited substance or method or over the premises in which the prohibited substance or method exists. This form of constructive possession can only be established if the person charged knew about the presence of the prohibited substance or method and intended to exercise control over it.

Under each formulation of the violation, the tribunal will examine the facts established by the evidence (and any inference which can be drawn from the facts) in order to determine whether the violation has been established to the required standard.[89]

While there is no need to prove an intention to use the prohibited substance or method or any intention to enhance performance, establishing the violation, whether by actual or constructive possession, will involve

---

89 For an example of the consideration of whether possession was established by 'control' on the facts, see *Marinov* v. *ASADA* at pages 252–4.

proof of knowledge of the existence of the prohibited substance or method and an intention to exercise control over it (if there is no actual possession), unless the situation is one where 'exclusive control' can be established. It is submitted that the requirement of exclusive control should be strictly approached where the consequences of finding that it has been established are that there is, in effect, deemed knowledge and possession of the prohibited substance or method. Where others have access to premises or to the prohibited substance or method, there will be no exclusive control and an anti-doping organisation will have to prove possession in the sense of knowing custody.

It is in the area of the proof of knowing custody that experience in the general criminal law in various jurisdictions shows that difficult questions can arise in determining whether possession has been established to the required standard of proof on the facts.[90]

Purchase over the Internet: Deemed Possession

The definition of possession was extended in the 2009 Code to cover the purchase of prohibited substances or prohibited methods by adding that the purchase (including by any electronic or other means) of a prohibited substance or prohibited method constitutes possession by the person making the purchase. This means that there can be possession in circumstances where the other requirements for possession in the definition are not met. The 2015 Code seeks to confirm this by a sentence added to the comment on the definition that the act of purchasing a prohibited substance alone, whether over the Internet or otherwise, constitutes possession even where the product does not arrive, is received by another or is sent to a third party. The conclusion of a purchase represents a form of deemed possession, which is treated separately from the other forms of possession covered by the definition. This has become a relatively common form of alleged possession in anti-doping proceedings, and the relative prevalence of such allegations reflects the facts that prohibited substances are advertised extensively on the Internet, that athletes are drawn to order prohibited substances online, and that increasing numbers of purchases are being intercepted by customs authorities.[91]

90 For an illustration of the proof of possession, both actual and constructive, of a prohibited method, see CAS 2007/A/1286, *Eder* v. *IOC* and the related cases at pages 172–7.
91 This was the position which applied under the 2009 Code. The addition to the definition removes any doubt.

Substances Prohibited only In-Competition

The violations under Article 2.6.1 against an athlete and Article 2.6.2 against an athlete support person each cover possession in-competition of any prohibited substance or method (whether banned in-competition only or both in- and out-of-competition) and possession out-of-competition of a substance or method which is prohibited out-of-competition. This means that possession out-of-competition of a substance or method prohibited in-competition only will not amount to possession in breach of Article 2.6. Whether possession is in-competition or not will depend on the application of the definition in the Code, or on the rules of the international federation or event organisation designating the period of competition if specific rules are applicable.

The violation can be committed by athletes (under Article 2.6.1) or by athlete support personnel where possession is in connection with athlete competition or training (under Article 2.6.2). Athlete support personnel are defined broadly to cover 'any coach, trainer, manager, agent, team staff, official medical or para-medical personnel working with or treating athletes participating in or preparing for sports competition'.[92]

To establish a violation of Article 2.6, an anti-doping organisation may need to establish knowledge of the presence of the prohibited substance or method which is said to be 'possessed' by the athlete or athlete support person under Article 2.6 as already outlined, but it is submitted that it is not necessary to prove that the person allegedly in possession knew that the substance or method was prohibited under the List.[93] Knowledge of the presence of the thing itself, as opposed to its status under the Prohibited List, is required. It is submitted that this violation cannot be committed where the substance or method in the possession of the athlete or athlete support personnel is not, in fact, on the Prohibited List, even if the person believes that the substance or method is prohibited under the List. This follows from the wording of the Article – the violation differs from a violation of attempted use in this regard because it requires possession as a matter of fact of a prohibited substance or method. It cannot be committed by attempting to possess prohibited substances.

The anti-doping organisation will have to prove that the substance or method in the possession of the person charged was in fact a prohibited substance or method unless there is other evidence which supports this

---

92 See the definitions in the Code.
93 It should be noted that the sole CAS arbitrator and the CAS Panel on appeal in *Marinov* proceeded on the basis that knowledge that the thing possessed was a prohibited substance or method was required. It is submitted that this is not a requirement of the violation.

conclusion. Admissions by the person charged that they ordered a prohibited substance or method or statements from a supplier that the substance or method is contained in a package are sufficient evidence, provided they are not rebutted by other evidence and/or shown to be unreliable.[94]

If it can be proved by the athlete or athlete support person subject to the allegation that the possession is pursuant to a TUE or other acceptable justification, then there will be no violation of Article 2.6. The athlete or athlete support personnel will have to prove this defence on the balance of probabilities. There will also be a defence if the athlete or athlete support personnel in possession of the prohibited substance or prohibited method has possession pursuant to some other 'acceptable justification'. The other acceptable justification would have to be some form of medically justifiable reason to have the prohibited substance or prohibited method.[95]

No anti-doping rule violation based on possession will be committed if, prior to receiving notification of any kind that a person has committed an anti-doping rule violation, the person has taken concrete action demonstrating that they never intended to have possession and has renounced possession by expressly declaring the possession to an anti-doping organisation. It would seem that the requirements for renouncing possession are cumulative. Whether such steps have been taken will be a question of fact and will be for the person alleged to have possession to prove on the balance of probabilities.

The violation of possession falls within the provisions of Article 10, which impose a four-year period of ineligibility as a sanction for a first violation. The imposition of the four-year period of ineligibility will depend on the question whether the violation is 'intentional' or not, as defined in Article 10.2.3.[96]

Illustrations

Consideration of the Concept of Possession under the 2004 Code

CAS A4/2007, ASADA v. Andrew Wyper Proceedings were commenced by ASADA on behalf of Cycling Australia against W. W was alleged to

94 See, for an example of the consideration of a range of documentary and other evidence to prove that a prohibited substance was administered to players and used by them, CAS 2015/A/4059, *Bellchamber and Others* v. *WADA* in Chapter 8, pages 417–20.

95 The notes to the Code refer to a person having a physician's prescription for, say, buying insulin for a diabetic child, or a team doctor carrying prohibited substances in order to deal with acute or emergency situations which may arise.

96 See further Chapter 8, page 443, note 90 on sanctions.

have had constructive possession of prohibited substances and to have attempted to use prohibited substances contrary to Articles 2.2 and 2.6 of the 2004 Code.

In 2005, hGH and EPO addressed to W were intercepted in Sydney by the Department of Customs. W was subsequently charged with the criminal offence of importing prohibited imports under customs legislation. He was fined after pleading guilty. The sentence was reduced on appeal. W admitted the facts as regards the criminal offence of importing prohibited imports but disputed that the admissions in the criminal court established the violations alleged by ASADA. The sole CAS arbitrator considered various statements made by W to customs officers in the investigation of the matter. Material which had been obtained by customs on the execution of a search warrant of W's parents' home was also produced. In the search, officers located a number of documents, including emails and a plastic bag of syringes. The emails showed W making inquiries to obtain hGH and EPO. W admitted sending various emails and making inquiries about the prohibited substances, and also sending an email asking for one of the shipments which was ultimately seized by customs. W admitted ordering the intercepted package. His initial answer in interview had been that he had intended to use the product. W admitted he had ordered hGH under the brand name Somatropin. When asked what his intention was in placing the order he said that it was, he supposed, to take the product.

Possession   The arbitrator considered whether there was constructive possession on the facts. He held that W did not have exclusive control over the prohibited substance where it was in the custody and control of the postal authorities. The arbitrator then considered whether the definition of constructive possession was fulfilled. He held that W did have an intention to exercise control but that the evidence was insufficient to establish knowledge of the presence of the prohibited substances for the purposes of exercising control over them. Accordingly, the allegation that W had been in possession of the prohibited substances was rejected.

Attempted Use   On the question of whether there was an attempted use, it was submitted that W's acts were merely preparatory and they were not substantial steps taken towards the use of a prohibited substance. This was based on the approach to attempt under the criminal law. The arbitrator found there was no need for W to have obtained possession of the substances before he could take substantial steps in the course of conduct planned to culminate in the commission of an anti-doping rule violation. The arbitrator held that W's conduct as a whole, when all the circumstances were examined, established that he intended to use the substances after they had been delivered to him and that he had purposely engaged in a series of acts which amounted to substantial steps in the course of conduct. This began with researching the effects of consuming hGH and EPO and continued with ordering and paying for them, and it would, the arbitrator held, have led to the consumption of those substances by W had they not been intercepted by customs.

On the plain, ordinary meaning of the words used in the definition of 'attempt' in the Code, the arbitrator found that the requirements of the definition were satisfied. The anti-doping rule violation had been made out and W was subject to a two-year period of ineligibility. The start date was put back by reason of some delay not attributable to the athlete in the results management process.

Proof of Possession on Facts

CAS A1/2007, *Australian Sports Anti-Doping Authority (ASADA)* v. *Sevdalin Marinov (Sole Arbitrator)* In November 2003, M was head coach of the Australian weightlifting team under the control of the Australian Weightlifting Federation (AWF). He was bound by the anti-doping policy of the AWF. ASADA had power to investigate possible violations of anti-doping rules. The AWF referred investigations and all related aspects to ASADA. M had been a successful competitor. He had, however, previously been suspended for two years for using a prohibited substance. He had retired and begun coaching.

In a police search of a house owned by another person, three packets each containing a prohibited substance were found on the top shelf of a wardrobe in a bedroom used by M. The three packets were labelled as steroids and, on analysis, the substances in them were identified as anabolic steroids. The owner of the house was charged with several criminal offences, including trafficking in the substances in the three packets. He pleaded guilty to the offences. There were no fingerprints on the packages and no DNA tests were conducted on them. There was no evidence that the packets were the property of M or that he had placed the packets on the shelf.

M was charged with the violation of trafficking in the prohibited substance under the AWF policy and faced a possible life ban for a second doping offence. The allegation was referred to CAS in its Ordinary Division under the AWF policy. The law relating to the substantive aspects of the matter was the law of the State of Victoria, Australia. The policy provided that a person committed a doping offence if they were knowingly involved in trafficking. Trafficking was defined by reference to conduct relating to prohibited substances, and this included 'accepting, possessing, holding …a prohibited substance …other than for personal use'.[97]

The anti-doping organisation contended that trafficking would be established under the policy by proof of possession of the prohibited substances. It submitted that, in the circumstances of the case, M was in possession of the prohibited substances.

The arbitrator held that the word 'possession' should be given its ordinary meaning in the contextual setting of the AWF policy and its obligations. He found that possession involved custody or control of the thing allegedly possessed, with knowledge of its presence. On the wording of the particular policy, only proof of 'possession' was required for the offence of trafficking to be established. There was no need to prove an element of distributing prohibited substances or methods to third parties in order to prove trafficking on the words of the policy.

The question for the arbitrator was whether the evidence could establish that M was in possession of the prohibited substances. There was no evidence as to how the packets came to be on the shelf and M denied having seen the packages during the period when he occupied the room. The anti-doping organisation put forward its case on the basis that, of the possible explanations for the presence of the prohibited substances, the only one which was properly available was that M knew of their presence at all times. The arbitrator found that M was in sole occupation of the bedroom at the time of the search and had not moved out as he contended. He found that M's exclusive occupation meant that he had custody or control (possession) of all the contents of the room, including the three packages. The arbitrator further found that M would have been able to see the packets on the shelf in the wardrobe, and that, if they were on the shelf when he first occupied the room in August 2003, he would have seen them and would have seen that they were marked as prohibited substances. The arbitrator relied on the control of the room and its contents to find that M knew that the packets were on the shelf of the wardrobe, that he knew they contained prohibited substances and that he had the power to remove them and was, as a consequence of these matters, in possession of the packages. He rejected the possible explanations put forward on behalf of M, namely, that either the packets had been there since he had moved into the room in

97 This 'deeming' definition must be contrasted with the definition in the Code, which more closely mirrors the meaning of the word 'trafficking'.

August 2003 and he had not seen them or become aware of them, or they were put there after he left the house to go to Canada on 11 November 2003, before being found in the police search on 14 November. As a consequence, the arbitrator found that the charge against M was made out. He held that the sanction of ineligibility for life under the policy was applicable and ordered M to contribute to the costs of ASADA under Rule 64.5 of the CAS Procedural Rules.

CAS 2007/A/1311, *Marinov* v. *ASADA* (on Appeal)   The CAS Panel sitting in the Appeal Division held that the sole arbitrator had held correctly that the particular doping policy only required proof of possession for trafficking to be established, and had correctly approached the application of the standard of proof. However, the Panel found that the arbitrator had fallen into error in finding that the manner in which M occupied the room could be described as giving rise to exclusive occupation so that he had custody and control of the prohibited substances in the room. M could not be described as exclusively controlling the room with the powers of control over its contents, including the prohibited substances, where he occupied as a bare licensee and others had access to it, most notably the occupier of the house, who had pleaded guilty in the criminal court to offences relating to the packages. The case advanced by ASADA that M knew of the packages at all times was not enough to establish the violation if control over the drugs by the exclusive occupation of the room could not be established. Even if there was the ability to control the drugs, the Panel found, on the totality of the evidence, that it could not draw the inference, which the sole arbitrator had drawn, that M must have known of the presence of the drugs on the shelf. There was insufficient evidence to support the conclusion that M must have been able to see the drugs on the shelf during the time he was in the room or that he must have been able to read the labels so as to know that the packages contained prohibited substances. Even if M had the ability to exercise control over the drugs (which the Panel found was not the case), the findings of fact relating to the knowledge of the presence of the substances required to establish possession could not be sustained. The appeal was allowed and the award of the sole arbitrator set aside.

Article 2.7: Trafficking or Attempted Trafficking in any Prohibited Substance or Prohibited Method

The definition of trafficking which applies to establish the requirements for a violation under Article 2.7 is contained in the definitions to the

Code. Article 2.7 itself (in contrast to the related violation of administration under Article 2.8) contains no specific provision setting out the elements of the violation. The definition remains largely unchanged in the 2015 Code. It states that the violation can be committed by any person who is bound by the Code and that trafficking carried out need not be with a person who is bound by the Code, but can be with any third party. The elements of the violation are:

- selling, giving, administering, transporting, sending, delivering or distributing (or possessing for any of these purposes) physically or by any electronic or other means
- a prohibited substance or prohibited method
- to any third party.

However, the definition is expressed not to cover the actions of bona fide medical personnel involved in the use of the prohibited substance for genuine and legal therapeutic purposes or with another acceptable justification. This exclusion from liability under Article 2.7 would have to be established by the person alleged to be in breach on the balance of probabilities.

The definition (and accordingly the violation under Article 2.7) is further expressed not to include actions (by the person potentially subject to an allegation under Article 2.7) involving prohibited substances which are not prohibited in out-of-competition testing unless the circumstances, as a whole, demonstrate such prohibited substances are not intended for genuine and legal therapeutic purposes or are intended to enhance sport performance. The scope of the exclusion from the violation of actions involving prohibited substances which are not prohibited in out-of-competition testing is problematic. This part of the definition starts with a general exclusion from the violation for all actions involving prohibited substances which are not prohibited in out-of-competition testing, with the result that generally those actions will not constitute trafficking. This would cover actions both in-competition and out-of-competition. However, the qualifications on the exclusion (which are expressed as alternatives) appear to mean that trafficking in substances or methods which are not prohibited out-of-competition will fall within the definition if the anti-doping organisation can prove that the substances were not intended for genuine and legal therapeutic purposes or that they were intended to enhance sport performance. The breadth of the first qualification tends to remove any qualification from the violation for actions in relation to substances which are not prohibited out-of-competition because rarely will dealing with such prohibited substances in- or out-of-competition have genuine and legal therapeutic purposes. The result of this approach is that even if the actions are in relation to substances not banned out-of-competition and not linked to sport performance at all, there could be a violation under Article 2.8 because dealing in the substances in- or out-of-competition will not have genuine and legal therapeutic purposes.

On its face, this definition would appear to mean, by way of example, that any person who carries out actions which fall within the definition in relation to a recreational substance which is prohibited in-competition only (such as cannabis or cocaine), with no intention to enhance sport performance, will commit the violation of trafficking (even where the actions are carried out at a time which is out-of-competition) because the circumstances do not show the substance is being used for genuine and legal therapeutic purposes. It is submitted that if the qualifications on the general exclusion for actions taking place in relation to substances not prohibited in out-of-competition testing are interpreted in this way, they remove any real meaning from the exclusion. While difficult on the wording of the definition, it is submitted that the definition should be interpreted as requiring either that both qualifications be established, so that both the absence of genuine legal therapeutic purposes and the presence of intention to enhance sport performance have to be established (by replacing 'or' with 'and' between the two qualifications), or that the first qualification is only for the situation where there is a purported medical use and the second only for a situation where the first situation cannot apply. This approach would allow the general exclusion for actions involving substances not prohibited in out-of-competition testing to have greater practical effect.[98]

This approach would be consistent with the approach under the violation of possession in Article 2.6 – there can be no violation of possession where a person has possession of substances or methods prohibited only in-competition at a time which is out-of-competition – and with the general provisions of Article 2.8, which specify that administration cannot be committed by administering a substance out-of-competition which is

---

98 This would be consistent with the approach in other violations where actions relate to substances prohibited only in-competition. There could be no violation under Article 2.1 or 2.2 for a positive test out-of-competition for a substance banned only in-competition, and, under Article 2.6, there could be no violation for possession where the possession was in an out-of-competition situation and related to a substance or method banned in-competition only. The concept of possession is referred to in the definition of trafficking and it would seem illogical if a person could be responsible for a breach of Article 2.7 where they would not be liable under Article 2.6.

prohibited only in-competition. The problem which arises under Article 2.7 is in part the result of not having a provision in Article 2.7 which limits the violation of trafficking out-of-competition to substances which are banned at all times, both in- and out-of-competition.

It is submitted that the scope of this violation and the application of the definition should be the subject of clarification and clearer articulation in the Code. This is all the more important where anti-doping organisations are increasingly concentrating their efforts on the investigation of violations of this kind.

In order to establish the violation, an element of intentional conduct, in relation to the distribution of prohibited substances or methods, must be proven. The definition of trafficking is narrower than the definition which was contained in the OMADC and does not deem trafficking to occur where simple possession is established.[99]

Together with the violation of administration under Article 2.8, this violation is the most serious under the Code, and carries under Article 10.3.3 a period of ineligibility of four years to life for a first offence. Article 10.5.2 will not be available as a defence to the violations because both have an element of intent.[100] In cases involving systematic doping, those involved may face allegations involving a number of violations, including trafficking and administration, and these violations are likely to be the most serious.

Illustrations

Planned Team Doping – Trafficking and Other Violations

USADA v. *Bruyneel Celaya Marti* **AAA 7190022512**   This case concerned doping allegations against the team director, team physician and team trainer of the US Postal/Discovery Channel cycling team. The allegations were made on the basis of evidence given by former team mates of Lance Armstrong (which also led to the sanctions against A). B, L and M faced allegations of possession, trafficking, administration and assisting others to commit anti-doping rule violations going back beyond the

---

99 See also *ASADA* v. *Marinov* at pages 252–4 for consideration of a broader definition than contained in the 2015 Code deeming trafficking to take place where a wide range of conduct is established.

100 See Article 10.5.2 revised notes in the 2015 Code, and for further consideration of the defence and sanctions, see Chapter 8, pages 395–401.

eight-year limitation period. The violations involved the supply of EPO, blood transfusions and the use of testosterone, hGH, corticosteroids saline plasma and glycerol infusions (all substances and methods prohibited at all times) in a cycling team.

B argued that USADA had no jurisdiction over the investigation or over them. The Panel held that USADA had jurisdiction as a result of its having discovered the violations. The Panel had jurisdiction over the individuals because they were bound to the Code as a result of participation in UCI cycling events, which meant that they had objectively agreed to the possibility of arbitration over anti-doping allegations. While USADA had broken the confidentiality obligations in the arbitration process in publishing details of allegations against B in the reasoned decision against Mr Armstrong, there was no prejudice which could support the claim to have the proceedings stayed, and B and others were still able to have a fair hearing.

B did not attend the hearing. The Panel did not rule on whether it could draw inferences against B because he did not attend (in circumstances where B claimed he was entitled to assert the privilege against self-incrimination and that it would be wrong to draw any inference against him in those circumstances) because it considered that other evidence against B meant that inferences were not required in order to establish the case against him.

Relying on the evidence from former team members, the Panel held that B had trafficked and had administered prohibited substances and that he had encouraged others to commit anti-doping rule violations. The team physician had had possession of the prohibited substances, had administered them and had encouraged commission of violations, but had not trafficked in the substances. The team trainer was held to have had possession, to have trafficked and to have encouraged the violations.

The Panel was not prepared to look back further than the applicable limitation period of eight years under the 2009 Code or to apply any equitable principle from national law allowing suspension of the limitation period for fraudulent concealment.

The Panel found that B had been at the apex of a conspiracy to dope over many years and that the doctor and trainer had been instruments in the conspiracy. B was ordered to serve ten years' ineligibility, the doctor eight years and the trainer six years. The riders who provided the evidence against the team management and Mr Armstrong received six months because they had given substantial assistance to USADA.

Article 2.8: Administration or Attempted Administration to any Athlete In-Competition of any Prohibited Method or Prohibited Substance, or Administration or Attempted Administration to any Athlete Out-of-Competition of any Prohibited Method or any Prohibited Substance that is Prohibited Out-of-Competition

This Article creates the violation of administration or attempted administration of a prohibited substance or prohibited method to any athlete. Previously in the 2009 Code Article 2.8 also included the violation of complicity but this violation has now been separated from the violation of administration. It should be noted that the violation under Article 2.8 carries a higher possible sanction than the violation of complicity under Article 2.9. The violation under Article 2.8 can be committed by any person who is subject to the Code.

There was no definition of administration under the 2009 Code. The 2015 Code has retained the components of the violation as set out in the 2009 Code but has added a definition of administration. The provision of Article 2.8 itself distinguishes between administration of substances prohibited at all times and substances prohibited in- competition only. The words of the violation mean that where the administration or attempted administration occurs in circumstances where the athlete is in-competition the administration of any prohibited substance or method will bring about a violation. Where the administration or attempted administration occurs where the athlete is out-of-competition, only the administration of a prohibited method or a substance which is prohibited out-of-competition will give rise to a violation. Accordingly on the wording of Article 2.8 the administration of a substance out of competition to an athlete which is prohibited in competition only will not give rise to a violation. The definition of administration which has been added to the 2015 Code contains terms which exclude certain actions from the violation which are in similar terms to those found in the trafficking definition.

Under the 2015 Code administration is defined as follows:

> Administration: Providing, supplying, supervising, facilitating, or otherwise participating in the use or attempted use by another person of a prohibited substance or method. However, this definition shall not include the actions of bona fide medical personnel involving a Prohibited Substance or Method used for genuine and legal therapeutic or other acceptable justification and shall not include actions involving Prohibited Substances which are not prohibited in Out of Competition testing unless the circumstances

as a whole demonstrate that such Prohibited Substances are not intended
for genuine and legal therapeutic purposes or are intended to enhance
sport performance.

The first part of the definition is expressed to cover a wide range of conduct which is linked to the use or attempted use of prohibited substances
('providing, supplying, supervising, facilitating or otherwise participating'). This will cover all conduct by those who work with athletes which
has the effect of facilitating the use of prohibited substance or methods.
Those who are part of an athlete's entourage are most likely to be subject
to investigations relating to administration and trafficking and allegations
under Article 2.7, 2.8 and 2.9 (provided they are subject to the Code).

The reference to the use or attempted use of prohibited substances or
methods by reference to the defined terms for the violation under Article
2.2 has the consequence that the violation under Article 2.8 can only apply
to conduct which involves administering to athletes because only athletes
can commit the violation of use or attempted use.

The definition contains the same general exclusion as the definition of
trafficking for the actions of *bona fide* medical personnel involving the use
or attempted use of a prohibited substance or method for genuine legal and
therapeutic reasons or other acceptable justification. This will potentially
apply whether the administration occurs in competition or out of competition and will be for the person against whom the allegation is brought to
prove on the balance of probabilities.

Again, as with the trafficking the definition of administration further
provides for a general exclusion from the violation of actions which are
concerned with prohibited substances which are not prohibited in out of
competition testing unless the circumstances as a whole demonstrate that
the prohibited substances are not intended for genuine and legal therapeutic purposes or are intended to enhance sport performance. It is unclear
whether this part of the definition is intended to qualify the terms of Article 2.8 itself in some way and apply to all actions involving substances not
prohibited in out of competition testing. Read broadly the definition could
mean that the administration of a substance out of competition which is
not prohibited in out of competition testing could give rise to a violation
if the qualifications on the general exclusion are established. It is submitted that the exclusion and qualifications should be read consistently with
the terms of Article 2.8 which provides that only the out of competition
administration of substances prohibited out of competition constitutes a

violation of Article 2.8 and that the definition is concerned to delimit the actions in competition in relation to substances prohibited in competition only which will give rise to liability under Article 2.8. This means that the administration of some recreational substances in competition will only be within the violation under Article 2.8 if the anti-doping organisation proves that the circumstances of the alleged violation show either that the use of the prohibited substances was not for genuine legal or therapeutic purposes or was intended to enhance sport performance. Even if the operation of the definition is approached in this way and is limited by the express provisions setting out the scope of the violation, the terms of the qualifications appear to mean that that most if not all actions involving the administration of prohibited substances in competition which are not prohibited out of competition are likely to fall within the violation under Article 2.8. By way of example facilitating the use of recreational substances in competition where the substances are not prohibited out of competition is likely to be caught because, while the circumstances relating to the actions taken might well show that the substances were not intended to enhance sport performance, the circumstances would be likely to show that the use was not for genuine and legal therapeutic purposes thereby taking the circumstances outside the exclusion. It is submitted that even where the exclusion and qualifications in the definition are limited on their proper interpretation to the administration of substances prohibited in competition during competition, it may be preferable to interpret the qualifications in the definition as providing alternatives (as set out in the discussion of the violation of trafficking under Article 2.7) meaning that if the circumstances established either qualification there would be no violation under the Code. However it may well be that the intention of the definition in the context of Article 2.7 was to make it difficult for a person who has administered a substance in competition which is only prohibited in competition to escape possible sanction even where the administration was not intended to enhance sport performance. Again the terms of the definition and its relationship to the provisions of Article 2.8 should be clarified.

To a certain extent, the violation may overlap factually with violations under Articles 2.2 and 2.5. The difference lies in the severity of the sanction, with a first violation under Article 2.8 attracting the same period of ineligibility as a violation under Article 2.7. The provision for the reduction of the period of ineligibility under Article 10.5.2 will not be applicable because the violation involves intentional conduct.

Illustration

CAS 2009/A/1817, *WADA and FIFA* v. *Cyprus Football Association, Marques, Medeiros, Eranosian and Others*

E was the coach of a team in which M and M and others were players. E began providing certain pills to his players before games. The pills were unlabelled and were produced by the coach from a clear plastic box. E said that the pills were caffeine or vitamins. The pills were administered openly in the dressing room. Some players took the pills. Others did not. The players trusted the coach, particularly as several doping controls produced no positive tests. After a test following a match, M and M tested positive for a prohibited substance: oxymesterone, an anabolic steroid. The Cyprus Football Association (CFA) investigated the circumstances. The investigation uncovered the basic facts of the administration of the pills. As a result of the investigation, the CFA commenced disciplinary proceedings against E, M and M, but decided not to proceed against the other players, who had not been tested. Its Judicial Committee decided that M and M should be subject to a ban from matches of one year and that E should be subject to two years' ineligibility from coaching. The basis for the reduction in the standard period of two years' ineligibility for the players and of four years for E was that they had given substantial assistance to the investigation.

WADA and FIFA appealed the decisions of the CFA in relation to E, M and M and in relation to the decision not to pursue proceedings against the other players to CAS. It sought orders that the period of ineligibility of E, M and M be increased to four and two years, respectively. It sought orders that the players who had been found by the investigation to have taken the pills be subject to the same two-year period of ineligibility as M and M on the basis that the evidence from the investigation showed that they had used or attempted to use a prohibited substance.

CAS held that the applicable rules were those of FIFA which were in force at the time of the alleged violations. It found that there was no basis for M and M to establish no significant fault given that the pills had been taken blindly and without question, but found that the reduction in their sanction could be justified under the FIFA cooperation rule (which had different wording from the WADC substantial assistance provision) and that their role in being the first individuals to provide evidence to the investigation of the practice of E in supplying the pills did amount to help in exposing a doping offence by E. The CAS Panel upheld the one-year reduction applied by the CFA Judicial Committee.

As regards E, CAS held that the investigation report provided clear evidence that E had administered the prohibited substance. E had administered pills to the players where he had obtained them from a source unrelated to the producer and had made no inquiries or investigations with a doctor or any other specialist as to their content. E could not establish no significant fault where he had been extremely negligent. CAS found that the matters relied on by the Judicial Committee to reduce the sanction imposed on E did not support such a course. The fact that E had opened a civil case against the CFA in the civil courts, which he abandoned in exchange for a lesser penalty, was irrelevant. E's conduct in assisting with the investigation, providing pills for testing and having explained all the circumstances in which he had supplied the pills did not trigger the cooperation rule. He had not provided help leading to the exposure or proof of doping by another. He had not named the supplier of the pills. There was no justification for any reduction in the period of ineligibility for a violation under Article 2.8, and the period was increased to four years.

As regards the allegations against the other players, CAS held that WADA could not establish on the evidence that the players had used a prohibited substance. There was no evidence that the pills taken by the other players contained a prohibited substance. While M and M had tested positive after taking pills, other players who had taken pills had not. The Panel was not prepared to infer from the fact that M and M took pills and tested positive that all the pills administered by E contained a prohibited substance. Indeed, the possible explanation referred to in the evidence that the pills were caffeine pills contaminated with the prohibited substance meant that it was not possible to follow the process of inference relied on by WADA. Accordingly, the appeal against the decision not to open disciplinary proceedings against the other players was rejected.

Article 2.9: Complicity – Assisting, Encouraging, Aiding, Abetting, Conspiring, Covering Up or Any Other Type of Intentional Complicity Involving an Anti-doping Rule Violation, Attempted Anti-doping Rule Violation or Violation of Article 10.12.2 by Another Person

This violation is broadly worded and will cover any intentional conduct which assists another to commit an anti-doping rule violation or to attempt to commit an anti-doping rule violation or to break the terms of the prohibition against participation under Article 10.12.1 which apply when a person is subject to a period of ineligibility. The reference in the violation should be to Article 10.12.3, which contains the violation of the prohibition from participation during ineligibility.

The conduct potentially covered will be any physical or psychological encouragement or assistance, any agreement to further the commission of or any conduct designed to cover up a violation or attempted violation under Article 2 or Article 10.12.3.[101] The violation, if established, attracts a significant period of ineligibility of from two to four years, depending on the seriousness of the violation. It is submitted that some form of knowing active conduct which assists in the commission of a violation should be required to establish liability.

It is submitted that a failure to report the violation of another would not give rise to liability under Article 2.9 (although it might give rise to liability under the rules of a particular sport) unless it was accompanied by some other intentional conduct which provided support for the violation. Whether an athlete who works with a coach who is subject to a period of ineligibility knowing this to be the case is liable under Article 2.8 on the basis that the coach is only able to commit a violation under Article 10.12.1 by reason of the involvement of the athlete is more difficult. It is submitted that this kind of conduct – associating with a coach who is ineligible – is intended to be covered by the prohibited association provisions of Article 2.10 and that Article 2.8 (and the increased sanction applicable) will only be applicable where the circumstances show that the athlete did more than associate with the banned coach and was actively involved in encouraging the breach of a period of ineligibility by a coach or in covering it up. It is submitted that this approach to the interpretation and application of Article 2.8 and its relationship to Article 2.10 can be further supported on the grounds that it produces a more proportionate outcome as regards sanctions for breach.

Illustrations

Complicity of a Coach in Violations of Athletes

CAS 2012/A/2791, *WADA* v. *Jamaludin and Ors* Six athletes were advised by a coach acting on the instructions of the Vice President of the Malaysian Athletics Federation (MAF) of a test the next day and were told to avoid the test. The athletes were also told to present the urine of friends

---

101 For consideration of the violation of complicity under Article 2.8 of the earlier Code, see CAS 2007/A/1286, *Eder* v. *IOC* in Chapter 4, pages 172–7, in particular pages 174–5.

for analysis at a subsequent medical examination. The athletes avoided the test and left to train overseas on a flight which had been rescheduled by the coach. One athlete made a recording of a meeting with the coach, which was handed over to the anti-doping organisation. After an internal inquiry into the circumstances, the vice president was given a six-year ban for complicity in trying to prevent tests. The athletes were given a stern warning, essentially because they had acted under the direction of the coach. No action was taken against the coach. WADA appealed to CAS.

CAS held the athletes had no defence to the violation under Article 2.3 – they had deliberately avoided the doping control. The fact the refusal was under the orders of the coach could not amount to compelling justification. This defence was for the athlete to prove on the balance of probabilities. The defence had been restrictively interpreted and 'wherever physically hygienically and morally possible', the sample has to be provided.

The anti-doping system was predicated on personal responsibility, and many personal reasons for not submitting to a test would not suffice – pressure of work, uncertainty about DCO authority, feeling unfairly disturbed.

CAS held all the athletes should be subject to a standard period of two years' ineligibility save for the athlete who had provided a CD of the recording of the meeting with the coach and vice president which provided evidence of their violations, who was given a reduction in the period of ineligibility to eighteen months. Where none of the athletes could show compelling justification for the refusal, they were found to have acted intentionally and could not rely on the defence of no significant fault.

The coach was found to be clearly in breach of Article 2.8 (complicity) by advising athletes not to bring their own urine to the medical examination and to avoid testing and by rescheduling flights to avoid tests. This was a very serious intentional violation by a coach, carried out to hide the fact that athletes were involved in a doping programme. A lifetime ban could have been imposed, but ten years' ineligibility was ordered partly because of the need for parity with the six-year period of ineligibility imposed by the MAF on the vice president after the internal inquiry.

Article 2.10: Prohibited Association

This violation was added in the 2015 Code. It attempts to address the problem of athletes working with coaches, trainers, physicians and other athlete support personnel who are ineligible under the Code on account of an anti-doping rule violation or who have been subject to findings by a criminal court or professional disciplinary body which would have amounted to violations under the Code if they had been subject to Code-compliant rules. While the violation can only be committed by a person who is subject to the Code, the application of the violation to association with a person who is not and may never have been subject to the Code raises particular issues because the application of Article 2.10 is likely to have an effect on activities which represent the work or profession of the person with whom association is prohibited.[102]

An athlete or any other person subject to the Code will commit a violation if he or she associates with any athlete support person who is subject to a period of ineligibility under the Code or who, while not sanctioned under the Code, has been the subject of a criminal conviction or a finding in a criminal court or disciplinary or professional proceeding which would have been an anti-doping rule violation if the Code-compliant rules had applied to the person.

An athlete or other person cannot associate with a person subject to a ban under the Code for the duration of the period of ineligibility. Nor can the athlete or other person subject to the Code associate with an athlete support person who has been subject to a criminal, disciplinary or professional finding which would have constituted a violation under the Code for a period of six years from the time of the finding.

In addition, an athlete or person bound by the Code cannot associate with a person who acts as a 'front' or intermediary for an athlete support person who is subject to the prohibition on association under Article 2.10. The Code contains no definition of 'front' or 'intermediary', but in this context the term will cover those who act on behalf of an athlete support person in providing assistance and guidance to an athlete, whether under formal or informal arrangements. Deciding whether someone acts as an intermediary in this way will be a matter of fact for the anti-doping organisation to establish.

For Article 2.10 to have potential application, an anti-doping organisation with jurisdiction over the athlete or person bound by the Code or WADA has to have given notice in writing to the athlete or person of the disqualifying status of the athlete support person and the consequences of

---

102 The issues arising under Article 2.10 were considered in the opinion prepared on the draft revision of the Code by Jean-Paul Costa, a former member of the highest French administrative court and former judge of the ECHR. See Costa, 'Legal Opinion', pp. 12–15.

association with him or her. The anti-doping organisation will also have to show that it is reasonably possible for the athlete or person bound by the Code to avoid the association. Athlete support persons can include parents and family members, and it may be difficult for an athlete to avoid some general association with them. However, it will generally be possible for an athlete to avoid working with parents and family members in preparing for sporting competition, and in most cases it would seem that an athlete should be able to avoid an association which involves parents or other family members assisting in a formal way with preparation for sporting competition.

In addition, the anti-doping organisation (or WADA) has to use reasonable effort to inform the athlete support person who is the subject of the notice in writing that they are the subject of the prohibited association notice given to the athlete.

It is submitted that the giving of notices will be governed by any specific provisions in the applicable rules on the giving of notices. Provided a written notice has been given to the athlete or person of the disqualifying status of the athlete support person in accordance with any requirements of the applicable rules, it will not be necessary for the anti-doping organisation to prove that the notice has been read and understood. With the advice to the athlete support person who is the subject of the notice to the athlete, the question whether the anti-doping organisation has used reasonable effort to give the advice will be a matter of fact. It is clear on this provision that the advice does not have to be shown to have in fact reached the athlete support person provided a reasonable effort to give the advice has been made.

There is no definition of 'association' in the Code. In the normal meaning of the word, there will be an association where there is a link between an athlete and an athlete support person. The aim of the provision is to catch the broad range of associations which are possible in the sporting world when working with athletes bound by the Code, from the work required to prepare an athlete for competition to work representing an athlete as an agent. Where some kind of contact or link which amounts to an association has been established (and that association cannot reasonably be avoided), the burden lies on the athlete or other person to show that the association is not professional or sport-related.

The notes to the Article provide some examples of prohibited association: obtaining advice relevant to sporting performance, by way of prescriptions or therapy, analysis of body products or allowing an athlete support person to act as an agent or representative. The aim of the provision overall would appear to be to catch any association which is concerned with helping the athlete in his or her sporting life, whether as regards performance or remuneration.

As previously noted, this provision has effects beyond those persons who are subject to the Code in that if applied, it may affect the work of a person giving coaching or otherwise supporting athletes (or, indeed, a person acting on behalf of such a person) who has not agreed to the application of the Code. It seems likely that an athlete support person who is subject to a notice of prohibited association given to athletes who does not succeed in persuading an anti-doping organisation that the criteria for prohibited association do not apply to him or her and/ or who wishes to challenge the legality of the application of Article 2.10 to his or her business would bring any claim for recourse to a national court. The claim would presumably be that the application of Article 2.10 to the work of the athlete support person for the period of time stipulated represents an unlawful limitation on personal freedom and the right to carry on work or an unlawful interference with those rights. The precise formulation of such a claim will be a matter for national law.

For anti-doping organisations, the notice provisions are important preconditions for bringing any allegation against an athlete that there has been a breach of Article 2.10. The requirements may be difficult to fulfil in a practical sense where a number of persons are likely to associate with a person who is subject to a period of ineligibility or is otherwise subject to a finding which makes Article 2.10 potentially applicable. It is submitted that the requirement for written notice to be sent to the athlete and the requirement for reasonable effort to be made to allow the athlete support person to explain why the criteria do not apply to him or her (where this is potentially applicable) will be considered to be mandatory requirements before any proceedings alleging a breach of Article 2.10 can be brought. These steps can be taken either when a period of ineligibility is initially imposed on an athlete support person under the Code (or when an athlete support person is subject to a finding which would have amounted to a Code violation) or when an anti-doping organisation becomes aware that particular athletes are associating with an athlete support person who is disqualified under Article 2.10. If the latter course is taken, only conduct which takes place after notification can support a possible violation under Article 2.10. Where an anti-doping organisation does not give notice under Article 2.10, it may still be able to bring allegations that an athlete support person has acted in breach of the terms of the period of ineligibility under the Code under Article 10.12.3 and/or that athletes or other persons have been complicit in assisting the athlete support person to breach his or her period of ineligibility in breach of Article 2.9.

While it can be contended that an athlete support person cannot break the prohibition against participation without working with an athlete and that the athlete thereby provides assistance to the athlete support person and amounts to complicity, it is submitted that in order to establish complicity under Article 2.9 an anti-doping organisation must establish conduct which goes further than simple association with the banned athlete support person (which is conduct that Article 2.10 appears to be intended to cover) and must demonstrate some form of deliberate conduct by the athlete which was intended to encourage or cover up the breach of the prohibition against participation.

Article 10.12.3: Violation of Prohibition of Participation during Ineligibility

Although this violation is placed in Article 10, which deals with sanctions, it effectively creates a further violation where a person who has had a period of ineligibility imposed on him or her breaches the terms of the prohibition against participation applicable in the period of ineligibility.

Such a breach of the prohibition against participation, if established, will lead to the imposition of a further period of ineligibility equal in length to the period of ineligibility initially imposed. The further period of ineligibility will commence at the end of the original period of ineligibility. The length of the further period of ineligibility may be adjusted depending on the fault of the athlete or the circumstances of the case. There is no provision providing any further guidance on the extent of any adjustment, and it is submitted that the adjustment can lead to the imposition of any period of further ineligibility which the tribunal finds reflects the fault of the athlete and the particular circumstances of the case.[103]

It will be for the anti-doping organisation to prove to the comfortable satisfaction of the tribunal that a person subject to a period of ineligibility has broken the terms of the prohibition against participation applicable

---

103 This provision amends the 2009 Code, which provided for the application of the defence of no significant fault to the violation of the prohibition on participation. It is submitted that the provision means that the defence of no significant fault is not available for breaches under Article 10.12.3.

under Article 10.12.[104] It will be for the person in breach to establish the facts in support of any claim for adjustment of the further period of ineligibility on the balance of probabilities.

The prohibition against participation during ineligibility prevents an athlete or other person who has been declared ineligible from participating in any capacity in a competition or activity authorised or organised by any Signatory, Signatory member organisation, club or other member organisation of a Signatory member organisation, in competitions authorised by any professional league or any international- or national-level event organisation or in any elite or national-level sporting activity funded by a government agency. The notes to the Article explain how this provision extends to competing in non-Signatory professional leagues and events organised by non-Signatory national-level event organisations: such participation will trigger a breach of Article 10.12.3. The notes explain that the scope of prohibited activity will extend to serving as an official director, office employee or volunteer at an organisation described in the Article. This appears to mean that any work for a sporting organisation as referred to in Article 10.12.1, whether or not the work is directly linked to sporting competition, will be within the prohibition.

While Article 10.12.1 does not expressly refer to the activities of athlete support persons who work with athletes to prepare them for participation in sporting competition, the provision is expressly applicable to any person who is subject to a period of ineligibility under the Code (as it must be if the Code is to apply to all bound by it in an effective way). Where an athlete support person is subject to a period of ineligibility, the effect of Article 10.12.1 will be to prevent them from participating in any capacity in organised competition or activity. Athlete support persons participate in competition and organised activities by providing support for athletes to prepare for sporting competition.[105] Where an athlete support person is subject to a period of ineligibility for breach of the Code, the prohibition against participation will, it is submitted, be interpreted as prohibiting the athlete support person from providing any kind of assistance to an athlete participating in or preparing for a sporting competition or activity organised, authorised sanctioned or otherwise under the jurisdiction of any organisation which is within the provision under Article 10.12.3. This

104 See Chapter 10, pages 486, note 6 for Article 10.12 Status during Ineligibility. This provision seeks to address the perceived unfairness of the effect of periods of ineligibility to those who need to enter a specific training environment in order to be ready to resume sporting activity at the end of a period of ineligibility.
105 See the definition of 'athlete support personnel' in the Code.

is the form of participation which is prohibited where athlete support persons are subject to the prohibition. This interpretation reflects the broad wording of the terms of the prohibition against participation, which bars participation 'in any capacity' in a competition or activity, and is consistent with the overall aim and purpose of the Code, which is to provide an effective sanctions regime where violations are committed by athletes, athlete support persons and others who are bound by the Code.[106]

Where an athlete or other person is subject to a period of ineligibility which is longer than four years, he or she may, after completing four years of the period of ineligibility, participate in local sports events not sanctioned or otherwise under the jurisdiction of a Code Signatory or member of a Code Signatory, but only so long as the local sport event is not at a level which would otherwise qualify the athlete or person directly or indirectly to compete in (or accumulate points towards) a national championship or international event, and so long as it does not involve the athlete or person working in any capacity with minors.[107]

An athlete or other person who is subject to a period of ineligibility remains subject to testing and, it is submitted, by necessary implication from this provision, to the provisions of the Code generally.

Article 10.12.2 permits athletes who are subject to a period of ineligibility to return to train with a team or use facilities at a club or other member organisation during the last two months of the period of ineligibility or the last one-quarter of the period of ineligibility, whichever is shorter.

Article 2.9 makes it clear that any person who is bound by the Code who assists or encourages another to breach Article 10.12.3 or conspires with another to breach the provision or who covers up a breach of the provision or otherwise is intentionally complicit in a breach of the provision will potentially be liable for complicity under Article 2.9. It is submitted that some form of intentional conduct which goes beyond simply associating with a person who is subject to a period of ineligibility will be required in order to establish a breach of Article 2.9.[108]

General Approach to Consideration of Violations

In considering allegations that anti-doping rule violations have been committed, tribunals will have to consider the proof of the contents of the

---

106 See SDRCC DT 12–0177 *Russell* v. *CCES*, paragraphs 59–61 for discussion of 'any activity' under the prohibition.
107 See Chapter 8, page 453 for further consideration of the scope of this exception.
108 See pages 263–4 for further discussion.

elements of the alleged violation. Where an anti-doping policy has chosen the law of a particular legal system to govern the application of the policy, the tribunal may be referred to decisions from the courts of that legal system which are said to be relevant to the meaning and operation of the violation provisions (particularly decisions under the criminal law).[109] While such decisions may assist in a general way, tribunals should bear in mind that the Code has to be interpreted and applied as a free-standing, independent text, and that it is not intended to be subject to the general legal principles of criminal law applicable in a particular jurisdiction.

Limitation

Article 17 of the 2015 Code extends the period of limitation for bringing anti-doping rule violation proceedings from eight to ten years. No anti-doping rule violation proceedings can be brought unless the person alleged to have committed the breach has been notified of the alleged anti-doping rule violation as set out in provisions of the Code relating to results management in Article 7 of the Code within ten years of the date on which the violation is alleged to have occurred. The limitation provision in the 2015 Code will be applied retroactively because, under Article 25.2, it is expressly termed a procedural rule. There can, however, be no retroactive application of the extended period of limitation in the 2015 Code if the period of limitation of eight years applicable under the 2009 Code had already expired by 1 January 2015, when the new limitation period came into effect, because the expiry of the period of limitation under the 2009 Code would have given rise to substantive rights.[110]

Like the provisions which set out the requirements for violations, Article 17 has to be implemented without substantive change by Signatories. The Article represents an agreed procedural time limit under the Code and would not be affected by time limits under national law or the approach to limitation under national law. There is no annotation to Article 17 in the Code. While there have been decisions at national level in which the running of the limitation period of eight years under earlier versions of the Code has been held to have been suspended by reason of fraudulent concealment of the violation in accordance with principles recognised under national laws on limitation, it is submitted that the application of such principles to Article 17, which provides on its wording for an unqualified contractual time bar, is, on a proper approach to the Code,

---

109 This was the approach adopted by counsel in *Marinov*; see pages 252–4.
110 See Article 25.2 of the Code.

incorrect.[111] While this approach to the Code might be said to increase the possibility of a person who conceals breaches of the Code escaping allegations of breaches of the Code, the terms of the Article and the extension of the period to ten years both point, clearly, it is submitted, to the absolute nature of the contractual time bar.

111 See e.g. AAA Case No. 7719016811 *JENF USADA* v. *Hellebuyck* (with the same approach to the application of the time limit being applied in the reasoned decision by USADA on ineligibility and disqualification in the Lance Armstrong case).

6

Article 3 of the Code: the Proof of Anti-doping Rule Violations under the Code

Introduction

Article 3.1 of the Code provides for both the burden and the standard of proof in proceedings before tribunals or CAS under the results management process under the Code, which has to be implemented by anti-doping organisations. In a regime which contains many provisions where either an anti-doping organisation or the person facing an allegation has to prove a particular relevant fact or facts, it is important to have a clear provision allocating the burden of proving the facts in issue and the standard of proof which is applicable to proving them. While the Code is sometimes silent in certain provisions on the standard of proof, Article 3.1 provides for the general position which will apply where there is no particular provision. With the removal of Articles 10.4 and 10.6 of the 2009 Code in the 2015 Code – both provisions which imposed the higher standard of proof, usually only applicable to the proof of a violation by an anti-doping organisation, on athletes – the 2015 Code now provides for a uniform position on the standard of proof which will apply whenever the athlete bears the burden of proof. This mirrors the position taken in the Code since it was first adopted that one uniform standard of proof should be applicable where an anti-doping organisation has to prove a violation of the Code.

As has been outlined in Chapter 5, the proof of the violations contained in Articles 2.2 and 2.4–2.8 of the Code will usually cover a wider range of factual circumstances than will be the case with violations under Articles 2.1–2.3. A much wider range of potentially relevant probative material is often produced after an investigation conducted by a NADO. As a result, in hearings involving the proof of violations under Articles 2.2 and 2.4–2.8, national and international tribunals and CAS, whether at first instance or on appeal, are more likely to be required to consider and assess a range of documentary and oral evidence on relevant issues, as opposed to the more limited relevant evidence on whether a test result has been reached and is valid after following the proper process. In such hearings, there is likely to be a greater focus on the proper application of the principles concerning the burden and standard of proof to the evidence presented in support of the alleged violations, and questions over the relevance, reliability and admissibility of evidence are more likely to arise.

The Code contains a number of provisions relating to the burden and standard of proof on anti-doping organisations and those against whom anti-doping rule violations are alleged, but it is generally silent on questions of the admissibility of evidence. Such matters will be governed by the rules of the particular arbitral tribunal considering the question and by any principles of law which are properly applicable to the proceedings of the tribunal in relation to such an issue under national law.

The General Burden of Proof

Burden on the Anti-doping Organisation

Article 3.1 provides that the burden of establishing that an anti-doping rule violation has occurred lies on the anti-doping organisation bringing the allegation. The organisation will have to establish the elements of the anti-doping rule violation alleged to have been committed. The process of proving an allegation will range from the presentation of the evidential material required to support an adverse analytical finding after sampling and analysis to the proof of the factual matters required to establish a violation such as trafficking in a prohibited substance or method. Apart from the consideration of a violation under Article 2.1, the violations under the Code do not require an adverse analytical finding in relation to a bodily sample taken from the person against whom the allegation is made. While the general focus of doping investigations and, accordingly, hearings has largely been on the allegations which arise regularly from doping control – namely, either the presence of a prohibited substance in a bodily sample or evidence of the use of a prohibited substance or method, or a refusal to submit to doping control – that focus has moved to a considerable degree as the investigatory activities of WADA and NADOs have expanded. Anti-doping organisations investigating the conduct of persons bound by the Code and assessing whether to advance allegations of breaches of the Code and tribunals hearing allegations brought both face the challenge of considering the more complex evidence often required to establish anti-doping rule violations under Articles 2.2–2.8 of the Code.[1]

1 See Chapter 5 for the components of the various violations under Article 2.

In addition, under the amendments in the 2015 Code, tribunals will also have to consider the significant question whether a breach of Article 2.1, 2.2 or 2.6 is 'intentional' as defined under Article 10.2.3, either on a claim by the athlete seeking to prove that a violation was not intentional or on a claim by an anti-doping organisation that a violation was intentional where it would ordinarily be presumed not to be. The burden and standard of proof in such cases will be of particular relevance.

Burden on the Athlete

In certain circumstances, an athlete or other person who faces an allegation that they have committed an anti-doping rule violation will carry a burden of proof. The range of situations in which this applies has gradually increased as the Code has been amended by the 2009 and 2015 Codes. In particular, under the 2015 Code, the athlete who faces certain violations will have to prove a violation was not 'intentional' to avoid the application of a four-year period of ineligibility. Generally, an athlete or other person facing an allegation will carry a burden of proof under the Code where he or she has to rebut a presumption or prove specified facts to support a reduction or elimination of the applicable period of ineligibility under Article 10:

- where the athlete seeks to rebut the presumption that sample analysis and custodial procedures have been carried out by a WADA-accredited laboratory in accordance with the International Standard for laboratory analysis;[2]
- where the athlete alleges a departure from the ISTI or that a testing method is unreliable from a scientific perspective;[3]
- where the athlete or other person seeks to prove a departure from any other International Standard which could reasonably have caused an adverse analytical finding or other anti-doping rule violation;[4]
- where the athlete seeks to establish 'compelling justification' for his or her refusal to submit to sample collection under Article 2.3;
- where the athlete seeks to establish that a violation of Article 2.1, 2.2 or 2.6 is not 'intentional' under Article 10.2.1;

---

2 See Chapter 3 and Articles 3.2.1 and 3.2.2 of the Code for the burden which falls on the anti-doping organisation if such a departure from the procedures under the Standard is established.
3 Article 3.2.1 was added in the 2015 Code. The Article imposes specific requirements as to notice where an athlete seeks to rebut the presumption that analytical methods or decision limits are scientifically valid.
4 Article 3.2.2 of the Code.

- where the athlete seeks to rebut the presumption of negligence relating to a missed test or filing failure under the whereabouts rules in Annex I ISTI;
- where the athlete or athlete support personnel seeks to establish that possession of a prohibited substance or method was pursuant to a TUE or other acceptable justification under Article 2.6;
- where the athlete seeks to prove a circumstance or a fact under the Prohibited List which will provide a defence to a positive test – such as that an abnormal result for salbutamol was the consequence of a therapeutic dose or that a treatment by intravenous infusion or injection was a legitimate medical treatment;
- where the athlete has to establish how a prohibited substance came to be in his or her body or, in the case of an athlete or other person, how a substance came to be his or her possession, in order to rely on the provisions in Articles 10.2.3, 10.4, 10.5.1 and 10.5.2 of the Code;[5]
- where the athlete seeks to establish that the use of a substance was out-of-competition in a context unrelated to sport performance under Article 10.2.3;
- where the athlete seeks to establish that the use of cannabinoids was unrelated to sport performance;
- where the athlete or other person seeks to eliminate or reduce the period of ineligibility which would be imposed for a violation on the grounds that the defences under Article 10.4 and 10.5 apply, by establishing either that he or she was not at fault or negligent or that he or she bore no significant fault or negligence.[6]

The Standard of Proof

Standard for the Anti-doping Organisation

Where the burden of proof lies upon an anti-doping organisation to establish an alleged violation, the standard of proof required is that the alleged violation has been established to the 'comfortable satisfaction of the hearing body, bearing in mind the seriousness of the allegation which is made'.

5 See Chapter 8 for consideration of the Articles and case summaries on the proof of intention and the defences of no fault and no significant fault.
6 The athlete will have to establish how a prohibited substance entered his or her system on the balance of probabilities where the violation in issue is under Article 2.1 or 2.2 before seeking to establish the facts upon which it is claimed that Article 10.5.2 should apply. This requirement to establish how the substance entered the athlete's system does not now apply where the athlete is a minor, by reason of an amendment to the definition of 'no significant fault'.

In Article 3.1, this standard is expressed to be higher than the standard of mere balance of probability which generally applies in civil proceedings, but less than the general criminal standard of proof, namely, proof beyond a reasonable doubt.[7] The notes to Article 3.1 refer to the standard of proof as being comparable to the standard which is applied, in most countries, to cases involving professional misconduct.

This 'intermediate' standard of proof appears to have its origins in the approach adopted by CAS before the Code,[8] the approach in some jurisdictions to the proof of allegations of professional misconduct and certain common law authorities which have been said to support the imposition of an intermediate standard of proof where allegations with serious consequences for an individual are made in civil proceedings. In common law jurisdictions, it was always doubtful whether there was room for an 'intermediate' standard of proof as a matter of law, and it is submitted that there are, as a matter of legal principle, only two operative standards of proof at common law – proof beyond a reasonable doubt and proof on the balance of probabilities.[9] However, with a serious allegation in a civil context, while the standard of proof remains the balance of probabilities, clear and cogent evidence will be required to meet the standard and satisfy the burden of proof. This follows from the general proposition that it is inherently less likely that a person will commit serious deliberate misconduct than, say, make a careless error.

The time for debate over whether an intermediate standard of proof is appropriate for doping allegations under the Code and is available as a matter of law is long past. The standard is well established as a feature of the Code (and, by extension, other sport rules) and its application seems to create little practical difficulty in hearings. Arguments that in certain circumstances in serious doping cases the standard of proof should be closer to or be the criminal standard have been rejected in CAS awards. There is one applicable standard of proof, as set out in Article 3.1 of the Code. While the standard which will be applied by tribunals is clearly provided for, as with serious allegations in civil proceedings, the application of that standard of proof under the Code means that anti-doping organisations have a significant burden to discharge. This is to be expected where allegations, if proved, can have a significant effect on a sporting career.[10]

---

7 See Article 3.1 and the notes to the Article.   8 See Chapter 1, pages 46–50.

9 See the clear statement to this effect by Lord Hoffmann in In Re B (Children) [2008] UKHL 35.

10 As was pointed out by the CAS Panel in *Montgomery* v. *USADA*: see Chapter 5, pages 170–2.

Certainly, where under the 2015 Code the standard period of ineligibility for breaches of Articles 2.1, 2.2 and 2.6 will be four years, tribunals should require cogent evidence to be comfortably satisfied that the violation has been committed. However, the burden and standard of proof should be approached sensibly and with common sense, and should be applied in a realistic manner. Tribunals should be wary of elevating the requirements of proof to a level which requires complete certainty. The central question is simply whether the tribunal determining the allegation considers that it is comfortably satisfied that the elements of the violation have been established by the evidence. This burden of proof will apply to the proof of each component part of the violation as outlined in Article 2. Unless the Code specifically places a burden of proof on the athlete, an explanation put forward by the athlete to support innocence (or perhaps that his or her conduct was not intentional) will have to be rebutted by the anti-doping organisation to the comfortable satisfaction of the tribunal. The athlete will have to provide an evidential foundation for an exonerating explanation if it is to be credible, but will not have to prove it (unless there is a specific provision for a factual circumstance which the athlete has to prove). This kind of situation may arise where anti-doping organisations seek to establish violations or intentional conduct by the drawing of inferences from facts proved or where an alleged violation is based on the expert analysis of an athlete's physiological profile and the athlete asserts that there is an innocent explanation for the abnormality.[11]

To date, CAS Panels have treated the standard of proof in Article 3.1 as reflecting the general common-sense proposition that, while the anti-doping organisation does not have to eliminate all possible explanations consistent with innocence, good reliable evidence will be required before a tribunal can find that a serious allegation which will have a significant effect on an athlete's or other person's career has been established to its comfortable satisfaction.

Standard of Proof where the Burden is on the Athlete

Where an athlete or other person carries a burden of proof, the standard of proof required is the standard of the balance of probabilities, which is the standard of proof applicable in many jurisdictions in civil proceedings.

---

11 For an example of a case where the athlete put forward an innocent explanation for an abnormal profile in a biological passport case, see *UKAD* v. *Tiernan-Locke* in Chapter 5, pages 214–17.

This involves the party on which the burden rests establishing the relevant matter or event as more likely than not to be correct or to have occurred. In the CAS award relating to the WADA and UCI appeals in the case against Alberto Contador, the CAS Panel held that applying the standard of proof of the balance of probabilities could enliven a related obligation on a party seeking to contest a matter which another party sought to prove to cooperate in order to bring out the relevant facts. This would apply where the proof of the factual matters under dispute involved the party carrying the burden of proof in establishing that certain matters had not occurred.[12] This qualification of the burden of proof was based on the approach to the standard of proof under Swiss law, because Swiss law was applicable to the issue in the arbitration. It is submitted that the Code should as far as possible be read and applied without qualification of this kind based on national law.[13] While the established burden on the athlete is the balance of probabilities, in the 2009 Code the burden on the athlete to establish the absence of intent to enhance sport performance under Article 10.4 was the higher standard of the comfortable satisfaction of the tribunal usually applicable to the proof of an allegation by an anti-doping organisation. This higher standard was also applicable where an athlete or other person sought to establish that they did not knowingly commit the violation so as to avoid the consequences of a finding of aggravated circumstances under Article 10.6. These specific provisions imposing a higher standard of proof on athletes or persons facing allegations have been removed by the 2015 Code, and there are no express provisions imposing a higher standard of proof on athletes. It is submitted that the standard of proof applicable whenever an athlete has to establish facts or circumstances under the Code is as set out in Article 3.1. This more consistent approach to the standard of proof on the athlete is to be welcomed.[14]

Departures from the International Standards: the Shifting Burden

As previously noted, the Code contains specific provisions concerning alleged departures from the International Standards. In the context of

12 See CAS 2011/A/2384, *UCI* v. *Alberto Contador Velasco* in Chapter 8, pages 385–90.
13 How far this gloss on the approach to proof on the balance of probabilities is appropriate is questionable where the Code is, so far as possible, to be interpreted without reference to the provisions of national law under Article 24 (and Swiss law recognises the force of this provision).
14 The approach in Article 10.4 was the subject of challenge on the grounds that it infringed fundamental rights protected by EU law in *Gibbs*, but this challenge was rejected. See Appendix 1, pages 557–9 for case summary.

a violation under Article 2.1, a presumption operates to the effect that WADA-accredited laboratories have conducted sample analysis and custodial procedures in accordance with the ISL. This presumption can be rebutted by the athlete by establishing on the balance of probabilities that there has been a departure from the Standard which could reasonably have caused the analytical finding. If the presumption is rebutted, the anti-doping organisation will have the burden of establishing that the departure did not cause the analytical finding. It will have to do this to the standard of 'comfortable satisfaction' under Article 3.1 in order to prove the violation. The proof that a departure was not causative to this high standard may be very difficult.[15] Departures from other International Standards or other anti-doping rules or policy which did not cause a positive test or other anti-doping rule violation will not invalidate results. Again, if an athlete or other person establishes a departure which could reasonably have caused the positive test or other anti-doping rule violation, the anti-doping organisation will have the burden of establishing that the departure was not causative of the positive test or other violation to the standard of the comfortable satisfaction of the tribunal hearing the allegation. The requirement that the person facing the violation establishes that the departure from the International Standard 'could reasonably have caused' the anti-doping rule violation or other violation has been interpreted as requiring that the athlete shows that it was reasonable to conclude that the violation could have been caused by the departure from the International Standard.

Article 3.2.1 of the 2015 Code now provides that analytical methods and decision limits which have been approved by WADA after consultation in the scientific community and which have been peer-reviewed are presumed valid. Where an athlete or person seeks to rebut this presumption of validity, he or she must notify WADA of the challenge and the reasons for it. CAS may also notify WADA of such a challenge. Where such a notice of challenge is given, WADA has the right to intervene in the proceedings and either appear to assist CAS or provide evidence. This amendment is only expressed in terms which relate to CAS proceedings,

---

15 See Chapter 5, pages 190–3 for the kinds of breach which will be considered where there are challenges to the results of testing and analysis. See the decisions summarised in Chapter 5, pages 193–204 – including *USADA* v. *Landis*, which is an example of consideration by a CAS Panel of the discharge of this burden in connection with a range of arguments relating to defects in the process of analysis under the ISL. For a recent successful challenge based on the failure to follow collection procedures under the ISTI, see *Campbell Brown* v. *JAA* in Chapter 5, pages 203–4.

but it is submitted that the presumption and a similar procedural process should be applied by other tribunals which have to apply the Code.[16]

The Evidence which can be Admitted in a Hearing

The Code contains very limited provision concerning the evidence which may be admitted by a tribunal or CAS in order to prove an anti-doping rule violation. Article 3.2 introduces the specific rules of proof for establishing certain facts and presumptions referred to previously, by saying that the facts relating to anti-doping rule violations may be established by any reliable means, and the notes to Article 3.2 refer generally to a range of evidence which may be called to prove an allegation of using a prohibited substance: admissions, evidence from third parties, reliable documentary evidence, reliable data from either an A or a B sample and conclusions drawn from the profile of a series of the athlete's blood or urine samples, such as data from the ABP. The admissibility of evidence will be a matter for the tribunal hearing the allegation to decide, in accordance with its rules, any particular legal principles applicable to the issue and, quite possibly, the general discretion of the tribunal (subject to the limits imposed by the system of law applicable to the arbitration, if the proceeding is an arbitration).

Article 3.2 places the emphasis on the reliability of the evidence which is submitted by the party seeking to prove facts in issue and contains no further specific provisions relating to questions of admissibility. Tribunals which hear allegations in relation to anti-doping rule violations, whether they have been established by a sporting organisation as an internal domestic tribunal or by a NADO or under State legislation as an independent tribunal, are likely to have a broader discretion to admit evidence under their rules than courts of law under applicable national law. Where national tribunals are concerned, they may have to decide questions of admissibility by reference to principles of national law. Where the national tribunal is arbitral in nature, admissibility will be determined by the national law applicable to arbitration if there are no specific agreed rules relating to the admissibility of evidence in the tribunal's rules. As an arbitral forum, CAS will determine questions of admissibility in

---

16 The amendment appears to be a response to the successful challenge to the limits and method applied in detecting hGH in CAS 2011/A/2566, *Veerpalu v. ISF*. After changes to the testing methods, further challenges to the method of detecting hGH were rejected in CAS 2012/A/2857, *NADA v. Sinkewitz* and CAS 2014/A/3480, *WADA v. Lallukka*.

accordance with any procedural rules applicable to the arbitration. The CAS Procedural Rules contain no detailed provisions relating to admissibility, but a CAS Panel will have a general discretion to rule on the admission and relevance of evidence. An international arbitral tribunal is not bound to the general legal rules of national law on questions of the admission of evidence, apart from any legal rules specifically relating to the conduct of international arbitration. Proceedings before a CAS Panel will be subject to Swiss law regulating domestic or international arbitration by reason of the location of the seat of CAS. Like the CAS Code, the relevant provisions of Swiss law contain no detailed provisions on the admissibility of evidence in an arbitration. Arbitrators have a broad discretion as to the admissibility of evidence under general principles relating to international arbitration, and it is submitted that the main considerations in relation to such questions will be the relevance and reliability of the evidence in question. Ultimately, the discretion of the arbitrators to admit evidence will be limited by the Swiss legal concept of procedural public order and any procedural rights of the parties. Under Swiss law, procedural public order will only be infringed in exceptional circumstances where generally recognised fundamental principles have been violated and this leads to an outcome which is entirely inconsistent with basic principles of justice, so that the decision appears to be incompatible with the values recognised in a law-abiding State. This approach gives arbitrators a very wide power in relation to the admission of evidence, which is consistent with the general approach in international arbitration.[17]

It is submitted that, while arbitrators and tribunals hearing allegations under the Code will have a broad general discretion in relation to the admissibility of evidence, given the serious nature of anti-doping rule violations the relevance and reliability of evidence tendered in support of an allegation should be carefully weighed and considered. By way of general example, evidence from a witness which seeks simply to endorse the veracity of another witness should be held to be inadmissible because it is irrelevant – it is the job of the tribunal to assess whether a witness is telling the truth or not.

17 See, for an example of a consideration of the admissibility of evidence considering the position before CAS and under Swiss law, TAS 2009/A/1879, *Valverde* v. *CONI* in Chapter 2, pages 82–7. Here, the evidence obtained by the Italian authorities from the Spanish authorities was held to be admissible. The conclusion was that the admission of bags of blood into evidence and the comparison of the blood in the bags with samples obtained from V did not infringe his fundamental rights or offend the principle of public order.

Admissions

The specific reference to proof by 'admissions' in the notes to Article 3.2 of the Code should be noted. Properly established admissions by those who face allegations are a well-known exception to the admissibility of hearsay evidence, in the context of both civil and criminal proceedings in most jurisdictions. The general inappropriateness of analogies drawn from the principles of criminal law has been noted on many occasions by CAS Panels (and is confirmed in the Introduction to the Code). Given this, the treatment of admissions in the doping context is likely to be relatively straightforward, with the emphasis being placed on the reliability and relevance of the admission. Only where the introduction of an admission was likely to infringe the principle of public order outlined here because of the way in which it was obtained would a CAS Panel rule that the admission was inadmissible. Evidence of admissions given to other competitors, or to investigators, is becoming a more common feature in doping cases where the allegations are the result of investigations. The early CAS awards in *USADA* v. *Montgomery* and *USADA* v. *Gaines*[18] provide good examples of proof by means of evidence of an admission made to another athlete, which the Panel hearing the allegations found was credible, and sufficient to establish one of the serious allegations brought against the athletes. The provisions of the 2009 Code provided for considerable credit to be given against the otherwise applicable period of ineligibility where an athlete or other person promptly admitted a violation. This provision has been significantly amended in the 2015 Code, but the presence of such provisions seems likely to result in more evidence of admissions being presented before tribunals to support allegations of breach of the Code.[19]

The Drawing of Inferences

The drawing of inferences from primary facts which have been established by admissible evidence is often an essential part of proving facts which are in issue between the parties in adversarial proceedings. This process will not be required in simple testing cases but, with other violations, the

18 See pages 289–90.
19 See Chapter 8, pages 436–8 for Article 10.6.1 on substantial assistance. The role of persons who act as 'whistleblowers' and report on activity which involves breaches of the Code has been highlighted by the circumstances which caused WADA to commission the independent reports released in late 2015 and 2016 in the period before the Rio Olympics. See Chapter 10, pages 530–4.

drawing of inferences from established facts may be a central part of the decision-making process. In many situations, given the nature of conduct involved in some violations and the limited powers of investigation available, it may not be possible for an anti-doping organisation to prove the violation by direct evidence. In such circumstances, a tribunal will have to be asked to draw an inference that a person committed the violation from the evidence which has been introduced.[20] It is important that inferences are drawn from facts established by the evidence and that the process does not become one of speculation or conjecture which is not based on proven facts from which an inference can properly be drawn.[21] A tribunal will need to be comfortably satisfied that an inference which it is asked to draw follows from the given facts as something which is probably true.[22] Similarly, where an athlete seeks to rely on the Articles in the Code which may allow a tribunal to remove or reduce a period of ineligibility, the athlete will have to prove how the prohibited substance came to be in his or her system by cogent evidence – tribunals cannot rely on speculation where an athlete has to establish such matters.

Silence in the Face of Allegations

An important issue in the proof of anti-doping rule violations may be whether a tribunal is permitted to draw an inference from the fact that an athlete or other person who faces an allegation is silent in the face of the allegation or takes no part, after requests, in the investigation. In criminal matters in many legal systems, it may well not be permissible to draw inferences against a defendant from such failures to answer questions or to testify, because a defendant has a right not to incriminate him- or herself. However, in professional disciplinary matters, a person facing an allegation of professional misconduct – an allegation which might be said to be broadly analogous to a doping allegation in the context of a sporting career – has been held, in many jurisdictions, to have a duty to explain his or her position in relation to the allegation or risk having adverse

20 See Chapter 5, pages 252–4. The cases used to illustrate the violation of tampering with doping control under Article 2.5 provide examples of tribunals drawing simple inferences from primary facts in order to find that the allegations had been established.
21 For an example of a case where CAS was not prepared to draw inference from facts said to support an attempt to commit an anti-doping rule violation, see *Gibilisco* in Chapter 5, pages 217–19.
22 There are observations on the drawing of inferences by the CAS Appeal Panel in CAS 2007/A/1311, *Marinov v. ASADA*. See Chapter 5, pages 252–4.

inferences drawn from his or her failure to explain.[23] Similarly, in civil cases, a failure on the part of a person to give or call evidence on an issue which a party would be expected to be able to give or call can lead to the drawing of an adverse inference against the party which fails to call the evidence. Where proceedings in relation to alleged breaches of the Code are expressed not to be criminal proceedings (and that is generally considered to be the case in the context of the application of the ECHR) but rather to be disciplinary or civil proceedings, it is submitted that it is permissible to provide for inferences to be drawn from a failure to appear and answer questions. The extent of the inferences which can properly be drawn and their probative value will depend on the circumstances of the case and the factual matters which the person responding to the allegation might be expected to be able to give evidence on. It may also be possible for a person facing an anti-doping rule violation to contend that it would not be appropriate to draw any inference against him or her on the basis that giving evidence in the tribunal hearing the allegations under the Code would incriminate him or her in other proceedings.[24]

In *Montgomery* – a decision under the 2004 Code – the CAS Panel indicated that it was prepared to draw adverse inferences against Mr Montgomery on the basis that he had remained silent in the face of allegations and had not given evidence when the matters relied on by the USADA in support of the allegations were matters upon which he could be expected to give evidence if he had an explanation consistent with innocence. Ultimately, in the final analysis, the Panel did not need to rely on the drawing of such an inference, because it found that the allegation of using a prohibited substance was established by the evidence given by another athlete, which amounted to an admission of use by Mr Montgomery and his co-defendant, Ms Gaines. The 2015 Code contains express provision in Article 3.2.5 permitting a tribunal hearing an anti-doping rule violation to draw an inference adverse to an athlete or other person facing an anti-doping rule violation where the athlete or other person refuses to appear at the hearing to answer questions from the hearing panel or anti-doping organisation. The provision is limited to a failure to attend and answer questions at a hearing, presumably because any earlier failure to attend an interview will be followed either by non-attendance at a hearing (from

23 See pages 290–1, where the decision in *Collins* provides an example of the willingness of a tribunal to draw inferences from the failure of an athlete to testify.
24 See, for example, *USADA* v. *Bruyneel* in Chapter 5, pages 257–8, where this argument was advanced but the Panel did not consider that it had to consider drawing inferences from non-attendance at the hearing where other evidence established the violations in any event.

which an inference might be drawn) or attendance (where any earlier failure to attend an interview might be the subject of questions).

Article 3.2.4 of the 2015 Code expressly provides for facts established by a court decision or professional disciplinary tribunal of competent jurisdiction which is not the subject of appeal to be irrebuttable evidence of the facts against an athlete or other person unless the athlete establishes that the decision was made in contravention of the principles of natural justice. The application of this provision will depend on what is established as a matter of fact in a court or tribunal decision. This may require a careful consideration of the facts which are accepted by the athlete in criminal or disciplinary proceedings and those which are not.

Where an athlete or other person pleads guilty in criminal proceedings, the plea of guilty will usually, in most jurisdictions, involve accepting a formal statement of facts relating to the criminal charges. These admitted facts will, it is submitted, be irrebuttable evidence against the person in anti-doping rule violations proceedings under Article 3.2.4, unless the person can prove in the anti-doping proceedings that the proceedings in the criminal court proceeded in a manner which was contrary to natural justice – a very unlikely possibility.[25]

The Burden and Standard of Proof in Action

As anti-doping investigations evolve, many more hearings are taking place which do not involve either the proof of the presence of a prohibited substance in an athlete's bodily sample or the question of a refusal to submit to doping control. Some decisions illustrate the difficulties which face anti-doping organisations when they investigate the wider range of anti-doping violations under Article 2 of the Code and gather and present the wider range of evidence which will need to be examined by tribunals under the Code's burden and standard of proof provisions. On a practical level, the investigation and proof of violations such as trafficking, where there are no clear admissions, represent a major challenge for anti-doping organisations under the Code. In carrying out investigations as they are required to do under the Code/ISTI, anti-doping organisations have to be conscious of the need to adduce cogent evidence before tribunals in order to satisfy the burden of proof, and to gather that evidence in a manner which ensures that it can be admitted before the tribunal and will be considered to be reliable.

---

25 For an example of an athlete who pleaded guilty to a customs offence but asserted that his plea in the criminal court did not amount to an admission of facts which proved the alleged anti-doping rule violation, see *Wyper* at pages 250–2.

The recent decision in CAS 2015/A/4059, *WADA* v. *Bellchambers et al.*,[26] in which thirty-four AFL players were held to have used a prohibited substance, provides an example of a CAS Panel reviewing a range of documentary evidence and actions by players (in the absence of direct evidence from those who administered the substances and testing of the substance administered) to determine whether the substance administered was prohibited under the List.[27] The Panel focussed on actions and documents which were contemporaneous with the administration of the substance which supported the conclusion that the players were administered with a prohibited peptide as part of a plan to improve performance. It is submitted that such an approach is appropriate where contemporaneous statements and actions are likely to be reliable indications of what was happening at the time.

Illustrations

Early Problems of Proof

CAS 2004/A/651, *French* v. *Australian Sports Commission & Cycling Australia*

F faced a range of allegations that he had breached various provisions of the doping policy of Cycling Australia in force at the time (2004) (which was in similar terms to the Code). He was found, at the initial hearing before a sole CAS arbitrator, to have breached the Cycling Australia anti-doping policy by committing some of the alleged breaches. The violations were similar in substance to the Code violations and concerned doping, aiding and abetting others to dope or being concerned in doping by others, trafficking by buying or holding prohibited substances and assisting doping or aiding or abetting doping by others. Cycling Australia sought to prove the violations by means of evidence in the form of admissions, statements from lay witnesses and scientific evidence linking Mr French to doping products which had been found. (The evidence did not involve a positive test of the athlete for a prohibited substance.)

The allegations had arisen after a bag of used syringes, needles and waste products and a bucket containing used syringes and needles had been found in a room which F had occupied at the Australian Institute of Sport in South Australia. The allegations of use and trafficking were found to have been established at the first hearing, and a two-year period of

26 See Chapter 8, pages 417–20.
27 Those who were responsible for developing the plan to administer the prohibited substance and for its administration refused to provide evidence. The Supreme Court of Victoria declined to issue subpoenas under the legislation regulating commercial arbitration.

ineligibility was imposed before the 2004 Olympics. F's appeal was heard by CAS in May 2005. The two banned substances which, it was alleged, were involved in the violations were glucocorticosteroids and equine growth hormone (egH).

On appeal, the CAS Panel was not satisfied to the required standard by the evidence adduced that the allegations had been established. The CAS Panel approached the matter as requiring proof somewhere between the balance of probabilities and beyond a reasonable doubt (see paragraph 42 of the Award). This standard of proof was said to be based on the Australian case of *Briginshaw* v. *Briginshaw*[28] (because the parties to the anti-doping policy had chosen Australian law) and CAS jurisprudence. Mr French had made admissions that he had used a substance called 'Testicomp' but, in the absence of scientific evidence proving that this product contained the prohibited glucocorticosteroid, the Panel found that the violations involving use of the prohibited substance were not made out.

While one set of allegations failed because no appropriate testing for the presence of glucocorticosteroids in the substance which the athlete admitted using had been carried out, problems in the chain of custody of the needles before they were tested and the possibility, on the Panel's analysis of all the evidence given by various witnesses, that the traces of egH on the needles in the bucket were the result of another cyclist, not French, injecting himself, meant that the allegations against French involving the use of egH were also found not to have been proved. The appeal was allowed.

BALCO Cases

Consideration of the Standard of Proof and Proof by Admissions and Inferences

USADA v. *Montgomery* **and** *USADA* v. *Gaines*   Two prominent American sprinters faced allegations, brought by USADA and arising from the BALCO inquiry,[29] that they had used prohibited substances or techniques,

---

28 *Briginshaw* v. *Briginshaw* (1938) 60 CLR 336, 362 (HCA). *Briginshaw* does not, on examination, appear to be authority for a different standard of proof, but rather confirms that, with a serious allegation, while the civil standard of the balance of probabilities is applicable, the evidence required to prove the allegation and tip the balance needs to be clear and cogent. As noted, the different formulations may make little practical difference to the consideration of allegations under the Code. See also e.g. *Hornal* v. *Newberger Products Ltd* [1957] 1 QB 247; *Re H and others (Minors) (Sexual Abuse: Standard of Proof)* [1996] 1 All ER 1, 16 (HL); and *In Re B (Children)*.
29 The inquiry led to criminal proceedings against various individuals, including Mr Conte, who ran the BALCO business, and to anti-doping proceedings against several athletes who were on Mr Conte's books.

assisted and incited others to do so and trafficked in prohibited substances contrary to IAAF Rules. The IAAF violation provisions were similar to the violations under the Code. In the course of the hearing, the charges relating to assisting, inciting or trafficking were either dismissed or dropped. A significant amount of documentary material produced by the BALCO investigation on the business run by Mr Conte from his San Francisco laboratory was presented before CAS by USADA,[30] but, ultimately, the CAS Panel found that the charge of using prohibited substances was established by the evidence given by another athlete, W, before the Panel. W had admitted to doping and had earlier accepted a two-year sanction. She gave evidence that G and M had admitted to her that they had used the prohibited substance, the designer steroid tetrahydrocannabinol (THC), provided by Mr Conte. The Panel found that this testimony was credible, and that the admission alone established the doping violation.

While the parties had contended for different applicable standards of proof at the interlocutory stage by reason of the change in the IAAF Rules to adopt the Code, the Panel did not consider that the standard of 'beyond reasonable doubt' or the standard of 'comfortable satisfaction' made any significant difference to the practical exercise of considering whether the allegations brought against M and G were made out. The Panel found that USADA bore the burden of proving, by strong evidence commensurate with the serious claims it made, that the Respondents had committed the doping offences in question. The Panel found that USADA had met this standard by reference to the admission given by the Respondent G to W.

Admissions and Inferences

AAA No. 30 190 00658 04, *USADA* v. *Collins* C was found by the AAA hearing to have been involved in the BALCO doping conspiracy as a long-standing client of Mr Conte. Mr Conte ran the BALCO business and was alleged to have distributed several types of banned substance to professional athletes in track and field, baseball and football in a 'large-scale doping conspiracy'. This conspiracy involved the use of the steroid tetrahydrogestrinone (THG) and a steroid cream in a manner which avoided detection by the drug-testing regime then in use.

C had never tested positive, and this was the first case in which USADA had sought to prove a doping violation against an athlete other than by a positive test or by evidence of refusal. As a result of the BALCO investigation and tests carried out as a consequence of it, several track and field

---

30 See *USADA* v. *Collins*, next, for the kind of evidence presented.

athletes ultimately accepted sanctions imposed by USADA under its Protocol, while others were found to have committed doping violations. At the time of the hearing, the cases against M and G were pending. The matter was dealt with under old IAAF Rules. USADA carried the burden of proving that C intentionally used a prohibited substance. The Panel considered the various documents produced by USADA, which included emails from C containing statements by her which, the Panel found, amounted to admissions of being involved in the use of prohibited substances and in a long-running conspiracy to take prohibited substances. The written admissions were supported by an analysis of the results of various tests carried out on the athlete during her career, which, while never producing a positive test, when read with the documents setting out the taking of substances and a calendar for the testing of the prohibited substances, were consistent, USADA claimed, with a managed doping programme. While the athlete submitted that no single test which she had taken had been found to show doping, the tribunal found that the results of the tests over her career, which showed significant variations in haematocrit levels and T/E ratios, could only be explained by regular doping. Expert evidence from USADA supported this conclusion, and no expert evidence or other evidence was presented by C to provide an alternative explanation. While it found that it did not have to take this step, in the light of the evidence which it had before it, the Panel was prepared to draw an adverse inference against C on the basis of her refusal to testify to explain her position in the face of the evidence. This was based on the approach in the professional disciplinary area under American law, where adverse inferences can be drawn against a person facing a disciplinary charge who refuses to testify in response to probative evidence offered against them.

The Panel found that USADA had proved the allegation that C had taken a testosterone/epitestosterone cream, THG and EPO over a considerable period of time in order to enhance her sporting performance and to elude the drug testing which was carried out at the time. She had not admitted her wrongdoing and had been involved in a scheme which was elaborately designed to hide the doping offences being committed by the athletes involved. The Panel did not accept the request by USADA for a life ban, but imposed a ban of eight years to mark the serious nature of the violations (in addition to the loss of all awards and trust fund payments arising in C's competitive career from February 2002 until the date of the award, 9 December 2004).

7

Responsibility for Testing and Investigations, Results Management and Hearings

The Responsibility for Testing and Results Management

Athletes and others bound by the Code may be subject to the jurisdiction of various anti-doping organisations operating under the Code. Where the jurisdiction in respect of such matters as testing and investigation as between different anti-doping organisations is unclear, this can lead not only to inefficiencies and possible disputes between anti-doping organisations, but also to athletes and others contending that the agreement by which they are bound to the Code does not extend to provide for the exercise of jurisdiction by the particular anti-doping organisation conducting an investigation or bringing an allegation. This makes clear allocation of responsibility between anti-doping organisations on the terms of the Code and Standards which will bind any person agreeing to their application an important requirement for the efficient, harmonised operation of the regime.

The 2015 Code and the ISTI contain revised provisions which seek to clarify the position on the allocation of responsibility for testing and investigations, and for related processes such as applications for TUE and management of whereabouts information, between anti-doping organisations.

The provisions of the Code and ISTI further regulate the processes which are to be followed by the anti-doping organisation which has responsibility under the Code and which initiates testing or carries out an investigation. These provisions cover the process of initial review of results, further investigations, notification to the person involved, provisional suspension and hearing of allegations. The Code further provides for the publication of decisions made in relation to allegations and for the mutual recognition of decisions. Publication and recognition are both fundamental aspects of the anti-doping regime under the Code, given its aim of establishing a harmonised system across all Signatories and those bound to the Code.[1]

The Code's provisions concerning results management generally establish standards which the Signatories must meet, but the relevant Articles are not among the Articles which have to be adopted without significant amendment into anti-doping policies. This means that anti-doping organisations have to establish and implement their own procedures to meet the mandatory requirements of the Code. The ISTI contains provisions relating to the general conduct of investigations, specific provision for the investigation of a possible failure to comply at sample collection and, in particular, specific provisions for results management for apparent filing failures and missed tests under the whereabouts regime in the ISTI.[2] It must also be borne in mind that the International Standards – the ISTI and ISL – contain the detail of the process by which samples are taken and analysed, and that the application of the Standards is a mandatory part of the testing and investigation process for Signatories.[3]

As already noted, after testing or investigation, the results obtained will be managed in order to conduct any further investigation required, and to bring any allegation arising from the investigation to a hearing. Generally, the hearing process must be conducted to the standards set out in Article 8 of the Code. Related matters, such as confidentiality during the investigative and hearing process and the reporting of decisions after a hearing, are also the subject of Articles in the Code (primarily Article 14).

Generally, anti-doping rules which implement the Code will bind those who agree to them to the processes required to carry out the necessary testing and investigations, manage results and bring them to hearing before a national tribunal. It is important that, at national level, those who have to implement the Code's provisions provide appropriately for the required procedures to bring results arising from the procedures under the Code through to allegations, hearings and decisions. While implementing the core Articles of the Code brings about agreement to the jurisdiction of CAS and its procedures for certain appeals under the Code, perhaps the most important tribunals for most anti-doping organisations and athletes are those which operate at first instance at national level (and any national

---

1 Articles 5 (scope of testing, event testing), Article 7 (results management responsibility for process, and process), Article 8 (right to fair hearing), Article 14 (confidentiality and reporting) and Article 15 (recognition of decisions). See Chapter 3.
2 See ISTI Annex A (possible failure to comply). Annex I.5 (whereabouts failures results management) is set out in more detail in Chapter 3, pages 138–41 and Chapter 5, pages 233–41.
3 See Chapter 3 for the operation of the International Standards in more detail.

appeal tribunal) or under the authority of the international federation. It is these first-instance tribunals which bear the responsibility for hearing the majority of allegations under the Code, and perhaps the most important factor in the operation of the Code across the sporting world is the fair and efficient operation of national-level and international federation tribunals. This means that careful consideration should be given by Signatories to the composition of the tribunal which will occupy this role, and the procedural rules which it will operate under, when anti-doping rules implementing the Code are drafted and adopted. Anti-doping rules should include express agreement to the jurisdiction of the tribunal chosen to hear allegations under the rules and to the applicable tribunal procedures.

Article 7: Clarification of Doping Control Responsibilities

The Code proceeds on the basic principle that the anti-doping organisation which initiated and directed the collection of samples or, in a case where no sample collection is involved, the anti-doping organisation which first gave notice to the athlete of an alleged anti-doping rule violation (and diligently pursued it) will be responsible for the management of results and the conduct of hearings.[4] This presumption does not apply where a NADO does not have jurisdiction under its rules over an athlete or person who is not a national resident license holder or member of a sport organisation in the country of the national anti-doping organisation. Where a national anti-doping organisation declines to exercise jurisdiction under its rules, results management has to be carried out by the athlete's international federation or the third party directed by the rules of the international federation. This makes the international federation the anti-doping organisation of last resort for results management.

WADA can carry out testing and its own investigations into possible anti-doping violations on its own initiative,[5] and where this occurs results management will be carried out by an anti-doping organisation nominated by WADA. Where the IOC, IPC or a major event organiser carries out testing, it will deal with the consequences insofar as they relate to results at the event (forfeiture of medals and such like), but otherwise the athlete's international federation will manage the results.[6]

---

4 Article 7.1 of the Code.   5 Articles 5.2.4 and 20.7.
6 The position at the recent Olympic Games in Rio was changed by the establishment of the CAS Ad Hoc Doping Division. This took on the role of the IOC in adjudicating on anti-doping rule violations committed during the Games. See further Chapter 1, pages 43–4.

Where there is a dispute between anti-doping organisations over which anti-doping organisation has results management responsibility, WADA has to decide the dispute. WADA's decision can be appealed to CAS within seven days of notification by the anti-doping organisations who are party to the dispute.[7] If a national anti-doping organisation elects to collect additional samples when contracted to carry out testing by another anti-doping organisation, it will be considered to be the anti-doping organisation which initiated sample collection for the purposes of results management.

There are specific provisions in Annex I ISTI for the management of possible whereabouts breaches which can lead to a breach of Article 2.4. Results management will be carried out by the national anti-doping organisation or international federation with which the athlete files his or her whereabouts information. Where a missed test or filing failure is determined to have occurred by that organisation, it has to be submitted to WADA through ADAMS and thereby made available to other anti-doping organisations.[8]

Testing In-Competition at Events

Where sample collection is carried out at an event, generally only a single organisation will be responsible for testing during the period of the event. At international events, the collection of samples should be initiated by the organisation which is the governing body of the event. An international event is an event where an international sport organisation such as the IOC, the IPC, an international federation or a major event organiser (e.g. the Commonwealth Games Federation) is either the ruling body of the event or provides the technical officials for the event.[9] The event organiser may enter into a contract with a NADO to provide testing services. This will usually not change the results management position. At national events, the national anti-doping organisation of the country where the event takes place will be responsible for sample collection. A national event is an event involving national- and international-level athletes which is not an international event. An anti-doping organisation

---

7 Article 7.1 – the appeal has to be heard in an expedited manner and has to be heard by a single arbitrator.
8 For a more detailed outline of results management in relation to whereabouts breaches and relevant anti-doping rule violations under Article 2.4, see Chapter 3, pages 138–41 and Chapter 5, pages 233–41.
9 See the definitions in the Code.

which would usually have testing authority but is not responsible for test-ing at an event may ask the ruling body of the event for permission to carry out testing. If the anti-doping organisation is not satisfied with the response of the event ruling body, it can ask WADA for permission to carry out testing and how testing should be coordinated. If so requested, WADA has to consult with the ruling body of the event. WADA's decision on a request to carry out testing is final and not subject to appeal. WADA has published a Protocol which sets out the process by which a request may be made in relation to proposed additional testing.[10] Tests carried out at events under this process are considered to be out-of-competition tests.

Testing Out-of-Competition

As has been outlined, out-of-competition testing is central to the World Anti-Doping Program. It can be initiated and directed by both national and international organisations and may also be initiated and directed by WADA, the IOC and the IPC (in connection with the Olympic Games and Paralympic Games).

The overall aim of the Code (and the ISTI) is to provide the basis for wide-ranging out-of-competition testing to be initiated and directed by Signatories so that athletes can be readily tested on a no-notice basis. This process depends for its effectiveness, to a significant degree, on Signatories obtaining and maintaining accurate whereabouts information for athletes within their registered testing pools and making this information available to other anti-doping organisations. The process of obtaining this informa-tion begins with NADOs and international federations identifying athletes for inclusion in their registered testing pool for out-of-competition test-ing. The collection of whereabouts information from athletes is governed by the ISTI, and the information collected will be submitted to WADA through its database management tool, ADAMS. WADA can, in turn, make the information available to other organisations with authority to test the athlete. WADA developed ADAMS so that information collected could be held in accordance with established data privacy principles and the International Standard on Privacy.

Test Results and Other Data

Where tests are carried out, WADA acts as a central clearing house for the results of international and national athletes included in their

---

10 See Protocol relating to Code Article 15.1.1 on the WADA website.

NADO's registered testing pool. All tests, whether in-competition or out-of-competition, must be reported to WADA to allow for the coordination of testing and to facilitate the planning of testing by anti-doping organisations. ABP data for international- and national-level athletes who are in ABP programmes will also be reported to WADA. WADA must maintain the information provided in the strictest confidence. The information must also be made accessible to the athlete in question and to other specified organisations.[11] The specific rules and policies under which the information is obtained from athletes must be developed by the relevant Signatories under the Code and Standards, namely, the international federations and NADOs. These bodies must ensure that information is collected in a manner which complies with privacy laws in the States where the information is collected. The ISTI contains detailed provisions relating to the supply of whereabouts information, which are of mandatory application.[12] That whereabouts information is also held by WADA in ADAMS. WADA has to hold all information in ADAMS (which is subject to supervision by Canadian privacy authorities) in strict confidence and in accordance with the ISPPPI.

Investigations into Anti-doping Rule Violations other than Doping

The 2015 Code and ISTI contain additional provisions[13] which refer to the conduct of investigations by anti-doping organisations into those violations under Article 2 which may be established without the taking of samples and analysis by WADA-accredited laboratories.[14] Previously, the IST and the 2009 Code contained scarcely any provision of this nature, and even the newly introduced amendments remain general in nature. While the results of such investigations will be managed by the organisation which notifies the potential violation, the Code makes limited detailed provision concerning the process by which investigations are conducted and results managed, and this is mainly left to the rules and policies of the anti-doping organisation carrying out the investigation.

11 See Article 14.5 of the Code.
12 For an early decision involving an argument that the whereabouts requirements under the British Athletics Federation (BAF) rules were an unjustifiable restriction on the rights to privacy of the athlete, which was rejected by the BAF Tribunal and CAS, see *Ohuruogu* v. *UK Athletics Lt*, summarised in Chapter 5, pages 236–7.
13 Articles 5.1.2 and 5.8 make mandatory provision for anti-doping organisations to carry out investigations. ISTI, Part 3, 11.0 makes general provision for the processes of gathering and using intelligence in investigations.
14 The ISTI also contains a general guideline setting out the process for investigation of a refusal to submit to doping control; see Annex A of the ISTI.

At a fundamental level, in order to conduct an investigation under the Code, an organisation must itself be subject to and function under the Code, and must have authority to carry out the investigation by agreement with the athlete or other person who is subject to the investigation. Generally, unless an anti-doping organisation is given statutory powers of detention, search and seizure or powers to summon for interview or demand documents under applicable national law, an investigation under the Code cannot employ any coercive power, and attempts to act in a manner which purports to use such power is likely to result in illegal conduct under national law. Generally, an athlete who does not comply with a request to answer questions or assist in an investigation faces no sanction under the Code, although athletes are subject to clear obligations to cooperate in an investigation under Article 21 of the Code, and often under the rules of the national anti-doping organisation implementing the Code in this regard. The rules of sporting organisations may contain additional provisions penalising such failures to cooperate in investigations. By contrast, an athlete who refuses to submit to doping control who has agreed to the application of the Code is, of course, subject to liability under Article 2.3 for the refusal. Where an athlete deliberately seeks to subvert an investigation by providing false or misleading information, he or she may commit the violation of tampering under Article 2.5 and/or be complicit in any violation committed by any other person who is under investigation, in breach of Article 2.9. There have, to date, been relatively few large-scale investigations by anti-doping organisations into anti-doping rule violations such as trafficking,[15] but investigations of this kind are becoming more common as international anti-doping organisations and NADOs expand their operations.[16] Anti-doping organisations are responsible for

15 The best example of such an investigation is still perhaps the BALCO case. A good deal of the investigation was carried out by US federal authorities, which made the information they obtained available to the USADA. The investigation resulted in criminal penalties for the individuals who were running the operation and disciplinary sanctions for athletes under the Code. This kind of exchange of information between those investigating for State agencies, such as the police and customs, and those investigating for NADOs is becoming more common.

16 Wide-ranging investigations have been carried out in cycling. Recently, WADA has carried out an extensive investigation into the running of the doping control process by Signatories in Russia, including at the Winter Olympic Games in Sochi in 2014. The investigation came about because of information supplied by 'whistleblowers' from within the organisations under investigation and has led to action against sporting organisations and athletes which is ongoing. See Chapter 10, pages 530–4. For the possible reduction of periods of ineligibility for the provision of substantial assistance, see Chapter 8, pages 436–8.

establishing the rules, policies and protocols which will apply to the conduct and management of such investigations.

Article 7: the Results Management Process

After providing for the responsibility for managing testing in Article 7.1, Articles 7.2–7.8 of the Code set out, in general terms, the process by which anti-doping organisations review adverse and atypical analytical findings, review and follow up adverse and atypical biological passport findings, review whereabouts failures and review and follow up other investigations. The provisions provide for the process of review of findings in a general way, and in most areas the detail of the process required will either be set out in the ISTI (e.g. whereabouts results management) or in Technical Standards and Guidelines (atypical findings, atypical passport findings and adverse biological passport findings).[17]

After it has carried out the review process, if an anti-doping organisation decides to proceed to bring an allegation, it will have to give notice to the athlete or person involved and to other relevant sporting organisations as required by the Code and Standards. The Article is not intended to replace the detailed systems of results management adopted by Signatories which produce the outcome required by the Code.[18] However, while the exact words of Article 7 (and 8) do not have to be adopted in rules or policies, the general standard for the process of results management and hearings is, as with other processes in the Code, mandatory. A process by which decisions under the Code are referred to an independent tribunal is an important feature of the Code in ensuring that its provisions are compatible with fundamental rights protected under Swiss law (or other legal systems) and whether they comply with public policy.[19]

Article 7.2 provides for the initial review of an A sample adverse analytical finding to check for any applicable TUE (which would lead to the test being declared as negative) or to determine whether there has been any departure from the ISTI or ISL which undermines the validity of the finding. After the initial review, the anti-doping organisation responsible must then notify the athlete promptly of the adverse analytical finding and the

---

17 See Athlete Biological Passport Operating Guidelines January 2017. Appendices A–E set out the Technical Documents relating to reporting from the ISTI and ISL which are relevant to reporting under the ABP.
18 See Article 7 of the Code.   19 See Chapter 10.

anti-doping rule violated, of the right of the athlete promptly to request the analysis of the B sample and the deemed waiver if no request is made, of the right to attend on the opening of the B sample in the time period specified in the ISL and of the right to request copies of the A and B sample laboratory documentation package containing the information required by the ISL.[20] At the same time, notice must also be given by the anti-doping organisation managing the result to the athlete's NADO, the international federation and WADA, giving details of the analytical result.[21]

Article 7.4 provides specifically for the review of atypical findings. Such findings will be made where the substance detected may be produced endogenously, as is the case with endogenous steroids such as testosterone. As with an adverse analytical finding, if the initial review does not reveal an applicable TUE or apparent departure from the ISTI or ISL that caused the finding, the anti-doping organisation has to conduct the required investigation in order to determine whether the substance detected was produced endogenously or not. Generally, this further investigation, which may take a number of different forms, will be confidential and will be carried out without notice to the athlete until the anti-doping organisation has completed it and decided whether to bring the atypical finding forward as an adverse analytical finding. If a decision to bring forward an adverse analytical finding is made, the athlete and other anti-doping organisations will be notified in the same way as with an adverse analytical finding. Notice may be given to the athlete before a final decision where the anti-doping organisation decides in the course of its investigation that the B sample should be analysed or where the anti-doping organisation receives a request from a major event organisation or sport organisation which has to meet a selection deadline for a major event to disclose whether any of a list of athletes has any pending atypical finding. In the second situation, the anti-doping organisation may only identify an athlete to the event or sport organisation after first notifying that athlete.

The mandatory notice provisions relating to the B sample rights of the athlete reflect the importance of the rights to the athlete. As previously noted, the B sample rights of an athlete have been held by CAS to be of such importance that a failure to provide an athlete with the rights will invalidate the result of the A sample for the purposes of establishing a

20 See Article 7.2 of the Code. The requirements are also set out in the Guidelines for the results management of tests provided by WADA (see the WADA website).
21 See Article 14.1.2 and pages 314–15.

doping violation under Article 2.1.[22] Similarly, failures in the proper test-ing of the B sample may also see an adverse analytical finding set aside because, if the B sample analysis is rejected, the A sample analysis will not be confirmed. The anti-doping organisation managing an adverse analyt-ical finding may itself have to decide that it cannot bring an anti-doping rule violation where B sample rights have not been properly afforded to the athlete. Such a decision would be notified to other parties under the Code and would give rise to appeal rights under Article 13.

Article 7.5 provides that the review of atypical passport findings and adverse passport findings will take place as provided for by the ISL and ISTI. The process for this review is largely set out in the Operating Guide-lines for the ABP. The detail of the process for the review of passport find-ings is set out in Chapter 5, pages 210–17 in relation to the use of evidence from this source to prove an anti-doping rule violation under Article 2.2. At the end of this process, if the anti-doping organisation is satisfied that a prohibited method has been used in contravention of Article 2.2, it will notify the athlete and other anti-doping organisations in the same way as for other allegations.

Results Management for Whereabouts Failures and Missed Tests

Article 7.6 of the Code provides that the review of possible filing failures and missed tests will take place as provided for in the ISTI. Article 7.1.2 of the Code provides that the results management of a potential whereabouts failure will be administered by the international federation or national anti-doping organisation with which the athlete files his or her where-abouts information. Filing failures or missed tests which are determined to have occurred will be submitted to WADA through ADAMS and made available in this way to other anti-doping organisations. If an athlete ceases to be in the registered testing pool of one anti-doping organisation but remains in the testing pool of another, or if another anti-doping organi-sation begins to receive the athlete's filings, that anti-doping organisation will become responsible for results management.

The detailed results management process for whereabouts failures is set out in ISTI Annex I.5. Anti-doping organisations with responsibility for results management have to work through a detailed process in a system-atic manner, which involves a process of review in relation to each failure.

22 See Chapter 5, pages 191–3 in relation to B sample rights and failures in the B sample process.

When the international federation or national anti-doping organisation is satisfied that a violation of Article 2.4 has occurred, it will give notice to the athlete and other anti-doping organisations in the manner stipulated in Article 14.1.2, as for other alleged violations. The determination by the anti-doping organisation of each failure relied on to establish a violation can be the subject of challenge in any hearing of the alleged violation. Where such a challenge is made, a tribunal hearing the allegation of a breach of Article 2.4 will reconsider the alleged failure and make a fresh decision on whether the requirements under the ISTI have been made out.

Results management will be carried out by the anti-doping organisation with which the athlete filed the whereabouts information. The process of results management involves obtaining any reports, reviewing the documentary file and deciding whether the requirements for a filing failure or missed test are established. If the anti-doping organisation decides that one of the requirements has not been met, it has to notify WADA, the relevant international federation or anti-doping organisation and the anti-doping organisation which uncovered the whereabouts failure. Reasons have to be given for the decision, and a decision not to record a breach of the whereabouts requirements can be appealed under Article 13 of the Code.[23]

If the organisation with results management authority decides that the requirements for a whereabouts failure are met, it has to give notice to the athlete within fourteen days, providing details of the alleged failure and giving the athlete a reasonable time-frame in which to decide whether to reply admitting the breach or to say why he or she does not admit it. The notice has to advise of the consequences of three whereabouts failure in a twelve-month period and note the position as regards any other failures. With a filing failure, notice has to be given that the athlete must file any missing whereabouts information by a given deadline.

If the breach is admitted or the athlete does not respond, the notified whereabouts failure has to be recorded against the athlete. If a response is provided, the anti-doping organisation has to consider whether the athlete's explanation changes the decision that the requirements for recording a whereabouts failure have been established. If the anti-doping

---

23 See ISTI Annex I 5.2 (c). For appeals generally, and for decisions in respect of which appeals lie, see Chapter 9, pages 470–4. This appeal against a failure to record an individual whereabouts breach (as opposed to a decision not to bring forward an alleged breach of Article 2.4) is not expressly provided for in Article 13 of the Code, but the appeal right is clearly set out in ISTI Annex I, which binds all signatories to the Code.

organisation changes its original decision, it has to advise WADA and the international federation or NADO, and the decision can be appealed under Article 13 of the Code. If, after considering the explanation from the athlete, the original decision stands, the anti-doping organisation has to notify the athlete of the right to request an administrative review of the decision. If no administrative review is requested, the whereabouts failure will be recorded. If a review is requested, it will be carried out by one or more persons not connected with the assessment of the failure. The review is on the papers only, and its purpose to consider afresh whether the requirements for a whereabouts failure have been met. Again, if the review concludes that the requirements have not been met, WADA and the relevant international federation or NADO which found the whereabouts failure have to be notified. Each notified organisation has a right of appeal against the decision under Article 13 of the Code.

If the review decides that the requirements for the whereabouts failure have been met, the athlete has to be notified and the failure recorded against the athlete. Decisions to record a whereabouts failure will be reported to WADA and all other anti-doping organisations under the Code by putting the information into ADAMS or another similar system approved by WADA. Information concerning apparent whereabouts failures can be given to other anti-doping organisations at an earlier stage of the results management process on a strictly confidential basis where the anti-doping organisation responsible considers this appropriate for anti-doping investigation or testing. There can be no public disclosure of whereabouts failures, whether by reference to individual athletes or to particular sports, before a decision in respect of an alleged breach of Article 2.4 has been made.

As noted, the organisation with results management authority must bring proceedings for a breach of Article 2.4 against an athlete who has three whereabouts failure recorded against him or her within any twelve-month period. If this step is not taken within thirty days of WADA receiving notice of the recording of the third whereabouts breach, the inactivity will mean that there is a deemed decision that no violation has occurred for the purposes of appeal rights under Article 13.2.

Where an athlete is alleged to have committed an anti-doping rule violation under Article 2.4 of the Code, he or she is entitled to have the allegation heard at a full hearing in accordance with Article 8 of the Code. Previous decisions on the earlier whereabouts failures do not bind the hearing body. The burden remains on the anti-doping organisation to establish all the required elements for any whereabouts failure. Where the Panel decides that a third alleged whereabouts failure has not been established to the required standard under the Code, there will be no violation under Article 2.4. However, if the other whereabouts breaches remain fresh, proceedings may be brought if a further whereabouts failure is committed in the relevant twelve-month period established by the first whereabouts breach.

Results Management for Other Anti-doping Violations

In relation to anti-doping rule violations not covered by Articles 7.1–7.6 (which will be those violations not established by testing and analysis or whereabouts breaches, namely violations under Article 2.3 and 2.5–2.10), Article 7.7 of the Code provides that an anti-doping organisation has to carry out any follow-up investigation required by the rules adopted under the Code or which the anti-doping organisation considers appropriate – often the anti-doping organisation will have rules which provide for the process of investigation. If the anti-doping organisation is satisfied that an anti-doping rule violation has been committed, it has to give notice to the athlete or person alleged to have committed the violation and to other anti-doping organisations, as for other allegations.

Part 3 of the ISTI establishes general standards for the conduct of investigations by anti-doping organisations. The conduct of investigations will be an internal process conducted by anti-doping organisations, which has to be carried out confidentially (although information produced in such investigations may be the subject of disclosure under privacy legislation). Where investigations are commenced, WADA has to be informed and updated on their status on request. The anti-doping organisation has to come to a decision efficiently and without undue delay as to whether proceedings should be brought as a result of information obtained in an investigation. WADA can impose a deadline for this decision. If the anti-doping organisation does not make a decision whether to bring proceedings or not, WADA can choose to bring an appeal to CAS as though a decision not to proceed had been made, provided it consults with the anti-doping organisation before taking this step. If the anti-doping organisation decides not to bring proceedings based on the result of its investigation, it has to notify WADA and the relevant international federation and national anti-doping organisation of its decision, providing reasons for the decision and other such information as is reasonably required to allow the organisations notified to decide whether to appeal. The anti-doping organisation has to consider whether any intelligence obtained should be used to inform the development of its testing plan or to plan target testing, and whether it should be shared with any other law enforcement or statutory agencies.

While the provisions relating to investigations are expressed in mandatory terms (and a failure to carry out investigations will amount to non-compliance with the obligations under the Code), they are generally expressed and do not provide a detailed process which anti-doping organisations have to follow. That is understandable, given the range of possible investigations and the need for anti-doping organisations to develop confidential internal processes for investigating doping activities which may be undertaken on a large-scale clandestine basis in breach of the Code and national criminal law.

Anti-doping organisations are obliged to develop detailed rules and policies governing the conduct of investigations and the management of results obtained by them. Some NADOs, which are statutory in nature, have made rules and policies under statutory provisions;[24] others, which are bodies without statutory foundation, have developed protocols of procedure which are adopted by sporting organisations, thereby binding member athletes. Under either method, the rules will be binding on athletes by the agreement of the organisations which they belong to, or by specific individual agreement. In the United States, by way of example, the USADA is an independent body which is responsible for the conduct of testing, investigations and results management by agreement with the USOC. The procedures which it follows for the results management and hearing process before the AAA are set out in a Protocol which is binding on all US athletes by their membership of sporting organisations and/or through other participation agreements.[25] In New Zealand, by way of contrast, the NADO is statutory in nature, and has made rules in the form of delegated legislation – now the Sports Anti-Doping Rules (SADR) 2017 – under its statutory powers under the Sports Anti-Doping Act 2006 to implement the WADA Code and provide for the conduct of investigations

24 For an example of the legislative approach which creates rules that bind by agreement, see the New Zealand Sports Anti-Doping Act 2006 (and delegated legislation, SADR 2017) and the Australian legislation (the Australian Sports Anti-Doping Authority Act 2006), which has been amended to give ASADA statutory powers to require the production of information in investigations. For the purely contractual approach, see by way of example the USADA Protocol, which is an agreement with sporting organisations and their members, and the anti-doping policy produced by UK Sport for all NSOs in the United Kingdom.
25 See USADA Protocol for Olympic Testing, at www.usada.org, which sets out the process of testing, investigation and adjudication (including the applicable rules of the AAA).

under the Code. While the NADO functions under these statutory powers, the rules can only bind NSOs by agreement (in the same manner as the Protocol in the United States) – this follows from the nature of the Code. There is no need for NADOs or other anti-doping organisations to function under statutory powers, but in many countries a statutory legislative framework exists in the anti-doping area by reason of State involvement in the establishment and funding of the country's NADO.[26] The general process of results management is shown in Figures 2 and 3.

Anti-doping Organisations: Obligation to Bring Proceedings

Where an anti-doping organisation is satisfied after any process of review or investigation that a person bound by the Code has committed an anti-doping rule violation, it is required to bring forward proceedings. It is submitted that an anti-doping organisation has no general discretion not to proceed with an allegation if that position is reached. The language used in Article 7 regarding the giving of notices asserting anti-doping rule violation where the position is reached that the evidence supports that course is mandatory ('shall'). There is no provision allowing for any discretion under the Code. That is consistent with the purpose of the Code, which is to impose a harmonised system under which anti-doping organisations operate in a consistent manner in bringing allegations forward.

This position is also consistent with the terms of the provisions of the Code and ISTI relating to investigations into violations which are not based on testing and analysis or breach of whereabouts rules. While an anti-doping organisation may have reasons for not wishing to bring proceedings forward (e.g. a desire to reach an agreement in order to obtain evidence against others) there is, it is submitted, no general discretion to adopt this course. Again, the language in Article 7.7 regarding the giving of notice alleging a violation if an anti-doping organisation is satisfied that a violation has occurred is mandatory. This position is borne out by the obligation of an anti-doping organisation operating under the Code to pursue all potential anti-doping rule violations within its jurisdiction vigorously and to ensure proper enforcement of the consequences of violations (Article 20.5.7 of the Code). An anti-doping organisation also has to carry out

---

26 Similarly, in some jurisdictions, tribunals to hear anti-doping rule violations have been established under statutory provisions with government funding, while, in others, domestic tribunals or private arbitration bodies created by sporting organisations provide the hearing process.

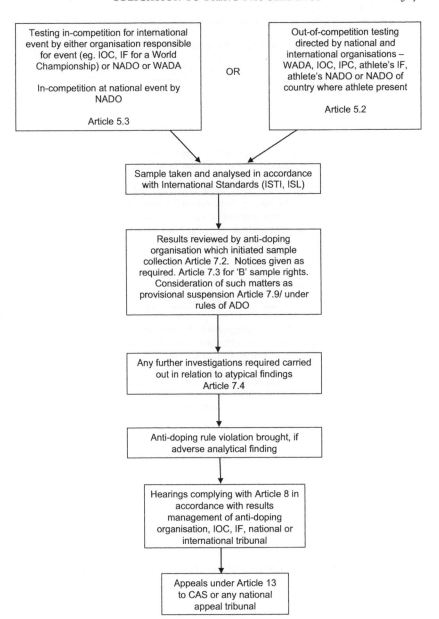

Figure 2 Testing for prohibited substances and methods – general process and results management

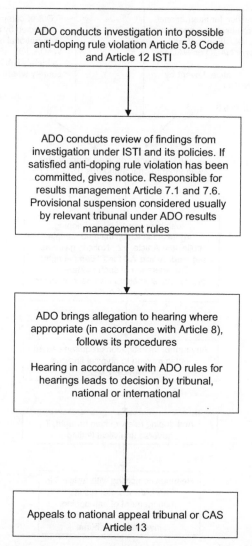

Figure 3 Results management where violation does not arise from sample collection

investigations in relation to all potential anti-doping rule violations and have the capability to do this under the ISTI (Articles 5.1.2 and 5.8 of the Code). ISTI 5.8.3 further provides that an investigation has to be carried out to either rule out a possible violation or develop evidence which would support bringing anti-doping rule violations. These provisions underline the role of the anti-doping organisation under the Code. Any form of residual general discretion not to proceed where the evidence supports the bringing of an allegation would be contrary to these obligations and would risk undermining the Code and its central purpose of creating a harmonised approach across all Signatories.

This position underlies the approach to the provision of substantial assistance under the Code. The Code provides specifically for those situations where substantial assistance can be considered in relation to sanctions under Article 10.6.1. The possible reduction or elimination of the period of ineligibility under this provision is expressly subject to the check of the approval of WADA and the applicable international federation and possible appeals under Article 13.[27] Any residual (unexpressed) discretion under the Code not to proceed with proceedings at all in order to obtain assistance would be at odds with this specific provision.

Overall, the Code should be interpreted as excluding any residual discretion not to bring proceedings where an anti-doping organisation is satisfied on the evidence which it has that a violation has occurred. This approach reflects the overall purpose of the Code, which is to create a uniform transparent system for the investigation of possible violations and the bringing of violations.

The position reached at the conclusion of an investigation which gives rise to an obligation to bring an allegation must be distinguished from the situation where the evidence obtained in an investigation is considered after evaluation by the anti-doping organisation not to be sufficient to support the bringing of proceedings. This kind of evaluation of evidence obtained to determine whether it will establish an anti-doping rule violation to the required standard of proof before the relevant tribunal is for the anti-doping organisation responsible for the investigation. If a decision is made not to bring proceedings after considering the evidence obtained, notice of this decision will have to be given, and this will give rise to appeal rights against the decision among the parties notified. In

27 See Chapter 8, pages 436–8.

this way, the integrity of the processes required under the Code can be protected by the exercise of appeal rights where that is necessary.[28]

Article 7.9: Provisional Suspensions

The question whether a provisional suspension should be imposed on an athlete pending a final decision on an alleged anti-doping rule violation is an important aspect of any results management process. Where there is an adverse analytical finding for a non-specified prohibited substance or prohibited method against an athlete, a provisional suspension must be imposed after the initial review and notice process under Articles 7.2, 7.3 and 7.5. The rules of Signatories to the Code have to provide for a provisional suspension to be imposed. This mandatory provisional suspension can be eliminated where the athlete proves that the violation is likely to have involved a contaminated product as provided for in Article 10.5.1.2.[29] A decision not to eliminate a provisional suspension on the basis of the athlete's assertion that the violation involved a contaminated substance is not appealable.

Where there is an adverse analytical finding for a specified substance or a violation involving a contaminated product or another violation under Article 2 is alleged, the imposition of a provisional suspension after the review under Article 7 is optional and a Signatory may adopt rules for the imposition of a provisional suspension before the analysis of the B sample or final hearing. The rules made for provisional suspension will apply to any event for which the Signatory is the ruling body or for any team selection for which the Signatory is responsible or where the Signatory is responsible for results management. The Code makes general provision to ensure a fair hearing process in relation to the imposition of a provisional suspension. It provides that a provisional suspension may not be imposed unless the athlete is given the opportunity for a provisional hearing in relation to the provisional suspension before or after the imposition of the provisional suspension, or an expedited hearing of the substantive allegation (in accordance with the principles for a fair hearing under Article 8) after the imposition of the provisional suspension.

28 In addition, WADA has the central role of monitoring compliance with the Code under Article 20.7, and decisions not to proceed with allegations may lead to investigation by WADA under this power.
29 See Chapter 8, pages 398–400 for more on this basis for reducing the standard period of ineligibility, which was added by the 2015 Code.

It should further be noted that where a provisional suspension is optional, the anti-doping organisation is obliged to offer the imposition of a provisional suspension to the athlete or person facing the allegation. This will allow the person facing the allegation to accept the imposition of a provisional suspension and obtain the credit for a period of provisional suspension against any period of ineligibility imposed provided for in Article 10.11.3.

Where the provisional suspension is based on the A sample analysis, if the B sample does not confirm the A sample, the provisional suspension has to be set aside. Where a provisional suspension is imposed, the athlete or other person facing the allegation under the Code will receive credit for the period of provisional suspension against the period of ineligibility ultimately imposed. Generally, given the importance of ensuring fair competition which the Code seeks to uphold, it would seem appropriate for Signatories to implement rules which have the result of imposing a provisional suspension in most cases unless the athlete or person facing the allegation can show that the case for breach has no proper basis or that it is likely that he or she will not be subject to a period of ineligibility (because a compelling case for no fault can be shown).

The criteria for deciding whether to impose a provisional suspension where the suspension is optional under the Code will be a matter for the rules of the anti-doping organisation. In many situations, the athlete or person facing the allegation will be advised to accept the imposition of a provisional suspension when the anti-doping organisation makes the offer of provisional suspension, which it must make under the 2015 Code. Where the imposition of a provisional suspension is disputed, the rules of the anti-doping organisation, if specific, are likely to be determinative. If the rules simply refer to the provisional suspension as being optional, the principles which will be applied are likely to be similar to those applied by CAS in deciding whether to make orders for provisional measures.

Where there is an appeal to CAS against a finding that an anti-doping rule violation has been committed, the person appealing may apply for provisional measures in order to compete pending the hearing of the appeal. Such an application will involve consideration of the grant of provisional measures under Rule 37 of the CAS Rules. This involves the tribunal considering whether the applicant for provisional measures will suffer irreparable harm if the suspension is not stayed, the likelihood of success on the claim and whether the interests of the applicant outweigh the interests of the Respondent. This can be a difficult balancing exercise, involving the consideration of the particular circumstances of the individual case.[30] In carrying out the exercise of weighing the interests of the athlete and the respondent sporting organisation or anti-doping organisation, CAS has to consider the public interest in the fight against doping.[31]

The imposition of a provisional suspension will often raise questions concerning the confidentiality of the process of investigation and hearing. It may often be impossible to maintain confidentiality effectively where an athlete is withdrawn from competition under a provisional suspension pending a final hearing. Again, Signatories must make their own rules to govern the position on the reporting of decisions imposing provisional suspensions. These rules should be consistent with the rules adopted for the results management and hearing process overall. It is suggested that the better approach is to seek to maintain the confidentiality of the processes wherever possible under the rules implementing the Code, save where the tribunal hearing the case determines that the particular circumstances make publication the better course in the overall interests of the sporting organisation involved.

Notice of Results Management Decisions

Article 7.10 confirms that in all cases where an anti-doping organisation has asserted that a violation has been committed, where it has withdrawn an allegation, where it has imposed a provisional suspension by order or agreement or where there has been an agreement to the imposition of a sanction without a hearing, the anti-doping organisation has to give notice to all anti-doping organisations with rights of appeal under Article 13.2.3. This is an important provision in triggering appeal rights whenever they might apply.

---

30 For a discussion of substantive requirements for the grant of provisional measures under Rule 37 of the CAS Rules, including on anti-doping allegations, see Mavromati and Reeb, *The Code*, pp. 207–44.

31 For an award considering an application for provisional measures pending the hearing of an appeal by the sporting organisation which had brought the appeal, see CAS 2007/A/1370 & 1376, *FIFA* v. *STJD* v. *Dodô* and *WADA* v. *STJD and Dodô* (Mavromati and Reeb, *The Code*, pp. 222–4), where FIFA appealed against a decision not to impose a sanction on a player and requested provisional measures in the form of immediate orders to suspend the player pending hearing of his appeal. The application was declined because FIFA had not satisfied the requirements, primarily because the short period of time before a final award would not damage FIFA's position on doping and would not diminish the punitive effect on the player.

Retirement

Under Article 7.11, where an athlete or person subject to the Code retires during a results management process, the anti-doping organisation retains jurisdiction and the process will continue to its conclusion. Where an athlete or person retires before the beginning of the results management process, the anti-doping organisation which would have had authority over the athlete or person will have the authority to conduct results management to a conclusion. These provisions prevent an athlete or person from avoiding the consequences of a breach of the Code after the commission of acts which constitute a violation under the Code by the simple expedient of retiring and asserting that he or she is no longer subject to the Code.

Article 14: Reporting and Confidentiality

Article 14 refers in its introduction to the principles of coordination of anti-doping results, public transparency and accountability and of respect for the privacy of athletes and other persons. These introductory words reflect the balance, or tension, which exists under the Code between the recognition of the privacy rights of the athlete or other person who is subject to an investigation or allegation under the Code, the need to inform other specified interested parties of the process and, ultimately, the need to report publicly on the final outcome of the process. The Code can be seen, on one hand, as a private disciplinary process, and, on the other, as a process which produces a result and reasoned decision which, in the world of sport at least, should be publicised and made accessible to all who are subject to the Code or who work under it. In some cases, an athlete may choose to make the case against them public notwithstanding provisions making the process until a formal decision on the allegation is made confidential.

As regards public reporting in the period of time between the end of the initial review of an adverse analytical finding or initial investigation and the hearing and decision on the allegation, the Code contains no mandatory approach and leaves anti-doping organisations to deal with the difficult balancing exercise which exists in this period themselves. The conflict between the individual interest in privacy and the wider interest in publication is perhaps most apparent in the results management process and after decisions have been made. Article 14 seeks to provide a balance in the approach in its mandatory provisions while leaving certain aspects of publication to the specific rules of anti-doping organisations.

Article 14 of the Code provides specifically for the giving of notices to particular individuals and organisations. These notices aim to keep relevant parties informed of the process of investigation and hearing, and are given on the basis that the process is confidential. While the Code is specific concerning the particular parties which have to be notified, the provisions on public disclosure are general in nature.

While the provisions of the Code leave a considerable amount to the rules of the particular organisation handling an investigation in relation to the public reporting of allegations and investigations, it should be noted that the process of sampling and laboratory analysis is strictly confidential under the ISTI and ISL.[32]

Notices

Whenever an anti-doping organisation with results management responsibility asserts that an anti-doping rule violation has occurred, it has to notify the anti-doping organisation of the athlete or person who is alleged to have committed the violation, the relevant international federation and WADA at the same time as it gives notice to the athlete or person. With violations arising from sample collection, the notice has to include the athlete's name, country, sport and discipline and competitive level, the date of sample collection, the analytical result from the laboratory and any other information required under the ISTI. With other violations, the notice has to set out the Article of the Code violated and the basis for the alleged violation. In addition, if after the process of initial review of a positive A sample, the anti-doping organisation responsible for the results management process decides not to bring forward the adverse analytical finding as an anti-doping rule violation, it has to notify the athlete and the same organisations it would have to notify on a decision to proceed with a violation. Where a notice of an asserted anti-doping rule violation has been given, the parties notified have to be regularly updated on the status and findings of any review or proceedings under Articles 7, 8 and 13

---

32 Under the ISL, the WADA laboratory, which will not know the name of the athlete who gave a sample which it analyses, must keep the process strictly confidential. Notwithstanding these obligations, leaks from WADA laboratories have been alleged in high-profile cases. Breaches of the obligations of confidence can lead to civil claims before national courts; see Chapter 10, pages 517–23 for general consideration of such civil claims and pages 526–7 for a relevant case summary.

and have to be given a prompt written reasoned explanation for the resolution of the allegation notified.[33] As already outlined, there is a specific confidential regime for the review of an atypical finding under Article 7.4 and the carrying out of any necessary investigations, with no notice to be given until the completion of any necessary investigation and until a decision is made to bring the atypical finding forward as an adverse analytical finding, save where specified exceptional circumstances arise while an atypical finding is being reviewed or investigated. There is also a specific results management process for the review of atypical and adverse biological passport findings by the anti-doping organisation responsible for the passport. Again, this process is a confidential internal process carried out by the responsible anti-doping organisation in communication with the athlete.[34]

The organisations which are notified cannot disclose the information provided beyond those persons who have a need to know it. This may include personnel at the applicable national Olympic Committee or national federation or on a team in a team sport. Notices given should emphasise the confidential nature of the process and of the information notified. This obligation applies until the anti-doping organisation with results management responsibility has published the information as provided for in Article 14 or has failed to meet the mandatory requirement for public disclosure under Article 14.3. Anti-doping organisations subject to the Code have to comply with the ISPPPI and national privacy law. The note to Article 14.1.5 also provides that they have to include in their rules procedures for the investigation and punishment of improper disclosure of confidential information by an agent or employee. Such improper disclosures are likely to lead to actions under national law with respect to privacy legislation or under common law.

Article 14.3: Public Disclosure before a Final Hearing

The process of notifying particular Signatories must be distinguished from the public reporting of the investigation process and of decisions reached at hearings. As previously noted, the Code does not make specific provision for public reporting during the course of an investigation, but it states that the anti-doping organisation responsible for results management may

---

33 Article 14.1.
34 See Article 7.5 of the Code for the general provision. The detail of the review process under the ABP Guidelines is outlined in Chapter 5, pages 205–10.

publicly disclose the identity of athletes or other persons whose samples have produced relevant adverse analytical findings or who face allegations that they have committed other anti-doping violations only from the time of the completion of the initial review and of the giving of notice to the athlete or person and to the relevant anti-doping organisation as required by the Code.[35] Signatories are left to make specific rules relating to possible public disclosure in this period after the initial period of review and the giving of notice, and there would appear to be different approaches to the question of publication. Given the arbitral nature of hearings (whether the hearing is before a domestic tribunal or CAS) and the essentially confidential disciplinary nature of the investigation process under the Code (which is reflected in the initial notification process), it is submitted that the correct approach during the period when an allegation is being brought forward to a hearing is for anti-doping organisations to adopt rules and policies which provide generally for confidentiality (subject to the obligation to give notices and provide reports as required under the Code) until such time as a decision on any alleged violation has been made. It would seem that many anti-doping organisations have adopted this approach in their rules and policies relating to the investigation of violations, with provision permitting public comment only in exceptional circumstances.[36]

Where a provisional suspension is imposed after the initial review of an adverse analytical sample or other investigation, it may, as noted, be difficult from a practical perspective to maintain confidentiality concerning the identity of the athlete facing the allegation, notwithstanding the making of confidentiality orders. Rules adopted by Signatories should, it is submitted, provide that there may be public reporting of decisions to impose provisional suspensions, if the tribunal imposing the suspension considers that this is in the general interests of the sport to which the allegations relate.

Public Reporting after a Decision

Where an anti-doping rule violation has occurred, the Code expressly provides in Article 14.3.2 that the disposition of the anti-doping matter *must* be publicly reported no fewer than twenty days after a final appellate

---

35 Article 14.2.1 of the Code.
36 By way of example, the anti-doping organisation may wish to provide for the possibility of public comment where the athlete makes public comment on the detail of the case before the hearing.

decision under Article 13.2.1 or 13.2.2 or after such an appeal has been waived (or where an appeal has been waived or a hearing under Article 8 has been waived or the allegation has not otherwise been challenged in time). The reference to final appellate decisions extends the period of time before the mandatory obligation to report a decision applies. Earlier public disclosure before a final appeal decision is optional. Generally, where an anti-doping organisation establishes a national-level tribunal for the hearing of anti-doping rule violations, it is submitted that the appropriate option on public disclosure given the role of the tribunal where a decision finds that an anti-doping rule violation has been committed is for the tribunal to report its decisions publicly under its rules, regardless of possible appeals. However, the amendments in the 2015 Code mean that it is no longer mandatory to disclose a decision publicly before the time for an appeal has passed or, where an appeal is brought, until the appeal has been determined. It is submitted that the rules of any first-instance tribunal should make clear provision for the position on publication.

Where publication is mandatory, the anti-doping organisation responsible for results management must report the disposition of the matter, the anti-doping rule violated, the name of the athlete or other person committing the violation, the prohibited substance or method involved and the consequences imposed. Publication has to be carried out by, at a minimum, placing the required information on the anti-doping organisation's website and leaving it there for either one month or the length of any period of ineligibility imposed, whichever is the longer. This mandatory automatic public reporting is confirmed as a mandatory part of the sanction under the Code by Article 10.13 of the 2015 Code (and by the inclusion of public disclosure or public reporting in the definition of consequences of anti-doping rule violations). It is not required where the athlete or person who has committed the violation is a minor. Public reporting in decisions involving minors is optional, and Article 14.3.6 provides that public reporting in such cases has to be proportionate to the facts and circumstances of the case.

Decisions under the Code generally have to contain full reasons, including, if applicable, the reasons why the maximum potential sanction was not imposed. The provision of proper reasons is also an essential aspect of the obligation to provide a fair hearing process. However, it is not mandatory to publish the full reasons for a decision under Article 14.3.2 – only the information required by the provision is necessary. This means that the extent of final publication will be a matter for the rules of the anti-doping organisation responsible for results management. On appeal before CAS, full awards will be published. International federations and NADOs have established independent tribunals to hear allegations under the Code. Generally, these tribunals will publish their reasoned decisions. It is submitted that this is the better course where many if not most anti-doping allegations are decided by tribunals at national level without appeals being brought, and it is important that those who are bound by the Code have ready access to a body of decisions applying the Code at national level. National-level tribunals will have to consider the extent and duration of publication required by their rules in the light of the provisions introduced in the 2015 Code and the need for publication to be a proportionate response as part of the sanction in cases involving minors. However, it is submitted that the appropriate approach where decisions at a national level are published should mirror that in CAS, where full publication of the award is made, because, at national level, tribunals carry out the same task as CAS in interpreting and applying the Code. Where a decision is published, the tribunal may publish the text in redacted form in order to protect sensitive personal information which is recorded in the decision.

Where it is determined that an athlete or other person did not commit an anti-doping rule violation, the decision can only be publicly reported with the consent of the athlete or other person who is the subject of the decision. Where consent is given, the decision may be published with the consent of the athlete or other person in a redacted form.

Article 14.3.5 specifically provides that no anti-doping organisation or WADA laboratory shall make public comment on the specific facts of a pending case, save in response to public comments attributed to the athlete or other person or their representative.

The process before CAS in its Appeal Division will be confidential, but final decisions by CAS Panels on appeals holding that violations have been committed will be published, with the athletes identified in accordance with the requirements of the Code.[37] Where a challenge is made to the

---

37 For the most part, awards in doping matters where allegations are proved identify the individuals involved when the awards are published on the CAS website. In international arbitration, while generally the confidentiality and privacy of the arbitration process has been confirmed by the rules of arbitration institutions, there are differences of approach on the question of publication where arbitral institutions produce decisions which may be of broader interest to those trading in the market served by the arbitral institution which produces awards. By way of example, in maritime law, there has been a long-running controversy concerning the publication of arbitration awards. Maritime arbitration awards in New York have been published for many years, while London maritime arbitration awards are not published. The publication of CAS awards, and the naming of those involved, which

courts regarding a CAS award, the question of confidentiality will be considered by reference to the procedural rules of the legal system governing the court which hears the appeal.

CAS hearings make specific provision concerning the question whether the hearing of alleged violations under the Code before CAS tribunals should be open to the public. In sporting tribunals, this will be a matter for the rules adopted by the tribunal, but a disciplinary tribunal is essentially a private arbitral process, which should, it is submitted, remain private, unless the parties have otherwise agreed. The CAS Procedural Code provides that proceedings, hearings and decisions in the Ordinary Division will remain confidential. Awards are not to be made public unless the award itself so provides or all the parties agree. By contrast, in the CAS Appeal Division, which will hear doping appeals under the Code, the CAS Procedural Rules contain no specific provision regarding confidentiality. The proceedings and the hearing are confidential, as is the case with arbitration proceedings generally. However, the CAS Procedural Rules for appeals provide that the award, a summary and/or a press release giving the outcome of the proceedings must be made public by CAS unless both parties agree that it is to remain confidential.[38] Where a challenge to a decision made by a tribunal under the Code is made to the national courts, the question of confidentiality and public access to a hearing will be considered under the procedural rules of the court hearing the appeal.

Claims for Breach of Confidence

The Code, while it imposes clear obligations to keep information in the strictest confidence, contains no provision relating to claims for breach of obligations of confidence and non-disclosure owed by Signatories or others operating under the Code. While breaches of the obligations under the Code may lead to a Signatory being found to be not in compliance with the Code, with the possible consequences of that non-compliance, claims for breach of the obligation to keep information in strict confidence will generally be left to the general law of the State which has jurisdiction over

---

is a well-established and necessary practice given the aims of the Code, illustrates the tension between the public element of doping cases and the private disciplinary aspect of the process.

38 See Chapter 1, pages 38–41 for Rule 43 on the Code of Sports Related Arbitration for Ordinary Division and Rule 59 on the Appeal Division.

the breach.[39] The wrongful release of confidential information concerning an athlete or other person under investigation may give rise to significant claims for loss and damage, where the information released has the effect of causing the general public and commercial parties to consider that the athlete is a drug cheat or is involved in doping. Where a subsequent inquiry or a hearing establishes that this is not the case, those responsible for the wrongful release may well face claims for significant sums by way of damages before national courts.[40]

Mutual Recognition

The goal of global harmonisation which underpins the Code requires that Signatories to the Code respect those processes and decisions of other Signatories which are consistent with the Code and are under the authority of the other Signatory (subject to the rights of appeal of Signatories under Article 13). Article 15.1 makes general provision for this mutual recognition. The recognition of TUE decisions is specifically provided for in Article 4.4 and ISTUE.

Where a Signatory fails to recognise a decision by another Signatory, the remedy is to complain to WADA, which monitors compliance with the Code, in relation to the failure.[41] There are no other specific remedies available under the Code for the failure of a Signatory to recognise the decisions of another Signatory.[42] WADA can report the non-compliance to the IOC, the IPC, international federations and major event organisations, and there would be possible consequences for non-compliance on the part of a government or national Olympic committee as determined by the ruling body of the Olympic Games, Paralympic Games, world

---

39 A breach of confidentiality might possibly be relied on to support an argument that proceedings under the Code before a tribunal or CAS should be stayed as an abuse of process if it meant that there could be no fair hearing.

40 For an example of an unsuccessful claim for the wrongful release of confidential information regarding an initial adverse analytical finding, see *Lagat* v. *IAAF* in Chapter 10, pages 526–7. There have been a number of situations in which athletes have complained of leaks of the details of an investigation by laboratories in breach of the obligations owed under the Code and International Standards, but, as yet, there has been no successful claim for damages. Claims of this nature are unlikely to fall within agreements to submit disputes under the Code to tribunals established by sporting organisations and CAS, and specific arbitration clauses in the rules of a sports organisation would be required to achieve this. This means that claims are more likely to be made before national courts. The subject has come to the fore recently with the release of confidential TUE files obtained by hacking into WADA databases. The ISPPPI has specific provisions relating to the notification of cyber security breaches.

41 Article 23.4.   42 Article 23.5.

championship or major event. Ultimately, exclusion from major events as a result of non-compliance is a possible sanction. The obligation to respect the decisions of other Signatories does not extend to decisions which are inconsistent with the Code. The appeal rights under Article 13 of the Code[43] are available to an anti-doping organisation (which could have imposed a sanction in the matter which is the subject of an appeal) or WADA, and these rights can be exercised in relation to a decision which is not consistent with the Code. A successful appeal would remove any doubt about the need to recognise a decision which is, in the view of a Signatory or WADA, inconsistent with the Code.

Article 15.2 makes further provision for the recognition of decisions made by bodies which have not accepted the Code, provided those decisions are otherwise consistent with the Code. Where a decision is, in some ways, compliant with the Code, Signatories have to try and apply the decision in a way which is consistent with the principles of the Code. This may involve a hearing to determine whether a period of ineligibility under the Code should be applied where a decision has been made which is generally consistent with the Code but which does not apply the period of ineligibility under the Code. Where a decision is recognised, it will have all the consequences of a decision under the Code. Difficult questions may arise where a decision by a body not bound by the Code comes to light some time after the making of the decision and the imposition of consequences. Under the 2015 Code, an athlete has an obligation to disclose a finding by a non-Signatory that he or she had committed an anti-doping rule violation within the previous ten years to their national anti-doping organisation or international federation.[44] This provision appears to cover decisions in the nature of an anti-doping rule violation by bodies not bound by the Code. Generally, where there is a delay in the consideration of recognition of a decision and where the athlete has not disclosed the decision, it is submitted that if the decision is recognised, the period of ineligibility should run from the time of recognition and any results earned in the period between the commission of the violation which is subsequently recognised and the date of recognition should be disqualified.

Article 8: Hearings

Fairness and Due Process

Article 8 of the Code provides for the general standards which must be met by Signatories to the Code in hearing alleged violations and giving

43 Article 13.2.3.   44 Article 21.1.5 of the Code.

decisions on them. The wording of Article 8 has been amended and short-ened in the 2015 Code to be consistent with the provisions of Article 6.1 of the Convention for the Protection of Human Rights and Fundamental Freedoms. Again, it should be noted in connection with this Article that, while the words of the Article do not have to be incorporated without significant amendment into anti-doping policies, the general standard required for the conduct of hearings under Article 8 is mandatory. The requirement is that the person facing an anti-doping rule violation must be given, at a minimum, as part of the results management process, a fair hearing within a reasonable time by a fair and impartial hearing panel and that a timely reasoned decision (including an explanation of the reasons for any period of ineligibility) must be publicly disclosed as set out under Article 14.3. The anti-doping organisation will have its own rules for hearing, but they must be consistent with these general principles in order to comply with the Code. The general process for hearings under the Code is set out in Figure 4.

The principles in Article 8 reflect the principles for fair hearings which are generally accepted in international law and in both common law and civil legal systems. These principles are contained in international conventions such as the ECHR and in various State constitutions which safeguard fundamental rights before courts and tribunals. Under Swiss law, as in many other legal systems, a proper hearing process is essential if the Code and its processes are to comply with general public policy (this is termed 'procedural public policy' under Swiss law). Article 8 is formulated on the basis that Article 6.1 of the ECHR, which applies where a person faces a claim in relation to rights and obligations of a civil nature, is applicable to proceedings under the Code and that Code proceedings are not criminal in nature.

Article 8 of the 2015 Code has abbreviated the previous provisions to provide simply for a fair trial. The components of a fair hearing and their content may vary to an extent with different hearing processes, but the key components would be a hearing in good time, before an independent impartial tribunal, at which the person facing an allegation has a proper opportunity to present his or her case and after which a reasoned decision will be provided in reasonable time.[45] A fair hearing will also generally involve the right to appeal the decision. While requiring that any

---

45 See the text of Article 8 of the Code. It is submitted that the earlier provisions in the 2009 Code provided a reasonable summary of some of the components of a fair hearing in the context of an allegation under the Code.

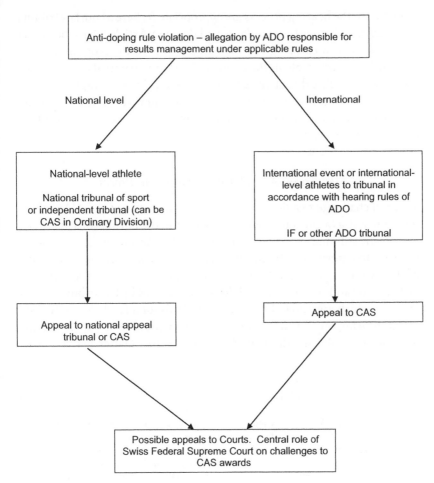

Figure 4 Hearings under the Code

hearing respects these fundamental principles of fairness, the Article (and the notes to it) does not seek to lay down the specific rules by which the fair hearing rights are provided and anticipates that Signatories will meet the standard required in different ways.

In certain areas, the list of principles might be said to go further than would be required in some jurisdictions under the established principles of natural justice and common law, but, in the context of an allegation which may, if established, end an athlete's career, and which carries significant stigma in both the sporting and the wider community, the standards required for the hearing process are appropriate. Where a court or tribunal has to assess whether the standards laid down in Article 8 have been met, it is important in carrying out such an assessment to recognise that the standards are applicable in the context of sporting tribunals. In considering appeals alleging defective hearing processes, CAS has emphasised that the standards required by Article 8 may be met in various ways – sporting tribunals should not generally be judged by the processes which would be expected in courts.[46]

Powers on Appeal: Curing Defects in Process

Where a challenge to a hearing process is made before CAS, CAS will, in the same way as a court reviewing challenges to the fairness of a hearing in a domestic tribunal, examine the totality of the hearing process in context in order to determine whether it is fair.[47] CAS has often used the scope of its review under the CAS Procedural Rules[48] to re-hear a matter on fact and law and so 'cure' alleged defects in process by the tribunal at first instance which are said to breach the standards for a fair hearing. If either a CAS hearing on appeal or a hearing by a national-level appeal tribunal does not meet the standards under Article 8, this matter may be raised

---

46 See e.g. *USA Shooting and Q* v. *UIT* in Chapter 1, pages 50–2, where the CAS Panel observed that a party could be afforded a fair hearing by being given the opportunity to make written submissions as opposed to being granted a full oral hearing.

47 There are many CAS awards where Rule 57 of the CAS Procedural Code has been relied on to allow CAS to review the facts and law fully on an appeal so that the re-hearing cures defects in the earlier process. In common law jurisdictions, this general approach is set out in *Calvin* v. *Carr* [1979] 2 All ER 440, where the Privy Council emphasised that the question on an appeal from a flawed first hearing is often whether there has, at the end of the day, been a fair result at the end of the appeal process. In the context of domestic tribunals, there may be situations where a properly conducted initial hearing is an indispensable part of the hearing process, so that a defective process at first instance cannot be cured by a later proper re-hearing on appeal. In appeals from sporting disciplinary tribunals (whether in general disciplinary matters or in anti-doping cases), CAS has consistently applied the principle that an untainted appeal process in which the facts and law are reviewed afresh will cure earlier defects and produce a fair result overall. On a proper hearing being granted on appeal, the fairness of the first-instance hearing 'fades to the periphery'. See e.g. CAS 2006/A/1175, *Danuite* v. *IDSF*, para. 61; *B* v. *FINA*, CAS Digest II, p. 255; *USA Shooting and Q* v. *UIT*, CAS Digest I, p. 187; *S* v. *FINA*, CAS Digest II, p. 339; and *A* v. *FILA*, CAS Digest III, p. 159. The Swiss Federal Tribunal has found that a CAS hearing has remedied defects alleged in the initial hearing.

48 See Chapter 9, pages 479–81 for CAS powers on appeal and the confirmation of the unlimited power of review in Articles 13.1.1 and 13.1.2 of the Code.

on an appeal against the decision to the courts.[49] As noted, the nature of the agreement to refer disputes relating to allegations under the Code to tribunals with an appeal to a national appeal tribunal or CAS means that, in many jurisdictions, a challenge to the decisions will be subject to the law governing the challenge of arbitration awards. A failure to afford fairness in the hearing process will provide grounds to set aside the award on the basis that a party was not given a proper opportunity to present its case, or that the award was contrary to the public policy of the legal system to which appeals against the award were subject. Similarly, a failure to provide a fair hearing process will potentially provide the grounds for the award not to be recognised or enforced by the courts or other competent authorities of the country where it is sought to have it recognised where the New York Convention on the Recognition and Enforcement of Foreign Arbitral Awards is applicable.[50]

Impartiality

The concept of impartiality contained in Article 8 will cover the different kinds of bias which might be alleged against a decision-maker under the principles established in administrative law in many jurisdictions. This would cover actual or apparent bias. Actual bias involves establishing that a decision-maker is, in fact, biased against a person facing allegations, in the sense that the decision-maker comes to decide a dispute with a predisposition to decide it one way or another. The legal test for apparent bias varies between jurisdictions, but, in common law jurisdictions at least, it involves the court or tribunal which is reviewing the question of possible apparent bias in an inferior tribunal asking whether a fair-minded and informed observer, having considered the facts, would conclude that there

---

49 A challenge of this kind, brought on the basis that CAS Panels are affected by bias or lack of independence in the general sense, because CAS is aligned with the IOC and specifically regarding the appointment of particular arbitrators, failed in *A and B* v. *IOC and FIS* (see Chapter 10, page 509). A challenge to the Swiss Federal Tribunal on the grounds that one of the Panel of arbitrators was affected by apparent bias in *Valverde* (see Chapter 2, pages 82–7) was rejected. Recently, a challenge brought by Claudia Pechstein against the CAS process was rejected by the German Federal Tribunal (see Chapter 10, pages 513–17).

50 See UNCITRAL Model Law, Recourse against Award, and Article V of the New York Convention on the Recognition and Enforcement of Foreign Arbitral Awards. For more on the limited grounds on which a CAS award (whether domestic or international) and a decision by a national-level tribunal may be challenged as an arbitration award, see Chapter 10, pages 464–7.

was a real possibility that the tribunal was biased.[51] It is again important to bear in mind that the assessment whether an impartial hearing has been provided for the person facing the allegation has to be made in the context of a sporting tribunal which may well have been established by a sporting organisation with the specific task of hearing allegations against its own members and imposing sanctions where the allegations are established. Depending on the particular rules of the sporting organisation, appointments to such tribunals may well be made from a small pool of qualified people often within the organisation itself. The fact that sporting tribunals are established in this way should not mean, of itself, that there is an appearance of bias or lack of independence. Indeed, such disciplinary structures are an expected and established aspect of voluntary membership of private associations. Something more will be required, it is submitted, to found a claim that the tribunal was, in fact, biased or lacking in independence, or that there was an appearance of bias.[52]

An anti-doping organisation which is responsible for investigating anti-doping rule violations cannot, as a matter of fairness, permit persons who were involved in the investigation itself to adjudicate on allegations if an impartial process is to be provided. Generally, allegations will be referred either to a tribunal established by the sporting organisation to carry out judicial functions (where members have no interest in the matter which they hear) or to a separate, independent tribunal established to hear such matters, which has been given jurisdiction by agreement with the sporting organisation.[53] It is suggested that the importance and seriousness of

51 See e.g. the decision of the English House of Lords in *Porter* v. *McGill* [2002] 2 AC 357, where this test was adopted under English law. There are nuances between the tests used in different common law jurisdictions, but the essence of each formulation is that there should be an objective inquiry into the conclusions on possible bias which a reasonable bystander would draw. The assessment must be made in the particular factual context.

52 See *Modahl* v. *BAF and IAAF* in Chapter 10, pages 525–6 for an example of a civil claim made against a sporting disciplinary tribunal for, among other things, actual or apparent bias. The claim was dismissed on the facts. See also *Valverde* in Chapter 2, pages 82–7.

53 In the United Kingdom, the need for doping allegations to be considered by an independent tribunal led to the establishment of an independent tribunal to hear doping matters. In the United States, doping allegations which are under the jurisdiction of USADA are referred to a hearing before the AAA under specific rules for such cases, with an arbitration hearing at first instance, and an appeal to CAS in its Appeal Division. In New Zealand, NSOs have agreed that anti-doping matters will be heard by the Sports Tribunal (a statutory tribunal continued by the Sports Anti-Doping Act 2006). Under SADR 2017, the Sports Tribunal will hear and determine matters brought before it by the NADO Drug Free Sport New Zealand. Athletes and other persons who have, through their NSOs, agreed to the application of SADR agree under SADR to the jurisdiction of the Sports Tribunal. The

anti-doping allegations makes a hearing before a tribunal which is wholly independent of the sporting organisation (and any investigating organisation) desirable where such a hearing structure can be adopted.

CAS at First Instance

The notes to Article 13 of the Code make it clear that there is nothing to prevent a sporting organisation bound by the Code from implementing a rule which selects CAS as the tribunal in which allegations will be heard at first instance, or as the appeal tribunal for national-level disputes. If this approach is adopted for first-instance hearings, allegations will be heard under the CAS Procedural Rules applicable to the CAS Ordinary Division.

Where an international athlete is concerned, there must be an appeal to a CAS Panel (in the Appeal Division) to satisfy the requirements of Article 13 of the Code. Where a national-level athlete is concerned, there must also be a right of appeal to satisfy the Code (and general principles of fairness and natural justice). If CAS is chosen to hear the allegation at first instance, there should be a further appeal to CAS sitting in its Appeals Division. Where the first hearing for a national athlete takes place before a national-level tribunal, there can be an appeal either to a national appeal tribunal or to CAS.

As already outlined, the power of CAS to re-hear a case *de novo* on appeal has played an important part in addressing allegations that a hearing before a tribunal has been unfair and in breach of Article 8. Part of the reason for this full power of review on appeal is that CAS may be the first tribunal independent of a sport to hear a case. The independence of CAS was challenged in a claim brought before the German courts by Ms Pechstein. That claim has recently been rejected by the GFT, and the role of CAS as a true arbitral court hearing appeals affirmed.[54]

---

establishment of CAS and its place under the Code recognise the importance of having a tribunal which is independent of sporting organisations hear anti-doping allegations if a fair hearing process is to be established.

54 See Chapter 10, pages 513–17 for summaries of the decisions in the German courts.

Articles 9 and 10 of the Code: Sanctions for Anti-doping Rule Violations

Introduction

Since the implementation of the 2004 Code, the rules relating to the imposition of sanctions under Article 10 have received the most attention from sporting tribunals and CAS. This is a natural consequence of a system where the athlete is strictly liable for the presence of prohibited substances in a sample (or for using prohibited substances or methods) but is provided with possible grounds, under Article 10, upon which to have the prescribed sanction eliminated or reduced. While the investigation and prosecution of anti-doping rule violations not involving evidence from positive tests is increasing and will continue to do so, and this will require more frequent consideration by tribunals of sanctions for violations such as administration, complicity and trafficking, the focus for many hearings and in revising the Code has remained on the provisions relating to the imposition of sanctions for the violations under Articles 2.1 (presence), 2.2 (use) and 2.6 (possession).

The provisions of Article 10 have also been the subject of much debate and amendment in the two reviews of the Code. This reflects the difficulty in providing for harmonisation in this area across all sports and participants.[1] The 2015 Code (which resulted from a review of the 2009 Code[2]) makes radical changes to Article 10 in pursuit of an approach to sanctions which is tougher on 'real cheats' and provides an appropriate balance between predictability and certainty on one hand, and a measure of flexibility on the other. This flexibility is intended to allow tribunals to consider the circumstances relating to the violation in order to vary the

---

1 The difficulty in this area is referred to in the comment on Article 10 in the notes at the end of the Article. The comment emphasises the overall need for harmonisation, sometimes at the expense of differing effects from sanctions across different sports and participants.
2 The summary from WADA of the amendments made in the final version of the 2015 Code records that over 300 separate submissions were received and some fifty working drafts produced.

standard period of ineligibility and so arrive at an appropriate response on a principled basis by considering the degree of fault of the athlete.

This process of review and amendment[3] throughout the relatively short history of the Code has in large measure involved an ongoing search for the right balance between certainty and flexibility. The result has been significant changes in the provisions, allowing for the elimination and reduction of periods of ineligibility by reference to the fault of the athlete or person in breach of the Code, as well as, in the 2015 Code, a change in the standard period of ineligibility from two to four years for breaches of Articles 2.1, 2.2 and 2.6. While the text of the Code has, since the first version in 2004, indicated that the Code is intended to evolve and improve under the direction of WADA, with WADA initiating proposed amendments and ensuring a consultative process in relation to proposed amendments, and while stakeholders have engaged wholeheartedly in that process,[4] a consequence of this evolution is that those bound by the Code have had to address significant regulatory change on a regular basis. Both the process of transition in the rules themselves (which may involve tribunals having to consider the possible operation of two different sets of rules in order to decide which set or rules should apply as being the more lenient as regards sanctions in accordance with *lex mitior* principles) and the interpretation and operation of new rules in themselves represent a significant challenge for those operating under and administering anti-doping regimes. Such challenges seem likely to arise with certain provisions of the 2015 Code.[5]

Overview of the History of Code Amendments and Summary of Key Amendments in the 2015 Code

The 2004 Code contained a standard period of ineligibility of two years for the violations of presence, use, refusal, tampering and possession, with limited provision for the reduction of that period when the person who had committed the anti-doping rule violation could establish either the

---

3 For the obligation of WADA to oversee the evolution and amendment of the Code, see Article 23.7. For comment on the development of the Code and its possible future development, see Chapter 11, pages 535–7. For the comments in earlier editions of this book on the development of the Code see Appendix 3, which contains the Chapter 11s from the first two editions.

4 See Article 23.7 – the global commitment to the Code and its processes is underlined by the acceptance of the UNESCO Convention.

5 For further comment on the effect of changes to the Code following review, see Chapter 11.

requirements for a reduced sanction where the violation involved a specified substance under the Prohibited List or the criteria for the application of the no fault or no significant fault defences. Overall, the regime
in the 2004 Code sought to place strict limits on any discretion in relation to sanctions in the interests of certainty, consistency and fairness
across sports and athletes worldwide.[6] This was an understandable reaction to the inconsistent, differing treatment of doping violations by different sporting organisations and different tribunals which the Code sought
to address. However, the central concern reflected in early CAS pre-Code
decisions remained – the need to strike the appropriate balance in the
rules between strict certainty and the interests of harmony and flexibility, aimed at producing just and proportionate outcomes across the wide
range of circumstances in which doping violations occurred. For many
stakeholders, the limited circumstances in which the standard period of
ineligibility could be reduced or eliminated under the defences in Articles 10.5.1 and 10.5.2 of the 2004 Code and the narrow ambit of the category of specified substances under the Prohibited List, which limited the
possible application of Article 10.3 of the 2004 Code, were productive of
too much unfairness. While the need for as much consistency and harmony as possible in the imposition of sanctions was acknowledged, many
considered that a more flexible system which took greater account in a
wider range of cases of the nature of the violation and the fault of the athlete in arriving at the period of ineligibility to be imposed was required.
The general criticism of the sanctions regime in the 2004 Code was, perhaps, that it imposed the standard two-year period of ineligibility on too
many who tested positive or used prohibited substances as a result of negligent mistakes, often with little real fault on a general understanding of
that term. For many, the 2004 Code did not distinguish sufficiently or at
all between the athlete who acted carelessly and the athlete who took prohibited substances deliberately, intending to cheat – both were often the
subject of the standard period of ineligibility of two years. After the review
process relating to the 2004 Code, amendments were made to allow for
more flexibility in the imposition of periods of ineligibility under the 2009
Code.

6 The most obvious statements in this regard were in the comments to the defences under
  Articles 10.4 and 10.5 of the 2004 Code, which stated that both no fault and no significant fault defences are for exceptional circumstances. Although reduced and diminished in
  length, the comment relating to the defences in Articles 10.4 and 10.5.2 of the 2015 Code
  retains much of the same text and contains the same general reminder – see pages 374–84
  and 395–401 for further consideration of the defences.

The 2009 Code

The 2009 Code made significant changes to the sanctions regime under Article 10, while retaining the same general framework for defences based on fault in Articles 10.3, 10.5.1 and 10.5.2 of the 2004 Code. Generally, the amendments to Article 10 sought to provide, on one hand, for a possible increase in the period of ineligibility for a first violation to four years where aggravating circumstances could be proven by the anti-doping organisation (in the general sense of the person charged being shown to be in a concerted intentional plan to cheat) and, on the other, for the broadening of the circumstances in which a tribunal would be able to reduce the standard period of ineligibility of two years by reference to the fault of the athlete. In general terms, the 2009 Code sought to differentiate more clearly between more serious violations and careless mistakes. Greater flexibility was achieved primarily by extending the range of substances designated as specified substances under the Prohibited List, with the consequence that an amended Article 10.4 in the 2009 Code (which replaced Article 10.3 of the 2004 Code) had increased potential application. Article 10.4 allowed for a reduction of the standard period of ineligibility of two years for violations of doping, use and possession where specified substances were involved, to anything from a warning to a period of ineligibility of two years. This Article could apply if the person who had committed the violations could show to the comfortable satisfaction of the tribunal (with corroborating evidence) that he or she did not intend to enhance sport performance. If this was established, the period of ineligibility had to be determined by reference to the fault of the athlete in relation to the violation. The category of specified substances under the Prohibited List was extended to cover all substances apart from those which are generally closely associated with the use of prohibited substances to gain unfair advantage in sport performance (to cheat) – steroids, peptide hormones, growth factors (such as EPO and hGH) certain stimulants and various prohibited methods.[7]

As already outlined, the 2004 Code and the 2009 Code sought to achieve the same goal – an appropriate (and elusive) balance between certainty and flexibility. The 2009 Code introduced a larger measure of flexibility and discretion for tribunals in imposing sanctions, provided the applicable preconditions were established. The focus in sanctions cases under the

---

7 For the Prohibited List 2017 and the specific categories in more detail, see Chapter 3, pages 96–106.

2004 Code tended to be on the possible application of no fault or no significant fault defences under Articles 10.5.1 and 10.5.2. The changes made by the 2009 Code saw much more consideration of sanctions under Article 10.4.[8]

The changing provisions between the 2004 and 2009 Codes reflected the continuing debate about the right approach to the imposition of sanctions. To an extent, this debate has been ongoing since the time of early pre-Code CAS decisions, when some CAS Panels held that they had the power to vary fixed sanctions in anti-doping regimes according to their assessment of the degree of fault of the person who had committed the anti-doping rule violation. With the 2009 Code, the pendulum can be said to have swung towards the Code providing for a greater measure of flexibility in the imposition of periods of ineligibility. This debate remained central in the process of reviewing and revising the 2015 Code.

The 2015 Code: Main Changes

The 2015 Code contains significant changes to the sanctions regime in Article 10. Articles 10.2–10.6 of the 2009 Code have been largely deleted and re-written in the 2015 Code. In general terms, the amendments in the 2015 Code primarily seek to impose longer periods of ineligibility on athletes or other persons who intend to compete unfairly and commit anti-doping rule violations to do this, to simplify the approach to the assessment of fault as a basis for reducing the period of ineligibility, to provide specifically for violations arising as a result of the use of contaminated products and recreational substances and to simplify the position in relation to the imposition of sanctions for multiple violations.

The most significant changes involve the introduction of the concept of 'intentional' conduct into the Code for the first time in respect of violations for the presence of a prohibited substance, use of a prohibited substance or method and possession of a prohibited substance or method, which are expressed to be strict liability violations under Article 2, in order to regulate the imposition of a longer four-year period of ineligibility for first violations, the removal of Article 10.4 of the 2009 Code (which governed the possible reduction of the standard period of ineligibility for violations involving specified substances), and its replacement with a defence based on 'no significant fault'.

---

8 See Appendix 1 for the operation of Article 10.4 of the 2009 Code and relevant case summaries.

In summary, the main amendments in the 2015 Code are:

- Article 10.2 Code provides for a four-year period of ineligibility for the presence, use and possession of a non-specified substance, unless the athlete proves that the violation was not 'intentional'. Article 10.2 provides for the same period of ineligibility of four years where the violation involves a specified substance, if the anti-doping organisation proves that the violation was 'intentional'. While expressed in terms of the requirements for the imposition of sanctions and included in the Code's Articles on sanctions,[9] the amendment has the practical effect of introducing further violations into the Code – the intentional taking of prohibited substances, the intentional use of prohibited substances and the possession of prohibited substances with intent – which attract longer bans.[10]
- The defences of 'no fault' and 'no significant fault' (with the same definitions) are still used in Articles 10.4 and 10.5 to regulate the possible elimination or reduction of the applicable period of ineligibility. However, the no significant fault defence is now applied both as a general defence under Article 10.5.2 (as previously) and in specific circumstances – to anti-doping rule violations involving a specified substance which are not 'intentional', to violations arising from contaminated products and, as a result of a note to the definition, to the taking of cannabis where it is taken in circumstances not related to sport performance. In each situation, the no significant fault defence, if the requirements for its application are established, opens up the range of sanctions from reprimand and no period of ineligibility to two years' ineligibility, with the period of ineligibility being arrived at by reference to the fault of the person in breach. The no significant fault defence is still applicable in the same way as under the 2004 and 2009 Codes in other individual cases not within the specified new 'no significant fault' defences where it will provide the basis for a reduction of the period of ineligibility down to one-half of the applicable period of ineligibility, with again the period of

---

9 The question whether there is intentional conduct will be considered at the time when a decision as to the applicable sanction is made, but the anti-doping organisation or the athlete will have to decide on the approach they will take to the violation at the time when proceedings are commenced or when a defence is filed. See pages 353–60 for further details.

10 Article 10.6 of the 2009 Code, which allowed for the imposition of a four-year period of ineligibility on proof of aggravated circumstances by the anti-doping organisation (and was rarely invoked by anti-doping organisations), has been removed.

ineligibility being determined by reference to the degree of fault of the athlete.

• The prompt admission and substantial assistance provisions, which allow for elimination or reduction on grounds other than fault, have been significantly revised (Articles 10.6.1–10.6.3).

• The provisions relating to multiple violations have been simplified, and the detailed table for periods of ineligibility for multiple violations in the 2009 Code has been removed (Article 10.7).

Effect of Changes

The changes to Article 10 of the 2015 Code will require tribunals to consider the imposition of sanctions differently and will produce significantly different substantive results on sanctions in certain circumstances. The most obvious change is that a 'standard' case involving a breach of Articles 2.1–2.3, 2.5 or 2.6, which previously attracted a two-year period of ineligibility, will be subject to a sanction of four years' ineligibility.

Tribunals will need to be alert to the changes in considering the imposition of sanctions under the 2015 Code, because either the approach will be new, as with the sanctions for 'intentional' violations, or familiar provisions with established definitions will be used in different circumstances, with different possible results. While the amendments continue to use defined provisions from the earlier versions of the Code in order to determine whether a tribunal can exercise a discretion to reduce the standard period of ineligibility – the familiar 'no significant fault' defence – the range of possible periods of ineligibility which the defences can open up may well be different. While under the 2004 and 2009 Codes the task of a tribunal, if an athlete established 'no significant fault', was to further assess the 'fault' of the athlete in order to determine a period of ineligibility of between twelve months and two years, under the 2015 Code the 'no significant fault' defence is applicable in a different way according to certain provisions under Article 10 of the 2015 Code, and if there is no significant fault the degree of 'fault' has to be considered in order to determine the level of sanction between a warning and no period of ineligibility and the maximum of two years' ineligibility. Article 10.4 of the 2009 Code, with its particular requirements[11] for determining whether a sanction for a violation involving a specified substance could be reduced by

---

11 The interpretation of the requirements caused significant uncertainty about the application of the Article, as set out in Appendix 1.

reference to the 'fault' of the athlete, has been repealed and replaced with the requirement to prove no significant fault before any reduction in the period of ineligibility of two years can be considered. This represents a significant change in approach. Further, whenever fault has to be considered in assessing periods of ineligibility, a tribunal now has to carry out the assessment by reference to the specific general definition of 'fault' which was introduced in the 2015 Code, which is of general application where fault has to be considered.[12] The different threshold tests for the application of the defences under the 2009 and 2015 Codes mean that an athlete who could show that he or she had no intention to enhance sport performance in taking a prohibited substance and rely on Article 10.4 of the 2009 Code might not be able to show no significant fault as required by the 2015 Code (and vice versa).

The changes in the 2015 Code make earlier decisions assessing periods of ineligibility by reference to the degree of 'fault' under Article 10.4 of the 2009 Code of limited direct relevance to the task of setting periods of ineligibility under the 2015 Code, although some decisions provide general observations relevant for considering 'fault', which can be of assistance.[13]

---

12 The 2009 Code contained no separate definition of 'fault'. The approach to the assessment of 'fault' under Article 10.4 was described in the notes to the Article as requiring a consideration of the circumstances which were 'specific and relevant to explain the Athlete's or other Person's departure from the expected standard of behaviour'. The definition of fault in the 2015 Code contains this consideration. In the context of liability for the presence of a prohibited substance in a sample or the use of a prohibited substance, the standard of behaviour generally involves the exercise of all reasonable care by the person bound by the Code to avoid a violation – the regime is one which requires the athlete to exercise the utmost caution. See Chapter 5, pages 183–6 for the nature of the violations and the personal duty of the athlete to ensure no prohibited substance enters his or her body under Article 2.1.1.

13 In CAS 2013/A/3327, *Cilic* v. *ITF*, CAS set out some general principles relevant to the consideration of the degree of fault under Article 10.4 of the 2009 Code, which have been referred to in considering the question of the degree of fault under the 2015 Code in CAS 2016/A/4371, *Lea* v. *USADA*, and most recently in CAS 2016/A/4643, *Sharapova* v. *ITF*. The awards are summarised at pages 420–3. While the *Cilic* award contains useful general guidance and observations on factors which affect an assessment of fault under the Code (where a positive test is produced by a substance prohibited in-competition only and taken out-of-competition) and sets out the general framework for establishing the degree of fault (under the 2009 Code) which can assist a tribunal, the highly fact-specific nature of the exercise of finding the degree of fault in a case means that the essence of the exercise for a tribunal (whether at first instance or at CAS on appeal) is to apply the rules in the Code – in particular, the definition of 'fault' – to the particular facts in the case, as the Code itself directs. Tribunals should, it is submitted, be wary of an approach which is based on specific points made in other decisions. Such an approach detracts from the essential nature of the exercise of arriving at findings on the degree of fault in a particular case. It is submitted

Decisions under Article 10.4 of the 2009 Code can only have any direct relevance if a case involves allegations which have to be considered under the 2009 Code because they arose before 1 January 2015.[14] Cases on the defence of no significant fault remain of relevance under the 2015 Code in showing the operation of that provision in different circumstances, but it must be borne in mind that situations in some earlier cases might well produce different results under the 2015 Code.[15]

Overall, where CAS awards often emphasise the fact-specific nature of the exercise of establishing the appropriate period of ineligibility by reference to the fault of the athlete, care should be taken that fact-specific decisions are not treated as determining periods of ineligibility in other cases or used in a way which distracts from the exercise of applying the provisions of the Code to the particular case before the tribunal. It is submitted that submissions and decisions should generally refer to the basic principles which are found in the text of the Code provisions themselves and to the key factual circumstances relating to the violation which are relevant to decide on the degree of fault of the athlete in the particular case. Where the relevant facts relating to a violation have been determined, an anti-doping organisation should be in a position to assist a tribunal by indicating the period of ineligibility or range of periods of ineligibility which it considers appropriate, referring where necessary to any CAS awards or tribunal decisions which are of general assistance or particular relevance in supporting the period of ineligibility and/or ensuring consistency.

Case summaries concerning the application of Article 10.4 have been removed from the main text and placed in Appendix 1. Some case summaries on the application of Article 10.5.2 of the earlier versions of the Code have been retained in the text because the defence under the 2015 Code is still based on the same definitions (with the addition of the general definition of 'fault').

Generally, the changed regime in the 2015 Code should, perhaps, be treated as providing the opportunity for tribunals considering the possible application of the defences in Articles 10.4 and 10.5 to adopt an approach

that this exercise can properly be carried out with limited reference to other cases, unless the cases can properly be regarded as considering very similar circumstances.

14 Given the time which investigations (particularly those involving non-analytical violations) can take it is quite likely that decisions will continue to be required under the 2009 Code.

15 For example, cases involving contaminated products will need to be considered under the specific contaminated products defence under the 2015 Code, which provides for a different range of sanctions than was available under the 2009 Code.

which focusses primarily on the application of the provisions of the Code interpreted according to the ordinary meaning of the words used, treating the Code as an autonomous independent text and using the comments as an aid to interpretation, as directed.[16]

Suggested General Approach to Sanctions

The general approach to the imposition of sanctions should involve establishing a clear understanding and interpretation of the provisions in the Code applicable to the particular case, then applying those provisions to the facts of the particular case. In most situations, the Code's provisions can be interpreted and applied without extensive reference to previous decisions and awards, and will be applied after the relevant facts and circumstances have been determined. While reference to other decisions may clarify interpretation in cases of real doubt or provide general guidance on the framework for considering fault and factors which might be relevant in determining the level of fault, the focus should remain on the interpretation and application of the Code's provisions (in accordance with the natural meaning of the text of the Code and its purpose).

Tribunals at first instance (and on appeal) which adopt this basic approach are likely to produce concise decisions which may be more readily produced in the short time-frames often required and in a form which will be readily understood by those who are bound by the Code. The comments in this chapter on the sanctions provided in Article 10 are made with these aims in mind – they seek to provide guidance on the requirements under the Code which can be readily used by a tribunal. The case summaries are intended to provide examples of the Code applying in different circumstances by way of general guidance. They should not be regarded as providing the 'answer' in a particular case and should

---

16 Case summaries of decisions under earlier versions of the Code concerning the approach to the determination whether 'no significant fault' can be established have been retained in the text. See pages 401–16. Case summaries and text on Article 10.4 from the second edition relating to the interpretation and application are set out in Appendix 1. That material will remain relevant where violations are considered which were committed when the 2009 Code was in force. The CAS award in *Cilic*, which provides more general guidance on the approach to finding the degree of fault and has been referred to in decisions under the 2015 Code, is summarised at pages 423–8. As previously noted, any general guidance of this kind must be kept within limits, given the fact-specific nature of the exercise of assessing the fault involved in a particular case.

not be approached in that way (absent, of course, truly striking factual similarity).

Appendix 2 to the 2015 Code contains examples of the operation of the Article 10 sanctions regime in arriving at the final sanction under the 2015 Code. These examples provide for a four-step process to arrive at a sanction. Generally, it is submitted that the process of arriving at a sanction involves the steps set out in Figure 5. There does not seem to be any good reason to consider the fault-based reductions in Articles 10.4 and 10.5 first where there is a violation under Article 2.1, 2.2 or 2.6 involving a non-specified substance or where a NADO alleges that a violation involving a specified substance was 'intentional' (on the basis that the fault-based reductions and intentional violations are mutually exclusive[17]). It is suggested that the better approach is for tribunals to work through Articles 10.2–10.5 in sequence (as the ordering of the Code and the example cases in Appendix 2 to the Code suggest), starting with the question whether the violation is intentional or not (if that issue arises) in order to arrive at the basic sanction, followed by the possible application of the provisions for any further reduction due to admission or substantial assistance and the disqualification of results and any further financial sanctions, in order to arrive at the result in the case. While the disqualification of results may often be considered last, at the end of the sanctioning process, this chapter follows the provisions of Article 10 in sequence for ease of reference.

The provisions of Articles 9 and 10 are considered in more detail later in the chapter, after the next section, which provides a general explanation of the role of the concept of proportionality in the history of the development

---

17 As to this suggested approach to fixing the applicable sanction, see the interesting article on the provisions of Article 10 of the 2015 Code by Antonio Rigozzi, Ulrich Haas, Emily Wisnosky and Marjolaine Viret, 'Breaking Down the Process for Determining a Basic Sanction under the 2015 Code' *International Journal of Sport Law*, 15 (2015), 3–48. The suggested approach elevates the mutual exclusivity between the violations involving intentional conduct and violations where the defences under Article 10.4 and 10.5 may apply in a manner not provided for in the Code, which has been ordered on the basis that the question of intentional conduct should be addressed first. It is suggested that the procedure put forward in the article would only further complicate the process of arriving at a sanction for tribunals and is unnecessary. It is suggested that it is better for tribunals to hear all the relevant factual evidence concerning the circumstances of the violation, then work through the provisions of Article 10.2–10.5 sequentially to arrive at the basic sanction with the assistance of the submissions by the parties. That approach has been adopted by tribunals in early hearings under the 2015 Code and is consistent with the ordering of the Code and its provisions and with the examples in the appendices.

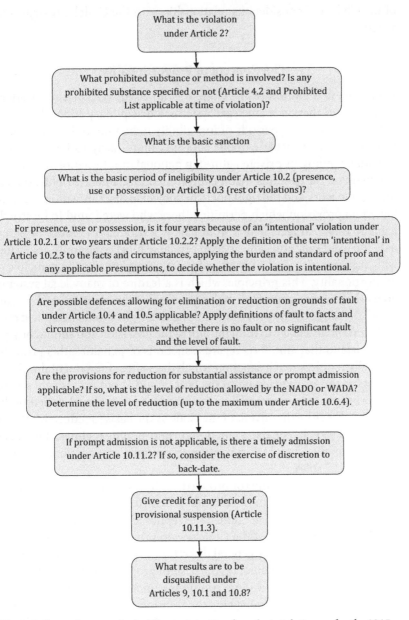

Figure 5 General process in deciding on sanction for a first violation under the 2015 Code

of the Code and considers its relationship with the Code's provisions on sanctions.

The Concept of Proportionality

Before the first edition of the Code was finalised, WADA and its advisers perceived that, in many legal systems, a disciplinary code which provided for rigid, fixed periods of ineligibility to be imposed upon athletes who were strictly liable without fault was more likely to be challenged (notwithstanding its private nature) in national or international courts or tribunals, on the grounds that it contravened fundamental rights, such as the right to work and the right not to be subject to discrimination, if it contained no provision which permitted those who were found to be strictly liable to establish facts which would allow a tribunal to reduce or eliminate the fixed sanction. The general principle most commonly associated with arguments against such a fixed sanction regime was the principle of proportionality. This principle, which is a feature of many legal systems, holds that, where a fundamental right such as the right to work is curtailed, the scope of any provision limiting that right should be upheld only to the extent necessary to fulfil the aim of the provision and should be proportionate to that aim.[18] As regards sanctions or penalties, this principle generally requires that a sanction which does affect fundamental rights is necessary and proportionate to the breach and is not excessively severe. The principle of proportionality was, as has been outlined, relied on by CAS Panels before the advent of the Code as the basis to reduce what they considered were harsh, fixed sanctions in anti-doping regimes. It has been generally applied by CAS in relation to disciplinary sanctions imposed under sports' rules.

An element of flexibility (or proportionality) was introduced into Article 10 of the 2004 Code (in Articles 10.5.1 and 10.5.2) to allow for the elimination or reduction of sanctions in exceptional circumstances. It would seem that the intention of the Code was to provide fully for proportionality, and leave no further general discretion to CAS Panels and tribunals as regards sanctions, whether on the basis of proportionality or otherwise. However, there remained some continuing uncertainty in this regard. In a case which the CAS Panel giving the decision described as 'exceptional', where the provisions of the Code appeared not to provide properly for

18 See further Chapter 10, pages 492–3 for a summary of the doctrine.

the particular circumstances arising where a second violation had been committed, with consequent perceived injustice in the result under the sanctions regime, the principle of proportionality was applied to reduce the period of ineligibility applicable on the face of the Code.[19] Similarly, in a case decided just before the 2009 Code came into force, the concept of proportionality was used in a broader (possibly unprincipled) way to reduce a period of ineligibility where Articles 10.5.1 and 10.5.2 could not apply.[20] The provisions of the 2009 Code increased the degree of flexibility as to the sanctions imposed for breach of the Code's provisions, and it seemed much less likely that there was any place for the general application of the concept of proportionality to be invoked where the outcome of the regime under the Code was perceived as being too strict, whether as regards the period of ineligibility or the burden of proof which falls on a person against whom an allegation is brought. Generally, challenges to the Code itself or the outcomes under the Code based on the concept of proportionality have met with very little success, whether they have been brought before the courts (in particular, the Swiss Federal Supreme Court, which is the Court of Appeal for CAS awards of an international nature) or CAS Panels.[21] Sanctions under the Code have been held not to infringe the fundamental principle of proportionality because they have been found to be necessary for the pursuit of the legitimate objective of combating doping in sport and are proportionate in their length, given their aim.

19 See *Puerta* v. *ITF* at pages 406–7.
20 See CAS 2007/A/1252, *FINA* v. *Oussama Mellouli and TSF* at pages 408–9. The decision would appear to have anticipated the greater discretion under the 2009 Code brought about by the broadening of the category of specified substances.
21 See e.g. CAS 2010/A/2230, *IWBF* v. *Gibbs* in Appendix 1, pages 557–9. where arguments in relation to fundamental rights and proportionality under EU and UK law were raised in relation to this aspect of the Code. For a recent example where CAS set aside a one-year period of ineligibility imposed by a sporting tribunal which relied on the principle of proportionality as expressed under national law as a basis to replace the two-year period of ineligibility provided by the Code, see CAS 2009/A/2012, *Doping Authority Netherlands* v. *Nick Zuijkerbuijk* (where the athlete tested positive in-competition for cocaine taken for recreational purposes outside competition). In CAS 2010/A/2268, *I* v. *FIA*, CAS held that a twelve-year-old go-karter could not establish the source of a prohibited substance and could not rely on Article 10.4 of the 2009 Code to reduce the sanction of two years as a result. The Panel held that this was an exceptional case where the period of ineligibility produced by the application of the provisions of the Code should be reduced on the grounds of proportionality and imposed a one-year period of ineligibility. Minors no longer have this obligation under the 2015 Code. For further consideration of the legal grounds under which awards under the Code may be challenged under Swiss law, see Chapter 10.

The greater flexibility available under the 2009 Code by reason of the extended availability of the discretion under Article 10.4 meant that reliance on proportionality was even less likely to be successful as a means of further reducing a period of ineligibility provided for in the Code.

Proportionality under the 2015 Code

As outlined, the 2015 Code imposes a new longer standard period of ineligibility for a first violation of four years for the violations under Articles 2.1–2.3, 2.5 and 2.6. This may increase the possibility that sanction under the Code will be challenged on the basis that they contravene fundamental principles of human rights protecting individuals because they do not represent a necessary and proportionate response to the problem of doping in sport which the Code seeks to address when the circumstances of a particular case are considered.

Changes in the introductory parts of the Code refer expressly to fundamental rights for the first time. The section setting out the Purpose of the Code states that the Code 'has been drafted giving consideration to the principles of proportionality and human rights'. The Introduction to the Code also confirms that the rules in the Code are intended to be 'applied in a manner which respects the principles of proportionality and human rights'.[22] The intention of these statements appears to be to confirm that the Code has been drafted with fundamental principles in mind and that its operation and application as drafted will apply those principles. However, the express reference to the Code being applied in a manner which reflects those principles does, perhaps, make it more likely that parties will advance arguments which seek to reduce penalties arrived at under the terms of the Code further by reference to the principles of law protecting fundamental rights. It is submitted that there is, in fact, very little or no room for such contentions and that arguments based on proportionality or infringement of fundamental rights to reduce sanctions under the

---

22 Other amendments to the 2015 Code are said to reflect proportionality and human rights in the explanation of the changes to the Code provided by WADA – the changes to the public disclosure provisions, the fact that a minor does not have to establish how a prohibited substance entered his or her system in order to establish no significant fault and the change to the definition of 'athlete' which allows a NADO not to apply the full range of Code obligations to an athlete who is neither an international- nor a national-level athlete where it applies anti-doping rules to him or her. As with earlier versions of the Code, WADA obtained an expert opinion on the compatibility of the Code with principles of human rights and proportionality, and dialogue with the expert is said to have influenced the drafting of several Articles of the Code.

Code could only possibly apply in very exceptional circumstances, most likely where it could be established that there is a gap in the provisions of the Code.[23] As a result, tribunals applying the Code should approach the task of arriving at the sanction to be imposed on the basis that the application of the provisions of the Code produces outcomes which are in accordance with the fundamental principle of proportionality and that no separate application of that principle is required or available.[24] However, where the Code expressly makes the principle of proportionality relevant (the publication of decisions where a minor is involved), a tribunal has to consider whether the intended sanction, when considered overall, is proportionate to the breach of the Code. In addition, where the Code provides for a wide range of possible sanctions in respect of certain violations, such as trafficking and administering, tribunals will wish to consider whether the period of ineligibility to be imposed is proportionate to the seriousness of the violation. Generally, however, the principle should only be considered to be potentially applicable in very exceptional circumstances in the context of sanctions under the Code. It is difficult to conjecture as to the claims which might be made, but a possible example is an athlete who intentionally refuses to submit to doping control for genuine religious reasons, who defends the alleged violation but who cannot establish the defence of compelling justification for the refusal at a hearing because of the established narrow approach to any justification advanced on this basis. Such an athlete would appear to have no basis to reduce the four-year period of ineligibility on the terms of the Code.[25] Where a tribunal considered that, on the evidence, the athlete was genuine and was not trying to avoid the detection of doping, could there be grounds for a

23 The view of the expert engaged by WADA to provide a legal opinion on the compatibility of the Code with international law and human rights was that the four-year period of ineligibility introduced under the 2015 Code is compatible with principles of proportionality and human rights. See Costa, 'Legal Opinion', pp. 6–9. referred to in Chapter 10, page 486, note 6.

24 In CAS 2016/A/4643, *Sharapova* v. *ITF*, the Panel rejected (at para. 99) a plea to reduce further the player's period of ineligibility applying the principle of proportionality because the Code had been 'found repeatedly to be proportional in its approach to sanctions'. See summary at pages 420–3.

25 Articles 10.4 and 10.5 would not be applicable to an intentional violation, and the athlete would not have made a prompt admission under Article 10.6.3, which would give WADA and the anti-doping organisation responsible for results management the discretion to reduce the period of ineligibility. Article 10.3.2 only allows a reduction to two years for a breach of Article 2.3 where the breach involves failing to submit to sample collection and the athlete proves that the violation was not intentional. It would not apply where intentional refusal or evasion is involved, as would be the case in the hypothetical example.

possible reduction on the basis that a four-year ban infringes the principle of proportionality, particularly where the four-year period of ineligibility is intended to identify those who 'cheat' as it applies to violations under Articles 2.1, 2.2 and 2.6?

Article 9: Strict Liability, Automatic Disqualification of Results

Notwithstanding the increase in flexibility relating to sanctions which has taken place as the Code has developed, the Code remains based on strict liability for doping where violations are committed in- competition. This fundamental principle of the Code (and of anti-doping regimes before the Code) is reflected in Article 9, under which any anti-doping rule violation in connection with an in-competition test in individual sports[26] automatically leads to the disqualification of the athlete's individual result in the competition in question, with all resulting consequences, including forfeiture of any medals, points and prizes won.[27] A competition is defined as a single race, game or singular contest. It should be contrasted with an event, which is defined as a series of individual competitions conducted together under one ruling body, such as the Olympic Games or FINA World Swimming Championships.[28] An individual who commits an anti-doping

---

26 Under the definitions in the Code, an individual sport is any sport which 'is not a Team Sport'. A team sport is a sport in which 'the substitution of players is permitted during a competition'. A competition is 'a single race, match, game or singular athletic contest'. Whether a race is a single race and thus a 'competition' or an event consisting of many races will be a matter of interpreting the rules of the particular sport. Where an individual sport is concerned, only the individual result in the particular competition will be disqualified under Article 9. The results in an event in an individual sport may also be disqualified, but this will depend on the rules of the sport involved. Where a violation under the Code involves a team sport as defined by the Code, the sanction under the Code will apply to the individual team member, and the provisions of Article 11 and the rules of the sporting organisation will govern the situation of the team. Where a sport involves 'teams' which do not fall within the definition of 'team' in the Code, the individual's result will be disqualified and the position of other individual athletes in the 'team' will be a matter for the rules of the sport in question. For two cases where the disqualification of the results of others within a team was considered under the rules of a sport where one team member had committed an anti-doping violation, see CAS 2008/A/1545, *Anderson and Others* v. *IOC* and CAS 2004/A/725, *Johnson and Others* v. *IOC*. The cases involve the effect of a doping violation being established against one member of a track and field relay team under the then IAAF Rules.

27 The priority for orders for the payment of CAS costs, awards and forfeited prize money is set out in Article 10.9. See pages 448–9.

28 See Article 9 and the definitions of 'competition' and 'event'.

violation in a team sport will lose his or her individual results. The disqualification of the team results will be considered under Article 11. Article 11 generally provides for the application of the rules of the event in which the team was competing to apply to sanctions on teams. These team sanctions are in addition to the consequences imposed under the Code upon individual team members who commit anti-doping rule violations under the Code.[29]

The disqualification of individual results under Article 9 will potentially apply not only to doping and use violations under Articles 2.1 and 2.2, but to any other violation which occurs in connection with an in-competition test. Violations such as evading, refusing or failing to submit to sample collection under Article 2.3, tampering or attempting to tamper with doping control under Article 2.5 or complicity by an athlete in an anti-doping violation which takes place in connection with an in-competition test under Article 2.9 will lead to the disqualification of results obtained by an athlete committing the violations under Article 9.

Article 9 reflects the well-established general principle behind the automatic disqualification of results, namely that an athlete with a prohibited substance in his or her system should not be able to maintain a position ahead of other athletes in a competition who have competed 'clean'.[30] This approach applies regardless whether the athlete who commits the anti-doping rule violation does so with fault or not. Similarly, it is irrelevant that an athlete may be able to show that there was, in fact, no possible benefit to sporting performance in taking the substances found in his or her system. This strict liability leading to the loss of results under Article 9 is unaffected by the provisions of Article 10, and cannot be removed or mitigated if the athlete establishes the basis for removing or reducing the sanction. Article 10 can, however, apply to sanctions which affect results in events beyond the particular competition in relation to which the violation occurred, the results of which must be disqualified under Article 9.

The general principle of strict liability and its effect on competition results have been upheld by CAS on many occasions, both before and after

29 See Article 11 at pages 457–8.
30 See the well-known dictum in *USA Shooting and Quigley* v. *UIT* in Chapter 1, pages 50–2. The same reasoning can be applied to the other violations which lead to the automatic disqualification of a result. All can be said to involve the possibility that the athlete has competed with a prohibited substance in his or her system.

the implementation of the Code (and also by the Swiss Federal Court on appeal from CAS).

Illustration

Strict Liability: Loss of Result, Medal – an Early Example

CAS Ad Hoc Division OG Sydney, 2000/000111, *Raducan* v. *IOC*, Award of 28 September 2000 R competed as a gymnast at the Sydney Olympic Games. She was prescribed a flu tablet by the team doctor. R won the gold medal but had taken a second tablet during warm-up. The tablet contained pseudoephedrine, which was detected on the doping test. A minor irregularity in the testing process did not set aside the test result. Notwithstanding reference to the case of an Australian swimmer who was[31] given 'a mere warning' when she took a headache pill from a coach which contained a prohibited substance, the CAS Panel was not prepared to depart from the principles of strict liability. While there was, in fact, no competitive advantage involved, under the relevant rules of the International Gymnastic Federation, R had to lose her medal. This was a consequence of the automatic disqualification. No further disciplinary sanction was put in place by the IOC. The decision of the IOC was upheld by CAS and R lost her medal.

Article 10

Article 10, the main provision of the Code relating to sanctions, lays down the periods of ineligibility for first, second and third anti-doping rule violations under the Code and contains the provisions which allow for the elimination or reduction of periods of ineligibility. The distinction based on the Prohibited List between violations involving 'specified' substances and violations involving prohibited substances not so specified or prohibited methods is central to the imposition of sanctions under Article 10 for violations of Article 2.1 (presence of a prohibited substance), Article 2.2 (use of a prohibited substance) and Article 2.6 (possession of a prohibited substance). Whether a violation concerns a specified or non-specified substance will determine the approach to the question whether the violation was intentional and thus subject to a four-year period of

---

31 Erroneously, it is suggested.

ineligibility.[32] The categorisation of a substance is also relevant to the operation of defences which provide for the possible reduction of the standard period of ineligibility of two years if the violation is not intentional.

The categories of substances under the Prohibited List are outlined in Chapter 3. Broadly speaking, non-specified substances and prohibited methods represent the substances and methods which are usually associated with attempts by athletes to gain an unfair advantage in-competition (unapproved substances, anabolic steroids, hormones growth factors including EPO and hGH, certain hormones, a limited number of listed specified substances and methods for manipulating blood, intravenous infusions and gene doping). Violations involving these substances are presumed to involve 'intentional' conduct under Article 10.2 for the purpose of applying the four-year period of ineligibility.

The first provisions under Article 10.1 follow on from the automatic disqualification of results under Article 9 and provide for disqualification of results where an anti-doping rule violation has been committed. The Articles are probably placed before the provisions on sanctions because they reflect the central feature of strict liability under the Code and because they may be applied in decisions made by sporting organisations responsible for events before any final hearing which determines sanctions and other consequences. Generally, however, the question of the disqualification of results will be determined in a sanctions hearing at the end of the process, after a decision on the appropriate period of ineligibility has been made.

Article 10.1: Disqualification of Further Results

Article 10.1 provides for the possible disqualification of all an athlete's individual results in an event during which an anti-doping rule violation occurs.[33] Article 9 is concerned with disqualification in a single competition.[34] Article 10.1 provides for the position of the other competitions during the event in which the violation occurs. As previously noted, a competition is a singular sporting contest, while an event is a series of such contests conducted together under one ruling body (e.g. the FINA

32 Whether a substance prohibited in-competition only is involved can also be relevant in certain circumstances in respect of liability for violations under Articles 2.6–2.8 of the Code. See further Chapter 5, pages 246–50.
33 The violation can be any of the violations under Article 2 of the Code.
34 See pages 344–6.

World Swimming Championships).[35] An anti-doping rule violation during or in connection with an event may lead to the disqualification of all the athlete's results at the event. Unlike the disqualification under Article 9, however, this is not an automatic consequence arising from strict liability, and whether disqualification occurs will depend on a decision by the ruling body of the event.

Article 10.1 refers specifically to certain factors which might be considered by the ruling body in considering whether to disqualify other results at an event: the seriousness of the violation and whether the athlete tested positive at other competitions at the event. Any decision on the disqualification of other results will involve considering the circumstances relevant to the anti-doping rule violation which has been committed at the event.

Article 10.8 should also be noted at this point. This Article provides for the retroactive disqualification of all competitive results from the time of sample collection or the time when any other anti-doping rule violation occurred 'unless fairness requires otherwise'. Article 10.8 is expressed to apply in addition to the automatic disqualification of competition results under Article 9. Both Article 10.1 and Article 10.8 are potentially applicable to results obtained after a doping violation has been committed at an event. However, Article 10.1 is specifically directed to results at an event, while Article 10.8 refers generally to results obtained after the time of sample collection or the time of the commission of an anti-doping rule violation. A CAS Panel has held that Article 10.1 is applicable to results obtained in competitions both before and after the competition in which a positive test was returned, so long as they were obtained at the same event. This decision is based on Article 10.1 being the provision which is specifically directed at results at an event. Where both Articles are potentially applicable, the provisions should produce the same outcome in relation to the disqualification of other results at an event, because the question whether for reasons of fairness results should not be disqualified should be approached broadly and in the same manner as a decision to disqualify results under Article 10.1.[36] Neither Article 10.1 nor Article 10.8 provides for any burden of proof, although Article 10.8 imposes a mandatory requirement to disqualify results unless fairness requires otherwise. It is submitted that absent any specific provision in the rules relating to

---

35 See the comment in the notes to Article 10.1.
36 CAS 2013/A/3274, *Mads Glasner v. FINA*, summarised at pages 349–50.

the particular event, the Articles provide for a broad discretion to make a decision on the disqualification of results based on fairness (assuming that the athlete subject to the potential disqualification raises matters for consideration), with no allocated burden of proof.[37]

CAS 2013/A/3274, *Mads Glasner* v. *Federation Internationale de Natation (FINA)* – Articles 10.1 and 10.8 – Disqualification of Results – CAS Full Power of Review

G, a professional swimmer, competed at the FINA World Swimming Championships from 12 to 16 December 2012. On 14 December, after finishing third in the men's 400 metre freestyle final, G underwent an in-competition doping control. On 16 December, he won the gold medal in the 1500 metres freestyle final. Another in-competition doping control test was conducted after this final.

After analysis, the sample given on 14 December returned a positive test for a prohibited substance, namely phenpromethamine, a specified stimulant prohibited in-competition. However, the test carried out after the 1500 metre final on 16 December was negative for all prohibited substances. The FINA Doping Panel found that the athlete had committed an anti-doping rule violation. It imposed a period of ineligibility of three months under the FINA Rules, applying Article 10.4 of the 2009 Code. It also decided that all G's results from 14 December, including the gold medal won on 16 December, should be disqualified.

The FINA decision was to the effect that all G's results at the World Swimming Championships were so related to the World Championships in the eyes of the public that the disqualification of all his results was a fair and clear sanction.

G appealed to CAS, solely against the disqualification of the gold medal result. CAS held that the proper approach to the appeal was to re-hear and reconsider the matter and that it was not appropriate to give any deference to the FINA decision. This followed from the terms of Rule 57 of the CAS Code and the need to provide a full hearing on appeal.

The CAS arbitrator rejected FINA's submission that the provision in Article 10.8, and not the position in Article 10.1, was applicable to the

---

37 The absence of any provision placing the burden of proof on the athlete makes it difficult to apply the general provision on the burden of proof under Article 3.1 and the provisions of both Articles reflect a broader consideration of factors relating to the fairness in disqualifying other results at an event.

possible disqualification of the results in the competitions at the event after the positive test, with Article 10.1 only possibly applying to results at an event before a positive test. He held that, on the proper interpretation of the FINA Rules/Code, Article 10.1 covered results in competitions at an event whether before or after the competition in which the anti-doping rule violation was committed. In any event, the arbitrator considered that the approach to the disqualification of results under Articles 10.8 and 10.1 would produce the same result. Article 10.8 should be interpreted to provide for a broad approach to the question whether fairness required that results should not be disqualified. Similarly, the approach to Article 10.1 involved the exercise of discretion as to the disqualification of results in the circumstances of the particular anti-doping rule violation, which should be exercised on the same basis.

In the circumstances of this case, where the fault of the athlete was rather 'minor or light', and it was not a case of intentional doping, the arbitrator found that the anti-doping rule violation was not sufficiently severe to justify the disqualification of the result subsequently obtained in the competition. He concluded that there would be no different conclusion if the question was dealt with under the Article 10.8.

Disqualification of Results where No Fault is Established

Under Article 10.1.1, if an athlete establishes that he or she bore no fault or negligence in relation to a violation under Article 10.4 (which will require exceptional circumstances), the individual results in other competitions apart from the competition in which the anti-doping rule violation occurred will not be disqualified, unless the results in the other competitions are likely to have been affected by the athlete's anti-doping rule violation. This will apply to all competitions, whether they are part of the same event in which the anti-doping rule violation occurred or not. While the Article contains no express provision as to the burden of proof, the application of this proviso, which qualifies the position where the athlete has established a no fault defence, should be for the anti-doping organisation seeking the disqualification of results apart from the result in the competition in which the anti-doping rule violation was committed to establish to the standard of the comfortable satisfaction of the tribunal, in accordance with the general standard of proof applicable under Article 3.1.

The general effect of the provision in Article 10.1 (and the other provisions under which a period of ineligibility may be eliminated or reduced) is to limit the application of strict liability in its absolute form to disqualification in the competition in which a violation occurs.[38]

Before considering the various situations in which the standard period of ineligibility may be reduced, the straightforward case should be kept in mind. While the 2015 Code provides for various routes by which a person who has committed an anti-doping rule violation may seek to reduce the sanction applicable, in many situations where an anti-doping rule violation has been committed, the standard fixed sanction will be applied, Articles 10.4, 10.5 and 10.6 will not be applicable and the consequence of the violation will be that all competitive results obtained from the time of the violation have to be disqualified. Often, an athlete or person facing an allegation after reviewing the allegation and relevant information and evidence with his or her advisers may only be able to contemplate any reduction in the period of ineligibility if he or she makes a prompt or timely admission or, more rarely, is in a position to provide substantial assistance to the anti-doping organisation.[39] The position which may well be reached with violations under the 2015 Code involving non-specified substances is that the potentially career-ending standard period of ineligibility of four years will be applicable.

Similarly, the sanctioning exercise in relation to violations such as whereabouts breaches, trafficking, administration and complicity, while presenting difficulties arising from the range of conduct[40] covered and the associated difficulty in arriving at the appropriate period of ineligibility, which reflects the fault of the athlete or seriousness of the violation, may well not be complex in terms of the interpretation of the provisions of Article 10. Cases involving these violations are more likely to traverse more detailed and contested factual evidence if the violation or the basis for the imposition of sanctions is contested. Again, however, the benefit of athletes or others facing allegations under the Code making a clear early assessment of the case against them with their advisers in order to consider the possible benefits of an early admission should be kept in mind.

---

38 See Article 10.8 at pages 447–8. See *WADA* v. *ASADA, AWF and Karapetyn* in Chapter 9, pages 475–6 for a decision involving a consideration of the application of Article 10.8 and an appeal on the approach taken. The approach taken on the appeal does not accord with the established position that a CAS appeal involves a hearing *de novo* and that there should be no deference to the decision of the first instance tribunal (now confirmed by Article 13.1.2 of the 2015 Code).

39 For these provisions, see pages 436–8.

40 For case summary examples of tribunals arriving at sanctions for these violations, see further pages 432–4.

Articles 10.2 and 10.3: Periods of Ineligibility

In summary, Articles 10.2 and 10.3 provide for periods of ineligibility for first violations under the Code as follows:

- First violations of Articles 2.1(presence), 2.2 (use) and 2.6 (possession): four years' ineligibility or, if the violation is not 'intentional' as defined in Article 10.2.3, two years' ineligibility.
- First violations of Articles 2.3 (refusal, evasion, failing to submit) and 2.5 (tampering): four years' ineligibility, unless in the case of a violation under Article 2.3 the athlete can show that there was no intentional conduct in relation to a violation involving failing to submit to sample collection, where the period of ineligibility will be two years.
- First violation of Article 2.4 (breach of whereabouts requirements): two years' ineligibility, subject to reduction down to twelve months depending on the degree of fault of the athlete.
- First violations of Articles 2.7 (trafficking) and 2.8 (administration): a period of ineligibility of between four years and life, depending on the seriousness of the violation.
- First violation of Article 2.9 (complicity): between a minimum of two years' and a maximum of four years' ineligibility, depending on the seriousness of the violation.
- First violation of Article 2.10 (prohibited association): two years' ineligibility, subject to reduction to a minimum of one year depending on fault and other circumstances of the case.

The New Four-Year Period of Ineligibility

Articles 10.2 now contains, for the first time, a standard period of ineligibility of four years for breaches of Articles 2.1, 2.2 and 2.6.

Article 10.3.1 further provides that the period of ineligibility for breaches of Articles 2.3 and 2.5 will be four years unless (only), in the case of a violation of failing to submit to sample collection, the athlete can establish that the commission of the violation was not intentional.[41]

The essential common requirement for this four-year period of ineligibility for breaches of Articles 2.1, 2.2 and 2.6 is the presence of 'intentional

---

41 Article 10.6.3 also contains a specific prompt admission provision which can reduce the period of ineligibility down to a minimum of two years for intentional violations sanctionable under Article 10.2.1 (violations under Article 2.1, 2.2 or 2.6) and Article 10.3.1 (Article 2.3 (evading or refusing only) and Article 2.5 (tampering)), at the discretion of WADA and the anti-doping organisation concerned. See pages 440–1.

conduct' (whether presumed and not disproved or proved) as that concept is defined in Article 10.2.3.

Articles 2.3 and 2.5 attract the four-year period of ineligibility and are equated with violations under Articles 2.1, 2.2 and 2.6 because, if established, the violations also involve intentional conduct which undermines the doping control process (apart from the violation of failure to submit to sample collection, which can be committed negligently and for which the period of ineligibility can be reduced by the athlete showing that the violation was not committed intentionally as defined in Article 10.2.3).

It should be noted that violations under Articles 2.4 and 2.7–2.10 are not affected by the provisions on 'intentional conduct' or subject to the standard four-year period of ineligibility. For these violations, the task of a tribunal is to arrive at the applicable sanction within the stipulated range by reference to the seriousness of the violation (Articles 2.7, 2.8 and 2.9) or the fault of the athlete (Articles 2.4 and 2.10, and also Article 10.12.3).[42]

Article 10.2.3: Intentional Conduct

Whether intentional conduct has to be proven by an anti-doping organisation in violations under Articles 2.1, 2.2 and 2.6 or whether a violation is presumed to involve intentional conduct unless the athlete disproves this element depends on whether the violation involves a specified substance or not. This makes the checking of the status of substances involved in any anti-doping rule violation by reference to the Prohibited List applicable at the time of the alleged violation an essential first step in considering the application of Article 10 (see Figure 5 for the steps in the process of arriving at the sanction).

Article 10.2.1.1 provides that a violation of Article 2.1, 2.2 or 2.6 will attract a period of ineligibility of four years where it does not involve a specified substance under the Prohibited List unless the athlete or person who committed the violation can establish that the violation was not intentional. Under Article 10.2.1.2, where the violation involves a specified substance, the period of four years for intentional breach will only apply

---

42 Different phrases for the consideration of sanctions are used in the relevant Articles – Articles 10.3.2 (sanction for Article 2.4), 10.3.3 (Articles 2.7 and 2.8), 10.3.4 (Article 2.9 (complicity)), 10.3.5 (Article 2.10) and 10.12.3 (breach of terms of ineligibility). It is difficult to ascertain what substantive difference is made, but where the sanction is to be arrived at by reference to the degree of fault, the tribunal will have to consider the circumstances by reference to the definition of 'fault'. For further consideration of this in relation to sanctions under these Articles, see pages 346–72 and 372–4.

if the anti-doping organisation bringing the violation can establish that it was 'intentional'. Specific rules which follow the definition of 'intentional' in Article 10.2.3 apply which make it easier to establish that the use of certain prohibited substances in certain circumstances should not attract the four-year period of ineligibility. Where the violation involves a specified substance which is only prohibited in-competition and the athlete can establish that the substance was used out-of-competition, the violation will be rebuttably presumed to be not 'intentional'. This will mean that if out-of-competition use of a substance prohibited in-competition has given rise to the violation, the anti-doping organisation will have to rebut the presumption that the violation was not 'intentional' as defined in Article 10.2.3 to the required comfortable satisfaction standard.[43] Where a violation involves a positive test for a prohibited substance which is not a specified substance and which is only prohibited in-competition, the violation will not be considered 'intentional' if the athlete proves that the substance was used out-of-competition in a context 'unrelated to sport performance'.[44]

Where there is burden of proof on the anti-doping organisation to prove intentional conduct, the standard of proof will be the 'comfortable satisfaction' standard under Article 3 of the Code. Where an athlete or other person has to prove that a violation was not intentional or prove circumstances which give rise to a presumption in his or her favour, the standard of proof will be the balance of probabilities.

If an athlete or other person proves that a violation involving a non-specified substance on the Prohibited List was not intentional or an anti-doping organisation does not prove that a violation involving a specified substance was intentional, the period of ineligibility will be two years under Article 10.2.2 and the defences allowing for the reduction or elimination of the period of ineligibility by reference to fault under Article 10.4

---

43 It is unclear what exactly this rebuttable presumption adds when the anti-doping organisation has to prove that a violation involving a specified substance was intentional under Article 10.2.1.2. The provision does generally serve to underline the difficulty for an anti-doping organisation in attempting to prove that taking such a substance out-of-competition involved 'intentional' conduct.

44 This would cover the use out-of-competition in circumstances which are not related to sport performance of non-specified stimulants which are banned in-competition, like cocaine and methamphetamine, where these substances produce a positive in-competition test. Both requirements have to be established to establish that the use cannot be considered to be intentional. If the requirements cannot be established, the athlete can still seek to prove that the conduct was not 'intentional' as defined by Article 10.2.3.

and 10.5 will be potentially available.[45] The defences will not be available where the violation is intentional under Article 10.2.[46]

What Constitutes 'Intentional' Conduct?   While the definitions in the Code contain no definition of 'intentional conduct', Article 10.2.3 contains a definition of the term 'intentional'. Consistent with the expressed aim of the 2015 Code, which is to provide for longer periods of ineligibility for 'real' cheats, Article 10.2.3 starts by referring to the aim of the term 'intentional' in identifying 'those Athletes who cheat', then goes on to provide for a broad definition of what amounts to 'intentional' conduct:

> the term 'intentional' is meant to identify those *Athletes* who cheat. The term, therefore, requires that the *Athlete* or other *Person* engaged in conduct which he or she knew constituted an anti-doping rule violation or knew that there was a significant risk that the conduct might constitute or result in an anti-doping rule violation and manifestly disregarded that risk.

This definition requires a consideration of two alternative bases for a finding that a violation was intentional: first, whether the athlete or person who carried out the acts which resulted in the violation had actual knowledge that the conduct would amount to an anti-doping rule violation; and, second, whether the person who carried out the acts which constituted the violation knew that that there was a significant risk that his or her conduct might lead to a violation and manifestly disregarded that risk.

In terms of the general principles of criminal law in many jurisdictions, this definition involves an athlete or person responsible for a violation having a 'guilty mind', whether that involves actual direct intent to break the rules with knowledge or recklessness involving conduct which involves consciously taking a significant risk of breaking the rules.

The first part of the definition involves establishing actual knowledge on the part of the person who has committed the violation that his or her conduct would break the rules under the Code – specific direct intent involving knowing breach of the rules. The second part is broader in its potential application. While the definition requires actual knowledge of the significant risk of breach (in the subjective sense) involved in engaging in the

---

45 The decisions in the *Sharapova* case by the ITF Tribunal and CAS illustrate the consideration of the question whether a violation was 'intentional', followed by the consideration of the possible 'no significant fault' defence under Article 10.5.2 where an athlete shows that a violation was not intentional. See case summary at pages 362–6.
46 See further Comment to Article 10.5.2 in note to Code at pages 400–1.

conduct amounting to the violation, this will cover a wide range of possible circumstances in which an athlete or person might be found to have the required knowledge of a significant risk of breach of the Code. The second part of the definition broadens the scope of intentional conduct beyond the kind of specific direct intent required by the first part, and the boundaries may be difficult to determine.[47] The scope of liability imposed by the mental requirement for recklessness of this kind has caused difficulties in criminal law in many common law jurisdictions. It can be difficult to determine whether liability of this kind should be entirely subjective, requiring proof of the athlete's actual knowledge that a risk is significant and that his or her conduct might result in a breach of the rules, or whether liability should also involve an objective element, which might mean that a person who is aware of the circumstances involved in their conduct but does not appreciate that there is a significant risk of breaking the rules should be liable when a reasonable person in that situation would have appreciated the risk. It can also be difficult to determine the magnitude of risk and the degree of likelihood of a violation occurring which a person must be aware of for liability to be imposed. Generally, where the application of the definition will mean that an athlete or person is subject to a four-year period of ineligibility and it will be for the athlete or person facing the violation to rebut the presumption of intentional conduct, it is submitted that the definition should be interpreted as involving both actual subjective awareness of significant risk of a breach of the rules – in the sense that it is probable that the conduct will result in a breach (not that a reasonable athlete should have been aware of the risk) – and conscious risk-taking. This is borne out by the terms of the definition, which refer to knowing that there was a significant risk. While the presence of an obvious significant risk of breach in the circumstances of the violation will make it more likely that an athlete knew of the risk, the question which is relevant will be whether the athlete in fact knew of the risk that the conduct would probably result in a breach of the rules.

While it seems very likely that the interpretation and application of the definition will be debated in hearings and decisions, it is suggested that the test in the definition might be approached as follows. The tribunal

---

47 It is submitted that it does not have the limitations which CAS Panels found applied to Article 10.4 of the 2009 Code, and the earlier divided jurisprudence on the interpretation of Article 10.4 is not relevant to the interpretation and application of this provision. The question is simply whether in the factual circumstances the person facing the allegation was aware of a significant risk that the conduct would result in a breach of the rules.

decides first whether there was in fact a significant risk that the conduct was likely to lead to a breach of the rules in the particular circumstances. If objectively there was no such risk, there can be no intentional conduct under this part of the definition. The tribunal then decides whether the particular athlete or person who has committed the violation was aware of the significant risk that his or her conduct would result in a breach of the rules and, with that knowledge of risk, deliberately engaged in the conduct which resulted in the breach. The questions arising under the definition will have to be addressed in the manner dictated by the burden and standard of proof which apply in the particular situation.

This provision seems likely to lead to contested hearings, where tribunals have to assess the credibility of an athlete and decide whether it is appropriate to draw inferences from other evidence as to the athlete's state of mind and awareness of risk, which may often be of a circumstantial nature, in order to decide whether the athlete or the anti-doping organisation has proven the absence or the presence of intentional conduct. Cases where a jury or trier of fact has to draw inferences from proven facts in order to determine whether the required mental element of a criminal charge has been established to the required standard of proof are a familiar aspect of criminal law. Contemporaneous oral or documentary statements by athletes and others are likely to be important in providing evidence from which the mental element of intention may be assessed or inferred.[48] In many cases, it may be difficult for an athlete who is bound by the Code and the obligations under it and who has committed a violation under Article 2.1, 2.2 or 2.6 involving a non-specified substance (which will be a substance with well-known associations with performance enhancement) to rebut the presumption of intentional breach by showing that the circumstances of his or her conduct did not give rise to a significant risk that the conduct would lead to a breach and that he or she was not aware of the significant risk that the conduct might constitute a breach of the rules. This is a natural consequence of the increasing levels of general awareness of the obligations under the Code and of greater levels of anti-doping education. Each case will, however, depend on the particular circumstances and conduct involved, the findings on the risk present and the awareness of the particular athlete or person of the risk, as assessed by the tribunal on the factual circumstances established by the evidence – in many cases, an assessment of the credibility of the athlete is likely to be central to the exercise of determining whether conduct is intentional or

48 For discussion of proof and the admissibility of evidence, see Chapter 6, pages 282–4.

not. Naturally, statements by an athlete, whether in communications with others, in interviews or in giving evidence, will be important evidence on the question whether his or her conduct was intentional at the time of the conduct which amounted to the alleged violation. Where the onus is on the athlete to rebut the presumption that a violation has been committed intentionally, he or she will have to give evidence in support of his or her case – this is a necessary consequence of the athlete carrying the burden of proving that he or she did not have the necessary intent. Where the anti-doping organisation seeks to prove that a violation was intentional and an athlete does not give evidence or chooses not to attend a hearing and answer questions, the anti-doping organisation may seek to have a tribunal draw adverse inferences against the athlete (relying on Article 3.2.5) in respect of the intentional nature of the conduct (assuming a request has been made for the athlete to attend and answer questions at the hearing, as is required before any adverse inference can be put forward).[49]

'Meant to Identify those Athletes who Cheat'   The first line of the definition underlines that the purpose of the term 'intentional' is to identify those athletes who cheat. There is no definition of 'cheat' in Article 10.2.3, and although the phrase is situated within the definition (and is linked to it), it does not appear to form part of the provisions which define 'intentional'. To cheat in sport might be said in general terms to refer to acting dishonestly or unfairly in order to gain an advantage, but the question whether particular conduct should be regarded as 'cheating' can be hard to answer. It is difficult to say, for example, whether cheating has to involve dishonesty.[50] Certainly, cheating covers a potentially wide range of conduct and there will often be different opinions on whether conduct can be described as cheating. A person who knowingly breaks the doping rules will usually readily be described as a cheat, but a person who knowingly takes a significant risk that they will break the rules may not so readily be described as cheating. The question which arises is whether the definition should be interpreted as meaning that the requirements define what an

---

49 See Chapter 6, pages 284–5 and 289–91 on the drawing of inferences.
50 See, for example, in the context of deciding whether the conduct of a gambler in a card game against the house is 'cheating' under the relevant legislation, the recent decision in *Philip Ivey* v. *Genting Casinos UK Limited trading as Crockfords* [2016] EWCA Civ 1093, where the Court of Appeal of England and Wales held by majority that cheating under the Gambling Act did not require dishonesty but simply an unfair departure from the way in which the game was usually played and that the method employed by the gambler was cheating as a matter of civil law under the Gambling Act.

intention to cheat is, or whether a tribunal which finds that the conduct in relation to a violation involves the kind of knowing or reckless breach of the Code required by the definition could still conclude that the conduct was not 'intentional' because the athlete or person was not 'cheating' in the sense of acting dishonestly to gain an advantage.

It is submitted that an approach which makes proof of 'cheating' a further requirement for a finding that a violation was intentional is not available on a proper approach to the definition and that the requirements for intentional conduct in the definition are the criteria for identifying a person who cheats.[51] It is likely that that decisions on the application of the definition under Article 10.2.3 will have to consider this issue. It may be that tribunals rely on the link of the definition to cheating to assist in interpreting the requirements in the definition, in particular those which provide that conduct involving conscious risk-taking will amount to 'intentional' conduct. Such an approach would, it is submitted, lead to the requirements for reckless liability being interpreted as requiring clear evidence of the presence of an obvious risk that the conduct was likely to lead to a violation of the Code, clear proof of knowledge of that significant risk on the part of the athlete and clear evidence of deliberate conduct manifestly disregarding the significant risk. The presence of the phrase setting out the purpose of the definition of intentional conduct might possibly be relied on where the conduct in issue meets the requirements of the definition in a technical sense but clearly does not justify the imposition of a period of ineligibility of four years, which is intended to sanction those who breach the Code in a serious manner.

While the provisions in Article 10.2 do not specifically require that the athlete or person who seeks to rebut the presumption of intentional conduct has to show how the substance came to be in his or her system (as is the case with the defence of no significant fault), it is submitted that this will generally be a necessary part of rebutting the presumption of intentional conduct. Where the inquiry under the definition of 'intentional' conduct refers to the conduct which produces the alleged violation, any athlete seeking to establish that a violation was not 'intentional' has to provide evidence of the nature of the conduct undertaken. Where the violation concerned involved a positive test for the presence or use of a prohibited substance, the relevant conduct involves the way in which the

---

51 See CAS/A/4512, *WADA* v. *Turkish Football Federation (TFF) and Ahmet Kuru*, where the arbitrator held that the phrase 'intention to cheat' did not impose a further requirement to prove an intention to cheat under the definition. See case summary at pages 368–9.

athlete took the substance. This position has been reached in decisions considering this question in national tribunals.[52] It is not possible for an athlete to establish that conduct was not intentional by providing general evidence asserting that he or she has never and would not cheat and that accordingly the only explanation must be spiking or sabotage.[53] Concrete evidence which explains how the violation occurred is required. In the same way, the proof of an intentional violation by an anti-doping organisation will require proof by specific evidence of the way in which the conduct of the athlete or person who is the subject of the allegation brought about the violation.

Some early decisions on intentional conduct, illustrating some of the considerations under the definition, are summarised here. Four of the decisions reach differing conclusions on whether the athlete was aware of significant risk on the particular facts, while *Bevan* (page 370) considers the question of intentional conduct where the conduct in question occurred before the 2015 Code came into force. In the first case, the experience of the athlete and the extent of doping education received were significant factors in assessing the athlete's case that he was not aware of the risk in taking some tablets given to him by a friend. Notwithstanding the level of the experience of the athlete, the decision reaches what might perhaps be seen as a surprising conclusion on the facts of the case concerning the knowledge of significant risk of committing a violation on the part of the athlete. The important general point in this area is that the question of the presence of subjective intent or not has to be decided on the particular facts of the case, and often by considering the credibility of the evidence given by the person facing the violation.

Gaelic Athletic Association v. *Connolly* – **National-level Tribunal** – **Intentional Conduct** – **Article 10.3.2** C was tested at training. The sample returned a positive test for stanozolol, a steroid and non-specified substance. There was a breach of Article 2.1 of the 2015 Code. The period of ineligibility was four years unless C could show that the anti-doping rule violation was not intentional under Article 10.2.1.1.

---

52 See, for example, *UKAD* v. *Graham* SR 0000120259, paras 35–45.
53 For CAS awards rejecting claims that positive tests were the result of sabotage or of contaminated supplements or food, such that the violation was not intentional, where the case advanced for the athlete was not founded in cogent evidence, see CAS 2016/A/4439, *Tomasz Hamelak* v. *IPC* and CAS Ad Hoc Division 16/025, *WADA* v. *Narsingh Yadav and NADA*. In both cases, a period of ineligibility of four years was imposed.

C had been invited to train at national league level and had been selected for a game and played some minutes. He gave evidence before the Gaelic Athletic Association (GAA) tribunal. He admitted taking tablets which had been given to him by a friend at work. He produced a container of tablets. While initially the trade name on the container did not explain the steroid in his sample, after testing it was found that the tablets did contain stanozolol.

C gave evidence that his friend had said that the tablets would relieve stiffness and pain he was suffering from as a result of training. He took four tablets a day for four or five days. C said he took the tablets to relieve pain, not to enhance performance. He was not aware that they contained a prohibited substance. He never thought that the tablets contained anabolic steroids. He also gave evidence that he had never been told of the anti-doping rules, their application to him or the sanctions for a breach – he had received no anti-doping education. C's evidence was challenged in cross-examination. The GAA submitted that C knew he was taking steroids or that he had taken a risk he was clearly aware of with a view to enduring pain to allow him to compete at higher level. C had at very least been reckless.

Argument on Jurisdiction   C contended first that he was not subject to the authority of the GAA for testing and that this authority was limited to senior inter-county players. He relied on the fact that the national testing pool included senior inter-county players to support the contended limit on the authority to test. C also argued that the nature of the anti-doping rules in the GAA rules meant that the Association had to draw them – and the consequences of their breach – specifically to his intention if he was to be bound by them. The tribunal held that the anti-doping rules were part of the rules of the GAA which bound all athletes who were members, like C, whatever the athlete's level. There was no need to have reached the level of senior inter-county player to be tested, and C was a senior inter-county player anyway by reason of his participation in training and in a game. As a result, C was bound and had committed the violation.

Intentional Conduct   On the question of sanction under the 2015 Code, C had to show that the anti-doping violation was not intentional if a four-year period of ineligibility was not to be applied. The GAA found that the lack of knowledge of the rules was relevant to C's state of mind and that he had not acted with intention or been reckless on the facts of the case. This was shortly stated, but it was presumably based on a finding that the athlete's evidence that he was not aware of a significant risk of breaching the Code was credible. The GAA found that a two-year period of ineligibility should be imposed. There was no proper basis for the plea of no significant fault because, while the conduct was not reckless as required by the definition of 'intentional' conduct, it did involve a high degree of fault, in that the athlete had made no effort to check the status of the tablets with anyone.

UKAD v. *Riddiford* **SR 26 May 2015 – Whether an Athlete can Show a Violation is Not Intentional – Clear Recklessness** R, a twenty-six-year-old weightlifter, tested positive for clenbuterol and stanozolol. R claimed that the positive test was a result of his taking supplements. He said that he did not intentionally dope and that he took the supplements without any intention to cheat. The tribunal stated that an athlete will be found to have acted intentionally if they knew the risk that their conduct might constitute or result in a violation under the Code and manifestly disregarded that risk.

R had been made aware of the risk of taking supplements and had chosen to ignore that risk. He also did not identify the supplement source, but simply referred to the source as supplements generally. On the facts, he could not show that his conduct was not intentional in terms of the Code. He had plainly, on his own case, ignored a significant risk, which he had been informed of and knew of, that his conduct would give rise to a violation.

A period of ineligibility of four years was imposed. On the scope of his ban, UK Anti-Doping (UKAD) made it clear that R could not carry on his work as a video analyst on rugby games, although other kinds of employment within the professional rugby club for which he worked were possible.

Independent Tribunal of International Tennis Federation ITF v. *Maria Sharapova* **6 June 2016 – Sanctions – Article 10.2.3 Intentional Conduct and Article 10.5.2 No Significant Fault under the 2015 Code** S tested positive for meldonium after giving a urine sample following a quarter-final match at the Australian Open on 26 January 2016. Meldonium had been added to the Prohibited List under S4.5 of the List as a metabolic modulator on 1 January 2016, after it had been in the 2015 Monitoring Programme.

S admitted the anti-doping rule violation under Article 2.1 as a result of the presence of the prohibited substance in her sample. She was provisionally suspended from 2 March 2016.

The International Tennis Federation (ITF) Panel hearing had to determine the applicable sanction under the 2015 Code. Under the Prohibited List, meldonium was prohibited at all times and was not a specified substance. As a consequence, the applicable period of ineligibility for a first violation under Article 10.2.1 was four years unless the athlete could establish that the anti-doping rule violation was not intentional as defined in Article 10.2.

S contended that her use was not intentional. She had been taking a medicine called Mildronate, which contained the active ingredient of meldonium, for over ten years and did not know that the product contained meldonium or that meldonium had been added to the Prohibited List 2016. S further contended, while admitting some fault, that the period of ineligibility of two years (which would apply where the anti-doping rule violation was not intentional) should be reduced on the grounds that she could establish no significant fault or negligence because she had taken due care in her use of Mildronate over ten years and because ITF had failed to take reasonable steps to publicise the inclusion of the substance on the Prohibited List 2016. S further claimed that the ITF should be estopped as a result of failing to warn her of the inclusion of meldonium on the Prohibited List from alleging any fault on her part and that the principle of proportionality should be applied to avoid or reduce the period of ineligibility under the Code.

Meldonium is a prescription drug in Eastern European and Commonwealth of Independent States (CIS) countries but is not approved for use by humans in the United States or the European Union. It has been reported to have cardioprotective effects and is used in the management of heart and cerebrovascular disorders. Meldonium is marketed under the name 'Mildronate' as having a positive effect on energy, metabolism and stamina. While the ITF called evidence from WADA that the substance enhanced sporting performance, it was not necessary for the Panel to rule on this, and it did not do so. The Panel did record that there was a widely held belief among athletes that the substance did enhance performance, as evidenced by the fact that 8% of the samples taken at the 2015 European Games (when the substance was on the monitoring list) were positive for the substance.

S explained her use of Mildronate throughout her career. S had used the substance from the age of seventeen as part of a detailed medicinal and nutritional regime directed by her doctor to address immune deficiency, mineral metabolism disorder and loss of energy. The use of the substance was directed as a cardioprotective agent and as a means of preventing diabetes, which the doctor regarded as risks for S given her family history. The doctor provided detailed instructions in relation to the regime, including directing the use of Mildronate before games by email, with increased doses before games of special importance. The doctor checked that the substances he recommended were not on the Prohibited List. S continued with this regime under the doctor, who continued to receive reports from the WADA lab certifying that the substances he was recommending were not on the Prohibited List, until 2012.

At the end of 2012, S decided not to continue working with the doctor and replaced him with a nutritionist. S continued to use three substances from the previous regime, but did not tell the nutritionist this. Nor did she tell other members of her team – her coach, her physio, the medical adviser she consulted through the Women's Tennis Association (WTA). Only her father and her manager – a vice-president of the global management group IMG – knew she continued to take the three substances from the previous regime, including Mildronate.

Apart from one consultation in the period between 2012 and 2015, S did not consult with any medical practitioner over her continued use of Mildronate. She did not look at a wallet card. She did not check the ITF website or ask the WTA for advice on taking Mildronate. She continued to use Mildronate up until the 2016 Australian Open without disclosing its use on any doping control forms.

The tribunal rejected evidence that her manager had failed to check the List for 2016 against the substances S was using as he had done in 2013 and 2014 as not credible, and the Panel concluded that S had no system in place to check on the substances which she continued to take from the earlier regime which were not disclosed to other members of her team. There was no medical diagnosis and no therapeutic advice supporting the use of Mildronate in 2016, and the manner of its use led the Panel to conclude that S used the substance to enhance her performance in matches.

Was the Use Intentional under Article 10.2?   On the question whether this use was 'intentional' under Article 10.2, the ITF accepted that S did not know that the product Mildronate contained a prohibited substance when she took it and that she would not have taken it if she had done. This meant that S's conduct could not be found to be intentional under the first limb of the definition of 'intentional' in Article 10.2.

The question was whether under the second limb of the definition S could establish that she was not aware that there was a significant risk that meldonium might have been banned and that she had not manifestly disregarded that risk. The Panel found that the proof of intentional conduct required actual knowledge on the part of the player. Where the ITF accepted that S did not know that Mildronate contained the prohibited substance, it had to follow that S could not have the necessary knowledge of risk under the definition. S's failures to check the changes to the Prohibited List might be relevant in considering whether S disregarded a known risk but were not relevant to the first subjective question whether she was in fact aware of the risk. Article 10.2.3 should not be extended to allow a finding of intention on the basis that the player ought to have been aware of a possible change in the rules which might make the taking of a substance a breach. Further, a player who made a genuine mistake as to the rules was not someone who 'intended to cheat', which was the aim of the definition of intentional conduct.

Was this a Case of No Significant Fault?   On the defence of no significant fault, S submitted that, given the failure of the ITF to warn her properly that meldonium would be included on the Prohibited List 2016, her fault was not significant. S also relied on the fact that she had taken the substance under medical supervision for many years and had taken reasonable steps to check on its status at least until 2010.

The Panel found that the ITF did not know that the player was using the substance nor, given the confidential nature of test results under the monitoring programme, ought it to have known that she was using it. It could not in those circumstances come under an obligation to warn S specifically. Nor had the ITF failed in its duty to take reasonable steps to publicise the changes to the List. Publication on its website of the summary of modifications to the List in December 2015, before the changes came into effect, discharged its duty. It also distributed the List by publishing it on the website and distributing wallet cards. Even if it had failed in these duties, S was still under a fundamental obligation to be familiar with the most current version of the List and to make annual checks, so the cause of the violation would still have been S's failure to meet her responsibilities. On the facts of the case, the change in the status of the substance after S had checked its status initially through her doctor did not render her fault not significant. Her failures in not checking at all on the substance which she was taking regularly were serious, and S could not come close to discharging her duty of utmost caution.

Estoppel Where the ITF did not know that S had tested positive for meldonium in 2015, when the substance was on the monitoring programme, and there was no basis to say that the ITF ought to have known she was regularly using it in 2015, there was no factual basis for any representation or assurance by ITF that S could safely continue taking the prohibited substance in 2016, assuming that the principle of estoppel could apply to the operation of the Code.

Proportionality The tribunal did not accept that the principle of proportionality could give rise to any inherent authority to reduce the applicable sanction under the rules. There was no basis for the claim that the period of ineligibility would operate unfairly on S because she would lose far more than another player – the rules expressly provided for this. The principle of proportionality could only operate in exceptional circumstances, probably where there was a gap in the rules. The Panel proceeded on the basis that the rules, by providing for a reduction in sanctions due to lack of intent, no fault or no significant fault, properly reflected the principle of proportionality.

S was entitled to have the commencement of the two-year period of ineligibility back-dated to the time of sample collection by reason of her prompt admission under Article 10.6.3 in March 2016.

The Panel concluded by saying that S was solely responsible for her breach and bore very significant fault in failing to take any steps to check whether she could continue taking the substance. If she had not chosen to conceal the use of the substance from her team and doctors and had sought advice, she would have avoided the breach. S was 'the sole author of her own misfortune'.

This decision was the subject of an appeal to CAS solely on the question whether S could show no significant fault. CAS reversed the decision of the ITF tribunal on the application of the no significant fault defence under Article 10.5.2 and held that, in the circumstances of the case, S had established that her fault was not significant. CAS set aside the period of ineligibility of two years and replaced it with a period of fifteen months.[54]

UKAD v. *Bevan* SR 00001202241 – Positive Test for Steroid – Relevance of Pre-2015 Conduct to 'Intentional' Conduct B took steroids by injection in late 2014, when he was playing rugby union and interested in

---

54 The CAS award on the appeal is summarised at pages 530–3, in the section of case summaries which are relevant to the no significant fault or negligence defence.

body-building. At that time, he was bound by anti-doping rules implementing the 2009 Code. B stopped taking steroids late in 2014. In February 2015, he was approached by a rugby league club and signed a contract with them. He did not read the declaration, which incorporated the 2015 rugby league anti-doping rules implementing the 2015 Code. After signing the contract, he did some short Internet research on the substances he had been taking, which led him to believe that he would not test positive. Two days after signing the contract, he was tested at a training session and the sample returned a positive test for steroids. Expert evidence was to the effect that the steroids taken could remain in the player's system for up to three months.

The positive test meant that B committed a violation for the presence of a prohibited substance at the time of the positive test in February 2016. The presumption that his conduct was intentional applied, as provided for in Article 10.2 of the 2015 Code. While the presence of the prohibited substance constituted the violation under the 2015 Code, the conduct which led to the violation took place before the 2015 rules came into effect. The tribunal held that this was not conduct which could be considered in relation to Article 10.2.3 as regards the question whether the conduct was 'intentional', because the rules were not expressed to apply to conduct which took place before the rule came into effect. Nor could the act of signing the contract in 2015 (at a time when the player knew he had taken steroids) be relevant conduct for the purposes of intent under Article 10.2.3, because it was the act of becoming bound to the rules, not conduct under them, that led to an anti-doping rule violation. In those circumstances, on the interpretation of the 2015 Code, where there was no relevant conduct to consider, the player could establish that he had not acted with the required intent under Article 10.2.3 of the 2015 Code. This meant that the standard period of ineligibility was two years.

The player further raised the defences of no fault and no significant fault. By contrast to its finding on relevant conduct under Article 10.2.3, the tribunal found that conduct before the player agreed to the application of the 2015 rules was relevant to the general consideration of the defences of fault as part of the circumstances relating to the violation. The tribunal referred to the unchanged definitions for no fault and no significant fault and the added definition of fault in the 2015 rugby league rules. Where the player had taken steroids while bound to anti-doping rules in 2014, when playing rugby, without doing any research or other investigation, and where he had only conducted cursory research relating to the steroids he had taken (which ought not to have satisfied him that he would not test positive) after signing the contract in 2015, the player had, notwithstanding his lack of anti-doping education and naivety, been significantly at fault. The defences failed and a two-year period of ineligibility was imposed.

CAS 2016/A/4516, WADA v. *Turkish Football Federation (TFF) and Ahmet Kuru* – Proof of Intentional Conduct – No Additional Requirement to Prove Intention to Cheat K was a professional football player in Turkey. He filed an application for a TUE in order to take clomiphene and proxeed as a treatment for infertility. The application was declined by the Turkish Football Federation (TFF) Therapeutic Use Committee, which warned K of the consequences if he continued to take the substance.

K tested positive for clomiphene, a prohibited substance under S4.3 of the Prohibited List 2015. K admitted that he had taken the medications which had been the subject of his TUE application in order to treat infertility at a time when no football matches were being played. K attributed the positive test to taking the medication. The TFF tribunals at first instance and on appeal imposed a period of ineligibility of six months from official games. After being notified of the decision, WADA appealed to CAS. The case was heard by a sole arbitrator and was determined on the written submissions without an oral hearing.

Clomiphene was a specified substance under the Prohibited List. The sole arbitrator held that the taking of the specified substances in the circumstances of the warning was intentional under Article 10.2. The phrase in the definition of intentional conduct in Article 10.2 which states that 'the term "intentional" is meant to identify those Players who cheat' did not create an additional burden in establishing intentional conduct. The anti-doping organisation had to establish that the athlete knew that his conduct would or was likely to constitute an anti-doping rule violation and disregarded the risk. It did not have to show that the athlete sought to gain an unfair advantage in-competition.

The arbitrator held that K knew, after being clearly warned of the risks associated with the medication, that his conduct would constitute an anti-doping rule violation and disregarded the significant risk associated with this. This met the requirements under Article 10.2.3. On its proper interpretation, Article 10.2.3 did not require a specific intent to cheat in sport, but only required proof of the elements set out in the provision. The arbitrator had sympathy with K, if the medication was indeed solely aimed at treating infertility, but the rules on plain reading imposed a four-year period of ineligibility. K could have resubmitted a TUE application meeting the requirements but chose instead to 'roll the dice, in full knowledge of the risks that he was taking for his career'.

A four-year period of ineligibility was imposed in terms of the Code (with no limitation to 'official matches', as had been the case in the orders made by the TFF tribunals, which were also in this regard contrary to the Code). TFF was responsible for the decisions which were incompatible with the Code and was ordered to bear the costs of the arbitration. TFF and K were ordered to pay jointly a reasonable contribution to the appellant's legal costs.

Possible Reduction of the Period of Ineligibility   Applicable periods of ineligibility may be subject to reduction under Articles 10.4, 10.5 and 10.6. These grounds can be split between elimination or reduction on the basis of the degree of fault of the athlete or other person (Articles 10.4 and 10.5) and reduction for reasons other than fault – admissions and substantial assistance (Article 10.6). Where both provisions are potentially applicable, the basic period of ineligibility is determined under Articles 10.4 and 10.5, before any possible reduction is considered under Article 10.6, with special provision regulating the application of multiple grounds for reduction of a sanction in Article 10.6.4.[55]

Fault, No Fault and No Significant Fault   For the first time, the Code contains a general definition of 'fault' in the definitions section. The comment to this definition says that it is applicable under all Articles where fault has to be considered. This amounts to a clear direction to consider every situation where fault has to be assessed by reference to the definition. In arriving at sanctions, an assessment of fault is required to arrive at the period of ineligibility for various violations and for the possible application of the defences of no fault and no significant fault in relation to violations of Articles 2.1, 2.2 and 2.6 (where they are not intentional under Article 10.2). The definitions of no fault and no significant fault remain the same under the Code and, while shortened, the comment to Article 10.4 remains similar to earlier comment in the 2004 and 2009 Codes in stating that the defences under Articles 10.4 and 10.5.2 are only intended to apply in exceptional circumstances.

The definition of 'fault' is broad and is directed to a fact-specific inquiry – 'any breach of duty or any lack of care appropriate to the particular situation'. It contains a range of factors which have to be taken into

55 See further page 441.

consideration in assessing an athlete or other person's fault and the degree of fault involved in a violation. The definition retains the importance of the strict obligations of the athlete under the Code by requiring that the fault be specific and relevant to explain the athlete or other person's departure from the expected standard of behaviour under the Code. Although the inquiry into the degree of fault is broad, the comment to the definition in the notes makes it clear that, while the general criteria apply whenever the degree of fault of the athlete has to be considered, there can only be a reduction under Article 10.5.2 when the degree of fault or negligence assessed is not significant. This new definition provides a clear starting point for any inquiry into the degree of fault of an athlete or other person.

Under the 2015 Code, the 'no significant fault or negligence' defence is introduced in two specific circumstances in addition to the possible general application of the defence under Article 10.5.2. Notwithstanding the changed application, the unchanged nature of the definitions of 'no fault' and 'no significant fault' indicates that the application of the defence should generally be approached in the same way as under the earlier versions of the Code. In relation to violations involving specified substances, the application of the no significant fault defence represents a significant change in approach to that which was provided for by Article 10.4 of the 2009 Code, which required an athlete to establish that he or she had no intention to enhance sport performance in order to put forward a case for a reduction in the period of ineligibility based on his or her degree of fault.

New Specific No Significant Fault Defences   The no significant fault requirement is used in Article 10.5.1.1 of the 2015 Code to provide the basis for the possible reduction of the two-year period where an anti-doping rule violation involves a specified substance. Article 10.5.1.2 follows and provides specifically for the possible reduction of the period of ineligibility where a prohibited substance is detected which came from a contaminated product where the athlete can establish no significant fault.

Apart from these specific new defences, Article 10.5.2 provides for the defence of no significant fault to apply in the range of possible circumstances beyond the specific no significant fault defences in Article 10.5.1. Article 10.5.2 retains the main provisions of the Article in the 2004 and 2009 Codes, including the maximum reduction to one-half of the applicable period of ineligibility.

Articles 10.4 and 10.5.2 refer to establishing the defences or no fault and no significant fault or negligence 'in an individual case'. Under the

2004 and 2009 Codes, the position was uncertain, but there were cases in which the defence of no significant fault was applied to violations involving intentional conduct, such as refusal under Article 2.3. The 2009 Code stated in the comments to the defences that they could potentially apply 'in any case' but that it was especially difficult to meet the criteria where knowledge was an element of the violation committed.

The note under Article 10.5.2 in the 2015 Code provides that 'Article 10.5.2 may be applied to any anti-doping rule violation, except those Articles where intent is an element of the anti-doping rule violation (e.g. Articles 2.5, 2.7, 2.8 or 2.9) or an element of particular sanctions (under Article 10.2.1) or a range of ineligibility is already provided for in an Article based on the athlete's or person's fault'. This note seeks to clarify the application of Article 10.5.2 and has to be considered in interpreting the Code under Article 24.3.[56] The effect of this note on the application of the defences is, it is submitted, that the defence of no significant fault should be interpreted and applied as only being available for breaches of Articles 2.1, 2.2 and 2.6 where there is no intentional conduct under Article 10.2. There is specific provision in Article 10.3.1 for the possible reduction of the four-year sanction for a violation under Article 2.3 down to two years where that violation is committed by failing to submit to sample collection (as opposed to evasion or refusal) and the athlete can show that the conduct which led to it was not intentional under Article 10.2.3. The defence under Article 10.5.2 can, it is submitted, apply to this form of the violation under Article 2.3 where an athlete establishes that his or her violation was not intentional because Article 10.2.3 does not provide for a range of ineligibility based on fault. This would allow an athlete facing a violation under Article 2.3 involving a failure to submit to sample collection to seek a further reduction down to a minimum of one year (if he or she showed that the violation was not intentional) by establishing no significant fault under Article 10.5.2. The other forms of the violation under Article 2.3 involve intentional conduct, and the defence is not applicable.[57] This application

---

56 As a matter of drafting style, the inclusion of important substantive provisions in explanatory notes to the Code is, it is suggested, unsatisfactory.

57 The presence of this specific provision for reduction where non-intentional conduct is established on one kind of breach of Article 2.3 and the specific provision for reduction to a minimum ban of two years depending on the athlete's degree of fault by prompt admission under Article 10.6.3, which applies where an athlete is alleged to have committed a violation subject to a four-year ban under Article 10.2.1 or 10.3.1 (refusing or tampering), indicates, it is submitted, that the defence of no significant fault or negligence is not

of the no significant fault defence arises either because all other violations have an element of intent in the sense of deliberate conduct or because the sanction provision for the violations contains an assessment which is made on the basis of fault. The other violations do not require proof of an intention to cheat or intentional conduct in terms of Article 10.2, but they do have an element of intentional or deliberate conduct, as the note to Article 10.5.2 makes clear.

Article 10.6 provides for a reduction in periods of ineligibility for reasons other than fault (prompt admissions and substantial assistance) and will, as noted, only be applied after the period of ineligibility has been determined by applying the provisions under Articles 10.2–10.5 (where the latter are applicable). Consistent with its aim – the obtaining of admissions and assistance generally – Article 10.6 is potentially applicable to any violation, whether involving intentional conduct or not, although the seriousness of the violation is a relevant factor in determining the amount of any suspension of the period of ineligibility. The making of a timely admission under Article 10.11.2 can reduce the length of the period of ineligibility for any alleged violation (where Article 10.6.3 on admissions has not been applied).

Fault

Assessment Generally

The assessment of fault, and in particular the degree of fault of a person who has committed a violation, is relevant to the exercise of arriving at an appropriate sanction under several violations – Articles 2.3 (in certain circumstances, as already explained), 2.4 and 2.10 – and in assessing whether the defence of no fault or no significant fault or negligence has been proven. Where no significant fault has been established, a tribunal will have to consider the degree of fault again in order to arrive at the period of ineligibility within the range specified by the particular defence. In any assessment of fault under the Code, the terms of the definition should be applied.

---

intended to apply to those forms of breach of Article 2.3 which involve deliberate conduct in refusing or evading sample collection. The approach in refusal cases under which the no significant fault defence was applied under the 2004 Code, which were summarised in previous editions of the text, should not now be followed – SDT 12/04, *New Zealand Rugby League v. Tawera* and CAS 2007/A/1416, *Wada v. Scherf*.

As has been outlined, the definition of fault in the 2015 Code is expressed in broad terms by reference to the risks in the circumstances of the violation which should have been perceived by the athlete or other person, the level of care and investigation taken by the athlete or person given the level of risk present, the experience of the athlete or person and any relevant special characteristics of the athlete or person. The circumstances which are considered in assessing the degree of fault have to be directly relevant to explain the athlete or person's departure from the expected standard of behaviour under the Code.

The reference to the expected standard of behaviour under the Code is important. This standard of behaviour includes the obligation on an athlete to ensure that no prohibited substance enters his or her body. In the context of assessing the degree of fault present in a breach of Article 2.1, 2.2 or 2.6 for the purposes of considering a plea to rely on the defences of no fault or no significant fault, a tribunal has to make the assessment with that duty in mind. It is submitted that this definition emphasises important points which provide the framework for an inquiry into the degree of fault present in a breach of the Code. Such an inquiry is intensely fact-specific. It must be concerned with examining the conduct which led to the violation and the reasons which led to the athlete departing from the conduct required by the Code. The inquiry is concerned with both objective and subjective considerations, but it is primarily objective (in contrast with the inquiry into whether conduct is intentional under Article 10.2.1) and involves considering what a reasonable athlete aware of his or her obligations under the Code would have done in the circumstances of the violation and comparing that with what the athlete who committed the violation in fact did to arrive at the level of fault. Particular personal characteristics which affect perception of risk may also be considered in arriving at the degree of fault.

The linked definitions of no fault and no significant fault, which are in the same terms as under the 2004 and 2009 Codes, underline the generally high duty placed on athletes under the Code. As previously noted, the comment to the 'fault' definition makes it clear that assessing the degree of fault under the definition does not allow a tribunal to apply the defence of no significant fault unless the tribunal concludes that degree of fault is not significant. The definition of 'fault' included in the 2015 Code is as follows:

> Fault is any breach of duty or any lack of care appropriate to any particular situation. Factors to be taken into consideration in assessing an Athlete or

other *Person's* degree of *Fault* include, for example, the *Athlete's* or other *Person's* experience, whether the *Athlete* or other *Person* is a *Minor*, special considerations such as impairment, the degree of risk that should have been perceived by the *Athlete* and the level or care and investigation exercised by the *Athlete* in relation to what should have been the perceived level of risk. In assessing the *Athlete's* or other *Person's* degree of *Fault*, the circumstances must be specific and relevant to explain the *Athlete's* or other *Person's* departure from the expected standard of behaviour. Thus for example the fact that an *Athlete* would lose the opportunity to earn large sums of money during a period of *Ineligibility* or the fact that the *Athlete* only has a short time left in his or her career or the timing of the sporting calendar would not be relevant factors to be considered in reducing the period of *Ineligibility* under Article 10.5.1 or 10.5.2.

It is suggested that the inquiry should be directed by the following questions:

- In the specific circumstances in which the violation was committed, what risk of committing a violation should a reasonable athlete, mindful of his or her obligations under the Code, have perceived?
- Given that level of perceived risk, what would a reasonable have done?
- How does the conduct of the athlete who committed the violation compare with what a reasonable athlete would have done?
- Does the athlete have any personal characteristics which should reduce his or her degree of fault?
- Overall, can the fault be described given the obligations under the Code as low, moderate or significant?

Definitions of No Fault and No Significant Fault

The definitions of no fault and no significant fault remain substantially as set out in the 2004 and 2009 Codes, with additional wording confirming the well-established general position under CAS awards that in order to rely on these defences an athlete or person in a case involving the presence of a prohibited substance in breach of Article 2.1 has to establish how the substance entered his or her system. There is a new exception to this rule in the case of minors, who do not have to establish the requirement before a defence of no fault or no significant fault can be considered.[58]

---

58 See the CAS award under the 2009 Code in CAS 2010/A/2268, *I* v. *FIA*, where a twelve-year-old go-karter could not establish the requirement but an eighteen-month period of ineligibility was imposed on the basis of proportionality principles.

No fault or negligence is defined as follows:

> The *Athlete* or other *Person's* establishing that he or she did not know or sus-
> pect, could not reasonably have known or suspected even with the exercise
> of the utmost caution that he or she had *Used* or been administered the
> *Prohibited Substance* or *Prohibited Method* or otherwise violated an anti-
> doping rule. Except in the case of a *Minor*, for any violation of Article 2.1,
> the *Athlete* must also establish how the *Prohibited Substance* entered his or
> her system.

No significant fault or negligence is defined as:

> The *Athlete* or other *Person's* establishing that his or her *Fault* or negligence,
> when viewed in the totality of the circumstances and taking into account
> the criteria for *No Fault or Negligence*, was not significant in relationship
> to the anti-doping rule violation. Except in the case of a *Minor*, for any
> violation of Article 2.1, the *Athlete* must also establish how the *Prohibited
> Substance* entered his or her system.

The exercise of assessing fault will always be highly fact-specific. This is
reflected in the breadth and generality of the definition of 'fault'. However,
the definitions of 'fault', 'no fault' and 'no significant fault' also emphasise that the assessment must take into account the underlying obligations
of those bound by the Code – namely, to be aware of their obligations
generally and to take all reasonable care to avoid taking or using prohibited substances or prohibited methods or committing violations under the
Code. An assessment of fault will involve considering the particular factors which are relevant to explain why the particular athlete or person did
not meet the obligations under the Code in the particular circumstances
of the violation.

No Significant Fault or Negligence?

Perhaps the most difficult exercise in assessing the degree of fault involves
deciding whether the fault of an athlete or person is 'not significant' for
the purposes of the application of the defences. In most legal systems,
assessments of fault are generally limited to such questions as whether
there is fault which amounts to a breach of a legal duty giving rise to a
claim, or possibly whether the degree of fault or negligence can be characterised as very serious or gross. It is unusual to require an assessment
to determine whether a level of fault is 'not significant' then require a
further assessment of the degree of fault within the range covered by

non-significant fault in order to arrive at a sanction which reflects the degree of fault. In civil or criminal law, this kind of penalty-setting exercise is often left to the general discretion of a judge, perhaps with sentencing guidelines applicable for various forms of offending or breaches.

Assessing the degree of fault under the Code and its level is a highly fact-specific task. The comments to the defences and decisions from CAS and tribunals considering the defences in various situations illustrate the general difficulty in establishing either the no fault or the no significant fault defence, given the framework of fundamental duties owed under the Code. The defences are intended to apply only in cases which can be said to be exceptional in the sense of falling outside the range of normal cases, although, as a matter of logic, cases of no fault must be more exceptional or out of the range of normal cases than those where no significant fault defences can apply. The nature of the defences means that athletes who have been careless with no intention to compete unfairly with prohibited substances in their systems will not be able to obtain a reduction of the standard period of ineligibility applicable. If anything, where those bound by the Code are increasingly well educated concerning their personal responsibilities under the Code, much more likely to have been instructed on specific risks such as workout supplements and much more likely to have been given information by medical professionals when they are prescribed with drugs, those who commit violations by ingesting prohibited substances or using prohibited methods will find it more difficult to show that their degree of fault was not significant. In making this general observation, the important point made in a number of CAS awards that the bar for the application of the defence of no significant fault should not be set too high because this would render the defence of little value should be kept in mind. While there will always be steps which might have been taken to avoid a positive test or other violation, the conduct of the athlete should be assessed reasonably in the context. An athlete who has taken some reasonable steps to meet his or her obligations but not others may still establish that his or her fault is not significant in the particular circumstances. In assessing the degree of fault, an approach which seeks to allocate the fault to bands of fault will assist,[59] but again there is no precise

---

59 In CAS 2013/A/3327, *Cilic* v. *ITF*, the CAS Panel referred to the objective and subjective considerations in assessing fault under Article 10.4 of the 2009 Code and divided fault into bands: light, moderate and considerable. The same approach is referred to in CAS 2016/A/4371, *Lea* v. *USADA* and *Sharapova* v. *ITF* in dealing with assessments of fault for the purposes of applying no significant fault defences under the 2015 Code. This

science in an exercise which is an evaluation by the tribunal in the particular circumstances of the breach of the Code by the individual athlete or person.

Where fault is being more generally considered in assessing the sanction to be imposed where the athlete's degree of fault is the criterion stipulated in the Code (Article 2.3, 2.4 or 2.10), the general factors set out in the definition will be applicable. Again, the explanation for the breach has to be relevant to explain the departure from the expected standard of behaviour. Both on the clear terms of the provisions themselves and generally as a matter of common sense, the assessment of fault cannot be concerned with the effects of a period of ineligibility, but rather must concern itself with the circumstances of the breach of the Code and the reasons which explain why the athlete or other person failed to meet his or her obligations under the Code.

The approach taken by a tribunal if an assessment of fault is required should be as straightforward as possible. The tribunal should find the circumstances of the violation in either the process of the violation being proven or in any sanctions hearing (applying the relevant burden and standard of proof to any disputed issues) before considering the fault of the athlete or person who has committed the violation by reference to the factors which are relevant in the case. If the exercise involves assessing fault or the seriousness of the violation under Article 2.4 or Articles 2.7–2.10 (where the defences in Articles 10.4 and 10.5 are not applicable), the degree of fault will be used to arrive at the period of ineligibility within the range provided for the violation. If the no significant fault defence is held to be applicable because the tribunal considers at the end of its assessment of fault that the fault is not 'significant', the degree of fault is again to be used to arrive at the sanction in the range provided.

While other decided cases provide examples of the provisions of the Code in action and show that in certain circumstances an athlete may or may not be able to establish no significant fault, it is submitted that the exercise of establishing the degree of fault can generally be carried out in a straightforward manner by referring to the provisions of the Code and the fundamental obligations of an athlete or person bound by it and applying the definitions and the requirements under those provisions to the

approach provides some general assistance in establishing a framework. However, the fact-specific nature of the exercise, which is also emphasised in many awards and is underlined by the Code provisions, makes any attempt to provide detailed guidance somewhat artificial.

relevant circumstances relating to the failure of the athlete or person to meet his or her obligations under the Code. The notes to the 2015 Code generally, and Article 10 in particular, have been reduced, and this encourages the appropriate focus on the words of the relevant provision and the applicable definitions and facts of the particular case.

Article 10.4: No Fault or Negligence, Potential Availability

The defence of no fault has been present in each version of the Code in largely unchanged terms. It is expressed to apply where an athlete or person establishes no fault in an individual case. The comment to Article 10.4 does not limit the possible application of the defence in the same way as the note to Article 10.5.2, and the definition refers to establishing the criteria for no fault where the athlete has used or been administered with a prohibited substance or otherwise violated an anti-doping rule. However, it is submitted that the Article should only apply to violations where the athlete is strictly responsible for a state of affairs – Articles 2.1, 2.2 and 2.6[60] – and not where the violation involves any element of intentional conduct under Article 10.2 or otherwise, or where an assessment of fault is required to arrive at the sanction. This approach is consistent with the approach to the availability of the no significant fault defence which is specifically set out in the 2015 Code. It can be contended that the defence should be applied more broadly on its wording and definition to any violation in exceptional circumstances. A possible example might be where an athlete or person has been forced by physical duress to commit a violation so that, while the violation is intentional and quite deliberate, the athlete or person can in the particular circumstances be said to carry 'no fault' because he or she could in reality do nothing to avoid committing the violation due to the operating duress. It is suggested that sanctions in such rare cases might be better considered under principles of proportionality, rather than trying to apply the no fault defence. The possible application of the defence in exceptional circumstances of this nature does not appear

60 The defence is applicable to a violation under Article 2.6 because the violation falls within the provisions imposing four years for an intentional anti-doping rule violation. Presumably if intentional conduct is not shown, a breach should be treated as potentially allowing the application of Article 10.4 or 10.5.1 and 10.5.2, in the same way as with violations under Articles 2.1 and 2.2. This follows even though the violation requires some element of intent to control, because the relevant intentional conduct which might prevent the defences applying is apparently the intentional conduct defined under Article 10.2 (see note to Article 10.5.2).

to have been the subject of any consideration by a tribunal. The no fault defence has the effect of removing all consequences of a violation apart from the disqualification of results in the particular competition in which the violation was committed. The defence is reserved for exceptional circumstances and involves the athlete or other person who has committed the violation proving that 'he or she did not know or suspect and could not reasonably have known or suspected even with the exercise of utmost caution that he or she had used or been administered the prohibited substance or prohibited method or otherwise violated an anti-doping rule'. In addition, unless the athlete is a minor, he or she has to establish how the prohibited substance entered his or her system or came into his or her possession. Cogent evidence will be required in this regard, and speculation and/or general assertion by the athlete that he or she would never take a prohibited substance supported by evidence of good character. This will not discharge the burden of proof on the athlete who asserts, by way of example, that, given the general evidence as to his or her innocent good character, the only explanation for a violation must be sabotage or spiking by a third party. The underlying rationale of this rule is that without such evidence, the fault of the athlete cannot be assessed.[61]

If the athlete succeeds in establishing that he or she is not at fault or negligent, the effect of the application of Article 10.4 is that, in addition to the elimination of the sanction and the removal of the disqualification of results in-competition,[62] apart from the result of the competition in which the violation occurred, the anti-doping rule violation will not be considered as a prior violation for the purpose of determining the period of ineligibility for multiple violations.[63]

The Notes to Articles 10.4 and 10.5.2

The notes applicable to Articles 10.4 and 10.5.2 have been cut down in the 2015 Code. However, they still contain passages intended to confirm that the defences are generally for exceptional circumstance and for use in relation to particular violations. The note to Article 10.5.2 is not expressly applied to the specific defences under Article 10.5.1, which contains the new specific 'no significant fault' defence for specified substances

---

61 See e.g. CAS 2006/A/1032, *Karatancheva v. ITF* at pages 383–4; CAS 2006/A/1067, *IRB v. De Keyter*; and CAS 2006/A/1130, *WADA v. Stanic & Swiss Olympic Association*, at pages 384–85.

62 Unless the results were affected by the violation as provided by Article 10.1.1; see pages 350–1.

63 Article 10.7.3 of the 2015 Code.

and contaminated products. This might lend some support to the position that the approach to the application of the specific defences in Article 10.5.1 is intended to be different or in some way less strict and confined than that which applies to the defence of no fault and the general no significant fault defence under Article 10.5.2 (which applies where the athlete or other person seeks to rely on the defence outside the circumstances in Article 10.5.1). It is submitted that this approach is not properly available as a matter of interpreting the Code where the definition of fault and, more important, the linked definitions of 'no significant fault' and 'no fault' are common to all defences under Article 10.5. The omission of a reference in the note is better understood as indicating that the defences in Article 10.5.1.1 and 10.5.1.2 are applicable in specific exceptional circumstances and have specific requirements which a tribunal must consider.

The notes to Article 10.4 explain that sabotage could be a basis for a plea of no fault where the athlete had taken all reasonable care. However, they then provide examples of situations which would not support the defence of no fault. These limitations arise from the strict nature of the regime under the Code and the obligations which it imposes on those bound by it.

The situations which the note says *cannot* be the basis for a finding of no fault or negligence under Article 10.4 are:

- a positive test resulting from mislabelled or contaminated vitamin or nutritional supplements;
- administration of a prohibited substance by the athlete's personal physician or trainer without disclosure to the athlete; and
- sabotage of the athlete's food or drink by a spouse, coach or other person within the athlete's circle of associates.

The reason these circumstances cannot provide a basis for a claim that the athlete was not at fault or negligent at all is that they will generally all involve some element of athlete fault, given the nature of the responsibilities and obligations of an athlete under the Code, which involve a duty to take all reasonable steps to avoid a positive test. Under this regime, the comment explains, athletes have to take responsibility for the use of nutritional supplements, the choice of medical personnel and the conduct of those persons they trust to have access to their food and drink. While the comment seeks to explain the operation of the no fault defence, it cannot limit the role of a tribunal in considering whether the terms of the defence apply to a particular case. All inquiries into fault are fact–specific, and the particular factual considerations raised by an athlete on the evidence must be considered by a tribunal in each case in order to decide whether, on the particular facts, a defence can be relied on. That said, the nature of the duties under the Code and the comment to Article 10.4 mean that a successful plea of no fault will be very rare.

The nature of the regime under the Code can properly be described as one under which athletes have a very high degree of responsibility for what they ingest and must exercise the utmost caution to avoid a positive test or committing other violations of the Code. This means that generally, depending on the actual circumstances, only situations where an athlete can truly be said to have been prevented by the circumstances prevailing at the time of the violation from taking the precautions which a reasonable athlete would have taken to prevent the violation occurring will permit the application of Article 10.4. However, the circumstances which the notes say cannot fall within Article 10.4 may provide grounds for a reduction of the period of ineligibility under Article 10.5.2 on the basis of no significant fault or negligence.[64] This means that, depending on the particular circumstances, where a member of the athlete's entourage such as a trainer, coach or doctor fails to take steps to avoid an athlete committing a violation, the athlete may be able to raise a no significant fault plea. While the actions of a third party who brings about or contributes to a violation will, in effect, be attributed to the athlete for the purposes of liability under the Code, an athlete may in certain specific circumstances be able to claim that his or her personal responsibility should be assessed in the context of a reasonable decision to place trust in a competent third party. In the recent decision in *Sharapova* v. *ITF*,[65] the CAS Panel held that it was reasonable for the athlete to delegate an annual check of the Prohibited List to her experienced manager and that the athlete could, to an extent, rely on that delegation as part of the circumstances relevant to a consideration of her personal fault. While the fault of the athlete had to be considered by reference to the steps which she had taken or had failed to take to meet her obligations under the Code, the failings of the manager could not be considered as her fault in assessing her degree of fault. The player had acted properly in delegating the task to the manager, and her degree of personal fault had to be assessed by the steps which she had not taken herself and her failure to instruct and supervise the manager correctly.[66]

---

64 See the notes to Article 10.5.2.   65 See case summary at pages 420–3.

66 Both parties to the appeal agreed that delegation of aspects of compliance with obligations under the Code was permitted and relevant in assessing the no significant fault defence.

The strict personal responsibility of an athlete to ensure that he or she does not ingest prohibited substances or commit anti-doping rule violations is expressed in very clear terms in the Code. While this does not mean that an athlete cannot rely on others to assist him or her in fulfilling the obligations under the Code and that such reliance is irrelevant in assessing fault (the notes to Article 10.4 make this clear), it will be a rare case where an athlete can establish no significant fault by relying in part on the failure by a third party in his or her entourage, because usually there will be steps which the athlete should have taken to avoid committing the violation, whether by him- or herself or in instructing the third party. It will generally be rare that an athlete will be able to show that an aspect of his or her personal responsibility under the Code can be delegated to a third party, but this will depend on the particular circumstances.

Articles 10.4 and 10.5: No Fault or Negligence, Potential Availability

Where a violation of Article 2.1 is concerned, the definition of no significant fault in the 2015 Code now expressly states that the athlete first has to establish how the prohibited substance entered his or her system. This basic principle had previously been underlined by many CAS Panels before its express inclusion in the Code. Cogent evidence will be required as to the way in which the prohibited substance came to be in the athlete's bodily sample (or from which that can properly be inferred), not speculation or guess work based on sworn statements by the athlete that he or she would never have taken a prohibited substance deliberately. The reason is simple common sense. Without such evidence, the fault of the athlete cannot be assessed.[67] It can be difficult for an athlete to prove how

This was based on a CAS award in CAS 2014/A/3591, *Al Nayhan* v. *FEI* concerning sanctions under the FEI rules, which implement the Code in the context of equine sport. Under those rules, CAS had held that a rider whose horse tested positive was entitled to have a plea of no significant fault assessed on the basis that he had acted reasonably in delegating the care of the horses to expert veterinary staff. After assessing the personal acts and omissions of the rider, the Panel held that the no significant fault defence had been established and reduced the period of ineligibility to eighteen months. It is submitted that the *Al Nayhan* award does not establish any general principle of delegation for anti-doping responsibilities by an athlete and should be limited to its particular context. The *Sharapova* decision, like other awards where an athlete has succeeded in showing no significant fault in circumstances where a violation was brought about in part at least by the failings of a trusted third party, should be considered an exceptional case on its facts.

67 See e.g. CAS 2006/A/1032, *Karatancheva* v. *ITF*; CAS 2006/A/1067, *IRB* v. *De Keyter*; and CAS 2006/A/1130, *WADA* v. *Stanic & Swiss Olympic Association*, as per page 379, note 61.

a substance came to be in his or her body even on the applicable balance of probabilities standard. While the burden of establishing the way in which a prohibited substance or method came to be in an athlete's sample remains on the athlete throughout, where information relevant to this issue lies with the anti-doping organisation, an athlete who requests that information and does not receive it may able to ask a tribunal to draw inferences in his or her favour in relation to the way in which the substance came to be in his or her system from the failure of the anti-doping organisation to assist. This point can be described in terms of a general legal rule imposing an obligation on the part of the anti-doping organisation to cooperate in assisting the party to prove its case (a concept under Swiss law referred to in the *Contador* decision), but it is submitted that it is better approached as a practical approach to the question of proof.

It is submitted that this requirement applies to any breach under Articles 2.1, 2.2 and 2.6 where the defences under Articles 10.4 and 10.5 are potentially available – the athlete or person must establish how he or she came to have the prohibited substance or method in his or her system or possession.

The following extracts from decisions (which are set out in *IWBF* v. *Gibbs*)[68] emphasise this requirement and its important role in considering any claim to rely on the Articles of the Code which can allow for a reduction in the period of ineligibility.

CCES v. *Lelievre*, SDRCC 7 February 2005, para. 51:

> While recognising that obtaining such evidence might be difficult, if not impossible, mere speculation as what may have happened will not satisfy the standard of proof required.

Karatancheva v. *ITF*, CAS 2006/A/1032, para. 117:

> If the manner in which the substance entered an athlete's system is unknown or unclear, it is logically difficult to determine whether the athlete has taken the required steps to prevent any such occurrence.
>
> In the absence of proof as to how the substance entered the player's body, it is unrealistic and impossible to decide whether, in those unknown circumstances, what steps he or she did take to avoid the commission of the doping violation.
>
> The provision must ensure that mere protestations of innocence and disavowal of motive or opportunity to cheat by a player, however persuasively asserted, will not serve to engage these provisions if there remains any doubt as to how the prohibited substance entered his body. This provision is necessary to ensure that the fundamental principle that a player

68 See Appendix 1, pages 557–9.

is responsible for ensuring that no prohibited substance enters his body is not undermined by an application of mitigating provisions in the normal run of cases.

The burden can be difficult for an athlete to discharge where there are a number of possible explanations for the presence of a substance in a sample, and the nature of the strict liability regime under the Code means that there may well be cases where the athlete is liable and simply cannot discharge the burden on him or her. Where this is the outcome of a consideration of the evidence, the result will be that the athlete is liable to the mandatory sanction (usually two years).

Illustrations from the 2004 and 2009 Codes: Burden on the Athlete to Show How a Positive Test Came About

Burden of Showing how Prohibited Substances came to be in the Athlete's Body, Applicable to Both Defences

CAS 2006/A/1130, WADA v. *Stanic & Swiss Olympic Association* S, a professional handball player, tested positive in-competition for cocaine metabolites. The doping violation was heard by a tribunal constituted by the Swiss Olympic Committee (SOC). S gave evidence that he had come to the conclusion that he had unknowingly smoked a cigarette containing cocaine in a discotheque when he was out with a friend four days before the positive test. S had asked the friend for a cigarette. The friend had run out of cigarettes and asked another group of men for one. S was given a cigarette, which he smoked, and felt strange. No other evidence was given. The SOC imposed a six-month ban on the basis that S had shown no significant fault or negligence and on the basis of his personal circumstances. WADA appealed to CAS on the basis that the SOC had misapplied its doping statute and should have imposed a fixed two-year period of ineligibility.

CAS held that S had not established by cogent evidence how the cocaine had entered his system. This was a precondition for the application of the Articles of the Code which permitted the elimination or reduction of the period of ineligibility. S had to establish the facts on the balance of probabilities, and on the evidence it was improbable that unknowing inhalation of cocaine was the manner in which the substance got into S's system. There was also, the Panel noted, no scientific evidence to show how long the cocaine could stay in his system which might support the finding that it entered his system at a discotheque four days before the in-competition test, as S suggested.[69]

Establishing the Way in Which Prohibited Substances came to be in an Athlete's Sample – the 2009 Code

CAS 2011/A/2384, *UCI* v. *Alberto Contador Velasco & RFEC*; CAS 2011/A/2386, *WADA* v. *Alberto Contador Velasco & RFEC* C tested positive for clenbuterol in a urine doping test carried out on the rest day of the 2010 Tour de France, on 21 July 2010. Analysis of the B sample confirmed the presence of clenbuterol, an anabolic agent under the Prohibited List, at a low level of 50 pg/ml. As a result of the low concentration of clenbuterol found in the samples, UCI and WADA conducted a series of investigations in order to understand the finding and to investigate whether other anti-doping violations might have been committed. Reanalysis showed low levels of clenbuterol in other urine samples taken from C on 22, 24 and 25 July 2010.

After the investigation, UCI concluded that there was evidence to support anti-doping rule violation proceedings and requested the Spanish Cycling Federation to commence proceedings against C in accordance with its rules. The national tribunal responsible, the CNCDD, considered the allegations against C. It received a large amount of technical, medical and scientific evidence from C in support of his defence that the positive test had occurred as a result of his unknowingly eating meat contaminated with clenbuterol on the day before the test. The examining judge of the CNCDD sought technical assistance and reports from UCI and WADA and the Spanish NADA. UCI indicated that it would not be able to provide the information requested in the time-frame given. WADA sent the CNCDD a letter indicating that it would not deal with the request because it was not under its jurisdiction.

As a result of the position of UCI and WADA, after CNCDD had initially proposed a one-year suspension, which C refused, the CNCDD gave a decision on 14 February 2011 finding that the clenbuterol detected in C's sample might, with a high percentage of probabilities, be due to the ingestion of contaminated meat. It found that other possibilities considered by UCI, namely, a blood transfusion or the injection of microdoses of

---

69 This decision demonstrates how scientific evidence concerning the quantity of a prohibited substance detected and the relationship of that quantity to body retention times may be relevant and important where an athlete seeks to establish the requirements for the application of Articles 10.5.1 and/or 10.5.2.

clenbuterol, were not the most likely causes of the positive test. CNCDD held that the most probable cause for the adverse analytical finding was the ingestion of contaminated meat. It found that C had no way of knowing or suspecting, even exercising the utmost caution, that he would eat meat contaminated with a prohibited substance in this way. It accordingly found that the athlete carried no fault.

UCI and WADA appealed against this finding. The appeals were consolidated. The case became more complex as the parties filed more evidence. There were a number of procedural delays before a hearing took place in November 2011. The CAS decision was given on 6 February 2012.

The parties produced a significant amount of expert evidence and submissions dealing with the three possible explanations which were put before the Panel to explain the presence of clenbuterol in C's sample:

- contaminated meat;
- blood transfusion; and
- contaminated supplement.

Procedural Issues   WADA sought to present evidence from a witness who was to remain anonymous. The tribunal considered this question by reference to the principles of a fair trial under Article 6 ECHR and decisions (although the ECHR was not directly binding on CAS as an arbitral tribunal). It relied on principles of admissibility in Swiss law, which required there to be clear evidence to show that the witness had to be protected before a party could be deprived of its rights to know the name of a witness and ask questions of a witness whose identity was known. In the circumstances of this case, the Panel denied WADA's request for the Panel to hear the witness without the disclosure of his or her identity.

The Panel accepted the well-established position that the burden of showing how the prohibited substance came to be in the athlete's sample remained at all times on the athlete. However, in discussing the standard of proof, the Panel drew upon Swiss law and found that, where a party has to prove a negative fact, a party contesting the disputed fact might come under a duty of cooperation in relation to the evidential issue. Although this principle did not change the allocation of the burden of proof, if the contesting party failed to cooperate, that could be taken into account in assessing whether the party has proved the negative fact.

In assessing the material before it and the explanations put forward by C and by WADA and UCI, the Panel held that C could only succeed in discharging the burden of proof by showing that, in his particular case, meat contamination was possible and that the other ways in which it was suggested the prohibited substances might have entered his body (blood transfusion and taking a contaminated supplement) were either impossible or less likely than the explanation advanced. The Panel emphasised that the burden remained on C throughout, even though WADA had put forward the two alternative scenarios explaining the presence of the substance, the likelihood of which the Panel had to take into account when determining whether C had established, on a balance of probabilities, that the source which he put forward was more likely.

The Panel found that proof by C that other scenarios by which the prohibited substance might have entered his body did not occur was a form of negative fact and that as a consequence, under Swiss law, UCI and WADA had a duty of cooperation in advancing relevant evidence on this issue. UCI and WADA had fulfilled this duty by submitting and putting forward two other possible routes by which the prohibited substance might have entered C's system. The overall approach which the Panel adopted in assessing the possible causes of the positive test was as follows:

> 264. This implies that if, after carefully assessing all the alternative scenarios invoked by the parties as to the source of entry of the Prohibited Substance into the Athlete's system, several of the alleged sources are deemed possible, they have to be weighed against one another to determine whether, on balance, the more likely source is the one invoked by the Athlete. However, in the extreme situation that multiple theories were held to be equally probable, the burden of proof, i.e. the risk that a certain fact upon which a party relies cannot be established, would rest with the athlete.
>
> 265. Thus, it is only if the theory put forward by the Athlete is deemed the most likely to have occurred among several scenarios, or if it is the only possible scenario, that the Athlete shall be considered to have established on a balance of probability how the substance entered his system, since in such situations the scenario he is invoking will have met the necessary 51% chance of it having occurred.

The Panel examined the evidence on each possible cause and made findings on the likelihood that each explained the positive test. It was accepted that C had consumed meat purchased from a butcher in Spain on 20 July 2010. C contended that the meat had been contaminated by clenbuterol, which had been illegally used in fattening the animal from which the meat came. The meat could not, of course, be produced. C based his position in part on the fact that the brother of the farm owner from which the animal was likely to have come had been involved in a clenbuterol-fattening case in 1996. Alternatively, he suggested that the meat had, in fact, come from another source outside Spain, where it had been contaminated. The Panel found it highly unlikely that the meat in question was imported from South America and considered it very likely that the supply chain of the meat could be traced back to the farm in Spain. The Panel was not convinced that there was any relevance in the argument that the brother of the farm owner had been found guilty of illegal fattening in 1996. Since that time, EU regulations dealing with the use of clenbuterol and Spanish law had been significantly tightened.

WADA provided statistics which showed there had been no positive test for clenbuterol in animals in 2008. There had only been two non-compliant samples in the EU in 2008, both in the Netherlands, and neither involving clenbuterol. On the statistics, it was, WADA submitted, extremely unlikely that there was contamination with clenbuterol where animals in Spain were concerned. The Panel's conclusion on the contaminated meat theory was that the meat consumed came from a calf reared in Spain, which was likely to be from the farm identified. While it was possible that a contaminated piece of meat could have caused the adverse analytical finding, the Panel found that there were no established facts that would elevate the possibility of meat contamination to an event that could have occurred on balance of probabilities. The position within Europe was that there was now no known contamination problem with clenbuterol in meat. There were no other cases of athletes having tested positive for clenbuterol in relation to Spanish meat.

While the meat contamination scenario was a possible explanation, it was very unlikely to have occurred. Where the contaminated meat scenario was not the only possible explanation, other possible explanations had to be assessed in assessing the athlete's case. The Panel considered the explanation advanced by WADA, namely that the presence of clenbuterol was the result of a blood transfusion and subsequent injection of plasma which contained clenbuterol. WADA sought to rely on the fact that positive tests for clenbuterol for doping reasons were much more common than positives caused by contaminated meat. It also sought to rely upon the athlete's background, which showed that he had been in a team where others had carried out blood doping and that he had a possible link to the Operatión Puerta investigation. The Panel found no relevance to the allegations of 'bad company' in assessing the likelihood that a blood transfusion explained the presence of clenbuterol, and considered that consideration of such matters would be a breach of fundamental principles of Swiss law.

The blood parameters of the athlete were said to be atypical and irregular by an expert called by WADA. This was not accepted by an expert called on behalf of C. The Panel found that the athlete's blood parameters did not support evidence of a blood transfusion. The Panel further considered the fact that traces of phthalates were found in the samples. These are additives widely used in plastics and other materials. WADA submitted that the presence of these plasticisers was evidence of a blood transfusion, because they came from plastic bags which were used to store blood and plasma. C provided evidence of a polygraph test which was to the effect that he was telling the truth when he said he had not undergone a blood transfusion. The Panel held that this test result was admissible to corroborate the athlete's statement. The Panel held, after considering the expert evidence, that while the blood transfusion was a possible explanation for the adverse analytical finding, it was very unlikely to have occurred. The Panel accordingly concluded that both the meat contamination scenario and the blood transfusion scenario, while possible explanations, were equally unlikely.

The Panel then considered the food supplement scenario. It pointed to the high incidence of positive tests caused by contaminated food supplements and referred to the *Hardy* case, where the athlete tested positive for clenbuterol from a tainted supplement. C provided the full list of food supplements used by his team, although no analysis of the products was presented. Other riders on the team had undergone at least two anti-doping control tests during the tour and only C had tested positive. C had provided evidence from the six manufacturers which had provided supplements to the team and had received confirmation that none of them had used or stored clenbuterol in their warehouses, none had ever been blamed for an athlete's positive test and all of them carried out extensive testing of their products, none of which had ever revealed the presence of clenbuterol.

Having considered the material before it, the Panel concluded that the supplement theory was possible. It noted that, in the same way as quality checks on livestock could not guarantee that there was no contamination in meat, quality checks on supplements would not guarantee that they were not contaminated.

The Panel considered that, after weighing the possibilities, it was more likely that the substance came into the athlete's system through a contaminated food supplement than through contaminated meat. Accordingly, after weighing all the evidence, the Panel accordingly held that the athlete had not discharged his burden of proof of showing how the prohibited substance came to be in his system. The decision of the CNCDD was set aside and C was found to have committed an anti-doping rule violation.

On the commencement of the period of ineligibility, the Panel held that the case might well have been dealt with more rapidly and, possibly, differently if UCI and WADA had responded to the initial request for assistance from CNCDD. There had also been delays in the CAS process, which had lasted over nine months, with the hearing being twice postponed. Taking into account these elements, the Panel held that the period of ineligibility would commence as of the date on which C had been offered the one-year period of suspension by CNCDD: 25 January 2011. The period of provisional suspension would also be credited against the period of ineligibility.

C submitted that it would be unfair and disproportionate to disqualify results obtained after he had returned to race following the decision of CNCDD to exonerate him. He had undergone approximately twenty tests since he had resumed competing, which had all been negative. C relied on other CAS decisions where athletes had been allowed to keep results obtained before the commencement of the sanction. Those cases were distinguished because C was, in fact, requesting that results obtained after the commencement of ineligibility be maintained. The Panel concluded that it would be unfair to other athletes (and those who were subject to provisional suspensions which were not lifted) to allow those results to stand. The earlier starting of the period of ineligibility could not mean that results obtained after the beginning of the period were unaffected.

Article 10.4: No Fault – Examples of (Rare) Successful Pleas of No Fault

Hospital Treatment in Emergency

CAS 2005/A/990, *P* v. *IIHF* P was a professional ice hockey player participating in the IIHF senior hockey championships in Vienna as a member of the national hockey team. After a game at the championship, he was drug tested and his A sample showed the presence of norandrosterone, a metabolite of the anabolic steroid nandrolone. The IIHF Disciplinary Committee found that an anti-doping rule violation had been committed and imposed a two-year period of suspension.

P's case was that, during a championship game in March 2005, he had been body checked and had hit the boards hard. He had been taken to the changing room, had had his hockey gear removed and then had been taken to hospital. At hospital, he had been treated for acute heart failure in the emergency room and given intravenous and intramuscular injections.

P contended that, unknown to him, one of the injections contained the steroid found in his sample when he was tested. P had not been accompanied by his team doctor to the hospital. At the hospital, P had been in very bad physical and mental condition, which made it impossible for him to monitor or even ask questions about the treatments being supplied. He was in severe pain and only cared about saving his life. His physical condition improved rapidly in hospital and he was allowed to leave the next day. He resumed training for the national team. He paid no further attention to the incident.

After the positive test on 1 May 2005, P conducted his own investigations and requested the hospital documentation. Only after he received further documentation was he able to establish the giving of the injection. P submitted that he bore no fault.

The CAS Panel concluded, after hearing the evidence, that there was clear evidence that the drug had been administered in the hospital and that the player had had no means of preventing its administration. P discharged the burden of proof in relation to no fault or negligence. The Panel found P's explanation credible. The Panel did not consider that it needed to address a further submission, which was that, even if P had not been at fault or negligent at the time the injection was given, he still had an obligation to take care after that to find out what substance he had received, to disclose his medical treatment and to obtain a retroactive TUE, if necessary. The Panel did not have to decide whether the Code imposed an ongoing obligation in respect of the substance staying in an athlete's body because it was satisfied, in the unique circumstances of the case, that the player could have no fault or negligence for failing to disclose his treatment and to apply for a retroactive TUE. P had no reason to suspect that he had been treated with a prohibited substance in hospital and so could not have any reason to check on the position after his discharge.

Cocaine in a Kiss

CAS 2009/A/1926, *ITF* v. *Richard Gasquet*; CAS 2009/A/1930, *WADA* v. *ITF and Richard Gasquet*   G, an international tennis player, arrived in Miami on 22 March 2009 with the intention of taking part in an Association of Tennis Professionals (ATP) tournament. G was not scheduled to play until Saturday, 28 March, although the tournament began on 25 March. In the period immediately before the tournament, the player was hampered by a shoulder injury. On the Friday before the tournament, after treatment and consultation with a doctor, he decided not to play. As he had decided to withdraw, he went out to a club in Miami that night. Before going on to the club, he socialised at a restaurant with four young women, including a woman called Pamela. At about midnight, the group went to a nightclub. The player consumed a vodka and apple juice. He also drank from Pamela's glass. At some point, the player and Pamela kissed. They kissed mouth to mouth about seven times during the time at the club. They attended a further club until about 5.00 am.

The next day, G went to the tournament and withdrew. He was required to provide a urine sample and underwent drug testing. The A sample contained a cocaine metabolite and a very small amount of unmetabolised cocaine. The player was charged with a doping offence.

Before the independent anti-doping tribunal of the ITF, G submitted first that there was no doping offence because the sample had been taken out-of-competition; or, if the sample had been taken in-competition, he could establish no significant fault or negligence. After deciding that the test was in-competition, the ITF Tribunal held that it was more likely than not that the source of the cocaine was kissing the woman, Pamela. However, the tribunal found that the player could not establish no fault or no negligence under Article 10.5.1 by reason of his behaviour during that night in drinking from open bottles and kissing a woman who was unknown to him, who might, for all he knew, have been a cocaine user. The ITF Tribunal found that he could establish the defence of no significant fault or negligence under Article 10.5.2. It went on to find that the minimum sanction of one year was disproportionate and a serious injustice and infringement of the player's right to practise his profession. As a consequence, it reduced the period of ineligibility to two and a half months.

On appeal before CAS, the explanation for the presence of the prohibited substance in the player's system, namely kissing the woman Pamela, was again accepted. In the circumstances in which the contamination had taken place, the player could not have reasonably done anything, notwithstanding the nature of the anti-doping regime as one of utmost caution, to avoid the positive test. There was no reasonable basis for him to think that he would ingest a prohibited substance in kissing Pamela. G bore no fault. Usually, the consequence of a no fault or negligence finding would be that the decision of the tribunal would be overruled. However, in the player's appeal, no formal pleading had been filed asking for the ITF Tribunal's sanction of two and a half months to be set aside. In those circumstances, the Panel could not do more than dismiss the appeals with the ITF and WADA against the decision in the ITF Tribunal.

Poppy Seeds in Bread

Drug Free Sport New Zealand v. *O'Grady*, ST 01 O'G tested positive in-competition at the New Zealand half ironman championships. His test showed a concentration of morphine of 1.4 µg/ml, which is just above the threshold for reporting of morphine of 1.2 µg/ml. Morphine was a prohibited substance under the 2011 List. There was no challenge to the test results.

The athlete relied solely on the no fault defence under Article 10.5.1 of the Code. The defence put forward on behalf of the athlete was that the positive test was caused by the consumption of poppy seeds in standard, commercially produced bread. After considering the evidence, which included expert evidence, the tribunal accepted that poppy seeds were a potential source of morphine and that poppy seeds could have produced the positive test for morphine where a combination of unfavourable variables had occurred. The tribunal then considered other possible sources for the positive test. On the evidence, the tribunal found that the positive test could not be attributed to the consumption of a codeine-based medicine (which could metabolise into morphine) and that the athlete did not take heroine or morphine.

In the circumstances, the tribunal was satisfied, having heard the evidence and the witnesses, that the source of the positive test was the consumption of poppy-seed bread. There was no other credible explanation and the tribunal was satisfied 'well beyond the balance of probabilities' as to the source of the positive test. In those circumstances, the tribunal concluded that the athlete could not reasonably have known or suspected that consuming normal bread products might produce a positive test. In the circumstances, there was no fault on the part of the athlete. The finding that a violation had occurred stood, together with the automatic disqualification of the results in the competition.[70]

Article 10.5: Reduction of the Period of Ineligibility Based on No Significant Fault or Negligence

The 2015 Code provides for a defence of no significant fault or negligence in three different forms. As has been outlined, two specific provisions have been introduced relating to violations involving specified substances and

---

70 For a further no fault case involving morphine produced by codeine metabolising into morphine, see *Softball New Zealand* v. *CindyPotae*, ST 04/07, 27 February 2008.

contaminated products in Articles 10.5.1.1 and 10.5.1.2. A general no significant fault defence, which reflects the defence in Article 10.5.2 of the 2004 and 2009 Codes, is retained in Article 10.5.2. The defence under Article 10.5.2 will apply where the substance involved is not a specified substance and does not come from a contaminated product as defined. These defences have different requirements, and if they apply they operate to provide for different ranges of sanctions. They do have common general features:

- The athlete carries the burden of establishing the defences on the balance of probabilities standard.
- The defences, while expressed as applying in any individual case, are not available where a violation has an element of intention or intentional conduct under Article 10.2.3 or where fault is part of the assessment of the period of ineligibility.
- The athlete (unless he or she is a minor) has to show how a prohibited substance entered his or her system (or how the violation occurred, for violations under Articles 2.2 and 2.6) to rely on these defences. This involves proof of the route by which the substance entered the body on the balance of probabilities, not proof of possible alternatives or general speculation.
- The defences only apply where the fault is held, after considering the circumstances of the violation by reference to the factors in the definition of 'fault', to be not 'significant'.
- The Code places a high level of personal responsibility on those bound by it to ensure that they do not ingest prohibited substances or commit violations. However the bar for establishing no significant fault should not be placed too high, because if it is, the defence will have little purpose. The duty of the athlete is to take all reasonable steps to avoid a violation. The extent of the athlete's failure to do this should be approached in a realistic way by assessing the fault in the circumstances at the time of the violation. It should be kept in mind that whenever a violation has been committed, hindsight is likely to show that there was something which could have been done to avoid a violation.
- The application of the defences involves a two-stage approach – first an assessment of the circumstances of the violation and an explanation for it, applying the general definition of fault in order to determine whether the fault or negligence is not significant, and second an assessment, if the fault is not significant, of the degree of fault within the range of fault which is not significant, to arrive at the sanction.

The significant difference between the provisions in Article 10.5 (apart from the specific requirements for the application of the defences in Article 10.5.1) is that the range of sanctions where the defences under Articles 10.5.1.1 and 10.5.1.2 apply runs from a reprimand and no period of ineligibility to two years, while under the general defence under Article 10.5.2 the provision can only reduce the period of ineligibility to not less than one-half the given period of ineligibility (or, if the period of ineligibility is life, to no less than eight years). This means that the exercise of arriving at the period of ineligibility under the defences, if they are found to apply, is concerned with arriving at a sanction within different ranges.

Articles 10.5.1.1 and 10.5.1.2: New No Significant Fault Defences

The specific defences under Article 10.5.1 were introduced in the 2015 Code to replace Article 10.4 of the 2009 Code where a violation of Article 2.1, 2.2 or 2.6 involves a specified substance (Article 10.5.1.1) and to provide for a specific defence where a violation of Article 2.1, 2.2 or 2.6 involves the detection of a prohibited substance which can be shown to come from a contaminated product (Article 10.5.1.2), whether the substance is specified or not. While the defences are not expressed to be mutually exclusive, where a specified substance is involved in the violation, Article 10.5.1.1 provides a broader possible defence, which means, in effect, that the defences will operate separately. The defence under Article 10.5.2 is expressly for situations other than those which fall under the defences in Article 10.5.1.[71]

Both specific defences involve the athlete or person who has committed the violation establishing that their fault in relation to the violation is 'not significant'. It is submitted that the requirement that the athlete or person seeking to rely on the defence proves how a prohibited substance entered his or her system, which is expressly stated to apply in the definition where there is a violation of Article 2.1, also applies where the violation involves use or possession, with the result that the athlete or person seeking to rely on the defence must establish how the violation occurred. This principle behind this requirement applies with equal force in all circumstances where the defence can apply and should be applied (with the same express reservation for minors set out in the definition of no significant fault).

---

71 The heading of the defence under Article 10.5.2 and the text make the separate application of Article 10.5.2 clear.

As previously noted, the 2015 Code now includes a generally applicable definition of fault which has to be applied in assessing an athlete's degree of fault. The content of the definition and the factors which it highlights have been outlined already. It is submitted that in most cases the central consideration in assessing fault will be the level of care which should have been exercised by the athlete or person in the light of the circumstances relevant to the violation, in particular the level of risk of a violation being committed that the reasonable athlete should have perceived. Some circumstances will usually raise the risks – obtaining medicines or using supplements or boosters in-competition – others may diminish them – eating normal meals, taking supplements in out-of-competition circumstances – but it must be emphasised that assessing fault and the application of the defences is fact-specific. What a reasonable athlete would have done is an objective consideration, but the athlete's breach of duty has also to be considered in the light of any relevant personal special characteristics which might affect his or her perception of risk and exercise of care. A tribunal will have to weigh these objective and subjective considerations to make its assessment of fault in the circumstances of the case.

The aim of the examination of fault is first to decide whether, at the end of the assessment, the level of fault can be described as not significant. It is difficult to provide specific guidance on when fault should be regarded as 'not significant' – the exercise is one of finding the facts and asking whether in the context of the Code and the obligations of the athlete or person under it their fault can properly be described as 'not significant'. Other decisions can assist a tribunal, but once the framework of the Code's provisions is established and addressed, in particular the requirements for assessment under the definition of 'fault', a tribunal has to make its assessment based on close consideration of the facts of the particular case. In making this assessment, the tribunal has to have in mind that the person bound by the Code has an express clear duty to avoid committing violations. However, this not an absolute duty, but rather one which involves taking all reasonable steps in the circumstances. In every case, there is likely to be something which might with hindsight have been done to avoid the violation, and a tribunal needs to be wary of adopting a position which is driven by hindsight – this is likely to set the bar for the defence too high.

From this starting point, the tribunal may first have to identify whether the case is wholly exceptional where the athlete can prove no fault – by showing that he or she exercised utmost caution in the circumstances at the time and could not have reasonably known or suspected that he or she had taken or used the prohibited substance or broken an anti-doping rule.

This will be a rare case. After this point, there will be some fault present, and the tribunal has to assess the degree of that fault. While the reference point is a negative 'not significant', the meaning of 'significant' can be equated with 'considerable' or 'noteworthy' and would indicate fault which is at the higher end of the range of fault or negligence that will be involved in the commission of violations under Articles 2.1, 2.2 and 2.6. Where the degree of fault assessed is found not to be at this level, the defence of no significant fault can apply. The difficulty lies in the reference in the notes to Article 10.4, which retain the reference to Articles 10.4 and 10.5.2 applying only in exceptional circumstances. This suggests that both defences will apply very rarely, presumably because those bound by the Code carry a high level of personal responsibility, which makes it almost impossible to establish no fault and very difficult to establish no significant fault. If the defence is for exceptional circumstances, this would suggest that it can only apply where the degree of fault might be considered to be exceptionally low, but that is not the natural meaning and effect of the term 'not significant' when used across a range of fault. While it may result in the defence applying more often than the term 'exceptional circumstances' might suggest, it is submitted that it is reasonable to apply the defence given its terms where it can be shown that the fault involved is not considerable or significant (in the sense of showing a significant departure from the standard expected under the Code) or, perhaps, obvious carelessness in the particular circumstances of the violation. This means that where fault can be described as low or moderate in the circumstances given the standard of behaviour expected under the Code, the defence is potentially applicable.

With an exercise of this nature, the tribunal's assessment and evaluation on the facts occupies an all-important position. A tribunal ultimately has to be mindful of the need to maintain a balance between upholding the strict personal responsibilities under the Code and allowing the defences to operate in a manner which allows them to function and provide a measure of relief from the standard consequences in appropriate circumstances. While the Code contains a number of provisions and definitions, the reality is that a good deal depends on how particular circumstances strike a particular tribunal, whether at first instance or a CAS Panel on re-hearing.

Cannabis

Since the adoption of the Code, there have been many cases where athletes have tested positive in-competition after recreational use of cannabis. The decision limits for reporting an adverse analytical finding for cannabis have been raised, which means that positive tests will be rarer. The problem with violations arising from the deliberate taking of cannabis is that often those who commit them often know well that they run the risk of a positive test and thus have a high level of fault given their responsibilities under the Code.[72]

The notes to the definition of no significant fault now contain a specific comment providing that the defence under Article 10.5.1.1 can be established by clearly showing that cannabinnoids were used in circumstances which were unrelated to sport performance. This provision seeks to allow for the application of the defence and the range of possible sanctions under it where it might not be applicable on its terms in order to allow for appropriate periods of ineligibility to be imposed for violations involving cannabis. In the context of cannabis use, this represents a form of deemed no significant fault, provided the athlete establishes the requirement that the use was clearly unrelated to sport performance.[73]

Contaminated Products

This defence in Article 10.5.1.1 was introduced to make specific provision for situations where a violation involves the detection of a prohibited substance which came from a contaminated product. Its introduction reflects the prevalence of violations since the adoption of the Code where an athlete takes a supplement which turns out to contain a substance not listed in its ingredients – often a banned stimulant or steroid. The defence can apply to a violation of Article 2.1, 2.2 or 2.6 (by reason of the use of the term

72 While there is a rebuttable presumption under Article 10.2.3 that out-of-competition use of a specified substance like cannabis which is only prohibited in-competition is not intentional, use of cannabis out-of-competition with knowledge of the risk that the use is likely to produce a positive test would appear to potentially fall within the definition of intentional conduct. It is submitted that this is not the intent of Article 10.2.3, and perhaps in this kind of situation a tribunal would be entitled to determine that the conduct could not be intentional where taking the substance was not linked to the enhancement of sporting performance in the circumstances of the case. In such circumstances, the definition in Article 10.2.3 would be applied in the light of its expressed aim – to identify those athletes who cheat – even though this is not generally a requirement which has to be proved to establish intentional conduct.

73 This remains an uncertain (and, it is submitted, unprincipled way) of dealing with the issues surrounding the fault involved in deliberately taking cannabis. Tribunals will handle fewer cases involving the taking of cannabis in any event because the change to the reporting level for a positive test means that there will be far fewer reported tests. But the analysis of the degree of fault in circumstances where the conduct may be deliberate and carried out with knowledge that it is likely to lead to a positive test is problematic. For the decision limits for cannabis and other substances, see WADA Technical Document Decision Limits 2017.

'detected'), but it will normally be relied on where an athlete tests positive for a prohibited substance which is found to have come from a contaminated product. The prohibited substance can be either a specified substance or a non-specified substance. A 'contaminated product' is defined as a product that contains a prohibited substance that is not disclosed on the product label or in information available in a reasonable Internet search. While the defence appears to have been added to address positive tests arising from contaminated supplements, it is potentially applicable to any product which an athlete consumes which meets the requirements of the definition and produces a positive test. It is submitted that it could possibly apply to any labelled product where the definition was met.

In order to rely on the defence, the athlete or person has to establish that the prohibited substance in his or her system (or detected in the product involved in the violation) came from a contaminated product as defined and that his or her fault was not significant in terms of the definition of 'fault' and the responsibilities of the athlete under the Code. The definition of 'contaminated product' contains some elements which are not in fact concerned with the contamination of the product, but rather with the steps that an athlete might take to check on the contents of a product, namely the conduct of a reasonable Internet search, which is more a consideration relevant to fault. The normal meaning of 'contaminated product' would be a product which contains something which should not be in the product and is not a usual ingredient of the product. The absence of the ingredient from the label would be an indication of contamination. Whether a person might detect the foreign ingredient by carrying out an Internet search is not properly relevant to the question whether the product is in fact contaminated.

In practical terms, the athlete or person who has committed the violation has to show, first, that the prohibited substance is not disclosed on the label of the product. It is submitted that this requires that the substance was not listed in terms which made it apparent to a reasonable athlete that it was in the product. Second, the athlete has to show that the presence of the substance would not be disclosed by a reasonable Internet search (regardless of whether the athlete did or did not carry out such a search). While in most cases falling within this defence, it will be reasonable to carry out an Internet search, there might be circumstances where it is not reasonable to expect a reasonable athlete to carry out an Internet search for the product which produced the positive test. It is submitted that if the athlete can show that this is the case, then a tribunal would be entitled to proceed to consider the possible application of the defence. It is uncertain under this definition whether the athlete can claim that it was not reasonable to expect him or her in his or her particular personal circumstances to carry out an Internet search and that, as a result, the second part of the definition should not be applied. It is submitted that the definition should be approached objectively and that it applies where it is reasonable for a reasonable athlete to have carried out a search.

It is important to note again that the athlete has to establish no significant fault for the defence to apply. This will involve the process of applying the definition of fault to the circumstances in which the contaminated product was taken. This comes down to the steps which the athlete took to ensure that the product did not contain prohibited substances before taking (or possessing) it in the particular circumstances of the violation. Generally, in order show that the fault was not significant, athletes are likely to need to show that they have taken significant steps to check on them, including quite possibly obtaining statements/guarantees from manufacturers.

Article 10.5.1.1: Specified Substances

Where violations of Article 2.1, 2.2 and 2.6 concern specified substances (and intentional conduct under Article 10.2.3 is not present), the defence under Article 10.5.1.1 can apply. The process for arriving at a sanction where a violation involves a specified substance and the athlete or person seeks to rely on the defence of no significant fault has already been set out. This defence replaces Article 10.4 of the 2009 Code with a no significant fault defence. It is important to note again that the threshold for a reduction of the standard period of ineligibility is no significant fault, and it is only if after assessing the degree of fault the tribunal reaches the view that the fault is not significant that the range of sanctions between a warning and two years is available. The appropriate sanction in that range will be established by reference to the degree of fault.

General No Significant Fault Defence

The general no significant fault or negligence defence under Article 10.5.2, which is available beyond the specific situations involving specified substances and contaminated products under Article 10.5.1, remains substantially in the form used under the 2004 and 2009 Codes (with shortened comment to the same effect). This defence may have more limited use given the specific defences in Article 10.5.1 and the clear limit on the application of the defence preventing its application where there is an element of intent or where there is an assessment of fault involved in arriving at the period of ineligibility (e.g. as in breaches of Article 2.4). If this defence is established, as was the case under the earlier Codes, the period of ineligibility has to be arrived at by reason of the degree of fault of the athlete or person. A reduction under this provision cannot be for more than one-half of the period of ineligibility which would otherwise be applicable.

As already noted, decisions considering the no fault and no significant fault defences under the 2004 and 2009 Codes remain of general relevance as examples of tribunals considering the requirements of the defence and applying them in differing factual situations. Generally, as noted, other decisions on the application of the defences on different factual circumstances should be approached with care. The need for care is further underlined by the fact that the 2015 Code provides for a wider range of sanctions under the specific defences in Article 10.5.1, and cases would now have different results. Certain awards, such as *Knauss* and *Cilic*, contain general observations on assessing fault which provide a useful framework for consideration of no fault and no significant fault defences.

As previously noted, given the many awards which might be referenced with limited direct benefit, tribunals should focus on interpreting and applying the defences in the Code on their wording in the specific context of the obligations under the Code, applying the burden of proof and assessing the fault of the athlete in the particular circumstances relating to the violation.

The summaries which follow contain two rare cases where, under the 2004 Code, sanctions were reduced on the application of the principles of proportionality. The cases provide examples of CAS applying the doctrine but have no direct application to the 2015 Code. However, as already outlined, the principles of proportionality are now referred to in the 2015 Code, and it is possible that they might be relied on in exceptional circumstances to reduce the period of ineligibility which would apply on the terms of the 2015 Code.

Early Cases on No Fault, No Significant Fault and Negligence Claims – 2004 Code

CAS OG 04/003 *Torri Edwards* v. *IAAF and USATF*

The Ad Hoc Division of CAS, sitting at the Athens Olympic Games, rejected an appeal by E from the decision of an AAA panel, which had imposed a two-year period of ineligibility upon her following a positive test and had ordered the disqualification of all her results obtained after the test. The disqualification included the results from an athletics meet where she qualified for the Olympic Games. She sought the right to compete at the Olympics by her appeal to CAS sitting in its *ad hoc* jurisdiction at the Games.

E had tested positive for nikethamide, a stimulant on the IAAF Prohibited List, after a doping control at an IAAF meet in Martinique. The evidence established that the stimulant had come from two glucose tablets which E had taken after they had been given to her by her physical therapist. The glucose tablets were labelled 'coramine glucose'.

The proceedings were brought under the Anti-Doping Rules of the IAAF. The jurisdiction on appeal arose from the IAAF Rules and Rule 74 of the Olympic Charter. After initially deciding that CAS had full power to review the matter on facts and law (notwithstanding more limited provisions in the IAAF Rules), the Panel considered the central argument put forward by E, namely, that the circumstances in which she had taken the stimulant constituted exceptional circumstances under the IAAF Rules (which were based on the Code). It was submitted that E had no reason to believe that the glucose tablets would contain any stimulant. E had explained in a written statement that she had asked her physical therapist for glucose. He had had some powdered glucose, but E had asked him to purchase new glucose because the older glucose had been used by other athletes. She had taken two tablets of glucose from the therapist and had not thought that the name 'coramine' had any significance.

Failure to Take Appropriate Precautions in the Circumstances The Panel heard from E and was satisfied that she conducted herself with 'honesty, integrity and character' and that she had not sought to gain any improper advantage or to 'cheat' in any way. The evidence demonstrated that she had been a diligent and hard-working athlete who gradually reached the pinnacle in her chosen sport. However, the Panel rejected her argument that there were exceptional circumstances in that it was reasonable for her to take the sachet of glucose and not check further. The product had been purchased in a foreign country earlier that day, and no one had examined it or the leaflet which accompanied the sachet within it. It would have been obvious from the examination of the leaflet that the product contained more than glucose. The leaflet said that it contained the stimulant and offered a warning for athletes. The Panel agreed with the finding of the Doping Review Board of the IAAF that it would have been 'clear to any person reviewing the tablets that there was more than one ingredient in the tablets' and that there was negligence in not finding out whether there was any prohibited substance in the tablets.

In considering the situation, in light of the duty of an athlete to ensure that no prohibited substance enters his or her body, the Panel found that there was negligence in failing to inquire into what the product contained. The Panel found that the circumstances did not meet the test for exceptional circumstances and, while acknowledging the harshness of the regime, agreed that the two-year period of ineligibility had to stand. There were difficulties with the particular IAAF Rule which made it virtually impossible to establish exceptional circumstances, but, on the facts, E had been careless in any event.

CAS 2004/A/690, *Hipperdinger v. ATP Tour, Inc.*

H, a tennis player, tested positive for cocaine and its metabolites. H gave evidence that he had drunk cocoa tea and eaten cocoa leaves to alleviate altitude sickness while at 3000 metres in South America. He had done this for three or four days and had continued to drink the tea and chew the leaves after departing from altitude. He testified that he did not know he was chewing cocoa leaves. Nor was he aware that sipping cocoa tea or eating cocoa leaves was a source of cocaine.

No Fault   The Panel relied on the concept of strict liability to find that the athlete was responsible for what was in his body without having regard to the reasons for its presence and the degree of any respective fault of the athlete. It then went on to consider whether the athlete could be said not to be at fault. The Panel found that the player should have and, indeed, would have suspected that he was consuming cocaine or a related substance. He had not been careful in what he did. The sanction could not be eliminated under the ATP Rule which is the equivalent of Article 10.5.1 of the Code on the ground that H was not at fault.

No Significant Fault   The Panel then considered whether the penalty could be reduced on the basis that the player had shown there was 'no significant fault or negligence on his part'. The Panel found that, if the player had only consumed tea made from cocoa leaves, it might have been prepared to accept the claim because it would not be right to insist that a player should investigate the source of a common drink such as tea. The Panel was of the opinion that the player was not significantly negligent in drinking the tea that was offered to him without enquiring about its nature or source. Drinking the tea without enquiry was a reasonable step for an athlete to take. However, the Panel was not prepared to accept the plea of no significant fault in relation to the less common act of chewing cocoa leaves. The athlete had chewed the leaves, which were of unknown origin, purpose and effect, for a number of days. It found that the player had not exercised the caution expected of him in the situation and that he had acted with significant negligence. Accordingly, the two-year ban was upheld.

Proportionality   The Panel also considered the principle of proportionality as a general principle of law stating that a reasonable relationship must exist between legally protected interests and measures taken which affect those interests. The Panel was of the view that the passing of the WADA Code had changed the situation in relation to the potential application of the doctrine of proportionality in assessing sanctions. It found that the Panel had no choice other than to apply the sanction set down under the Code when it did not find that there was either no fault or no significant fault. In any event, the Panel did not consider that the two-year fixed suspension was totally disproportionate to the behaviour of the player, and so there was no reason to bring the principle of proportionality into play. The Panel found that, as a matter of fairness, the period of ineligibility should start on the date of sample collection and not the date of the hearing. It felt justified in taking into account some of the mitigating matters which did not establish no fault or no significant fault in relation to the commencement of the penalty.[74]

Article 10.5.2: Reductions for No Significant Fault

CAS 2005/A/830, *Squizzato* v. *FINA*

S was a swimmer who tested positive for a low concentration of clostebol, an anabolic andronic steroid, at the European Open Water Swimming Cup competition. FINA Rules were based on the WADA Code. Under FINA Rules, a one-year period of ineligibility was imposed by FINA. The decision was appealed to CAS. The main issue before CAS was whether the

---

74 It is submitted that this is not the correct approach. The discretionary factors which may lead to the period of ineligibility starting earlier in time should not include matters of general mitigation or fairness but should be matters which relate directly to the date on which it is appropriate to commence the period of ineligibility.

one-year suspension was correct. The standard period of ineligibility under the 2004 Code was two years. The FINA Rules were based on the Code and provided for the elimination or reduction of the period of ineligibility based on exceptional circumstances where there was no fault or negligence or no significant fault or negligence. The FINA Doping Panel had considered that no fault or negligence was not applicable in this case, where the athlete was responsible for the presence of a prohibited substance in her bodily sample, was aware of doping in sport (although she was only seventeen years old) and had applied a cream containing the banned substance without the advice of a doctor. It had, however, ruled that the no significant fault or negligence provision was applicable. It did this on the grounds that, as an athlete, S was not very experienced in international competition and had relied on her mother's advice, the quantity of clostebol detected was very low and the application of the cream had had no enhancing effect on her performance.

Lack of Care   The CAS Panel found that the swimmer had not exercised the level of care required. She could, at least, have asked her doctor or coach, or any other competent person, to check the contents of the cream bought by her mother. Her age was not a relevant factor in establishing exceptional circumstances. The CAS Panel held, however, that no significant fault or negligence had been established on the facts.

Proportionality   The Panel then considered whether the WADA Code reduction from two years to one year was consistent with the principle of proportionality. After considering the various pre-Code CAS authorities on the application of proportionality, the Panel found that the adoption of the WADA Code does not 'force the conclusion that there is no other possibility for greater or less reduction of sanction than is allowed under the Code'. The rules of an association, whether based on a code or not, cannot replace 'fundamental and general principles like the doctrine of proportionality ... for every thinkable case'. The WADA Code had, however, closed the door somewhat to reducing fixed sanctions, and the principle of proportionality could only apply if an award were to constitute 'an attack on personal rights which was serious and totally disproportionate to the behaviour penalised'. The Panel, not without hesitation, decided that there could be no further reduction of the penalty. This award is an early example of the reluctance of a CAS Panel to find that there is no further discretion to reduce a fixed sanction on the ground of proportionality.

WADA Code 2004: Continuing (Limited) Role for the Principle of Proportionality?

CAS 2006/A/1025, *Puerta* v. *ITF*

P was an international tennis player who played in the French Open final. He tested positive for the prohibited substance, etilefrine. He had been waiting to play the final in the players' area in the company of his wife and other members of his family. The game had been delayed. He was drinking water, as were others in the group. There were glasses on the table. P's explanation for the presence of etilefrine in his sample was as follows. He had left the room and, unknown to him, his wife, who was taking the drug for a medical condition, had taken some etilefrine in water and drunk from one of the glasses on the table. P's wife, and other members of his family, then left the room. P came back into the room and took a drink of water from what he thought was his glass. P said that the result was that a small quantity of the prohibited substance was ingested. The analysis at the laboratory confirmed a very small quantity of the prohibited substance in P's sample, in an amount which would not enhance sporting performance.

The major problem for P was that, before the ITF had adopted the Code, he had committed an earlier inadvertent doping offence under the previous anti-doping rules by taking an asthma drug when he did not have a TUE for it. He faced a possible life ban for a second offence as a result.

The ITF Tribunal did not accept that the etilefrine had come from the player drinking from the wrong glass, as put forward by P. The tribunal decided that P had, in some manner, inadvertently taken a prohibited substance in the day or two before the game. Although P's wife was taking the drug and he was always careful not to inadvertently take it, the risk of accidentally taking the substance was present. The tribunal concluded that he must have mistakenly ingested the substance.

The effect of having the two doping offences was that P was potentially liable to a lifetime ban. Under the Code, if there was no fault or no significant fault in relation to the second offence, a reduced sentence would be available. The tribunal did not accept that there was no fault, but found that there was no significant fault in the second offence. The effect of this was that an eight-year period of ineligibility and not a lifetime ban was the sanction under the Code.

On appeal, CAS agreed with the ITF Tribunal on the conclusion that there were two relevant violations. The pre-Code violation could not be disregarded.

'Nearly No Fault' The CAS Panel did not agree with the ITF Tribunal's conclusion that the player had not established how he had taken the substance, and instead accepted the explanation that drinking from the wrong glass had led to his ingesting the prohibited substance. This was supported by the small amount of etilefrine detected by the testing process. The CAS Panel found that this was 'nearly' a no fault case but 'not quite'. The true question was whether there was any jurisdiction in the Panel to reduce the period of ineligibility below eight years where there were, as here, two inadvertent doping offences. The problem was that the Code did not provide for a reduction below eight years where a first violation was inadvertent as well as the second one. However, CAS held that this was a situation in which the absence of a specific provision in the Code to deal with a situation where there were two inadvertent violations meant that the period of ineligibility could be reduced by the application of the general principle of proportionality.

Accordingly, CAS allowed the appeal and reduced the period of ineligibility to two years on the basis that an eight-year ban was not proportional to the conduct, and that two years was a just and proportional outcome. The Panel emphasised that, in most situations, the WADA Code creates a proportionate result, but it found that this was a case in which there was no specific provision in the Code, and there was a need to fill the 'gap' and ensure that there was a proportionate sanction for two inadvertent doping violations. The Panel recognised that generally the doctrine of proportionality would only apply if an award constituted 'an attack on a personal right which was serious and totally disproportionate to the behaviour penalised'. The Panel also noted that there was little law on reducing lifetime bans on the basis of proportionality and that the weight of earlier awards had been to uphold such bans.[75] The Panel referred to earlier decisions in which the limited possible application of proportionality had been noted:

> [O]nly if the sanction is evidently and grossly disproportionate in comparison to the proved rule violation, and if it is considered as a violation of fundamental justice and fairness, would the Panel regard such a sanction as abusive and, thus, contrary to mandatory Swiss law.[76]

The Panel found that the sanction which the 'gap' in the Code would have led to was such a disproportionate result.

75 See Chapter 1, page 59 for an example.
76 CAS 2005/C/976, *FIFA and WADA* (see Chapter 10, pages 499–501).

Proportionality: Continued Reliance by Certain CAS Panels Pre-2009 Code

CAS 2007/A/1252, *FINA v. Oussama Mellouli and Tunisian Swimming Federation (TSF)*

M, an elite swimmer on a scholarship at the University of Southern California, took a tablet called 'Adderall' which was given to him by a fellow student. Adderall was apparently regularly taken by students to increase wakefulness while studying. M took it so that he could complete an assignment for his course. He was assured by his fellow student that there would be no ill effects from the tablet. After finishing his assignment, M attended the US Open Championships on 28 November 2006 and tested positive for amphetamine. This was two days after taking the tablet. When M received the result, he immediately explained the circumstances to the Tunisian Swimming Federation (TSF), which was responsible for its management. The TSF decided that M should be warned but not banned, on the basis that the amphetamine should be considered as a specified substance under Article 10.3 of the Code. FINA appealed this decision to CAS. After the November test, M submitted to doping control at several meets, always with negative results. TSF gave its decision in March 2007, and after that M competed in the World Championships, winning gold and silver medals in distance freestyle events. The appeal was heard on 18 July 2007.

CAS held that the amphetamine was not a specified substance, but a stimulant falling within the substances for which the period of ineligibility for a first violation was two years, unless M could show no fault or no significant fault under Article 10.5. In the circumstances where M had taken a tablet on the recommendation of a fellow student without knowing what was in it and without further inquiry, the Panel found that the requirements for the application of Article 10.5 could not be made out. However, where M had admitted taking the tablet immediately after the test result had been received, had agreed to assist with schemes for educating athletes in doping matters, had said that he was prepared to give up his World Championship medals although he had tested negative at those events (and many others) and where the imposition of a two-year ban from the time of the appeal hearing would mean that M would not be able to compete in the Olympics, the Panel considered that the period of ineligibility was disproportionate in all the circumstances. It decided to substitute a period of ineligibility of eighteen months, dating back to the time when the sample was taken. The results obtained in the period before the appeal hearing were disqualified. To an extent, the Panel appears to have recognised the change in approach which will apply when the amended Code comes into force in reaching this decision.

No Significant Fault and Nutritional Supplements

Careless Taking of Supplements – an Early Case

CAS 2003/A/484, *Kicker Vencill* v. *USADA*   A CAS Panel rejected an appeal by the US swimmer, Kicker Vencill, from the decision of an arbitration panel to impose a two-year period of ineligibility for a doping offence under the pre-Code FINA Rules. A urine sample given out-of-competition by the swimmer tested positive for the presence of norandrosterone at a concentration greater than 2 ng/ml (4 ng/ml). The USADA Review Board recommended the imposition of a four-year ban under the FINA Rules which were applicable at the time. After a hearing, an AAA Arbitration Panel found that a doping offence had been committed under FINA Rules, and a four-year period of ineligibility was imposed from the date of the collection of the sample. Before CAS, the argument advanced by V was that the positive test was the result of some capsules which he was taking by way of supplement at the time of the test, containing, unknown to him, anabolic agents.

The CAS Panel decided that the circumstances in which V had taken the capsules over a number of years did not fall within the exceptional circumstances which were intended to bring either Article 10.5.1 or 10.5.2 into play, and that there were no grounds to eliminate or reduce the sanction. There had been many warnings about the risk of contamination of supplements, yet V had taken the supplements without any medical advice, and without checking or testing the products, so that his conduct amounted 'to a total disregard of the positive duty to ensure that no prohibited substance entered his body'. His conduct involved significant negligence, and there was no basis to reduce the period of ineligibility. The result was that a two-year ban was imposed (from the time of the hearing), with credit for a period of provisional suspension.

Early Examination of No Significant Fault Requirements – Nutritional Supplements

CAS 2005/A/847, *Knauss* v. *FIS*   K was an Austrian international skier. He tested positive at an Alpine World Cup Downhill in Canada for the prohibited substance noran-drosterone. The source of the prohibited substance (as is often the case)[77] was a nutritional supplement taken by the athlete. The athlete had established that he did not know the nutritional supplement contained a prohibited substance. However, warnings had been issued to athletes to exercise utmost care in taking nutritional supplements because they could contain prohibited substances. K had personally chosen to use supplements which were not part of the supplements recommended by his association. He was an experienced athlete taking part in several major international events, including the Olympic Games. As a result of the positive test, he had filed a criminal complaint against the importer of the nutritional supplement. The FIS Panel found that the athlete had not acted without fault, but also found that there was no significant fault or negligence and reduced the period of ineligibility from two years to eighteen months under Article 10.5.2.

On appeal, K submitted that there should be a further reduction of the ban. The CAS Panel discussed the interpretation and application of the provisions of the Code. This Panel found that the doctrine of proportionality was contained within Articles 10.5.2 and 10.5.3, and that there was no further discretion in the tribunal other than that which was contained in those Articles. The Panel concluded that there was no doubt in this case that K had acted with fault and with negligence. The Panel then found that the requirements for 'no significant fault or negligence' must not be set excessively high. This followed from the language of the provisions and the doctrine of proportionality. Once the requirements were met, the Panel then had to examine the level of fault or negligence and establish an appropriate period of ineligibility between one and two years. In this way, the element of fault or negligence was doubly relevant.

Neither the packet containing the nutritional supplement nor the leaflet that came with it stated that the product contained a prohibited substance. The athlete took 'normal' precautions. He also made direct inquiries with the distributor of the product as to its compliance. The Panel found that, on all the evidence, K was not significantly at fault or negligent. This was further underlined by the fact that he had not acquired the product illegally on the 'grey' market or in some other dubious manner. He had obtained the product from a reputable supplier, and the product was distributed throughout the country. The Panel upheld the decision by the FIS Panel that there were exceptional circumstances justifying a reduced period of ineligibility.

77 There have been many positive tests resulting from contaminated supplements, and the risks are now so well known that an athlete will have to show that he or she took significant steps to be careful in order to show that a case is exceptional so as to support the application of Article 10.5.2.

Reduction for Assistance to Authorities – Article 10.5.3 The CAS Panel further considered whether the period of ineligibility should also be reduced because the athlete had provided substantial assistance to FIS in discovering or establishing an anti-doping rule violation by another person involving possession of a prohibited substance, trafficking or administration of a prohibited substance to an athlete under Article 10.5.3. The Panel found that the fact that K had reported the matter to the police, and that this had caused criminal proceedings to be issued against the supplier, resulting ultimately in the seizure of the remaining stocks of the contaminated nutritional supplements, was a matter which could be considered in reducing the sanction. It did not matter that those who might be subject to criminal prosecution might not be subject to the FIS Rules. The provisions of Article 10.5.3 were not limited, given the aim of the Article, to assistance which led to the pursuit of allegations under the Code. The fact that the information provided by the athlete resulted in criminal proceedings against the third party, rather than a doping-related procedure by a sporting federation, did not make Article 10.5.3 inapplicable. That would have been contrary to the spirit of the Code. The Panel pointed out that there was no clear guidance as to how the two possible sources for a reduction (Articles 10.5.2 and 10.5.3) might function together. The Panel found that this did not require an answer in this particular case, because it considered that the penalty of eighteen months imposed was fair and reasonable.

The Panel did not regard personal matters, such as the blameless past of an athlete over a long career, as relevant in determining the applicable sanction.

To be sure, the purpose of introducing the WADA Code was to harmonise, at the time, a plethora of doping sanctions to the greatest extent possible and to uncouple them both from an athlete's personal circumstances (amateur or professional, old or young) and from circumstances relating to the specific type of sport in which they competed (individual or team sport etc.).

The Panel maintained the period of ineligibility of eighteen months which had been established by the FIS tribunal.

Later Decisions on No Significant Fault or Negligence with Nutritional Supplements

CAS 2008/A/1489 & 1510, *WADA* v. *Serges Despres* D, a member of the Canadian Bobsleigh team, tested positive for nandrolone at 2.8 ng/ml (more than the 2 ng/ml reporting threshold). He admitted that he had committed an anti-doping rule violation but claimed that there were exceptional circumstances under Article 10.5.2 which justified reducing the standard period of ineligibility of two years.

The source of the positive test was shown to be a supplement called HMB, produced by a company called Kaizen, which D had taken to help him recover from a severe hip injury. Further testing revealed that the product had been contaminated, presumably in the manufacturing process. D took the supplement on the recommendation of the nutritionist contracted to the team. The nutritionist recommended various supplements but did not recommend particular brands.

D had been taking several other supplements which he purchased from stores. He bought the Kaizen HMB along with other supplements recommended by the nutritionist from one of the stores which he used. He examined the label of the HMB, which said that the product contained only HMB and certain other listed ingredients. He asked the sales person about the reputation of Kaizen and was told that it was a good company with strict guidelines to provide clean products. He made some short Internet inquiries. The store's website gave an assurance that all supplements met its highest standards. D gave evidence that after making these inquiries, he did not think that this supplement would be suspect for contamination.

The Canadian Centre for Ethics in Sport (CCES) referred to evidence on the Internet showing that bodybuilders were a marketing focus for HMB on the part of Kaizen, and to further evidence which should have alerted D to the high-risk nature of the product. D had not made appropriate enquiries of the nutritionist or other team personnel and had not acted with proper care given the well-known risk of contamination in nutritional supplements and the various ways in which CCES alerted athletes to the risk of using supplements and discouraged their use. On consideration of the evidence, the Sports Dispute Resolution Centre of Canada (SDRCC) arbitrator found that D just met the requirement to show no significant fault and reduced the standard period of ineligibility to twenty months.

CAS Appeal   WADA and CCES appealed to CAS, and the Panel found that D had not shown a proper degree of care in relation to the taking of the supplement. He had not made any direct approach to the manufacturer for an assurance as to the purity of the product (as the athlete in *Knauss* had done). He had not contacted the nutritionist or his team doctor to ask about the Kaizen brand or carried out any adequate research on the Internet. While an athlete did not have to take every conceivable step (such as having the product tested himself), D had not taken steps to leave no reasonable stone unturned. His conduct could not be regarded as showing no significant fault. Any general principle allowing a reduction on grounds of proportionality was inapplicable. As a result, CAS set aside the SDRCC decision and imposed the standard period of ineligibility of two years. While an earlier start date for the period of ineligibility could not be set in order to allow D to try and qualify for the Olympics, the start date could be moved back on grounds of fairness arising from the athlete's confusion over whether he should continue to compete after the initial positive test.

Contaminated Supplements Again

CAS 2009/A/1870, WADA v. *Jessica Hardy and USADA* H competed at the US Olympic trials for swimming. She qualified for the Beijing Olympics. At the trials, she underwent doping controls and tested positive for clenbuterol. She withdrew from the Olympic team. USADA determined that an anti-doping violation had been committed. A panel of arbitrators was appointed to hear her case in the first instance, in accordance with USADA procedures. The AAA Panel found that there had been a violation of Article 2.1 of the Code. It found that the athlete had established no significant fault or negligence in connection with the violation and imposed a one-year period of ineligibility. The athlete established on the balance of probabilities that the clenbuterol in her sample came from a supplement she was taking prior to the doping control. The Panel considered the steps taken by the athlete in relation to the supplement and found that there was no significant fault or negligence.

FINA appealed to CAS, as did WADA. H raised the further question of the effect of Rule 45 of the Olympic Charter (see Chapter 10). Before CAS, the Panel was asked by H to rule on the enforceability of this by-law. FINA and WADA sought the imposition of the standard period of ineligibility of two years. H sought the joinder of the IOC to the arbitration. She also sought the reduction of the one-year period of ineligibility to a period of six months so that the IOC Rule would not be applicable, because otherwise, it was submitted, the resulting penalty of one year's ineligibility would be grossly disproportionate and in violation of Swiss law.

The Panel held that there was no basis upon which the IOC could be joined without its agreement. The CAS Panel agreed that the circumstances in which H had taken the supplement did amount to a truly exceptional situation, notwithstanding the well-known risks with supplements. H had had personal conversations with the maker of the supplement before taking it and had been told by the maker that the products were tested by an independent company for purity, and the company website confirmed that the products were formulated with quality ingredients. H had obtained the supplements directly from the producer and not from some unknown source, and the supplements were not labelled in a way which would have raised suspicion. H had also obtained an indemnity from the manufacturer with respect to its products and had consulted with various swimming personnel, including team nutritionists, the team sports psychologist and her coach. She exercised care and had made good-faith efforts 'to leave no reasonable stone unturned' before taking the product. She had taken the steps which could be reasonably expected of an informed athlete.

The CAS Panel then considered what the appropriate period of ineligibility was. The Panel did note that H's positive test occurred many years after risks connected to the use of nutritional supplements had first become known to athletes. The level of diligence due from an athlete had risen over the years, and an athlete's behaviour had to be considered with care in this area. The Panel concluded that a one-year period of ineligibility was appropriate.

The Panel did not consider that it could make a declaratory judgement on the IOC Rule. No declaration could protect H because neither the IOC nor the USOC was bound by the arbitral award. Other proceedings were necessary to determine the applicability of the IOC Rules. The Panel further considered that the sanction could not be altered to reflect the effect of the IOC Rule. Accordingly, the one-year period of ineligibility remained.

No Significant Fault Cases where a Medical Prescription is Taken Relying on the Team Doctor

CAS 2006/A/1133, *WADA v. Michael Stauber and the Swiss Olympic Committee*

S was a handball player who tested positive for a prohibited substance. He was taking the medicine Co-Diovan, which had been prescribed for him by his doctor. After the positive test, he requested, and obtained, a TUE for the prescribed medicine. The prohibited substance was not a specified substance. The question was whether the player could establish no fault or negligence or no significant fault or negligence.

He was prescribed the medicine for high blood pressure. He was unaware that the medicine contained the prohibited substance. He had been treated with Diovan for some time and had always tested negative. His doctor admitted having committed an error when he changed the prescription to Co-Diovan, which did contain a prohibited substance. At the time of the control, there was no doping information site available for the athlete. S had simply placed his confidence in the doctor, who was his team doctor. The CAS Panel held that S could not discharge the burden on him of showing no fault. This required that the athlete show that he had exercised utmost caution. Given his responsibilities, he could not hide behind his doctor's failing. He was not relieved of his responsibility to check whether the medicine contained a prohibited substance. He had never tried to check the contents of his prescription.

On no significant fault, the Panel found that S had taken the medicine for medical reasons and that it had not enhanced his performance. He had relied on a sports medicine practitioner who was the official doctor of his team. The doctor had recognised that he had made a mistake in not checking the medicine and requesting a TUE. The fact that a TUE had been obtained afterwards showed that a positive test could have been avoided. The CAS Panel held that S had shown no significant fault and imposed a one-year period of ineligibility. The Panel made an observation directed at the then review of the Code and observed that the case before it represented a sign that the present system had serious questions from the point of view of proportionality in specific cases.

Prescription for Another Player – 2004 Code

CAS 2005/A/951, *Guillermo Canas* v. *ATP Tour*

C, a professional tennis player, appealed the imposition of a two-year period of ineligibility by the ITF Anti-Doping Tribunal for a positive test for a substance called HCT, which is identified as a prohibited substance under the Prohibited List. The tribunal imposed a two-year period of ineligibility under the Code. This was initially confirmed by CAS on appeal, but, after a successful appeal to the Swiss Federal Supreme Court, which held that C's rights had been disregarded by the Panel by its not hearing all his points, the question of the appropriate sanction was reconsidered by CAS.

C contended that he had ingested the drug Rofucal, which contains HCT, after he received a prescription from the tournament doctor –

intended for another player – in error. He submitted that he was entitled to trust the tournament doctor in such matters, and that the standard of care on him as a player was reduced where he received the medicine from the tournament doctor.

Fundamental Rights Argument   C also contended that the sanctions regime under the Code was contrary to the law of Delaware (which applied to the ATP anti-doping policy) in imposing disproportionate penalties, that the sanctions were void as forfeitures and against public policy and that the sanctions represented an abuse of a dominant position or were anti-competitive under the Sherman Antitrust Act. He also contended that the same arguments were available under Swiss law – the law applicable as a result of the seat of the arbitration.

The CAS Panel found that C had discharged the onus on him to establish how the prohibited substance had entered his system, and that he had mistakenly received the medication prescribed for another player. It then had to consider C's level of fault in the context of his responsibility to act with utmost caution under the Code. While C did not check the medication, and was clearly at fault to a degree, the medication was purchased from a source with no connection with prohibited substances and on the guidance of a medical professional. There was no intention to cheat. The Panel found, while emphasising that the finding was made on the totality of the circumstances in this case, and that the decision was not meant to absolve all competitors from a duty of care when being cared for by their sport's medical personnel, that C had made a reasonable (insignificantly negligent) mistake in picking up the wrong medicine.

The Panel (by a majority) rejected the argument to strike down the provisions of the doping policy based on the fundamental principles of Delaware law and EU law.[78]

The Panel considered earlier decisions of CAS Panels on reducing the period of ineligibility, such as *Knauss*, and found that the standard period of ineligibility of two years should be reduced to fifteen months. As a matter of fairness, results at a subsequent tournament, at which there was a negative result on testing, were not disqualified, but all other results from the time of the tournament at which the sample was given, and before the time when C voluntarily ceased to compete, were disqualified.

---

78 For the Swiss Federal Tribunal decision on a challenge to an earlier CAS award in the case
   on the basis that arguments under Delaware law as to the validity of the Code sanction
   provisions had not been properly considered, see Chapter 10, page 494.

Recent Decision on No Significant Fault or Negligence

CAS 2015/A/4059, WADA v. *Thomas Bellchambers and Others,*
Australian Football League, Australian Sports Anti-Doping
Authority – Proof of Use of a Prohibited Substance – No
Significant Fault under the 2009 Code

WADA appealed to CAS from a decision of the AFL Anti-Doping Tribunal. That decision had dismissed charges against thirty-four players from Essendon Football Club that they had used a prohibited substance during the 2012 AFL competition. The prohibited substance was the peptide hormone thymosin beta-4 (TB4), which is prohibited at all times both in-competition and out-of-competition and is not a specified substance. The allegation of use arose from a programme of injections given to the players by a Mr Dank, who was employed as a sports scientist by Essendon. The AFL Anti-Doping Tribunal concluded that the evidence put forward by ASADA did not prove the allegations to the required standard of comfortable satisfaction. The players further submitted before CAS that if the allegation of use was established, the players were able to rely on the defence of no significant fault under Article 10.5.

Procedural Issues   On appeal, CAS permitted WADA to adduce further expert evidence on the analysis of certain urine samples from the players in the 2012 season, but ultimately did not find that evidence probative and did not rely on it to reach its decision.

CAS approached the appeal on the established basis that the hearing was *de novo* (in accordance with the CAS Procedural rules and established practice) and involved a full reconsideration of the allegation on the evidence before CAS. It did not accept submissions that it should give deference to the decision of the AFL Anti-Doping Tribunal. It further held that Rule 56 of the CAS Procedural Rules did not prevent WADA from reformulating its arguments on the approach to the evidence and that in any event the CAS Panel was entitled to review a case *de novo* and pursue its own analysis of the evidence.

Standard of Proof   The CAS Panel held that WADA had to establish the violation to the comfortable satisfaction standard under Article 3.1, which it described as a 'term of art' developed before the Code in sports law and applied since then under the terms of the Code. It did not accept the submission made on behalf of the players that this standard was not materially different to the criminal standard of 'beyond reasonable doubt' or that

WADA had to eliminate all possibilities which could point to the innocence of the players.

Decision on Facts   The central issue on the alleged use of TB4 was whether the programme of injections had in fact involved administering TB4 to the players. The case relied on circumstantial evidence. Mr Dank and those involved in the programme did not give evidence (and could not be compelled to.)

The contemporaneous documents available on the administration of the injections and various statements against interest by the players, Mr Dank and others were to the effect that the injections did involve the administration of TB4. The players had blood tests before the injections, which was a recommended step before receiving injections for peptides like TB4, and signed consent forms referring to thymosin injections. Six players said in interviews that Mr Dank had identified the substance injected as thymosin, and two players saw the word 'thymosin' on vials. On an appeal to the Australian Administrative Appeals Tribunal (AAT), the tribunal had found that Mr Dank had used TB4 on another NRL player. Mr Dank had made statements in documents and in a media interview concerning the use of TB4. The programme devised by Mr Dank was aimed at enhancing players' recovery rates, which is a benefit associated with the use of TB4. In addition, the officials who were aware of the programme were careful to ensure that the club doctor was not informed, and the players were instructed to keep the programme secret.

On this evidence, the Panel concluded that it was comfortably satisfied that the injections contained TB4 (the prohibited substance), not one of the other forms of thymosin, and that the programme, which was designed to cover the whole squad, involved administration to all of the players.

While there was a credible chain of evidence tracing the TB4 back to its manufacture and subsequent delivery to Mr Dank, this was not a matter which had to be proven to establish the violation – the source of the prohibited substance used was not a necessary component of the violation.

The Panel did not consider that the expert evidence given in relation to a sample from one player which showed elevated levels of TB4 could support a finding of use to the required standard given that it was possible that an elevated level of TB4 could be present in a sample for natural, innocent reasons.

The Panel concluded that the evidence presented proved to the required standard that the players had used TB4. One Panel member would not have found the allegation proved in relation to all players on the evidence produced before the tribunal.

No Significant Fault   The Panel referred to the definition of 'no significant fault' and to the commentary in the Code which refers to the assessment of fault as requiring the consideration of evidence which is relevant to explaining the player's departure from the expected standard of behaviour under the Code. It found that the general approach to assessing fault under Article 10.4 of the 2009 Code could equally well be applied to the exercise of assessing fault under Article 10.5. It referred to the CAS award in CAS 2013/A/3327, *Cilic v. ITF* and the general approach to the assessment of fault outlined in that case. In *Cilic*, the Panel referred to the objective and subjective considerations relevant to the assessment of fault. This involved considering the conduct of the athlete against that of a reasonable athlete with obligations under the Code, as well as any personal considerations which would have affected the athlete's perception of risk in the conduct which produced the violation.

The Panel referred to the oft-repeated statement by CAS Panels that it is an athlete's personal responsibility to ensure that what goes into his or her body does not contain a prohibited substance and that it is not generally open, for example, for an athlete to say that he or she trusted a doctor in order to establish no significant fault. At the very least, the athlete has to specifically ask whether the medicines contain prohibited substances and obtain written confirmation from the doctor that they do not.

The players submitted that they had reasonably assumed that the club doctor had approved the programme, that the consent form confirmed that the injected substance was not prohibited, that in a team they could take additional comfort from the fact that the senior official approved the programme, that in some cases the players' youth and inexperience was relevant and that the CEO of ASADA, in recommending the issue of infraction notices, had referred to a maximum reduction of fifty per cent under the no significant fault defence as being appropriate on the information which it had at the time.

The Panel concluded that none of the matters advanced came close to providing a 'platform for the submission that ineligibility should be reduced on account of the display of due care'. The players' assumption that the club doctor knew of the programme was ill-founded and wholly inadequate because none of the players sought even to inform the club doctor. The consent form should have triggered inquiry rather than being an excuse for not making inquiry given the detailed explanation by

Mr Dank of the programme to players. Reliance on senior officials was less impressive than reliance on the assumed approval of the club doctor. All players had doping education. ASADA's position at a particular time could not be determinative of the degree of fault in fact present in committing the violations.

None of the points advanced could meet the requirements of the defence given the personal responsibility under the rules. No player had made any inquiry into the injections and, in addition, in breach of the AFL rules, none had made disclosure of the use of the substance when tested, at any point during testing. The players had in effect gone along with the programme after being told at a meeting that it was like going to the edge of a cliff 'but not going over it'.

The Panel agreed that the defence of no significant fault could not be made out and imposed two years' ineligibility on all the players. The Panel exercised its discretion to back-date the period of ineligibility for delay which, considered objectively, could not be attributed to the athletes, back to the date of the decision by the AFL Tribunal – March 2015. The Panel noted the potential application of the return to training provision in Article 10.12.2 of the Code, which was a matter for the AFL to work out with each player. There was no power to disqualify results under the applicable AFL rules.

Subsequently, the players appealed against the CAS award to the Swiss Federal Tribunal, as they were entitled to under Swiss law relating to international arbitration. The appeal was based on CAS not having had jurisdiction to hear the case *de novo* on the proper construction of the AFL rules. The Swiss Federal Tribunal dismissed the appeal, essentially because the players had accepted the *de novo* jurisdiction of CAS when they signed and accepted the procedural orders for the appeal.

CAS 2016/A/4643, *Maria Sharapova* v. *International Tennis Federation* – No Significant Fault under Article 10.5.2 2015 Code – Reasonable Delegation of Some Doping Responsibilities

S appealed the decision of the ITF Independent Tribunal to CAS.[79] She contended that in the circumstances of admitted violation of Article 2.1, she could show that she had no significant fault under Article 10.5.2. This would support a reduction of the period of ineligibility of two years to a minimum of twelve months. S further submitted that CAS should further reduce the sanction beneath the minimum sanction available on the

79 See case summary at pages 362–6.

application of Article 10.5.2 on the grounds that a sanction of eight months would be proportionate.

The ITF did not challenge the finding of the ITF Tribunal that the violation was not intentional under Article 10.2.1 on the appeal. It submitted first that CAS should not interfere with the decision of the ITF Tribunal that S could not show no significant fault as required by Article 10.5.2. It further submitted that if CAS did consider the case *de novo*, S could not show no significant fault under Article 10.5.2 to support any reduction in the period of ineligibility in the circumstances of the violation when her conduct was considered in the context of her obligation to exercise the utmost caution to avoid a positive. ITF submitted that the two-year period of ineligibility imposed by the ITF Independent Tribunal should be maintained in the circumstances of the violation.

The CAS Panel confirmed that its power on appeal under Article 57 of the CAS Code was to examine the case on a *de novo* basis. The Panel noted that CAS jurisprudence should not be considered to limit this power, although CAS would not 'would not easily "tinker" with a well-reasoned award on sanctions by, say, replacing a sanction of 17 or 19 months with one of 18' (CAS 2011/A/2518, with reference to CAS 2010/A/2283).

The Panel further held applying Article 187.1 of the Swiss Private Law International Law Act and Article 58 of the CAS Code that English law was the system of law applicable to the Tennis Anti-Doping Programme (TADP), which implemented the provisions of the Code. The Panel noted that it was contended that Swiss law should apply because the TADP implemented the World Anti-Doping Code and the Code is governed by Swiss law. This did not need to be further explored because the Panel was not directed to any difference which might arise from applying Swiss not English law.

The Panel considered the totality of the circumstances relating to the violation arising from the evidence. It emphasised the factual nature of the inquiry relevant to the consideration of the application of the defence. It noted that the period of ineligibility could only be reduced where the circumstances were truly exceptional and not in the vast majority of cases. It noted that the bar should not be set too high for the application of the defence and that the defence could not be excluded because the athlete had not taken some steps she should have taken to discharge the duty of utmost caution. Not taking some possible steps did not invariably mean that the fault was significant, because if an athlete had to take all possible steps in every circumstance, the defence would be rendered meaningless.

The parties agreed that the approach in an earlier award in CAS 2014/A/ 3591, *Al Nahyan* v. *FEI* was applicable. This decision concerned the application of FEI rules for equine sport (based on the Code), under which the rider was the person responsible for a prohibited substance in a sample from his or her horse. CAS held that the mistakes of third parties which caused a horse to return a positive test were attributed to the rider for the purpose of liability, but not for the purpose of assessing the degree of personal fault of the rider. Where the rider had established a system to care for his or her horses and to comply with his or her duties under the anti-doping rules which was reasonable and involved the appointment of properly qualified veterinary personnel, his or her fault should be assessed by his or her personal fault in the particular circumstances of the case.

The CAS Panel held that S was entitled to delegate the monitoring of the substances which she was taking and their status under the Prohibited List to her manager. The failures of the manager did not become part of her personal fault – S's fault had to be assessed by reference to her personal fault in the selection and oversight of the third party and her own negligence in not checking on the ingestion of a controlled substance. A person who chose to delegate his or her anti-doping responsibilities to another would be at fault in choosing an unqualified person to carry out the duties, in failing to instruct the delegate properly, in failing to provide clear procedures or in failing to supervise or control the delegate.

Applying this approach, the Panel decided that S's fault was not significant. S was entitled to rely on her manager and his organisation (one of the largest athlete management companies) in respect of aspects of her anti-doping responsibilities. That system had operated and provided satisfactory compliance with anti-doping rules for a long time. Although the Code emphasised the personal duty of the athlete to avoid violations, S, as an athlete involved in demanding sporting activities throughout the world, was not prevented from delegating regulatory compliance to her manager. S chose an experienced manager, who made a mistake in checking the List on an annual check. S had failed in her responsibilities in not giving the manager instructions as to how to check the List properly, in not putting him in touch with the doctor who had prescribed the substance and in not instructing him to consult with WADA, ITF or WTA or to call the IFT hotline in relation to substances newly included in the List. S was at fault in passing everything to her manager and in not establishing any proper procedure to supervise or control the manager.

The Panel further found that S had a reduced perception of risk in using Mildronate and that this was justified because she had used the product for ten years with no issue, the product had been used for medical reasons on prescription from her doctor for many years and no specific warning had been given as to the change in status of Meldonium in 2016.

Although an athlete or his or her delegate could have found reference to Meldonium and its inclusion in the Prohibited List by following links on the ITF website, the notices to athletes referred only to significant procedural changes, not to adding new prohibited substances.

In the totality of the circumstances, the Panel concluded that the defence of no significant fault had been established. The Panel then assessed the fault for the purposes of arriving at the period of ineligibility. It referred to the award in *Cilic* (and CAS 2016/A/4371, *Lea* v. *USADA*) as being relevant to an assessment of the degree of fault. It found that the failures lay in S's not properly monitoring and supervising her manager and discussing with him what was required in checking the List. The Panel determined that the fault was higher than the minimum degree of fault and imposed a period of ineligibility of fifteen months. It found that the Code was proportional in its approach to sanctions and that there was no basis to rely on the principles of proportionality to reduce the period of ineligibility further.

The Panel emphasised that the case was not about an athlete who cheated but about the fault of an athlete in failing to make sure that the status of a substance which she had been taking for a long time had not changed.

Assessing Degrees of Fault

CAS 2013/A/3327, *Cilic* v. *ITF* – General Comment on the Approach to Assessing Fault

C was a highly ranked international tennis player on the ITF circuit. He broke into the top 20 of the ATP singles ranking in 2009. He was familiar with anti-doping measures and had been tested on many occasions. From about 2011, he had been working with a particular nutrition adviser, H. H recommended C take electrolytes, protein and glucose. C obtained the first two products from the Croatian Olympic Committee (COC), which usually supplied his supplements. The COC did not stock the glucose, so H recommended that he purchase it from a reputable chain store. C bought a product called Traubenzucker, which included a vitamin called nicotinamide in its listed contents. A little later, he began taking creatine on H's advice, mixing the glucose powder with the creatine to reduce the bitter taste.

In late 2012 and early 2013, C was under pressure in his professional circumstances due to tense relationships with his coach and entourage. In April 2013, he went to play in the Rolex Masters at Monte Carlo. At some time during his preparations between 15 and 18 April, he realised that he was running low on glucose and asked his mother to go to a pharmacy and purchase some for him. She purchased a packet of Coramine glucose tablets. The label listed the ingredients, including nicethamide. C did not focus on the label until about 22 April, when he had been knocked out of the tournament. At this time, there was increasing tension between the athlete and his coach, which was upsetting his father. The athlete gave evidence that his mother had told him that the pharmacist had said that the glucose tablets were safe for a professional tennis player like C to take. When C looked at the label, he thought that 'nicethamide' on the glucose tablets was French for 'nicotinamide' which was the ingredient of his usual glucose powder. As a result, he looked no further at the box or label and made no further checks. C took a photo of the box of Coramine glucose and sent it to H to check that it was okay to take. C took two of the tablets each morning for three days before going back to his usual glucose powder, which H had brought to his next tournament. At this tournament, C was tested after his first match. The test returned a positive test for a metabolite of nicethamide, which is a specified substance banned in-competition only.

The violation of Article 2.1 of the 2009 Code was admitted before the ITF tribunal. On sanctions, the relevant provision was Article 10.4 of the 2009 Code, which allowed for the period of ineligibility to be assessed according to the fault of an athlete if the athlete could establish that he or she did not intend to enhance his or her sport performance by taking the tablets. The tribunal held that the tablets had not been taken to enhance sporting performance. In assessing fault, the tribunal found that C's fault was quite high. He had had considerable anti-doping education and had easy access to professional advice. He took no steps to check on the ingredients of the tablets by reading the packet or the leaflet inside, which would have informed him that the tablets contained the prohibited substance. He made highly careless linguistic mistakes in assuming that the substance on the label was the same as in his normal glucose. He did not use Google or Wikipedia to do any checks. He was under stress, but this was not a factor of great weight because his stress did not prevent him from discussing his situation with others, sending the package to H or engaging in text conversations about the product. This doping offence was not at the most serious end of the scale, but nor was it a 'venial offence'.

Weighing the various factors, the ITF Tribunal imposed a period of ineligibility of nine months. C's results, ranking points and prizes from the time of the positive test until the beginning of his provisional suspension (he had served three months) were forfeited.

C appealed to CAS. He sought an annulment of the ITF decision and orders that the sanction be limited to a warning and reprimand and that only his results in the tournament at which the positive test was returned be disqualified. The ITF asked CAS to impose a period of ineligibility which was commensurate with C's fault and to confirm the loss of results. The ITF submitted that a longer period of ineligibility should have been imposed in light of the degree of fault. It characterised the mistake of the athlete as highly careless. In closing (after not suggesting range in opening), the range suggested was between twelve and twenty-three months.

CAS considered the appropriate sanction on a *de novo* basis and heard evidence from C, H, a consultant psychiatrist and the ITF anti-doping manager. C gave evidence as to his mistake regarding the contents and how he had been sure in his head that the tablets had contained nicotinamide. He said he had only seen the leaflet in the box in June, after he received the results of the test and double-checked the tablets. It had not occurred to him that the tablets were a supplement. He accepted that he knew that prohibited substances could be found in supplements and medications. The scientific evidence was that the nicethamide would not have given any noticeable stimulating effect and that its effect would have lasted one or two hours.

For the athlete, it was submitted that the breach was of a technical nature. The relevant circumstances leading up to the violation supported this: glucose was an everyday natural sugar product which was commonly used on the tour by players, not a suspiciously named supplement; C had been taking tablets for about two years without incident; the names of the legal vitamin in C's usual glucose – nicotinamide – and the prohibited substance – nicethamide – were extraordinarily close; the substance was taken out-of-competition five days before C played; and the tablets tasted the same as C's normal glucose tablets. The tablets had come from a reputable pharmacy, C's mother had checked with the pharmacist, C had checked the packaging and made an understandable mistake, C had sent a picture to H, his trainer, who raised no concerns and C had not noticed the leaflet in the package which said that the product contained an active product which could produce a positive test until after the test result had been given. C was also in the midst of a very stressful period of his career regarding his relationship with his coach.

The ITF characterised the level of fault as high. It submitted that the key questions were the extent to which C had departed from his duty to use utmost caution to avoid taking prohibited substances and the reasons for that departure. C had only read the list of ingredients on the package (and made a mistake in his understanding of the ingredient listed) and taken no other steps to check on the product, such as reading the side panels or the leaflet inside, contacting the ITF or his national Olympic committee or searching the Internet. Although this was not a suspiciously marketed product, it was not just glucose but a medication taken to help C absorb creatine – C's duty of care had to reflect this. C could not claim lack of experience or education – he had only vague reassurances from his mother, and the advice from H was not anti-doping advice. It was unreasonable for C to assume that the tablets were the same as his normal tablets where they looked different and the box said the tablets were a 'medicament'.

The CAS Panel set out some principles relating to the exercise of determining the length of the period of ineligibility under Article 10.4 by reference to the athlete's degree of fault. The Panel noted three general degrees of fault: significant or considerable fault, normal fault and light fault. Given the range under Article 10.4 of the 2009 Code, the Panel arrived at a range of sanctions of between sixteen and twenty-four months for significant fault (with a 'standard' significant fault case leading to twenty months' ineligibility), between eight and sixteen months for normal fault (with 'standard' normal fault leading to twelve months) and between zero and eight months for light fault (with 'standard' light fault leading to four months).

In considering how to place a case in a category, the Panel submitted that it was useful to consider fault from both an objective and a subjective perspective. An objective consideration involved examining what degree of care could have been expected of a reasonable athlete in the circumstances of the violation. A subjective consideration involved examining what could have been expected of the particular athlete in the light of his or her personal capacities. The objective element was foremost in deciding on the category, with the subjective element being used 'to move a particular athlete up or down within that category.' Exceptionally particular personal characteristics might change the allocated category of fault.

Objectively, it is always possible to say that almost all doping offences could be prevented by taking a range of steps – reading the label, cross-checking all ingredients on the label, doing an Internet search, ensuring that the product is reliably sourced and consulting relevant experts before consuming the product. But an athlete cannot be expected to do all this in every case. The particular circumstances are all-important. In some circumstances, where the substance involved is prohibited at all both times in- and out-of-competition, the full range of precautionary steps should be taken. Where substances are prohibited in-competition only, the difference between taking the substance in-competition and taking it out-of-competition is important. Where a substance is taken in-competition, it is appropriate for the full standard of care to be required, but where the substance is taken out-of-competition, the doping violation is not the taking of the substance but taking part in competition with the substance or its metabolites still present in the athlete's body. The athlete cannot be under the same duty in such circumstances, and the level of fault must be lower because the fault lies primarily in deciding to compete when the substance or its metabolites are still in the athlete's system. Generally, for this kind of breach, the level of fault will not be significant and the range of sanctions should be between zero and sixteen months. The exceptions are where the product which is banned in-competition only is advertised as 'performance-enhancing' or where the product is a medicine for therapeutic use. In both situations, there is a particular risk associated with obtaining and using such products, and the athlete will be under a higher duty of care and the degree of fault may be considerable or significant. The subjective factors which may be relevant are youth, experience, particular environmental or language problems on the part of the athlete, the extent of anti-doping education of the athlete, reduced awareness because of stress and a careless mistake.

In this particular case, C had taken the substance out-of-competition and did not commit a violation at the time. The Panel considered that the product was not sold as performance-enhancing. Nor was it a medicine on the expert evidence. C had bought an ordinary glucose product. The fault could not fall within the significant fault range, so the period of ineligibility was between zero and sixteen months. On the objective approach, the Panel noted that C did take some precautions, even if he could have done more, and the subjective factors of stress, having taken glucose for a long time without problems and making an initial careless error in assuming that the listed ingredient was the same as the one in his normal glucose tablets reduced C's capacity to take further steps to prevent the violation. Weighing the various factors, the Panel found that this was a standard case of light fault, justifying a four-month period of ineligibility. The key difference between the ITF Tribunal's decision and the decision by CAS was that CAS accepted that the fault was not 'quite high', as the ITF Tribunal had found. This was mainly due to CAS accepting that the initial careless mistake in thinking that the tablet had the same substance in it as his normal table meant that it was not reasonable to impose on the athlete the duty to take the usual precautions in relation to the substance.

The Panel considered that overall C had prevailed, and held that the ITF should make a contribution to C's expenses and legal fees in the circumstances of the case, particularly where the ITF had not assisted CAS by putting forward a specific sanction or a narrower range of sanctions.

CAS 2016/A/4371, *Robert Lea* v. *USADA* – Specified Substance
– Fault under the 2016 Code – Applying *Cilic*

L tested positive in-competition for a metabolite of oxycodone. Oxycodone is s specified substance prohibited in-competition only. L had been prescribed a medication called Percocet, which contains oxycodone. This was primarily for pain relief after crashes. The positive test resulted from L taking a Percocet tablet the night before a competition. He took the tablet because he had run out of his other medication for sleep difficulties. In the past, he had taken Percocet about ten times as a sleep aid and once for pain relief. In the period when he took Percocet, he tested negative eight times in-competition and four times out-of-competition.

The AAA Panel decided that L had acted with significant fault. He had taken a known pain-relieving medicine and had failed to check the ingredients of the pill against the Prohibited List. The Panel considered that, applying *Cilic*, the period of ineligibility was between sixteen and twenty-four months, and after weighing the various factors, it placed the athlete at the lower end of the range and imposed a period of ineligibility of sixteen months.

L appealed the sanction to CAS and requested that the AAA decision be annulled and any period of ineligibility limited to a maximum of three months. USADA did not appeal the findings of the AAA that L took the substance out-of-competition, that L did not commit an intentional violation, that L took the tablet to sleep well not to gain any sporting advantage and that L had established no significant fault, so that the defence under Article 10.5.1.1 applied. CAS heard evidence on a *de novo* hearing. L took Percocet to help with sleep. He knew that it contained oxycodone but did not check how long the metabolites would remain in his system. The doctor who had prescribed the Percocet had given him no warning on this.

The Panel referred to the classes of case in *Cilic*. This was a case of use of a substance out-of-competition which produced a positive test for metabolites in-competition. The absence of an appeal by USADA on the question whether the use was in fact in-competition meant that the out-of-competition use had to be accepted. Similarly, the finding that L met the requirement that he show no significant fault before he could rely on the defence in Article 10.5.1.1 could not be reconsidered because USADA did not contest the point.

While the CAS Panel considered the heightened standard of care which will usually apply under *Cilic* where medicines are obtained and ingested, it held that this did not apply in the particular case where the pills had been prescribed by a long-time trusted sports doctor without any warning of a possible in-competition positive test where the pills were taken out-of-competition. The Panel emphasised that the case had to be considered on its particular facts. The degree of fault to be considered was not the fault in not checking on the ingredients of the medicine but the fault of not taking reasonable steps to check how long the oxycodone would stay in the athlete's system. There was no evidence that this information was available. The Panel found that this was moderate fault. The Panel then found that the subjective factors relating to the athlete's fault – the pills were prescribed without any warning as to the risk of metabolites remaining in the athlete's system and giving rise to a positive test by a long-trusted physician, USADA had not followed up to warn L of the risk when he had disclosed use on a doping control earlier, L had taken the product for a long time without incident – justified moving the athlete's fault to the lower category of light degree of fault and imposing a six-month period of ineligibility. The Panel based its approach on *Cilic*, but ultimately focussed on the individualised exercise of arriving at the appropriate sanction.

Sanctions for Violations apart from Violations of Articles 2.1, 2.2 and 2.6

As already outlined, the defences under Articles 10.4 and 10.5 are not generally available for violations under Articles 2.3–2.5 and 2.6–2.10. The comment to Article 10.5.2 states that the defence does not apply to violations in which intent is an element or where a range of ineligibility is already provided for in the relevant Article based on the athlete or other person's degree of fault. With the exception of one form of the violation of Article 2.3, all the violations under Articles 2.3–2.5 and 2.7–2.10 (and the violation under Article 10.12.3) fall within this statement. The defences in Article 10.5.1 are specifically limited to violations under Articles 2.1, 2.2

and 2.6 by the introductory words of the Article. The period of ineligibility for other violations is arrived at by reference to the fault of the athlete and/or the seriousness of the violation committed by the athlete or other person subject to the Code.

Articles 2.3 and 2.5

There are some specific provisions in relation to sanctions for violations of Articles 2.3 and 2.5 which, if applicable, reduce the standard period of ineligibility for these violations, which has increased to four years in line with the period of ineligibility for doping violations under Articles 2.1, 2.2 and 2.6. Where the violation under Article 2.3 consists of failing to submit to sample collection, if the athlete can establish that the commission of the violation was not intentional (as defined in Article 10.2.3), the period of ineligibility will be two years.[80] Where the violation under Article 2.3 has been committed by refusal or evasion, the period of ineligibility will be four years, unless the prompt admission provision under Article 10.6.3 applies. Under this Article, the period of ineligibility for a violation of Articles 2.3 and 2.5 may be reduced with the approval of WADA and the anti-doping organisation with results management responsibility, down to a minimum of two years. The amount of the reduction will be assessed depending on the seriousness of the violation and the athlete or other person's degree of fault. As with any such assessment of fault under the Code, the degree of fault will be assessed by applying the definition of 'fault' to the circumstances of the case. The interaction of this exercise with the assessment of the seriousness of the violation is not amplified. It is submitted that the tribunal will have to examine all the circumstances of the case and the athlete's explanation for his or her conduct in order to arrive at the period of ineligibility. In considering the question of the seriousness of the violation in the particular circumstances of the case, the tribunal will have to keep in mind that both evasion and tampering

---

80 The express limitation of this provision to the form of the violation under Article 2.3 which can be committed negligently shows that the other forms of violation under the Article are considered to involve intentional conduct falling outside the operation of the no significant fault defences. The prompt admission provision applicable to Articles 2.3 and 2.5 contains an assessment of fault which also takes the violations outside the scope of the operation of Article 10.5.2, as set out in the comment to that Article. The circumstances involved in the earlier decisions *SDT 12/04 NZRL* v. *Tawera* and *CAS 2007/A/1416, WADA* v. *USADA and Scherf*, which were summarised in earlier editions of the text, would not attract the possible application of the no significant fault defence under the 2015 Code.

are serious violations which involve conduct that undermines the testing system which is a central element of the Code.

Article 2.4

The period of ineligibility for a whereabouts failure is two years, with a possible reduction down to a minimum of one year depending on the degree of fault. Article 10.3.2 further qualifies this possible reduction by providing that it will not be available to athletes where there is a pattern of last-minute changes of whereabouts information or other conduct which raises a serious suspicion that the athlete was trying to avoid being available for testing. This additional requirement will be for the anti-doping organisation to establish to the comfortable satisfaction of the tribunal if it wishes to remove the possible reduction based on the athlete's degree of fault. The anti-doping organisation may investigate whereabouts failures involving a persistent pattern of last-minute changes and any explanation by the athlete for them with a view to establishing the violations of refusal or tampering.

Where the possible reduction down from the standard two-year period of ineligibility is considered, the tribunal will have to consider the circumstances of the three breaches of the whereabouts requirements and any explanation of the athlete for them in order to assess the fault of the athlete by reference to the definition of 'fault' under the Code. In assessing fault, the importance of the whereabouts regime in the context of anti-doping programmes and the responsibilities of the athlete (which have to be notified to the athlete on joining a registered testing pool and are likely to be repeated often to him or her by anti-doping organisations) will need to be borne in mind. Cases under the 2009 Code provide examples for tribunals operating under the 2015 Code, although the provision that three inexcusable breaches means that there can be no reduction in the period of ineligibility which was present in the 2009 Code has been removed. As with other assessments of fault, a tribunal has to consider the facts of the case and apply the definition of 'fault' to the whereabouts breaches in light of the expected standard of behaviour of the athlete in order to arrive at an appropriate period of ineligibility within the range.

The 2015 Code makes it clear that it is not possible to apply the defence of no significant fault in addition to making the assessment of fault in arriving at the sanction.[81]

---

81 For a CAS award making the same point under the 2009 Code, see CAS 2013/A/3241, *WADA v. CONI*.

Sanctions for Breach of Articles 2.7 and 2.8

For the violations of administering a prohibited substance or method and trafficking in prohibited substances or methods, the period of ineligibility is between four years and life, depending on the seriousness of the violation. This requires the tribunal to assess the circumstances of the particular violation and seek to impose a sanction for it within the range which reflects its seriousness according to the range of circumstances covered by the Article. Whether the sanctioning process can consider the effect of the sanction on the person in breach in his or her particular personal circumstances is not clear, but it is submitted that, in contrast to breaches of Articles 2.1, 2.2 and 2.6, a tribunal is able to consider such matters in arriving at the appropriate sanction. Such an approach makes it more likely that a tribunal will arrive at a proportionate sanction within the wide range available. However, the seriousness of the violation should, as stipulated by Article 10.3.2, be the main consideration. Where either administration or trafficking involves conduct involving a minor (a person who had not reached the age of eighteen), the violation must be considered as particularly serious, and where committed by an athlete support person (as it is defined in the Code – most likely a coach or trainer), it will attract a lifetime period of ineligibility (unless it involves specified substances). The provision is mandatory, and a lifetime period of ineligibility is automatically applicable where it applies.

There are no guidelines for sanctions for these violations under the Code, and a tribunal imposing a sanction will have to consider all the circumstances in assessing the seriousness of the breach of the rules. Relevant factors will be the position of the person who has acted in breach of the rules, the extent to which the administering and/or trafficking has made use of a position of trust and responsibility, the scope and duration of the conduct in breach of the rules, whether the operations involved a doping system or programme and/or were of a commercial nature and whether they were a 'one-off' occurrence. A lifetime period of ineligibility (if not mandatory) should be reserved for the most serious breaches by persons who are involved in and lead large-scale systematic doping schemes.[82] As previously noted, tribunals are only specifically directed by the provisions

---

82 For an example of sanctions in this area in the context of a doping scheme, see *USADA* v. *Bruyneel and Others* in Chapter 5, pages 257–8. The same doping programme led to the imposition of a lifetime period of ineligibility on Lance Armstrong. Evidence from former team members was central to the case against Mr Armstrong, and they received reduced bans for providing it.

of Article 10.3.3 to consider the seriousness of the violation in assessing the period of ineligibility. There is no further provision to take into account more general factors such as the effect on the particular athlete of the period of ineligibility. While the focus should be on the nature of the violation and the conduct of the person in breach in relation to the breach (factors which make up the seriousness of the violation), it is submitted that tribunals are able to consider a wider range of factors in arriving at the period of ineligibility, which is likely to have very significant effects on an athlete or other person, often in terms of their full-time occupation. This will allow the tribunal to arrive at an appropriate sanction which best reflects the principle of proportionality. This principle requires that a period of ineligibility which cuts down the rights of a person to work for an extended period should be necessary to meet the purpose of the Code and should be a proportional response to the need to fulfill that purpose. There is no general provision to discount the period of ineligibility for an admission of responsibility if the specific provisions for timely and prompt admissions are not applicable.

In addition to imposing a period of ineligibility, violations by athlete support personnel which also violate the general law have to be reported to the relevant administrative professional or judicial authorities. The comment to this provision confirms that bringing violations involving coaches and others who support athletes to the attention of competent authorities is important if doping is to be deterred.

Illustrations

DFSNZ v. Milne, NZ Sports Tribunal ST 11/14 – Sanction for Attempted Trafficking

M admitted attempted trafficking and possession. He suggested the use of steroids to a young weightlifter he was coaching and offered to obtain them for him. He showed the weightlifter bottles of the drugs and indicated how the substances would be injected. The young weightlifter reported the offer and provided a statement to the anti-doping organisation. He was not a minor, but was nineteen at the time of the offer.

The tribunal was referred to various other tribunal decisions and CAS awards.[83] It considered that the decisions showed that the imposition of

---

83 *UKAD* v. *Tinklin* SR/18201, *UKAD* v. *Colclough* SR/120105, *USADA* v. *Stewart* 77109 170
    10 JENF, *RFU* v. *Peters* 27 May 2012 and *CCES* v. *Gariepy* SDRCC DT 11–0162 19 January
    2012 provide a range of cases involving the imposition of sanctions for violations. The

sanctions was a fact-specific exercise. The aggravating factor was that this could not be described as a 'one-off' incident. It was a deliberate attempt to supply prohibited substances to a young athlete by a coach. The conduct of M at this time indicated that he had the wrong attitude to the use of prohibited substances. The mitigating factors included his remorse and his acceptance of the violations, which meant that the young weightlifter did not have to give evidence (his name was suppressed in the published decision). After considering these factors, the tribunal imposed a six-year period of ineligibility.

UKAD v. *Tinklin* SR/180201 – Sanction for Attempted
Trafficking and Other Related Charges

T's daughter was an amateur boxer with the Welsh Boxing Association. T was not a registered coach (and his application was not likely to have been accepted because of a previous criminal conviction). T took his daughter and other amateur boxers to competitions and assisted them at the competitions.

When police raided T and his daughter's family home, they found prohibited substances (steroids) in significant quantities. Documentary evidence showed that T had ordered steroids overseas and was arranging distribution to others in South Wales. He involved his daughter in this business. He gave her packages of steroids to take to the Post Office for distribution.

T and his daughter were charged with possession, complicity and trafficking. The tribunal held that the evidence showed that both were in possession of steroids and that both were involved in trafficking.

In carrying out the distribution of the steroids, T had given possession of the substances to his daughter when she was a minor and, as a result, a lifetime period of ineligibility had to be imposed on T. His daughter was young and had been under his influence – a four-year period of ineligibility was imposed.

Article 2.9 – Sanction

For the violation of complicity under Article 2.9, which has been split off and separated under the 2015 Code, the period of ineligibility will be

---

increase in investigative work by anti-doping organisations into the increasing trade in prohibited substances over the Internet is likely to produce more such cases.

between two and four years, again depending on the seriousness of the violation. In this context, the seriousness of the violation will, it is submitted, involve considering both the nature of the conduct which amounts to the violation (the extent of actions given in support of the breach by another person) and the seriousness of the violation committed by another person to which the complicity relates.

Article 2.10 – Sanction

For a breach of the prohibition association violation, the period of ineligibility is two years, with possible reduction down to one year depending on the fault of the athlete or other person and the other circumstances of the case. The process of arriving at a period of ineligibility between twelve months and two years involves applying the definition of 'fault' to the circumstances in which the athlete or other person has associated with the athlete support person whose prohibited status has been notified to the athlete or other person. There have, as yet, been few, if any, Article 2.10 violations before tribunals. It would seem likely that an important consideration in many cases in assessing the fault of an athlete or other person will be the nature of the relationship between him or her and the athlete support person who is the subject of the notice and the extent to which he or she was under the influence of the athlete support person. In assessing the fault and seriousness of the case, the tribunal will have to keep in mind the expected standard of behaviour under the Code, which is that an athlete or other person will not associate or continue to associate with an athlete support person having been given express notice of his or her status as required by the Article.

Article 10.12.3 – Sanction

Where an athlete or other person breaches the prohibition against participation during his or her period of ineligibility,[84] the length of the new period of ineligibility will be the same as the original period of ineligibility and will start at the end of the original period of ineligibility. The length of this new period of ineligibility may be adjusted based on the fault of the athlete or other person and other circumstances of the case. Again, this possible adjustment of the period of ineligibility (which replaces the possible adjustment for no significant fault in the 2009 Code) means that a

---

84 For the terms of the prohibition, see pages 454–5.

tribunal will have to examine the circumstances of the breach and the fault of the athlete as provided for in the definition of 'fault'. Where an athlete or other person has the terms of the period of ineligibility communicated to him or her in clear terms (as will normally be the case where a tribunal decides that an athlete or person has committed a violation and imposes a period of ineligibility), the expected standard of behaviour under the Code is obviously that the athlete or person will obey the terms of the prohibition against participation. If a decision or other communication from an anti-doping organisation does not explain the effect of the period of ineligibility clearly or provides misleading information about it, the person in breach may be able to establish a lower degree of fault. In general terms, where an athlete or other person is considering participating in a sporting activity which may breach the prohibition on participation, he or she should make proper inquiry of the relevant anti-doping organisation before participating. If this step is not taken, the athlete or person is likely to have a high degree of fault. Matters such as the nature of the breach and its duration are also likely to be circumstances which will be important in determining the sanction.

Article 10.6: Eliminating, Reducing or Suspending the Period of Ineligibility for Reasons other than Fault

Article 10.6 provides for periods of ineligibility to be reduced for reasons other than fault: providing substantial assistance and making prompt admissions. An important feature of these provisions is that they involve the discretion to reduce, or in certain circumstances eliminate, the period of ineligibility, which is for WADA, the anti-doping organisation carrying out results management and the applicable international federation to exercise. While decisions to suspend a period of ineligibility have to be notified to other anti-doping organisations with rights to appeal, the discretion to apply the provisions is in the first instance for the specified organisations to exercise on the wording of the Articles and is not, it is submitted, a matter to be adjudicated by tribunals hearing alleged anti-doping rule violations.[85] Those tribunals might, in appropriate circumstances, make recommendations as to the exercise of discretion

---

85 The specified obligation to notify other organisations with rights of appeal of a decision to exercise the discretion so that they can appeal in fact supports the interpretation of the Article (which is clear in its terms) that a tribunal determining a sanction is not intended to make decisions on whether the discretion is to be exercised.

where the relevant organisations have not considered the application of the Articles at the time of hearing, but they cannot, it is submitted, make decisions on the exercise of the discretion themselves.

Article 10.6.1 provides for the reduction of periods of ineligibility where an athlete or other person provides substantial assistance to an anti-doping organisation. This provision is directed at the provision of an incentive in the form of a reduced or suspended period of ineligibility for those who have committed anti-doping rule violations to provide information and evidence which leads to anti-doping organisations, criminal authorities or professional disciplinary bodies bringing forward anti-doping rule violation proceedings, criminal charges or professional disciplinary charges. A person providing substantial assistance is required by the terms of the definition of 'substantial assistance' to provide a signed statement setting out all the information he or she has in relation to anti-doping rule violations and to cooperate fully with any investigation and adjudication of any case arising as a result of the provision of the information, including appearing at a hearing if requested to do so. The information provided has to be credible and form an important part of any case which arises from it. If no case is initiated as a result of the provision of the information, the information has to have provided a basis for a case to be brought.[86] The information supplied does not have to lead to the successful bringing of anti-doping rule violation proceedings. Generally, the provisions place a significant obligation on a person who seeks a reduction for substantial assistance to provide full and probative information to the anti-doping organisation involved.

If substantial assistance is provided to an anti-doping organisation, the organisation may suspend up to three-quarters of the period of ineligibility before any final appeal decision is made under Article 13. After a final appeal decision has been given, or the time for an appeal has passed, any suspension of the period of ineligibility can only take place with the approval of WADA and the relevant international federation. The extent to which the period of ineligibility is suspended depends on the seriousness of the anti-doping rule violation and the significance of the assistance given. These will be matters for the particular anti-doping organisation or WADA and the relevant international federation to assess.[87] No more than

---

86 See the definition of 'substantial assistance' in the Code.
87 As already noted, it is submitted that the exercise of this discretion is not something to be referred to a tribunal which is given jurisdiction for results management, given the terms of Article 10.6.1.1. This provides for the discretion to be exercised by the organisations

three-quarters of the period of ineligibility otherwise applicable can be suspended. If the period of ineligibility would otherwise be life, the minimum period of ineligibility has to be eight years. If the athlete or other person fails to continue to cooperate and to provide the substantial assistance which was the reason for the suspension, the original period of ineligibility will be reinstated. The decision to reinstate a period of ineligibility (or not to do so) is capable of appeal under Article 13.

Specific Further Power of WADA

In addition to the power to suspend the period of ineligibility given to anti-doping organisations with the approval of WADA, WADA also has a separate power to agree to an appropriate period of suspension of the otherwise applicable period of suspension. This power is given to WADA with the purpose of further encouraging athletes and other persons to provide substantial assistance to anti-doping organisations. The discretion available to WADA goes further than that given to anti-doping organisations under Article 10.6.1. WADA can agree to periods of suspension of more than three-quarters of the period of ineligibility, and even to no period of ineligibility. Again, a period of ineligibility which WADA has agreed to suspend may be reinstated if the athlete or other person does not provide the substantial assistance upon which the decision is based.

Where an anti-doping organisation decides to suspend any part of a period of ineligibility under Article 10.6.1.1, it has to give notice providing justification for the decision to other anti-doping organisations with a right of appeal under Article 13.2.3. These anti-doping organisations will be the organisation of the person's country of residence and the organisations of countries where the person is a national or a license holder. The notice has to be in terms of Article 14.2.1 and must include reasons for the decision, including a justification for the decision not to impose the maximum potential sanction. Other parties identified in Article 13.2.3 will be entitled to appeal to CAS from such a decision. There is, it is submitted no right of appeal from a decision not to exercise the discretion under Article 10.6.1.1 or 10.6.1.2 available to an athlete. Where WADA decides to agree to a suspension of the period of ineligibility in the exercise of its powers

with the role of investigating violations, which are best placed to assess the value of assistance. For consideration of the related discretion under Article 10.6.2, which takes this approach (which would, it is submitted, apply to the discretion under Article 10.6.1), see *UKAD* v. *RFU and Dan Lancaster RFU Anti-Doping Appeal Panel* 9 February 2016.

under Article 10.6.1.2, there is no right of appeal by any other anti-doping organisation.

There have been several recent examples of anti-doping rule violations arising from the provision of evidence by 'whistleblowers'. The recent inquiries involving international athletics relating to alleged systemic doping in Russia and the findings that the international federation has been involved in the corrupt suppression of results management processes have arisen as a result of evidence provided by an athlete that potential doping violations were not proceeded with after payments had been made to the IAAF and the Russian anti-doping organisation. The WADA Foundation Board has recently agreed to strengthen the WADA whistleblower programme.

Admissions

In the Absence of Evidence

Under Article 10.6.2, where an athlete or other person voluntarily admits the commission of an anti-doping violation before having received notice of sample collection or before receiving notice of an anti-doping violation, the period of ineligibility for the violation may be reduced by up to half. The terms of the provision indicate that it is intended to apply where there is an immediate admission by an athlete or other person before the process of obtaining evidence has advanced (whether the collection of a sample or the collection of evidence to support another violation) and where that admission provides evidence against his or her interests which amounts to the only evidence against him or her. The requirement that the admission be the 'only reliable evidence' against the athlete or person necessitates that the anti-doping organisation has no evidence which it might have relied on to support an allegation when the athlete or person comes forward. The comment to the Article refers to the provision not being intended to apply to circumstances where the athlete or other person makes an admission when he or she 'is about to be caught'.

In most investigations, an anti-doping organisation is likely to have some evidence. Where the purpose of the Article is to encourage the making of admissions, it can, it is submitted, be applied where the anti-doping organisation has some evidence but that evidence would not have been sufficient to be capable of being relied on to support an allegation before a tribunal. The added reference in the note to the Article which refers to the amount of any reduction in the period of ineligibility being based on the likelihood that the athlete or person would have been caught had he or she not made the voluntary admission suggests that the provision is intended to apply where the admission provides the evidence which allows the anti-doping organisation to bring forward the allegation and where any evidence which it does have at the time of the admission would probably not support a successful claim for breach at the time when the admission is made. This provision is not described as a discretion exercisable by an anti-doping organisation, but appears to be a ground for reduction which can be raised before a tribunal in the results management process. A tribunal will be best placed to assess the application of this provision in the context of the particular case before it.

When Confronted with a Violation

Article 10.6.2 should be contrasted with the situation where admissions are made when an athlete or other person is confronted with a violation which is provided for by Article 10.6.3. Under Article 10.6.3, where an athlete or other person who is potentially subject to a four-year sanction under Article 10.2.1 (four years for violations of Articles 2.1 (presence), 2.2 (use) and 2.6 (possession)) or 10.3.1 (violations of Articles 2.3 (evading or refusing) and 2.5 (tampering)) promptly admits the violation after being confronted by an anti-doping organisation, he or she may receive a reduction in the period of ineligibility down to a minimum of two years, depending on the seriousness of the violation and his or her degree of fault. The possible reduction has to be approved by WADA and the anti-doping organisation responsible for managing the results.

The requirement to consider the degree of fault appears somewhat anomalous because fault-based assessment is not generally applicable to situations where there is intentional conduct (as the note to Article 10.5.2 states). This provision amounts to a discretion available to the anti-doping organisation and WADA to reduce the significant sanction for intentional breaches for an early admission of guilt.

An admission under Articles 10.6.2 and 10.6.3 should be contrasted with the further admission provision under Article 10.11.2, which allows for the earlier commencement of the period of ineligibility where a timely (or prompt) an admission is made. This provision expressly states that it will not apply where the period of ineligibility has been reduced under Article 10.6.3.[88] The timely admission provision in Article 10.11.2 is applicable to any violation and regardless of the evidence which the anti-doping

---

88 An admission under Article 10.6.2 has the same maximum effect as the timely admission provision. It is submitted that Articles 10.6.2 and 10.11.2 are mutually exclusive.

organisation has. It is the provision which is most frequently relied on to reduce the period of ineligibility, by back-dating the start date, although the extent of any back-dating will depend on the exercise of discretion by tribunals, and that discretion can only be exercised in the circumstances set out in the Article. In deciding whether to back-date the starting date of the period of ineligibility, a tribunal may consider the activity which the athlete was engaged in during the period over which the period of ineligibility may be back-dated.

Article 10.6.4: Application of Several Grounds to Reduce Sanction

Where an athlete or other person establishes grounds to reduce the period of ineligibility under more than one provision of Articles 10.4, 10.5 and 10.6, the period of ineligibility under Articles 10.2–10.5 has to be established before any further reduction or suspension for giving substantial assistance or making admissions under Article 10.6 can be applied. In no circumstances can the application of Article 10.6, after the period of ineligibility has been established by the application of Articles 10.2–10.5, reduce or suspend the period of ineligibility below one-quarter of the period of ineligibility which would otherwise be applicable under the operation of Articles 10.2–10.5. (See Appendix 2 to the Code: Examples of Application of Article 10 – Example 1, Example 6.)

Article 10.7: Multiple Violations

The 2015 Code simplifies the provisions relating to multiple violations. For violations to count as multiple violations, they must all take place within the same ten-year period. This period of time reflects the lengthening of the limitation period in Article 17 of the 2015 Code from eight to ten years. In effect, violations become 'stale' for the purposes of imposing a period of ineligibility if they were committed outside the ten-year period. Such violations cannot be directly relevant to the imposition of a sanction, although they could be relevant to establishing the knowledge possessed by an athlete of such matters as doping control procedures and the risks in taking supplements, which might be relevant in establishing the athlete's degree of fault.

Is There a Second Violation?

Article 10.7 is concerned with the imposition of sanctions for multiple violations. Under Article 10.7.4, a violation will only be considered a second anti-doping rule violation for the purposes of imposing sanctions if the organisation bringing the allegation establishes that the athlete or other person committed the second anti-doping rule violation after the athlete or other person had received notice, or after the anti-doping organisation had made a reasonable attempt to give notice, of the first anti-doping rule violation.[89] The burden of establishing these requirements for a second violation will be on the anti-doping organisation asserting that there is a second anti-doping rule violation, and the standard of proof for the giving of notice or a reasonable attempt to give notice will be the 'comfortable satisfaction' of the tribunal, as provided by Article 3.1. If the conditions in Article 10.7.4 cannot be established, the violations are considered as a single first violation for the purposes of imposing the sanction under the Code, and the sanction imposed for the deemed single first violation is based on the violation which carries the more severe sanction. This Article is commonly applied where investigations reveal several violations have been committed over a period of time.

Where more than one anti-doping rule violation results from the same doping control, the athlete is considered to have committed a single anti-doping rule violation, but the sanction imposed must be based on the violation which carries the more severe sanction.

Under Article 10.7.4.2, if, after a sanction for a first anti-doping rule violation has been imposed, an anti-doping organisation discovers facts which involve an anti-doping rule violation that occurred before notice was given in respect of the first violation, a further sanction must be imposed by the anti-doping organisation, reflecting the sanction that could have been imposed if the later discovered violation and the first violation had been heard together. It is submitted that this provision will only lead to different periods of ineligibility where the anti-doping rule violation which is discovered after the sanction has been imposed for the first violation is a more serious violation which would have increased the initial penalty if both violations had been heard together under Article 10.7.4.1.

Where an earlier violation is subsequently discovered, the disqualification of results has to be further back-dated to the time of the subsequently discovered violation unless fairness requires otherwise, as provided by Article 10.8.

The provisions requiring the giving of notice for a violation (or reasonable attempts to do so) before a second violation can be dealt with

---

89 For consideration of the giving of notice, see CAS 2008/A/1572, *Gusmao* v. *FINA* at pages 445–6.

separately (and the provisions for dealing with a later discovered violation) indicate that Article 10.7.4 is intended to cover all situations in which there may be further violations after a first violation. It does not appear to be limited to violations of a similar nature to the first violation notified, but is expressed to cover any circumstances which can give rise to a further alleged violation under the Code. It does not seem appropriate to treat a violation which is of a different kind to that which has been notified or resolved as if it had been committed at the same time as the first violation (as opposed to dealing with the violation as a distinct separate violation) if notice has not been given, but this is the meaning of the provision.

Although Article 10.7.4 makes no specific provision on when to treat violations as third violations for the purposes of sanctions, it is submitted that the position under Article 10.7.4 applies in determining whether there was a third violation or whether violations have to be considered together as a second violation.

Period of Ineligibility for a Second Violation

Under Article 10.7, where a second violation has been committed, the period of ineligibility is the greater of six months, one-half of the period of ineligibility imposed for the first anti-doping rule violation (without taking into account any reduction under Article 10.6) or twice the period of ineligibility otherwise applicable to the second anti-doping rule violation, treating the second violation as if it were a first violation (again without any reduction under Article 10.6 for substantial assistance or admissions). When the period of ineligibility for a second violation has been established, it may be reduced under Article 10.6 if the provisions on substantial assistance or admissions apply. It would appear that, in certain circumstances, the provisions of Article 10.7.1 of the 2015 Code can lead to periods of ineligibility for second violations which are lower than those that would have been imposed under the 2009 Code and which may not reflect one of the central purposes of the 2015 Code.[90] There is no power

---

90 See, for example, the sanction in *DFSNZ v. Ciancio*, which is summarised in Chapter 5, pages 240–1, and the consent award on appeal to WADA in CAS 2014/A/3498, *IAAF v. Asli Cakia Alptekin*, where the agreed sanction of eight years was reached after it was acknowledged that the athlete could argue that the period of ineligibility for a second serious violation of the Code should be eight years under the 2015 Code, as opposed to life under the 2009 Code (applying *lex mitior* principles).

under the Code to make a period of ineligibility imposed for a second violation run consecutively after the end of a period of ineligibility for a first violation.

Third Violations

Article 10.7.2 provides that a third anti-doping rule violation will always result in a lifetime period of ineligibility unless the third violation meets the requirements for a reduction under Article 10.4 or 10.5 or involves a breach of the whereabouts provisions under Article 2.4. In these cases, which all involve reductions for fault or a fault-based violation, the period of ineligibility will be between eight years and life, presumably set by reference to the seriousness of the violation and the circumstances of the case. It is submitted that a tribunal may take into account the personal situation of the athlete in order to arrive at a proportionate sanction.

If no fault is established on a third violation, no period of ineligibility can be applied. If the athlete or other person successfully invokes one of the defences under Article 10.5 or if the third violation was under Article 2.4, the period of ineligibility is between eight years and life. There are no criteria expressed for deciding on the appropriate period of ineligibility within this range in these cases, but it is submitted that the tribunal should assess the athlete's degree of fault in connection with the third violation in the same way as under the no significant fault defence or in accordance with the provisions relating to the violation of Article 2.4 on a first violation. It is submitted that a tribunal should be able to examine the circumstances more broadly, and in particular the effect of the period of ineligibility on the athlete or other person, in arriving at an appropriate sanction.

It is now generally accepted that lifetime bans from sport are not incompatible with fundamental principles of human rights where serious misconduct is seen as disqualifying a person from continued participation in sport. This is reflected in the consensus of sporting organisations expressed in the Code and by the broad support for the Code at State level evidenced by the high level of acceptance of the UNESCO Anti-Doping Convention.

Similar sanctions are found in the context of professional disciplinary rules where serious breaches of professional standards occur. The provisions on mandatory lifetime bans for third violations in the Code are clear, and it is submitted that there is no proper basis for a tribunal to consider the proportionality of a lifetime period of ineligibility for a third violation where that consequence is the fixed sanction for a third violation.

Examples of Lifetime Bans for Repeat Violations

Nature of Notification of Earlier Violation

CAS 2008/A/1572, *Gusmao* v. *FINA* G was a Brazilian swimmer who appealed three decisions of the FINA Doping Panel determining that she had committed doping violations. Two of these decisions related to a positive test and the third to an allegation of tampering with doping control. The positive tests were for elevated testosterone levels. The third violation arose from irregularities in the testing process at the time of the second positive test, conducted by the medical director of the swimmer's team. The sample was taken in the athlete's room and not in a specific designated doping control station. DNA analysis showed that the samples collected were from different donors. In a criminal investigation in relation to an allegation of making a false statement on the doping control form, the team doctor refused to provide a DNA sample for analysis, relying on her constitutional rights under national law. The athlete made submissions in relation to the positive test and the DNA analysis in relation to the tampering allegation.

The athlete claimed that she had not been notified of a first anti-doping rule violation at the time of the alleged commission of a second anti-doping rule violation. The Panel found that the IRMS analysis showed the presence of exogenous testosterone in the samples taken. They found that doping violations had been committed on both occasions.

As regards the tampering allegation, the Panel found the evidence of the DNA analysis and differing steroid profile in the samples meant that the only explanation was that there had been some form of collaboration between athlete and doctor to provide different urine samples. The CAS Panel found that the fact that the Brazilian court had found that there was not enough evidence to bring criminal proceedings was not relevant to its determination. It was comfortably satisfied that the athlete had tampered with doping control.

Notice of the First Violation Having concluded that the athlete had committed three anti-doping rule violations, the Panel had to consider whether there was a second anti-doping rule violation for the purposes of the 2004 Code. The question was whether the competitor had received notice of the first anti-doping rule violation before the commission of the second. The Panel held that formal notice of the first violation was not required and that knowledge of the results management process for the violation was sufficient for the athlete to have notice. This was based on the wording of Article 10.6.1 of the 2004 Code in the light of its objective and purpose.

Under the 2004 Code, the second violation led to a lifetime period of ineligibility. The Panel further considered whether, under the principle of *lex mitior*, the 2009 Code provided for a lesser period of ineligibility. Considering the nature of the violation, the Panel took the view that, even if the 2009 Code could apply to sanctions as a *lex mitior*, it had no other option but to impose a lifetime ban for the second violation. G was banned for life and her results obtained in May 2006 and from 12 July 2007 were disqualified.

Non-analytical Violation – Lifetime Period of Ineligibility and Disqualification of Results

USADA v. O'Bee, AAA No. 77 190 005 1509   O'B, a professional cyclist, had tested positive for an anabolic steroid in 2001 and had served a period of ineligibility. He gave a positive test for EPO in May 2009. USADA initially brought charges of use or attempted use, but also sought to raise possession, trafficking and administration of rhEPO and hGH. After dismissing the allegations of possession, trafficking and administration because they were not within the USADA charging letter, the Panel held that O'B had used or attempted to use EPO going back to at least 3 October 2005. This was based upon his admissions to USADA and his team manager, and on documentary evidence in the form of emails. Challenges to the admissibility of the emails were rejected on the grounds that an arbitration does not have to apply the strict rules of evidence which would apply under national law.

As a result of the finding, O'B was held to have committed a second violation under the 2004 Code, and a lifetime period of ineligibility was imposed. The Panel noted that the same result would apply given the nature of the violation if the 2009 Code were invoked under *lex mitior* principles.

As a result of the evidence showing that his use or attempted use went back to 3 October 2005, O'B's results were disqualified from that time forward.

Third Violation for a Specified Substance under the 2009 Code

Drug Free Sport New Zealand v. Whare ST 11/09   W was a rugby league player who committed a third violation of the New Zealand SADR, which implemented the Code. All three violations related to positive tests for cannabis, a specified substance. Previously, W had been reprimanded and fined for his first violation under the earlier SADR 2004, which implemented the 2004 Code, and had been the subject of a two-year period of ineligibility for his second violation. The third violation meant that, under Article 10.7 of the 2009 Code (SADR 14.7), if the requirements of Article 10.4 were established, the period of ineligibility was between eight years and life. The tribunal found that the requirements for a consideration of the athlete's fault were made out. It was submitted that the fault of the athlete in relation to the breach had to be assessed. The athlete had quite deliberately smoked cannabis. The tribunal adopted a broader approach and concluded that the assessment of fault should include the explanation offered in order to put the use in context, where there was social use with no performance-enhancing elements that could be taken into account. In the circumstances, the tribunal imposed a period of ten years' suspension.[91]

Article 10.8: Disqualification of Results

Where a violation is established at a hearing, in addition to the disqualification of the results in the competition in which the violation occurred, the results obtained after the date on which a positive sample was collected or after the date when the violation was committed are also disqualified, up until the imposition of a provisional suspension or the start of a period of Ineligibility. This retroactive disqualification applies 'unless fairness requires otherwise'. The same approach should be applied to this provision as is applied to the operation of Article 10.1 relating to the disqualification of results in other competitions at the event at which a violation occurred.[92] The starting point is that all results will be disqualified. The question whether fairness to the athlete or person who has committed the violation requires a different outcome falls to be considered on the facts of the particular case. Where delay in pursuing an anti-doping violation and/or obtaining an order for provisional suspension leaves an athlete free to compete, a tribunal which ultimately decides that an anti-doping violations has been committed may consider that, given the period of ineligibility imposed, it would be wrong for results over a considerable period

---

91 This approach would appear to be similar to that which would be adopted if a third violation involving similar circumstances was considered under the 2015 Code.

92 See pages 347–50 for discussion of Article 10.1 and a case summary.

of time to be disqualified and decide to limit the period of disqualification of results. It is submitted that the fact that an athlete tested negative in competitions which took place after the time of the sample collection or occurrence of the violation is not necessarily a proper basis on which to find that fairness requires the results to stand. The disqualification of further results is part of the sanction and reflects the fundamental principle that an athlete who has committed a violation should be treated as if they were not able to compete after the commission of the violation. The discretion to allow results to stand has to be exercised in the circumstances of the particular case. It is submitted that results should only be allowed to stand where the athlete has been allowed to compete in the results management process in circumstances where it is unfair to impose the sanction of disqualification of results and ineligibility given the seriousness of the violation and where a decision to not disqualify results would not undermine the principle that an athlete who has committed a violation should not generally be able to compete against clean athletes who comply with the Code after committing the violation.

Articles 10.9 and 10.10: Costs and Financial Orders

The Code's primary sanctions involve imposing periods of ineligibility removing those who breach the Code from competition, with financial orders left to the rules of the particular sport. The policy behind this approach is that financial orders, if available alongside or as alternatives to ineligibility, might see the dilution and reduction of sanctions imposing periods of ineligibility. Articles 10.9 and 10.10 have been included in the 2015 Code to make some provision in this area while maintaining the primacy of the sanction of ineligibility.

Article 10.9 provides for the priority of repayment orders between awards of CAS costs and forfeiture of prize money. The first priority is the payment of any costs awarded by CAS, and the second the payment of prize money, if the rules of the relevant international federation provide for this. The lowest priority for financial orders is the reimbursement of the anti-doping organisation which carried out results management. This does not affect the sanctions imposed under Article 10.

Article 10.10 provides that anti-doping organisations may provide for financial sanctions in relation to anti-doping rule violations which provide for a proportionate recovery of cost or impose a financial penalty. Financial sanctions can only be imposed where the maximum period of ineligibility has been imposed and the imposition of financial sanctions or costs awards cannot be considered as a basis for reducing the period of ineligibility. This expressly maintains the primacy of the imposition of periods of ineligibility as the sanction under the Code. The Article emphasises the need for any financial sanctions to be proportionate. This is no doubt a response to the decision of the Swiss Federal Tribunal in *Matuzalem*, where a FIFA-ordered financial sanction against a player which had the effect of preventing the player from playing indefinitely in the event of default was struck down by the Swiss Federal Tribunal.[93] It should be noted that nothing in these provisions prevents an athlete who has sustained loss and damage as a result of a doping violation committed by another athlete from bringing a civil claim for compensation. If a sport's rules do not provide for the reallocation of prizes, a civil claim could include a claim for this as part of any claim for loss and damage.

Article 10.11: Commencement of the Period of Ineligibility

Under Article 10.11, the period of ineligibility imposed by way of sanction under the Code starts from the date of the hearing decision providing for ineligibility, or, if the hearing is waived or there is no hearing, from the date ineligibility is accepted or otherwise imposed. Together with the disqualification of results obtained from the time of violation under Article 10.8, this provision operates to provide that the standard position is that an athlete who commits a violation loses all results going back to the time of the violation and is subject to the full period of ineligibility going forward from the time when the commission of a violation is established. In combination, the provisions ensure that the Code has full effect where a violation has been committed. They operate to prevent delay benefiting an athlete who has committed a violation and to ensure that athletes who compete when other athletes would expect that they would not do not retain results. In order to uphold the general effect of the sanctions and disqualification regime, Article 10.11 makes express provision for the only circumstances which may allow for the period of ineligibility to start earlier than as provided by Article 10.11 and thereby shorten the period of ineligibility: delays not attributable to the person facing the allegation, timely admission or the imposition of a provisional suspension.

Under the 2004 Code, some tribunals used the power relating to the commencement of a period of ineligibility to move back the starting date as a means of imposing a proportionate sanction. This was, it is submitted,

93 For the case summary, see Chapter 10, pages 501–2.

an unprincipled approach. The provisions in Article 10.11 are now clearly expressed to provide for the only possible exceptions from the standard position and prevent the power to move back the starting date of a period of ineligibility in an unprincipled way. Article 10.11 provides the specific, relatively narrow set of circumstances in which a period of ineligibility can be ordered to start at an earlier date. Any period of provisional suspension will be credited against the total period of ineligibility. If there are substantial delays in the hearing process, or in other parts of the doping control process, which are not attributable to the athlete or other person facing the violation, the tribunal imposing the sanction may decide that the period of ineligibility shall commence at an earlier date. This can be as early as the date of sample collection or the date on which the anti-doping rule violation last occurred. Many investigations into doping violations will take significant periods of time. The comment to Article 10.11 makes it clear that where an anti-doping organisation is conducting an investigation in a reasonable way that should not be considered to be delay for the purposes of the application of Article 10.11. Alleged delays in investigations will need to be considered with this comment in mind, but ultimately whether there has been a delay not attributable to the athlete will be a question of objective fact in the particular case. A decision in relation to the starting date for a period of ineligibility involves consideration of the exercise of a discretion, but this discretion is narrowly circumscribed and must be related to the delays in the process, not to any other factors. As noted, the usual starting point for the commencement of a period of ineligibility will be the hearing date, with the person seeking an earlier commencement date carrying the burden of showing that an earlier date should apply. If the starting date is moved back, all competitive results in the period of ineligibility, including the period of retroactive ineligibility, have to be disqualified.

Article 10.11.2: Timely Admission

A timely admission by an athlete when confronted with an anti-doping rule violation by an anti-doping organisation also gives the tribunal hearing the allegation the discretion to order that the period of ineligibility should start as early as the time of sample collection (or the time the violation was committed). Article 10.11.2, while headed 'Timely Admission', refers to the athlete or other person 'promptly' admitting the violation, and the same approach would apply to this as under Article 10.6.3. This provision does not apply where the admission by the athlete has led to a reduction of the period of ineligibility under Article 10.6.3.

Article 10.11.3: Provisional Suspension

Where a provisional suspension is imposed, the athlete will always receive credit for the period of any provisional suspension against the period of ineligibility. A provisional suspension involves the imposition of an order on a provisional basis prohibiting the athlete or other person from participating, in the same way as a final order of ineligibility. A written voluntary acceptance of a provisional suspension put forward by an anti-doping organisation will have the same effect (and is not to be treated as an admission by the athlete). Whether imposed or accepted, a formal provisional suspension is required, and there can be no credit for a voluntary decision not to compete or a suspension by a team.

Article 10.12: Status during Ineligibility

Article 10.12 provides expressly for the status of an athlete or other person who is subject to a period of ineligibility. The definition covers all orders of ineligibility under the Code (including provisional suspensions) and all persons who can be subject to those orders under the Code. It should, it is submitted, be interpreted broadly so as to fulfil the purpose of the Code and the purpose of imposing orders for ineligibility: the imposition of effective sanctions on those who breach their obligations under the Code.

The consequence of ineligibility is broadly expressed, and a person subject to a period of ineligibility is not able to participate in any capacity in a competition or activity (other than authorised anti-doping education or a rehabilitation programme) organised by any Signatory, any Signatory's member organisation or any club or other member organisation of a Signatory's member organisation, or in competitions authorised or organised by any professional league or international- or national-level event organisation or in any elite or national-level sporting activity funded by a government agency. Ineligibility applies across all sports which are subject to the Code.

The notes to Article 10.12.1 make it clear that this prohibition is intended to be extended to cover the sporting activity of a person subject to an order for ineligibility in events organised by bodies which are outside the Code, such as non-Signatory professional leagues and non-Signatory international- and national-level event organisers. The scope of this extension is unclear (and it could be argued that in order to fulfil the purpose of the Code, any sporting activity which is analogous to those which are within the Code should be within the scope of the prohibition on participation), but it is submitted that the extension would not cover sports which are not under the Code at all or the competitions which they organise, because those sports cannot be said to run competitions which are within the scope of the Code (examples might be eSports or CrossFit competitions).

'Activity' is not defined in the Code, but the comment to Article 10.12 gives examples of serving as an official, director, officer employee or volunteer of a sporting organisation of the kind referred to in the Article. The provisions should, it is submitted, be given a broad interpretation so that they cover any work which contributes to the running of a sporting organisation. However, it seems possible that a tribunal might conclude (notwithstanding the comment on activity in the notes to the Article) that the provisions of Article 10.12 should not be construed to prevent an athlete or other person from working in certain roles in a sporting organisation which are not directly connected to sporting activity. Such an approach would be consistent with upholding the fundamental right to work and common law principles of restraint of trade. As yet, the application of Article 10.12 has not been subject to examination in this context. The scope and effect of the ineligibility provision will have to be determined on the facts in individual cases. A person who contemplates continuing in a role with a sporting organisation during a period of ineligibility should seek to clarify the position with the anti-doping organisation responsible for the results management process which led to the imposition of the period of ineligibility.

The prohibition on participation by an athlete will apply to any form of organised training in a club setting.[94] Article 10.12.2 provides for athletes to be able to return to training with a team or use the facilities at a club

---

94 See notes to Article 10.10.1. See also Antonio Rigozzi, 'Legal Opinion: On the Conformity of the Exclusion of Team Athletes from Organised Training During their Period of Ineligibility with Swiss Law, including the General Principles of Proportionality and Equal Treatment', 9 July 2009, where the author concludes that it is permissible to exclude athletes who compete in team sports from organised training during their period of ineligibility as a matter of Swiss law (as provided for in Article 10.9 of the 2009 Code). Rigozzi concludes that the effect of a period of ineligibility in relation to attendance of team/club training over the period of ineligibility does not infringe the protections afforded to personality rights under Articles 27 and 28 of the Swiss Civil Code, the principles of legality, proportionality and equal treatment or the principles of public policy under Swiss law. Article

during the shorter of two periods: the last two months of the period of ineligibility or the last quarter of the period of the ineligibility.

Where an athlete or other person is subject to a period of ineligibility of longer than four years, Article 10.12 provides that he or she can compete after four years in local-level sport events not sanctioned or otherwise under the jurisdiction of a Code Signatory or member of a Code Signatory, as long as the participation does not allow the accumulation of points for a national championship or international event and does not involve the athlete or person working in any capacity with minors. This exception is difficult to interpret. It must be referring to participation which would otherwise be within the prohibition imposed on the athlete by the period of ineligibility, as opposed to participation which would not be caught. It is submitted that the exception is intended to permit participation in events organised by organisations which are outside the Code at a local level which involve competitions that would otherwise be within the general prohibition (events which are organised by non-Signatories such as professional leagues and non-Signatory international and national event organisers taking place at local level), provided they are not qualifying events for higher-level national or international competitions and do not involve working with a minor.

The prohibition in Article 10.12.1 is expressed to cover any person who has been declared ineligible under the Code. The provision covers all those who are bound by the Code and may commit violations under it – athletes, athlete support personnel and other persons. The prohibition prevents 'participation in any capacity in a competition or activity'. This should, it is submitted, be interpreted to cover all the various activities in sport which may be carried out by those who are bound by the Code. 'Athlete support personnel' is defined as 'any coach, trainer, manager, agent, team staff, official, medical, paramedical personnel, parent or any other person working with, treating or assisting an athlete participating in or preparing for sports competition'.

Under the prohibition, an athlete support person who is subject to a period of ineligibility will be prevented from participating in the activities carried out by athlete support personnel, namely any work helping an athlete participating in or preparing for sports competition, provided the sports competition is one organised by an organisation which brings

10.12.2 of the 2015 Code is a response to this issue. On the grounds to challenge the Code under Swiss law, see further Chapter 10.

ARTICLES 9 AND 10 OF THE CODE

it within the scope of the Code. This will cover all assistance given to athletes preparing for such competition, both at the time of competition and before. This interpretation accords with the plain meaning of the Code and supports the purpose of the Code overall. It provides for the sanction of ineligibility to have the effect on athlete support personnel which is required if the Code is to function effectively and provide an effective anti-doping regime. The precise boundaries of the prohibition are unclear. However, it is submitted that it would cover any work by way of preparation or training carried out by an athlete support person for organised competition which falls within the scope of the events which are within the prohibition in Article 10.12.1. It would generally not cover work as an athlete support person with an athlete not bound by the Code who is not preparing for sporting activity within the prohibition against participation. It might, however, be interpreted as covering work as an athlete support person with an athlete who, while not bound by the Code, is to the knowledge of the athlete support person being prepared for competition which falls within the prohibition.

Where an athlete or person is subject to a period of ineligibility, he or she remains subject to testing. It is submitted that a person who is subject to a period of ineligibility remains, by necessary implication, generally subject to the provisions of the Code.[95]

Article 10.12.3: Violation of Prohibition against Participation

Under Article 10.12.3, an athlete or other person who violates the prohibition of participation under Article 10.12.1 will have any competitive result obtained in the period of violation disqualified and a new period of ineligibility equal to the original period of ineligibility imposed starting at the end of the period of ineligibility originally imposed. The length of the new period of ineligibility may be adjusted by reference to the degree of fault of the person in breach and the other circumstances of the breach.[96] The decision whether an athlete or other person has violated the prohibition against participation will be made by the anti-doping organisation which was responsible for the results management process which led to the imposition of the initial period of ineligibility (or the tribunal to which the anti-doping organisation refers results management). It is submitted that a violation under Article 10.12.3 has to be established to the

---

95 Signatories should, it is submitted, expressly provide for this in implementing the Code.
96 See pages 436–8 for more on the assessment of the new period of ineligibility.

standard of 'comfortable satisfaction' under Article 3.1 and that such a decision must be made after a hearing process which fulfils the principles in Article 8. A violation should be treated like other violations under Article 2.

In order to regain eligibility at the end of the period of ineligibility, an athlete has to be available for out-of-competition testing and provide whereabouts information if requested. Where an ineligible athlete retires during the period of ineligibility and then wishes to return to active competition, the athlete cannot return to international or national events until he or she has made him- or herself available for testing by giving six months' notice as provided in Article 5.7.

Transitional Situations

As has been explained, the anti-doping regime under the Code has been amended significantly at regular intervals since the adoption of the 2004 Code under the process of evolution and amendment provided for by the Code itself. The changes in the Code mean that the rules may change in the time between the commission and hearing of violations. The Code contains transitional provisions, and from the early days of CAS the principle of *lex mitior* has been employed to determine which of two sets of rules is to apply to the imposition of a sanction.[97]

Article 25 of the Code confirms the basic position that the 2015 Code came into full effect as of 1 January 2015 and that its provisions (apart from the procedural rules relating to limitation[98] and the periods for the consideration of multiple violations) do not have retroactive effect unless the principle of *lex mitior* applies. Where an anti-doping rule violation proceeding has started before the 2015 Code came into effect and was pending as at the start date for the 2015 Code, it will be subject to the version of the Code in force at the time when the alleged anti-doping rule violation occurred, unless the tribunal hearing the case determines that the principle of *lex mitior* applies in the circumstances of the case.[99] This means that violations occurring before 1 January 2015 which have not been the subject of a final decision before that date will be governed by the

---

97 See Chapter 1, pages 46–57.
98 Unless the limitation period under an earlier version of the Code has expired, giving rise to accrued substantive rights which the change in Article 17 cannot alter.
99 Given the effect of limitation periods.

2009 Code unless the 2015 Code provides for a more lenient position on sanctions.[100]

Article 25.3 extends the possible application of the 2015 Code's provisions to cases where a final decision has been made on a violation which occurred before 1 January 2015. Such cases could not fall within the *lex mitior* principle because they would have been heard and decided by the time the 2015 Code came into effect and there could be no question of a different set of rules being in force at the time of hearing from that which applied at the time of the violation (as is required for the *lex mitior* principle to apply). As a matter of general principle, such cases might properly be regarded as complete and finally determined under the rules which were in force at the time when the violation was committed. Article 25.3 can, however, be seen as reflecting the desire to provide for a possible reduction in sanction where an athlete dealt with under harsher rules is likely to have feelings of unfairness as a result of new rules introducing more lenient penalties for the same or similar violations. The scope of the application of this provision is uncertain. It is simply expressed as allowing the consideration of a possible sanction imposed under earlier rules 'in light of the 2015 Code'. This can be interpreted as allowing for such a consideration where the *lex mitior* principle would have applied had the case not been the subject of a final decision before the 2015 rules came into force or as allowing a broader discretion whenever the 2015 Code can be relied on to support a possible reduction of the period of ineligibility imposed on grounds of fairness. This broader interpretation was favoured by the Sports Tribunal of New Zealand on the wording of the Article in a recent decision.[101] The discretion to consider reducing a period of ineligibility in

---

100 Although the 2015 Code is generally intended to provide for a more stringent regime as regards those athletes who cheat, in some circumstances the sanction under the 2015 Code may be lighter. For the example of sanctions for second violations, see pages 443–4.

101 See *Gemmell* v. *TriNZ* ST 01/15, where the New Zealand Sports Tribunal adopted the broad view of the jurisdiction under Article 25.3 and modified a period of ineligibility of fifteen months imposed by CAS on appeal. The period of ineligibility was reduced to twelve months where the 2015 Code changed the substantive requirements to prove a whereabouts breach to three breaches in twelve months. The reduction was allowed in order to reflect the fact that the sporting community had decided, since the imposition of the period of ineligibility by way of final decision in the case, that the Rule under which the athlete had been found to have breached the Code was too onerous – under the new Article 2.4 in the 2015 Code, the athlete would not have committed a violation. The period of twelve months was set on the basis that it represented the minimum period of ineligibility under the 2009 Code. It is submitted that the discretion under Article 25.3 should be limited in its application to situations where, but for the fact that the final decision was made before the rule change, the *lex mitior* principle would have allowed

light of the 2015 Code cannot be relied on where the period of ineligibility has been completed – in such a case, the violation must be considered to have been decided and dealt with under the rules applicable at the time of the violation.

Article 25.4 provides that, for the purposes of assessing the period of ineligibility where a second violation is committed under the 2015 Code and the first violation occurred under the pre-2015 Code rules, the period of ineligibility for the first violation has to be determined on the basis of the application of the 2015 Code rules. This provision gives some limited retroactive effect to the Code, presumably to achieve a measure of consistency.

Article 10.13: Automatic Publication

Article 10.13 has been added to the 2015 Code to confirm that the automatic publication of the disposition of an allegation that an athlete or other person has committed an anti-doping rule violation as provided for in Article 14.3 is part of the sanction under the Code. Article 14.3 sets out the requirements for publication (content and duration of publication).[102] Mandatory pubic reporting is not applicable where a case concerns a minor, and optional public reporting in such cases has to be proportionate to the facts and circumstances of the case.

Article 11: Consequences to Teams

Article 11 provides for the target testing of a team during the period of an event where more than one member of a team has been notified of an anti-doping rule violation in connection with the event. The obligation to target test is imposed upon the ruling body of the event. Where more than two members of a team are found to have committed an anti-doping rule violation in the period of an event in a team sport,[103] the ruling body of the

for a reduction – that is, where the 2015 Code has introduced a more lenient sanction. This would mean that Article 25.3 could not apply to cases where the substantive law had changed and a final decision had been made in the case. It is submitted that this accords with the general fundamental principle that violations are dealt with under the rules which apply at the time of the commission of the violation and that exceptions to this principle should be consistent with the principle of *lex mitior*, which is expressed to be the exception to the general principle in Article 25.2. For more on the *lex mitior* principle generally, see Chapter 1, pages 46–57.

102 See Chapter 7, pages 315–19 for further consideration of publication of decisions.
103 As 'team sport' is defined under the Code – see pages 344, note 26 for definition.

event has to impose the appropriate sanction on the team: loss of points, disqualification or other sanctions. It is important to note that team sanctions will be in addition to the sanctions under the Code which will be imposed on the individual athletes who have committed the violations. Again, the appropriate sanction will be a matter of the rules applicable at the event. Generally, where one athlete commits an anti-doping rule violation and is a member of a team, whether that falls within the definition of 'team' under the Code or not, the consequences for other athletes in the team will depend upon the rules of the sporting body concerned.[104] There is nothing to prevent the ruling body of an event choosing to have rules in place which are stricter than those set out in this section. Nor are Signatories or governments which accept the Code prevented from enforcing their own rules which have the purpose of sanctioning bodies over which they have authority. A Signatory's own rules cannot, however, have the effect of adding to the sanction which can be imposed upon an individual athlete under Article 10 of the Code, because this would amount to a breach of Article 23.2.2 of the Code.[105] The application of Article 11 is limited to violations by team members connected with events (a series of individual competitions which are organised under the rules of one ruling body). Violations by team members which are committed or discovered outside events (e.g. in training camps) will be dealt with under the Code and under any further rules which apply in the sport concerned in relation to sanctions on teams.

Reallocation of Results and Medals

The Code contains no provision relating to the possible reallocation of results and medals awarded where a competitor is disqualified under the

---

104 For a well-known example of a case concerning team disqualification where the specific rules of the international federation had to be interpreted and applied, see CAS 2004/A/725, *USOC and Johnson* v. *IOC and IAAF*. On the interpretation of the particular IAAF Rules then in force, CAS held that the members of a relay team should not lose their Olympic gold medals where one member of the team (who did not run in the final) was found to have committed an anti-doping rule violation a long time after the event and ought therefore to have been subject to a ban at the time of the Games. The same approach to the same IAAF Rules was adopted by the CAS Panel in CAS 2008/A/1545, *Anderson and Others* v. *IOC*. For the application of rules providing for strict consequences as a result of a violation by a team member, see CAS 95/122, *NWBA* v. *IPC*, CAS Digest I, p. 173, where, under the applicable rules, a team lost its Olympic gold medal where one team member tested positive for doping during the tournament.

105 For consideration of this issue, see Chapter 10, pages 517–23, where the IOC regulation is discussed.

Code. The Code's sanctions relate to the individual who has committed the violation, and there is no provision for other aggrieved athletes to bring claims to be awarded the medals and prizes of an athlete who commits an anti-doping rule violation. The Code makes it clear in the comment to Article 10.8 that nothing in the Code prevents athletes or others who have been caused loss and damage by breaches of the Code from bringing ordinary civil proceedings for compensation in the courts. Whether medals and prizes will be reallocated in such a claim will be a question of the interpretation of the rules under which the particular competition took place. In many situations, the disqualification of the results obtained by an athlete who is found to have committed an anti-doping rule violation will lead to the reallocation of placings and prize moneys under the rules of the event and/or the international federation or major event organiser responsible for the event, but difficult questions may arise in this area where a doping violation is established sometime after an event. Such matters will be determined under the rules which apply to the event in question. Further issues may arise where competitors seek to challenge a decision not to bring forward an allegation that a violation has been committed and claim that a competitor should have been found to have committed a violation and been the subject of a period of disqualification and ineligibility. The Code does not provide for appeals by individual athletes who are aggrieved by decisions made under the Code, but nothing in the Code prevents individual athletes from seeking redress in the courts or before tribunals with jurisdiction by relying on any contractual or other rights which they may have in this regard. Again, such claims will be decided on the interpretation and application of the rules relating to the event.[106]

Illustrations

Appeals and Claims to Change Results

CAS 2002/O/373, *Canadian Olympic Committee and Beckie Scott* v. *IOC*
S had represented Canada at the 2002 Salt Lake City Winter Olympics and placed third in the 5 km pursuit cross-country skiing competition. The gold and silver medal winners were D and L. L had tested positive for darbepoetin (a mimetic of EPO) before the Olympics, but took part in the Games because the FIS heard the matter and imposed a two-year sanction beginning after the Games. At a test before a later race at the Games – the cross-country relay – D and L were asked to provide blood

---

106 This is expressly stated in the notes to Article 13 of the Code.

and urine samples and withdrew from the race. Both D and L subsequently competed in the 30 km cross-country race at the Games, and D won the gold medal, while L came eighth. After this race, tests were administered and returned positive results for darbepoetin, a mimetic of EPO. Under the Olympic Charter (and OMADC), the IOC had the responsibility of holding an inquiry commission into the positive test. The IOC disqualified D from the 30 km event, excluded her from the Games and annulled her result in the race. After the Games, FIS banned L for two years, and the IOC then decided that all the results obtained by L at the Games would be annulled. By reason of the decision relating to L, S became the silver medal holder for the 5 km race. However, the IOC decision in relation to D meant that D's result in the 5 km race still stood.

The Question of Construction   S challenged the decision made by the IOC which did not affect the earlier race at the Games – the 5 km pursuit – before CAS, and claimed that, on the proper interpretation of Rule 25 of the Olympic Charter, the IOC should have ordered the return of all D's medals, including the medal in the 5 km pursuit, when it decided that D should be excluded from the Olympic Games. The IOC had based its decision on the application of the OMADC, not the Olympic Charter. It submitted, before CAS, that the OMADC contained no provision allowing for the disqualification of results from another event apart from the one in which the athlete had tested positive, and that, as the OMADC was the specific set of rules relating to doping, it prevailed over the terms of the Olympic Charter. CAS had to decide whether S had standing to bring the claim, and, if she did, it had to determine the meaning of the rules which applied under the Olympic Charter and OMADC. CAS held that, as a matter of Swiss law (which applied by Rule 45 of the CAS Procedural Code), S had standing to bring the claim because she was invoking a contractual right to claim under the Olympic Charter, which was available to her as a result of the agreement she made on entering the Games. On the proper interpretation of the Olympic Charter, the IOC should have ordered the return of all the medals, including the gold medal in the 5 km race, when D was excluded from the Games. Accordingly, the IOC was directed to disqualify all D's results at the Games and to give the necessary orders to amend the ranking of the 5 km race, 'ensuring that Becky Scott was ranked first and awarded the Olympic Gold Medal'. While this decision was based on the interpretation of the Olympic Charter, and pre-dated the Code, the provisions of the Code relating to the disqualification of all results at an event under Article 10.1 were noted as supporting the interpretation of the Olympic Charter adopted by CAS, which led to the disqualification of all D's results at the Games.

CAS 2004/A/748, ROC and Ekimov v. IOC, USOC and Tyler Hamilton
The Russian Olympic Committee (ROC) and E, who had won the silver medal in the cycling time trial at the Athens Olympics, sought to appeal a decision made by the IOC not to pursue anti-doping rule violation proceedings against H, the gold medal winner. The IOC had decided not to continue with a doping investigation after H's B sample was frozen and could not be used to support an initial laboratory report that the A sample returned an adverse analytical finding showing two different red blood cell populations, evidencing blood doping. The B sample was considered by the IOC to be 'non-conclusive' because there were insufficient intact red blood cells present, and the IOC resolved that it would not be pursuing sanctions in the matter. The ROC and E appealed this finding to CAS, and sought orders for H's disqualification and the return of his gold medal and Olympic diploma, and for his result to be given to E. R, who was fourth in the time trial, appeared as an interested party, together with the Australian Olympic Committee.

CAS decided an initial question as to the jurisdiction to hear the appeal, which concerned the standing of E (and R) to bring an appeal. There were two main arguments: there was 'no decision', so that CAS was free to consider the question whether blood doping had been committed; and, if there was a 'decision', the limit on standing in the IOC Anti-Doping Rules was not applicable, because it was contrary to the Olympic Charter, was not mentioned on the entry form, constituted an unusual rule under Swiss law which needed express reference to be included in the contract formed when an athlete entered the Games, was an unlawful violation of the athlete's personality rights and was discriminatory under competition law, given the IOC monopoly over the Olympic Games.

CAS held that E had no standing to bring the appeal against a decision that no anti-doping rule violation had been committed. The case was contrasted with the *Beckie Scott* decision, where the applicant for relief was able to rely on the broad arbitration provision in the Olympic Charter to establish her right to request that CAS make orders adjusting the results and medals.

Where a sporting organisation fails to apply the Code to athletes in accordance with its responsibilities, particularly if the failure can be shown to involve deliberate actions made in bad faith by individuals acting for the sporting organisation and if this has led to athletes competing with pro-hibited substances in their systems when they should not have been, it will be possible for other athletes to bring claims for loss and damage caused. It seems possible that circumstances of the kind set out in the recent WADA reports into the IAAF and the Sochi Olympics might lead to such claims being brought, but as yet none has been put forward. Such claims would fall outside the Code and would be dealt with under the general law of the applicable national legal systems.[107]

107 For consideration of claims which fall outside the Code, see Chapter 10, pages 517–23.

Article 13: Appeals under the Code

Introduction

An appeal process is an important aspect of any court or tribunal system, and, in the context of tribunals established by private bodies such as sports organisations, a right of appeal may play an important role in providing a fair hearing overall to a member of an association who faces a serious disciplinary charge, such as a doping allegation.[1]

Under the Code, the right of appeal is provided for under Article 13. The fact that the key elements of Article 13 have to be included in their anti-doping rules without substantive change by Signatories in order to comply with the Code, that appeal rights are extended to parties with an interest in the uniform application of the Code (in particular WADA) and that an appeal before CAS proceeds as a full re-hearing on the facts and law, means that appeals have a central role in the overall operation of the anti-doping regime under the Code.

The nature of the hearing on an appeal to CAS – a full re-hearing on the facts and the law – is the most important feature of the appeal process. Unlike many appeal processes in court systems which are limited to correcting errors of law in approaching the facts of a case but not reviewing factual findings, or which allow only limited reconsideration of factual matters on a re-hearing, the appeal process before CAS, while having some limits on the presentation of new evidence on appeal which could have been presented to the tribunal that made the decision under appeal, is much more open. The appeal process allows an appellant to present its evidence and submissions on appeal afresh and have its case considered afresh by CAS without CAS being obliged to show any deference to the decision of the tribunal being challenged. The *de novo* scope of a CAS

---

1 While an appeal right is not expressly referred to in the right to a fair hearing under Article 8, it is submitted that the availability of a right of appeal is an essential aspect of the right to a fair-hearing process. See Costa, 'Legal Opinion' for the expression of this view.

Panel's review in appeal is set out in Rule 57 of the CAS Code. The scope of review is also confirmed by Articles 13.1.1 and 13.1.2 of the Code.[2]

On many occasions, in appeals from decisions of anti-doping tribunals under the Code, CAS has relied on this established approach to appeals to address and remedy[3] alleged defects in the hearing process before the tribunal which initially heard the allegations.

The appeal structure also plays another important role. By providing that Signatories have to adopt Article 13 without significant amendment in order to comply with the Code (with the exception of Article 13.2.2, which provides for the appeal structure at national level, and Articles 13.6 and 13.7, which concern the rights to appeal to CAS of a party subject to a report of non-compliance with the Code by WADA under Article 23.4.5 and to appeal the revocation of a laboratory accreditation), the Code reinforces the central role of CAS in interpreting and applying the Code. By this means, and by widening the range of parties which have a right of appeal to CAS to include WADA (and other anti-doping organisations), the provisions of Article 13 allow a process of appeal which can be used to foster a consistent approach to the application and interpretation of the Code by all Signatories.[4] WADA receives decisions made under the Code under Article 14 of the Code and can review decisions made at national level concerning international athletes (or indeed, decisions concerning other athletes bound by the Code where anti-doping policies adopting the Code provide for appeals in terms of Article 13 for those athletes) and decide whether it is in the interests of the proper harmonious application of the Code to bring an appeal to CAS.

Nature of the Process: Challenges beyond Code Appeals

As has been outlined,[5] CAS is an arbitral institution, and as a consequence, where a sporting organisation agrees to adopt the Code, the effect of that agreement, under most legal systems, will be to provide for an agreement

---

2 It is difficult to see that agreeing to Article 13 can regulate the jurisdiction of CAS under the CAS Code, because it is the CAS Code which must regulate the exercise of powers by CAS. However, the provisions of Article 13 are consistent with the position which has been reached by CAS in the exercise of its powers in hearing an appeal.
3 Rule 57 of the CAS Code for Sports Related Arbitration.
4 For cases where WADA has been a party to CAS appeals, see the WADA website's legal section.
5 See Chapter 1, pages 21–6. The status of CAS as a true arbitration court was confirmed in the decisions referred to there.

to submit disputes in relation to anti-doping allegations under the Code to the tribunals and appeal tribunals (national-level anti-doping appeal tribunals and CAS) which are provided for in Article 13. Under the legal systems to which the decisions of these tribunals may be subject, this agreement may well amount to an agreement to submit disputes arising in relation to the application of the Code to arbitration. If this is so, it will mean that any challenge to the decisions of the tribunals before national courts is likely to be considered under the principles governing appeals against arbitration awards (not under administrative law principles, as was formerly the case in many jurisdictions with challenges to decisions by tribunals in the anti-doping area).[6] A possible appeal to a national court by either party to an arbitration award lies outside the scope of the hearing process under the Code, which simply directs a fair hearing process under Article 8 as part of the results management process and provides for rights of appeal to CAS as stipulated under Article 13.

The CAS Code has been amended to confirm the position which would have applied under the Code previously. Rules 46 and 59 provide that CAS awards will be final and binding 'subject to recourse available in certain circumstances pursuant to Swiss law within 30 days from the notification of the original award'.[7] Where challenges are made to national courts against decisions made by national-level tribunals under the Code, the nature of the challenge available will depend on the nature of the tribunal process and the scope of appeal rights available under the particular rules. The Code only provides for a mandatory fair hearing at this national level, and for possible appeal rights to a national appeal tribunal or CAS to be put in place to meet the need for an appeal process. If the proceedings before the national tribunal were not found to constitute an arbitration process, a national court would have to examine any challenge under the principles of judicial review applicable to the decisions of domestic tribunals under the national legal system. If there were appeal rights from the first-instance tribunal decision, those rights would have to be exhausted before any challenge by way of judicial review could be entertained. If the tribunal hearing was found to be an arbitral process then, as noted earlier, the national laws relating to arbitration would apply. If there was an appeal to CAS from the first-instance tribunal decision under the rules in

---

6 For more on applications to national courts applying to set aside awards by CAS, see Chapter 10, pages 487–9.

7 See Chapter 1, pages 29–43 for an outline of CAS Code R46 and 59 as amended by Amendments to the Code of Sports Related Arbitration (2016).

question, this would mean that an appeal to CAS with possible recourse to the Swiss Federal Tribunal would be the only proper course for challenge. This would be the case unless a national court could be persuaded that the process of an exclusive appeal to CAS with recourse to the Swiss Federal Tribunal was in breach of fundamental rights in some way.[8]

In the field of arbitration, many countries have enacted domestic legislation implementing the UNCITRAL Model Law and the New York Convention on the Recognition and Enforcement of Foreign Arbitral Awards. Both international instruments seek to promote international uniformity in relation to the law relating to arbitration. Both support the choice of parties to submit disputes to arbitration, provide for stays of court proceedings where court proceedings are brought in breach of agreements to arbitrate disputes and provide for limited grounds upon which an arbitration award may be set aside, or upon which recognition and enforcement may be refused, by a national court.[9] The result of agreement to the appeal structure under the Code will generally be that, although the CAS Rules do not exclude the jurisdiction of the courts, and cannot do so,[10] there will

---

8 An example of a recent challenge to the agreement to the CAS process can be seen in the decision by the Munich Higher Regional Court 37 O 28331/12, *Pechstein v. DESG and ISU*, in which the Munich Higher Regional Court upheld a challenge to the jurisdiction of CAS on the basis that the requirement to submit to CAS arbitration, which the athlete had to enter into under the Code, involved a breach of German competition law, which made the reference to CAS of no effect. This decision has recently been reversed on appeal by the German Federal Court of Justice, which upheld the status of CAS as a genuine arbitration tribunal under German law and found that there was no breach of competition law by the international federation requiring agreement to the jurisdiction of CAS as a condition of athletes being able to compete. The Court held that the arbitration agreement was not invalid when various fundamental rights were considered. The result was that the period of ineligibility imposed upon the athlete in 2009 was valid. For a case summary, see Chapter 10, pages 513–17.

9 Generally, the trend in national legal systems since the coming into force of the New York Convention has been to move from distrust of arbitration as a method of dispute resolution, which ousted the jurisdiction of the courts, in breach of public policy, to active support for a private agreement to resolve disputes in a manner of the parties' choosing, which is to be encouraged by courts and legislatures. Support for arbitration as the means of resolving disputes under the Code is an obligation under the UNESCO Convention.

10 While the Code of Sports Related Arbitration provided that CAS decisions will be final and binding between the parties, this provision could not prevent the courts from considering whether an award may be set aside, or not recognised or enforced, under legislation which provides for the grounds contained in the Model Law or the New York Convention. The parties to an arbitration may seek to agree to an exclusion agreement which expressly ousts the jurisdiction of the courts. The enforceability of such an agreement will depend on the law of the legal system with jurisdiction over the agreement. A submission that

be only a limited basis for any further challenge after a decision on an anti-doping rule violation under the Code has been made on appeal by CAS, or, indeed, by an appeal tribunal at national level for appeals by national-level athletes.[11] In most jurisdictions where CAS has been chosen as the appeal tribunal for appeals by national-level athletes under the Code (and is the appeal tribunal for international-level athletes by the mandatory provisions of Article 13), the effect will be to limit any further appeal right in a case under the Code to an appeal to the Swiss Federal Tribunal under the Swiss PILA 1987 (as amended 2014).

Position of CAS in the Appeal Structure

The overall effect of Article 13 is generally to affirm the position of CAS in interpreting and applying the Code under the anti-doping policies of Signatories, and to place CAS at the apex of the appeal process for international-level athletes. For doping appeals, CAS will conduct the appeal under the CAS Procedural Rules for appeals, and agreement to the application of the Code will represent an agreement to the application of those rules. Where CAS is responsible for first-instance hearings under the rules or policies of a sporting organisation, or operates *ad hoc* at major events such as the Olympic and Commonwealth Games, it will conduct the hearings under the CAS Procedural Rules for first-instance hearings or the relevant CAS *ad hoc* rules.[12]

The fact that the mechanism for hearings and appeals, like the enforcement of the Code itself, requires agreement for its effect means that a threshold issue for a tribunal (whether a national-level tribunal or CAS) may be the question whether there is a binding agreement to submit an

there was a binding exclusion agreement under Swiss law was rejected in *X* v. *ATP Tour* (see Chapter 10, page 494). For a consideration of the argument that CAS arbitration is a domestic arbitration and subject to the provisions of Australian domestic law, which provides that an ouster agreement is unenforceable in a domestic arbitration, see *Raguz* v. *Sullivan*, decision of the New South Wales Court of Appeal (Chapter 10, page 506). Where a tribunal hearing is not an arbitration process, a clause purporting to exclude the jurisdiction of the courts will again be subject to the law of the legal system applicable to the rules, but it is unlikely to be enforceable.

11 For more detail on the grounds to challenge a CAS award before the courts (in particular the Swiss Federal Supreme Court), see Chapter 10.

12 See Chapter 1, pages 29–43 for more on CAS procedural rules. For the first time, ICAS created a separate CAS Anti-Doping Division, which sat in addition to the regular Ad Hoc Division, for the Rio Olympics.

alleged anti-doping rule violation to the tribunal or to CAS.[13] This issue
will be determined by the tribunal hearing the matter or by CAS under its
Procedural Rules (as will any dispute as to whether the particular dispute
falls within the agreement to submit disputes to the jurisdiction of the tribunal or CAS). Where the subject matter of the hearing is an alleged violation under the Code, there will usually be little doubt that the dispute falls
within the agreement to the process of hearings before a tribunal (with
appeal rights, as provided for by the Code).

Illustration

Is there a Binding Arbitration Agreement? An Early Example

CAS 2000/A/262, Preliminary Award, *R* v. *FIBA*, CAS Digest II, p. 377
R was banned by the International Federation for Basketball (FIBA) under
its regulations as a result of a drug test carried out by the US National
Basketball Association (NBA). R appealed to CAS. The suspension was
lifted on an interim basis by a German court. On the appeal to CAS, R
submitted that there was no binding agreement giving CAS jurisdiction
because he was not bound to the agreement to settle any dispute arising
from the FIBA regulations by way of arbitration before CAS.

R was a professional player in the NBA and had not entered a contractual relationship with FIBA, nor was he a member of any federation affili-
ated to FIBA. There was no arbitration agreement by contract until R was
given his right of appeal by FIBA. CAS held that the written procedure
which R agreed to was sufficient to form an arbitration agreement under
Swiss law, because it was in writing and contain sufficient reference to the
FIBA regulations relating to appeals to CAS to satisfy the agreements of
Swiss law that there be sufficient reference to the arbitration in the written
material agreed to. The global reference to the appeal process was sufficient to create a valid arbitration agreement where the parties were experienced in the field, and the arbitration clause was regarded as customary
to the sector of business.[14]

---

13 The CAS Procedural Rules expressly provide for the requirement that there be a binding
   agreement to refer a sports-related dispute to CAS, whether at first instance or on appeal
   (appeal arbitration proceedings): see Rule 27 of the CAS Procedural Rules.
14 See also *N* v. *FEI*, Swiss Federal Court, 31 October 1996, CAS Digest at Chapter 10, page
   509. By way of contrast, where the particular contractual provisions in a form signed by
   an athlete did not, on their proper interpretation, bring about a reference of the particular
   dispute to CAS, see *Busch* v. *IHG* in Chapter 2, pages 72–5. See also *Dodô* v. *FIFA and*

Scope of Review not Limited

Article 13 begins by stating that decisions made under the Code can be appealed as set out in Articles 13.2–13.4 or as otherwise provided in the Code or International Standards. Article 13.1.1 now expressly confirms that the scope of review on an appeal is not limited and that it includes all issues relevant to the appeal and is not limited to the scope to the issues before the first decision-maker. Article 13.1.2 further confirms the position reached under the majority of CAS awards, which is that CAS need not give deference to the discretion exercised by the body which made the decision being appealed against. These provisions appear to have been included in the 2015 Code to provide certainty as to the position on CAS appeals, because there were some CAS awards which did say that CAS should show a measure of deference to the decisions subject to appeal, particularly where a tribunal had arrived at sanction for a violation in a well-reasoned decision. While the provisions in Article 13 of the Code cannot provide for the jurisdiction of CAS, they do represent a procedural agreement between parties who are bound by the Code as to the process on appeal to CAS which CAS should follow (unless it is contrary to its own procedural rules). In fact, the provisions in Article 13 are consistent with most CAS awards on the nature of an appeal and the CAS Procedural Rules. Recently, a CAS Panel confirmed its full power to examine a case on sanctions *de novo* and observed that the idea of deference as expressed in some CAS awards only meant that CAS 'would not easily "tinker" with a well-reasoned award on sanctions by say replacing a sanction of 17 or 19 months with one of 18'.[15]

The implementation of an appeal system for allegations involving athletes who are not international athletes and events that are not international events is a matter for the Signatories at national level. Where a system of national-level appeals is implemented which does not involve a CAS appeal, the scope of review on appeal will be a matter for the applicable national system. It is submitted that such a national-level appeal system can provide for a more limited right of appeal where CAS is not chosen to hear appeals, because there is no mandatory requirement for the scope of these appeals.

WADA in Chapter 2, pages 75–7, where the particular sporting rules were held to establish jurisdiction over the player.

15 See CAS 2016/A/4643, *Sharapova v. ITF*, paras 62–63. For summary, see Chapter 8, pages 420–3.

Decisions which are Capable of being Appealed

Under Article 13.2, the following decisions at national or international level can be the subject of an appeal:

- a decision that an anti-doping rule violation has been committed, or has not been committed;[16]
- a decision imposing consequences or not imposing consequences for an anti-doping rule violation;
- a decision that an anti-doping rule violation cannot go forward for procedural reasons (e.g. limitation);
- a decision by WADA not to grant an exception to the requirement that a retired athlete give six months' notice before returning to competition under Article 5.7.1;
- a decision assigning results management under Article 7.1;
- a decision that an anti-doping organisation lacks jurisdiction to rule on an alleged anti-doping rule violation or its consequences;
- a decision not to bring forward an adverse analytical finding or atypical finding, or a decision not to go forward with an investigation under Article 7.7;
- a decision to impose a provisional suspension;
- a decision not to impose a provisional suspension as required by Article 7.9;
- a decision that an athlete or other person has violated the prohibition against participation under Article 10.12.3;
- a decision under Article 10.6.1 to suspend or not suspend, or to reinstate or not reinstate, a period of ineligibility for providing substantial assistance and
- a decision not to recognise a decision by another anti-doping organisation under Article 15.

Article 13.3 provides that where an anti-doping organisation fails to give a decision as to whether an anti-doping rule violation has been committed within a reasonable deadline set by WADA, WADA can appeal directly to CAS as if the anti-doping organisation had given a decision that no anti-doping rule violation had been committed. Where such an

---

16 For a consideration of what constitutes a decision under the Code with the result that an appeal is available, see *ROC and Ekimov v. IOC, USOC and Hamilton* in Chapter 8, pages 461–2.

appeal is brought and the CAS Panel determines that WADA acted reasonably in appealing directly to CAS, the anti-doping organisation has to pay WADA's costs and legal fees on the appeal.[17] There is no time limit for the exercise of this appeal right by WADA. The notes to Article 13.3 provide that WADA will give the anti-doping organisation the opportunity to explain why it has not given a decision before intervening and appealing directly to CAS.

Where WADA has a right of appeal and no other party has lodged an appeal against a final decision under the hearing process established by an anti-doping organisation, WADA can appeal direct to CAS and does not have to exhaust all other appeal rights under the hearing process under the rules of the anti-doping organisation.[18]

Illustration

Appeal by Wada to CAS under Article 13.3 Failure to Give a Timely Decision at National Level

CAS 2011/A/2435, WADA v. Thys, Athletics South Africa and South African Institute for Drug-Free Sport T tested positive for norandrosterone after the Seoul Marathon. The A sample result was confirmed by B sample analysis in April 2006. The analysis was carried out in a laboratory in Korea. Athletics South Africa (ASA) commenced disciplinary proceedings against T in September 2006, and gave a decision in December 2008 that T had committed a violation. No reason or analysis was given in its decision. T appealed to CAS, which upheld the appeal on the grounds that there had been a breach by the laboratory of the applicable provisions under the ISL which prevented the same analyst from carrying out elements of both the A and the B sample analysis. ASA appealed to the Swiss Supreme Court, which set aside the CAS award on the basis that the applicable rules provided on their proper interpretation for an appeal to the South African Institute for Drug-Free Sport (SAIDS), not to CAS. In May 2010, T filed an appeal against the ASA decision to SAIDS. T made numerous requests to SAIDS to proceed with his appeal, to no avail. After

---

17 Article 13.3. For an example of the use of this power by WADA, see *WADA* v. *Thys*, next.
18 Article 13.1.3.

eight months, WADA wrote to the minister responsible for SAIDS, asking for a hearing date to be set within twenty-one days. WADA wrote to the minister because he was responsible for appointing an Appeal Panel for SAIDS and no members had been appointed. The letter was copied to SAIDS. By the time WADA filed its appeal to CAS, no steps had been taken to set a hearing date. After the filing of the appeal, members of an Appeal Panel were appointed and procedural directions for the hearing of T's appeal by the Panel were made.

CAS held that it had jurisdiction to hear the appeal by WADA under Article 13.3. It interpreted and applied Article 13.3 in the light of its general purpose of safeguarding the rights of an athlete to a timely hearing while allowing internal procedures to operate, if possible. It rejected the submission by SAIDS that the letter from WADA did not trigger the appeal rights of WADA under Article 13.3 because it did not impose a deadline for a decision but simply referred to setting a hearing date. The fact that SAIDS could say that the failure to provide a hearing was the result of the failure of the minister to appoint panel members was irrelevant. The only relevant consideration was whether there had been a failure to provide a timely hearing process as requested. On the substance of the appeal, the Panel held after reviewing the documentary material which had been before CAS on the first hearing and the earlier CAS decision that there had been a breach of the ISL same-analyst provision which applied at the time of the testing that ASA and SAIDS could not establish that the breach of the ISL did not undermine the validity of the adverse analytical finding. As a result, the ASA decision was again set aside.

Appeals against Provisional Suspension

Article 13 provides for appeals against provisional suspension.[19] The only person entitled to appeal against the imposition of a provisional suspension is the athlete or person who is subject to the provisional suspension.[20] Where the decision appealed against is a failure to comply with Article 7.9 and impose a provisional suspension, the full range of persons entitled to appeal under Article 13.2.3 will be entitled to appeal – the position will differ depending on whether the appeal is to CAS or to a national-level appeal body, as set out later.

19 See Article 7.5 of the Code for the general provisions relating to provisional suspension. See also Chapter 7, pages 310–12.
20 Article 13.2.3.

Cross-appeals

Article 13.2.4 makes express provision that a Respondent named in an appeal which has rights of appeal under Article 13 is entitled to file a cross-appeal or an appeal in relation to the award appealed against. This right can be exercised at any time until the Respondent files its answer to the appeal. This provision was included to allow for a cross-appeal where CAS procedural rules did not permit a cross-appeal after the time for an appeal has expired.

Persons Entitled to Appeal

Where appeals involve international athletes, the following parties can appeal:

- the athlete or other person who is the subject of the decision;
- the relevant international federation;
- the NADO of the athlete's country or residence, or of the countries where the athlete is a national or licence holder;
- the IOC or IPC, where the decision may affect the Olympic Games or Paralympic Games; and
- WADA.

Where appeals are at national level and made to a national-level appeal body, the parties which may appeal are as provided in the rules established by the NADO, but they must, at a minimum, include the athlete or other person who is the subject of the decision, the other party to the case, the relevant international federation, the NADO of the country where the athlete or person resides, the IOC or IPC (as applicable) where the decision may have an effect on the Olympic or Paralympic Games and WADA. Where there is a national-level appellate body, WADA, the IOC or IPC (where the decision has an effect on their respective Games) and the relevant international federation have a further right of appeal to CAS against the decision by the national-level appeal body. This further right will not be required where the national-level rules provide for the national-level appeal to be to CAS, as will often be the case.

TUE Appeals

The 2015 Code now provides that all appeals against TUE decisions will be exclusively dealt with under Article 4.4 of the Code. In general terms, where a TUE is not granted to an athlete who is not an international-level athlete, he or she will have appeal rights to a national-level appeal body. In national systems which have established a tribunal for the hearing of allegations under the Code, the appeal will generally be to that tribunal. It is submitted that the approach of this tribunal to an appeal should be the same as that which would be undertaken by CAS – namely, a full reconsideration of the application *de novo*.

Where an athlete enters a major event, an application for a TUE or for the recognition of a TUE will be made to the TUEC of the major event organisation. Appeals by an athlete against the failure to grant or recognise a TUE will be to the body established by the major event for the hearing of appeals – this is likely to be CAS. Where an international athlete applies for a TUE or the recognition of a TUE to the TUEC of his or her international federation, after any decision to decline an application or any application to WADA for review has been made, the appeal will be made to CAS by the athlete, his or her national anti-doping organisation or the relevant international federation.[21]

Other Appeals

Decisions made under Parts 3 and 4 of the Code are concerned with compliance with the Code by Signatories. Where consequences are imposed on a Signatory for non-compliance with obligations under the Code, an appeal can be made to CAS.[22] Where a laboratory has its accreditation revoked by WADA,[23] the laboratory can appeal exclusively to CAS.[24]

The appeal rights under Article 13 are intended to cover all decisions which can be made by anti-doping organisations in relation to anti-doping rule violations under the Code and the International Standards. The definition of 'consequences' under the Code means that all aspects of a decision relating to sanctions are capable of being appealed under Article 13.[25]

---

21 See Chapter 3, pages 112–24 for detail, including the appeal and review of TUE decisions under the ISTUE.
22 See Articles 13.6 and 13.7 and Parts 3 and 4 of the Code.
23 See Chapter 3 on the ISL, and pages 142–6.
24 See CAS 2010/A/2162, *Doping Control Centre Universiti Sains Malaysia* v. *WADA*, where a Malaysian laboratory appealed to CAS against the removal of its accreditation by WADA for non-compliance with the ISL, lack of awareness of relevant Technical Documents and the use of inappropriate methodologies which brought about false-positive results. On the appeal, the laboratory failed to show that, on the balance of probabilities, the decision to revoke by WADA was wrong.
25 See e.g. CAS 2007/A/1283, *WADA* v. *ASADA, AWF and Karapetyn* at pages 475–6.

Illustration

Ambit of Appeal Rights under the Code: Disqualification
of Results Part of the Consequences of an Anti-Doping
Rule Violation

CAS 2007/A/1283, WADA v. ASADA, AWF and Karapetyn K was
tested on 26 June 2005 at a weightlifting competition. There was no
adverse analytical finding at the time, but a year later the sample was re-
tested by a WADA laboratory at UCLA and an adverse analytical finding for BZP was obtained. BZP is a stimulant which, while not specifically listed on the Prohibited List at the time, would have been prohibited
as a substance with 'similar chemical structure or biological effect' as a
category S6 Stimulant.[26] The test came about as a result of information
supplied in a general investigation into doping in Australian weightlifting
which had been commissioned by ASADA (the statutory body responsible
for the investigation of anti-doping rule violations under the Australian
Sports Anti-Doping Act 2006). Before the further analysis, K had competed in the 2006 Commonwealth Games and won a gold medal. There
was no adverse analytical finding at an in-competition test at the Games,
nor from tests a month before and after the Games, when a screen was run
for BZP.

K was interviewed in the course of the general investigation into doping in the AWF and it transpired that he had been using the same supplement as four other weightlifters who had tested positive for BZP at the
time of the test on 26 June 2005. This supplement was contaminated. The
conclusion reached by the investigation was that this was an inadvertent
ingestion of the prohibited substance. K was advised of the adverse analytical finding in November 2006. There was no B sample available, and,
accordingly, the determination by ASADA was that there had been use of
a prohibited substance, as established by the test result and other information gathered. Subsequently, K was informed that the decision by ASADA
was that a doping violation had been committed, and that a sanction of
two years' ineligibility had to be imposed starting from 22 March 2006.
His result at the competition in June 2005 was disqualified, but ASADA
decided that the results from the time of the initial test until 22 March

---

26 By way of example for a further decision in which BZP was identified in a sample and
led to the finding that there was a violation under Article 2.1 with no grounds for any
reduction in the sanction applicable under the Code, see SDT 11/05, *NZFBB* v. *Ligaliga*.

2006, which included the Commonwealth Games result, were not disqualified. This decision took into account the nature of the substance, the circumstances in which the BZP had been ingested, the fact that the use of BZP would have been of no use in later competitions and the fact that, after the initial test, there were no further positive tests. ASADA made this decision on the basis that 'fairness required that the results not be disqualified under Article 10.7 of the Code'. K had rights to appeal to an Administrative Appeal Tribunal under the statutory system in Australia and to CAS. He accepted the sanction. WADA exercised its right to appeal under Article 13.2.3 of the Code, and the only issue before CAS was whether all results after the competition in which the positive test was ultimately returned had to be disqualified.

Was there a Right to Appeal?   ASADA submitted, first, that WADA had no right of appeal on the proper construction of Article 13.2 and, second, that if there was a right of appeal, then its decision not to disqualify the results from June 2005 was discretionary in nature and should not be set aside, as it had properly assessed a number of factors which were relevant to the exercise of its discretion.

WADA submitted that it had a right to appeal on the proper interpretation of Article 13 because the disqualification of results under Article 10.7 of the Code was one aspect of a decision as to the consequences of an anti-doping rule violation. This followed from the definition of 'consequences' under the Code. WADA further submitted that the disqualification of results should be a rule where a violation was established, unless there were reasons such as a finding of no significant fault or a voluntary withdrawal from competition which would support a decision not to disqualify further results.

CAS held that WADA did have a right to appeal because the disqualification of results was one part of the decision as to the consequences of an anti-doping rule violation. However, there was no 'rule' governing the disqualification of results after a positive test as contended by WADA, and CAS decided that the decision by ASADA, which was an exercise of discretion based on a number of factors which could legitimately be considered as relevant to the question whether fairness required the disqualification of results after a positive test, should not be interfered with and set aside.[27]

27 This aspect of the decision would not now, it is submitted, be followed, given the many
    CAS awards confirming the *de novo* nature of CAS appeal hearings and the confirmation
    of the nature of the appeal hearing in Articles 13.1.1 and 13.1.2.

International-level Appeals: Tribunal

Where cases arise from an international event or involve an international athlete, any appeal against a decision by a tribunal at first instance is exclusively made to CAS under Article 13.2.1, wherever the first-instance hearing takes place. The hearing of the appeal will be by CAS in its Appeals Division, in accordance with the CAS Procedural Rules.

National-level Appeals: Tribunal

For national-level athletes, where there is no right of appeal available under Article 13.2.1 (which allows for an appeal to CAS by a national-level athlete where the decision appealed against, while involving a national-level athlete, was made in connection with an international event), a Signatory may provide for an appeal to an independent and impartial body established by the relevant NADO, provided the principles for a fair hearing set out in Article 8 of the Code are respected.[28] The notes to Article 13.2.2 Code provide that the national-level appeal right may also be given by appeal on the part of the national-level athlete to CAS.[29] This provision offers different ways in which an appeal right can be provided to athletes or other persons who do not have an appeal under Article 13.2.1. While the way that this appeal right is conferred is not set down, the obligation to provide this right to appeal to a tribunal which is impartial and independent of the NADO is mandatory. This appears to be confirmed by the notes to the Article, which say that anti-doping organisations 'may elect to comply' with the provision.

WADA Appeals

The extension of the appeal rights at national and international level to non-parties in a manner which would not usually be available in respect of a decision in the courts provides a mechanism by which anti-doping organisations, in particular WADA, may appeal decisions in the interest of the consistent application of the Code. WADA has exercised this appeal right to challenge decisions made by national and international tribunals which it considers have not properly interpreted and applied the Code.

---

28 See Article 13.2.2 and Chapter 7, pages 321–7 for the obligations in relation to hearings.
29 This approach has been adopted in some jurisdictions and in the rules of many sporting organisations, e.g. New Zealand, where the decisions of the Sports Tribunal are subject to appeal to CAS.

By way of example, WADA has brought several appeals against decisions concerning the application of Articles 10.5.1 and 10.5.2 of the Code by tribunals,[30] and has appealed against decisions relating to the interpretation of the International Standards.[31] This broadening of the scope of parties with appeal rights under the Code cannot, on its proper interpretation, be seen as providing a CAS Panel with jurisdiction to make orders binding on a party with such appeal rights which does not agree to be joined to a CAS proceeding on appeal between two other parties because such an exercise would be beyond the scope of the agreement by which participants are bound to the Code.[32]

As the notes to the Code make clear, there is nothing to prevent a sporting organisation which is bound by the Code from implementing a rule which selects CAS as the tribunal in which allegations will be heard at first instance. If this approach is adopted, the agreement to refer allegations under the Code to CAS will mean that they will be heard under the Rules of the Code of Sports Related Arbitration applicable to proceedings in the CAS Ordinary Division. Where an international athlete is involved in such a hearing, the athlete must, under the Code, have a right to appeal to a CAS Panel in the Appeal Division. Where the process concerns a national-level athlete, there must be a right of appeal to satisfy the Code (and, it is submitted, general principles of natural justice). If CAS is chosen by the NADO to hear the allegation in its Ordinary Division at first instance, there should, it is suggested, be an appeal to CAS in its Appeal Division in order to provide for a consistent approach. As has been noted, where the first hearing for a national-level athlete takes place before a tribunal established by the sporting organisation or NADO, an appeal right may be provided for by rules giving an appeal either to a national appeal tribunal (which respects the principles of a fair hearing set out in Article 13.2.2) or to CAS.

30 For some examples of WADA appeals in relation to the sanctions imposed under Article 10.4 of the 2009 Code and in relation to the consideration of the defences under Articles 10.5.1 and 10.5.2 of the 2004 and 2009 Codes, see case summaries in Chapter 8, e.g. *Contador* (pages 385–90), *Stanic* (pages 384–5); and *Hardy* (pages 413–14), as well as *Eder* in Chapter 10 (pages 510–11).

31 See e.g. CAS 2005/A/908, *WADA v. Wium* and *IPC v. WADA and Brockman* in Chapter 3, page 121. The legal section of the WADA website provides the full text of the decisions in which WADA has exercised its rights of appeal.

32 See CAS awards, such as CAS 2009/A/1870, *USADA v Hardy* (Chapter 8, pages 413–14), in which athletes sought to challenge the validity of IOC By-law 45 in proceedings where the IOC was not a party and expressly declined an invitation to be joined.

CAS Approach to Appeals

As already outlined, CAS Panels have approached appeals in relation to anti-doping violations under the Code as full re-hearings on both the facts and the law, relying on the powers contained in Rule 57 of the Code. This approach has been emphasised by CAS Panels in appeals where the appellant claims that that there has been a breach of rights to a fair hearing in the tribunal below. The approach to appeals in many court systems, which involves, in general terms, an appellant having to establish that the court below has proceeded in a manner which can be characterised as wrong as a matter of legal principle, has not been adopted by CAS in its appeal jurisdiction in doping matters. It is submitted that it is open for national-level appeals to be available on a more limited basis, with narrower grounds, if the national anti-doping organisation wishes to adopt such an approach in the relevant rules.

The approach taken by CAS to appeals in relation to the grant or refusal of TUEs appeared to be an exception to the approach which involved a full re-hearing. In such cases, CAS Panels appeared not to be prepared to interfere with what was considered an expert determination as to the appropriateness of the grant or refusal of a TUE, unless it could be shown that the expert determination had been made on a wrong principle (usually, in this kind of case, a wrong interpretation of the applicable International Standard). This approach was, however, not accepted by the CAS Panel in *Berger* v. *WADA*,[33] and the Panel held that it could and should consider and assess the medical evidence which was relevant to the grant of a TUE. That approach has been followed in a more recent CAS award and should now be regarded as the established approach on TUE appeals.[34]

The provisions of Articles 13.1.1 and 13.1.2 of the 2015 Code make it clear that the same approach based on full review should be applied on any appeal to CAS under the Code or International Standards. The approach adopted in some CAS awards, such as *WADA* v. *ASADA AWF and Karapetyn*,[35] where the CAS Panel adopted a more limited deferential approach to the appeal brought by WADA against a decision not to disqualify an athlete's results as a matter of fairness under Article 10.7 and considered whether the appellant had shown that the decision had been made on a wrong basis, cannot be adopted. Similarly, while there are

---

33 See Chapter 3, pages 122–4.   34 *CAS2013/A/3437 ISSF* v. *WADA*.
35 See pages 475–6 for a summary of the decision.

CAS awards which hold that a sanction imposed by a sporting disciplinary body properly exercising its discretion under the applicable rules can only be reviewed when the sanction is evidently grossly disproportionate to the offence, it is submitted that the proper approach to such appeals is for CAS to consider any appeal *de novo* under Rule 57 and consider whether the sanction is, in its view, correct.[36]

In the *Valverde* proceedings,[37] the CAS Panel, after deciding that a national body had wrongly decided not to start proceedings in relation to an anti-doping rule violation, went on to consider the evidence presented in support of the alleged violation and to decide that a violation had been committed by V. An appeal to the Swiss Supreme Court was dismissed and, on this aspect of the CAS decision, the court was of the view that the arbitration agreement which bound V to the CAS process and Code gave CAS complete discretion under Rule 57 to consider the facts and law in the case and to proceed to rule on the allegation, even though the Spanish sporting body had declined to commence proceedings and had not considered the facts and law relevant to the substantive allegation. The *Valverde* award and the decision in the Swiss Supreme Court were relied on by the CAS Panel in *WADA and UCI v. Ullrich*, where the Panel rejected the argument that continuing to determine the merits of an allegation (as opposed to directing the matter back to a national tribunal for further consideration) after a finding that there was no jurisdiction had been reversed was contrary to Swiss law.

Although the terms of Rule 57 of the CAS Procedural Rules do not make a re-hearing mandatory, but rather provide for the full power to re-hear a matter on the facts and law, the approach to CAS appeals in cases under the Code is well established and has been confirmed by the provisions introduced into Article 13 in the 2015 Code. The policy factors supporting this *de novo* approach to appeals are the need to ensure that an athlete has a hearing before a tribunal which is not established by his or her sporting body and is independent of it, and the need to ensure that CAS has the opportunity to review all facts and law on decisions on appeal in order to make sure that the Code is interpreted and applied correctly and consistently. The general approach to appeals

---

36 As noted earlier at page 469, note 15, any element of deference can only operate to prevent a CAS Panel making fine adjustments to a period of ineligibility which has been reached in a well-reasoned decision.

37 See Chapter 2, pages 82–7.

by CAS is now very well established. While it may come under some pressure as the CAS workload and the range and complexity of first-instance hearings increase, with tribunals considering more allegations relating to violations which do not require a positive test and involve a wider range of evidence on questions such as proof of intentional conduct, any change would require express changes to the CAS Procedural Rules and the Code. With the introduction of provisions in Article 13 of the 2015 Code which clearly underline the *de novo*, no-deference approach to appeals to CAS under the Code, any change at any stage involving specific amendment to the Code and/or CAS Procedural Rules is very unlikely.

Jurisdiction to Revise CAS Awards

As the Code notes, appeals beyond CAS are not the subject of provisions under the Code and will be governed by the law applicable to the annulment and enforcement of arbitration awards. Appeals from CAS will generally be to the Swiss Federal Tribunal, on limited grounds.[38] In addition to the right to appeal, it should be noted that it may be possible for a party to an award to seek to have a final CAS award reviewed and revised by CAS or the Swiss Federal Tribunal. While PILA contains no provision for the revision of arbitral awards, the gap has been filled by case law in the Swiss Federal Tribunal, which has recognised this extraordinary legal remedy of revision of an arbitral award.[39] Revision allows for the reconsideration of an award by a court in exceptional circumstances where the award would otherwise relate to matters which had been finally decided and were *res judicata*. A CAS Panel has also held that it is able to reconsider an award in the light of new factual material where the parties have entered into an agreement which provides for a review of the award. The jurisdiction of the Swiss Federal Tribunal will be available if the parties do not agree to CAS having jurisdiction to review and if CAS refuses to consider a request for a review. Revision will only be possible where the award is subsequently shown to be materially affected by criminal conduct (e.g. sabotage of the source of a prohibited substance by a third party, testimony by witnesses who have been bribed to give evidence, forged documents) to the detriment of the party applying for the review, or where relevant material evidence or facts are discovered after the award is given which could not have been found at the time of trial but which existed at the time of the first-hearing process.[40] The new material must be significant and must be capable of altering the award in favour of the party applying for revision. Where the court grants a request for revision, it will not decide the matter itself but will send it back to the arbitral tribunal for a decision in the light of the review.

40 For more on the jurisdiction to revise final CAS awards, see Antonio Rigozzi, 'Challenging Awards of the Court of Arbitration for Sport', *Journal of International Dispute Settlement* 1(1) (2010), 217–65, at 255–62.

10

Appeals to the Swiss Supreme Court from CAS, Challenges to the Code in the Courts and Civil Claims outside the Code

Challenges to Anti-doping Regimes before the Code

Before the advent and adoption of the Code, legal challenges were occasionally made by athletes to the enforceability of doping rules and regulations implemented by sporting organisations before national courts and before supranational tribunals and courts, such as the European Court of Justice. The challenges sought to invoke a range of arguments, which were united by the contention that the anti-doping rules in issue should not be enforced because they were contrary to the fundamental individual rights and freedoms which were protected by national or international constitutional provisions or by general principles of national and international law.

Fundamental rights such as the right of the individual to work, to privacy, not to be punished without fault, to equal treatment, not to be subjected to discrimination and to be protected by national legal rules were relied on to challenge the enforceability of the strict liability 'no fault' regime common in anti-doping rules.[1] Principles of competition law protecting individuals from anti-competitive conduct and agreements and from restrictions on the freedom to work and provide services, and

---

1 See e.g. the early decisions in the German courts, such as *Krabbe* v. *IAAF*, where K successfully challenged the then period of ineligibility under the IAAF Rules of four years before the German courts on the grounds that it was an unfair restriction on the ability of an athlete to earn his or her living and was a disproportionate response to a doping violation, or *Baumann* v. *IAAF*, OLG Frankfurt am Main, 2 April 2002, where the German court held that a competition ban on B was contrary to the same principles where B was suspended from his work without fault. B's appeal to CAS in the Ad Hoc Division to reverse the decision of the IOC not to permit him to participate in the Olympics (in which he relied on the decision of the German court) was unsuccessful. CAS noted that the result under the applicable sport rules could well be different from that which had been produced by the German court, and held that there was no proper reason to set aside a decision which was based on the anti-doping policy which the athlete was bound by in entering the Olympic Games (see CAS Ad Hoc OG Sydney 2000/006, *Baumann* v. *IOC, NOC of Germany, and IAAF*, CAS Digest II, p. 633).

common law contractual principles protecting individuals from restrictions in restraint of trade, were also relied on to contend that periods of ineligibility should be set aside.[2] Such challenges go beyond questions concerning the interpretation of the anti-doping rules in question (or, indeed, challenges to the fairness of the hearing process) and seek to set aside the provisions of rules on the ground that, while their terms may be clear and the subject of agreement, they infringe fundamental rights and should not, as a result, have legal effect.

Any regime, such as that implemented under the Code, which functions by agreements made at national and international level binding on individuals, cannot escape the possibility of challenge by reference to the legal principles which protect the fundamental rights of individuals under national and international law where those principles are potentially applicable to the regime. Challenges of the kind set out in the preceding paragraphs have been and continue to be made by athletes and others, both after they have been subject to a CAS award imposing the penalty under the Code and where they face the prospect of such an award being made against them.

The most recent significant challenge came before the German courts in *Claudia Pechstein v. DESG and ISU*.[3] Ms Pechstein brought a civil claim relating to the damage which she claimed had been done to her reputation and career. She claimed that the period of ineligibility imposed under the Code by a CAS award in 2009, which had been confirmed on appeal to the Swiss Federal Tribunal, was illegal under German law.

The Munich Higher Regional Court rejected an application to stay the civil claim on the grounds that it had been the subject of a CAS award which had been confirmed in subsequent appeals to the Swiss Federal Tribunal. It held that the agreement to CAS jurisdiction was contrary to EU competition law and that as a result, the arbitration award was unenforceable. On appeal, the German Federal Court of Justice allowed the appeal by the ISU. The court held that CAS was a court of arbitration under German law, that there was no breach of national competition law in requiring

---

2 See e.g. *Johnson v. Athletics Canada and IAAF*, 25 July 1997, Ontario Court (General Division) (restraint of trade at common law) and *Wilander v. Tobin* [1997] 2 Lloyd's Rep 296; *Meca-Medina and Majcen v. Commission of European Communities and Republic of Finland*, Case C-519/04 P, European Court of Justice. (See pages 503–4, where the fundamental freedoms of Articles 49 and 81–82 of the EC Treaty were held to be potentially applicable to anti-doping regimes; these are now Articles 101 and 102 of the Treaty on the Functioning of the European Community.)
3 See pages 513–17 for summary and comment.

an athlete to sign an arbitration agreement referring anti-doping issues to CAS and that the arbitration agreement was valid under German law. This long-running case has produced much comment. As with earlier challenges to the arbitral system applicable under the Code, the challenge was unsuccessful and the outcome has reinforced the important central role of arbitration before CAS under the Code. The decision and related comment did, however, highlight the need for the procedure before CAS to be reviewed regularly to ensure that it meets the expectations and needs of all users.[4]

It is submitted that the decision and reasoning in the *Pechstein* case generally reflect the consensus that a form of arbitral system such as that provided by CAS represents the best way for sport to administer the Code worldwide. States are fully committed to support the Code and CAS under the UNESCO Convention.

Before looking at the broader challenges to the operation of the Code which have been and may be made in national courts and supranational tribunals and courts, this chapter will consider the way in which the Code has been drafted and amended with fundamental rights in mind, and how decisions made under the Code by CAS can be challenged in the Swiss courts on the basis of principles protecting fundamental human rights under Swiss law.

The Code and Fundamental Rights Generally

To an extent, the provisions of the 2004 Code, in particular Articles 10.5.1 and 10.5.2, which introduced an element of flexibility into the sanction regime, were drafted with such possible challenges in mind. At the time of the development of the draft Code, WADA commissioned a legal opinion to consider the compatibility of the Articles of the Code with certain fundamental principles of international human rights.[5] Since the adoption of

4 As the *Pechstein* case proceeded through the courts, ICAS made some amendments to the system for appointing arbitrators. While the process of appointing arbitrators was not found to have insufficient guarantees to protect the rights of athletes, the amendments were a response to criticism of the appointment process. See Chapter 1, pages 26–7 for a summary of the role of ICAS and of recent amendments to the way in which it appoints arbitrators to the CAS List.
5 There are now five legal opinions on the WADA website which consider the compatibility of the Code with fundamental human rights. The most recent, by Jean-Paul Costa (a former judge and President of the ECHR), concerns the compatibility of certain provisions of draft 3.0 of the 2015 Code with accepted principles of international law and human rights (Costa, 'Legal Opinion'). This opinion examines the initial question whether the Code's provisions

the Code and its subsequent amendment by the 2009 Code, there have been further challenges relying on similar grounds, both before CAS and to the Swiss courts, in proceedings to annul CAS arbitration awards under Swiss law. In these cases, it has been contended that the Code's provisions are inconsistent with the fundamental protections under the legal system which applies to the substantive dispute before CAS or under the system which is applicable to a challenge to a CAS award.[6] It is to be anticipated that athletes (and others who are subject to allegations under the Code) will continue to resist findings and sanctions before tribunals and CAS on the basis that the processes under the International Standards and/or the provisions of the Code contravene fundamental human rights protected by law. An important difference, which has already been noted, is

are criminal or civil, then considers whether the amendments in the 2015 Code are compatible with fundamental rights in relation to eight questions. His opinion is favourable save in relation to the then draft of Article 10.9 (subsequently amended in the final 2015 Code). The earlier opinions were particularly concerned with the provisions for fixed periods of ineligibility regardless of fault, the principle of strict liability and the provisions by which the onus to provide evidence in support of matters justifying the reduction of the period of ineligibility falls on the athlete. See Gabrielle Kaufmann-Kohler, Giorgio Malinverni and Antonio Rigozzi, 'Advisory Opinion for WADA' on the compatibility of the draft 2004 WADA Code (in particular Articles 2.1, 9 and 10 of the Code) with commonly accepted principles of international law and human rights; see also the further opinion requested by WADA, Claude Rouiller, 'Opinion on the Compatibility of Article 10.2 with the Fundamental Principles of Swiss Domestic Law', 25 October 2005. This opinion concerns the question whether the Code would be contrary to Swiss law to the extent that a Swiss judicial authority considering the Code on an appeal would not apply it, even where the parties to the dispute had agreed to its application. The same approach was adopted by WADA in relation to the 2007 Code amendments which became the 2009 Code and their compatibility with fundamental rights. An opinion on the enforceability of Article 10.6 of the 2009 Code, which allowed for an increase in the standard period of ineligibility from two to four years, is on the WADA website; see Gabrielle Kaufmann-Kohler and Antonio Rigozzi, 'Conformity of Article 10.6 of the 2007 Draft World Anti-Doping Code with Fundamental Rights of Athletes'. For a further legal opinion concerning the specific question of the compatibility of the Code's provisions with fundamental general principles of law, see Antonio Rigozzi, 'Conformity of the Exclusion of Team Athletes from Organised Training during their Period of Ineligibility with Swiss Law, including General Principles of Proportionality and Equal Treatment', 9 July 2008 on the WADA website. See Chapter 8, pages 451–4 for the effect of ineligibility on athletes and other persons who commit anti-doping rule violations and for the specific provisions relating to athletes returning to training.

6 For examples of the arguments before CAS, see 2006/A/1102, *Eder* v. *Ski Austria* and 2007/A/131, *Adams* v. *CCES* (see pages 511–13). In the CAS hearings and court proceedings in the Swiss Courts concerning the positive test returned by the Swiss cyclist Daniel Hondo, H challenged the WADA Code provisions. The arbitration was domestic in nature because the parties were all resident in Switzerland. The Swiss courts dismissed the argument that the Code's provisions were in breach of fundamental rights and infringed the principle of proportionality, both at first instance and on appeal.

that where there has been agreement to the Code, challenges to decisions made by national-level tribunals or by CAS under the Code should generally be governed by the principles applicable to challenges to arbitration awards, rather than the general principles relating to the review of decisions by domestic tribunals. In many cases which come before CAS, Swiss law will be applicable to any argument that the Code's provisions breach fundamental rights, because most international sporting federations have their headquarters in Switzerland and will have rules which are expressly or impliedly subject to Swiss law. Appeals from CAS awards will be governed by the principles applicable to challenges to arbitration awards under Swiss law.[7] The adoption of the Code, which includes the mandatory provisions for appeals to CAS, has created a defined procedural structure, with challenges to decisions under the Code ultimately being by way of proceedings in the Swiss Supreme Court (the Swiss Federal Tribunal) to annul CAS awards (where the CAS award has the characteristics of an international arbitration award). This replaces the situation which existed before the Code, where challenges to decisions under sports anti-doping rules were made under various national legal systems.

Challenges to CAS Awards: Appeals to the Swiss Supreme Court

Proceedings before CAS, whether in the Ordinary or the Appeals Division, will, where there has been an agreement to submit anti-doping rule violations under the Code to CAS, be arbitral proceedings, and the seat of the arbitration will, under the CAS Rules, be Lausanne, Switzerland, wherever the tribunal in fact sits to hear the dispute.

Notwithstanding the seat of the arbitration, the principles of several legal systems may possibly be relevant to different aspects of the arbitration. Different legal systems may govern the capacity of the parties to enter into an arbitration agreement, the question whether there is an agreement, the performance of the arbitration agreement, the existence and proceedings of an arbitral tribunal, the substantive issues in dispute[8] and the law

---

7 See further pages 490–2.
8 In CAS hearings in the doping area, where disputes involve the interpretation and application of the Code, it is unlikely that the application of the principles of a particular legal system in this area will make a difference to the outcome. Principles of interpretation are broadly similar across many jurisdictions (both civil and common law), and in any event, as is outlined in Chapter 4, the Code expressly provides that questions of interpretation under the Code should not be approached by reference to the existing laws of Signatories or governments.

governing the enforcement of an award.[9] However, the legal system which will exercise jurisdiction over a CAS arbitration regarding procedure and challenges to an award will generally be the law of Switzerland, as the law of the seat of any CAS arbitration.[10] Challenges to CAS awards will generally be made to the Swiss Courts, whether the award is domestic or international. Where a CAS award is an international award, under Swiss law the Swiss Federal Supreme Court will hear any application to set the award aside.

In recent years, there has been a significant increase in the number of applications to the Swiss Federal Supreme Court seeking to set aside CAS awards. While the grounds for possible challenge are narrow under Swiss law, an application to the Swiss Supreme Court represents the last opportunity for appeal for a party subject to a CAS award which is an international award. The substantive grounds for an application to annul such a CAS award are contained in Part 12 PILA. The procedural requirements for an application to annul an award are set out in the Supreme Court Act (SCA).

Grounds to Set Aside a CAS Award

Under PILA, an international arbitration is defined as an arbitration where one of the parties does not have its place of residence or domicile in Switzerland.[11] An international arbitration award is final when communicated, and an annulment of the award can only be sought on the basis[12] that:

- a sole arbitrator was not properly appointed or the arbitral tribunal was not properly constituted;
- the arbitral tribunal wrongly held that it did or did not have jurisdiction;
- the arbitral tribunal went beyond the claims submitted to it or failed to rule on one of the claims;
- the principle of equal treatment of the parties or their right to be heard was violated; or
- the award is incompatible with Swiss public policy (*ordre public*).

9 See *Naviera Amazonia Peruana SA* v. *Compania Internacional de Seguros del Peru* [1988] 1 Lloyd's Rep 116 at 121.
10 See CAS Code of Sports Related Procedure, Rule 28.
11 Article 176 PILA 1987 amended 2014.   12 See Article 190 PILA.

Any application to set aside an international arbitration award can only be made to the Swiss Federal Supreme Court. The grounds to annul an award in PILA reflect the grounds in the UNCITRAL Model Law, which has been adopted by legislation in many jurisdictions. Similar grounds will be relevant in relation to the enforcement of foreign arbitral awards in States which have acceded to the New York Convention.[13] In considering an application to set aside an award, the Swiss Supreme Court will generally not enter into factual matters but will decide an application to annul an international award on the facts recorded in the award.

Recognition and Enforcement of Awards

Where the New York Convention applies, the courts of a country can only refuse to recognise or enforce an award where:

- a party to the arbitration agreement was acting under some incapacity;
- the arbitration agreement is not enforceable under either the law to which the parties have subjected it or, if there is no choice of law, under the law of the country where the award is made;
- the party against whom the award was made was not given proper notice of the appointment of an arbitrator or of the arbitral proceedings, or was otherwise unable to present its case;
- the award deals with a dispute not within the scope of the arbitration agreement;
- the composition of the arbitration tribunal or tribunal procedure was not in accordance with the agreement of the parties, or, failing such agreement, was not in accordance with the law of the country where the arbitration took place; or
- the award is not binding or has been set aside.

These matters have to be established by the person against whom it is sought to enforce the award.

The award will also not be recognised or enforced where the court finds that the subject matter of the dispute is not capable of settlement by arbitration under the law of the country where it is sought to enforce the award, or where the recognition or enforcement of the award would be contrary to the public policy of the country where it is sought to enforce

---

13 For a detailed consideration of the criteria for challenging CAS awards and the applicable procedural rules, see Rigozzi, 'Challenging Awards'.

the award. This last ground is of potential relevance in considering challenges to the enforcement of CAS awards, and it was the basis for the claim that the CAS award could not be relied on to stay the civil claim for damages brought in the German courts by the athlete in the *Pechstein* case. However, generally, CAS awards have immediate effect in the world of sport, and challenges at the stage of enforcement have been very rare.

Applications to Annul CAS Awards before the Swiss Federal Supreme Court

The challenges to CAS awards which have been made to the Swiss Federal Supreme Court have involved arguments that the CAS Panel lacked jurisdiction, that there were doubts about the independence of the arbitrators, that the Panel was not properly constituted, that there had been a breach of the rights of a party to be heard and that the award was incompatible with Swiss public policy. While applications have only rarely been successful, there has been a significant increase in applications to annul CAS awards, and the writer of a recent article on the topic estimated that applications concerning CAS awards made up over fifty per cent of the work of the court in relation to international arbitration.[14] Under Swiss law, an award will only be contrary to public policy if it is contrary to fundamental legal principles in a way which is incompatible with the Swiss legal and economic system. The concept of public policy covers fundamental principles of justice which are recognised as underlying any system of law according to the prevailing understanding in Switzerland. The notion of public policy has been held to encompass principles such as *pacta sunt servanda*, double jeopardy, *ne bis in idem*,[15] the principle of good faith, the prohibition of expropriation without compensation, the prohibition against discrimination and the protection of minors and other persons capable of legal acts. It is important to note that the principle of *pacta sunt servanda* in the context of public policy does not bring errors of contractual interpretation within the grounds for the annulment of an international arbitration award. The principle only provides a ground to set aside an award where a

---

14 Ibid.
15 In applications for the annulment of two CAS awards in the *Valverde* case, the Supreme Court held that an allegation that the tribunal had been improperly constituted failed, and rejected claims that there had been a breach of public policy because V had been subject to punishment twice for the same infringement by being subject to two CAS proceedings – one relating to competition in Italy, the other affecting his eligibility worldwide (see decision 4A 386/2010). See summary in Chapter 2, pages 82–7.

tribunal makes a decision which ignores a contractual provision which it has held to be applicable or where it applies a contractual duty where it has held that none exists. Athletes have also sought to challenge the application of provisions of the Code, in particular the sanctions imposed, on the basis that they infringe the prohibition on discrimination and the principle of proportionality under Swiss law. While these two principles fall within the notion of public policy as a matter of Swiss law, the definition of 'discrimination' adopted by the Swiss Supreme Court is narrow, and only sanctions imposed which are wholly at odds with the principle of proportionality might constitute a violation of public policy. The general narrow nature of the concept of public policy explains why there has never been a successful challenge to a CAS award applying the Code based on a breach of public policy. The very rare successful challenges to CAS awards have involved a failure to consider arguments advanced by a party (involving a failure under Article 190(2)(d))[16] and a failure to establish that CAS had jurisdiction over the dispute under Article 190(2)(b).[17]

Where a CAS award is domestic in nature because all the parties have their domicile in Switzerland, a challenge to an award can only be made under Swiss law before the local court of the canton where the arbitration takes place, with an appeal from that court being made to the Swiss Federal Supreme Court. An award in a domestic arbitration under Swiss law can be set aside if it is arbitrary in the sense of being manifestly insupportable or seriously in violation of clear and undisputed legal principles or norms. This concept of arbitrariness is a rule of general conduct under Swiss law. While broader than the idea of a breach of public policy, it can only be established in cases where an award is manifestly at odds with the law and facts, not where it simply contains clear errors of fact and law. Any further appeal from the local court of the canton to the Federal Supreme Court will be on narrow grounds in separate proceedings.[18]

The result of the application of the Code is that an arbitration system has been created for the handling of doping disputes arising under the Code.

---

16 *X* v. *ATP Tour*, ATF 133 III 235. See page 494.

17 See *Busch*, and compare *Dodô*, both case summaries in Chapter 2, pages 72–6.

18 The grounds for appeal against a domestic arbitration award are contained in Article 36(f) of the Intercantonal Concordat on Arbitration. In *X* v. *WADA*, *UCI*, *Swiss Cycling Federation*, 4P.148/2006, reported in the *ASA Bulletin*, the Swiss Federal Supreme Court held that the notion of arbitrariness, while broader than the concept of public policy as it is relevant to challenges to international arbitration awards, did not extend the general protection of personality rights under Swiss law to the application of doping sanctions, provided that the fundamental principles of law – proportionality and equal treatment – were complied with.

While in the past, in many jurisdictions, challenges to sporting tribunals in anti-doping matters (or other areas) were based on grounds derived from public or administrative law (and courts in some jurisdictions were reluctant to entertain challenges to what were termed the 'decisions' of domestic tribunals), such challenges are now likely to be met with an application for a stay founded on an agreement to arbitrate and/or a claim that the challenge is wrongly founded. If a court finds that there is a binding arbitration agreement and national legislation has implemented the UNCITRAL Model Law, then a stay will be available to enforce the agreement. It should be noted that there may be aspects of disputes which arise as a result of anti-doping procedures and investigations under the Code or International Standards which fall outside the ambit of the arbitration agreement on the proper construction of that agreement. Where this is the case, parties will be able to bring claims in the national courts.[19]

Proportionality

The fundamental principle most relied on to support the argument that an anti-doping regime or a sanction is contrary to fundamental principles of law is that of proportionality. This principle was initially developed in civil law jurisdictions, but the concept now has a central place in human rights and administrative law in many civil and common law jurisdictions. A long line of CAS awards has developed and applied the principle of proportionality in cases involving sanctions in sport in a general way, and in general terms the principle provides that sanctions must be proportionate to the offence committed under the rules of the sporting association.

The principle of proportionality has been regularly referred to in the context of challenges to the operation of the anti-doping regime under the Code, and is now specifically referred to in the Code in its Introduction and in certain substantive provisions.[20] The question referred to in the decisions of CAS and the Swiss Supreme Court is whether the limits imposed by the Code are a proportionate interference with fundamental individual rights. General arguments relying on the principle to contend that the Code's provisions breach individual rights in a fundamental way have been consistently rejected.

19 See pages 517–30 for civil claims falling outside the Code.
20 See *FIFA and WADA*, CAS Advisory Opinion at pages 499–501. See also the Opinion by Professor Claude Rouiller on the compatibility of Article 10.2 of the Code with Swiss law, available on the WADA website.

The test whether a measure or rule is proportionate in the sense of not contravening fundamental rights can be summarised as follows:

- the restriction on the individual's rights in the rule must be appropriate and fit to achieve the aim it pursues;
- the restriction must be necessary in the sense that no lesser intrusion would achieve the desired aim;
- the restriction must be proportionate in the sense that it does not affect the interest of the individual in a disproportionate manner; and
- the restriction must be necessary in the sense of fulfilling a pressing social need.

As we have seen,[21] the principle of proportionality was relied on by CAS Panels before the adoption of the Code to justify reducing fixed sanctions in anti-doping regimes, and by the Swiss Federal Supreme Court in assessing the enforceability of anti-doping policies under Swiss law. From time to time, the principle is still invoked in support of a submission that the mandatory period of ineligibility under the Code should be further reduced in the particular circumstances of a case. In such cases, it is contended on behalf of the athlete that the imposition of the standard period of ineligibility has such an effect that it amounts to a violation of the individual's right to health and life, to proportionality of sanction and to equal treatment under Swiss law. As has been noted, such arguments, whether directed at the legality of the Code overall or at the effect of particular provisions of the Code in the particular circumstances of a case, have consistently been rejected by CAS[22] and the Swiss Federal Supreme Court (with one or two exceptions). The Supreme Court held in early decisions challenging the Code that the strict liability principles and the automatic consequences of doping in terms of the imposition of a period of ineligibility and loss of results did not constitute a breach of public policy under Swiss law. In addition, the fact that athletes may perceive that they are treated unequally by the operation of the Code's provisions does not amount to discrimination giving rise to a claim for breach of public policy.

---

21 See Chapter 1, pages 46–50.
22 See e.g. CAS 2010/A/2307, *WADA* v. *Jobson*, where arguments based on proportionality were put forward to challenge the imposition of the standard period of ineligibility of two years. In the recent *Sharapova* award, the Panel endorsed the established position that the Code's provisions on sanctions provide for proportionality in rejecting a claim that the period of ineligibility imposed should be reduced beneath the minimum period of twelve months required under Article 10.5.2, to eight months. See Chapter 8, pages 420–3 for case summary.

Illustrations

Challenge to a CAS Award to the Swiss Federal Supreme Court – Breach of the Right to be Heard

X v. ATP Tour, ATF 133 III 235   X appealed to the Supreme Court to set aside a CAS arbitration award under Article 190 PILA. The CAS tribunal had imposed a fifteen-month period of ineligibility on X under the Code where he had tested positive for a prohibited substance contained in a prescription for another player which he had mistakenly picked up and ingested. X had contended that the sanction imposed on him was contrary to the protection given to him under the law of Delaware, which was applicable to the rules of the ATP Tour. On the application, X submitted that he had been denied a proper hearing because the CAS Panel had not considered the arguments arising under the law of Delaware. The ATP Tour alleged that X had agreed that there would be no further appeal to CAS. This was based on a provision of the rules of the ATP Tour to which X had agreed.

The court held that the consent in the rules was indirect rather than an express exclusionary agreement and not sufficiently voluntary given the hierarchical nature of sports rules to amount to an agreement barring an appeal to the Supreme Court under Article 192 PILA. The court emphasised that this finding on the binding nature of a waiver of an appeal did not affect the general validity of arbitration agreements in sports rules or the liberal approach adopted to their interpretation. Accordingly, the consent was not effective to bar the appeal by the player.

After considering the award of CAS, the court held that on the face of the award, the Panel did not appear to have considered the argument raised under the law of Delaware, and accordingly X's right to be heard had been breached under Article 190(2)(iv). The CAS award was set aside and the matter remitted to CAS.

Challenge to CAS Award under the Code as Domestic Arbitration Award under Swiss Law

Hondo v. WADA, UCI and Swiss Olympic Association   H, a Swiss cyclist, tested positive for the stimulant carphedon. Initially, the Swiss Olympic Association tribunal imposed a two-year period of ineligibility, with one year of the period suspended. The suspension was removed on appeal by WADA to CAS, because there is no basis for such a suspension of part of a period of ineligibility under the Code. H appealed the CAS award to the court of the local canton under Swiss law. The court of the canton held that the decision of CAS in applying the strict liability provisions of the Code was not arbitrary in failing to have proper regard to fundamental protection under Swiss law and dismissed the appeal. A further appeal to the Swiss Federal Supreme Court was also dismissed.

Protection of Individual Personality Rights under Swiss Law

While it is conceivable that an infringement of the fundamental personality rights protected under Swiss law could give rise to a claim for breach of public policy in particular circumstances and provide the grounds on which to challenge an international arbitration award, the narrow scope of the concept of the breach of public policy as a ground of challenge means that this is unlikely. It is perhaps more likely that the protection of fundamental personality rights under Swiss law will be relied on by a person subject to an anti-doping rule violation who seeks to argue before the relevant arbitral tribunal that the doping regime and sanctions which he or she is bound by infringe those rights and are invalid as a matter of Swiss law.

Under Swiss law, individual personality rights are protected by Articles 27 and 28 of the Civil Code. The concept of personality rights includes the fundamental rights of an individual, such as physical integrity and the right to exercise a trade or profession. Article 27 prevents a person from wholly or partially renouncing his or her capacity to have personality rights and to effect transactions. A person cannot alienate his or her personal liberty, nor impose restrictions on the enjoyment of personality rights in a manner which is contrary to the law. Article 28 provides that a person who suffers an illegal infringement of personality rights can apply to a judge for protection against any third party participating in the infringement. An infringement will be illegal unless justified by consent, by overriding private or public interest or by law. In summary, Article 27 prevents individuals from contracting to remove certain fundamental rights, while Article 28 provides for protection against third parties infringing or participating in infringing personality rights.

The free acceptance of rules constituting an infringement of personality rights may justify the infringement. However, such a consent can amount to an excessive commitment which is not valid under Article 27. It can be argued that the one-sided nature of the relationship between an athlete and a sporting organisation means that the athlete has no real choice but to accept the sport's rules and that this removes any true consent by the athlete to the rules. The position on the effect of a consent to sporting rules on the justification for an infringement of personality rights has not been settled in the Swiss Supreme Court, because the court has found when the issue is raised that any infringement of personality rights under an anti-doping regime is likely to be justified on grounds of public interest in having a clear set of rules aimed at keeping sporting competition fair.

On any challenge under Swiss law based on the infringement of personality rights, the determining factor is likely to be whether the rules and any sanction imposed by them are justified by an overriding private or public interest. The Swiss Supreme Court has, in the context of doping rules in horse racing, held that a sanction imposed under a strict liability regime can be justified from the perspective of both the private interests of the sporting body and the wider public interest in having doping-free sport.[23] While this decision did not concern the justification for the Code, it seems likely that any intrusion by the Code on fundamental rights will be justified on a similar basis.

Sports' rules must not infringe fundamental principles of due process or fundamental principles protected under Swiss law. Due process or legality requires that the imposition of a sanction be based on a clear regulatory basis and that any person facing an anti-doping rule violation must have a fair hearing process. Swiss law also maintains fundamental principles of law: the principles of equality and proportionality. Even where a rule can be justified by public or private interest, it still has to be proportionate to the objective which it seeks to achieve if it is to comply with fundamental principles of law. A challenge based on a breach of these fundamental principles of law would fall within the grounds for an appeal against an international arbitration award as a breach of public policy recognised under Swiss law.

Generally, as noted, the Swiss Supreme Court has held that the Code's anti-doping rules represent a proportionate response to the problem of doping in sport. The right to equality of treatment might also be invoked. However, while the Code will give rise to different outcomes for different athletes in different sports, a breach of the principle of equality of treatment will be justified by the need to have an effective harmonised anti-doping regime. Unequal treatment, where justified on grounds of

---

23 See Swiss Federal Supreme Court, *Schafflützel and Zöllig* v. *Fédération Suisse de Courses de Chevaux*, ATF 134 III 193, where a challenge to the strict liability regime for doping in horse racing based on the argument that its provision infringed public policy was rejected. For case summary, see pages 497–9.

overriding public and private interest by the need for harmonisation, will not breach public policy.

Recently, in *Matuzalem* v. *FIFA*,[24] which did not concern a sanction under the Code but the imposition of a financial penalty by a sporting organisation, the Swiss Federal Supreme Court held that a FIFA financial sanction which in effect potentially prevented a player from exercising his profession for life was contrary to Swiss law and unenforceable because it interfered excessively with the player's economic freedom and professional life. This decision illustrates the kind of measure which might be held to be invalid as being in breach of fundamental protections under Swiss law.

Illustration

General Challenge to Anti-doping Rules in Sport on the Basis of Protection of Personality Rights under Swiss Law – Proportionate Response

Schafflützel and Zöllig v. *Fédération Suisse de Courses de Chevaux*, ATF 134 III 193   S and Z were the owner and trainer of a horse. The horse had been treated with a medicine for colic. A veterinary surgeon had advised that the horse could compete in the Swiss Derby, notwithstanding the treatment, because the medical literature indicated that the substance would have been eliminated from the horse's system by the time of the race. The horse won the race, but afterwards tested positive for the substance in the medication at a low level. The horse was disqualified, the prize money of CHF48 000 was forfeited and the trainer was fined CHF2000. This decision was taken under the rules of the Fédération Suisse de Courses de Chevaux (FSC), which impose strict liability for the presence of a prohibited substance in a horse's sample. The decision of the council of the FSC was confirmed by the Sporting Jury – the relevant appeal body within the FSC.

Z and S then brought proceedings in the Swiss courts seeking to set aside the penalties imposed. The local civil court set aside the decision and the fine, and ordered that the results stand, with the prize money to be paid to Z. This judgement was set aside in the Cantonal Appeal Tribunal, which reinstated the initial decision by the FSC.

Z and S appealed to the Swiss Federal Tribunal, asking for the decision in the local civil court to be reinstated. Z and S argued that the

24 Swiss Federal Court – 4A_558/2011. For case summary, see pages 501–2.

sanctions imposed on them were an illegal infringement of their personality rights and contravened Swiss public policy. In deciding that the sanctions imposed did not infringe personality rights, the Cantonal Tribunal had relied, to an extent, on the decisions of private sporting bodies applying the WADA Code, under which the taking of prohibited substances alone justified disqualification, even though no influence on performance could be established. The Cantonal Tribunal had also decided that, by taking part in the race, the owner and trainer had impliedly accepted the rules of the FSC, which were known to them. As a result, they had consented to an infringement of their rights under Article 28.2 of the Code Civil, which did not constitute an excessive agreement under Article 27 of the Code Civil.

The Swiss Federal Tribunal accepted the autonomy of the FSC as a private body dealing with its members, but held that this autonomy was limited in that the private rules of the FSC could not infringe fundamental principles – in particular, they could not infringe the personality rights of members under Articles 27 and 28 of the Code Civil. A judicial authority was free (subject to a margin of appreciation) to examine whether the rules did amount to an infringement of personality rights. Fundamental rights in sport at the higher level include the right to health and bodily integrity, the right to reputation and the right to develop and build a working career. In this case, it was clear that the forfeiture of prize money, the disqualification of the horse and the fine were sanctions which damaged the trainer and owner in their professional standing. The finding against the owner and trainer created the impression that the results had been obtained by inappropriate behaviour or forbidden methods. A person's individual dignity and reputation were affected by such findings. The sanctions imposed would be an infringement of the personality rights of the owner and trainer under Article 28.2 of the Code Civil, unless justified by the consent of the victim or by private or public interest or the law.

The tribunal then examined whether the infringement of personality rights could be justified. It concluded that the strict liability and sanctions regime was justified by the public interest in fighting doping and by the private interest of the sporting organisation and its members in having clear, readily applicable rules. The examination in every case of the potential effects of the substance detected in order to arrive at a particular sanction would open the door to endless disputes and create different treatments in different situations. Strict liability was a way of avoiding such differences. The need for an efficient anti-doping system overall was a stronger interest than that of the trainer and the owner, who wished to see a sanction imposed which took into account the potential influence of prohibited substances on performance. The tribunal also rejected the submission that the implementation of a threshold value for the presence of a substance before sanctions could be imposed would protect their personality rights. Such an amendment was not a matter for the tribunal but for the sporting authorities, on the basis of their own expert knowledge and advice. The court upheld the strict liability rules and sanction on the basis of the overriding public and private interest, and held that there was no illegal infringement of personality rights. As a result, there was no need to consider whether there was a binding consent by the owner and trainer to the rules which also justified the restriction on personality rights.

Results on Challenges

Generally, challenges to anti-doping regimes have not succeeded, sometimes on the grounds that the anti-doping regime is a private disciplinary regime consented to by the athlete which is not subject to control by the State courts by reference to fundamental constitutional principles, sometimes on the grounds that, while fundamental constitutional principles may be relied on in relation to private contractual rules, anti-doping regimes represent a proportionate response to the problem of doping in sport. The strength of the arguments depends, to a significant degree, on the extent and nature of the protection offered for fundamental rights in the legal system which applies to the issue, but, in many systems, the fact that a private association's rules are in issue does not prevent consideration of the question whether those rules are compatible with certain fundamental individual rights. In such legal systems, the legal position may well be that, as is the case under Swiss law, the rules of private associations are subject to the limits imposed by certain mandatory principles protecting fundamental rights, with the result that consent to the rules of a private association cannot be a complete answer to a claim that fundamental rights have been infringed.[25]

In *FIFA and WADA*,[26] CAS gave the opinion that the freedom of private associations to impose sanctions in accordance with its rules on members who had agreed to the application of those rules was subject, as a

---

25 For an example considering the legality of delegated legislation in a sporting context by reference to the New Zealand Bill of Rights Act, see *Cropp* v. *Judicial Committee* [2008] 3 NZLR 774. This is a decision in a common law jurisdiction which is similar to the decision in *Schafflützel and Zöllig* in the Swiss Federal Supreme Court.
26 Advisory Opinion, CAS 2005/C/976 and 986.

500 APPEALS TO THE SWISS SUPREME COURT FROM CAS

matter of Swiss law, to the principles of proportionality and equal treatment, the requirement that there be a measure of fault before a penalty can be imposed and the right to be protected against excessive violations of an individual's personality rights and excessive penalties or sanctions. The Panel found that the mandatory prohibition on excessive penalties could only be applicable if the sanction was 'evidently and grossly disproportionate in comparison with the proved rule violation[; only if the sanction was] ...considered as a violation of fundamental justice and fairness would the Panel regard the sanction as abusive, and, thus, contrary to Swiss Law'. The Panel gave the opinion that the Code's two-year fixed sanction did not infringe this fundamental protection.[27] If the Code's provisions do, *prima facie*, infringe a fundamental right or protection under an applicable legal principle, there is, it is submitted, great force in the argument that the provisions are a proportionate justifiable response to the problem of doping in sport. This is supported by the international consensus (represented by the Code and the Doping Convention) that has developed in recent years, which has been widely accepted by those involved in sport.

It is submitted that future challenges to the enforceability of the Code and the Standards are generally likely to be successfully resisted on the ground that infringements of personal liberty, privacy and economic freedom or other fundamental rights which athletes and others agree to in order to participate in sport can be justified and are proportionate in the context of the fight against doping in sport. This has been the general approach in the courts of Switzerland and in the European Court of Justice to date.[28] It must, however, also be observed that the more investigations into doping violations can be said to intrude into personal privacy, the more likely it becomes that a court may find that the processes infringe fundamental rights in a manner which cannot be justified, even where considerable deference must be given to the rights of private associations to regulate their affairs, and where the reason for the measures can be shown to have widespread support.[29] In providing his opinion in

27 The sanctions regime was held to be in accordance with Swiss law apart from a finding that the then unlimited time-frame for the commission of a second offence which could lead to a potential lifetime ban was an excessive commitment contrary to the Swiss Civil Code.
28 See e.g. *Meca-Medina* at pages 503–4.
29 Similarly, arguments based on fundamental rights may have greater chances of success where sporting organisations seek to impose penalties on athletes in addition to those which apply under the Code. An argument based on proportionality under Swiss law was advanced (but not ruled upon) before CAS in relation to IOC Rule 45, which barred athletes from competing in the Olympic Games if they had received a sanction under the Code of more than six months for an anti-doping rule violation under the Code by reason of the IOC rules; see further pages 523–4.

relation to the draft 2015 Code, Jean-Paul Costa discusses the questions posed regarding the compatibility of the Code with fundamental human rights. While the opinion is generally favourable on the proposed changes in the 2015 Code, it highlights how the principles protecting human rights have greater potential relevance where the rules of the Code can be seen as significantly interfering in the rights of the individual, and underlines the need to ensure that the Code maintains a proportionate response in such areas as testing athletes at any time of the day, the imposition of financial penalties, the length of sanctions and the duration of publication of decisions. Where the Code represents a response to the acknowledged serious problem of doping in sport and has significant international support both within sport and at State level, it will, it is submitted, only be a significant interference with personal freedoms which will bring these principles into play. The following recent decision provides an example of excessive interference with fundamental personal freedoms by sports rules which impose financial penalties.

Illustration

4A – 558/2011, *Silva Matuzalem* v. *FIFA 27 March 2012 Swiss Federal Tribunal* – Challenges to Financial Sanction

M entered into a contract to play for Shakhtar Donetsk. He terminated the contract without just cause or just sporting cause. He entered into a contract to play for Real Saragrossa FC. Real Saragrossa agreed to indemnify him for his breach. After an appeal to CAS, Shakhtar was awarded damages for breach of contract against M and Real Saragrossa in the sum of €11 million, plus interest. Neither the club nor M paid the sum awarded.

In disciplinary proceedings, the FIFA Disciplinary Chamber fined M and ordered that if he did not pay the sum outstanding in a period of thirty days, he would, on the application of the creditor, be subject to a worldwide ban on playing until the sum was paid. CAS upheld the orders on appeal.

M appealed to the Swiss Federal Tribunal on the grounds that the CAS award violated his right to be heard and public policy under 190 (2) PILA. The claim in relation to the right to be heard was rejected because it related only to the hearing before FIFA, with the result that the CAS appeal hearing *de novo* cured any defect.

As to the claim based on the infringement of public policy, the Swiss Federal Tribunal confirmed that public policy had both substantive and procedural aspects. The concept was applicable 'only where it disregards some fundamental legal principles and consequently becomes completely inconsistent with the important generally recognised values which according to dominant opinions in Switzerland should be the basis of any legal order'.

The Swiss Federal Tribunal set out a non-exhaustive list of fundamental principles which, if infringed, could constitute a breach of public policy: *pacta sunt servanda*, prohibition on abuse of rights, acting in good faith, prohibition on expropriation without compensation, prohibition on discrimination and protection of incapables. The right to exercise a profession was protected from grave violation under Art 27(2), and excessive limitation on personal freedom could amount to breach of public policy if not proportionate and justifiable. The right of an individual to physical integrity, freedom of movement, economic freedom and free exercise of an occupation were all protected from unjustifiable infringement by State actors or private persons. A person was protected from total limitation on his or her freedom by contractual curtailment of his or her economic freedom. A limited curtailment was also considered to be excessive if the foundation of the person's existence was jeopardised.

These principles applied to disciplinary provisions by a body like FIFA, as well as contractual stipulations. Measures taken by a federation which infringed the rights of members were only enforceable if they could be justified.

The Swiss Federal Tribunal held that the unlimited worldwide ban on M from all professional activities which would be triggered upon a request by Shakthar Donetsk if M did not pay €11 million plus interest disregarded the limits on excessive commitments under Art 27(2) BGB and could not be justified by the interest of FIFA in enforcing compliance by players with their obligations as employees, particularly where the ban would prevent M from being able to pay and it was very unlikely that M would be able to pay. The CAS award was set aside on the basis that it was in breach of public policy.

Examples of Challenges in the Courts to Anti-doping Regimes before the 2004 Code

Application of EU Law to Doping Regimes

Edwards v. British Athletics Federation and IAAF [1998] 2 CMLR 363

E, an amateur athlete banned for four years by the IAAF for a positive test for steroids, applied for reinstatement which would have remitted the last two years of his ban under IAAF Rules. This was refused, and E brought proceedings challenging the lawfulness of the refusal. Such remission had been granted to other athletes in the EU in States where a ban of four years had been declared to be unlawful under national law. E contended that the refusal of his application amounted to discrimination on the ground of nationality, contrary to Article 59 of the EC Treaty.

The English High Court held that the drug control rules were not subject to Articles 59–66 of the EC Treaty, which prohibit discrimination in the freedom to provide services for remuneration in the European Union, because the anti-doping rules were said merely to regulate the sporting conduct of participants in sport.[30] It was further held that the fact that different periods of ineligibility were imposed in other EU Member States as a result of the application of national law did not mean that the IAAF could not adopt different approaches in relation to athletes depending on whether the period of ineligibility was lawful under national law. EU law respected the rights of national legal systems to declare the lawfulness of bans, and federations were permitted to decide on the appropriate length of ban to impose. In those circumstances, the IAAF could not be forced under EU law to adopt the shortest period available by national law to bring about uniformity across the European Union.

Wilander v. *Tobin* [1997] 1 Lloyd's Rep 195

Two professional tennis players challenged the ITF Rules on doping, alleging that the Rules were void as an unreasonable restraint of trade. The restraint-of-trade allegation was struck out on the ground that the factors relied on by the players to claim that the doping regime was an unreasonable restraint of trade (the strict liability under the Rules for the presence of a prohibited substance, the reverse onus of proof and the mandatory penalties) were not capable of founding such a claim at common law. This decision was upheld in the High Court, which held that the deficiencies in the ITF Rules might provide a basis to claim that the Rules were in restraint of trade or in breach of Article 59 of the EC Treaty, which protects the fundamental rights of plaintiffs to provide their services throughout the European Union. This argument arose from the absence of a proper appeal right in the ITF Rules. Other arguments based on other Treaty rights under Articles 85 and 86 were held to be 'hopeless'.

Case C-519/04 P, *Meca-Medina and Majcen* v. *Commission of the European Communities*

M-M and M were long-distance swimmers who tested positive for nandrolone (slightly over the limit) after a World Cup race in 1999. The

---

30 For the change in the position on this point, see again *Meca-Medina*.

swimmers were initially banned for four years by FINA under its Rules. This was subsequently reduced to two years by CAS at a further hearing, which had been granted after a study had suggested eating certain castrated boars' meat could lead to a positive test for nandrolone. CAS did not accept this explanation for the presence of the nandrolone, but reduced the fixed sanction on the basis of the proportionality principle. The swimmers did not appeal the award to the Swiss Federal Court, but took their case to the European Court of Justice. They filed a complaint with the Commission alleging that the FINA doping rules were in breach of Articles 49, 81 and 82 of the EC Treaty, which protected their economic freedoms in the European Union. The Commission found that the complaint could not be upheld because the anti-doping rules were not subject to EU law as being rules concerned with organising sport as opposed to economic matters covered by the Treaty. The Court of First Instance agreed with this. On appeal to the European Court of Justice, the court held that anti-doping regimes had an effect on the economic activities of those bound by them, and that, accordingly, the protections under the Treaty were applicable. The court relied on several cases, applying EU legal protection to sport on the basis that it is an economic activity within the meaning of Article 2 of the Treaty. The two swimmers were professional sportsmen providing services for remuneration, and were entitled to the protection of the freedom of movement and the freedom to provide services and to be protected from rules restricting competition or abusing a dominant position under the Treaty. The judgement of the Court of First Instance was set aside in this regard.

The court went on to hold that the doping rule which established the threshold for nandrolone was justifiable and did not go beyond what was necessary to ensure that sporting events could take place and function properly. The rules represented justifiable restrictions on rights protected under the Treaty and were not excessive in nature. The anti-doping rules were accordingly enforceable under EU law.

Common Law Doctrine of Restraint of Trade and Anti-doping Regimes

High Court, Chancery Division, *Gasser* v. *Stinson* (Unreported, 15 June 1988)

G, a Swiss 1500 m runner, challenged the testing process by which she had been found to have committed a doping offence by the IAAF, and also contended that the two-year ban imposed on her was void at common law as a restraint of trade. The High Court rejected the challenge to the testing process and to confirmation of the A sample by the B sample. The court further held that the IAAF rule which imposed strict liability for the presence of a prohibited substance in a sample, with a mandatory two-year ban, was subject to the doctrine of restraint of trade where competitors were able to exploit their ability for financial gain. However, the rules were held to be a reasonable restraint of trade in the context of the fight to eliminate doping in sport. Strict liability was a reasonable response to the difficulties which would be caused in the effort to prevent drug-taking if a defence of moral innocence were introduced.

Johnson v. *Athletics Canada and IAAF* [1997] Ontario Court (General Division) No. 3201

J was found to have committed a second doping offence, and, under the IAAF Rules, he was banned for life. He submitted that the ban was void under common law principles as being in restraint of trade, and that he had not been afforded natural justice. Complaints relating to the fairness of the proceedings, including an allegation of apparent bias in the tribunal which heard the allegation, were rejected. The court held that the ban was a restraint of trade at common law but found it to be justifiable as a reasonable measure to protect the health of athletes and the fairness of competition in sport.

Challenges to the Enforcement of Pre-Code Arbitration Awards

Mary Decker Slaney v. *IAAF and USOC*, 244 F 3d 580; 2001 US App Lexis 4923

S, an Olympic runner, challenged an award by the IAAF Arbitration Panel in the US courts. The award had found that S had committed a doping offence contrary to the IAAF Rules as a result of the detection of a raised testosterone/epitestosterone (T/E) level. S raised a number of state law claims and sought to set aside the IAAF award. The claims were rejected by the District Court for the Southern District of Indiana. The United States Court of Appeals (7th Circuit) dismissed the appeal and held that, as S had participated in the arbitration, she could not challenge the existence of an arbitration agreement which was binding on her, and that the award, as a foreign arbitration award, had to be enforced unless one of the grounds under the New York Convention, under which enforcement could be denied, applied. None of the grounds were made out. In particular, the presumption that an elevated T/E ratio gave rise to a doping offence, with the burden shifting to the athlete to prove that the heightened level was caused by pathological or physiological factors and not the taking of the prohibited substance, was not contrary to public policy in the United States so as to justify not enforcing the award. The IAAF rule was not 'in violation of the most basic notions of morality and justice', as required if it was to be contrary to public policy, but rather was regarded as a reasonable response to the problem of doping and the difficulty of proof. Other state law claims were dismissed, and the award was enforced.

New South Wales Court of Appeal, *Angela Raguz* v. *Rebecca Sullivan*, CAS Digest II, p. 783

Two judokas, R and S, disputed the selection for the Australian Under-52 kg category at the Sydney Olympics. CAS found against R, who sought leave to appeal the award to the New South Wales Supreme Court on the question of law arising out of the award under the relevant Australian legislation relating to appeals against arbitration awards, the Commercial Arbitration Act 1984 (CAA 1984). The proceedings were removed into the Court of Appeal, where it was argued that there was no jurisdiction for the appeal because there was an exclusion agreement as provided for under section 40 CAA 1984. R submitted that the exclusion agreement was not effective under CAA 1984 because the arbitration was domestic and the requirement for a signed exclusion agreement under CAA 1984 was not met. The Court of Appeal held that the exclusion agreement did not relate to a 'domestic arbitration agreement' because the agreed seat or place of the arbitration was Switzerland under the CAS Rules, and this made the arbitration international. The exclusion agreement was upheld, and the court held that there was no jurisdiction to hear the appeal. In reaching the finding that the jurisdiction of the local courts had been validly excluded, the court emphasised the change in the attitude to arbitration of the courts in common law countries from hostility to support, as reflected in the UNCITRAL Model Law and the local legislation, CAA 1984.

Pre-Code Public Law Appeals to Swiss Courts to Set Aside CAS Arbitration Awards: Swiss Federal Supreme Court Decisions Relating to CAS

1st Civil Division of Swiss Federal Tribunal, *G* v. *Fédération Équestre Internationale (FEI)*, 15 March 1993, CAS Digest I 1986–88, p. 545

G made a public law appeal under the Swiss Code on Private International Law to the Swiss Federal Tribunal from an award by a CAS Panel which imposed a sanction on the rider under the Rules of the FEI.

Under Swiss law, the requirement for an appeal was that the judgement of CAS must be an international arbitral award, must concern a point of law and could not have as its sole object a 'games rule' (a rule whose application is outside judicial control). The CAS arbitral award was found to be an international arbitration award because one of the parties – the appellant – was domiciled in Germany.

The court held that CAS was sufficiently independent to amount to an arbitral tribunal, so as to be amenable to appeal (in particular, where the IOC was not a party). The court also held that the penalties in the case, namely, the withdrawal of prize money and suspension, went beyond simple penalties intended to ensure the correct conduct of the game, and were true penalties prescribed by the regulations which prejudiced the juridical interests of the person whom they affect and could, as a result, be subject to judicial control by the courts. An argument that the matter was not properly capable of arbitration before CAS was rejected, because this point had not been taken below.

The appellant submitted that the award was contrary to public policy in various ways. It was submitted that, as a matter of principle, the penalty imposed under the FEI Rules was a matter of criminal law, and should be solely subject to the jurisdiction of State courts. This was rejected on the basis that the forms of penalty were fixed by contract and could properly be the subject of an arbitral award. Punishment under an anti-doping regime had nothing to do with criminal law.

A challenge on the basis that at least two of the arbitrators did not have sufficient independence because of connections to the FEI was rejected. The court further rejected an argument that the appellant's right to be heard had been violated in various ways.

The court also noted that a breach of public policy, in the context of this kind of appeal, had to involve breaches of the fundamental principles which underpinned the legal order to provide grounds to set aside an arbitral award and could not be made out by rulings of law on points of fact which were plainly wrong.

The court held that, in the context of an anti-doping regime, there was no breach of public policy in adopting strict liability and a reversal of the burden of proof. Such matters could not be approached by reference to the criminal law and corresponding guarantees under the ECHR.

> Nor was there a breach of public policy where the applicable rules of the FEI are characterised by great severity and operated to prohibit the presence of substances which would not be likely to affect the performance of the horse.

The anti-doping rules of the FEI were held not to infringe public policy as a matter of the Swiss legal order.

Swiss Federal Tribunal, *N, J, Y, W* v. *FINA* (Chinese Swimmers
Case), Judgement of Second Civil Division 31 March 1999

The Swiss Federal Tribunal again held that a CAS award was an international arbitration award and that CAS could be regarded as a genuine arbitration tribunal. The court held that the decision under challenge, namely, the decision to impose a two-year period of ineligibility on four swimmers for a doping offence, related to points of law and not merely the application of game rules, which would not be a matter for the court. The appellants argued that their right to a hearing had been violated in two main ways:

- the arbitrators had not properly been present in making the decision on the award; and
- the Panel had not properly entertained arguments on the process by which their samples had been analysed.

Both arguments were rejected on the facts. The appellants then further argued that the award was not compatible with Swiss public policy, in that it endorsed a discriminatory and retaliatory measure adopted against them (the sanction), constituted a serious and unwarranted violation of their personal liberties and personal rights or was a violation of procedural public policy contrary to the principles of good faith and fidelity. It was contended that the award should be set aside as involving a breach of public policy.

The court found that there was no violation of fundamental principles so as to make the award contrary to public policy:

- Any defects in the initial process before the FINA Doping Panel were cured by the CAS Panel hearing.
- The two-year suspension was not contrary to the principles of proportionality so as to be contrary to public policy. It could not be said that the penalty was totally disproportionate to the behaviour penalised.
- The argument that the FINA Anti-Doping Rules violated fundamental principles by reversing the burden of proof was rejected. Reversal of the burden of proof did not relate to public policy properly so-called, but to the duty of proof in the assessment of evidence, and criminal procedure was not relevant. There was no proper basis to say that the award was contrary to principles of good faith and contractual fidelity or otherwise in breach of public policy. The appeal was dismissed.

Swiss Federal Tribunal, *A and B* v. *IOC and FIS*, 27 May 2003

Four cross-country skiers made a public law appeal to the Federal Supreme Court in Switzerland, claiming that the CAS award imposing sanctions on them should be set aside on the basis of a lack of independence on the part of CAS where the IOC was a party to the dispute. This related to the earlier statements in *G* v. *FEI*. Since that decision, ICAS had been established as a body of international jurists with the task of ensuring the independence of CAS. The Swiss Federal Tribunal held that CAS was independent. The IOC had no means of influencing the composition of the list of CAS arbitrators drawn up by the ICAS. The complaint concerning the alleged unlawful general composition of the CAS List was unfounded. A complaint that the particular three arbitrators who made up the Panel were not independent in the particular factual circumstances of the case was also rejected.

The court considered further challenges on grounds of public policy in a substantive or procedural sense relating to the imposition of strict liability, the burden of proof and sanctions. These grounds to set aside the award were rejected on similar grounds to those which were applied in *N, J, Y, W* v. *FINA*.

Swiss Federal Tribunal, *N* v. *FEI*, 31 October 1996

N brought a challenge in the Swiss courts to a decision of the judicial committee of the FEI disqualifying the rider and his horse after a prohibited substance had been found in the horse's urine and blood. The decision had ordered the return of a trophy and prize money and imposed a suspension of six months on the rider.

N claimed that the dispute was not capable of being arbitrated and that the court should set aside the award. The Swiss Federal Court, on appeal, held that the established principle was that the Swiss court will decline jurisdiction unless it finds that an arbitration agreement has lapsed, become ineffective or is not applicable. The question in the case was whether the submission to CAS arbitration was effective to exclude the court.

The issue was whether the rider was bound to the CAS arbitration process. He had signed a model agreement which did not mention the arbitration clause contained in it. In the circumstances of the particular case, it was held that the plaintiff knew of the arbitration clause inserted in the FEI Rules when he signed the model agreement – indeed, he had made use of it in an earlier dispute. The matter was properly referred to arbitration and the court proceeding was dismissed.

Challenges to the Code on the Basis of Individual Rights Protected under National Legal Systems

CAS 2006/A/1102, *Eder* v. *Ski Austria*; CAS 2006/A/1146, *WADA* v. *Eder and Ski Austria*

E was a professional Austrian skier. At the 2006 Winter Olympics, he was nominated for the cross-country skiing relay. He was suffering from diarrhoea. He could not contact the team doctor, so contacted his private doctor, who recommended that he inject himself with a saline solution by infusion. Shortly after he had started to give himself the infusion, the premises where he and the Austrian team were living were raided by the Italian police under search warrants. The police searched the house and carried out doping tests. The police found a used infusion bottle and a used infusion needle. A test on E was negative. On an allegation that E had used or attempted to use a prohibited method, Ski Austria found that the violation had been established, and imposed a period of ineligibility of one year. Under the Prohibited List, 'intravenous transfusions are prohibited except as a legitimate acute medical treatment'. They are a prohibited method and, if use is established, there will be a violation under Article 2.2 of the Code.

Fundamental Rights Argument   On appeal, E contended that the Prohibited List and the Articles of the Code in issue were null and void because they infringed the basic human rights of athletes and were contrary to Austrian law, which governed the rules of Ski Austria. He also submitted that, on the facts, the intravenous infusion was a legitimate medical treatment, which meant that it was not a prohibited method under the Prohibited List. If the infusion was considered to be a prohibited method, it was submitted that he should have been found to bear no fault in the circumstances, with the result that the period of ineligibility should be removed. WADA exercised its right of appeal to contend that the decision to reduce the sanction to one year was wrong and involved misapplying Article 10.5.2 of the Code.

Applicable Law   The question of the validity of the rules relied on had to be determined under Austrian law because Ski Austria had its domicile in Austria and the parties had not chosen a law to govern the dispute. It was submitted, on behalf of E, that the prohibition of intravenous infusions was contrary to fundamental principles and should be of no effect. This was advanced on a number of bases under Austrian law and the ECHR.

CAS rejected the arguments primarily on the basis that arguments based on fundamental rights were not properly available in relation to disciplinary regimes established by private associations which regulated members by contract, and that, if they were applicable, the rule in the Prohibited List was a necessary and adequate response to the problem of athletes manipulating blood test results. The rule was proportionate and in compliance with *bona mores* and thus not contrary to public policy under Austrian or EU law. Similarly, the Articles of the FISA Rules which adopted the provisions of the Code on sanctions were not contrary to the principle of proportionality or in violation of the presumption of innocence under Article 6(2) of the ECHR by reversing the 'onus of proof'.

The Panel then considered whether an anti-doping rule violation had been committed. It applied the criteria in *Mayer et al. v. IOC*[31] to decide whether the infusion was 'legitimate acute medical treatment', and held that it was not, primarily because this could not apply where the 'treatment' was self-administered with no examination or attendance from any medical practitioner. The Panel accordingly determined that a violation had been committed.

No Significant Fault   On the sanction, CAS found that the circumstances, while not amounting to 'no fault', did amount to 'no significant fault or negligence' where the infusion was administered on the advice of a medical practitioner in a stressful situation for the athlete. It was not 'disposed to disagree' with the assessment of Ski Austria that there was no significant fault or change the assessment that the period of ineligibility should be reduced to one year under Rule 10.5.2 of the FIS Anti-Doping Rules.

Challenges to a Code Finding on the Basis of Fundamental Rights under Canadian Law – No Fault

CAS 2007/A/131, *Adams v. Canadian Centre for Ethics in Sport, Athletics Canada and Government of Canada*

A was an elite-level disabled athlete who tested positive for cocaine at the Ottawa Wheelchair Marathon. A contended that the positive test had come about because some residues of cocaine were present in a catheter which he had used to provide his sample to CCES. Some six days before the event, A had been in a bar when an unidentified woman had put cocaine

---

31 CAS 2002/A/389/390/391/393, CAS Digest II.

into his mouth with her fingers without his consent. This was the subject of evidence from A and two witnesses who supported A's evidence that he had been pretending to be asleep when the unknown woman had acted as she did. One of A's friends had intervened and the woman, who was carrying a small bag which A's friend confirmed contained cocaine, had left. The bar was across the street from a drug rehabilitation centre. After the incident, A had been upset and was taken home by one of his friends. He had used a catheter that night to urinate and had stored the catheter in the emergency pocket of his wheelchair. A gave evidence that he had carried out extensive online research and had spoken with the head of a US drug-testing laboratory to determine whether the cocaine would be out of his system by the time of the competition. He was convinced that this would be the case. After the competition, he had used the catheter used after the incident to provide his sample. At the time of the test, there was no discussion about the use of a used catheter. A sterile wrapped catheter was never requested or offered. The evidence was that CCES did not inspect catheters used by athletes or advise them to use a clean catheter. CCES was not aware at the time that a catheter could be a source of inadvertent contamination. A testified that CCES was aware of his need to self-catheterise. There was further evidence that it was common for disabled athletes to reuse catheters. The scientific evidence was not conclusive on whether it was possible that the positive test was caused by the contaminated catheter used to provide the sample.

A contended that his constitutional rights under the Canadian Charter of Rights and Freedoms had been violated in a manner which could not be justified and that he had been subject to unlawful discrimination under federal and Ontario human rights legislation. This was based on the failure by CCES to provide a sterile catheter or warn him about the risk of contamination in using a used catheter. A submitted that the appropriate remedy for the constitutional violation should be that he was not guilty of a doping violation. If the arguments based on the breach of his rights under Canadian law were not accepted, A submitted that there had been a violation of the sample collection rules in not providing a clean catheter and that this had caused the adverse analytical finding. If CCES had established a violation, A submitted that he bore no fault or no significant fault in the circumstances.

At first instance, the Doping Tribunal, after considering submissions from the parties – including the Attorney-General of Ontario – on the constitutional question, held that the Charter claim was not applicable and dismissed the further arguments on behalf of A. The Doping Tribunal found that the evidence on behalf of A did not credibly explain the source of the positive test, with the result that the plea of no fault or no significant fault could not succeed.

Before CAS, the Panel held that, as a matter of Canadian law, the claim based on the Charter and the Canadian Human Rights Act was not available where CCES, although created by statute, was a private body operating under contractual arrangements and did not exercise statutory authority so as to be subject to the legislation. Even if the Charter could apply, it would not be appropriate to decide the matter on constitutional grounds where protection under the Ontario human rights legislation was potentially applicable. On this aspect, the Panel found that there had been no actionable discrimination against A because the legislation did not impose an affirmative burden on CCES to provide sterile catheters or warn the athlete about using used catheters.

The Panel further held that the CCES collection rules did not contain an obligation to provide sterile catheters or warn athletes about the risk of contamination and that such an obligation should not be read into them. Accordingly, no breach of the rules had been established. As a result, the test result established an anti-doping rule violation by the presence of a prohibited substance in A's sample.

The Panel did not share the view of the Doping Tribunal on the credibility of the explanation for the presence of the prohibited substance in the sample. It found that A's evidence had not been contradicted and was supported by two witnesses, with the result that it accepted that the source of the positive test was the contaminated catheter. It found that the circumstances of the case were truly exceptional. By showing that the source of the test was the contaminated catheter, A had established that there was no prohibited substance in his body at the time of the test and that the presence of the cocaine was the result of an assault which led to the ingestion of cocaine. A could not be said to have been at fault or negligent in not preventing the ingestion of cocaine in this manner. He was entitled to a finding of no fault and the two-year period of ineligibility was set aside.

Recent Challenge to a CAS Arbitration Award in Civil Proceedings in German Courts – Claim for Abuse of Dominant Position in Requiring Arbitration Agreement under German Law

U 1110/14 Kart, *Claudia Pechstein v. Deutsche Eisschnellauf-Gemeinschaft e. V. (DESG) and International Skating Union (ISU)*, Munich Higher Regional Court

P brought proceedings in the German courts seeking a declaration that a doping ban imposed under the Code and confirmed on appeal to CAS (and after an appeal to the Swiss Federal Court) was unlawful.[32] P claimed compensation for the alleged illegal ban against the NSO and international federation responsible for ice skating in the sum of €3 584 126.09 plus interest. The defendants sought to stay the claim on the grounds that the doping ban had been imposed by CAS (and confirmed by the Swiss Federal Tribunal), which had been agreed as the arbitration forum for the doping allegation under the arbitration agreement entered into by P. P resisted this on the basis that the arbitration agreement was invalid under German anti-trust law.

At first instance, the Regional Court dismissed the claim on the grounds that the German courts did not have international jurisdiction over the claim and that there was no jurisdiction because the parties had entered into an arbitration agreement for CAS proceedings, with any appeal being to the Swiss Federal Court.

On appeal, P directed her appeal against the dismissal of the action against the ISU. The Munich Higher Regional Court held that there was international jurisdiction over P's claim against the ISU on the proper application of the Convention on Jurisdiction and the Enforcement of Judgments in Civil and Commercial Matters (the Lugano Convention).

On the argument based on the agreement to arbitrate the dispute before CAS which athletes had to agree to enter into in order to compete, the court held that the dispute was within the scope of the arbitration clause contained in the provisions of the rules of the ISU. The clause was apt to cover all claims, including claims for compensation or damages. This included claims under anti-trust law of the kind made by P.

However, the court held that the clause was ineffective because it violated fundamental principles or compelling norms of German law. These compelling norms included the principles of anti-trust law. The ISU was in the position of exercising a monopoly in offering services in a market – namely the market for world championship events in speed skating. As a monopolist, the ISU was prohibited under German anti-trust law from demanding business terms which would not exist if there was competition. Consequently, the ISU could not demand that P consented to the arbitration clause. The application of this competition law provision was not prevented by any requirement in the Code or UNESCO Doping Convention for arbitration before CAS. While the agreement to arbitrate was not

---

32 For a summary of the CAS award imposing a two-year period of ineligibility on P for use of a prohibited method based on the analysis of the athlete's ABP, see Chapter 5, pages 205–10.

per se ineffective because the athlete could not freely decide whether to enter into the agreement, the demand to enter into such an agreement did constitute an abuse of market power. While there were good grounds for the arbitration of sporting disputes which meant that athletes would agree to the arbitration of sporting disputes by a neutral arbitration court in a competitive market, the arbitration agreement for CAS which was demanded by the ISU would not have been agreed to in such a market because the CAS-appointed list of arbitrators was predominantly connected with the governing bodies of sport. This arose from the process for appointment to ICAS under the 2004 CAS procedural regulations. The result of this analysis was that the athlete who was forced to accept arbitration before CAS by the exercise of monopoly power by the ISU was deprived of rights of access to national courts and a properly appointed judge by the CAS process. This represented an abuse of market power, which meant that the CAS award could not be recognised on public policy grounds because it infringed compelling norms of German law. As a consequence, the appeal was allowed in part, and the claim by P against the ISU for damages was reinstated.

Federal Court of Justice DESG and ISU v. Claudia Pechstein, KZR 6/15 – 7 June 2016 – Decision of Higher Regional Court Reversed

On appeal, the Federal Court of Justice set aside the decision of the Higher Regional Court and reversed its decision that P's claim for loss and damage was admissible. This was because the arbitration agreement in favour of CAS was enforceable, which meant that the claim in the courts was inadmissible under German law.

The court held that by signing the registration for the competition, P entered into an arbitration agreement which was effective under German law because CAS was a true court of arbitration. CAS was such a true court of arbitration because it was an independent and neutral body, was not incorporated into any particular international federation and was independent of the sports federations and Olympic Committees which supported it.

The procedure for drawing up the list of arbitrators for CAS did not call into question CAS as a true court of arbitration. The fact that international federations would appoint twelve of the twenty members of ICAS responsible for appointing arbitrators to the closed CAS List from which arbitrators had to be drawn did not mean that the independence in a true court of arbitration was lacking, because it did not give rise to direct or predominant influence by one party over the appointment of arbitrators. No direct dominant influence which would remove the independence of CAS could be deduced from the ICAS appointment process. The process could not support such a conclusion where in general terms the federations and athletes would have the same goal of bringing about doping free sport. Other aspects of the CAS Rules also safeguarded the individual independence of the arbitrators. There was no basis to conclude that an award from CAS was not enforceable. This accorded with German law on the enforcement of foreign arbitration awards, which required that recognition could only be refused where there was a violation of impartial administration of justice which had actual consequences for the arbitral proceedings. After finding that the claim brought by P in the German courts fell within the terms of the arbitration agreement, the court held that the agreement between the parties was valid as a matter of German law. The court rejected the argument that the conduct of the ISU in requiring the signing of the arbitration agreement represented an abuse of its dominant position in the market under German anti-trust law. The requirement to sign the arbitration agreement was justified on the balancing of interests between the ISU and P. Looking at the interests of the parties subject to the Code, which included all athletes subject to the regime, the overall common interest in a uniform system of arbitration intended to implement the Code in an effective manner justified the arbitration agreement in favour of CAS. The agreement did affect some of P's fundamental rights, but it did not amount to a violation of those rights. The voluntary submission to arbitration was one way in which the guaranteed right of access to State courts could be waived.

Although P did not want the arbitration clause but had to sign to it in order to compete in the sporting event organised by the ISU, she entered into the contract without duress or misrepresentation. While the ISU did make use of its position to impose the arbitration clause (and it could be inferred that P would not have been permitted to compete without signing), this did not amount to an abuse of monopoly power when the interests of the parties in the clause were considered and balanced. P had fundamental rights to access the courts and to practise her profession, but those rights had to be balanced against the right of the ISU to ensure that its sport ran properly and that the rules were applied to all athletes and implemented everywhere in accordance with uniform standards. In the area of doping, the uniform application of rules was particularly important. This was evidenced by the obligation under the Code to require arbitration before CAS and the obligation at State level under the UNESCO Convention to support the Code, which meant that the Code was a set of contractual principles recognised under international law. This led to the conclusion that there was no abuse of a dominant position in requiring the arbitration agreement before CAS. The agreement meant that all athletes could benefit by competing in an environment where the uniform application of anti-doping rules was guaranteed by CAS. P's rights were sufficiently protected before CAS and by the appeal process under which arbitral awards might be challenged before the Swiss Federal Tribunal. This conclusion was further supported under German law by the terms of the recent anti-doping legislation, which provides that arbitration agreements are not invalidated merely because they have been signed involuntarily.

The fact that Germany had ratified the 2005 UNESCO Convention, which imposed an obligation on Signatory States to comply with the Code (including provision for arbitration before CAS), further supported the finding that the arbitration agreement was enforceable. Nor could the arbitration clause be invalidated under Swiss law, as the lower court had found Swiss law was applicable because the law before the Swiss Federal Tribunal was that an arbitration agreement would still be valid where an athlete had no choice but to sign it if he or she wished to exercise his or her profession. Agreements for arbitration before tribunals like CAS of the kind before the court were enforceable because the parties had sufficient guarantees of impartiality and independence, including rights of appeal under Swiss law.

Claims Outside the Code

The Code does not affect the general civil rights and liabilities which may arise where there are breaches of the Code or where actions under the Code give rise to possible liability under the general law. Civil claims may possibly arise in many different factual circumstances. Possible claims might be divided broadly into claims by athletes who were subject to allegations under the Code or were found to have committed violations under the Code and claims by athletes against other athletes and other persons bound by the Code. An athlete found to have committed violations under the Code may seek to recover loss and damage caused to him or her by the sanction imposed under the Code against third parties who, it is claimed, have caused the athlete's breach of the Code, while an athlete found not to have committed alleged violations may seek to recover loss and damage suffered as a result of the allegation from the anti-doping organisation responsible for bringing the allegation. Clean athletes may try to recover loss and damage from competitors who competed while in breach of the Code.

By way of example, an athlete who commits an anti-doping rule violation after ingesting a contaminated supplement or as a result of an error by a medical practitioner may seek to pursue the supplement manufacturer or medical practitioner, alleging that, notwithstanding the duties which the athlete had to fulfil under the Code, the negligence of the manufacturer or medical practitioner was at least partly the cause of the positive test and the loss and damage caused by the period of ineligibility imposed under the Code.[33]

An athlete who commits or is alleged to have committed an anti-doping rule violation may face consequences under his or her employment contract or under an agreement with the ruling sporting body. Such claims will involve the interpretation and application of the agreements in issue under the principles of the legal system applicable to the dispute. Where doping allegations are raised against an athlete, his or her sporting employers may be liable if they terminate his or her contract of employment on inadequate grounds. If, after such a summary termination, anti-doping rule violations are not subsequently brought or are not established, the athlete may have significant claims for damages for wrongful termination of the contract. Such claims will be determined in accordance with the legal system which governs the contract. Sporting employment contracts may contain arbitration clauses which provide for the jurisdiction of CAS in relation to disputes arising out of the contract. In addition to contractual claims of this nature, from time to time, defamation claims have been brought by athletes who have been wrongly described as 'drug cheats' in the media.[34]

Where an athlete or other person is subject to an adverse analytical finding or a finding that a violation has been committed which is subsequently set aside, possible civil claims against the anti-doping organisations

---

33 There have been a number of civil suits against supplement manufacturers in the United States.
34 See the finding in favour of the Australian cyclist, Mark French, who was awarded AUD175 000 against Australian newspapers in the Supreme Court of Victoria in 2008. He had earlier successfully sued a radio station for defamation, winning an award of AUD350 000 by way of damages after he had been described on-air as a 'dirty stinking dobbing cyclist' by the media reporting on Mr French's suspension in 2004, which was reversed on appeal to CAS.

responsible for testing, investigation or results management for improperly carrying out the processes may be available. Such claims will be rare, will face both substantive and jurisdictional issues and may be difficult to establish on the facts.

The range of possible claims which might be brought is wide, and they may be founded in contract or tort. In most jurisdictions, there would be no objection in principle to the existence of a concurrent duty of care owed in tort and in contract by the sporting organisation to the athlete in relation to the testing, analysis and results management process for which it is responsible.

Similarly, in the results management process, the wrongful release of confidential information in breach of an obligation to maintain confidentiality such as that imposed by many sporting rules and policies and by the ISL and ISPPPI could give rise to civil claims for breaches of confidentiality and privacy rights.[35] In some jurisdictions, it may also be possible to claim damages for the abuse of a dominant economic position by the organisations responsible for the testing and analytical process. This kind of claim is much more problematic, but, in light of the European Court of Justice decision in *Meca-Medina*, in which the potential applicability of EU law principles to anti-doping regimes was accepted by the European Court of Justice, it is potentially available in at least some jurisdictions. There have been very few civil claims arising from allegedly deficient testing or investigations.

Claims will be determined in accordance with the system of law (including the conflict of law rules) of the jurisdiction in which they are brought. Where the WADA Code has been adopted, there may, no doubt, be initial arguments as to whether the athlete or person bringing the claim has submitted to the jurisdiction of CAS or a national-level tribunal in relation to the claim, so that the claim cannot be brought in the ordinary courts. This will depend upon the construction and application of the relevant arbitration agreement entered into by the athlete. However, it would appear to be unlikely that civil claims for wrongly carried-out testing processes or for breach of obligations of confidentiality in the testing and investigation process will fall within the scope of an agreement under which anti-doping rule violations and sanctions under the Code are referred to a national tribunal or CAS. This does, however, depend on the scope of

---

35 These claims will be advanced on different legal bases in different jurisdictions, but the legal regimes in most jurisdictions recognise principles which protect these rights and provide the basis upon which to bring claims.

the particular agreement, and there is nothing to prevent sporting organisations adopting arbitration clauses which have this effect. In addition, CAS, which can decide on its own jurisdiction under the applicable Swiss legislation, generally adopts a broad approach to the interpretation of the scope of arbitration clauses.

It is also possible to envisage claims being made in the courts by athletes who have been affected by the conduct of other athletes who are found subsequently to have breached the Code. While the rules of the international federation are likely to provide for the reallocation of prizes and medals, it is quite possible that an affected athlete might wish to claim compensation for loss and damage caused by an athlete who was a fellow competitor. Indeed, this possibility is specifically recognised in the notes to Article 10.10 of the Code. As has been noted, such a claim would be governed by the requirements of the legal system applicable in the jurisdiction where the claim was brought (unless the claim was within the scope of an agreement to arbitrate before CAS, which is unlikely). In general terms, a claim seems most likely to be advanced on the basis that an athlete owes duties under the applicable law (whether in tort or in contract, by implying a term into the agreement under which the athletes compete or otherwise) to his or her sport and his or her fellow competitors to participate in a manner which conforms with the Code and to avoid causing loss and damage to those parties.

To the author's knowledge, no such case has yet come before the courts, and the scope and content of the possible duty owed to other competitors or other persons by an athlete competing has not been addressed. While it might be argued that there should be no separate independent duty owed to other competitors under the general law on policy grounds, because the remedy available should be limited to the circumstances expressly set out in the Code and any particular sporting rules applicable, it seems likely that many national legal systems might impose duties under the law not to act to cause loss and damage to other athletes by committing intentional breaches of the Code where the loss and damage is not recoverable under the applicable international federation rules. It is difficult to speculate, but it seems doubtful that a duty to avoid causing loss and damage by careless (as opposed to intentional) breaches of the Code would be imposed on athletes on policy grounds, namely that the consequences of such breaches should be limited to those contained in the Code and the applicable rules of the sporting organisation involved.

It is also possible to envisage civil claims for compensation being brought against a sporting organisation bound by the Code where the organisation fails to act in accordance with its obligation to comply with the Code and causes loss and damage to third parties in particular athletes. Of course, an organisation in breach of its obligations under the Code in this way is likely to face sanctions under the Code and may face financial claims because it has breached the terms of contracts with third parties by a failure to carry out obligations under the Code. It is, again, more difficult to speculate about the nature of the claims which might be brought by athletes and possibly others who are subject to the Code. By way of example, such a claim might arise where it could be established by relevant admissible evidence that an anti-doping organisation or international federation of another sporting organisation bound by the Code had failed to act in accordance with its obligations under the Code and this had allowed an athlete to compete when he or she should not have done. It seems possible to contend that a duty to carry out the obligations under the Code in a manner that avoids causing loss and damage to other athletes competing should be imposed on the sporting organisation under the general law. Again, the question of policy which would arise is whether the general law of a national legal system should recognise such a duty where the Code provides for remedies against participants and organisations.[36] Again, and as already outlined, it seems more likely that a duty to avoid causing loss and damage to third parties such as athletes would be imposed on a sporting organisation bound to implement the Code in the case of conduct which could be shown to be an intentional or a deliberate breach of the obligations under the Code. It seems less likely that a general duty would be imposed to avoid economic loss to third parties by careless breaches of the Code on the grounds that, as a matter of policy, the remedies for such breaches are better limited to the penalties imposed under the Code and any rules adopted by the sports organisation in question.

Athletes who commit anti-doping rule violations may sustain further consequences under contracts of employment or other contracts with third parties such as sponsors or under other sporting rules which bind them. Whether a commitment to a sporting body under which an athlete promises to forfeit a sum of money in the event that he or she commits an anti-doping violation will be enforced is a question of interpreting and applying the particular contractual provision.

---

36 While the note to Article 10.10 is concerned with claims by clean athletes against athletes who have breached the Code, the general point which can be made is that the Code is not intended to fetter the possible claims which might be made under national law where loss and damage is caused by the breach of obligations under the Code.

Similar questions will apply where an athlete is potentially subject to further consequences under the particular sporting rules of his or her sport. The Code expressly provides that the rules of a sport may impose financial penalties where there is a breach of the Code.[37]

A striking example of athletes being subject to further consequences where they commit an anti-doping rule violation was found in the Regulation made by the IOC under the Olympic Charter relating to the eligibility of athletes to compete in the Olympic Games. The IOC Regulation provides as follows:

1 Any person who has been sanctioned with a suspension of more than six months by any anti-doping organisation for any violation of any anti-doping regulations may not participate, in any capacity, in the next edition of the Games of the Olympiad and of the Olympic Winter Games following the date of expiry of such suspension.

2 These Regulations apply to violations of any anti-doping regulations that are committed as of 1 July 2008. They are notified to all International Federations, to all National Olympic Committees and to all Organising Committees for the Olympic Games.

This Regulation was challenged before CAS on the basis that it imposed a further penalty on an athlete which was disproportionate under the general principles of Swiss law where an athlete may, by reason of the strict nature of the Code, incur a period of ineligibility of six months or more for a relatively low level of fault and, as a result of the Regulation, be prevented from competing at the next Olympic Games after the period of ineligibility under the Code has been served. As previously noted, Article 23.2 of the Code contains the provisions relating to sanctions (Article 10) which must be included in the rules of a Signatory 'without substantive amendment'. Article 23.2 provides that 'no additional provision may be added to a Signatory's rules which changes the effect of the Articles enumerated in the Article'. In an advisory opinion, CAS held that the IOC Regulation was in breach of the Code.[38] Notwithstanding this opinion, the

---

37 See Chapter 8, pages 448–9 for Article 10.10 of the Code.
38 See case summary CAS 2011/O/2442 pages 523–4. Similarly, a UCI rule under which cycling teams were assessed in order to decide whether they would receive licences to compete was held to be incompatible with the Code in CAS 2012/A/3055, *Riis Cycling A/S v. Licence Commission of the UCI*. The rule was a specific provision which prevented the points earned by a rider who had been sanctioned with a period of ineligibility of more than two years from being counted in assessing the sporting value of a team for the purposes of applying for a professional licence for the team for a further two years after the

contractual nature of the Code and any additional rules means that the policy issues which arise from this kind of rule remain alive.[39]

Illustrations

Application of Additional Sports Rules – Advisory Opinion on IOC Regulation

CAS 2011/O/2442, *USOC* v. *IOC* The USOC and IOC agreed to obtain an advisory opinion from CAS concerning the IOC regulation made under Rule 45 of the Olympic Charter.

The IOC is a Signatory to the Code and had made it part of its statutes. The central question for CAS was whether the regulation was enforceable under the Code. The regulation had been considered in several decisions involving anti-doping rule violations against US athletes (see e.g. *USADA* v. *La Shawn Merritt*, AAA No. 77 190 00293) and if applied by the IOC would impact upon the eligibility of several athletes for the 2012 London Olympics. The Code provides, at Article 23, for those Articles which must be included by Signatories in their anti-doping rules 'without significant amendment'. The Articles prescribed in Article 23 include Article 10, relating to sanctions.

The central argument concerned the question whether IOC Regulation 45 imposed an additional sanction which, as a Signatory to the Code, the IOC could not include in its rules as it amounted to a 'significant amendment' to Article 10.

The IOC contended that the regulation was an eligibility rule which it could impose as a matter of contract in relation to entries to the Olympics. The USOC contended that the regulation could not properly be characterised as an eligibility rule but was, rather, a qualifying rule which imposed a sanction in relation to past behaviour. The USOC further contended that the regulation was in breach of the IOC statutes, because it violated certain specific provisions of the Olympic Charter concerning discrimination and the dignity of athletes. It also contended that the

---

end of the athlete's period of ineligibility. Although it was directed at teams, the effect of this provision was to punish the rider – as the rider's points would not count for a team's standing, it would be harder for him or her to obtain a contract even though his or her period of ineligibility had come to an end.

39 A further challenge to the rule of the BOA which imposes a lifetime ban on competing at the Olympics on athletes who commit violations of the Code was decided by CAS in April 2012. The BOA bye-law was found to impose a further doping sanction and to not be in compliance with the Code. See CAS 2011/A/2068, *BOA* v. *WADA*.

regulation violated principles of Swiss law, in particular the principle of proportionality, athlete personality rights, the principle of equal treatment and due process, the principle of double jeopardy and public policy. The USOC also contended that the rule was an unlawful restriction on competition.

The CAS Panel held that the rule could not properly be characterised as an 'eligibility' rule. On its proper interpretation, it had the effect of imposing an additional sanction and was therefore contrary to Article 23 of the Code. Where the IOC had adopted the Code as part of its statutes, it was acting illegally in breach of those statutes in making and imposing the regulation. The Panel further found that the effect of Regulation 45 was to impose a further sanction on athletes for the same behaviour which was in breach of the double jeopardy principle (*ne bis in idem*). It did not need to decide the further claims based on Swiss law and fundamental principles of law and competition rules.

Possible Civil Claims: Early Pre-Code Consideration of a Claim for Compensation by CAS

CAS 95/142, *L* v. *FINA*, Award of 14 February 1996, CAS Digest I L was subject to testing under FINA Rules. Salbutamol was detected in a test. On the Rules at the time, salbutamol had an exceptional status. Salbutamol was not completely banned and its use was permitted with prior notification. CAS interpreted the FINA Rules as meaning that the presence of salbutamol was not conclusive proof of a doping offence. L did not give notice of his use of salbutamol in his form, but established before CAS that he was considered a long-term asthma sufferer who had repeatedly informed authorities of his use of salbutamol. This was held to be the equivalent of declaring the use of salbutamol as required. The result was that there was, on the construction of the Rules, no doping offence.

L claimed damages for loss of grants and bonuses under sponsorship contracts, loss of further sponsorship contracts and violation of his personality rights arising from the wrongly declared doping offence. The claims were considered by the CAS Panel under Swiss law, because FINA had its headquarters in Switzerland. The claims were dismissed for lack of proof of causation and for failure to prove the damages claimed. The claim for damages for breach of personality rights was also dismissed because there was no evidence of a lasting negative image. There could be no general claim for unlawful conduct outside the contract under Swiss law because FINA had not acted in bad faith or arbitrarily in bringing the doping proceedings (see pp. 238–44 of the award for consideration of the damages claim).

Civil Claim in the English Courts Arising from the Testing Process

Modahl v. BAF and IAAF [2001] EWCA Civ 1447   M sought damages in the English courts for the conduct of the testing and hearing process by the British Athletic Federation (BAF). She was a successful British international 800 m runner who was suspended from competition by the BAF in September 1994 because of an allegation that she committed a doping offence under its rules. M was found guilty by a disciplinary committee, but her appeal to an independent appeal tribunal was successful some seven months later. The appeal tribunal found that there was a reasonable doubt as to whether the laboratory test on the urine sample was reliable. M was reinstated and sued BAF for damages. She sued in contract, claiming that the suspension and initiation of disciplinary proceedings were in breach of the contract between her and BAF. She claimed considerable damages for the financial loss she had suffered for nearly a year when she could not compete in international athletics.

Essentially, in her claim, M alleged that two members of the disciplinary committee were biased against her, and that the doping charge which was brought against her was brought in breach of the rules and the contract with her, because the laboratory which tested her urine sample was not officially accredited. Her claim on this last point was that, on a true construction of the BAF/IAAF Rules, 'only a doping finding from an accredited laboratory could justify the finding that a doping offence had been committed'. The House of Lords found that this argument was not available on the true construction of the BAF Rules. There was no express or implied term that only accredited laboratories could be used. In the House of Lords, Lord Hoffmann said:

> It seems to me, wrong to construe the rules to mean that an athlete is entitled to financial compensation, if proceedings against her are initiated on the basis of the test (which may well have been accurate) from a laboratory which had moved its premises but not a test which was wrong on any other ground.

The House of Lords agreed with the Court of Appeal and struck out the claim in contract based on the test being performed by a non-accredited laboratory. The claim which proceeded to trial was the allegation of bias against the disciplinary committee. M lost this claim for bias on the facts in the High Court and her appeal against this decision was dismissed by the Court of Appeal.

Civil Claim in the German Courts – Alleged Wrongful Testing and Wrongful Release of Confidential Information

Cologne Regional Court, *Lagat* v. *WADA and IAAF*, **13 September 2006**
The Cologne Regional Court considered the claim by L against WADA and the IAAF for allegedly improperly performed tests and results management. L was a leading Kenyan middle-distance runner. His reputation was impeccable, and he held high-value advertising contracts with Nike. In August 2003, he was preparing for the Paris World Athletic Championships when he underwent a doping test. He provided a blood and urine sample and signed the following confirmation when he provided the sample:

> I hereby declare that the above information is true and correct and I accept the test method and agree that all disputes arising from the doping test administered pursuant to the IAAF Rules shall be settled pursuant to the IAAF Arbitration Regulations, and that the doping test administered pursuant to the rules of any other sports organisation shall be settled pursuant to this organisation's arbitrations regulations.

The A sample reported as showing a positive test for EPO. This was notified to the Kenyan Athletics Federation on a confidential basis in Paris. The athlete was notified. He was asked to provide a declaration, which the IAAF found inadequate, and was suspended. A Kenyan newspaper published a report of an interview with a coach for the Kenyan athletics team in which the coach gave details of the positive test. L was provisionally suspended. He asked for the B sample to be opened and tested. A reliable analysis was not possible on the B sample and, as the B sample did not support the A sample, the athlete's suspension was lifted and no further proceedings were taken. By this point in time, all the athletics competitions for the year were over.

L brought a claim in the Cologne Regional Court for damages in the sum of $500 000 for his losses and for damage to his reputation. He alleged that WADA and the IAAF had used a faulty testing method for EPO, conducted the test in an inadequate manner and been responsible for breaching their duty of confidentiality to him.

The court found that the various claims fell outside the arbitration agreements which were relied on by WADA and the IAAF to claim that there was no jurisdiction in the court for L's claims. However, the court

found, on the application of conflict of law rules, that there was no jurisdiction in relation to significant elements of the claim. The court accepted,
as a matter of principle, contrary to the then state of EU law,[40] that there
was a potential claim for abuse of a dominant position under EU law and
that the plaintiff could potentially sue in contract and tort for the defective
performance of testing obligations. The court also accepted the potential
availability of a breach-of-confidence claim, but found that neither defendant was responsible for any breach of confidentiality.

> In turn, the defendants conducting the control were obliged to perform
> the analysis and all other steps preceding it with due diligence to ensure
> the plaintiff would not suffer any damage. The accessory obligation arising
> from the agreement was the obligation to protect, i.e. the duty to implement
> the provisions of the agreement in a way which did not injure or violate the
> other party's body, life, property or other legal interests. Specifically, the
> doping control procedure must be affected [sic] in a way which precludes
> errors or manipulations to the greatest possible extent and which, in all
> its stages, ensures that the control is conducted under the responsibility of
> competent, independent and impartial persons.

Enforcement of Penalties under Agreements and Undertakings with Sporting Bodies

CAS 2008/A/1458, *UCI* v. *Vinokourov and KCF* V was found to have
used a prohibited method, namely a homologous blood transfusion, in
the 2007 Tour de France. The Kazakhstan Cycling Federation decided to
disqualify V for a period of one year only. WADA appealed to CAS seeking
the application of the standard two-year period of ineligibility. The appeal
proceedings were suspended because V had communicated his desire to
end his career.

V later sought to return to competition. UCI sought an acknowledgement from V that he had violated UCI's anti-doping rules and that he
would accept a two-year period of ineligibility, as well as disqualification
of his results at the 2007 Tour de France. In addition, UCI sought a payment from V in accordance with the commitment which he had signed
on 27 June 2007. In the CAS proceedings, V admitted the anti-doping rule
violation and accepted a two-year period of ineligibility.

UCI made V's reinstatement conditional upon payment of a contribution in money terms under the rider's commitment to new cycling, signed
by V on 29 June 2007. The commitment provided for a payment of the

40 See *Meca-Medina* at pages 503–4 for the current position under EU law.

annual salary of 2007 in case a cyclist committed an anti-doping rule vio-
lation which attracted a sanction of two or more years. UCI submitted
that the commitment to make the contribution was valid under Swiss law.
V submitted that the commitment was null and void and unenforceable.
V submitted that the commitment violated his personality rights under
Swiss law and was not justified by consent or overriding public interest.
The commitment had been signed about seven days before the 2007 Tour
de France and was a condition for V's participation in the Tour.

Under Swiss law, the contract had to be interpreted and applied according to the true intention of the contracting parties. The Panel examined
the circumstances in which the commitment was publicised and put to
the riders before the Tour. The commitment was found to be a public
relations measure introduced for the benefit of the Tour and its organisers. At the press conference at which the commitment had been presented,
both the President and the Director of the anti-doping programme of UCI
disclosed their doubts as to the legal validity of the commitment.

The Panel held that, in the circumstances, V could legitimately have had
the belief that the rider's commitment was not intended to have binding
force, so that he did not have a separate legal obligation under the agreement. The Panel concluded that the commitment was non-contractual
and that V was entitled, in the circumstances, to believe that the commitment was not intended to be legally binding. Accordingly, there was no
intent to establish a valid binding penalty clause. UCI and V mutually did
not intend to establish a penalty clause, but rather to issue a declaration
of good will to the public. The Panel did not make findings on the various
further arguments made by UCI and V, such as non-conformity with the
WADA Code 2004, the signing of the commitment under pressure, the
violation of personality rights, the imposition of an excessive penalty, the
violation of the principle of proportionality and discrimination. The outcome was that no payment was due from V as a precondition of his reinstatement under the 'rider's commitment to a new cycling'.

Claims before CAS in Relation to Sporting Employment
Contracts – Wrongful Termination

TAS 2008/O/1643, *Gusev* v. *Olympus SARL*   G was a professional
cyclist under a two-year contract. The contract contained termination
clauses which applied if a cyclist violated the team's code of conduct or
anti-doping policy.

G's team summarily terminated his contract as a result of suspicious
values shown in his biological passport. Doping was not subsequently

established, and no proceedings were brought against G. The contract contained an arbitration clause for all disputes to be referred to CAS. Before CAS, applying the principles of employment law under Swiss law which applied to the contract, the Panel held that the contract of employment had been wrongly summarily terminated by the team. G was entitled to his lost earnings and a further sum to reflect the effect on him of summary termination (six months' pay). An award of €650 000 was made in G's favour. The tribunal did not accept a further claim for €5 000 000 by G for damage to reputation, finding that compensation for this head of damage was provided for in the award which it made.

Claim from Employer for Breach by Employee

CAS 2008/A/1644, *Mutu* v. *Chelsea Football Club* M was a footballer who had been held to have committed an anti-doping rule violation and whose contract was terminated by Chelsea Football Club (CFC). (The player's breach of his employment contract with the club without just cause and the validity of the termination by the club had been established by previous CAS awards.) The club claimed damages under the employment contract under the principles of English contract law and the relevant FIFA regulations which were incorporated into the contract. The FIFA regulations permitted an assessment of damages, not only on the basis of legal principles, but on the basis of broader considerations specific to the sport ('specificity of sport'). The claim, as originally formulated by the club, covered the various unamortised costs in acquiring the player, the costs of replacing the player and other benefits received by the player before termination, legal costs and damage to the club's brand. The FIFA regulation also allowed the remaining value of the contract breached to be considered. After considering the claim, the Disputes Resolution Charter (DRC) made an award based solely on the unamortised cost of acquiring the player in the sum of €17 173 990.

On appeal, it was contended on behalf of the player that the claim for reliance loss was not properly established under English law on grounds of remoteness and absence of effective causal connection, that the FIFA regulations were in breach of an EU agreement and EU law and, if the player were liable for damages, that the claim should be limited to the period during which he was unavailable to play for the club as a result of the anti-doping rule violation.

CAS held that English law was applicable to the contract in accordance with the parties' choice and that the regulations were properly incorporated into the player's contract. It determined that, as a matter of English law, the reliance cost in the form of the unamortised cost of acquisition of the player was recoverable. It assessed this head of loss in a greater sum than that awarded by the DRC, but, as the club's appeal only sought to uphold the award in the DRC, the award of €17 173 990 stood.

The loss of the benefit of the acquisition costs could be directly attributed to the breach by the player. While the DRC had considered various factors, including the specificity of sport, its decision was based upon the cost of acquiring the player's services. This claim was properly available as a matter of English law. The point on EU law was moot because it only related to the FIFA regulations, and even if the regulations could be struck down, the damages would have to be calculated on the principles of English law under the employment contract. In any event, the CAS Panel held that the application of the regulations was not discriminatory on grounds of nationality, nor contrary to EU competition provisions. The Regulations simply confirmed the binding force of an employment contract, and the obligation to pay compensation under the contract in the Regulations did not imply an unlawful restriction of competition in the European Union. The player could not invoke EU rules on the freedom of movement within the common market because he was not an EU citizen at the time of the breach. The CAS Panel also rejected arguments that the damages awarded were penal in nature. Nor did it accept that the player could succeed in reducing damages on any other basis.

Decisions Outside the Code but Arising from Issues of Compliance by Signatories: Rio Olympics and Paralympics

Following allegations of corruption within the IAAF and related allegations of systematic doping in Russia, WADA commissioned independent reports into the allegations. Reports by an Independent Commission released in November 2015 and January 2016 and a report by an Independent Person appointed by WADA (Professor McLaren) released on 18 July 2016[41] concluded that there had been systemic failures by Signatories to

---

41 The second McClaren Report was released on 9 December 2016 and confirmed the findings of the first report. It focussed on athletes who were alleged to have benefitted from the manipulation of doping control. It was accompanied by a package of evidence which is searchable on the WADA website. The allegations against individuals which arise from the report are being investigated and brought before the applicable tribunals, and presumably in due course the organisations with responsibility for results management will bring allegations before the applicable tribunals where the evidence supports the bringing of allegations against individuals.

the Code – the Russian Athletics Federation (RusAF), the Russian anti-doping organisation RUSADA and the IAAF – to act properly in accordance with their obligations as Signatories to the Code and that this had involved systematic doping and deliberate conduct to cover up doping.

After the release of the Independent Commission report in November 2015, WADA declared the RusAF to be non-compliant with the Code and the IAAF Council provisionally suspended RusAF under its Constitution. The full suspension of RusAF was confirmed in November 2015, and the conditions for its reinstatement were published in December 2015. In June 2016, following a report from a task force which had been monitoring RusAF, the IAAF decided not to reinstate RusAF, which meant that Russian athletes remained ineligible under the IAAF competition rules (as members of the suspended member). The IAAF passed an amendment to its rules to the effect that if an athlete could clearly and convincingly show that he or she had not been tainted by the system in which RusAF had been involved because he or she had been subject to other anti-doping systems and effective testing, the athlete could apply for special permission to compete as a neutral athlete in an individual capacity.

The first report of the Independent Person appointed by WADA (the 'McLaren Report'), released in July 2016, explained that the inquiry team had identified and verified evidence which led them to believe that the Russian government had developed and controlled a doping programme from at least 2011 until August 2015. The report concluded that this programme had involved various athletes (and had benefitted them by suppressing positive tests) and athlete support personnel, the key anti-doping organisations and key personnel in those organisations. The reports, in particular the McLaren Report, were followed by calls from WADA for the IOC not to invite any Russian athletes to the Rio Olympic Games.

The IOC did not do this, but it did make a decision on 24 July 2016 concerning the eligibility of Russian athletes for the Rio Olympics. The decision set out the conditions which had to be met before any entry for a Russian athlete or accreditation for a support person from the ROC could be accepted. The conditions involved the athlete's international federation being satisfied of the requirements set out in the IOC decision, including that the athlete should not have been sanctioned for doping in the past and that the athlete was not implicated in the circumstances set out in the McLaren Report.

In addition to the decision taken by the IAAF in relation to the suspension of its member, RusAF, in June 2016, after the publication of the McLaren Report the IPC decided to suspend the membership of the

Russian Paralympic Committee (RPC) because of its failure to comply with the WADC. This decision meant under the IPC Constitution that the RPC could not enter athletes in any competition sanctioned by the IPC, including the Paralympic Games in Rio. Both the decisions by the IAAF and the IPC were challenged before CAS.

The decisions on eligibility for the Rio Olympics made in relation to athletes by international federations under the conditions in the IOC decision produced a number of challenges before CAS, which were heard in the Ad Hoc Division at the Games or in specially agreed arbitration before the Games.[42]

It is important to note that the various CAS decisions were not concerned with adjudicating on possible violations committed by individual athletes, nor with the question whether it was appropriate to sanction athletes collectively without proving individual cases, but with the interpretation and application of the IOC decision and/or the rules of international federations put in place to decide on the eligibility of athletes and with the question whether particular sporting associations, the IAAF and the IPC had acted properly within their rules in suspending the membership of particular members. It should further be noted that the reports commissioned by WADA, while they made findings based on evidence obtained by those who wrote them, were not adjudicated decisions by a court or CAS. The material relied on to support the conclusions in the reports could be relied on as evidence if produced before CAS, and Professor McLaren did provide affidavit evidence before CAS. However, the hearings before CAS were largely concerned with the consideration of the validity of the rules and decisions under them relating to the eligibility of Russian athletes. While the independent reports made various findings of non-compliance by Signatories, the sanctions for non-compliance by Signatories under the Code are limited and various organisations were declared to be non-compliant, the cases were not concerned with sanctions under the Code but with the interpretation of specific rules made by sporting organisations.[43] The cases generally illustrate the

---

42 See Chapter 3 for the Ad Hoc Division of CAS and applicable rules. There were several CAS awards in relation to the eligibility of Russian athletes. CAS Ad Hoc Division (OG Rio) 16/011, *Andrienko and Others* v. *FISA and IOC*.

43 See Article 23.6 of the Code, which provides that non-compliance by a Signatory may result in consequences in addition to ineligibility to bid for international events, such as forfeiture of offices at WADA, ineligibility to be a candidate to hold international events and other consequences under the Olympic Charter. None of these consequences provide for the kind of response which was put in place by decisions/rules of the IOC and international federations as a result of the findings contained in the McLaren Report.

underlying point that sporting associations operate by making rules which are enforceable by contract and that if the rules made are not on their interpretation contrary to the Code, sporting associations have a broad power to make rules which bind their members. Very recently, the WADA Foundation Board has proposed that the Code be amended to include a more developed sanctions regime for non-compliance with the Code, and in this way compliance with the Code by Signatories will be brought directly under the Code.

In one respect, the IOC decision was caught by the Code. The condition that an athlete could not be eligible to be put forward for the Games if he or she had ever been sanctioned for doping was declared to be a denial of the individual rights of the athlete because it imposed an additional sanction in addition to the period of any sanction served under the Code.[44] This is contrary to the Code, which provides that Signatories have to implement sanctions provisions without substantial amendment and cannot change the effect of those provisions.

Other challenges to decisions by international federations that athletes did not meet the conditions for eligibility under the IOC conditions or rules put in place to meet those conditions were unsuccessful, with the exception of a challenge by the single Russian athlete originally permitted to compete as a neutral athlete, who challenged the decision to reverse that permission after the release of the McLaren Report.

A challenge to the competition rules made by the IAAF under which RusAF was suspended as a member was unsuccessful. This challenge came before CAS under a special arbitration agreement.[45] The CAS Panel stated that the appeal was not concerned with the collective responsibility of athletes or with the consideration of the question whether the individual athletes were directly or indirectly responsible for anti-doping rule violations. The appeal was concerned, rather, with the validity of the IAAF Rules under which IAAF suspended RusAF and provided for Russian athletes who met certain criteria to be allowed to compete. CAS held that the competition rule which provided that an athlete who was a member of a suspended national federation was not eligible for competitions was clear and enforceable. It was an eligibility rule arising from the way in which

---

44 CAS Ad Hoc Division (OG Rio) 16/004, *Yulia Efimova v. ROC, IOC and FINA*, where the condition was declared to be unenforceable. This decision followed the reasoning in the earlier CAS award on the Osaka Rule (see summary at pages 525–6). The result was that the international federation had to consider the other conditions in the IOC decision. Ultimately, E's entry for the Games was put forward by the ROC after the international federation had approved it under the IOC conditions, and E competed at the Rio Games.
45 CAS 2016/O/4684, *The Russian Olympic Committee, Lyukman and Others v. IAAF*.

international sport is structured and was imposed on RusAF because of what it had done. It was not a doping sanction imposed on individual athletes under the Code. It was in any event consistent with the Code. The Code obliged international federations to require national federations to have rules which complied with the Code, and nothing in the Code prevented a Signatory like the IAAF from enforcing its own rule on sporting bodies over which the Signatory had authority. There was no basis for any plea of estoppel, the principle of proportionality could not be engaged where the rule was not a sanction provision and there was no basis to say that the rule was applied in a way which breached the right to equal treatment. The competition rule and the rule which allowed for the IAAF Council to grant eligibility to an athlete who was not tainted by the failure of the suspended member and had been subject to full drug testing outside the country of the suspended federation were both held to be valid and enforceable.

Similarly, the challenge brought by the RPC to the decision to suspend its membership of the IPC on the grounds that it had not met its obligations under the Code (which had the effect of preventing the RPC from entering athletes to the Paralympic Games in Rio) was unsuccessful. CAS held that the suspension was properly made under the IPC Constitution and was within its power and not disproportionate in light of the findings in the McLaren Report. The CAS Panel expressly noted that the para-athletes were not parties to the appeal and that the question for decision was not the legitimacy of a collective sanction of the Russian para-athletes but whether the IPC was entitled to suspend one of its members – the RPC – under its rules.[46]

---

46 CAS 2016/A/4735, *Russian Paralympic Committee v. International Paralympic Committee.*

11

The Way Ahead for the Code

Amending the Code

WADA is responsible for overseeing the evolution and improvement of the Code and for initiating amendments to the Code under Article 23.7. Where WADA puts forward amendments, it must institute a consultation process under which athletes, Signatories and governments provide their comments on the proposed amendments. After the required consultation process has taken place, the proposed amendments must be approved by a two-thirds majority of the WADA Foundation Board, with a majority of the public sector and Olympic movement members casting votes, in order to be adopted. Amendments come into effect three months after approval, and Signatories to the Code must implement applicable amendments within one year of approval by the WADA Foundation Board.[1]

WADA initiated amendments to the 2004 Code in 2005, and a consultation process took place over the next eighteen months, which culminated in the meeting of the WADA Foundation Board in Madrid in November 2007 at the World Conference on Doping. At this meeting, amendments to the Code were approved, and the deadline for acceptance of the amended Code by Signatories was set at 1 January 2009. Also on 1 January 2009, the International Standard for Testing 2009 was implemented. The revised standard introduced the detailed requirements for the implementation and administration of the whereabouts regime.

The process of reviewing the 2009 Code commenced at the end of November 2011. The result of the first phase of consultation with stakeholders, which ended on 15 March 2012, was the production of a first draft of a revised 2015 Code. Eventually, the 2015 Code went through four published drafts, with the drafting team producing fifty different working drafts. The process of consultation with stakeholders produced some 315 separate submissions, and there were thousands of suggested changes.

---

1 See Article 23.6.3 of the Code.

Ultimately, the 2015 Code was the result, and it was submitted to the WADA Foundation Board for approval at the Fourth World Conference on Doping in Sport at the end of 2013. In summary, the main changes proposed in the first draft of the revised Code were:

- the inclusion in the Purpose of the Code of an express statement that the Code will be applied in a manner which reflects proportionality and human rights;
- the abolition of B sample analysis;
- the addition of two further anti-doping rule violations (complicity in an anti-doping rule violation and prohibited association with ineligible athlete support personnel);
- the requirement that potential performance enhancement be a necessary condition for the inclusion of a substance or method on the Prohibited List;
- the overruling of the approach to Article 10.4 in the *Oliveira* decision;
- more flexible sanctions where contaminated products are the cause of a violation;
- special provision for sanctions for substances of abuse allowing rehabilitation to form part of a sanction;
- the expansion of incentives for those who provide substantial assistance;
- a standard four-year-period of ineligibility where aggravated circumstances are established;
- provision for sanctions to include ineligibility in future Olympic Games;
- further provision for the consequences for teams;
- particular provisions concerning minors being persons who have not reached the age of 14; and
- an extension of the period of limitation under Article 17 from eight to fourteen years on a non-retroactive basis for the more serious anti-doping rule violations.[2]

As can be seen, many of the points in the initial draft were incorporated into the 2015 Code. Others were not, including the significant proposal to change the criteria for the inclusion of a substance or method on the Prohibited List, which aimed to narrow the focus of the Code. At the same

2 The process of further consultation and revision of the document until the finalisation of the 2015 Code could be followed on the WADA website in a section devoted to the process of review of the 2009 Code. The review of the Code was carried out at the same time as an extensive review and amendment of the International Standards; see Chapter 2 for the detail of the current International Standards.

time as the Code review, WADA initiated a review of the International Standards, with consultation. The current International Standards are the result.

In the past, this text was produced at the time when the process of reviewing the current Code was underway under Article 23. This edition of the text appears when the 2015 Code has been in operation for nearly two years and we are beginning to see tribunal and CAS decisions on the significant provisions of the Code. This is not the time to speculate on what changes a future review might produce, but it does seem appropriate to offer some comment on the challenges which face the Code and how well the Code has functioned as a set of anti-doping rules since its first version in 2004. (The concluding chapters from the first and second editions are included in Appendix 3 of this edition in order to reflect some of the views which have previously been expressed regarding the development of the Code.)

Recently, the operation of the Code has faced significant challenges. The first was before the German courts, where the enforceability of a CAS award was challenged on the grounds that the CAS system of arbitration infringed German competition law. While the legal grounds for the challenge were specific and ultimately unsuccessful, the case was at the time reported as showing wider dissatisfaction with the CAS system, particularly on behalf of athletes. The rejection of the challenge underlined important aspects of the arbitration system and the reasons for it. While any system which is based on agreement will remain open to challenge under national legal systems, the general acceptance of the need for an arbitral systems in sport at both national and international level and the affirmation of that system by national courts – in particular the Swiss Federal Tribunal – has confirmed CAS in its important central role under the Code. If CAS remains attentive to the needs of its users, the result should be a strengthening of the role of the Code and of CAS. The strong State-level support for the Code and for sports arbitration as the means of deciding on allegations under the Code, evidenced by the widespread acceptance of the UNESCO Convention, suggests that the Code and CAS will remain central to the anti-doping effort.

The Operation of the Code as a Set of Rules

At this point in the evolution of the Code, it seems appropriate to make some general comment on how well it operates as a set of rules and how it measures up to its stated aims and purposes. The Code has now operated

THE WAY AHEAD FOR THE CODE

for well over ten years and has been significantly revised twice, after wide-ranging consultation produced the first version in 2004.

My Perspective

My experience with anti-doping rules, as with the law generally, has been that of an independent lawyer working with the rules. This work with anti-doping rules goes back well before the acceptance of the first version of the Code in 2004. Where your general focus is day-to-day work and advice, it can be hard to take a broader view of the rules you work with. From time to time, when the Code was reviewed in the WADA review process and I was asked to help with comments or I sat down to write about the rules for this text (particularly this last chapter), I did have the opportunity to think more about the aim and formulation of the rules. But generally, my emphasis has remained on offering guidance for those who have to apply the rules. The name of the game is usually working out what the rules mean and how to operate under them in particular circumstances in particular cases, rather than thinking about whether rules might be better framed or reformed.

A Central Document in an Expanding Regulatory Field

The Code and the International Standards and Guidelines have to cover a wide field and include significant technical aspects (in particular the Standards and related Guidelines). The areas covered by the rules produced by WADA are extending, and this makes the rule-making and rule-drafting process ever more difficult and demanding. However, the focus for those who participate in sport and are subject to the rules is the Code itself, and it is to that document that participants will turn in order to understand the key elements of the anti-doping regime and their rights and obligations under them. The Code is the central document for the 'rules of the game' in doping regulation – a form of sports legislation that is binding by agreement. The core Articles are relatively few and are mostly found in Part One of the Code (see Article 23.2.2)

Against that background, I would like to make three points on the rules in the Code and their operation. These points are concerned with the practical operation of the Code and largely do not go into technical detail. A response to them would require a good deal of technical legal work, and from my perspective that work should form part of the path ahead for the Code and decision-making under it. Before I make these points, an important general observation about the path travelled so far should be made.

Looking Back Over the Path Travelled

The control of doping in sport worldwide has come a very long way in a short time. WADA was established to promote, coordinate and monitor the fight against doping in sport in all its forms in 1999. This was after the *Festina* doping affair in the 1998 Tour de France had highlighted the need for more coordinated global action against doping. The first version of the Code was adopted by the World Conference on Doping at Copenhagen in March 2003 and came into effect in January 2004. The Code has unprecedented support from sporting organisations, by their agreement to its application and enforcement, and from States, by their acceptance of the UNSECO Anti-Doping Convention 2005. While the Convention is best described as 'soft' international law, the high level of State support for the Code and CAS is obvious.

The fact that we can speak the same language on the regulation of doping and its core elements – burden and standard of proof, violations, sanctions and so on – as sports administrators, lawyers and athletes in considering doping and the problems which arise from it, when a little over a decade ago there was no standard approach across sports or nations, is a very significant achievement. So much hard work has been done to start this process and maintain impetus in a rapidly changing and challenging environment.

Every sport and national system will have its examples of the lack of uniformity which existed pre-Code. New Zealand, by way of example, has moved quickly from circumstances where it would often be unclear on looking at a sport's rules whether there were effective anti-doping rules in place, or whether, if anti-doping rules had been made, they were binding on a particular athlete, to the situation today under the Code, where the application of the provisions of the Code and the jurisdiction of a specialist tribunal to interpret and apply them is an established norm.

Rise of Sport-specific Arbitration

In addition, along with the development of the Code, a specific hearing system in the form of CAS has developed. As has been outlined, the development of CAS started before the Code, when CAS began to work in interpreting and applying anti-doping regimes as sports increasingly adopted exclusive appeal rights to CAS. CAS Panels sought to develop a coherent body of decisions relating to anti-doping rules, and some of those elements were taken up by the Code (including, of course, the somewhat idiosyncratic 'comfortable satisfaction' standard of proof).

CAS was given a central role in the interpretation and application of the Code. It is the mandatory appeal court for international-level athletes and an option for appeals by national-level athletes, and it is available to operate as a first-instance tribunal.

Since the adoption of the Code, CAS Panels have taken the lead in interpreting and applying the provisions of the Code. While CAS has its detractors, has had its challenges before the Swiss Federal Tribunal and before national courts – most recently in the *Pechstein* case – and will, like any institution of its kind, need to continue to develop in order to address the needs and concerns of its users, the existence of an independent arbitral tribunal for sports disputes standing outside the constraints and variations inherent in national legal systems and offering a re-hearing on appeal, has been a significant part of creating a binding harmonised approach to anti-doping regulation.

At the national level, in many jurisdictions, the rise of independent sport-specific arbitral tribunals has mirrored the development of CAS in the international arena. This is an important area, because most doping violations will be heard before first-instance tribunals, whether within international sporting federations or at national-level tribunals.

So, if you look back to the world before sport committed to a harmonised set of anti-doping rules, you can see that sport has taken a path which has created significant positive change and much greater harmony in the regulation of anti-doping across the sporting world. That movement has also contributed significantly to sport establishing its own arbitral tribunal systems to provide decisions in the way and in the time-frames it requires.

When the shift in New Zealand in dealing with sporting disputes is considered, it is striking how much the Code and its implementation are closely linked to the very significant movement towards sports arbitration, which sees disputes determined in a speedy and cost-effective manner, in keeping with the needs of sport.

The regime faces challenges and will continue to do so, but I believe that progress towards an efficient harmonised regime has been considerable and is undeniable.

But what of the central document itself as it stands in 2016, and the rules it contains – how well does it work? How well do the rules in the

COMMENTS ON THE 2015 CODE 541

Code meet the goals of legislation under the general law? Is the Code as understandable and accessible as it is practicable? How good a foundation does the Code offer for a harmonised approach to anti-doping? Can the Code be improved?

Comments on the 2015 Code

The Ongoing Quest for Simple, Understandable Rules

I think that it is worth asking how the Code measures up against its aims and how it might be improved as an operating set of rules.

What is sought after in a set of rules or regulations like this is clarity and certainty. Rules with these attributes can be readily understood by those they affect and are accessible. These aims are particularly important with a document like the Code which tries to establish an independent, fundamental set of rules and function in order to harmonise the core elements of the anti-doping regime across the world of sport. The purpose is similar to that of international conventions and agreements which establish common regimes in international trade and commerce. Simplicity and clarity are vital – agreements with such qualities are more likely to allow those affected to understand their obligations and order their affairs accordingly.

The law is sometimes described as an ongoing quest for clarity and certainty – Lord Cooke described administrative law as being about the 'search for simplicity'. But these *desiderata* are very elusive. They have a will-o'-the-wisp nature. Many task forces set up by governments to simplify legislation in complex areas such as tax do not reach their goal because those with the task (or those who pay them) decide that the law in the area just cannot be reduced to simple language!

Drafting rules can become a Sisyphean task – just when you think you have achieved certainty or clarity in expressing a required rule, circumstances show that you have not and you have to start again.

My observations on the Code need to be considered with all this in mind – drafting such a document is not easy.

How Does the Code Say it will Work?

In the Introduction to the Code, the text states that the Code is intended to be a set of anti-doping rules which function like the rules of sports competition themselves and can be treated by participants in the same way as the rules of the sport they play. These sport-specific rules and procedures aim to enforce anti-doping rules in a global and harmonised way and to be distinct in nature from criminal and civil proceedings. The Introduction strongly underlines the need for the Code to work and operate in a practical, understandable way across sport and to provide a set of core common rules.

First Point: the Key Rules in the Code have Changed Too Much

The Code has been reviewed and modified on two occasions (with significant consultation before the first version in 2004), and each time significant changes have been made to the rules. Under Article 23.7, WADA has the responsibility of overseeing the 'evolution and improvement' of the Code. This process of evolution and improvement is part of the agreement which Signatories to the Code have entered into. The result has been a wide-ranging review process leading to significant changes in core Articles (in particular Article 10 on sanctions) with each revision.

On one hand, this process can be seen as a laudably inclusive exercise which has been necessary as the Code has developed to maintain the confidence of all parties with an interest in the Code. On the other, where the balance between strictness and flexibility and harmonisation across sports in the area of sanctions is very difficult to arrive at, the result of the regular reviews has been significant unsettling change in the core Articles with each new version of the Code.

If the aim is to bring about certainty in the rules, there has been too much change and variation in core areas of the Code. International conventions and agreements which seek to harmonise rules in an area do not normally undergo this level of regular review and significant variation to core elements. While sports competition rules are reviewed regularly, their core elements do not change like this – if they did, the sport would be damaged.

The provisions of Article 10 on sanctions are the most obvious example of the significant changes on review. Take, as an example, the provisions for the process of imposing a reduced sanction for violations of Articles 2.1, 2.2 and 2.6 involving a specified substance. Article 10.3 of the 2004 Code, Article 10.4 of the 2009 Code and Article 10.5.1 of the 2015 Code provide for different approaches and will produce different results.

Generally, the 2015 Code introduces a much changed sanctions regime, increasing the standard period of ineligibility to four years where 'intentional' violations are involved and changing the regime for sanctions for violations involving specified substances. In this last area, the changes cannot be disguised by the application of familiar definitions such as 'no significant fault' to the exercise of arriving at a period of ineligibility because that definition is used in a different context and the sanctions provisions require a different inquiry into fault to arrive at the applicable sanction.

Significant changes to the rules which are central to the regime under the Code have been made at relatively short (five- and six-year) intervals. This is a brief period for a set of global rules to operate in before changing. Tribunals may just have become familiar with the operation of sanctions provisions under the Code when they have to apply a different Code (they may, indeed, in some cases have to work out which of two Code regimes should apply on *lex mitior* principles). Athletes and others subject to the rules will be dealt with differently (notwithstanding the inclusion of transitional provisions), affected for good or bad, by accidents of timing.

On one hand, this flexible changing regime is positive because it can be said to reflect the consensus of the changing wishes of Signatories, but on the other, it creates uncertainty, which risks undermining the foundation that the Code seeks to provide.

It must be acknowledged that the Code had to develop and change at the start. When the Code was first implemented, there was a widespread concern that a standard period of ineligibility of four years for doping would be vulnerable to attack under certain national legal systems. This made differentiation between real cheats and those who made negligent mistakes more difficult, and there was a widespread sense that the 2004 Code did not do this enough.

However, the basic point is that there has been too much change as a result of the extensive review process and the Code should, if possible, be changed less. If modification has been required up until 2015, perhaps now the framework of the Code has reached a state where it does not need significant substantive further amendment in the next review.

Second Point: the Drafting and Structure of the Code

From the first version in 2004, the Code has sought to prescribe in some detail for matters such as the operation of the defences to doping violations. With each successive review, the text has tended to grow by accretion. A highly prescriptive style with a good deal of explanation in the notes has been maintained. No doubt, the aim is to draft and explain the rules as fully as possible in order to assist tribunals to interpret and apply the Code as an autonomous document, as they are required to do. The extensive rules seek to underline the strictness of the regime and narrowness of the defences and any discretion under them.

Understandably, where the Code replaced a range of regimes where differing approaches brought about very different results, the aim was to provide as clearly as possible for standard outcomes. This approach has continued. Although the sanctions regime has been amended to provide more discretion to tribunals in certain areas, the relevant provisions of Article 10 have become more complicated and have remained very prescriptive. The result is that we now have a complicated document which may be very hard for a participant, or indeed a lay tribunal member, to follow.

It seems questionable whether the restricted approach to discretion in applying possible defences to reduce or eliminate a two-year period of ineligibility actually achieves the control over discretion which it aims at. Are tribunals and CAS applying the concepts of no significant fault by reference to the definitions in the Code in assessing the application of the defences, or do they tend to treat the provisions as supplying a more general discretion to arrive at an appropriate sanction by reference to the degree of fault anyway?

It is curious that in other, more serious violations (Articles 2.7–2.10), tribunals are left to arrive at a period of ineligibility across a wide range by reference to the fault or seriousness of the violation. Perhaps the time has now come to simplify the approach to defences which might reduce the two-year period of ineligibility where specified substances are concerned, and adopt simpler provisions.

In many areas, the Code contains over-elaborate definitions which should be simplified. Some definitions contain substantive or explanatory provisions which would be better understood if they were in the substantive provisions of the Code. For some examples, see the contents of the definitions of 'administration', 'trafficking', 'athlete' and 'contaminated product'.

Some important definitions relevant to serious violations are also difficult to apply, such as 'administration' and 'trafficking'. Sometimes the scope of an important definition lacks clarity in some aspects, such as 'ineligibility'.

The important definition of 'intentional', added in the 2015 Code in Article 10.2.3, which determines whether a violation of Article 2.1, 2.2 or 2.6 attracts four years' ineligibility or two (and effectively creates a further set of 'intentional' violations), is not contained in the definitions at all. It is also unclear how the phrase explaining that 'intentional is intended to identify those athletes who cheat' fits with a definition which provides that conscious risk-taking can be intentional conduct.

On a structural level, the Code has four parts, with most of the core elements of the anti-doping regime contained in Part One. For an athlete or other participant, the size of the document makes the key parts much less accessible.

Overall, the structure, the prescriptive drafting and the drafting style make the Code hard for participants (particularly athletes) to follow. It would be difficult, if not impossible, for an athlete to pick up the document and know where he or she stood.

Perhaps the time has come to retain the general framework of the violations and the applicable periods of ineligibility on any review but simplify the structure and drafting to create a standalone or sign-posted Part One which an athlete can turn to and readily understand.

The removal of the complex defence provisions in Article 10.5, which seek to control discretion on certain violations, and their replacement with a more general fault-based approach to discretion might be a part of this process.

In short, the next review should not involve significant changes, as has happened to date, but should be aimed at making the Code clearer and more accessible.

This is easy to say but hard to do, and will require a strong lead from WADA as the regulator. But if the Code is to provide a solid foundation in the interests of harmony, it should change less in its substantive essentials and be simpler and clearer. This desire for a simpler document is indirectly connected to my last point on the operation of the Code, which is concerned with improving hearing processes under the Code.

Third Point: Improving Hearing Processes under the Code

As has been outlined, Article 8 sets out the requirements for fair hearings under the Code in a general way which reflects the requirements of Article 6(1) of the ECHR. How the standard for a fair hearing is met is a matter for Signatories of the Code. While CAS has a central role as an appellate tribunal and re-hears decisions appealed on a *de novo* basis, most alleged violations under the Code will be heard at the first-tier level by a tribunal established by the particular sport involved (whether an international federation or NSO) or by an independent tribunal created for the purpose of hearing doping violations under the Code (and possibly other sporting disputes, as is the case with the Sports Tribunal in New Zealand). Most cases do not go to a re-hearing before CAS on appeal. This system places a heavy emphasis on the standard of first-instance hearings.

Establishing efficient and effective systems to hear alleged breaches of the Code in a manner which meets the requirements of Article 8 is a vital part of the Code system. Worldwide, it appears that a good deal of work is required in this area to improve the tribunal systems operating at national level and for international federations. The requirements for the hearing process will be evident – separation between the body investigating and making allegations under the Code and the tribunal deciding on allegations, an independent tribunal with experienced members, simple procedural rules which can be flexibly applied, a commitment on the part of the tribunal to produce reasoned decisions as quickly as possible expressed in a straightforward manner.

One of the key areas for work and development is in building up the standard and uniformity of first-instance hearing processes. While WADA's appeal right is one way of correcting erroneous approaches, it will be far better overall if first-instance tribunals can be expected to apply the Code properly and produce the required reasoned decisions quickly. Work in establishing and training independent tribunals at national level and for international federations is important in the process of building a common approach to the Code across all sport worldwide.

Improvement in tribunal processes and greater confidence in those processes is linked to the development of the Code. The simpler the drafting of the Code, the easier it will be for tribunals to apply. The more tribunals develop and provide consistent decisions – something which WADA can assess – the more tribunals might be left to exercise discretion in areas such as the imposition of sanctions.

As noted, the sanctions regime currently seeks to restrain the operation of discretion to reduce periods of ineligibility by providing for specific defined defences. In a more mature system, serious violations involving intentional conduct would attract fixed sanctions and longer periods of ineligibility in higher ranges, while other violations involving specified substances might have periods of ineligibility imposed within a range simply by reference to the fault of the athlete, assessed in the context of the athlete's obligations under the Code. Such an approach involves trusting the first-instance tribunal system to a significant degree, but perhaps the time to do this has come. It would certainly be easier to simplify the drafting of the Code if the exercise of imposing a sanction for certain violations was generally expressed to allow a discretion to the tribunal and removed most of the range of prescriptive defences in the Code.

These comments are general in nature, but they should provide some food for thought for those responsible for the rules. Pulling the strands together, the Code has probably reached a point of relatively mature development where the fundamental aim of creating harmony in anti-doping regulation is best served if further review concentrates specifically on simplifying the drafting of the document, particularly in those areas which represent the core obligations for athletes and participants. This will make the key elements of the Code more accessible for participants and allow the Code to function more as intended. This development of the Code as a set of rules should be linked to a concerted effort to provide for effective hearings of allegations under the Code in first-instance tribunals.

Appendix 1

Article 10.4 of the 2009 Code and Case Summaries

Article 10.4 of the 2009 Code has been removed from the 2015 Code. The 2015 Code contains different requirements (showing no significant fault) which an athlete must prove they meet in order to reduce the period of ineligibility for strict liability violations of presence, use or possession (where there is no intentional conduct as provided for in Article 10.2 of the 2015 Code). Although some decisions on Article 10.4 of the 2009 Code contain discussions on the general assessment of levels of fault which can provide some general insight into the process,[1] they are mostly of historic interest and should not, it is suggested, generally be referred to in considering the 2015 Code. The effective operation of Article 10.4 of the 2009 Code was to a significant extent hindered by debate over its meaning and application – in particular, the so-called '*Oliviera* debate', which concerned the question whether an athlete who ingested a prohibited substance in a product could show the required absence of intent to enhance sport performance if he or she could show no knowledge of the presence of the prohibited substance in the product, because the intent in question on the interpretation of Article 10.4 had to concern the particular prohibited substance. After the second edition, this debate between CAS Panels continued, with awards taking different views on the interpretation of Article 10.4.[2] Whether the interpretations made much substantive difference, the

---

1 See, for example, the discussion of assessing fault in CAS 2013/A/1327, *Cilic v. ITF*. However, tribunals should now, it is submitted, refer to the definition of 'fault' in the 2015 Code, which has to be referred to in any consideration of fault under the 2015 Code and provides general direction for the process.

2 See CAS 2013/A/3316, *WADA v. Bata*, where the award reviews the cases on the interpretation of Article 10.4 and follows the *Oliviera* line of authority supporting the preference for the interpretation in that award with a *contra proferentem* argument that Article 10.4, if unclear, should be interpreted against the drafter in favour of the position of the athlete. The award refers to the various awards in the debate. Most take the *Oliviera* side (although some of these were concerned with the further complication of indirect intent/recklessness, which would mean that an athlete who had no knowledge of the presence of a substance in a product but took obvious risk could not show the absence of intent required) – CAS

548

uncertainty and difficulty in applying Article 10.4 no doubt contributed to its removal and replacement with the provisions on sanctions in the 2015 Code, which, put simply, use the requirement of establishing no significant fault to open the possibility of reducing the applicable sanction to violations of presence, use or possession of a specified substance.

Article 10.4: Broadening the Category of Specified Substances

While the 2009 Code maintains the basic position that a two-year period of ineligibility is the standard sanction for most violations, Article 4.2.2 provides that, for the purposes of the application of Article 10, all prohibited substances, save those substances which are in the class of anabolic agents and hormones, as well as specific identified stimulants, hormone antagonists and modulators identified on the Prohibited List, will be 'specified substances'. As was the position under Article 10.3 of the 2004 Code, where a specified substance is detected in the bodily sample of an athlete (or a specified substance has been used by an athlete in breach of Article 2.2), the strict liability regime will apply as to disqualification of the result obtained in the competition where the result was obtained, but the athlete who has committed the violation has the possibility of establishing the grounds for a potentially more lenient sanctions regime to be applied. The text which follows is taken from Chapter 8 of the second edition. No further case summaries have been added – the principal CAS awards after the second edition are referred to in the footnote in this paragraph. (All page references which follow refer to the second edition of the text and do not apply to this current edition. They have been retained for completeness sake.)

Operation of Article 10.4

Under Article 10.4 where an athlete or other person can establish how a specified substance entered his or her body (or came into his or her

---

2010/A2229, CAS 2011/A/2645, CAS 2011/A/2677, CAS 2011/A/2615, CAS 2012/A/2756, CAS2012/A/2747, CAS 2012/A/2822 and CAS Bulletin 02/2013 18–27 – but there are significant awards on the other side, too – CAS 2012/A/2804, *Kutrovsky* and CAS 2013, *West*. These latter follow the approach in *Foggo*, which did seem to have the merit of simpler exposition and application. It is submitted that the debate showed the disadvantage of the absence of a doctrine of binding precedent in CAS and did not further the practical application of the regime under the Code. It has been resolved by replacing Article 10.4 with different provisions for the reduction of the period of ineligibility where violations of presence, use or possession involve a specified substance.

possession), and can show that the specified substance was not intended to enhance sport performance or mask the use of a performance-enhancing substance, the standard period of ineligibility for a violation of Article 2.1 (presence of a prohibited substance), 2.2 (use) and 2.6 (possession) under Article 10.2 is replaced by a possible range of sanctions from, at a minimum, a reprimand and no period of ineligibility to a maximum of two years' ineligibility. The increase in the maximum period of ineligibility from one year under the 2003 Code reflects the greater range of substances which now fall within the category of specified substances and provides for a wider range of possible sanctions depending on the fault of the athlete if the tribunal considers that the requirements for the exercise of discretion under Article 10.4 have been established.

To be able to take advantage of this provision and open up the broader discretion, the athlete or other person who has committed the violation must, in addition to the crucial threshold requirement of establishing how the prohibited substance came to be in his or her system or in his or her possession (which also applies to the defences under Articles 10.5.1 and 10.5.2), produce corroborating evidence, in addition to his or her word, which establishes the absence of an intent to enhance sport performance or mask the use of a performance-enhancing substance. Corroborating evidence will be evidence from another source (not the athlete) which supports the word of the athlete on the absence of an intent to enhance sport performance.

The Standard of Proof under Article 10.4

While the athlete must establish how the specified substance entered into his or her body or possession on the balance of probabilities, the absence of an intention to enhance sporting performance required under Article 10.4 has to be established to the higher standard of the comfortable satisfaction of the hearing body – a standard previously applied under the 2003 Code only to the proof of an allegation by an anti-doping organisation. This is a change from the approach in the 2003 Code (where an athlete never had to meet this higher standard of proof) and, in particular, the requirements of Article 10.3 of the 2003 Code. The more rigorous approach to the application of Article 10.4 was, no doubt, established because within the much wider range of 'specified substances' under the 2009 Code, there will be more substances which can be used intentionally to enhance sporting performance.

The application of Article 10.4 raises two significant issues for tribunals – how to approach the question whether the athlete has proved that he or she had no intention to enhance sporting performance and how to assess fault if the athlete proves the absence of such intent.

How to Assess the Intention to Enhance Sport Performance

Article 10.4 is unclear in the approach which is to be taken in the assessment of whether there was an intention to enhance sport performance. Plainly, a tribunal has to consider the circumstances in which the substance was taken (or came to be in a person's possession) in order to decide whether the athlete has shown that he or she did not intend to enhance sport performance. While this is an inquiry into the athlete's state of mind, it involves assessing the facts objectively to determine that state of mind. This inquiry can give rise to difficulties in assessing what amounts to enhancing sport performance. The question whether an athlete must know of the presence of a specified substance in the substance consumed before he or she can be said to have an intention of enhancing sport performance by taking the substance detected, has also caused some difficulties for tribunals and CAS Panels. While the first part of Article 10.4 refers to establishing that the specified substance was not intended to enhance performance, the second part simply refers to the absence of intent to enhance sport performance without reference to the specified substance. A CAS Panel has held[3] that the question is whether the athlete can show that he or she did not intend to enhance sport performance by taking the specified substance detected. As a result, where the athlete could not identify the prohibited substance as a constituent of the substance ingested from the product labelling, he or she was able to show an absence of intent to enhance sport performance. This approach was based on the premise that the intention of Article 10.4 was that the athlete had simply to establish the general absence of intent to enhance performance, with matters such as the athlete's failure to take proper precautions to avoid ingesting the particular specified substance being considered when deciding on his or her level of fault. It is to be noted that this decision has not been followed by another CAS Panel in *Foggo v. NRL*,[4] where the Panel held that the effect of the words in Article 10.4 when read in the context of the rules as a whole and their purpose is to require that the athlete show that the ingestion of the product which contained the prohibited substance was not intended

---

3 See CAS 2010/A/2107, *Oliveira* v. *USADA*, pages 268–9 below. See also CAS 2011/A/2465, *UCI* v. *Kolobonev*, where the CAS Panel followed the approach in *Oliveira*. There was a non-doping medical explanation for the use of the prohibited substance which supported the finding that there was no intention to enhance sport performance.

4 CAS A2/2011.

to enhance sport performance. This question is a matter of assessing the intention of the athlete at the time of the ingestion of the substance taken whether or not the athlete is aware that it contains a prohibited substance.

It is submitted that Article 10.4 directs a factual consideration of the circumstances in which the specified substance came to be ingested and does not require that an athlete knows specifically of the presence of the substance for there to be an intention to enhance sport performance in taking the substance. If the prohibited substance consumed was contained in a supplement where the athlete did not know of the contents of the supplement and the athlete cannot show in a general sense that he or she did not intend to enhance performance in taking the supplement containing the specified substance, it would not seem correct to say that there is no intent to enhance performance where the athlete does not know of the presence of the substance. It is suggested that the better approach to this requirement of Article 10.4 (as outlined in *Foggo*) is to ask whether in the circumstances in which the specified substance was ingested, the athlete has shown that he or she was not intending to enhance sport performance to the required standard with the required corroborative evidence. This more rigorous approach is consistent with the notes to the Article which refer to the specified substances including many substances which are capable of use as doping agents and the overall purpose of the Code.

The notes to Article 10.4 refer to various factual matters which may in combination lead a tribunal to find that the athlete had no intention to enhance performance – the nature of the substance, the fact that the timing of its ingestion would not have been beneficial to the athlete, the open use or disclosure of the substance, medical records indicating that there was a non-sport-related reason for taking the substance. Perhaps the greatest difficulties for tribunals have arisen in considering where to draw the line between those cases where the use of the product and taking part in competition are sufficiently remotely connected to allow the player to show that there was no intention to enhance his or her performance and those cases where the use of the product and sporting competition are too close to show this. Where an athlete explains the taking of a supplement which turns out to contain a specified substance by saying his or her aim was to be less tired after work so as to be able to train, some tribunals have found the question whether the athlete has no intention to enhance sport performance difficult. This is a factual question which comes down to assessing the degree of connection required under Article 10.4 between the taking of the prohibited substance and sport performance. It is submitted that the taking of any substance with the intention of improving training or racing performance should mean that an athlete cannot establish the requirement under Article 10.4.[5]

It should also be noted that what amounts to an intent to enhance sport performance will depend upon the particular circumstances and will need to be assessed by reference to the qualities required in the particular sport involved. By way of example in some sports, substances which may cause an athlete to lose weight or produce a slimmer appearance may be seen to enhance sport performance.

Enhancing Sport Performance: Wide Range of Possible Circumstances

CAS 2006/A/1175, Danuite v. International Dance Sport Federation

D, a competitive ballroom dancer, tested positive for a prohibited stimulant which had been taken to produce a slimmer appearance. Necessary under sports rules to determine whether a substance improved sport performance. In the context of the particular sport, CAS held that the effects of the product did produce an enhancement in sport performance.[6]

---

5 For examples of a national-level tribunal finding this question difficult and deciding by a fine margin that the requirements of Article 10.4 have been established, see the decisions of the NZ Sports Tribunal in *DFSNZ* v. *Prestney* ST 09/11 and *DFSNZ* v. *Jacobs* ST 24/10, where in each case the Tribunal held by a very fine margin that the requirements of Article 10.4 had been fulfilled (with the athlete having a high degree of fault). See also *DFSNZ* v. *Takerei* S/T 01/12, where the Tribunal held by a majority that the athlete could rely on Article 10.4 on the basis that the approach in *Oliveira* was applicable. The Tribunal notes the unsatisfactory uncertainty in the approach in the CAS decisions and expresses the hope that WADA will bring certainty to the position in the near future. See further *ITF* v. *Kutrovsky* 24 May 2012 (at www.itftennis.com), where ITF Anti-Doping Tribunal noted the conflict in approach to Article 10.4 in the CAS decisions but did not have to decide point in the circumstances of the case and found that player had not established absence of intention to enhance sport performance.

6 See observations in *USADA* v. *Frankie Caruso III*, American Arbitration Association (North American Court of Arbitration for Sport Panel) where C tested positive at Men's US Championship tournament in 2003. He was selected for drug testing and disclosed that he had taken two 'water pills' and a Centrum pill which contained furosemide. The athlete had obtained the pill from his mother, who had been prescribed it by her doctor. The Panel found no defence to an allegation of anti-doping rule violation or any ground to reduce the then applicable period of ineligibility of two years. While it was not necessary to show that the prohibited substance improved performance, the Panel observed that the boxer did obtain performance enhancement by taking the pill because it assisted him to make the weight for his fights.

Fault and the Discretion under Article 10.4

If the requirements for the application of Article 10.4 are established, the degree of fault of the athlete or person relevant to the commission of the violation has to be considered by the tribunal in determining the period of ineligibility to be imposed.[7]

The notes to Article 10.4 make it clear that an athlete who does not meet the criteria under Article 10.4 must receive the standard two-year period of ineligibility, and could, indeed, receive an increased period of ineligibility if aggravating circumstances are established by the anti-doping organisation under Article 10.6. Where Article 10.4 is applicable and the criteria are met so that a tribunal can assess the degree of fault of the athlete, Article 10.5.2 will not be applicable because Article 10.4 already involves assessing fault.[8]

Previously under the 2003 Code, the greater discretion given in relation to first violations involving the presence of a specified substance in an athlete's bodily sample or the use of such a specified substance by an athlete, led to differences in the sanctions imposed by various national tribunals and international federations, in relation to violations involving such specified substances as cannabis. However, over time, in various countries a common approach emerged which involved arriving at a period of ineligibility by reference to a range of factors.[9] Generally, tribunals around the world have imposed a period of ineligibility ranging from two months to twelve months on an athlete who tests positive for cannabis in-competition, and who establishes that the use of the drug was not intended to enhance sport performance, but does not establish particular circumstances justifying a reprimand and warning.[10]

---

7 The assessment of the athlete's or other person's fault is limited by the notes to Article 10.4 to a consideration of the circumstances which are relevant to explain the athlete's or other person's departure from the expected standard of behaviour under the Code. See further, pages 259–60 below. The Code tries to limit the exercise of discretion in arriving at the period of ineligibility under Article 10.4. However, maintaining an approach based on the exercise of a restricted discretion across sporting tribunals worldwide may prove difficult.

8 See notes to Article 10.5.2.

9 See e.g. various websites where decisions relating to the imposition of periods of ineligibility for cannabis can be viewed, see Introduction, page 11, note 19 above.

10 See the developments in the New Zealand Sports Tribunal, through its decisions, starting with SDT 13/04, *Boxing New Zealand, Inc.* v. *Alex Mene*, where a reprimand and a warning was seen as an appropriate penalty to its Minute to National Sports Organisations of 15 December 2006 and letter of 28 July 2010 to national sporting organisations published on the Tribunal's website increasing the starting point for a first anti-doping violation involving cannabis to four months' ineligibility. Generally applying a tariff in this way appears

In imposing a penalty for a violation involving a specified substance under Article 10.3 of the 2003 Code, tribunals examined a range of factors relating to both the violation and the general circumstances in which it was committed. Where such a wider range of factors is considered before arriving at the period of ineligibility, the difficulty is to ensure that a consistent approach is taken internationally by the many tribunals which are required to consider sanctions. Where a range of sanctions is potentially applicable, because the athlete establishes that there was no intention to enhance sport performance, aggravating and mitigating factors which relate to both the violation and the individual's circumstances concerning the commission of the violation, were treated as potentially relevant to the assessment of the appropriate sanction. These matters included factors such as the nature of the violation, whether it was knowing and deliberate or unknowing or careless, any particular circumstances which prompted the violation, whether there was a prompt admission, the general attitude of the offender to the allegation and the effect of any disqualification or period of ineligibility on the athlete. The discretion to be exercised in assessing fault under Article 10.4 of the 2009 Code is now expressed in more limited terms than the approach taken by some tribunals under Article 10.3 of the 2003 Code.

Assessment of Fault under Article 10.4

The notes to Article 10.4 in the 2009 Code provide that the fault of the athlete or other person committing a violation has to be considered in connection with the specific circumstances which are relevant to explain the athlete or other person's departure from the expected standard of behaviour under the Code, namely 'utmost caution'. Matters such as the effect of a period of ineligibility on an athlete's career or earnings are given as examples of factors which are not relevant to this assessment. Matters such as lack of experience, youth, lack of education in anti-doping matters or other personal characteristics which might explain why an athlete has not acted as he or she should, will be relevant.[11]

It can be difficult to apply this approach to the assessment of fault in some circumstances such as the deliberate taking of recreational drugs

at odds with the case-by-case exercise of discretion under the Code, but is the inevitable consequence of a high instance of similar violations involving cannabis. Generally, the requirements of Article 10.4 are difficult to apply to the deliberate taking of specified substances for recreational purposes (see Chapter 11, pages 379–80, 383).

11 See note to Article 10.5.2 of the Code.

such as cannabis out-of-competition which produce positive in-competition tests. Often, there will be no satisfactory explanation for the athlete's failure to adhere to the expected standards of behaviour. In imposing periods of ineligibility for such violations, tribunals have continued to adopt a practical approach to the appropriate period of ineligibility for violations which do not involve substances which enhance sport performance, which can be hard to square with the fault assessment directed by the notes under Article 10.4.[12]

Generally, assessments of fault where violations involve specified substances will cover a wide range of circumstances and, while decisions by other tribunals may provide useful guidance to tribunals, each case has ultimately to be determined on its own facts. However, tribunals considering the imposition of sanctions under Article 10.4 will need to keep a watchful eye on decisions in other jurisdictions to ensure that, as far as possible, there is a significant degree of comity in the imposition of sanctions where periods of ineligibility are imposed in broadly similar circumstances for the same or similar prohibited substances.

Any plea to invoke Article 10.4 requires the athlete to establish how the substance entered his or her system. This threshold requirement has often been emphasised by CAS Panels in connection with all the Articles of the Code which permit the standard two-year sanction to be reduced.

The General Requirement to Show how the Substance Came to Be in the Athlete's System

The provisions of Articles 10.4, 10.5.1 and 10.5.2 all require the athlete or person seeking to rely on them to show how the prohibited substance came to be in his or her system (or possession). The reason for this requirement is that, without the circumstances surrounding the positive test being established before the tribunal, there can be no proper basis upon which to assess the fault of the athlete or person. CAS Panels have often underlined the requirement in strong terms. Cogent evidence as to the way in which the prohibited substance came to be in the athlete's bodily sample is required, not speculation or guess work based on sworn statements by the athlete that he or she would never have taken a prohibited substance deliberately. The following extracts from decisions (which are set out in *IWBF* v. *Gibbs*)[13] emphasise this requirement and its important role in considering

12 See Chapter 11, pages 379–80 for further comment.   13 See pages 261–2 below.

any claim to rely on the Articles of the Code which can allow for a reduction in the period of ineligibility.

CCES v. Lelievre, SDRCC, 7 February 2005, para. 51:

> While recognising that obtaining such evidence might be difficult, if not impossible, mere speculation as what may have happened will not satisfy the standard of proof required.

Karatancheva v. ITF, CAS 2006/A/1032, para. 117:

> If the manner in which the substance entered an athlete's system is unknown or unclear, it is logically difficult to determine whether the athlete has taken precautions in attempting to prevent any such occurrence.
>
> In the absence of proof as to how the substance entered the player's body, it is unrealistic and impossible to decide whether, in those unknown circumstances, he did or did not exercise all proper precautions to avoid the condition of the doping offence.
>
> The provision must ensure that mere protestations of innocence and disavowal of motive or opportunity to cheat by a player, however persuasively asserted, will not serve to engage these provisions if there remains any doubt as to how the prohibited substance entered his body. This provision is necessary to ensure that the fundamental principle that a player is responsible for ensuring that no prohibited substance enters his body is not undermined by an application of mitigating provisions in the normal run of cases.

The burden can be difficult for an athlete to discharge where there are a number of possible explanations for the presence of a substance in a sample and the nature of the strict liability regime under the Code is that there may well be cases where the athlete is not able to discharge the burden on him or her. Where this is the outcome of a consideration of the evidence, the result will be that the athlete is liable to the mandatory sanction (usually two years).

Article 10.4 – the Requirement to Prove how the Substance Entered the Athlete's System – Failure to Meet the Requirement

CAS 2010/A/2230, International Wheelchair Basketball Federation
v. UK Anti-Doping and Simon Gibbs

G was a wheelchair athlete who tested positive for mephedrone in-competition. The National Anti-Doping Appeal Panel imposed a two-year period of ineligibility on G under the UK Anti-Doping Rules. G appealed to CAS. Before the tribunals below, G had argued that the presence of the prohibited substance in his system was the result of his drink having been spiked. The first tribunal did not believe the evidence and admission of another person to this effect. On appeal to CAS, the decision was upheld after a re-hearing before a sole arbitrator.

The substance in question was a specified substance which meant that Article 10.4 was potentially applicable. The sole arbitrator referred to the conditions which must be satisfied for Article 10.4 to provide an exception to the standard period of ineligibility under Article 10.2. He held that the process under Article 10.4 involved three conditions – how the substance got into the athlete's system, proof by the athlete that there was no intent to enhance sport performance and an assessment of fault if the athlete establishes the first two requirements. In seeking to establish how the substance had come into his system, the arbitrator emphasised that the athlete could not rely on a mere assertion, even supported by corroborative testimony, that he did not intend to enhance performance or would not take prohibited substances to do so, to provide a basis for the tribunal to conclude that the athlete had shown how the substance had got into his system. It was not sufficient for an athlete to say 'I never took and would never take such a specified substance'. In the circumstances, the arbitrator held that the athlete had not established how the substance came to be in his system.

In considering the second condition, the arbitrator emphasised that a sports-specific standard of comfortable satisfaction was applicable and that corroborative evidence was also required. Corroboration means no more than evidence tending to confirm other evidence. The arbitrator considered a legal argument that the meaning of Article 10.4 should be read down or departed from because it represented a limitation on a human right guaranteed under the ECHR or under EU law and was in breach of the fundamental principle of proportionality. He applied the following test to this challenge:

- were the measures designed to meet a legitimate objective and rationally connected to it?
- were the limits on the right or freedom more than necessary to accomplish the objective?
- did the measure strike an appropriate balance between the interests of society and those of individual groups?

The arbitrator concluded that the provisions of Article 10.4 and the requirements imposed before the degree of fault could be considered achieved a proportionate and appropriate balance when the context of the fight against doping in sport was considered. The arbitrator upheld the decision to impose a two-year period of ineligibility on Mr Gibbs because he could not establish how the substance got into his system.

Assessing Fault under Article 10.4

Degrees of Fault – High Degree of Fault

CAS 2010/A/2107, *Oliveira* v. *USADA*

O, a competitive cyclist, suffered from allergies and had taken over the counter and prescription medicines on a regular basis for several years. She conducted her own research and found a product called Hyperdrive. O obtained this product online from an online store called Vitamaker. She ran out of the product while training in Italy and ordered a further bottle which was shipped to the US then brought to her in Italy by her husband. After competing in a professional stage race in Italy, O was selected for doping control and tested positive for a specified substance called oxilofrine.

At the initial arbitration hearing, the arbitrator found, even if the requirements to the application of Article 10.4 were met, that O's degree of fault was sufficiently high to deny her any elimination or reduction in the period of ineligibility. This was based on her failure to carry out a proper and careful investigation of the product which she had purchased. There were warnings which the athlete had not heeded, namely, express marketing as a stimulant and advertising on manufacturer's web-site, together with other products, that made direct reference to anabolic agents and hormones. Further, twelve months before the sample, the US Food and Drug Administration had issued a public warning that Hyperdrive contained another drug that was banned and on the Prohibited List.

Before CAS on appeal there was no dispute as to the positive test. O's case was that she had ingested the prohibited substance from the dietary supplement where the substance was not disclosed on the label and she had made a reasonable, if not extensive, effort to research the product. It was accepted that the Hyperdrive product was the source of the positive test for the prohibited substance. The Hyperdrive label did list a substance which was on the Prohibited List (although not oxilofrine).

On the requirement that the athlete prove that she did not intend to enhance her performance, O submitted that she had to prove that she did not intend to take oxilofrine to enhance her performance. USADA submitted that, where it was admitted that O had taken Hyperdrive to prepare for a cycling race, this established an intent to enhance performance, even if the athlete did not know that the product contained a banned substance.

The CAS Panel discussed the provisions of Article 10.4 and concluded on its approach to Article 10.4 that O's testimony and other corroborating evidence established to its comfortable satisfaction that she did not intend to enhance her sport performance by (unknowingly) ingesting oxilofrine.[14]

Fault

In the circumstances, the athlete's degree of fault was significant. The nature of the website should have put the athlete on increased alert concerning the potential risks with the product. The risks of mislabelling and contamination were generally well known with nutritional supplements and had been for a considerable period of time (e.g. CAS 2009/A/1870, *WADA* v. *Hardy and USADA*). It was not reasonable for O to rely on the label as an accurate listing together with her limited research. She failed to check the label of the new supply of the substance delivered to her in the US carefully because that did contain a listed chemical which was a prohibited substance. The Panel considered other decisions in assessing fault – CAS 2008/A/1490, *WADA* v. *USADA and Thompson* – where lack of experience of athlete in doping matters, lack of formalised drug education and lack of guidance in support and lack of any intention to enhance athletic performance were all relevant to assessment of fault, *USADA* v. *Brunemann* where an intercollegiate swimmer negligently took her mother's prescription medicine. After considering the matter, the Panel imposed an eighteen-month period of ineligibility on the athlete which was set to run for the period during which the athlete had not competed by virtue of her timely admission under Article 10.9.2.

Article 10.4 Assessment of Fault – Low Level

CAS 2011/A/2495, 96, 97 and 98, *FINA* v. *Cielo Filho, dos Santos, Barbosa and Waked*

Four Brazilian swimmers tested positive for furosemide, a specified substance on the 2011 List. At a first hearing before a Brazilian Swimming Doping Tribunal it was accepted by each swimmer that they had

14 See pages 254–5 above for doubts about this approach to the application of Article 10.4.

committed an anti-doping rule violation, and the tribunal held that a violation had been committed and the event result had to be disqualified. It
found, however, that there was no fault or negligence on the part of the athletes and, apart from W, who had a previous anti-doping rule violation, all
should be given a warning. In applying Article 10.7 to W's case, the Doping
Panel concluded, as there was no fault or negligence, no period of ineligibility was to be imposed, notwithstanding the fact that it was a second
violation.

An appeal to CAS was heard as a matter of urgency before the World
Swimming Championships 2011. It was initially pointed out that the finding of the Doping Panel that there was no fault or negligence should have
meant that there could be no sanction at all, not even a warning and only
results obtained in the particular competition at the event should have
been automatically disqualified.

After a full *de novo* re-hearing, a CAS Panel considered the circumstances under which the prohibited substance came to be in the athletes'
samples. Dr M had worked with C since 2008. Under a sponsorship relationship, C had begun taking an energy drink. He consumed products
with doctor M's knowledge to assist in overcoming tiredness. The drink
contained caffeine which is not a prohibited substance. C experienced
some gastric problems from this drink and Dr M sought to find another
source of caffeine. On reading medical literature, Dr M decided the best
course was for him to prescribe pure caffeine in the form of capsules which
could be taken one or two at a time. Aware of the risk of contamination
and the responsibilities under the Code, C and Dr M sought out a particular pharmacy to produce the caffeine tablets in pure form. The pharmacist
was recommended by C's father, who was a paediatrician, as the best in the
area where he had been health secretary. Dr M visited the pharmacy on
a number of occasions to satisfy himself as to suitability to produce the
tablets.

C began using capsules prescribed by Dr M in January 2010. He used
them at various major swimming meets around the world and was frequently drug tested. He returned no adverse test results in 2010 and 2011.

DS visited C from university in US. He also began using caffeine pills
prescribed by Dr M. C formed a club of elite swimmers in Brazil. The
other swimmers who tested positive were members of that club. Dr M
became doctor to the club and would attend training sessions. The swimmers took the caffeine capsules prescribed by Dr M. The general process
was that C would take a prescription written by Dr M to the pharmacy and
obtain a bottle of capsules. Dr M would retain it and give the capsules to

swimmers. Each of the swimmers was informed by Dr M that the tablets were safe and fine to use. W was particularly anxious because he had an earlier inadvertent anti-doping rule violation.

From time to time, Dr M visited the pharmacy. He was shown a certificate showing the caffeine used to make the capsules was 100 per cent pure. Dr M remained very conscious of the risk of contamination. He believed he had done everything possible to ensure that the capsules contained only pure caffeine and were not contaminated. The reason for the positive test in May 2011 was discovered when the remaining capsules were tested. They were found to contain furosemide. The pharmacy admitted that contamination had occurred when a bottle of caffeine tablets was being made up at the same time as prescriptions for the treatment of heart disease which contained furosemide. Evidence as to how the contamination occurred was not seriously challenged.

It was accepted by FINA that the athletes had established how the specified substance had entered their systems and that they had not intended to enhance sport performance by taking the prohibited substance. The Panel considered the concessions were correctly made by FINA. The Panel held that this was not a case of 'no fault'. The notes to Article 10.5.1 in the Code are to the effect that taking a contaminated supplement could not give rise to such a plea. An argument that the caffeine capsules were a medication not caught by the wording in the notes on contaminated supplements was rejected.

In relation to Article 10.4, on the athletes' degree of fault, the Panel considered that the fault of the athletes was at the lowest end of the spectrum. They and their doctor had done all they could reasonably or practically have done to avoid the positive test results. It was not realistic to expect that they could test the product before they took it or conduct an audit or due diligence with the pharmacy on a regular basis. There was no evidence that supply from a large, reputable, multi-national drug company would have been more reliable. In the circumstances, the Panel determined that the appropriate sanction for the athletes with a first violation was a warning. W was in a different position. Under Article 10.7, for W with two anti-doping rule violations for specified substances, the mandated minimum period of ineligibility was one year with a range of up to four years. The Panel was not prepared to rely on the principle of proportionality to reduce the period beneath the mandatory minimum under Article 10.7. It imposed a period of ineligibility on W of one year. It allowed that period to start from the date of sample collection because W had effectively admitted the anti-doping rule violation at the time he waived the B sample.

The Panel expressed sympathy for W's position and said that but for the mandatory minimum in the Code, the majority would have imposed a much lesser period of ineligibility.

Fault Assessment – Mid-range

USADA v. *Emily Brunemann*, AAA No. 77 190
E 00447 08 JENF

B was a swimmer at the University of Michigan and a USA national swimming champion. She had been part of the college testing programme for three years and the USA national programme for one year. She tested positive for a diuretic that, at the time of hearing, was a specified substance under the Code. At the time of her test, the 2003 Code was in effect.

B took the diuretic to relieve stomach pains believing it was a laxative pill taken by her mother. She did not read the label on the pill which would have shown that it contained prescription medicine. She made no inquiry of USADA, nor did she use the USADA hotline to determine the status of the substance.

Applying *lex mitior* principles the substance was treated as a specified substance. The Panel held that the 2003 Code, in particular Article 10.3, applied because it had a lower maximum sanction (one year) than the 2009 Code under Article 10.4 for the taking of a specified substance. The Panel was satisfied that B did not intend to enhance sport performance. In considering her level of fault, the Panel referred to other decisions under Article 10.3 of the 2003 Code. B had not taken basic steps to avoid ingesting the specified substance. She was, however, relatively inexperienced in the out-of-competition doping testing system. She had received no formal individualised or group education or training in anti-doping matters. The Panel imposed a period of six months' ineligibility.

Fault in Relation to Specified Substance – Mistake by
Physician – Responsibilities of the Athlete

CAS 2005/A/828, *Koubek* v. *ITF*

K was an experienced international tennis player. He had been a professional for many years. He had consented to be bound by the ATP anti-doping testing programme. He had been given a wallet card which was designed to be carried in his player's wallet. The card contained a warning that they should give a copy to their physician, coach and personal trainer and also warned that the player had to apply for a TUE before using any bannedsubstance. It invited players to check with the ITF or ATP if there were any questions. A hotline and fax number were also given in the card. K did not keep his wallet card.

In March 2004, K experienced pain in his right wrist. He entered the French Open. On the advice of a friend, he decided to consult a doctor whom he had not previously seen. He obtained a number from a friend and went to an appointment. The doctor was an eminent hand surgeon specialising in sports injuries. He was also a doctor for international ice hockey teams. K did not have his wallet card and as a consequence, did not show it to the doctor, nor did he raise the question of a TUE. The doctor administered a glucocorticosteriod which contained a prohibited substance. K tested positive at the French Open.

The CAS Panel upheld the decision of the ITF which was to impose a three-month period of ineligibility. It agreed that the player could not show no fault or negligence. He had not acted in a completely diligent way as was required. He had ignored the risk present in taking medical treatment. He had not made inquiries of the ATP or ITF. He did not know of the possibility of obtaining a TUE. He had not been interested in listening to information about anti-doping. He did not keep his wallet card and accordingly could not give it the doctor. He relied entirely on the doctor's advice although he had never met the doctor before. He consulted with the doctor on short notice despite the fact that his injury had been affecting him for some time.

The CAS arbitrator agreed with the ITF decision that a three-month period of ineligibility was appropriate for the level of fault on the part of K in not taking appropriate steps to avoid the risk of medical treatment causing the positive test.

Appendix 2

Figures 5–8 of the Second Edition – Process for
Arriving at Appropriate Sanction under Earlier
Versions of the Code

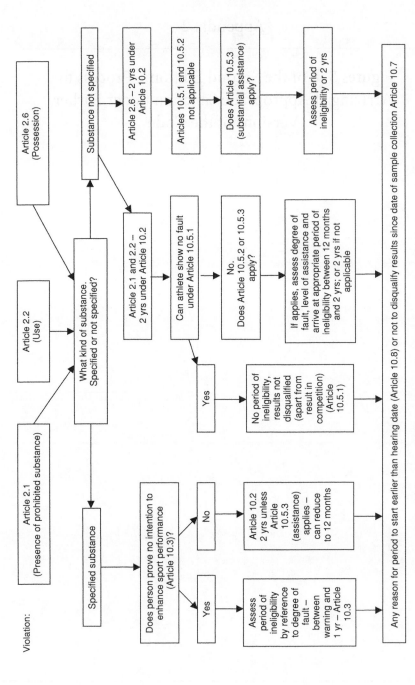

Figure 5 Determining periods of ineligibility under the 2003 Code: first violation

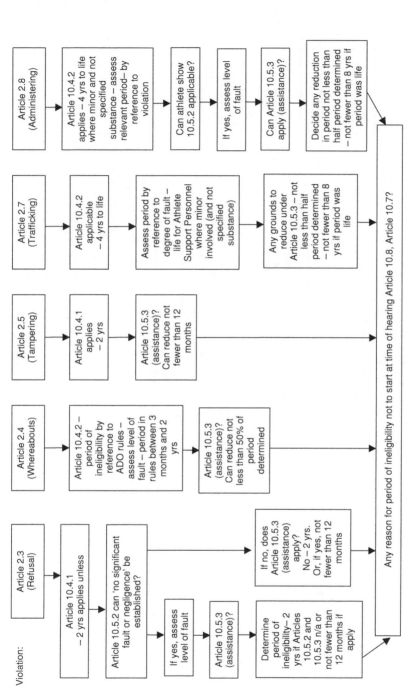

Figure 6 Determining periods of ineligibility under 2003 Code: first violation (continued)

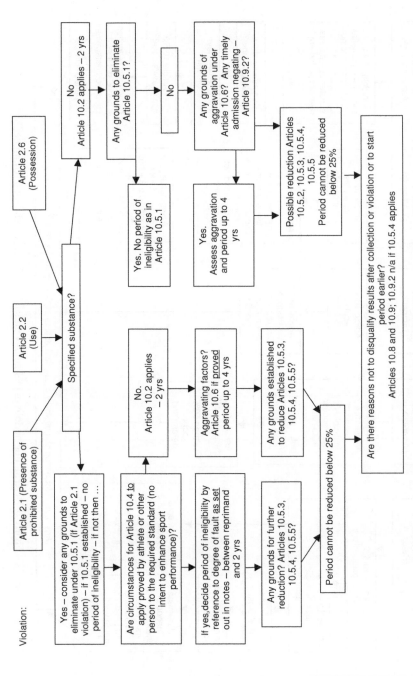

Figure 7 Determining periods of ineligibility for first violations under the 2009 Code

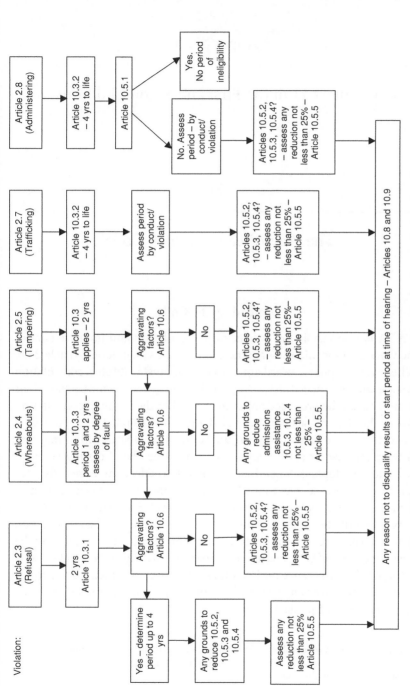

Figure 8 Determining periods of ineligibility under the 2009 Code (continued)

Appendix 3

Chapters 11 of the First and Second Editions

11

The Way Ahead: the 2009 Code[1]

Amending the Code

WADA is responsible for overseeing the evolution and improvement of the Code and for initiating amendments to the Code under Article 23.6. Where WADA puts forward amendments, it must institute a consultation process under which athletes, Signatories and governments provide their comments on the proposed amendments. After the required consultation process has taken place, the proposed amendments must be approved by a two-thirds majority of the WADA Foundation Board, with a majority of the public sector and Olympic movement members' casting votes, in order to be adopted. Amendments come into effect three months after approval, and Signatories to the Code must implement applicable amendments within one year of approval by the WADA Foundation Board.[2]

WADA initiated amendments to the Code in 2005, and a consultation process took place over the next eighteen months, which culminated in the meeting of the WADA Foundation Board in Madrid in November 2007 at the World Conference on Doping. At this meeting, amendments to the Code were approved and the deadline for acceptance of the amended Code by Signatories is 1 January 2009.[3]

---

1 All page references which follow refer to the first edition of the text and do not apply to this current edition. They have been retained for completeness sake.
2 See Article 23.6.3 of the Code.
3 For the 2009 Code in its final form, see WADA website, www.wada-ama.org.

Amendments to the Sanctions Regime in the Code

The area in which the most significant amendments to the Code have been made is the sanctions regime under Article 10. The part of the anti-doping regime created by the Code which has generated the most debate has been the limited flexibility in relation to sanctions, with many believing that greater flexibility should be available to tribunals and CAS in imposing sanctions where anti-doping rule violations have been established. It was perceived by many as unfair that, in most circumstances, the careless athlete who had no intention to cheat or enhance performance, who was caught by the strict nature of some violations under the Code, was likely to be subject to the same period of ineligibility as an athlete who had taken a prohibited substance, or used a prohibited method, in order to enhance sporting performance and cheat.[4] This debate has been ongoing from the time of early pre-Code CAS decisions, when some CAS Panels held that they had the power to vary fixed sanctions in anti-doping regimes, after considering the degree of fault of the person who had committed the anti-doping rule violation.[5]

The Code, by providing that athletes could only eliminate or reduce the fixed sanction in narrowly defined exceptional circumstances, seeks to place strict limits on discretion in relation to sanctions in the interests of global consistency and fairness. This was an understandable reaction to the inconsistent treatment of doping violations by different sporting organisations and different tribunals, which the Code sought to address. However, the tension between a strict harmonised approach, and the need to produce just outcomes across the wide range of circumstances in which doping violations occurred, remained. For many, the limited circumstances under which an athlete could rely on Articles 10.5.1 and 10.5.2 of the Code and the relatively narrow ambit of the category of specified substances which could attract a more flexible approach to the imposition of sanctions was productive of too much unfairness and, while the need to maintain a harmonised overall approach was acknowledged, many considered a more flexible system was required which took greater account of the nature of the violation, and the fault of the athlete, in arriving at the period of ineligibility to be imposed by way of sanction.

---

4 See for example, the cases of *USADA* v. *Montgomery* at Chapter 5, page 91 above, and *IAAF* v. *Edwards*, at Chapter 8, page 182, above both of whom received a ban of two years for very different conduct.

5 See Chapter 1, pages 32–3 above.

Proposed Changes to the Sanctions Regime

The result of the extensive consultation on the Code's operation has been the adoption of amendments to Article 10 which provide for a wider range of factors to be potentially applicable in deciding whether the fixed sanction for a violation is to be applied. It must be emphasised that, in many situations, the outcome as regards the sanction imposed under the 2009 Code will be the same as under the current Code, but there are, under the amendments, a number of provisions in Article 10 which, if applicable, can lead to the replacement of a fixed sanction with a discretionary sanction,[6] to the reduction of the fixed sanction by up to 75 per cent[7] or the increase of a fixed sanction of two years' ineligibility for a first violation to a period of four years' ineligibility.[8]

Article 10.4: Broadening the Category of Specified Substances

While the amendments maintain the basic position that a two-year period of ineligibility is the standard sanction for most violations, Article 10.4 provides that all prohibited substances, save those substances which are in the class of anabolic agents and hormones and specific identified stimulants in the Prohibited List, will be 'specified substances' for the purpose of the sanctions provisions in Article 10. As with the position under Article 10.3 of the current Code, where a specified substance is detected in the bodily sample of an athlete (or a specified substance has been used), the strict liability regime will apply as to disqualification of the result, but the athlete who has committed the violation will be able to establish the grounds for a potentially more lenient and discretionary sanctions regime to be applied.

Under the new Article 10.4, where an athlete or other person can establish how a specified substance entered his or her body, or came into his or her possession, and can show that the specified substance was not intended to enhance sport performance or mask the use of a performance-enhancing substance, the standard period of ineligibility for violation of Article 2.1 (presence of a prohibited substance), 2.2 (use) and 2.6 (possession) under Article 10.2 is replaced by a possible range of sanctions from, at a minimum, a reprimand and no period of ineligibility to a maximum of two years' ineligibility. The effect of this provision is to make the current

6 Amended Code, Article 10.4.   7 Amended Code, Articles 10.5.3, 10.5.4 and 10.5.5.
8 Article 10.6.

Article 10.3 applicable to a wider range of prohibited substances.[9] To be able to take advantage of this provision and open up the broader discretion, the athlete or other person who has committed the violation must produce corroborating evidence, in addition to his or her word, which establishes the preconditions for the application of the sanctions regime in Article 10.4. The athlete must establish on the balance of probabilities how the specified substance entered his or her body. The absence of an intention to enhance sporting performance has to be established by the person seeking to rely on Article 10.4 to the higher standard of the comfortable satisfaction of the hearing body. This is a change from the general approach in the current Code (where an athlete never has to meet this higher standard of proof) and the particular requirements for the application of the current Article 10.3. The change was, no doubt, intended to reflect the fact that, within the wider range of 'specified substances' in the 2009 Code, there will be more substances which can be used as agents to enhance sporting performance. If this precondition is established, the degree of fault of the athlete or person relevant to the commission of the violation will be considered by the tribunal in determining the period of ineligibility to be imposed.[10] The Notes to the amended Article 10.4 make it clear that an athlete who does not meet the criteria under Article 10.4 will be likely to receive the standard two-year period of ineligibility, and could receive an increased period of ineligibility if aggravating circumstances are established by the anti-doping organisation under Article 10.6.

The Continuing Role of Articles 10.5.1 and 10.5.2

The established grounds in the current Code under Article 10.5 to eliminate or reduce the period of ineligibility based on exceptional circumstances remain potentially applicable under the 2009 Code as the possible basis for reducing sanctions for violations involving anabolic steroids, hormones, amphetamines and prohibited methods (i.e. non-'specified substances'). Under the 2009 Code, Article 10.5.1 is potentially applicable only to a breach of Article 2.1, while Article 10.5.2 is now potentially

---

9 See Chapter 8, pages 173–5 above, for the operation of Article 10.3 in the current Code.
10 The approach will, no doubt, involve weighing the various factors relating to the fault of the athlete. The range of situations is likely to be much wider than under the current Article 10.3, given the wider range of substances and situations in which the substances may be taken and the approach taken by tribunals under that Article to anti-doping rule violations involving substances such as cannabis is likely to be only of limited assistance.

applicable to any violation.[11] As under the current Code, the Articles cannot be relied on to reduce or eliminate a period of ineligibility where a first violation for a specified substance is being considered, because the possible range of sanctions under that Article is considered to allow for sufficient flexibility in the imposition of a sanction. The Notes to the 2009 Code confirm that, while the status of an athlete as a minor is generally of no relevance to the commission of the violation, this factor maybe relevant in relation to the possible application of Articles 10.5.1 and 10.5.2. This, it is suggested, should be the approach to the application of Articles 10.5.1 and 10.5.2 under the current Code.

Reduction for Assistance and Admissions

The Code currently makes no provision relating to admissions by an athlete or a person facing an allegation that he or she is in violation of the Code, and, as was indicated by the CAS Panel in *Knauss*,[12] the application of the substantial assistance provision required some clarification both as to its scope and as to its relationship with other Articles (Article 10.5.2 under the current Code) under which a reduction in a fixed period of ineligibility is available. The 2009 Code makes detailed provisions for the consideration of admissions and assistance in assessing the period of ineligibility to be imposed for a violation.

Assistance for Anti-doping Organisations: Amended Article 10.5.3

Article 10.5.3 of the 2009 Code allows an anti-doping organisation to suspend part of the period of ineligibility before a decision on a final appeal under Article 13, where the athlete, or other person who has committed the violation, provides substantial assistance to an anti-doping organisation, or a criminal authority or a professional disciplinary body, and the assistance results in the discovery of a criminal offence, or a professional disciplinary offence or a breach of the Code.[13] After the final appeal, there can be a further suspension only with the approval of WADA. No more

---

11 The Notes to the 2009 Code provide that it will be very difficult to establish the criteria where knowledge has been established as an element of the violation; compare this situation with the current Code where Article 10.5.2 is potentially applicable only to violations under Articles 2.1, 2.2, 2.3 and 2.8.

12 See Chapter 8, pages 187–8 above.

13 This provision clarifies some uncertainty on the scope of application of Article 10.5.3 and reflects the position reached by the CAS Panel in *Knauss* (see above).

than 75 per cent of the period of ineligibility can be suspended for giving substantial assistance under this Article. The decision by an anti-doping organisation to suspend must be based on the seriousness of the violation and the nature of the assistance given. If a decision to suspend is made under Article 10.5.3, the anti-doping organisation making the decision to suspend must provide a written justification for its decision to the other anti-doping organisations which have a right to appeal the decision in relation to the violation. The anti-doping organisation may reinstate the period of suspended ineligibility if the substantial assistance anticipated is not provided. A decision to reinstate the period of ineligibility can be the subject of an appeal by the athlete or person who is subject to the order for reinstatement of the period of ineligibility. Overall, this provision is noteworthy because it is the first time that the Code has allowed for a suspension of part of a period of ineligibility in particular circumstances. A general power to suspend periods of ineligibility was provided for in some anti-doping regimes before the advent of the Code, but was not available under the Code, and a decision under the current Code suspending part of a period of ineligibility does not comply with the Code.[14]

Admissions where the Admission is the Only Evidence: Amended Article 10.5.4

Admissions made in various circumstances can be considered in relation to the imposition of sanctions under the 2009 Code. Under Article 10.5.4, a voluntary admission by an athlete or other person before notice of a sample collection that could establish an anti-doping rule violation, or before receipt of a notice of a violation under Article 2.1, can lead to a reduction in the period of ineligibility of up to 50 per cent. The admission given must be the only reliable evidence at the time it is given that an anti-doping rule violation has been committed. This provision is intended to apply where there is an immediate admission by an athlete or other person who confesses before the process of gathering evidence has advanced and provides evidence against his or her own interests by way of a confession, at a time when there is no evidence to support an allegation. An admission at the stage when the athlete or other person is confronted with an anti-doping violation can be considered under Article 10.9.2 which allows for the

---

14 See *WADA* v. *Hondo*, Chapter 8, page 235 above, where CAS set aside a decision by the Swiss Olympic Committee to suspend one year of a two-year fixed sanction imposed under the Code.

earlier commencement of the period of ineligibility where such an admission is made. An admission of this kind can also prevent the application of Article 10.6 and the possible increase in the period of ineligibility under that Article by reason of aggravating factors. The provision under Article 10.9.2 will not apply where Article 10.5.4 has applied.[15]

Admissions and Assistance Together

Article 10.5.5 specifically provides that, where an admission is made and substantial assistance provided both of which would bring about a reduction in the period of ineligibility, the period of ineligibility can be reduced by a maximum of three-quarters of the full period and no further.[16] The process of applying any reduction in the period of ineligibility must be carried out after the tribunal has assessed the period of ineligibility which would otherwise apply in relation to the anti-doping rule violation.

New Article 10.6: Aggravating Circumstances which may Increase the Period of Ineligibility

In addition to the Articles which provide for reductions in the period of ineligibility in a wider range of circumstances, Article 10.6 of the amended Code provides that an anti-doping organisation may establish, in relation to any anti-doping rule violation (apart from Article 2.7 (trafficking) and Article 2.8 (administration)),[17] that aggravating circumstances are present which justify the imposition of a period of ineligibility longer than the standard sanction. Examples of such aggravating circumstances are noted as follows:

- The athlete or other person committed the violation as part of a larger doping scheme involving a conspiracy or common enterprise to commit violations.[18]

15 For more detail on the provision in Article 10.9.2 of the 2009 Code, see page 247 below.
16 As noted above, it is unclear under the current Code whether substantial assistance and establishing no significant fault or negligence can together lead to a reduction of the period of ineligibility below twelve months. There has been no decision on the point, and it is submitted that a reduction of the period of ineligibility to less than twelve months is not available, unless, in all the circumstances, the period of ineligibility under the Code might be described as imposing a sanction which infringes the principle of proportionality (see e.g. *Puerta*, Chapter 8, pages 189–91).
17 These violations involve intentional conduct, and are already subject to a harsher regime with four years' ineligibility as the sanction for a first violation.
18 An example of this kind of case would be the *Collins* decision, see Chapter 6, pages 142–3 above.

- The athlete or other person used or possessed multiple or prohibited substances or prohibited methods, or used or possessed a prohibited substance or prohibited method on multiple separate occasions.
- A normal individual would be likely to enjoy the performance-enhancing effects of the anti-doping rule violation beyond the otherwise applicable period of ineligibility.
- The athlete or person engaged in fraudulent or obstructive conduct to avoid the detection or adjudication of an anti-doping rule violation.
- The athlete competed in violation of a provisional suspension.

Prompt Admission: Effect on Article 10.6.2 and Period of Ineligibility

If the anti-doping organisation establishes aggravating circumstances under Article 10.6, the fixed period of ineligibility will be increased from two years to four years, unless the athlete or person can prove that he or she did not knowingly violate the anti-doping rule. The application of Article 10.6 can also be avoided by an admission made promptly after being confronted with the violation. As has already been noted, this kind of admission is different from an admission to which Article 10.5.4 applies which can lead to the suspension of part of a period of ineligibility – it is made at the time when the athlete or other person is confronted with the evidence against him or her by the anti-doping organisation. It should also be noted that Article 10.9.2 of the amended Code provides that a timely admission by a person, when confronted by an anti-doping rule violation, will allow for the commencement of the period of ineligibility imposed in relation to the violation to be started from as early as the date of sample collection. If Article 10.9.2 is applied, the athlete or person must serve at least one-half of the period of ineligibility from the date the sanction is imposed. This provision does not apply where there has already been a reduction for an admission under Article 10.5.4. Article 10.9 has also been amended to make it clear that only delays not attributable to the athlete, provisional suspension and/or timely admissions can justify starting the period of ineligibility earlier than the hearing date.

Multiple Violations

Article 10.7 of the Code 2009 sets out a table by which the period of ineligibility for a second violation will be assessed. The increase in the range of outcomes for violations means, again, that, on the commission of a second

578 APPENDIX 3

violation, there will be greater consideration of aggravating and mitigating factors in order to fix the appropriate period of ineligibility. Articles 10.5.3 and 10.5.4 of the Amended Code can be applied where a second violation is committed. Article 10.7.2 explains that (as with a first violation) the tribunal must first fix the period of ineligibility which would otherwise be applicable before assessing any reduction. Any reduction cannot reduce the period of ineligibility below 25 per cent of the period of ineligibility which would otherwise be applicable. Article 10.7 also provides that only violations which occur within a period of eight years will count for the purposes of establishing multiple violations. This removes the possible objection to the apparently unlimited period for the occurrence of a second counting violation under the current Code.[19]

Summary of Effect of Amendments to Articles on Sanctions

Overall, the general result of the principal amendments to the Code is to provide for a more complex process by which tribunals will consider the imposition of a period of ineligibility for a violation of the Code. In this context, tribunals at both national and international level will have to step through a process before arriving at the appropriate sanction. They are likely to have to consider more frequently whether a relevant factual precondition has been met before applying the amended Articles, and this will inevitably produce a more complex hearing process. The notes to the 2009 Code contain useful examples of the process which will be followed in determining periods of ineligibility. Figures 7 and 8 outline the main steps involved in considering the imposition of a period of ineligibility for first violations of the various anti-doping rule violations under the 2009 Code.[20]

The most significant change lies in the range of substances which will now be regarded as specified substances, and the consequent opening up of the process of determining the appropriate period of ineligibility for the common violations under Articles 2.1, 2.2 and 2.6. Under the current Code, the main area of contested fact has, to date, been in relation to the application of Articles 10.5.1 and 10.5.2 to violations which can be committed without fault. Under the 2009 Code, tribunals will still have to

19 As identified by the CAS Panel in the advisory opinion for *FIFA and WADA*, see Chapter 10, page 226 above.
20 The tables are a general guide to the process. The position under the 2009 Code should be compared with that under the existing Code.

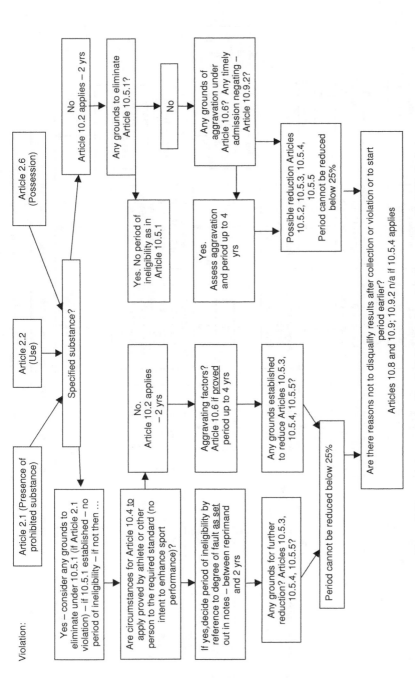

Figure 7 Determining periods of ineligibility for first violations under the 2009 Code

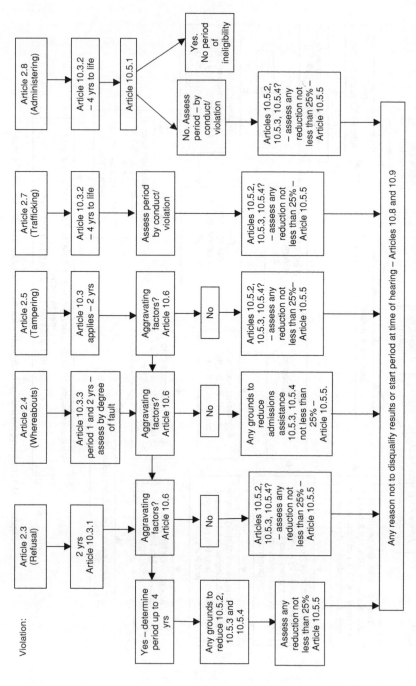

Figure 8 Determining periods of ineligibility under the 2009 Code (continued)

consider the application of these Articles in cases where non-specified substances are concerned, but, where one of the many substances is detected which will fall within the category of 'specified substances' under the Prohibited List, it seems likely that tribunals will have to consider difficult questions such as whether an athlete has met the burden of establishing that there was no intent to enhance sporting performance, and, if this is established, what the appropriate sanction is within the range permitted under Article 10.4. This, together with the likely increase of allegations relating to other violations, which are likely to require more wide-ranging evidential proof, will place increased responsibility on tribunals hearing cases under the Code.

Further Amendments

While the changes in the area of sanctions are, perhaps, the most significant amendment, there are several further amendments to the Code. Some are intended to remedy errors or clarify aspects of interpretation and application of the current Code. By way of example, Article 2.2 has been amended to provide clearly that this violation can only be committed by an athlete. Article 2.6 has also been amended to provide that the possession of substances prohibited in-competition will be a violation of the Code, where the athlete or athlete support personnel is in possession of the substance in-competition.

The Note to Article 4.2.2, which concerns the Prohibited List, explains the policy behind the broadening of the category of 'specified substances', and the increased flexibility in relation to sanctions in the amended Code. It records that there remains a strong consensus of stakeholders that the occurrence of a violation under Articles 2.1 and 2.2 should be based on strict liability, but says that the consensus was that the sanctions under the Code should be more flexible where the athlete or other person can clearly demonstrate that he or she did not intend to enhance sport performance.

Atypical Findings

Article 7 of the 2009 Code provides for laboratories to report an 'atypical finding'.[21] Such a finding will be reported where this is required under the International Standards and, generally, this will be where the

---

21 See Chapter 3, page 65 above, where the provisions in the Prohibited List 2008 relating to atypical findings are outlined.

laboratory detects the presence of a prohibited substance, which can be produced endogenously, in unusual parameters, in the athlete's sample where further investigation is required before an adverse analytical finding can be made. On receiving such a finding, the anti-doping organisation responsible for the initial review will conduct the required investigation. After that investigation, the athlete, the national anti-doping organisation, the international federation and WADA will be notified if the investigation reveals an adverse analytical finding. Significantly, no notice will be given to other signatories where there is an 'atypical' analytical finding (apart from advising the athlete of the further investigation where he has to participate in it). A notice will be given to the athlete if the anti-doping organisation determines that the 'B' sample should be analysed before the conclusion of its investigation. If the anti-doping organisation receives a request from a major event organisation or a sporting body selecting a team with an urgent deadline, asking it to disclose whether any athlete identified on a list has a pending atypical finding, the anti-doping organisation will identify the athlete after first giving notice of the atypical finding to the athlete. This provision is designed to allow for the confidential investigation of atypical findings, until such time as a decision has been made on whether to bring forward the atypical finding as an adverse analytical finding.

Violation for Breach of Ineligibility Order

Article 10.10.2 of the amended Code provides for a violation which consists of breaching an existing period of ineligibility. Where an athlete is found to have broken the prohibition against participation under a sanction, the period of ineligibility originally imposed will start again from the date of the breach. The question whether a breach has been committed will be determined by the anti-doping organisation which managed the results which led to the imposition of the initial period of ineligibility.[22] The violation under Article 2.4 relating to whereabouts information has been amended to refer to the rules set out in the International Standard for Testing. It was anticipated that the amended IST would be adopted when the amended Code was adopted but the rules relating to whereabouts information are to be the subject of further consultation with a view to the IST being adopted by the middle of 2008.

22 Amended Code, Article 10.10.2.

Sanctions of Teams

The 2009 Code contains further provisions for sanctions on teams. When two or more members of a team in a team sport are found to have committed an anti-doping rule violation during an event period, the ruling body of the event must impose an appropriate sanction on the team. No particular sanction is specified as mandatory, but the examples of loss of points and disqualification for the competition or event are given as examples of the sanctions which must be given in the Notes. A sanction of this nature is mandatory, and stricter sanctions can be imposed by an event ruling body if it so wishes.[23]

Appeals

Article 13 governing appeals has been slightly amended, so that WADA is not required to exhaust internal remedies within the hearing processes established by an anti-doping organisation, where it has a right of appeal and no other party has appealed a decision. This allows WADA to bypass an internal appeal process, where no other party appeals, and to bring its appeal direct to CAS. The range of decisions from which an appeal lies has been broadened to cover decisions that anti-doping rule violations cannot go forward for procedural reasons, a decision for a breach of Article 10.10.2, and a decision by an anti-doping organisation not to bring forward an adverse analytical finding or an atypical finding as an anti-doping rule violation, or a decision not to go forward with an anti-doping rule violation after an investigation under Article 7.4.

Provisional Suspension

At Article 7.5, the 2009 Code makes further express provision in relation to provisional suspensions. Where there is an adverse analytical finding for a prohibited substance (other than a specified substance), a provisional suspension must be imposed promptly after the initial review and notification process under the Code. The athlete must be given either an expedited hearing before the imposition of the provisional suspension, or a timely hearing after the provisional suspension has been imposed, whether in relation to the provisional suspension or the violation itself. In other situations, where there is an 'A' sample adverse analytical finding for a

---

23 Amended Code, Article 11.

specified substance, or some other anti-doping rule violation, Signatories can make specific rules in relation to provisional suspensions. Under the current Code, this aspect of results management is left entirely to anti-doping organisations to deal with under their rules but, under the amended Code, a provisional suspension is mandatory in some circumstances.

Whereabouts Information

As noted above, the specific requirements for the provision of whereabouts information by athletes in a registered testing pool and for the declaration of missed tests and failures to provide whereabouts information will be contained in the amended IST which will be of mandatory application. The current draft amended IST requires athletes to provide quarterly information concerning the athlete's place of residence, training locations, competition schedule and one specific location and one specific sixty-minute time slot during each day where the athlete will be available and accessible for testing. The athlete is also required to provide specific confirmation of the athlete's consent to the sharing of his or her whereabouts information with other anti-doping organisations.

The responsibilities of Signatories in Article 20 have been slightly amended to include a clear obligation to obtain consent to the application of the Code as a condition of participation, no doubt with a view to ensuring that there is, wherever possible, clear written agreement to the application of the Code.[24]

Article 25: Transitional Provision

The provisions of the amended Code are expressed to apply in full after 1 January 2009. Signatories will have to adopt the amended Code by agreement by changing their rules and policies. The provisions are not retroactive, unless the principle of *lex mitior* is applicable. This means that, where an anti-doping rule violation allegation is pending as at the date of the 2009 Code applying in full, it will be subject to the anti-doping rules in effect at the time of the alleged violation, unless the tribunal hearing the case determines that the provisions of the 2009 Code are more favourable

---

24 An agreement would include the International Standards and CAS Procedural Rules which are incorporated by reference into the Code, but express agreements to the application of the Code should also, where possible, refer to these aspects of the Code.

to the athlete or person facing the violation, and should apply. Where an athlete has commenced a period of ineligibility before the effective date for the entry into force of the 2009 Code, and is still serving the period of ineligibility, he or she can apply to the anti-doping organisation responsible for results management for the consideration of a reduction in the period of ineligibility in light of the 2009 Code. Given the changes to the sanctions regime in Article 10 of the 2009 Code, it is likely that there may be a number of applications under this Article when the amended Code comes into force, where athletes, who are serving periods of ineligibility under the current Code, seek to have the sanction reconsidered.

Possible Effects of the Amended Code

Throughout the history of anti-doping regimes and their consideration by tribunals, there has been considerable, largely unresolved, tension between a system based on strict liability and fixed sanctions, in the interests of consistency and harmony, and a system which permits tribunals to weigh a variety of factors before imposing a sanction which is considered appropriate in the particular circumstances of the case. In the formulation of the current Code, the urgent need for harmonisation was the dominant force, and the limited scope for reduction or elimination of the fixed sanctions was the result. At this stage in the development of the Code, the stakeholders have indicated a desire for a measure of relaxation in the strict standards to allow for differentiation between those who intentionally take or use prohibited substances for advantage, and those who are victims of carelessness or inattention and/ or admit their errors. The more complex sanctions regime is the result of this change.

As has been outlined above, one consequence of the approach taken in the 2009 Code is likely to be longer and more complex hearings where, by way of example, anti-doping organisations seek to prove an intention to enhance performance, and athletes seek to show that they did not have this intention. The consideration of the various factual considerations by reference to the standard and burden of proof imposed on the anti-doping organisation and on the athlete, is likely to become a much more difficult exercise for tribunals in certain cases. This, together with the possible increase in allegations involving the violations which are not connected with testing and analysis of samples, seems destined to put greater pressure on tribunals to provide fair hearings in an efficient and timely manner, in an increasingly complex area. Furthermore, tribunals, at both national and international level, will operate in a framework which allows greater flexibility as to sanctions in certain circumstances, and will face a greater challenge in maintaining a consistent approach. While the current Code is perhaps too rigid, there must be a risk that the greater flexibility under the 2009 Code makes consistency and harmony between different tribunals more difficult to achieve. Whether the demands on the hearing process which will be created by the amended Code can be met, and whether the entry into force of the 2009 Code will mark a return to a more uncertain, inconsistent environment in relation to the imposition of sanctions remains to be seen.

The Way Ahead: Review of the 2009 Code[1]

Amending the Code

WADA is responsible for overseeing the evolution and improvement of the Code and for initiating amendments to the Code under Article 23.6. Where WADA puts forward amendments, it must institute a consultation process under which athletes, Signatories and governments provide their comments on the proposed amendments. After the required consultation process has taken place, the proposed amendments must be approved by a two-thirds majority of the WADA Foundation Board, with a majority of the public sector and Olympic movement members casting votes, in order to be adopted. Amendments come into effect three months after approval, and Signatories to the Code must implement applicable amendments within one year of approval by the WADA Foundation Board.[2]

WADA initiated amendments to the 2003 Code in 2005, and a consultation process took place over the next eighteen months, which culminated in the meeting of the WADA Foundation Board in Madrid in November 2007 at the World Conference on Doping. At this meeting, amendments to the Code were approved and the deadline for acceptance of the amended Code by Signatories was 1 January 2009.[3] Also on 1 January 2009 the International Standard for Testing 2009 was implemented. The revised standard introduced the detailed requirements for the implementation and administration of the whereabouts regime.

The process of reviewing the 2009 Code commenced at the end of November 2011. The result of the first phase of consultation with stakeholders which ended on 15 March 2012 has been the production of a first draft of a revised 2015 Code. The second phase of consultation on the proposed revised Code is under way and will run until October 2012.

---

1 All page references which follow refer to the second edition of the text and do not apply to this current edition. They have been retained for completeness sake.
2 See Article 23.6.3 of the Code.
3 The current WADA 2009 Code can be seen on the WADA website (www.wada-ama.org).

Ultimately after a further phase of consultation a revised Code which will be scheduled to come into force in January 2015 will be submitted to the WADA Foundation Board for approval at the Fourth World Conference on Doping in Sport towards the end of 2013. In summary the main changes proposed in the draft revised Code are:

- the inclusion in the Purpose of the Code of an express statement that the Code will be applied in a manner which reflects proportionality and human rights;
- the abolition of B sample analysis, the addition of two further anti-doping rule violations (complicity in an anti-doping rule violation and prohibited association with ineligible athlete support personnel);
- the requirement that potential performance enhancement is a necessary condition for the inclusion of a substance or method on the Prohibited List;
- the overruling of the approach to Article 10.4 in the *Oliveira* decision;
- more flexible sanctions where contaminated products are the cause of the violation;
- special provision for sanctions for substances of abuse allowing rehabilitation to form part of a sanction;
- the expansion of incentives for those who provide substantial assistance; a standard four-year-period of ineligibility where aggravated circumstances are established;
- provision for sanctions to include ineligibility in future Olympic Games;
- further provision for the consequences for teams; particular provisions concerning minors being persons who have not reached the age of 14; and
- an extension of the period of limitation under Article 17 from eight to fourteen years on a non-retroactive basis for the more serious anti-doping rule violations.[4]

The first draft of the 2015 Code will, no doubt, be subject to further revision and amendment in the ongoing consultation process, but the current draft does seek to address some of the concerns in relation to the 2009 Code which are outlined below.

---

4 The process of further consultation and revision of the document until the finalisation of the 2015 Code can be followed on the WADA website, where there is a section on the site devoted to the process of the review of the 2009 Code. It is to be noted that the International Standards are also subject to a process of review in conjunction with the review of the Code.

It is difficult to assess the general impact of the Code to date, but there can be little doubt that it has been the centre of a coherent campaign against doping in sport and has been very important in providing a standardised anti-doping regime applicable throughout the sporting world which is based upon the fundamental obligation imposed on athletes to take the utmost caution to take all possible steps to avoid ingesting prohibited substances. There are, however, challenges for the Code if it is to retain the confidence of the world of sport.

Some Concerns

A general concern appears to be developing that the operation of the Code produces too many allegations and findings which arise as a result of positive tests for recreational drugs or for positive tests for substances which, while they are capable of enhancing sporting performance, have been taken in circumstances where the athlete had no intention of enhancing sporting performance but has failed to exercise the high standard of care imposed under the Code.

In the latter group of cases, the question which arises is what is the appropriate action for an athlete who, with no intent to enhance performance, may only carry 'fault' because of the high standard required under the Code.

In the other area involving recreational substances there seem to be two separate questions:

- Whether recreational substances should be included in the Prohibited List and thus be within the Code.
- Whether the Code's provisions (in particular, Article 10.4) work logically in relation to such substances.

Since its adoption in 2003, the Code has had to chart a path between setting out a clear, strict regime founded on strict liability with a standard sanction and providing for a measure of flexibility as to sanctions. The 2009 Code sought to provide increased flexibility as regards sanctions by increasing the range of circumstances in which Article 10.4 would be applicable.

Greater Flexibility – Greater Uncertainty?

The 2009 Code sought to introduce greater flexibility in imposing sanctions to address some of the concerns as to the harsh outcomes arising from mistakes by athletes under the 2003 Code but this comes at some cost in terms of certainty and may not be the best answer.

The broadening of the potential application of Article 10.4 has seen and will continue to see an increase in fact-specific decisions. Each case will ultimately have to be decided on its own facts with other cases only capable of providing limited assistance (see the observation of the CAS Panel in CAS 2011/A/2495, *FINA* v. *Cielo and others*). With many different sporting tribunals and CAS Panels dealing with differing factual situations worldwide it is inevitable that some of the certainty of outcome under the 2003 Code will be lost. The potential for more diverse outcomes is not, perhaps, a reason to revert to a stricter, more circumscribed approach, but it does underline the need to have a Code which works with as much global certainty as is possible.

The diversity of potential outcomes is the result of the broad range of substances contained on the List, some of which are either not performance enhancing or which occur commonly in other substances in a way which makes mistaken ingestion quite commonplace. If the focus of the Code can be tightened, it may be easier to maintain consistent, predictable outcomes.

Effect of Different Bases for Inclusion of Substances

The Prohibited List encompasses a wide range of substances included by reason of the application of the criteria in Article 4.3. The application of the criteria means that the category of prohibited substances encompasses substances which can enhance performance and those which cannot. The reason a substance is listed is not stated, but the different bases for the inclusion of substances create some difficulty in the operation of Article 10.4 which appears to be directed mainly at the consideration of substances which are capable of enhancing sport performance. The provisions of Article 10.4 are difficult to apply in a logical way where a substance is, in fact, not capable of enhancing sport performance.

Use of Recreational Substances and Article 10.4

Where an athlete uses a substance which is not performance enhancing in a private setting, he or she may have difficulty establishing the absence of intent to enhance sport performance in the manner required by Article 10.4. If this precondition is established (and inevitably tribunals occasionally resort to assuming this from the nature of the substance), on a proper approach to the assessment of fault (which the notes to the

Article explain must be specific and relevant to explain the athlete or other person's departure from the expected standard of behaviour), it is usually difficult to see how an athlete who intentionally or recklessly takes a recreational substance can bear anything other than a high level of fault. Of course, the difficulties with Article 10.4 can lead tribunals to adopt an approach which is not consistent with the provisions of the Article and impose sanctions which are considered appropriate for the taking of a substance which does not enhance performance rather than following the approach in the notes. In summary, the general point is that Article 10.4 does not work properly with these recreational substances.

Possible Solutions

One possible solution lies at a policy level – change the criteria under Article 4.3.1 and remove substances which are not capable of enhancing sport performance from the List and Code, leaving the social and sporting issues arising from the taking of recreational drugs to sports' rules and national law. Such an outcome may have seemed unlikely, given the history of the policy debate in this area and the long-standing nature of the provisions of the Code which are applicable to the decision whether to include a substance on the List.[5] However, a change in the criteria applicable to the decision whether to include a substance on the Prohibited List to make potential performance enhancement a necessary condition for the inclusion of any substance on the List is contained in the draft revised 2015 Code.

The alternative is to create a clear set of rules for those substances which are included on the List because under the Article 4.3.1 criteria they represent an actual or potential risk to the health of the athlete and are contrary to the spirit of the sport (as described in the introduction to the Code). If a substance is listed on this basis and this is identified, then it may be that a form of tariff system involving loss of result and a further standard penalty could be implemented. This would avoid tribunals having to apply an Article which does not work to decide on sanctions and would also provide a strong measure of consistency in an area where tribunals currently have different approaches.

---

5 For an article which sets out the scientific data to support the inclusion of cannabis on the Prohibited List from the WADA standpoint, see M. A. Huestis, I. Mazzoni and O. Rabin, 'Cannabis in Sport: Anti-Doping Perspective', *Sports Med.* 41(11) (2011), 949–66.

Substances which can Enhance Performance

The other area in which concern is expressed lies in those situations where athletes make negligent mistakes with substances which can be performance enhancing. While any strict system of the kind implemented by the Code will catch those who make mistakes, the general concern is that the process under the Code is catching and banning too many athletes who make negligent mistakes. With such violations the integrity of sport can only be safeguarded by having a hearing process at which an athlete, who is found to have a potentially performance-enhancing substance in his or her system, has to satisfy an independent body that there was no intent to enhance sport performance. Some suggest that it would be appropriate to introduce more stipulated minimum detection levels for some of the substances which can be performance enhancing with only findings above that level leading to consideration of the issues which arise under the Code as regards the appropriate sanction (usually Article 10.4). Detection of specified substances at lower levels might be dealt with by an administrative system of warnings and fixed penalties similar to that which should apply to the substances which are listed but which are not performance enhancing. To many this seems to go too far in permitting some use of performance-enhancing substances and while intended to allow for innocent ingestion in other products is likely to lead to some intentional use which should generally be discouraged by the Code.

Prohibited List

As outlined above, Section S0 of the Prohibited List provides as follows:

> S0. NON-APPROVED SUBSTANCES
> Any pharmacological substance which is not addressed by any of the subsequent sections of the List and with no current approval by any governmental regulatory health authority for human therapeutic use (i.e. drugs under pre-clinical or clinical development or discontinued) is prohibited at all times.

While the desire to include this kind of 'open-ended' provision is understandable where doping products are constantly being developed, the provision lacks certainty or predictability. 'Catch-all' provisions on the List are linked to specific lists of substances in parts of the List but this provision does not appear to identify prohibited substances in an appropriate way.

The section on endogenous steroids on the List might be amended to include a 'catch-all' provision, or, further metabolites and isomers specifically listed if the taking of metabolites synthesised from endogenous steroids is to be clearly prohibited.

Points on Some Articles of the Code

There are a number of points which might be made in relation to the various Articles of the Code. Some selected comments follow.

Article 2.1 or the notes to the Article might be amended to make it clear whether an athlete can commit the violation of the attempted use of a prohibited substance where, as a matter of fact, the attempt does not relate to a prohibited substance. While there is a CAS award[6] interpreting the violation under Article 2.2 as meaning that an athlete can attempt the impossible (by analogy with the criminal law in various jurisdictions) the argument to the contrary can also be made that the Code is concerned with prohibited substances as defined and should not be extended to those situations where, as a matter of fact, there is no prohibited substance involved. The notes (or text of the Article) could clarify the position.

Article 2.4 provides for a violation where there is a breach of the requirement to file whereabouts information or a missed test. The substance of the whereabouts regime is found in the IST. The notes to Article 2.4 might refer to the essential features of the regime and point any reader of the Code to the relevant IST provisions. The non-delegable nature of the obligation imposed on the athlete by the whereabouts regime should, perhaps, be referred to in the notes to the Article.

Article 7.3 makes provision for the review of atypical findings. While the technical document concerned with the detection of anabolic steroids (TDEAAS 2004) makes provision for further investigation where there is doubt about the origin of the substance which produces the positive test, there appears to be no specific reference to atypical findings in the International Standards at present. While the definition of atypical finding appears to permit any requirement for further investigation to be treated as an atypical finding, it appears possible to contend on the current wording that there can be no report of an atypical finding because there is no reference to such findings in any International Standard. It may well be that it was intended to produce a revised International Standard or Technical Document to specify the situations in which atypical findings might

6 See CAS *Troy v. ARU*, Chapter 5, pages 170–1 above.

be made. As things stand the circumstances where an atypical finding may be reported need to be specified in the Standards (or Code).

As previously noted, Article 10.4 does not operate logically where a substance is not one which is included on the List because it is capable of enhancing sport performance. Where Article 10.4 is applicable, the notes might provide more clarification of the nature of the inquiry which is required in respect of the question whether there was an intention on the part of the athlete to enhance sport performance. The discretion as regards the athlete's fault should perhaps not be limited as currently set out in the notes. While the desire to narrow the ambit of the inquiry into fault is understandable, once the exercise of discretion is allowed, it is hard to contain and trying to restrain the exercise of discretion may well be more likely to produce unfairness and inconsistency as some tribunals seek to expand the boundaries of the discretion. Overall it seems unnecessary to try to limit the discretion to provide a sanction for the particular individual in the manner in which the notes to Article 10.4 seek to do.

Articles 10.5.1 and 10.5.2 will continue to be less frequently relied on with the expansion of the category of specified substances. However, Article 10.5.2 is now expressly stated as being potentially applicable to any anti-doping rule violation. (As the notes say, it is difficult to see how this provision can be applied where there is any element of intentional conduct in the violation.) The definition of 'no significant fault' refers to the criteria for 'no fault or negligence' as defined and is not readily applicable to some of the violations because it refers to the utmost caution to avoid a positive test. If Article 10.5.2 is to remain more broadly applicable, then the definitions need amendment. The definition of provisional suspension also requires amendment so that it aligns the effect of provisional suspension with the effect of a period of ineligibility imposed by way of final sanction.

General Comment

The continuing challenge for the Code is to maintain a regime with sufficient certainty of outcome to create a harmonised global response to the problem of doping in sport (in particular as regards sanctions) while providing for some flexibility to allow for proportionate responses to violations in particular circumstances. There will always be a tension between these two objectives. The problem with too many substances requiring the flexible approach is that the benefit of a clear strict regime is lost. The Code seems likely to benefit from a narrowing of its focus, whether by refinement of the List or by clearly separating out the treatment of particular substances.

The Need for Timely Hearings

The Code faces other significant challenges. On the procedural front the problem of delay in arriving at final decisions on doping violations which will affect the career of the athlete facing the allegation and, quite possibly, the results of many other athletes competing in the same sport must be addressed. In the world of sport a period of three months is a long time in the career of an athlete and a long time for a sporting result to be subject to possible change. The recent example of the CAS appeal by WADA and UCI in the case involving the Spanish cyclist Alberto Contador in which a final decision on the appeal to CAS (which changed the results of several major events) was given about eighteen months after the initial positive test illustrates the problem. While it can be difficult to impose time-frames on parties in arbitration proceedings, the sporting context in which the hearing process operates under the Code requires that there be agreed mandatory time-frames which can only be departed from in exceptional circumstances. Those involved in the review of the Code should seek to reach a general agreement for such time-frames to be expressly provided for. Article 8.1 and Article 13.2.2 provide for 'timely' hearing but, it is suggested that the provisions should be amended to include fixed time limits for hearings. CAS will need to be involved in setting any time-frames because they will need to be realistic and achievable in a practical sense.

The Effect of other Sporting Rules

The rules of sporting organisations which seek to add to or reduce the effect of the Code's key provisions also pose a significant threat to the uniform regime which the Code seeks to create. Where they have the effect of amending the Code's key provisions in a significant way, the implementation of such rules will be a breach of the obligations of Signatories to the Code. However, the nature of the Code means that it is essential that sporting organisations are content with and respect the balance struck by the Code and do not seek to circumvent the Code's provisions. While an opinion or decision from CAS that a rule imposing an additional or indeed lesser sanction does not comply with the obligations of a Signatory declares the position which a Signatory should take, the contractual nature of the Code (and any other sporting rule) means that the ultimate answer to divisions of opinion as to the appropriate approach under the Code must be found in an agreed solution reached after debate and incorporated into the Code, which all parties agree to adhere to. The Code review process will be important in seeking to achieve a unified approach from Signatories on such matters as the length of sanctions which will, it is hoped, mean that we do not continue to see Signatories implement their own rules in the area covered by the Code. If a unified position is not reached, continuing development and implementation of separate rules by Signatories or other sporting organisations concerning such matters as sanctions will undermine the harmony which the Code has sought to establish.

Throughout the process of its development the Code will continue to face the challenge of balancing competing interests and aims. An effective process of regular review is an important aspect of maintaining acceptance throughout the sporting world for the harmonised position represented by the Code. The Code will always have to balance the competing requirements of certainty and flexibility which are hard to reconcile but the more effective and inclusive a review is undertaken, the more likely it is that the Code will continue its central role in the fight against doping in sport.

INDEX